MW01702055

Custom Textbook for CSEC 620

University of Maryland University College

WILEY Custom
LEARNING SOLUTIONS

To order books or for customer service, please call 1(800)-CALL-WILEY (225-5945).

Printed in the United States of America.

ISBN 978-0-470-92442-6

Printed and Bound by EPAC Technologies, Inc.

10 9 8 7 6 5 4 3 2

Contents

HANDBOOK OF INFORMATION SECURITY

Key Concepts, Infrastructure, Standards, and Protocols

Volume 1

Hossein Bidgoli
Editor-in-Chief
California State University
Bakersfield, California

WILEY
John Wiley & Sons, Inc.

This book is printed on acid-free paper. ♾

Published by John Wiley & Sons, Inc., Hoboken, New Jersey.
Published simultaneously in Canada.

Library of Congress Cataloging-in-Publication Data:

The handbook of information security / edited by Hossein Bidgoli.
p. cm.
Includes bibliographical references and index.
ISBN-13: 978-0-471-64830-7, ISBN-10: 0-471-64830-2 (CLOTH VOL 1 : alk. paper)
ISBN-13: 978-0-471-64831-4, ISBN-10: 0-471-64831-0 (CLOTH VOL 2 : alk. paper)
ISBN-13: 978-0-471-64832-1, ISBN-10: 0-471-64832-9 (CLOTH VOL 3 : alk. paper)
ISBN-13: 978-0-471-22201-9, ISBN-10: 0-471-22201-1 (CLOTH SET : alk. paper)
1. Internet–Encyclopedias. I. Bidgoli, Hossein.
TK5105.875.I57I5466 2003
004.67′8′03–dc21

2002155552

Printed in the United States of America

10 9 8 7 6 5 4 3 2 1

HANDBOOK OF INFORMATION SECURITY

Information Warfare; Social, Legal, and International Issues; and Security Foundations

Volume 2

Hossein Bidgoli
Editor-in-Chief
California State University
Bakersfield, California

WILEY
John Wiley & Sons, Inc.

This book is printed on acid-free paper. ♾

Published by John Wiley & Sons, Inc., Hoboken, New Jersey.
Published simultaneously in Canada.

Library of Congress Cataloging-in-Publication Data:

The handbook of information security / edited by Hossein Bidgoli.
p. cm.
Includes bibliographical references and index.
ISBN-13: 978-0-471-64830-7, ISBN-10: 0-471-64830-2 (CLOTH VOL 1 : alk. paper)
ISBN-13: 978-0-471-64831-4, ISBN-10: 0-471-64831-0 (CLOTH VOL 2 : alk. paper)
ISBN-13: 978-0-471-64832-1, ISBN-10: 0-471-64832-9 (CLOTH VOL 3 : alk. paper)
ISBN-13: 978-0-471-22201-9, ISBN-10: 0-471-22201-1 (CLOTH SET : alk. paper)
1. Internet–Encyclopedias. I. Bidgoli, Hossein.
TK5105.875.I57I5466 2003
004.67′8′03–dc21

2002155552

Printed in the United States of America

10 9 8 7 6 5 4 3 2 1

Cybercrime and the U.S. Criminal Justice System

Susan W. Brenner, *University of Dayton School of Law*

INTRODUCTION

Cybercrime, which is essentially the use of computer technology in the commission of criminal activity, presents many challenges for the U.S. legal system. On the one hand, state and federal law adequately criminalizes most of the basic cybercrime offenses; on the other hand, there is substantial disagreement as to the penalties that are appropriate for those who commit these offenses. The disagreement over penalties is exacerbated by the fact that many offenders are juveniles; the federal system, especially, is not equipped to deal with juveniles. Charging decisions can be difficult because it is not easy to parse cybercrime into offenses: Is the dissemination of a virus that damages a million computers one crime or a million crimes? As is explained below, these are only a few of the ways in which cybercrime challenges the basic assumptions that structured traditional criminal law.

DIFFERENCES FROM CIVIL JUSTICE SYSTEM

The criminal justice system in the United States—as elsewhere—differs from the civil justice system in several important ways. One difference is substantive: the goal of the civil justice system is to provide redress for accidental or conventional injuries or losses one "person," which can be an individual or a corporate entity, has suffered as the result of another's actions or failure to act (LaFave, 2003). The goal of the criminal justice system, on the other hand, is to allow the state—acting on behalf of the people in a specific society—to inflict punishment on those who inflict deliberate, serious injuries upon others. Technically, therefore, in the criminal justice system, the state is the injured party, and criminal proceedings are brought in the name of the appropriate government, which will be federal, state, or local (LaFave, 2003).

Another difference is procedural: the U.S. Constitution sets limits on what law enforcement officers can do when investigating crimes such as hacking or cyberfraud. State and federal officers must tender the *Miranda* warnings to anyone whom they take into custody for the purposes of interrogation (LaFave, Israel, & King, 1999). The Fourth Amendment requires that they either obtain a search warrant or invoke a valid exception to the warrant requirement to search for and seize evidence of a cybercrime; so, if officers believe child pornography is located in a suspect's computer in his or her bedroom, they must persuade a magistrate to issue a warrant allowing them to search the computer or convince the suspect to consent to such a search (consent being an exception to the warrant requirement) (LaFave et al., 1999).

There are other procedural differences that distinguish criminal trials from civil trials: In a criminal trial, the prosecution must prove its case "beyond a reasonable doubt," which is a far more demanding standard than the "preponderance of the evidence" standard used in civil trials (LaFave et al., 1999). If the civil standard were used in a hacking prosecution, the government would only have to prove it was "more likely than not" that the defendant engaged in hacking; under the criminal standard, the government must prove beyond a reasonable doubt that the crime of hacking was committed and that it was committed by the defendant (LaFave et al., 1999). This higher standard protects those who are accused of crimes and thereby helps to avoid wrongful convictions; other rules that work to the same end are the presumption that a defendant is innocent and an indigent defendant's right to appointed counsel (LaFave et al., 1999). The size of criminal juries also contributes to this goal; in the federal system and in most states, 12 jurors are required in criminal trials (LaFave et al., 1999). Civil trials often involve fewer jurors, frequently as few as six (LaFave et al., 1999). The size of the jury is important because studies have shown larger juries are more likely to result in fair deliberations (LaFave et al., 1999).

BASIC INSTITUTIONAL STRUCTURE

Law enforcement in the United States takes place at three distinct levels: federal, state, and local government (LaFave et al., 1999). At the federal level, the Federal Bureau of Investigation and the Secret Service actively pursue cybercrime investigations, but their efforts account for only a fraction of the total number of investigations; in the United States, state and federal law enforcement have traditionally been primarily responsible for pursuing criminal cases (LaFave et al., 1999). As a result, U.S. cybercrime laws can overlap: The federal system and all of the states have laws that criminalize hacking, cyberfraud, and other common cybercrimes (Ditzion, Geddes, & Rhodes, 2003). The default assumptions are that (a) state and local authorities have jurisdiction to prosecute and (b) federal authorities must be able to bring a hacking or other cybercrime case within a federal jurisdictional predicate to be able to prosecute (LaFave, 2003). The most common federal jurisdictional predicate used in cybercrime cases is an effect on interstate or foreign commerce; this is the predicate used in the general federal cybercrime statute, 18 U.S. Code §1030 (Ditzion, Geddes, & Rhodes, 2003). So, to prosecute someone for hacking in violation of §1030, federal prosecutors have to show that the hacking had an impact on interstate or foreign commerce, which is usually not difficult to do (American Bar Association Task Force, 1998).

When a cybercrime occurs, the investigation is undertaken by local, state, or federal law enforcement officers who may work in conjunction with a prosecutor and who often work in conjunction with computer forensic and other experts, such as forensic psychologists (LaFave et al., 1999). Given the complexity of cybercrime cases, these investigations are increasingly undertaken by task forces in which local, state, and federal officers collaborate with private investigators to pursue a cybercriminal (Miami Electronic Crimes Task Force, 2003). Indeed, one of the distinguishing aspects of cybercrime cases is the essential involvement of the private sector: cybercrimes are often committed against businesses, which must decide if they want to report the matter to the authorities or handle it in-house. There are disincentives for reporting a cyberattack; aside from anything else, news that a company has been victimized by a cyberattacker can undermine confidence in the business and in its ability to protect client or customer information (Brenner & Schwerha, 2002). If a business is attacked and decides to report the matter to the authorities, it will have to decide if it wants to contact federal, state, or local authorities (Brenner & Schwerha, 2002). There are certain advantages to seeking federal prosecution; federal agencies often have more resources and expertise in dealing with computer crime, and they are not hampered by the jurisdictional impediments that confront state authorities. A federal search warrant, for example, is enforceable anywhere in the United States; a state search warrant, a New York warrant, say, is enforceable only within the state of New York.

Because cybercrime cases can be difficult to investigate and prosecute, there is an emerging emphasis on avoiding the need for both by preventing cybercrime. Prevention is a major focus of the Secret Service's Electronic Crime Task Forces and the Federal Bureau of Investigation's Infragard program. Both initiatives bring together representatives from law enforcement, the private sector, and academia to share information and resources, thereby facilitating the prevention of cybercrime and the investigation of completed cybercrimes.

Prosecutor

The central figure in any cybercrime case is the prosecutor. In the U.S. justice system, prosecutors occupy a unique role; they serve as advocates for the state and in that sense play a role analogous to that of the defense lawyer. As advocates, defense lawyers are obliged to use every tactical advantage permitted under the law to obtain their client's acquittal, even if doing so keeps the jury from the truth (LaFave et al., 1999). Prosecutors are held to a higher standard; their duty is to ensure justice is done, not merely to win a criminal case (LaFave et al., 1999). But when a state or federal prosecutor does take a case to trial, his or her goals will generally be to obtain a conviction (LaFave et al., 1999).

Because crimes are considered a wrong against the government, prosecutions are undertaken in the name of the government, whether federal, state, or local, and victims consequently play a minor role (LaFave et al., 1999). Victims typically have little say in the charging or plea bargaining processes; their role is usually limited to that of witness (LaFave et al., 1999). Prosecutors control charging and plea bargaining; they have wide discretion in deciding (a) whether someone will be prosecuted and (b) if someone is to be prosecuted, what charges they will face (LaFave et al., 1999). In a hacking case, for instance, the prosecutor might decide not to prosecute the offender because he is a juvenile. This is particularly likely to occur in the federal system, which is not set up to deal with juvenile offenders (Esbenshade, 2002–2003). As a result, federal prosecutors tend to concentrate on adult offenders and turn juveniles over to the juvenile court of the appropriate state, pursuant to the Federal Juvenile Delinquency Act (Esbenshade, 2002–2003).

Another large class of cybercrime cases in the United States involves intellectual property (U.S. Department of Justice Computer Crime and Intellectual Property Section, 2001): "Legal regimes have created enforceable rights in certain intangibles that have become familiar as intellectual property, including copyrights, trademarks, patents, and trade secrets" (U.S. Department of Justice Computer Crime and Intellectual Property Section, 2001). At the federal level, various statutes are used to prosecute the unlawful appropriation of intellectual property: 18 U.S. Code §2320 makes it a crime to counterfeit trademarks. 18 U.S. Code §§1831 and §§1832 make the theft of trade secrets a federal crime. And copyright infringement is criminalized by 17 U.S. Code §506(a) and 18 U.S. Code §2319. Patent infringement "is not generally a criminal violation" (U.S. Department of Justice Computer Crime and Intellectual Property Section, 2001). Federal law preempts state law governing copyright violations, so prosecutions can be brought only at the federal level (Nicholson et al., 2000). Federal law does not preempt state law governing trademark violations, except insofar as the state and federal statutory provisions conflict (Kahn, 2004).

In deciding whether to prosecute intellectual property crimes, such as criminal copyright infringement, federal prosecutors must consider the strength of their case, the person's culpability in connection with the crime(s), the person's history (if any) of prior criminal activity, current federal law enforcement priorities, and the extent to which such a prosecution would deter others from engaging in similar conduct (U.S. Department of Justice Computer Crime and Intellectual Property Section, 2001). These factors, and perhaps most notably the federal interest in protecting U.S.-based intellectual property rights, have prompted federal prosecutions of those who use the Internet to supply "warez," that is, pirated copies of software (U.S. Department of Justice Computer Crime and Intellectual Property Section, 2001). A study of federal cybercrime prosecutions found that in 2001 the Department of Justice declined to prosecute in 496 of 631 referred cases; 135 cases were prosecuted, resulting in 107 convictions and 28 dismissals or acquittals on all charges (National Association of Criminal Defense Lawyers, Electronic Frontier Foundation & Sentencing Project, 2003). The primary reason given for declining prosecution was lack of evidence or inadmissible evidence (National Association of Criminal Defense Lawyers, Electronic Frontier Foundation & Sentencing Project, 2003). The next most commonly cited reasons were (a) that the person would be prosecuted at the state level and (b) the lack of a federal interest in prosecuting (National Association of Criminal Defense Lawyers, Electronic Frontier Foundation & Sentencing Project, 2003).

Even when prosecutors decide to charge someone, the defense attorney may be able to arrange a plea bargain: in 1995, hacker Kevin Mitnick pled guilty to 1 of 23 counts brought against him in a North Carolina federal prosecution (Goldman, 1995). By pleading guilty, he was guaranteed a sentence of no more than 8 months and avoided prosecution on the remaining 22 counts (Goldman, 1995). Plea bargains offer defendants the opportunity to accept a lesser penalty in return for avoiding at least the possibility of a greater penalty, but they also offer certain advantages for prosecutors. Plea bargains let prosecutors resolve cases without having to go to trial, which alleviates the burden on a criminal justice system that is swamped with cybercrime and real-world crime cases; plea bargains also let prosecutors trade lesser sentences for a defendant's cooperation in prosecuting other, presumably more culpable, offenders. The potential for cooperation is one of the factors federal prosecutors consider in deciding whether to bring charges and whether to plea bargain charges that have already been brought (U.S. Department of Justice Computer Crime and Intellectual Property Section, 2001).

As noted, law enforcement in the United States operates on three levels: local, state, and federal. This is also true for prosecutors. Local prosecutors generally operate at the county or parish level; there is typically an elected prosecutor who is usually known either as the county prosecutor or the district attorney (LaFave et al., 1999). He or she functions with the aid of a number of assistants, who are known as assistant district attorneys, deputy county prosecutors, or similar titles (LaFave et al., 1999). Moving up a tier, each state has an attorney general whose jurisdiction varies from state to state: in some states, attorney generals are authorized only to prosecute certain, specialized crimes such as antitrust or organized crime cases; in other states, attorney generals have much more limited jurisdiction to prosecute and may be limited to substituting when a local prosecutor is disqualified (LaFave et al., 1999). Like local prosecutors, attorney generals function with the aid of assistants, who are usually known as deputy attorney generals or assistant attorney generals. Many state attorney general's offices have established cybercrime units and the National Association of Attorneys General has its own cybercrime initiative (National Association of Attorneys General—Computer Crime, 2003). Moving up to the third tier, the federal justice system is headed by an attorney general, who also functions with the aid of assistants and deputies (LaFave et al., 1999). The attorney general also heads up a nationwide organization of United States attorneys; a United States attorney is appointed for every federal judicial district in the United States; they function in a fashion analogous to county prosecutors; that is, they deal with federal crimes committed in a specified geographical area (LaFave et al., 1999). The Department of Justice, headed by the attorney general, also deals with federal crime on a more global level; the department has a specialized unit—the Computer Crime and Intellectual Property Section—which deals with cybercrime as a general phenomenon (Ditzion, Geddes, & Rhodes, 2003).

After a prosecutor has taken a case to trial and obtained a conviction or entered into a plea bargain with a defendant, the next step in the process is sentencing (LaFave et al., 1999). In all but a few U.S. jurisdictions, which allow for jury sentencing even in noncapital cases, the determination and imposition of an appropriate sentence are a matter for the court (LaFave et al., 1999). The U.S. system uses four types of sanctions: financial (fines, restitution), community release (probation, unsupervised release, house arrest), incarceration in a jail (for shorter sentences) or a prison (for longer sentences), and capital punishment (for murder) (LaFave et al., 1999). Courts can combine these sanctions; in one cybercrime case, for example, the court sentenced the defendant to 3 years' probation, a $40,000 fine, and the payment of $20,000 in restitution (U.S. v. Hicks, 1995). In the federal system and a number of states, sentences are determinate; that is, the offender serves the entire sentence imposed by the court (except for "good time" credit) (LaFave et al., 1999). The other states use indeterminate sentencing, in which the court sets a maximum period and a minimum period of incarceration and the state parole board decides how much time the offender will exactly serve (LaFave et al., 1999). Both systems are increasingly using sentencing guidelines, which are standards that limit the judge's discretion in imposing sentence (LaFave et al., 1999). Until recently, cybercrime offenders often received sentences of probation only, or, at most, a short period of incarceration (Beauprez, 2003). In November 2003, new sentencing guidelines went into effect in the federal system that will increase punishments in at least some cybercrime cases (Beauprez, 2003).

Defense Attorney

The defense attorney's role is to ensure that no conviction is obtained unless (a) the prosecution proves its case beyond a reasonable doubt or (b) the defendant accepts a plea bargain that is advantageous for him or her (LaFave et al., 1999). As noted, when charges have been brought, it is defense counsel's task to utilize every tactical advantage at his or her disposal to obtain the best outcome for the client (LaFave et al., 1999). Unlike the prosecutor, the defense attorney's advocacy is not constrained by external principles; in our adversarial system of justice, defense counsel is charged with pursuing the client's best interests without regard to other concerns (LaFave et al., 1999). That includes ensuring that the trial or the plea bargaining process is conducted in accordance with constitutional and other legal requirements; for that reason, ineffective assistance of defense counsel is a basis for setting aside a conviction (LaFave et al., 1999). But although defense counsel must represent his or her client zealously and loyally, defense attorneys, like prosecutors, are ethically obligated not to misrepresent matters of fact or law to the court, not to suborn perjury by one's client, and not to destroy, alter, or conceal evidence (American Bar Association, 2003).

The Sixth Amendment creates a right to counsel for those charged with the commission of crimes; the Supreme Court has held that this right attaches to all "critical" stages of a prosecution, such as the arraignment, plea negotiations, and trial (LaFave et al., 1999). In both the state and federal systems, defendants are represented either by privately retained attorneys or by attorneys provided by the government (LaFave et al., 1999). If a defendant cannot afford to retain private counsel, the court will arrange for appointed counsel to represent him or her (LaFave et al., 1999). States use three systems to accomplish this: in most counties, indigents are represented by public defenders—attorneys whom the county employs to represent those who cannot afford private counsel (LaFave et al., 1999). The second most commonly used system relies on private attorneys whom judges appoint to represent indigents; these private attorneys are paid at a rate determined by the local government (LaFave et al., 1999). Finally, a few counties use a system in which a private law firm or a bar association contracts with the county to provide representation for indigents (LaFave et al., 1999). In the federal system, federal public defenders represent indigents in a number of judicial districts, whereas the others rely on court-appointed private counsel (LaFave et al., 1999).

The defense of a cybercrime case is a difficult matter, because it requires special expertise as to substantive law [i.e., the offense(s) charged], procedural law (i.e., the legality of the tactics employed in the investigation), and the intricacies of computer technology. So far, there appears to be a serious scarcity of attorneys who specialize in cybercrime cases, no doubt because such cases are still relatively rare, considered in relation to the other types of criminal cases being brought. To date, many of those charged with cybercrime have relied on privately retained counsel, perhaps because hackers and others involved with computer technology are less likely to be indigent than, say, those charged with drug offenses. There have, however, been exceptions: Adrian Lamo, who became famous as the "homeless hacker," relied on a public defender when he was prosecuted federally for hacking into systems, including the *New York Times'* computer system (Reuters Wired News, 2003).

Adjudication

Perhaps the most critical decision the defense has to make, especially in a computer crime trial, is whether to have the case tried by a jury ("jury trial") or a judge ("bench trial"). The Sixth Amendment guarantees criminal defendants the right to trial by an impartial jury drawn from the state and district in which the crime(s) allegedly occurred (Right to Jury Trial, 2003). The right attaches when one has been charged with an offense which is punishable by a prison sentence of 6 months or more; as to crimes for which one can serve less than 6 months in prison, the right to jury trial does not attach unless the presence of additional statutory or regulatory penalties indicates that the legislature considered the offense a "serious" crime (Right to Jury Trial, 2003).

Usually, the jury in a criminal trial consists of 12 jurors, but the Supreme Court has held that 6 jurors are enough to satisfy the Sixth Amendment (Right to Jury Trial, 2003). Court rules, such as Rule 23 of the Federal Rules of Criminal Procedure, require the impaneling of 12 jurors in federal criminal trials, absent a written waiver executed by the parties and approved by the court (Right to Jury Trial, 2003). The Supreme Court has consistently held that jurors in federal criminal trials must return a unanimous verdict (Right to Jury Trial, 2003). As for state criminal trials, the jury must be unanimous if it consists of only 6 jurors; if the jury consists of 12 jurors, they can return a nonunanimous verdict (Right to Jury Trial, 2003). Traditionally, jurors were required to be purely passive spectators at a trial; they were not allowed to ask questions or otherwise participate in the proceedings (Hans, 2002). More and more, however, jurors are being allowed to ask questions, take notes, and discuss the case with each other during the trial (Hans, 2002).

A jury trial is a defendant's constitutional right, but it may or may not be the best choice, depending on the nature of the case. If the defense attorney believes the case is likely to inflame the passions of the jury against his or her client, the best course may be to ask for a bench trial. This can, for example, be an advisable tactic in a child pornography case: even though there may be valid evidentiary and/or legal reasons to acquit the accused, the jurors may be so disturbed by the images the prosecution presents that they will ignore those reasons and convict, leaving the matter to be appealed. In such an instance, the wiser course may well be for the defendant to waive his right to a jury trial and have the case tried by the court. The same can be true for crimes involving difficult legal and technical issues, such as actions under the Digital Millennium Copyright Act (*Universal City Studios, Inc. v. Corley*, 2001).

A defendant can waive his or her right to a jury trial by (a) obtaining the court's approval and the government's consent and (b) executing a written waiver that is knowing, voluntary, and intelligent (Right to Jury Trial, 2003). The government's consent is required because the Supreme Court has held that there is no constitutional right to a bench trial (Right to Jury Trial, 2003). Because there is no constitutional right to a nonjury trial, the prosecution can, in effect, veto a defendant's wish to have his or her case heard by the court instead of a jury; all that is required is for the prosecution to refuse to consent to a bench trial (Right to Jury Trial, 2003).

Once a criminal case has been tried to its conclusion, the defendant cannot be tried again for the crimes at issue in that proceeding, as the Fifth Amendment declares that one cannot be twice "put in jeopardy" for the "same offence" (LaFave et al., 1999). The double jeopardy clause not only prevents the retrial of cases that have produced a conviction or acquittal; it can also prevent retrials after a case has been begun and is then terminated before the matter goes to the jury (LaFave et al., 1999). The basic rule is that "jeopardy" attaches (a) after the first witness has been sworn in a bench trial and (b) after the jurors have been sworn in for a jury trial (LaFave et al., 1999).

The protections of the double jeopardy clause are subject to certain exceptions: for one thing, the government may be able to reprosecute a defendant even when a trial has been dismissed after jeopardy has attached; in certain circumstances, a retrial can occur after a mistrial has been declared (LaFave et al., 1999). For another, the protection only applies to a second prosecution by the same government; consequently, it is not a violation of double jeopardy for a state to prosecute someone for crimes that were at issue in a preceding federal prosecution that produced a judgment of conviction or acquittal (LaFave et al., 1999). Perhaps the most famous instance of this, in recent years, is the state prosecution Oklahoma has brought against Terry Nichols for his role in the bombing of the Oklahoma City Federal Building; Nichols, of course, has already been prosecuted and convicted in a federal proceeding arising out of the same event (Romano, 2004).

Another important constitutional protection is the Sixth Amendment right to speedy trial. The Supreme Court has explained that this right is essential to protect at least three basic demands of justice: "(1) to prevent undue and oppressive incarceration prior to trial, (2) to minimize anxiety and concern accompanying public accusation and (3) to limit the possibilities that long delay will impair the ability of an accused to defend himself" (*Smith v. Hooey*, 1969). Indeed, this right is considered so important that the Sixth Amendment guarantee has been supplemented by statutory and rule-based protections in both the state and federal systems (LaFave et al., 1999).

Basic Defenses

As to defending himself or herself, the substantive criminal law provides an array of theories defendants can use to argue that they should be acquitted of the charges brought against them. Analytically, these defenses fall into two categories: (1) failure of proof defenses and (2) affirmative defenses (LaFave, 2003).

Failure of proof defenses are not "true" defenses; they are merely a way of attacking the prosecution's case. As one scholar explains, a "failure of proof defense is one in which the defendant has introduced evidence at his criminal trial showing that some essential element of the crime charged has not been proved beyond a reasonable doubt" (LaFave, 2003). Because criminal liability requires a voluntary act (*actus reus*) done with the appropriate mental state (*mens rea*), defendants often argue that they cannot be held guilty because they either were not acting voluntarily or, if they were acting voluntarily, did not possess the mental state required for the offense (LaFave, 2003). Assume, for example, that an employee of a company is charged with hacking (i.e., with unauthorized intrusion into an area of the company's computer system); the premise of the charges is that although the employee had authorized access to part of the company's computer system, he exceeded the scope of that authorized access and explored parts of the system that he was not legitimately entitled to access (*United States v. Czubinski*, 1997). Assume, further, that the charge against the employee is that he "knowingly" gained "unauthorized access" to parts of his employer's computer system. The defendant can mount a failure of proof defense by claiming that, although he did exceed the scope of his authorized access to the computer system, he did not do so "knowingly"; he could argue, for example, that he believed he had full access to the entire system because no security measures prevented his exploring parts of the system beyond those he used in the course of his everyday tasks. If the employer did not have policies that made it clear that employees were not to exceed a specifically defined scope of access to the computer system, this failure of proof defense might well work. Predicating a failure of proof defense on the theory that one was not acting voluntarily at the time the offense was committed is much more difficult when computer crimes are involved: generally speaking, claims that one was not acting voluntarily require the defendant to show that he or she was in a state of unconsciousness at the time the offense was committed; such claims rest, for example, on assertions that the defendant was sleepwalking, suffering from an epileptic seizure, or in a fugue state induced, say, by brain trauma or a reaction to medication (LaFave, 2003). Claims such as these can be credible when the offense involves simple acts, such as driving a car; they are hardly likely to be credible when the offense involves complex activity requiring the application of specialized technical knowledge and skills.

Unlike failure of proof defenses, affirmative defenses do not involve attacking the prosecution's ability to prove the elements of its case (LaFave, 2003). One who asserts an affirmative defense is, in effect, saying "yes, but..."; that is, the defendant is saying, in effect, "Yes, I committed the crime but there are valid reasons why I should not be held liable for doing so." The basic affirmative defenses are (a) insanity, (b) self-defense, (c) defense of others, (d) defense of property, (e) duress, and (f) choice of evils (LaFave, 2003). Insanity and duress are "excuse" defenses; one who asserts these affirmative defenses is, in essence, saying "Yes, I committed the crime but I should not be held liable" because (a) I was insane and therefore did not know right from wrong or (b) I was forced to commit the crime by threats or violence from another person (LaFave, 2003). The other four are "justification" defenses; one who asserts these affirmative defenses is, in essence, saying "Yes, I committed the crime but I did the right thing in doing so" because I acted to protect myself, to protect someone else, to protect property or to avoid some harm greater than that resulting from the commission of this crime (LaFave, 2003). Although the prosecution bears the burden of proving every element of the crime beyond a reasonable doubt, the defendant bears the burden of producing evidence that is sufficient to raise a cognizable claim that the affirmative defense applies; a defendant must, for example, produce evidence that supports his or her claim of having acted in self-defense (LaFave, 2003).

Generally speaking, these traditional affirmative defenses tend to have little applicability in cybercrime prosecutions. One who seeks to raise an insanity defense will encounter some of the same logical obstacles as a defendant who tries to argue that he or she was not acting voluntarily at the time the crime was committed; although it might be possible to show, say, that the defendant was acting under the influence of command hallucinations when he or she hacked into NASA, both juries and judges are likely to be skeptical of such claims when the charges involve crimes the commission of which necessarily entails a course of structured, sequenced conduct. The same is true of duress: to qualify for the duress defense, a defendant must show that he or she committed the crime(s) at issue because he was forced to do so by another person, who threatened him with death or serious bodily injury if he did not comply with that person's demands (LaFave, 2003). It is, of course, quite possible that someone could use force or the threat of force to coerce a person with computer skills into hacking into a system, releasing a virus or otherwise violating state or federal cybercrime laws. The likelihood of this happening seems, however, rather remote; the duress defense is often raised when one participant in criminal activity (A) is coerced by another participant in that activity (B) to "go further" than A had intended or desires (LaFave, 2003). It is exceedingly rare for the defense to be raised in an instance of "stranger danger" (i.e., when a stranger forces an otherwise law-abiding citizen to commit a crime by using or threatening force). Because computer crimes tend, so far, to be committed by those who have no history of violent criminal activity, it is unlikely that the duress defense will be successfully asserted in cybercrime prosecutions for the foreseeable future.

It may be somewhat easier to raise a justification defense. Self-defense requires a use of "force" that the defending party deemed was necessary to protect himself or herself from another's use of force, either deadly or nondeadly (LaFave, 2003). Historically, "force" has meant physical force, but there is no reason why we could not expand the concept to encompass "virtual force" (i.e., an assault using computer technology). Even if we did so, however, the assault would have to threaten a human being with death or serious physical injury for the defending party to be able to utilize self-defense as the justification for retaliative actions; an attack focusing solely on a computer system would not suffice as the basis for invoking this defense (LaFave, 2003). In 2001, a Chinese man claimed to have hacked into a computer system in self-defense: he said he hacked into the other system because he thought the operators of that system had attacked his computer (Ying-Cheng, 2001). Even if this gentleman had been correct in that belief, he would not, under U.S. law, have been able to claim self-defense because the attack was not a personal attack (i.e., was not directed at causing physical harm to him) (LaFave, 2003).

The same would be true if this gentleman had tried to assert the related affirmative defense of defense of others; defense of others requires that one has acted because such action was necessary to prevent another person or other persons from death or physical injury (LaFave, 2003). It is of course conceivable that such a defense could be asserted successfully in the context of a cyberassault: assume, for instance, that during the dead of winter a cyberterrorist is in the process of attacking a computer system that controls electrical power to a midwestern city; if the cyberterrorist succeeds in taking over the system and shutting down power to the city, people will be without light, heat, and other services. Many will die from exposure; others will die from panic, from their inability to gain assistance, from emergency services, and for other reasons. A computer technician discovers that the attack is in progress and knows it will succeed before he would have time to contact the authorities and secure official intervention; if this technician hacks into the cyberterrorist's computer or otherwise takes defensive measures to prevent the attack, he should be able to assert a claim of self-defense in the improbable instance he is charged with hacking into the computer which is the cyberterrorist's target. In this example, the computer technician is using a type of "force," virtual force, to prevent injury to other persons and is, therefore, justified in attacking the cyberterrorist's computer.

This brings us to defense of property; like self-defense and defense of others, defense of property has traditionally required that one use physical force. In this instance, the force is used to preserve one's possession of, or the integrity of, real or personal property (LaFave, 2003). The Chinese gentleman discussed above, who hacked into a computer system because he believed the operators of that system had attacked his system, was really asserting a defense of property theory (Ying-Cheng, 2001). He claimed he had to take affirmative action against those whom he believed were attempting to harm his computer system (Ying-Cheng, 2001). Because he believed he was acting to protect his property from unlawful conduct, he could, subject to the qualifications discussed below, assert a defense of property claim when he was charged with unlawful hacking.

The final justification defense is choice of evils. Choice of evils justifies the commission of a crime when one commits that crime to avoid a harm or evil greater than the harm or evil resulting from the commission of this offense (LaFave, 2003). The choice of evils defense would, for example, be available to one who cut a hole in a dam that was about to burst to prevent the dam from collapsing and flooding a town; the defense is available even if, by cutting the hole in the dam, the actor caused a nearby farm to flood, killing livestock or even a person (LaFave, 2003). As long as the harm sought to be avoided (i.e., flooding the town, which would cause great loss of life and property) is greater than the harm inflicted (i.e., damage to the dam plus the loss of a single life and property damage at the farm), the actor is entitled to the choice of evils defense (LaFave, 2003). This defense could therefore serve as an alternative basis for justifying the actions of the computer technician discussed earlier: the one who frustrated the efforts of the cyberterrorist. His actions could be characterized either as defense of others (if we focus on the threat coming from another person) or as choice of evils (if we focus on the harm to be avoided versus the harm resulting from his hacking into the computer system).

As this discussion of justification defenses should demonstrate, they raise difficult issues of law and policy. When we allow someone to assert a justification defense, we are, in effect, saying that they did the right thing by taking the law into their own hands; because the legal system cannot tolerate people's taking the law into their own hands as a matter of general practice, the law imposes restrictions on the assertion of the justification defenses to ensure that they can be successfully asserted only in truly compelling cases (LaFave, 2003). The restriction that is common to all of the justification defenses is that the actor believed it was "necessary" to, in effect, take the law into his or her own hands (LaFave, 2003). "Necessary" in this context means that there were no viable, lawful alternatives (LaFave, 2003). To use the examples given above, the computer technician who hacked into a computer system to prevent the cyberterrorist's attack from succeeding would no doubt qualify for a justification defense (defense of others or choice of evils) because it seems he had no lawful alternatives; if he had contacted the authorities and asked for their assistance, the attack would have succeeded (LaFave, 2003). Conversely, the Chinese gentleman who hacked a computer system he thought was being used to attack his own system would not qualify for a justification defense because it was not "necessary" for him to take the law into his own hands; he could have gone to the authorities, reported the attacks on his system, and given them the information that led him to believe a particular computer system was being used in the attacks. The authorities could have handled matters from there.

Hack Back Defense

The above discussion of justification defenses logically leads to the issue of vigilante action—what the law calls "self-help"—as a response to cybercrime. Some argue that because the law enforcement response to cybercrime is likely to be ineffective given the limited resources law enforcement has for this purpose plus the fact that many cybercrimes are transnational in nature, it is only reasonable to allow victims of hacking and other computer crimes to "strike back" at the offenders (Loomis, 2001). Those who advocate this approach claim that "you can't reason with attackers and you can't coddle them—the only language they understand is force" (Loomis, 2001). Those who take this position believe that if a victim strikes back at his/her attacker with sufficient force, this will deter that attacker and similarly situated attackers from launching future assaults on the victim's system (Loomis, 2001). This argument has an undeniable visceral appeal, because of the apparent impunity with which many cybercriminals operate. Indeed, it has even led to the introduction of proposed federal legislation that would legitimize self-help against those who engage in criminal copyright violations (H.R. 5211, 2002).

Society, however, cannot tolerate vigilante behavior. This was true in the 19th century, when vigilantes were active in the American West, and it is still true today (Hine, 1998). The drift toward vigilantism as a response to cybercrime is not surprising; vigilantism tends to appear in "frontier" situations (i.e., when law enforcement is ineffective or absent; Hine, 1998). This is, of course, true of cyberspace, which is often analogized to the Wild West. The problem is that although self-help can be a viscerally satisfying approach to one's victimization, it creates more problems than it solves: for one thing, vigilantes commit crimes. In the examples given in the previous section, both the computer technician who is responding to the cyberterrorist's activities and the Chinese gentleman who is responding to the attacks on his system are violating the law by hacking. It is a fundamental premise of every legal system that citizens are not privileged to commit crimes (LaFave et al., 1999). It is true that, as the previous section explained, the law does absolve citizens who take the law into their own hands under certain, very limited, situations; however, this is very different from a blanket authorization for online retaliative behavior. Aside from anything else, such behavior is objectionable because of the risks that innocent parties will be targeted for retaliation; the consequences of this risk are particularly intolerable in cyberspace, where it can be impossible to know precisely from which system an attack was launched (Loomis, 2001). It is to avoid the possibility of harm to an innocent actor that the legal system has developed a complex structure of rules and processes governing the imposition of sanctions upon those who are believed to have committed crimes (LaFave et al., 1999).

Evidentiary Issues

Cybercrime cases present a variety of evidentiary issues, which can be broken down into two categories: (1) the process of gathering evidence and (2) the process of introducing evidence at trial.

The process of gathering evidence differs depending on whether the evidence is located in a stand-alone computer (desktop or laptop) or is on a network. If the evidence is located on a stand-alone computer, the basic principle governing law enforcement's gaining access to the evidence is the Fourth Amendment, which protects citizens from "unreasonable" searches and seizures (LaFave, Israel, & King, 1999). If a seizure is "reasonable," it does not violate the Fourth Amendment (LaFave, Israel, & King, 1999). To be "reasonable," a search or seizure conducted by law enforcement agents must be carried out either under the authority of a search warrant or under one of the exceptions to the warrant requirement, such as consent (LaFave, Israel, & King, 1999). So, assume federal agents are investigating allegations that John Doe has child pornography on his home computer. In scenario 1, they have gathered enough information to establish probable cause to believe there is child pornography on his computer. They take that information to a magistrate—in the form of an application for a search warrant and a sworn affidavit attesting to their probable cause—and obtain a warrant to search for and seize child pornography (LaFave, Israel, & King 1999). They take the warrant to John Doe's house and conduct the search either onsite, at his home, or seize his computer and take it away for an offsite search. In scenario 2, the agents either do not have enough information to establish the probable cause they need to get a warrant or prefer to proceed without a warrant. They approach John Doe and ask him if they can search his computer; if he consents, he waives his Fourth Amendment rights and surrenders his ability to object to the search at a later date (LaFave, Israel, & King, 1999).

The process of gathering evidence is far more complex when the evidence is located on a network or on several networks (Dean, 2003). Continuing the example used above, assume the agents have received information that John Doe is corresponding online with minors whom he sends child pornography and whom he arranges to meet for the purposes of having sexual relations. The agents could proceed as outlined above with regard to evidence located on John Doe's computer, but they also need information about his e-mail contacts with the minors. To learn about that, they need information from Doe's Internet service provider (ISP). Because the Supreme Court has held that the Fourth Amendment does not apply to records held by a third party, the agents are not constitutionally required to get a warrant to obtain the information they need from the Internet service provider (LaFave, Israel, & King, 1999). But because Congress was concerned about unrestricted law enforcement access to records, it adopted a series of statutes—the Electronic Communications Privacy Act of 1986 (ECPA)—which require law enforcement to go through certain procedures to get evidence from an Internet service provider and others who provide electronic communications services (Electronic Communications Privacy Act). Under ECPA, the agents will have to use a search warrant, a subpoena, or a court order to obtain the information they need from the Internet service provider (Dean, 2003). ECPA sets up different requirements for different types of information, but the critical difference between it and the Fourth Amendment is that agents can often use either a subpoena or a court order, neither of which requires probable cause, to get the information they require (Electronic Communications Privacy Act).

The process of introducing electronic evidence, such as that described above, at trial is a very complex one which is quite beyond the scope of this chapter. Generally, for evidence to be admissible at trial it must be (a) relevant, (b) authentic, and (c) reliable (*Daubert v. Merrell Dow Pharmaceuticals, Inc.*, 1993). The issue of relevance is seldom problematic; evidence is "relevant" when it tends to prove the fact for which it is offered (i.e., child pornography was found on John Doe's computer) and when that fact is material to an element in the case (i.e., John Doe is being prosecuted for possessing child pornography; Mueller & Kilpatrick, 2003). Authenticity can be problematic, because digital evidence can be altered easily, the party offering digital evidence must be able to establish that it is what it is claimed to be (U.S. Department of Justice Computer Crime and Intellectual Property Section, 2002). To establish this and rebut defense claims that evidence has been altered, the prosecution will typically establish a chain of custody for the evidence; that is, the prosecution will typically trace the processes that were used to find the evidence and retrieve it from a computer or from a network (U.S. Department of Justice Computer Crime and Intellectual Property Section, 2002). Establishing a chain of custody authenticates digital evidence by showing that it was never left unsecured in conditions that would have permitted its alteration (U.S. Department of Justice Computer Crime and Intellectual Property Section, 2002) Reliability raises similar concerns; the defense may, for example, claim that a computer-generated record that the prosecution is offering as evidence is not reliable because the program used to create it contained serious programming errors (U.S. Department of Justice Computer Crime and Intellectual Property Section, 2002). For the prosecution to overcome such a challenge and establish the reliability of the record in question, it will have to establish that the computer program did, in fact, meet the requisite standard of reliability (U.S. Department of Justice Computer Crime and Intellectual Property Section, 2002).

Sentencing

As explained, sentencing is done by a judge; in imposing sentence, a judge is guided by a set of rules that define either the required sentence or an allowable range of sentences (LaFave et al., 1999). There are four basic rationales for inflicting punishment on offenders: incapacitation (to physically prevent this person from reoffending), deterrence (to discourage this person and others from committing similar crimes), rehabilitation (to educate the person so that he/she no longer desires to commit crimes), and retribution (to retaliate for the harm the offender has caused) (LaFave, 2003). Since the 1980s, sentencing in the federal and state systems has been based on deterrence, retribution, and incapacitation, a reaction against rehabilitation, which had been the primary rationale for sentencing since the 19th century. A new approach began in the 1970s and culminated in the adoption of new sentencing provisions that emphasize the need to deter and incapacitate offenders and society's need for retribution (Vitiello, 1991).

Victims and their families have increasingly been given input into the sentencing process; the federal system and most states either permit or require the use of victim impact statements, which assess a crime's impact on the victim and the victim's family at sentencing (LaFave et al., 1999). This practice extends to cybercrime cases; in the federal system, for example, victims of criminal copyright infringement are statutorily guaranteed the right to submit a victim impact statement documenting their losses prior to sentencing (U.S. Department of Justice Computer Crime and Intellectual Property Section, 2001).

In 2003, three groups submitted a statement to the U.S. Sentencing Commission arguing that those convicted of computer crimes are already being punished more severely than those convicted of similar crimes that do not involve the use of computer technology (National Association of Criminal Defense Lawyers, Electronic Frontier Foundation & Sentencing Project 2003). The statement argued against increasing penalties for federal computer crimes (a) because the incidence of computer crime is low, (b) because loss calculations currently in use lead to disproportionate sentences that do not accurately reflect the offender's culpability, and (c) because harsh penalties can "chill legitimate computer research, business development, and reporting on security vulnerabilities" (National Association of Criminal Defense Lawyers, Electronic Frontier Foundation & Sentencing Project, 2003). The Sentencing Commission ultimately responded by increasing the penalties for certain of the cybercrime offenses defined by federal law (U.S. Sentencing Commission, 2003). The Commission found that the amendments reflected the "serious and risky nature of many computer offenses" (U.S. Sentencing Commission, 2003).

RELATIONSHIP BETWEEN STATE AND FEDERAL CRIMINAL JUSTICE SYSTEMS

The United States has over 50 legal systems, each with its own definitions of "crimes." The federal system traditionally dealt with a limited set of "crimes" that protected special federal interests, such as the integrity of the currency (counterfeiting), the safety of federal officials (assassination), the viability of the taxing scheme (tax fraud), and the nation's security from its enemies (treason and espionage) (American Bar Association, 1998). There has been a tremendous expansion in federal crimes over the past century. The primary basis for this expansion has been the commerce clause of the Constitution, which lets the federal government regulate matters that can negatively affect the country's ability to sustain and engage in interstate or foreign commerce (American Bar Association, 1998). Using this power, the federal system has criminalized hacking and related crimes and has used more generic offenses (such as wire fraud and the interstate transportation of stolen property) to pursue cybercriminals (American Bar Association, 1998).

The federal government's exclusive power to criminalize conduct is limited to a few areas, including those noted above; except for these areas, both the federal and state governments can outlaw certain types of activity (American Bar Association, 1998). The drafters of the Constitution intended that criminal activity be prosecuted primarily at the state level; they saw federal criminal jurisdiction as an exception to this principle that should be carefully restricted in scope (American Bar Association, 1998). Consequently, notwithstanding the expansion in substantive federal criminal law, states still retain primary responsibility for defining and prosecuting criminal activity (American Bar Association, 1998).

Because both the federal and state governments can outlaw certain types of activity, including cybercrime, a defendant can be prosecuted by the federal government and a state government for offenses rising out of the same course of conduct; as noted, prosecutions by separate governments do not violate the prohibition on double jeopardy (LaFave et al., 1999). To prevent unfairness, the Department of Justice has adopted a policy—known as the *Petite* policy—which bars federal prosecution after a state prosecution unless certain conditions are met (LaFave et al., 1999). Basically, a subsequent federal prosecution will be barred unless the case involves a substantial federal interest that was not vindicated in the prior prosecution and unless an assistant attorney general approves the prosecution (LaFave et al., 1999).

CRIMINAL JUSTICE SYSTEM AND CYBERCRIME

Federal Cybercrime Law

The basic federal cybercrime statute is 18 U.S. Code §1030. Section 1030(a) makes it a federal offense to (1) knowingly access a computer without authorization and obtain information that can be used to the disadvantage of the United States and deliver it to someone not entitled to it; (2) intentionally access a computer without authorization and obtain information contained in a financial record; (3) intentionally and without authorization access a computer used exclusively by a federal agency; (4) knowingly with the intent to defraud access a computer without authorization and obtain anything of value unless the thing obtained is only the use of the computer and does not exceed $5,000 in any 1-year period; (5) *either* (a) knowingly cause a program, information, or code to be transmitted and intentionally damage a computer, intentionally access a computer without authorization and recklessly cause damage, *or* intentionally access a computer without authorization and cause damage *and* (b) cause or attempt to cause physical injury, modification of a medical diagnosis, loss aggregating $5,000 in 1 year, a threat to public health or safety or damage to a computer used in furtherance of the administration of justice, national security, or national defense; (6) knowingly and with intent to defraud traffic in a password if the trafficking affects interstate commerce or the password can be used to access a federal government computer; and (7) transmit a threat to damage a computer with the intent to extort any thing of value.

Another important area is copyright law; copyright gives the author of a creative work the exclusive right to control its use for a fixed period of time (U.S. Department of Justice Computer Crime and Intellectual Property Section, 2001). Copyright derives from the Constitution and is therefore exclusively federal (U.S. Department of Justice Computer Crime and Intellectual Property Section, 2001). It is a crime for someone willfully to infringe a copyright for purposes of commercial advantage or private financial gain or by reproducing or distributing one or more copies of one or more copyrighted works having a total retail value in excess of $1,000 during any 180-day period (U.S. Department of Justice Computer Crime and Intellectual Property Section, 2001).

Child pornography is another priority: federal law has long criminalized obscenity, which is considered to be outside the First Amendment's protection of free speech; in 1982, the Supreme Court held that pornography portraying minors engaging in sexually explicit activity can be criminalized even though it is not obscene (*New York v. Ferber*, 1982). The *Ferber* Court held that child pornography can be criminalized because its production inflicts physical and emotional abuse on the children involved. In 2002, the Supreme Court struck down a federal statute—18 U.S. Code §2252A—that criminalized the possession and distribution of "virtual" child pornography (i.e., pornography created using morphed or other artificial images of children) (*Ashcroft v. Free Speech Coalition*, 2002). The Court found that the statute violated the First Amendment because (a) the material was not obscene and (b) no real children were harmed in its creation (*Ashcroft v. Free Speech Coalition*, 2002). Congress has since adopted legislation reinstituting the ban on virtual child pornography; its constitutionality is uncertain (Feldmeier, 2003).

State Cybercrime Law

Every state prohibits hacking (unauthorized access to a computer system) and cracking (unauthorized access to commit theft, damage, or other offenses) (Brenner, 2001). States tend to distinguish between basic unauthorized access (simple hacking) and unauthorized access that results in the commission of some further criminal activity, such as copying or destroying data (aggravated hacking), defining the two as distinct crimes (Brenner, 2001). They generally make simple hacking a misdemeanor and aggravated hacking a felony (Brenner, 2001).

A number of states outlaw the dissemination of viruses, worms, and other types of malware (Brenner, 2001). Many lump varieties of malware into one category: "computer contaminant" (Brenner, 2001). California, for example, defines it as "any set of computer instructions that are designed to modify, damage, destroy, record, or transmit information within a computer, computer system, or computer network without the intent or permission of the owner of the information" (California Penal Code, 2003).

States vary widely in how they criminalize the use of computers to commit traditional crimes, such as theft and forgery (Brenner, 2001). Some states outlaw computer forgery as a distinct offense. New Jersey makes it a crime to possess "forgery devices," which include computers, computer equipment, and computer software "specifically designed or adapted to such use" (Brenner, 2001). A substantial number outlaw using computers to commit fraud. Instead of making computer fraud a separate crime, a few states increase the penalties for aggravated hacking if the offense was committed for the purpose of devising or executing a scheme to defraud (Brenner, 2001). Many states outlaw "computer theft," which encompasses several different crimes, including information theft, software theft, computer hardware theft, and theft of computer services (Brenner, 2001). A number of states have "identity theft" or "identity fraud" statutes and some make it a crime to traffic in stolen identities (Brenner, 2001).

Cyberstalking is using computer technology to stalk or harass someone. A number of states outlaw cyberstalking (Brenner, 2001). Some criminalize "computer invasion of privacy," which typically consists of using a computer to examine "employment, salary, credit or any other financial or personal information" pertaining to another person (Brenner, 2001). A few make it a crime to introduce false information into a computer for the purpose of "damaging or enhancing" someone's "financial reputation" (Brenner, 2001). Some states have a "misuse of computer information" offense that prohibits copying, receiving, or using information that was obtained by violating a hacking or cracking statute (Brenner, 2001).

A surprising number of states have an "offense against computer equipment or supplies," which consists of modifying or destroying "equipment or supplies that are . . . intended to be used in a computer" (Brenner, 2001). A number make it a crime to deny or disrupt computer services or access to a computer and a few make it a crime to destroy computer equipment (Brenner, 2001).

Defenses

As explained, defendants in cybercrime cases can avail themselves of traditional "failure of proof" and "affirmative defenses" to the extent the facts of the case support the assertion of such a claim. This means, for example, that one who has been charged with hacking can defend on the basis that (a) his access to the computer in question was authorized, (b) he did not know his access to the computer in question was not authorized, or (c) he knew his access to the computer in question was not authorized but believed his hacking was justified.

Cybercrime defendants also raise less traditional defenses, two of which merit discussion here. One involves the nature of theft: in an Oregon case, a defendant was charged with computer theft for copying a password file belonging to Intel, his employer; he challenged the legal sufficiency of the charge, claiming that *copying* the file did not constitute *stealing* the file (*State v. Schwartz*, 2001). He pointed out that the essence of "theft" is depriving the rightful owner of property of its possession and use and argued that because Intel still had the file he had not deprived Intel of its property (*State v. Schwartz*, 2001). The court disagreed, holding that he did commit theft, albeit theft of intangible property (*State v. Schwartz*, 2001). This argument illustrates how computer technology can challenge the assumptions that have historically animated criminal law; with intangible property, theft ceases to be a zero-sum event. Therefore, instead of drafting theft statutes to reach a deprivation of tangible property, it becomes necessary to utilize a diminution theory (i.e., that the defendant deprived the rightful owner of some quantum of the value of his property, such as the right to its exclusive use).

Another approach is the Trojan horse defense, which as been notably successful in the United Kingdom. In 2003, Aaron Caffrey, a 19-year-old British hacker, was prosecuted for launching a denial of service attack that shut down computer systems at the Port of Houston (Questions cloud cybercrime cases, 2003). His defense was that a hacker had used a Trojan horse program to take over his computer and launch the attack. Even though experts found no trace of a Trojan on the computer, a jury acquitted Caffrey of the charges against him (Questions cloud cybercrime cases, 2003). The same theory was used successfully in several child pornography prosecutions in the United Kingdom (Bean, 2003). An American accountant was acquitted of charges of filing false tax returns because he convinced the jury that a computer virus was responsible for the errors on the returns (Auditor acquitted, 2003). These cases raise a difficult issue for prosecutors: how is it possible to prove beyond a reasonable doubt that no Trojan horse or virus was responsible for the crime charged? Some argue that the solution lies in scanning the computer to determine if it contains a Trojan horse or other type of malware; if it does, then it would be necessary to determine if the malware could do what it is claimed to have done (The Trojan horse defense in child pornography, 2003). If the computer does not contain malware capable of having committed the crime, so the argument goes, then the jury should convict (The Trojan horse defense in child pornography, 2003). Of course, Aaron Caffrey was acquitted even though experts found no trace of a Trojan on his computer. The Trojan horse and related defenses illustrate the difficulties that can be involved in presenting highly technical evidence to a lay jury; some have suggested that the solution lies in bench trials, but because of the Sixth Amendment, that option remains solely with the defendant ("Trust me, I'm an IT expert," 2003).

Other Problematic Areas

Clearly, the most challenging aspect of cybercrime as far as law enforcement is concerned is its pronounced tendency to cross borders, especially national borders (Brenner & Schwerha, 2002). Law is territorially based, whether it is national or the law adopted by a component state in a federal system like the United States (Brenner & Schwerha, 2002). Cybercrime's ability to transcend national borders created problems for cybercrime investigators and prosecutors.

There are two ways to obtain evidence from another country. One is informal cooperation; the other is relying on the formal mechanisms that have traditionally been used to gather evidence (Brenner & Schwerha, 2002). A 1994 case illustrates informal cooperation: in 1994, system administrators at the Rome Air Development Center in New York found hackers had installed password sniffers on the Rome Labs networks (Brenner & Schwerha, 2002). The Air Force's Office of Special Investigations (AFOSI) used informants to identify one of the hackers, a 16-year-old from the United Kingdom (Brenner & Schwerha, 2002). Having established a relationship with New Scotland Yard, AFOSI agents contacted them (Brenner & Schwerha, 2002). Working together, AFOSI and New Scotland Yard developed probable cause to believe evidence of the intrusions would be found at the juvenile's home; New Scotland Yard used this information to get a warrant to search his residence (Brenner & Schwerha, 2002). They executed the warrant and seized incriminating evidence; Pryce was prosecuted and eventually pled guilty to 12 counts of hacking (Brenner & Schwerha, 2002).

Traditionally, informal cooperation depended on networking; few local police officers had the opportunity to network with officers from abroad (Brenner & Schwerha, 2002). In cybercrime cases, officers who have never had the opportunity to network with officers from other countries may find they need assistance from abroad. To meet this need, two entities—Interpol and the G8—have established 24 networks officers can use to obtain assistance from officers in other countries (Brenner & Schwerha, 2002). These networks qualify as informal cooperation because they bypass the processes discussed below (Brenner & Schwerha, 2002). As is explained below, informal cooperation is usually the most expeditious way to proceed.

The basic formal devices are requests for assistance submitted under mutual legal assistance treaties (MLATs) and letters rogatory (Brenner & Schwerha, 2002). An investigator's first step is determining if an MLAT encompassing the evidence to be sought is in effect between the United States and the country where the evidence is located. Using an MLAT is much faster than the letter rogatory procedure (U.S. Department of Justice, 1999). If an MLAT is in effect, the investigator must prepare a request for assistance pursuant to the treaty; it contains essentially the same information as that used for a letter rogatory, which is described below, except for the promise of reciprocity (U.S. Department of Justice, 1999). If an MLAT is not in effect, the investigator will have to resort to the letter rogatory process.

A letter rogatory is a request from a U.S. judge to a judge in another country requesting the performance of acts that would be illegal without local judicial approval (U.S. Department of Justice, 1999). The investigator must complete the letter rogatory and have it transmitted to authorities in the country from which assistance is being sought (U.S. Department of Justice, 1999). Letters rogatory are usually transmitted through diplomatic channels, which is one reason why they are such a time-consuming method of obtaining assistance; the Department of Justice warns federal prosecutors it may take a year or more to obtain assistance through a letter rogatory (U.S. Department of Justice, 1999).

Formal methods of obtaining evidence are far too time consuming to be effective in cybercrime cases, and informal methods, even when supplemented by the efforts of Interpol and the G8, can be unreliable (U.S. Department of Justice, 1999). This is part of a larger problem, namely that the laws of varying nations are inconsistent.

That was the problem in investigating the Love Bug virus, which spread around the world in May 2000 (Brenner & Schwerha, 2002). U.S. experts traced the virus to the Philippines; when FBI agents arrived there, they worked with local authorities to investigate Onel de Guzman, the primary suspect. Informal cooperation between the officers worked splendidly; the problem came with the Philippine legal system (Brenner & Schwerha, 2002). At that time, the Philippines criminal code did not criminalize hacking or the dissemination of viruses; laws to that effect were enacted after this incident. This presented several problems: investigators had difficulty getting a warrant to search de Guzman's apartment because warrants authorize searches for evidence of "crimes" and virus dissemination was not then a crime (Brenner & Schwerha, 2002). The officers eventually got the warrant and conducted the search, but then they had to decide what to charge de Guzman with. He was charged with fraud and theft, but the charges were dismissed (Brenner & Schwerha, 2002). Because de Guzman could not be prosecuted locally, he could not be extradited for prosecution elsewhere; no one was ever prosecuted for the damage caused by the Love Bug (Brenner & Schwerha, 2002).

Many believe the only way to achieve an internationally effective response to cybercrime is to harmonize national laws so they are consistent in how they (a) define cybercrime offenses and (b) specify what law enforcement officers can and cannot do in gathering evidence in cybercrime investigations (Brenner & Schwerha, 2002). So far, the most notable achievement in this effort is the Council of Europe's Convention on Cybercrime. Parties to the Convention, which is not limited to European nations, agree to take such "legislative or other measures" as are necessary to outlaw certain types of computer-facilitated criminal activity (Brenner & Schwerha, 2002). They also agree to take similar measures to ensure that they can preserve and collect evidence and provide assistance in cybercrime investigations even when no MLAT is in force between the requesting country and the requested country (Brenner & Schwerha, 2002). So far, 34 countries, including the United States, Canada, and Japan, have signed the Convention (Brenner & Schwerha, 2002). It goes into effect when it has been ratified by 5 countries, 3 of which are members of the Council of Europe; it has been ratified by 3 countries, all of which are members of the Council of Europe (Brenner & Schwerha, 2002).

CONCLUSION

Cybercrime presents challenges not only for the U.S. legal system: because cybercrime so easily and so often transcends national borders, cybercriminals can take advantage of gaps or inconsistencies in national law in an effort to evade apprehension and/or prosecution. It will not be easy to resolve the challenges cybercrime presents for the criminal justice system, here and abroad. As this chapter demonstrates, cybercrime requires the extrapolation of legal principles that were developed to deal with activity occurring in the real, tangible world; it will also, no doubt, require the articulation of new principles that are especially designed to deal with the novel ways criminal activity can manifest itself in the online world.

GLOSSARY

Affirmative Defense A legal doctrine that lets a defendant avoid liability even though he or she committed a crime; self-defense is an example.

Bench Trial A trial in which the judge, not a jury, acts as the finder of fact; in a bench trial the judge decides whether the defendant is guilty or innocent.

Beyond a Reasonable Doubt The standard of proof in criminal trials; the prosecution must prove beyond a reasonable doubt that the defendant committed the crime(s) charged; if the prosecution fails the finder of fact must acquit the defendant.

Computer Virus Computer program code that copies itself and spreads by attaching itself to a another computer program; a virus can alter or delete data or interfere with the operation of a computer.

Council of Europe Created in 1949, the Council of Europe brings together 45 European countries; among other things, the Council works to standardize social and legal practices across its member countries.

Cyberstalking The use of a computer and the Internet to stalk or harass someone, often by sending them harassing e-mails.

Double Jeopardy A constitutional prohibition that bars a government from trying someone more than once for the "same offence."

G-8 The major industrial democracies (the United States, Britain, Germany, France, Japan, Italy, Canada, and Russia) have joined together to address the political and economic issues they all face; officials from the member countries meet periodically to discuss these issues and formulate policies.

Hacking Gaining access to a computer or computer system without authorization; hacking is analogous to trespassing in the real world.

Intellectual Property In most countries, laws give the creators of intangible products—such as books, movies, and software—property rights in those products; the property rights can be sold or licensed, but they have the same legal status as ownership of tangible property, such as a house or a car.

Intellectual Property Crime In most countries, it is a crime to take someone's intellectual property without their permission or to use intellectual property in a way that is not authorized by the owner.

Interpol Interpol is an international police organization that was created in 1923; it is financed by its 181 member countries and coordinates law enforcement efforts around the world.

Jury Trial A trial in which a group of civilians, usually twelve in number, act as the finder of fact; in a jury trial these jurors decide whether the defendant is guilty or innocent.

Plea Bargain An arrangement in which a defendant pleads guilty, usually to a crime of lesser severity than that charged in the indictment; typically, plea bargains include a requirement that the defendant cooperate with the government by providing evidence against others.

Preponderance of the Evidence The standard of proof in civil trials; in civil trials, the plaintiff must present proof that establishes that her case is "more likely than not" to be true.

Sentencing Guidelines Rules adopted in the federal system and in most states that guide what judges can do in sentencing someone for an offense; they tend to require that a judge impose a specific sentence, based on various factors, instead of setting a range of time someone must serve.

Victim Impact Statement A statement submitted as part of the sentencing process; it is designed to show how the crime impacted on the victim's life and, where appropriate, on the victim's family.

CROSS REFERENCES

See *Cyberlaw: The Major Areas, Development, and Information Security Aspects; Cyberterrorism and Information Security; Law Enforcement and Computer Security Threats and Measures; Online Stalking; Privacy Law and the Internet.*

REFERENCES

American Bar Association. (2003). *Model rules of professional conduct*. Washington, DC: American Bar Association.

American Bar Association Task Force. (1998). *The federalization of criminal law*. Washington, DC: American Bar Association.

Ashcroft v. Free Speech Coalition. 535 U.S. 234. (2002).

Auditor Acquitted. (2003). *Computer cops*. Retrieved December 18, 2003, from http://www.computercops.biz/article2946.html

Bean, M. (2003). The Trojan horse: A viral defense? Retrieved December 18, 2003, from http://www.cnn.com/2003/LAW/08/12/ctv.trojan/

Beauprez, J. (2003, November 3). New rules cut hackers less slack. *Denver Post*. E01

Brenner, S. W. (2001). State cybercrime legislation in the United States of America: A survey. *Richmond Journal of Law & Technology, 7*, 28–36.

Brenner, S. W., & Schwerha, J. J., IV (2002). Transnational evidence gathering and local prosecution of international cybercrime. *John Marshall Journal of Computer and Information Law, 20*, 347–394.

California Penal Code. §502(b)(1). (2003).

Daubert v. Merrell Dow Pharmaceuticals, Inc. 509 U.S. 579. (1993).

Dean, S. W. (2003). Government surveillance of Internet communications: Pen register and trap and trace law under the Patriot Act. *Tulane Journal of Technology and Intellectual Property, 5*, 97–113.

Ditzion, R., Geddes, E., & Rhodes, M. (2003). Computer crimes. *American Criminal Law Review, 40*, 285–336.

Electronic Communications Privacy Act, Pub. L. No. 99-508, 100 Stat. 1848. (1986).

Esbenshade, P. W. (2002–2003). Hacking: Juveniles and undeterred recreational cybercrime. *Journal of Juvenile Law, 23*, 52–64.

Federal Bureau of Investigation, Infragard, http://www.infragard.net/.

Feldmeier, J. P. (2003). Close enough for government work: An examination of congressional efforts to reduce the government's burden of proof in child pornography cases. *Northern Kentucky Law Review, 30*, 205–227.

Goldman, A. (1995, July 2). Computer hacker agrees to plea bargain, lawyer says. *Los Angeles Times B3*.

Hans, V. P. (2002). U.S. jury reform: The active jury and the adversarial ideal. *St. Louis University Public Law Review, 21*, 85–96.

Hine, K. D. (1998). Vigilantism revisited: An economic analysis of the law of extra-judicial self-help. *American University Law Review, 47*, 1221–1253.

H.R. 5211. (2002). A Bill to Amend Title 17 of the U.S. Code (107th Congress, 2d Session).

Kahn, M. A. (2004). May the best merchandise win: The law of non-trademark uses of sports logos. *Marquette Sports Law Review, 14*, 283–317.

LaFave, W. R. (2003). *Substantive criminal law*. St. Paul, MN: West Group.

LaFave, W. R., Israel, J. H., & King, N. J. (1999). *Criminal procedure*. St. Paul, MN: West Group.

Loomis, C. (2001). Appropriate response: More questions than answers. Retrieved December 16, 2003, http://www.securityfocus.com/infocus/1516

Miami Electronic Crimes Task Force. (2003). Retrieved December 10, 2003, from http://www.facci.org/usss_ectf.htm

Mueller, C. B., & Kilpatrick, L. C. (2003). Federal evidence.

National Association of Attorneys General—Computer Crime. Retrieved December 12, 2003, from http://www.naag.org/issues/20010724-cc_list_bg.php

National Association of Criminal Defense Lawyers, Electronic Frontier Foundation & Sentencing Project. (2003). Commentary on Homeland Security Act of 2002. Retrieved December 18, 2003, http://www.eff.org/Legislation/CFAA/1030_Comments_3-17-03.pdf

New York v. Ferber 458 U.S. 747. (1982).

Nicholson, L., Shebar, T., & Weinberg, J. (2000). Computer Crimes, *American Criminal Law Review, 37*, 207–259.

Questions cloud cybercrime cases. (2003). BBC News. Retrieved December 18, 2003, from http://news.bbc.co.uk/1/hi/technology/3202116.stm

Reuters Wired News. (2003). Helpful hacker will surrender. Retrieved December 12, 2003, from http://www.wired.com/news/privacy/0,1848,60334,00. html

Right to jury trial. (2003). *Georgetown Law Journal, 91*, 489–512.

Roberts, P. (2003). Homeless hacker heads to court. PC World.com. Retrieved December 11, 2003, from http://www.pcworld.com/news/article/0,aid,112442,00.asp

Romano, L. (2004, February 29). New Trial of 1995 Oklahoma Bombing to Open. Washington Post A15.

Smith v. Hooey 393 U.S. 374. (1969).

State v. Perry 83 Ohio St.3d 41, 697 N.E.2d 624. (Ohio 1998).

State v. Schwartz 173 Or. App. 301, 21 P.3d 1128 (Or. App.). (2001).

The Trojan horse defense in child pornography. (2003). NewsMax.com. Retreived December 18, 2003, from http://www.newsmax.com/archives/articles/2003/8/12/204345.shtml

Trust me, I'm an IT expert. (2003). Silicon.com. Retrieved December 18, 2003, from http://www.silicon.com/ comment/0,39024711,10006460,00.htm

United States Constitution, Amendment IV.

U.S. Department of Justice. (1999). U.S. Attorney's Manual. Retrieved December 17, 2003, from http://www.usdoj.gov/usao/eousa/foia_reading_room/usam/title9/1mcrm.htm

U.S. Department of Justice Computer Crime and Intellectual Property Section. (2001). Prosecuting intellectual property crimes manual. Retrieved December 10, 2003, http://www.cybercrime.gov/ipmanual.htm

U.S. Department of Justice Computer Crime and Intellectual Property Section. (2002). Searching and Seizing Computers and Obtaining Electronic Evidence in Criminal Investigations. Retrieved from http://www.cybercrime.gov/s&smanual2002.htm

U.S. Sentencing Commission. (2003). Increased penalties for cyber security offenses. Retrieved December 18, 2003, from http://www.ussc.gov/r_congress/ cybercrime503.pdf

United States v. Czubinski 106 F.3d 1069 (1st Circuit). (1997).

United States v. Hicks 46 F.3d 1128 (4th Circuit). (1995).

United States Secret Service. (2004). Electronic crime task forces. Retrieved March 18, 2005, from http://www.ectaskforce.org/Regional_Locations.htm

Universal City Studios, Inc. v. Corley 273 F.3d 429 (2d Circuit 2001). (2001).

Vitiello, M. (1991). Reconsidering rehabilitation. *Tulane Law Review, 65*, 1011–1054.

Ying-Cheng, J. (2001, February 21). Man pleads "self-defense" after hacking. *Taipei Times*.

Cyberterrorism and Information Security

Charles Jaeger, *Southern Oregon University*

INTRODUCTION

In the past several years, the world has come face to face with terrorists who are becoming more extreme. At the same time, the world has become increasingly dependent on using computers and networks to manage the way we work, communicate, and live. Terrorism, used throughout human history in one form or another, has found a powerful new weapon.

Although most terrorist organizations remain either national or regional, cyberspace gives them tools to become global in reach and coordination. A cyberattacked nuclear power plant meltdown, a massive air traffic control shutdown, a dam spillway opened to flood downstream cities, or other cyber-based terrorist acts could entail even greater loss of life than the September 11, 2001, attacks. Cyberterrorists—an unknown, unseen enemy who strike from anywhere, anytime, and disappear like a vapor trail and is difficult to trace and bring to justice, with devastation potentially as destructive as poison gas, deadly diseases, truckloads of explosives, and atomic radiation—may evoke even more dread and terror than the conventional terrorist.

This chapter asks whether it is reasonable to conclude that global terrorism and cyberspace will converge in this deadly intersection. It attempts to present a balanced view of what constitutes cyberterrorism and the extent of the threat. It addresses how cyberattacks are possible on physical infrastructure or other vital facilities and explores the support role of cyberspace in conventional terrorism. It discusses how government, businesses, institutions, schools and universities, private interest groups, and individuals can each play a role in combating cyberterrorism.

Academic research on cyberterrorism is in its early stages. In the fast-moving world of cyberspace, formal research lags behind current events. Information sources for this chapter include scholarly journals and survey data where available, with up-to-date information from news reports and government or institutional Web sites.

The chapter begins by introducing potential terrorist acts and assessing sometimes confusing levels of threat. It asks whether fears of cyberterrorism are exaggerated and proceeds to formulate working definitions of cyberterrorism, which set a foundation for discussing how terrorism in cyberspace occurs and its relationships to asymmetric response and cyberwarfare. It follows this by showing some of the things individuals, companies, organizations, and government can do and how they can work together to help control the cyberterrorism threat.

The Cyberterrorism Threat

On August 14, 2003, 50 million people in the northeastern United States lost electrical power—the biggest electrical blackout in U.S. history—including the core of America's financial network. Police responded to 80,000 emergency (911) calls on September 11, 2005 (9/11), more than double the usual number, and firefighters made more than 800 elevator rescues (Kaplan, 2003). Some in the media speculated that Al Qaeda and other terrorists were beginning a wave of cyberattacks to disable the country's physical infrastructure; 50 million victims would be a big story. It played on conspiracy theory in a post-9/11 world.

On September 14, 2004, an air traffic blackout in the Los Angeles Air Route Traffic Control Center created chaos in much of the western United States, including reported near misses and "almost near-mid-air collisions . . . as helpless controllers watched in disbelief" (Associated Press, 2004). Communication was lost with some 800 airplanes in flight (Wald, 2004). Could cyberterrorists be on the attack?

Responsible news organizations soon ruled out terrorism in both cases. The electrical blackout was attributed to faulty tree trimming and vulnerable design deficiencies in an aging grid infrastructure (Reuters, 2003). The air traffic problems resulted from neglected computer maintenance. In the long term, however, these incidents make people think: Was there a reasonable basis for concern that terrorists could compromise the power grid or other vital physical infrastructure through cyberattacks? Could they do something even worse?

Acts That May Be Cyberterrorism

In 1996, Barry C. Collin, who takes credit for coining the term *cyberterrorism* in the mid-1980s, wrote, "This enemy does not attack us with truckloads of explosives, nor with briefcases of Sarin gas, nor with dynamite strapped to the bodies of fanatics. This enemy attacks us with ones and zeros." He listed some potentially deadly acts of the cyberterrorist:

- Remotely changing the pressure in gas lines, causing valve failures, explosion, and fire.
- Placing computerized bombs around a city, all simultaneously transmitting unique numeric patterns, each bomb receiving each other's pattern. If any of the set of bombs stops transmitting, all the others detonate simultaneously, which effectively prevents disarming any of the bombs.
- Attacking future air traffic control systems to cause civilian jets to collide.

Cyberterrorists might open a dam's spillway to inundate downstream communities or cause a meltdown of a nuclear power plant. They might cause trains to crash into each other. These "ones and zeros" attacks, Collin said, could have violent and fearful physical effects equally or more devastating than those caused by truckloads of explosives, dynamite, or poison.

Collin included several acts in cyberspace that do *not* have devastating physical effects on a large scale but clearly have the potential to create widespread chaos and fear in offices, homes, and on the streets:

- Remotely accessing the processing control systems of a cereal manufacturer to alter the formula and sicken children.
- Disrupting banks and international financial institutions and stock exchanges, with resulting loss of confidence in the economic system.
- Remotely altering formulas of medication at pharmaceutical manufacturers, resulting in ineffective or potentially harmful medications.
- Shutting down the electrical grid, causing widespread chaos.

"In effect," Collin (1996) concluded, "the cyber-terrorist will make certain that the population of a nation will not be able to eat, to drink, to move, or to live. In addition, the people charged with the protection of their nation will not have warning, and will not be able to shut down the terrorist, since that cyber-terrorist is most likely on the other side of the world."

In 1998, Michael Vatis, director of the National Infrastructure Protection Center (NIPC), reportedly told a Senate subcommittee, "Tracing cyber-attacks is like 'tracking vapor'" (Christensen, 1999). Unknown and unseen, an enemy difficult to bring to justice connotes a lack of control that may make people more fearful.

Parks (2003) notes that attacks need not be confined to critical infrastructure, offering the example that a hacker could change the composition of vitamins at manufacture to include increasing an ingredient to a lethal level, and asks, "What if the cyber-terrorists were able to . . . attack . . . several hundreds of common products at the same time?"

Haimes (2002) separates cyberterrorism risks into three categories: (a) risk to critical cyberphysical infrastructure; (b) risk to organizational/societal infrastructures; and (c) risk to human lives and to individual property, liberty, and freedom. Physical infrastructure includes "manmade engineered systems that include telecommunications, electric power, gas and oil, transportation, water treatment plants, water distribution networks, dams, and levees." Threats include a list of potentially crippling adverse effects on society and loss of confidence in government institutions that could create chaos.

Other Warnings about Cyberterrorism

These warnings raise questions about our vulnerability to cyberterrorism. Fears were heightened by the September 11, 2001, attacks. In December 2001, a Luntz Research survey reported that 74% of Americans were concerned that a cyberattack could target critical infrastructure assets such as telephone networks or power plants. Harris Miller, president of the Information Technology Association of America (ITAA) said, "The attacks of Sept. 11 . . . destroyed peace of mind for many people using the Internet [and] is generating high anxiety in cyberspace" (Greenspan, 2002a; CyberAtlas, 2001).

In June 2002, the *Washington Post* published an article titled "Cyber-attacks by Al Qaeda Feared, Terrorists at the Threshold of Using Internet as Tool of Bloodshed." It reported that the FBI, working with experts at the Lawrence Livermore National Laboratory, had been tracing a "suspicious pattern of surveillance against Silicon Valley computers by unknown browsers," mostly emanating from the Middle East and South Asia, targeting digital systems used to manage Bay Area utilities and other physical infrastructure. "Routed through telecommunications switches in Saudi Arabia, Indonesia and Pakistan, the visitors studied emergency telephone systems, electrical generation and transmission, water storage and distribution, nuclear power plants and gas facilities." The article said that additional information turned up on computers seized from Al Qaeda and on sympathetic Web sites. Roger Cressey, then chief of staff of the President's Critical Infrastructure Protection Board reportedly said, "Al Qaeda spent more time mapping our vulnerabilities in cyberspace than we previously thought. An attack is a question of when, not if" (Gellman, 2002).

The same article reported that in 1998 a 12-year-old hacker had taken "complete command" of Arizona's Roosevelt Dam and the system controlling floodgates holding back 489 trillion gallons of water, enough to flood Phoenix, Mesa, and Tempe (accurate facts are given later in this chapter). In a separate incident in the early 1990s, a man reportedly had "turned his vehicle into a pirate command center" for the sewage treatment center in Queensland, Australia, and used the digital controls to release thousands of gallons of sewage into parks and streams. Manuals for the digital control systems, the article said, were available on the Web, and "nearly identical systems run [U.S.] oil and gas utilities and many manufacturing plants." The North American power grid, described as "the most complex machine ever built," was identified as a potential target.

In October 2001, Richard Clarke, then White House security advisor and chairman of President Bush's Critical Infrastructure Protection Board, had claimed that cyberattacks on the nation's critical information technology infrastructure could cause "catastrophic damage to the economy" akin to the "functional equivalent of 767's crashing into buildings" (Johnson & Radcliff, 2001). In February 2002, testifying to the U.S. Senate, Clarke had warned, "Every sector of the U.S. economy and government has moved onto network systems . . . and nothing can operate unless the networks are functioning correctly. However, none of these things were designed with 'security in mind'" (Wynne, 2002).

In July 2002, the U.S. Naval War College and Gartner had carried out a "digital Pearl Harbor" war game to test the vulnerability of the U.S. infrastructure to a cyberterrorist attack. In a postgame survey, 79% of the participants said that a strategic cyberattack is likely within the next 2 years (Gartner, 2002).

Clarke had used the term *digital Pearl Harbor* in 1997 during operation "Eligible Receiver," a military exercise in which 35 hackers hired by the National Security Agency simulated attacks on the U.S electronic infrastructure and reportedly achieved "root-level" access in 36 of the Department of Defense's 40,000 networks, "turned off" sections of the U.S. power grid, "shut down" parts of the 9-1-1 emergency response network in Washington, DC, and other cities, and broke into computer systems aboard a Navy cruiser at sea (Christensen, 1999).

At the National Cyber Security Summit in December 2003, Secretary Tom Ridge of the Department of Homeland Security (DHS) cautioned, "A vast electronic nervous system operates much of our nation's physical infrastructure. Everything from electricity grids to banking transactions to telecommunications depends on secure, reliable cyber networks. These networks and the infrastructures they support present an attractive target for terrorists. They know, as we do, that a few lines of code could ultimately wreak as much havoc as a handful of bombs" (CERT, 2003b).

A leading journal reported a finding by the Center for Strategic & International Studies that "all it would take to decimate the technological infrastructure of the U.S. economy is fewer than 30 computer hackers strategically placed around the world and a budget of less than $10 million." It noted that research firm IDC estimated "there are 1.3 million people worldwide who possess the skills needed to launch a cyber attack" (*Information Management Journal*, 2002b).

This background, Collin's warnings, and incidents such as the electrical grid failure in 2002 and the shutdown of the air traffic control in 2004 raise questions about our vulnerability to cyberterrorism. But a media hungry for attention, agencies seeking increased budgets, and security products vendors all have something to gain. Other voices question whether the cyberterrorism threat is exaggerated.

Exaggerated Threats?

In an overview of the cyberterrorism threat, Lemos (2002) investigated facts surrounding the *Washington Post* story about the 12-year-old hacker who allegedly had control of Arizona's Roosevelt Dam and its 489 trillion gallons of water. Lemos reported that the hacker was 27, not 12, and the incident occurred in 1994, not 1998. Furthermore, "While clearly trespassing in critical areas, the hacker never could have had control of any dams—leading investigators to conclude that no lives or property were ever threatened." The Australian incident, it turns out, involved a former employee with access to a stolen copy of the control software.

Lemos (2002) notes that experts agree that it is easier to bomb a target than hack into a control system, and the results are more dramatic. He points out that the Digital Pearl Harbor exercise team determined that a successful effort would need significant resources—$200 million, high-level intelligence, and 5 years of preparation time—and may not result in enough high-value devastation. Those same participants who predicted a likely strategic cyberattack within the next 2 years finally concluded that "such an offense could cripple communications in a heavily populated area but would not result in deaths or other catastrophic consequences."

Denning (2001) supports that logic. "Although cyber terrorism is certainly a real possibility, for a terrorist, digital attacks have several drawbacks. Systems are complex, so controlling an attack and achieving a desired level of damage may be harder than using physical weapons. Unless people are killed or badly injured, there is also less drama and emotional appeal."

Lemos (2002) concludes that cyberterrorism "has become a catch-all buzzword that evokes nightmare images that can be exploited to support political agendas," including increased police power and funding for government departments and programs. He adds, "While warnings pervade government and the media, doomsday scenarios of cyberterrorism that result in massive deaths or injury remain largely the stuff of Hollywood scripts or conspiracy theory."

The *Wall Street Journal* used the term *terrorism-industrial complex* in reporting on the Digital Pearl Harbor exercise, saying, "It is the aim of this cluster of interests both to define 'terrorism' as a technological problem . . . and to convince everyone that various tech tools hold great promise in combating terrorism. Billions of dollars of federal 'homeland security' dollars are at stake" (Gomes, 2002).

Green, commenting on Richard Clarke's statements of alarm, Collin's predictions, the *Post* article, and other dire warnings says:

> There's just one problem: There is no such thing as cyberterrorism—no instance of anyone ever having been killed by a terrorist (or anyone else) using a computer. Nor is there compelling evidence that al Qaeda or any other terrorist organization has resorted to computers for any serious destructive activity. . . . It is virtually impossible to use the Internet to inflict death on a large scale, and many scoff at the notion that terrorists would bother trying. (Green, 2002)

He quotes a former Clarke colleague: "Dick has an ability to scare the bejusus out of everybody."

So, should cyberterrorism be considered a serious threat?

Lemos (2002) concedes that, although Collin's more extreme scenarios are unlikely, the threat of a cyberattack is real. "Many power companies and water utilities are operated with networks of computer-controlled devices, known as supervisory control and data acquisition (SCADA) systems, which could be hacked." These systems, which can dramatically lower the cost of network maintenance, provide a window for hackers and cyberterrorists, who might use them to attack the network and the devices attached to it.

Academic researchers support the media reports and heighten the concern. "Some of these [computer hackers] are aligning themselves with terrorists like bin Laden. While the vast majority of hackers may be disinclined towards violence, it would only take a few to turn cyber terrorism into reality. Further, the next generation of terrorists will grow up in a digital world, with even more powerful and easy-to-use hacking tools" (Denning, 2001).

In a typical lottery, although the odds of winning are very low, someone eventually gets the right numbers. Hackers, even with the odds stacked against them, sometimes succeed. Cyberterrorists, using common hacking techniques or soliciting hacker help, could penetrate secure systems, too. In a comprehensive discussion of risk assessment applied to cyberterrorism, Haimes (2002) asserts that the traditional paradigm of expectancy value risk assessment does not apply to potential cyberterrorism acts. A high-probability event with a low negative effect is far different than a low probability event with a high-negative effect, even though the two might score identically in a multiplicative model. "Because terrorism is asymmetric, it defies conventional benefit–cost analysis." Thus, if the potential negative effects are devastating, it is critical to bring the probability to near zero (Haimes, 2002).

Hensgen, Desouza, Evaristo, and Kraft (2003), in a game theory article calling cyberterrorism a "bastard stepchild to physical terror attacks [in a] 'virtual,' non-real world," note that "the virtual is transformed to actual by the execution of a keystroke" (Hensgen et al., 2003). Following the 2002 electrical grid failure, Kaplan (2003) called it an "overloaded, archaic, unevenly managed electrical-transmission system." He cited a spokesman for the North American Electric Reliability Council saying, "Hackers try to intrude on some aspect of the grid's computer network on a daily basis" (Kaplan, 2003). We could be a keystroke away from disaster. Gordon and Ford (2002) conclude, "Unless steps are taken to significantly reduce risks, disaster is inevitable."

At the National Security Summit in December 2003, Tom Ridge, Secretary of the DHS said, "Eighty-five percent of our nation's critical infrastructure, including the cyber network that controls it, is owned and operated by the private sector" (CERT, 2003b), and there is little oversight to their direct and indirect paths to the Internet. Lemos (2002) cited a survey of 50 utilities that found that 40% of water facilities allowed their operators direct access to the Internet, and 60% of them could be dialed into by modem. Even after 9/11, many of these systems have not been updated. Newer technologies, such as KVM (shared keyboard, video, mouse) that simplify network management and make SCADA attacks even more attractive, may increase the risks by encouraging wider adoption of network access.

DEFINING CYBERTERRORISM

Definitions are required for counting and quantifying incidents of cyberterrorism, or the numbers are difficult to interpret. Laws and regulations depend on specific underlying definitions, otherwise they are unenforceable. This section explores some formal definitions used by government, private organizations, and academic researchers. Many of these definitions are inconsistent and imprecise. It gives examples of incidents in cyberspace that might be considered when defining cyberterrorism and leads to an extended definition of cyberterrorism. It also discusses how terrorists use the Internet in support roles. Multilevel operational definitions are presented, including a five-layer model. Later in the chapter, the ideas of asymmetric response and cyberwarfare are discussed in relation to the definitions.

Definitions in Use

In the United States, government agencies implement laws by formulating regulations, which may define specific terms such as *cyberterrorism*. Ultimately, a court establishes a case law determination for a given situation. Changes require new legislation or regulations, and the process begins anew. In the coming years, cyberterrorism issues and definitions will be clarified as case law evolves, but they are likely to be made more complex as new threats and other unforeseen activities arise outside precedents.

Government departments and agencies use the term *cyberterrorism*, but none have formulated a definition that is binding outside their sphere of influence. In 2001, the NIPC called cyberterrorism an "evolving concept" and stated, "the definition of terrorism must evolve to reflect the type of activity that goes beyond traditional physical violence" (NIPC, 2001b; Vatis, 2001).

Howard Schmidt, then vice chairman of the Critical Infrastructure Protection Board, defined cyberterrorism at a conference early in 2002 as "anything that disrupts or causes mistrust about the security of computers and networks" (Moran, 2002). This is a broad definition, as terrorism is usually thought of as including some element of politically motivated coercion, intimidation, fear, confusion, uncertainty, or violence directed at civilians or other noncombatants.

In congressional testimony, J. T. Caruso, deputy executive assistant director of the FBI's Counterterrorism and Counterintelligence unit, defined cyberterrorism as "*the use of* cyber tools to shut down critical national infrastructures . . . for the purpose of coercing or intimidating a government or civilian population" (emphasis added; Caruso, 2002; Greenspan, 2002b).

The NIPC's Analysis and Information Sharing Unit (2001b) proposed the following:

> Cyberterrorism is a criminal act perpetrated by *the use of* computers and telecommunications capabilities resulting in violence, destruction and/or disruption of services to create fear by causing confusion and uncertainty within a given population, with the goal of influencing a government or population to conform to a particular political, social, or ideological agenda. (emphasis added)

Mark Pollitt (2002), of the FBI Laboratory in Washington, DC, constructed a "working definition" as follows:

> Cyberterrorism is the premeditated, politically motivated attack *against* information, computer systems, computer programs, and data which result in violence against noncombatant targets by sub national groups or clandestine agents. (emphasis added)

The definitions have important differences. The NIPC and Caruso emphasize *the use of* computers in creating terror, focusing on the act itself. Pollitt emphasizes the *target* or victim(s) of the act. They generally agree on some element of politically motivated coercion, fear, confusion, uncertainty, violence, intimidation, or intent. Gordon and Ford (2002), in a comprehensive review of government definitions, make a similar distinction between the "tool" and the "target" and introduce "the concept of 'pure' cyberterrorism," which is carried out "entirely (or primarily) in the virtual world."

Hensgen et al. (2003) in discussing definitions and game theory, include both the use of computers and the target of the act in a working definition for cyberterrorism:

> A purposeful act, personally or politically motivated, that is intended to disrupt or destroy the stability of organizational or national interests, through *the use of* electronic devices which are *directed at* information systems, computer programs, or other electronic means of communications, transfer, and storage. (emphasis added)

Their definition is relatively broad. It can apply to both national and organizational interests in the virtual or physical worlds. However, it does not include elements commonly associated with terror.

More research needs to be done on establishing a definition of cyberterrorism that is consistent with definitions of conventional terrorism. Dictionary definitions of *terror* commonly include intense fear, extreme fright, dread, or panic. Terrorism includes violence or threatened violence, an ideology intended to cause harm, and some form of collective intent, usually with a political or ideological objective, directed at noncombatants.

The CIA's Counterterrorist Center refers to Title 22 of the U.S. Code, Section 2656f(d), in defining terrorism as "premeditated, politically motivated violence perpetrated against noncombatant targets by sub national groups or clandestine agents, usually intended to influence an audience" (DCI Counterterrorist Center, CIA, 2002). The FBI defines terrorism as "the unlawful use, or threatened use, of violence by a group or individual . . . to intimidate or coerce a government, the civilian population, or any segment thereof, in furtherance of political or social objectives" (Watson, 2002). The FBI's definition of terrorism could include *threats*, whereas the CIA specifies actual *acts*. Both involve political motivation or activities.

Dorothy Denning (2001), director of the Institute for Information Assurance, Georgetown University, offers a discussion of cyberterrorism that includes many of the elements that would lead to terror: fear, confusion, uncertainty, violence, or intimidation. "The attack should be sufficiently destructive or disruptive to generate fear comparable to that from physical acts of terrorism. Attacks that lead to death or bodily injury, extended power outages, plane crashes, water contamination, or major economic losses would be examples."

Compared to conventional terrorism, defining cyberterrorism is complicated by the nature of cyberspace. Traditionally, laws deal with acts that are defined to occur in time and space. Acts in cyberspace may have physical effects in time and place, but some of their causal factors reside in a virtual reality, mostly independent of time and space. Defining (and prosecuting) cyberterrorism acts will need to take these factors into account, and it will take time to develop applicable case law. Many other nations have similar interpretation problems, and work needs to be done to reach international consensus. A more detailed discussion of problems in formal cyberterrorism definitions is given in the *Internet Encyclopedia* (Jaeger, 2003).

Extended Definitions

Cyberterrorism often is defined loosely. President Clinton, in December 2000, said, "One of the biggest threats to the future is going to be cyberterrorism—people fooling with your computer networks, trying to shut down your phones, erase bank records, mess up airline schedules, do things to interrupt the fabric of life." Clinton's examples include many acts that do not qualify under FBI, CIA, and other definitions that include the terror component.

Gordon and Ford (2002) discuss extended definitions of cyberterrorism, which involve wide-ranging means of using cyberspace to further terrorism. They cite self-interest motives (media attention, budget, power) in a section on "terrorism as theater." Arguing for an extended definition, they maintain, "those who do insist on treating only 'pure cyberterrorism' as cyberterrorism are completely missing the true threat posed by the addition of acts in the virtual world to the terrorists' playbook."

Making a definition too restrictive may omit acts that should qualify. An overly broad definition, in contrast, will include so many acts that "terrorism" would become meaningless. Many ordinary crimes, vandalism, and hacking would be classified as terrorism. Even repeated "spam" might be terrorism if it intimidates or coerces people into purchasing or otherwise acting on an offer. Let us consider some examples.

In November 1999, a Tampa, Florida, man was charged in federal court with using the Internet to threaten to destroy the reputations of six young women and girls unless they engaged in phone and cybersex, charges investigated by a task force that included the FBI (FBI, 1999). Also in 1999, U.S. Web government sites were defaced in the name of China. The White House Web site was shut down for 3 days by massive amounts of e-mail. Pro-Chinese hackers hacked 165 Taiwanese Web sites to protest the Taiwanese presidential elections (Jane's Information Group Ltd., 1999). In 2000, pro-Pakistani hackers defaced more than 500 Indian Web sites. In 2001, U.S. Web sites were attacked after a Chinese fighter jet collided with a U.S. reconnaissance plane (Tang, 2001). Pro-Korean hackers attacked computers and Web sites of various Japanese organizations following their approval of a new history textbook (NIPC, 2001a). In July 2002, CNN reported that Yale University experienced 18 unauthorized Web site log-ins—traced back to computers at Princeton (CNN.com, 2002c). The Terrorism Research Center's Information Warfare Database lists over 50 "incidents" dating back to 1982 targeting the North American Air Defense Command, NASA, U.S. military sites, the White House, the U.S. Department of Defense, and others vital to U.S. and world security (Information Warfare Database, 2002).

These acts, and many other activities in cyberspace, are annoying and may cause monetary or other damages, but are they cyberterrorism? Some are intended to punish a country or other political entity for the purpose of influencing policy, but many do not involve large-scale or otherwise disastrous physical consequences.

In fact, only the cybersex case resulted in charges of cyberterrorism. That event had no political motivation or unauthorized break-ins, affected relatively few people, and created virtually no property damage or direct monetary losses. (The FBI called the attacks "large scale," and Frank Gallagher, special agent in charge of the Tampa division, described them as "cyberterrorism" because of the fear created in the recipients.) The case was resolved on charges other than cyberterrorism (FBI, 1999).

There is general disagreement on whether using the Internet in a support role should be considered cyberterrorism, especially where the objective is not immediately destructive and is designed to influence public policy or further a political cause.

In a 1999 article, Denning explored how Internet users can influence public policy. She separates their usage into three categories: activism, hacktivism, and cyberterrorism. Activism refers to the normal, nondisruptive use of the Internet for persuasion or information dissemination. Hactivism is where the activist uses hacking techniques for activities such as Web sit-ins or denial of service attacks, "with the intent of disrupting normal operations but not causing serious damage" against a target's Internet site. Cyberterrorism refers to a "convergence of cyberspace and terrorism [that is] politically motivated [and] intended to cause grave harm such as loss of life or severe economic damage" in influencing policy (Denning, 1999).

Support for Conventional Terrorism

Many experts believe that the most likely future attack scenario is for the cyberterrorists' bits and bytes to be combined with terrorists' bombs. This leads us to consider extended definitions of cyberterrorism, including support for conventional terrorism.

Gellman (2002) quotes Ronald Dick, then director of the FBI's NIPC, "The event I fear most is a physical attack in conjunction with a successful cyber-attack on the responders' 911 system or on the power grid," meaning that "the first responders couldn't get there . . . and water didn't flow, hospitals didn't have power. Is that an unreasonable scenario? Not in this world. And that keeps me awake at night."

The Digital Pearl Harbor study group dealing with the electrical network "envisioned a two-pronged attack: first, the physical destruction of key transmission bottlenecks, followed by sabotage through the Internet of the digital systems that allow supervisors to switch transmission flows, . . . thus blocking them from restarting the power after the attack" (Kaplan, 2003). With simultaneous attacks on water, rail, highway, air traffic, and other physical infrastructure and digital control systems, the cyberterrorist would compound and prolong physical attacks. Disruptions of banks, stock exchanges, and pharmaceutical and food manufacturing and distribution would compound the effects.

At the 2003 National Cyber Security Summit, Amit Yoran (2003), then director of the National Cyber Security Division of the DHS, warned "America's economic engine is fueled by efficiency . . . though the use of technology. . . . When we look at the vulnerability of cyberspace, there's no doubt in my mind that what we've seen so far in attacks is just the early stage of what could become a critical national weakness—if we don't aggressively address it."

Does the use of cyberspace to support conventional terrorism qualify as cyberterrorism? To the extent that it is premeditated, politically motivated, perpetrated against noncombatant targets to influence an audience, there is a reasonable argument for including such activity.

Communication in Terrorism

Under broad definitions, communication between terrorists and other cyberspace support for terrorist acts may be considered forms of cyberterrorism. The Web is a fast, easy, cheap, and powerful communication tool. Just as businesses, governments, military forces, and other individuals use the Internet to communicate and transfer files, so do terrorists. A December 2003 Al Qaeda video appeared on the Web to recruit new terrorists (Arena, 2003), and terrorists have used the Web for disseminating information about the Iraq war.

In February 2003, a University of Idaho graduate student was arrested and charged in U.S. district court with using his computer expertise between 1994 and 2003 to foster terrorism. Specifically, *United States of America vs. Sami Omar Al-Hussayen* charged that he "provided and conspired with others to provide material support and resources... by, among other things, creating and maintaining internet websites and other internet media designed to recruit mujahideen and raise funds for violent jihad in Israel, Chechnya and other places" (details are on www.findlaw.com).

After a 7-week trial and 7 days of deliberations, Al-Hussayen was found not guilty on three terrorism counts and a mistrial was declared on several other counts. The government agreed to drop the remainder of the charges after the defendant agreed to deportation to Saudi Arabia.

As early as 1999, Denning concluded, "It appears that virtually every terrorist group is on the Web," such groups are actively establishing alliances and coalitions via the Web, and this support role is the most common use of the Web in terrorism. She adds, "Forcing them off the Web is impossible, because they can set up their sites in countries with free-speech laws."

Cyberspace can become a conduit for terrorist intelligence gathering and calls-to-action, often using unprotected, hacked computers as open relays, planting spy devices, and reading the contents of computer hard drives in homes, businesses, or institutions anywhere in the world (security is covered in other chapters of this *Handbook*). Some of this activity is criminal, even if it does not result in terrorism.

A Five-Level Operational Model

Although a formal definition of cyberterrorism may remain obscure, it is useful to address the problem with a multilevel operational model that describes behavior. Tavani and other writers on ethics in cyberspace have separated cyberspace activities into variations of subsets, such as cybervandalism, cybertrespass, and cyberpiracy. Together, these activities capture a part of cyberterrorism, at least in the extended definition, but they are only elements in the destructive acts described by Collin and others. (Cybercrime, cybervandalism, hacking, and related topics are covered in other chapters of this *Handbook.*)

Conway (2002) described a general three-tiered schema, categorizing "fringe" activity on the Internet as "use, misuse, and offensive use." Use is normal and legal Internet usage—the same for terrorists as for anyone else—similar to Denning's activism. Misuse includes acts that disrupt or otherwise compromise other sites, including protests and vandalism typically associated with hackers. Most of the incidents described in this chapter fall into this category, similar to Denning's hacktivism. Offensive use entails actual damage, theft, fraud, extortion, or commercial espionage. Not all of these offensive uses are crimes. Some of them may be cyberterrorism.

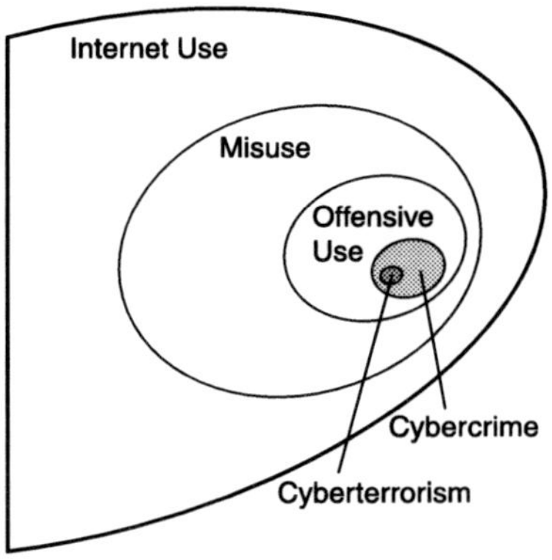

Figure 1: Categories of Internet usage related to terrorism.

Expanding Conway's general schema would include two additional subsets of offensive use: cybercrime and a subset of that, cyberterrorism. Cybercrime would be criminal acts using cyberspace that can be prosecuted. Cyberterrorism would include crimes with political motivations, grave harm, severe economic damage, and so on, consistent with dictionary definitions of terrorism, definitions of cyberterrorism in common use, and Denning's operational hierarchy (see Figure 1).

Many of what would be misuse and offensive use "incidents" are tracked by the Carnegie Mellon CERT Coordination Center. The incidents counts have increased exponentially since 1988 (CERT, 2004b) (see Figure 2).

Cyberterrorists seldom would engage in ordinary misuse or offensive use, unless such use supported their larger goals, as the potential risk of discovery would be counterproductive. Conversely, ordinary use of the Internet by terrorists to communicate and coordinate activities that support conventional terrorism is likely to be common.

HOW CYBERTERRORISM OCCURS

This section outlines how the convergence of the physical and virtual worlds creates vulnerabilities to cyberterrorism. It presents some of the tools and techniques available to cyberterrorists. It addresses the distributed nature of the generally unregulated Internet, which increases its vulnerability and creates limitations to how regulation can be applied. It discusses the concept of asymmetric response, its role in cyberwarfare, and its relationship to cyberterrorism.

Convergence of the Physical and Virtual Worlds

Cyberspace is a virtual world of combinations of ones and zeros with no appreciable mass, time, or space. Digits can represent the physical world but are not the physical object(s). With the attachment of stimuli and sensory interface devices, however, the flow of ones and zeros can

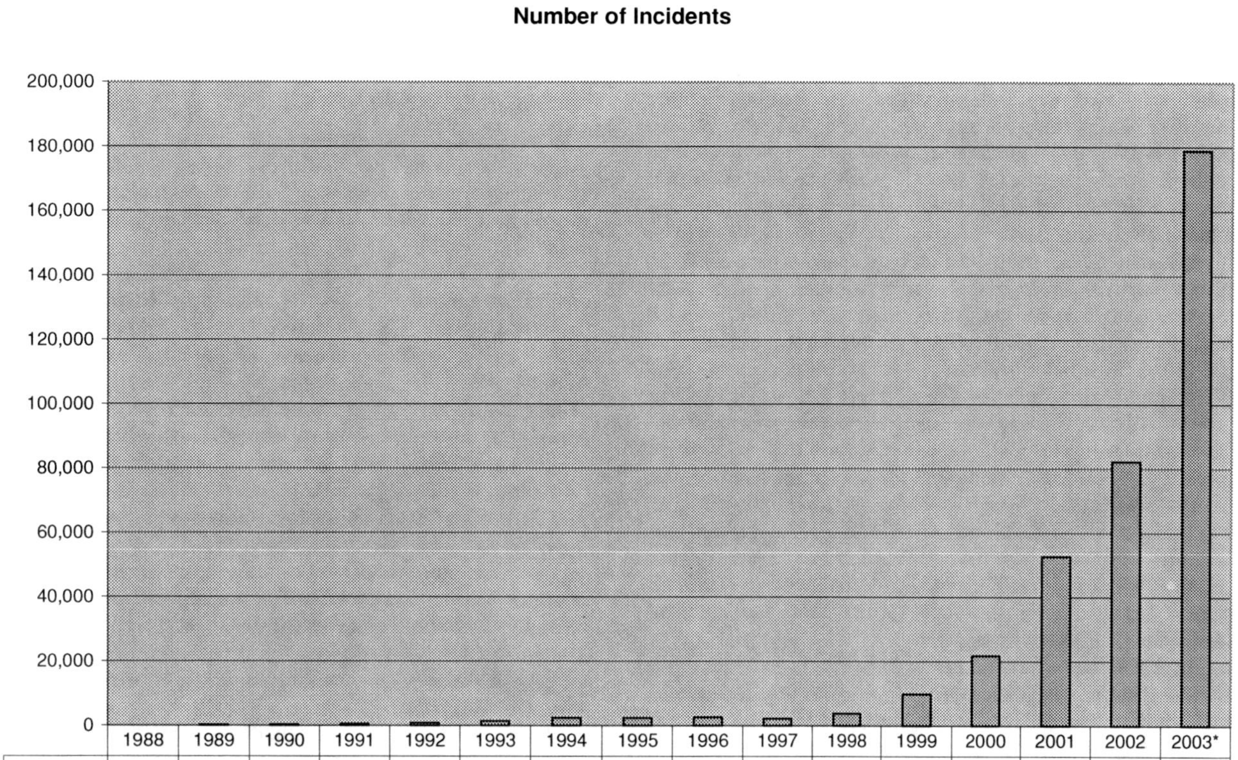

	1988	1989	1990	1991	1992	1993	1994	1995	1996	1997	1998	1999	2000	2001	2002	2003*
Incidents	6	132	252	406	773	1,334	2,340	2,412	2,573	2,134	3,734	9,859	21,756	52,658	82,094	178,788

Figure 2: Number of incidents (from www.cert.org/stats/). Asterisk indicates the 2003 estimate is based on 137,529 incidents reported through Q3.

control physical objects that exist in time and space. "It is now the intersection, the convergence, of these two worlds that forms the vehicle of cyberterrorism, the new weapon that we face" (Collin, 1996).

Collin (1996) discusses activities in the physical world that intersect with cyber-based systems through these vulnerable convergence points. Examples include food and pharmaceutical processing plants, electric and natural gas utilities, train crossings and traffic control systems, air traffic control systems, virtually all modern military equipment, and military, public safety, and civilian communications. Using readily available digital tools and freely available information from Internet Web sites, the cyberterrorist may exploit this "point of convergence" to achieve one or more of three goals: destruction, alteration, or acquisition and retransmission.

An electronic signal can be attacked if its rule-based behavior of ones and zeros can be determined and accessed. When remote administration of the physical device is used, illustrated by the discussion of SCADA devices at the beginning of this chapter, the Internet can be a conduit to the target device through standardized Internet rules [Internet protocols (IPs) and transmission or transfer control protocols (TCPs)] that enable worldwide communication. Each device has a unique IP address. Once terrorists access the IP address and learn the rules controlling the device itself, they have the potential to control it through cyberspace.

Hackers and terrorists may not need to know details of the physical structures in which the ones and zeros reside—usually a computer or system of computers with its associated network—or even the physical location of the device itself. If they know the processes used to maintain and control its action(s), the IP or other electronic address "where" it resides in cyberspace, and how its internal structure responds to electronic stimuli, the device is vulnerable.

The Internet was designed to be decentralized and unregulated, except through technical protocols, so there is little control over individual installations. There are no effective committees with official authority or tracking oversight based on content (although some countries such as China and France have laws regulating forbidden content). The terrorists' servers can reside in any country, sometimes in difficult-to-discover physical locations, and they can be moved easily.

Vulnerabilities: External, Internal, Other

Kevin Mitnick, "the condor," is perhaps the world's most notorious cybercriminal and the first to appear on the FBI's Most Wanted list. Mitnick stole tens of thousands of credit card numbers and copied millions of dollars worth of computer software beginning in the 1980s. He eventually served 5 years in prison and now is a consultant (Meriwether, 1995; Sargent, 2001).

Mitnick breaks vulnerability into four "access points": host, network, physical security, and people. He says the most common sources of vulnerability today are unpatched and misconfigured systems, their associated networks, and insufficient systems management education (*eWeek*, 2003). Hosts and networks can be protected with firewalls, improved passwords, encryption, and other technological shields, discussed later in this chapter and elsewhere in this book.

Mitnick says that systems operators—particularly those controlling physical infrastructure with SCADA devices—need more education, training, and awareness of the issues. "Unfortunately, a lot of enterprises believe that buying a firewall or an [intrusion detection system] is all they need to do. And they're lulled into a false sense of security." He is concerned that companies and organizations are not making the required commitment to long-term security. "A lot of our clients want a one-time... test to satisfy an auditor... or to get buy-in to get a security budget."

The 2004 "State of the CIO" survey found that the highest *technology* priority, after enhanced system performance, was ensuring data security and integrity. Data security did not make the top 10 of the CIO's *management* priorities (*CIO Magazine*, 2004).

In 2004, Deloitte's annual Global Security Survey of worldwide financial services firms reportedly found that 83% of respondents "acknowledged that their systems had been compromised in the past year, compared to only 39% in 2002." However, although 59% of the respondents "indicated security is a key part of their solution, only 10%... reported that their general management perceives security as a business enabler" (CCNMatthews, 2004).

Hinde (2003) supports the idea that technical solutions and other measures to keep outsiders from unauthorized access is only one part of the problem. "Internal security breaches and backdoors are a growing problem. Insider hacking represents about 70% of all malicious attacks, and costs US business over $1 billion annually in damages," he says. "Firewalls will not help against this." He recommends a 10-point plan for implementing an advanced intrusion detection system (IDT) that would address both internal and external threats.

There are conflicting estimates. The Carnegie Mellon CERT Coordination Center reports that a *CSO* magazine survey found 71% of attacks coming from outsiders, compared with 29% from insiders. Hackers were listed as the greatest security threat, followed closely by current or former employees or contractors (CERT, 2004a).

The CERT Center has tracked technical vulnerabilities since 1995. They have shown exponential growth until 2002, but there has been a gradual decline since then (CERT, 2004b) (see Figure 3).

Physical network architecture is vulnerable to traditional terrorism from the outside, too. In 2002, a story about Internet physical vulnerability reported how in San Jose, California, "any visitor can walk into the building and board the elevator unchallenged" and exit on the fifth floor location of MAE West, one of "about a dozen major U.S. peering points... where the wires of thousands of data networks intersect [in a] clustering effect" (Wylie, 2002). In a facility of this kind, a well-placed bomb might be coordinated with a cyberattack. Physical security at this and many similar facilities has been upgraded, but other locations have not.

Tools of Cyberterrorists

Hackers and cyberterrorists use similar tools and techniques: hardware, sophisticated software, and detailed knowledge of the technology, the targets, and the procedures used to maintain and control operations at target sites.

Today, hacking tools are more powerful, easier to use, and more plentiful than ever. Hacking software and documentation are easily obtained on the Internet. In discussing "the democratization of hacking," Christensen (1999) said, "The tools of mayhem are readily available. There are about 30,000 hacker-oriented sites on the Internet, bringing hacking—and terrorism—within the reach of even the technically challenged." He quotes a manager of technical security at a company that does business with the Pentagon: "You no longer have to have knowledge, you just have to have the time."

Hacking into secure sites may simply mean millions of iterations of new trial-and-error algorithms that ultimately discover the target device's secret passwords or defeat its other protective barriers. Even with a low probability of success, the documented cases of unauthorized entry are common.

In tracking attack sophistication versus intruder technical knowledge, Lipson (2002) asserts that in 1980, attack sophistication was low, but it required high intruder knowledge. By 2000, attack sophistication had become high, but the required intruder knowledge was low, and there was "widespread availability of exploit tools." An excellent graphic is included, showing the development of this relationship over time (Lipson, 2002).

Hackers typically work alone, but can gain power by working together. Obtaining the knowledge, hardware, software, and access to targets in cyberspace can be complex. Specialists can focus on a tiny problem that unlocks success in the broader venture. Acting together, even informally in loosely knit alliances, cyberterrorists can defeat barriers that would be impossible for any single individual. Networks of cyberterrorist hackers working together, perhaps in widely separated parts of the world, may one day unlock the keys to making Collin's doomsday scenarios reality.

BGP Tables, DNS Poisoning, and DDoS

Vulnerabilities exist in network traffic routing and in methods to track users. Snyder (2002) points out that the entire Internet depends on huge border gateway protocol (BGP) tables that detail the more than 100,000 routes information can travel. BGP4 is the protocol used to exchange routing information among providers and to propagate external routing information through autonomous networks. BGP-speaking routers "peer" with each other to exchange information about routes and improve data flow efficiency:

> In the early days, these tables were validated against routing registries that ensured bogus information could not be injected into the tables.

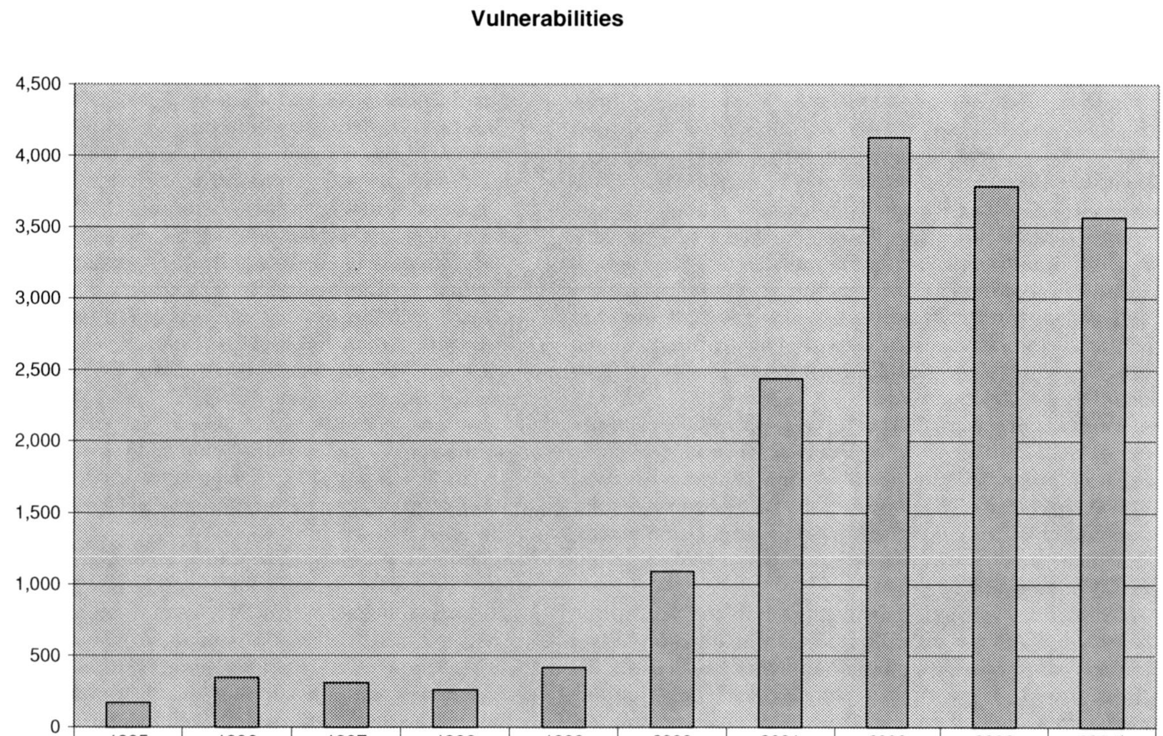

	1995	1996	1997	1998	1999	2000	2001	2002	2003	2004*
Vulnerabilities	171	345	311	262	417	1,090	2,437	4,129	3,784	3,568

Figure 3: Number of vulnerabilities (from www.cert.org/stats/). Asterisk indicates 2004 estimate is based on 1,740 vulnerabilities reported through Q2.

> Nowadays, that doesn't happen. Keeping those routing registries updated and synchronized is just too expensive and inconvenient. The lack of a global routing registry means that it's fairly easy to create routes to nowhere.... If a determined attacker were to start injecting routes into the BGP tables, the ripple effects could be enormous.... [It] could cripple routers around the world.

Craig Labovitz, a border gateway protocol researcher, reportedly identified a 1997 event where a "serious weakness was discovered" by a network technician who changed two lines of code and "nearly brought down the global network" (Lemos, 2002).

The University of Oregon Route Views Project studies variations in core route table sizes and growth rates through regular BGP sessions with many routers spread throughout the world. They found that the number of routes in the Internet increased from approximately 15,000 in 1994 to approximately 115,000 by mid-2002, magnifying their vulnerability (Meyer, 2002).

Chakrabarti and Manimaran (2002), in their comprehensive taxonomy of Internet infrastructure security, say, "So far, the research in Internet security primarily focused on securing the information rather than securing the infrastructure itself." They note that attacks on BGP tables could create a "large amount of service disruption" and "are very difficult to detect because the attacker is hidden," adding, "Such service disruption has already been noticed with ... routing flaps due to Nimbda/Code Red" (their taxonomy discusses domain name system (DNS) hacking, routing table poisoning, packet mistreatment, and denial of service (DoS), using "masquerading," "cache poisoning," and other techniques).

Reviewing the DHS's National Strategy to Secure Cyberspace, Fisher (2003b) says, "While there is considerable space given to the need for reducing the number of vulnerabilities in... BGP (border gateway protocol), the Domain Name System and IP, the strategy makes little mention of how to go about fixing these problems, a key shortcoming."

Attacks on the are common. In March 2003, after Al-Jazeera's Web site showed pictures of dead or captured soldiers in Iraq, hackers posted the U.S. flag and the message "Let Freedom Ring" on Al-Jazeera's site. The suspected technique is called "DNS poisoning," which fools traffic-directing computers across the Internet (Associated Press, 2003a). A creative cyberterrorist might combine an attack on the DNS servers with BGP routing. If it is possible to use BGP tables to redirect messages by acquisition and retransmission to random or unknown locations, it might be possible to redirect them to a specific destination—its own control station—where the terrorist might alter the message contents and redirect it, thus taking control of critical physical devices without discovering the secret passwords and other barriers to these devices. A technique of this kind is unlikely but perhaps not impossible.

Internet DNS servers track users, referencing millions of user names. It is common to "ping" these and other address nodes by sending packets with a short query message that maintains communication with them and detects abnormalities. Normally, this traffic is minimal.

DoS attacks use packet flooding to overwhelm servers. In distributed denial of service attacks (DDoS), once a vulnerable computer is compromised, the worm infects that target, randomly or systematically selects new targets, and resends the exploit and propagation code to that host, which in turn launches coordinated attacks from their distributed locations.

On October 21, 2002, an estimated 6,000 computers worldwide swamped the Internet's 13 root servers in Japan, Europe, and the United States that control most of the Net's traffic. Eight were disabled to some degree. This massive "ping flooding" was part of a DDoS attack, "the biggest ever hacking attack on the Internet" (Naraine, 2002; Vickers, 2002).

These relatively new and effective tools in the cyberterrorist's toolkit are difficult to track. In the old days, it was possible to trace a message or command back to a guilty IP address. Today, with distributed attacks, the offending packets may originate in an otherwise innocent computer. (Details of DoS and DDoS attacks are in other chapters in this *Handbook*.)

The attacks may have resulted in no direct or lasting damage, but they are unsettling. One expert maintains that although there were few direct effects on Internet users, "as nations and critical infrastructure become more dependent on computer networks for their operation, new vulnerabilities are created—a massive electronic Achilles' heel" (Lewis, 2002).

On January 25, 2003, much of the Internet was shut down with a similar attack that used the "Slammer" worm (discussed later in this chapter and in other chapters of this *Handbook*). A security firm official predicted, "Slammer variants could emerge which are capable of being used in a blended threat scenario alongside physical attacks by radicals. This could achieve a significant multiplier effect" to prolong or worsen conventional terrorist attacks (Greenspan, 2003b).

RMA and Asymmetric Response

Asymmetric response (one sided; does not follow "rules") is a way for the weak to attack the strong. A rag-tag, poorly trained militia that is no match for a powerful state's army may use guerilla tactics, sneak attacks, bombings, or sniper attacks to harass and demoralize the superior force. As the balance tilts more and more toward the camp of the powerful adversary, asymmetric response becomes more likely. It can be highly effective, as witnessed by Russia's withdrawal from Afghanistan and the United States' departure from Somalia.

The industrialized nations have highly developed electronic infrastructure that drives knowledge-based economies and gives them advantages in business, government, and military power. Loren Thompson, a defense analyst with the Lexington Institute in Arlington, Virginia, says, "Warfare is less and less about pushing men and machines around the battlefield and more and more about pushing electrons and photons" (CNN, 2003a). Attacking those assets through cyberspace, as a guerilla army might use suicide bombers and beheadings, to the degree that it creates chaos and panic, can be cyberterrorism.

The National Intelligence Council (NIC) has predicted asymmetric responses to an expected overwhelming military superiority brought about by a paradigm shift in the nature of warfare. This "revolution in military affairs" (RMA) will employ "a small, information-intensive, professional armed force [as] the model for a 21st century military," largely based on strength in information technology and smart weaponry (NIC, 1999). In October 2003, ministers from 19 NATO nations met to discuss "transformation of their armies" and held an exercise named Dynamic Response '07, designed to help formulate such a force of 5,000 international troops by October 2006 (CNN, 2003b).

When the U.S. military captured Saddam Hussein, they used digital technology, the Force 21 Base and Command Brigade and Below (FBCB2) system, for commanders to monitor and direct equipment and other war assets in real time. The Army Battle Command System (ABCS) helped run the war room to monitor the big picture. Voice radio, Internet controllers, and the global positioning system (GPS) added efficiency (Van Marsh, 2004). This expensive technology saves lives and gives the military a significant tactical advantage in physical warfare. Cyberterrorism—as an asymmetric response—may be the only way for an opposing force to counteract this overwhelming advantage.

Overill (2003), discussing the nature of asymmetric information warfare, observes that "the cost of defending an asset from attack is many orders of magnitude greater than the cost of attacking it." Regan (1999) points out, "Cyberterrorism allows terrorists... to inflict damage with no harm to themselves and little chance of being caught. It is a way for the 'weak' to attack the 'strong'."

The Associated Press reported that then-White House Technology Advisor Richard Clarke warned a Senate Judiciary subcommittee on cyberterrorism, "A serious cyberattack is almost inevitable because it is cheaper and easier for a foreign country or a terrorist group than a physical attack" (Holland, 2002).

Cyberspace Warfare

Governments are becoming more interested in electronic warfare. In 2002, in testimony before a Senate Judiciary subcommittee on cyberterrorism, Richard Clarke named Iran, Iraq, North Korea, China, Russia, and other countries as "already having people trained in Internet warfare" (Holland, 2002). Previously, the NIC (1999) had said, "Iraq and Iran are examples of states that will likely explore the usefulness of information technology in pursuit of asymmetric conflict... including through the employment of information warfare and cyberterrorism."

The United States is not backing away from defensive—or offensive—use of cyberspace warfare tools. Fisher (2003a) cites the National Strategy to Secure Cyberspace:

"When a nation, terrorist group or other adversary attacks the United States through cyberspace, the U.S. response need not be limited to criminal prosecution. The United States reserves the right to respond in an appropriate manner, including through cyber warfare. The United States will be prepared for such contingencies."

The *Washington Post* reported that President Bush signed a National Security Presidential Directive 16 in July 2002, under which "The United States would launch cyber-attacks against enemy computer networks." The article said, "The Pentagon has stepped up development of cyber-weapons, envisioning a day when electrons might substitute for bombs and allow for more rapid and less bloody attacks on enemy targets" (Rasmussen, 2003). Mark (2003) reports that "the Pentagon is actively developing cyber-weapons to disable enemy radar, electrical grids and telephone systems."

In the 2003 buildup to the Iraq war, a CNN article had predicted a "fierce cyber war," saying, "Imagine Iraqi commanders getting misleading text messages on their cell phones. They appear to contain orders from Saddam Hussein but are actually sent by the U.S. military in disguise, directing Iraqi troops to a trap." CNN likened this to the Civil War, when signal flag messages were diverted, and in World War II, when German forces were deceived by "leaking" battle plans involving nonexistent troops. The article concluded that "the Internet makes deceptions easier" (CNN, 2003a).

SPONSORS AND SUPPORT

Terrorism traditionally has been sponsored by nations who provide financial resources and a safe haven. Cyberterrorism requires less funding. It uses fewer physical assets, so it is more mobile and can cross physical borders or operate simultaneously in many locations. Thus, nations that sympathize with cyberterrorists can support them without becoming a sponsor in the traditional sense. This section addresses different forms of terrorist groups and explores what it means to sponsor them in cyberspace. Cyberterrorism is an international issue, and perspectives from other parts of the world are explored.

Cyberterrorism Sponsors

Hackers and cyberterrorists can operate out of almost any physical location on Earth. Many undeveloped or emerging nations have daunting problems such as hunger, disease, political unrest, or traditional war, often to the extent that they are unable to address security issues or exert effective control over cyberspace. Although the number of computers may be relatively few in these countries, many offer adequate electronic infrastructure and sometimes—knowingly or not—harbor terrorists.

In simpler times, conventional terrorists required a sponsoring organization, often state sponsorship, to obtain sufficient funding and connections. Traditional organizations and state sponsors had a fixed infrastructure. They were comparatively easy to monitor to determine who was pulling strings and causing consequences. Today, terrorists can pursue extreme agendas with more powerful tools than ever before, leaving no easy-to-follow trail. Low-cost cyberspace tools reduce the need for large-scale money transfers, and because physical currency need not be exchanged, following a money trail is more complex.

CNN quotes M. J. Gohel of the Asia-Pacific Institute in London, who describes many of these terrorist organizations as "autonomous with their own leadership, with their own funding, their own personnel. And they have their own plots, as it were. But they're all bonded together by a common ideology" (Arena, 2003). This fragmentation makes them and their funding difficult to track.

Caruso separated the international terrorist threat into three categories: (a) traditional, clearly defined terrorist organizations; (b) the radical international jihad movement; and (c) state sponsors of international terrorism, specifically identifying Iran, Iraq, Sudan, and Libya (Iraq subsequently has changed governments, and Libya has taken steps to limit terrorism; this list will likely undergo continual change). Many of the terrorist groups are not identified with a sponsoring country (Caruso, 2002).

Cyberterrorists acting alone or in small groups can pursue extreme agendas either through volunteer labor or by relatively small amounts of money disbursed from wealthy individuals, foundations, fund raising organizations, or almost any rogue country's intelligence unit. Regan (1999) quotes Dr. Harvey Kushner, chairman of the criminal justice department at Long Island University:

> We have moved away from state-sponsored terrorism. The old model of the hierarchical or "organized crime" group, no longer exists. These days, terrorists move in loose groups, constellations with free-flowing structures. So these days terrorism—both the traditional kind and cyberterrorism—is more the act of the freelancer or the individual. This is true both internationally and nationally.

The Associated Press, reporting on a London-based study, quotes author Kevin Rosser, "What we're beginning to see is a much more disparate movement of people who are sometimes coordinating and sometimes not, but who are inspired by the example of Al Qaeda, . . . so we see the threat becoming much more elusive and . . . much harder to track" (Associated Press, 2003b). However, if these groups coalesce into relationships with each other through Al Qaeda or other known organizations, better visibility could result, and tracking, with worldwide participation, could become more effective.

The Worldwide Perspective

Although there are differences between the way individual nations and the world community view cyberterrorism, there is general agreement that it is a global problem. Nations have become more aware of their vulnerability and are beginning to work together to counter the threat.

In 2003, European Union (EU) ministers agreed to "require all 15 EU member states to adopt a new criminal offence: illegal access to, and illegal interference with an information system," recommending "jail terms of at least two years in serious cases" (*The Information Management Journal*, 2003).

A Manila conference of Southeast Asian telecommunications ministers reported "facing a computer security threat following the 11 September terror attacks in the United States." They implemented "stricter measures to counter cyberterrorism" and "urged the United Nations to come up with a universally accepted definition" (BBC Worldwide Monitoring, 2002).

The United Nations (UN) understands the cyberterrorism connection. "The same Internet that has facilitated the spread of human rights and good governance norms has also been a conduit for propagating intolerance and has diffused information necessary for building weapons of terror" (Annan, 1999). Following the September 11, 2001, attack on the World Trade Center, the 56th regular session of the UN General Assembly declared that cyberspace threats are a weapon against UN goals and unanimously passed a resolution condemning terrorism and cyberterrorism.

On November 23, 2001, the first-ever international treaty on criminal offenses committed against or with the help of computer networks was signed in Budapest, Hungary, by 26 member states of the Convention on Cyber-crime, a part of the Council of Europe. Four nonmembers who helped draft the document, Canada, Japan, South Africa, and the United States, also signed to pursue "a common criminal policy aimed at the protection of society against cyber-crime" (Convention on Cyber-crime, 2001a). Christian Kruger, deputy secretary general of the council, announced that "the Convention would give national legal systems ways of reacting together to crimes committed against or through computer networks, especially those related to terrorism" (Convention on Cyber-crime, 2001b).

Although struggling to cooperate, some nations of the world are reluctant to give up sovereignty. Beyond prosecuting international war criminals charged with physical atrocities, international justice efforts have made only minimal progress. International law and bilateral treaties rarely adjudicate conflicts between companies, individual entities, or public/private disputes. Entities such as the World Trade Organization set rules for engaging in trade and commerce, but their judicial branch only settles differences in trade matters between nations. Formal international agreements usually deal with physical presence and events, not cyberspace activities.

Many developed nations have their own international security agencies, many of which operate anywhere in the world—and often in the virtual world. Nations with such agencies generally work with each other through informal agreements. Since the mid-1990s, cooperation has been on the upswing, and the 9/11 attacks and other international terrorism incidents have added urgency. Although it is rarely discussed publicly, this is a very active area of international relations.

CONTROLLING CYBERTERRORISM

This section begins with general strategies for fighting back against unauthorized attacks, including cyberterrorism. Subsections follow that focus on specific actions that government, businesses, organizations, higher education institutions, and individuals can do. Privacy concerns, especially where government regulations may limit freedom of speech or use confidential information, are addressed.

General Strategies

Many general steps can be taken by individuals, businesses, organizations, and government to reduce the risk of unauthorized intrusion into computer systems and electronically controlled infrastructure. Many of these are technical. Scholarly journals have raised issues of how we view the problem strategically.

Overill discusses the "protect, detect, and react" paradigm and outlines strategic issues associated with various types of reactive strategy. He separates defenses into technical possibilities, legal aspects, and ethical considerations. Technical responses range from benign (notifying the system operator) to aggressive (launch a retaliatory malicious software strike). Many of these are becoming part of built-in computer system "active defense" capabilities in organizational settings (Overill, 2003).

Marcella, Roth, and Espersen (2003) advocate moving "from a reactive posture to a proactive approach to crisis management," adding, "Assessing an organization's weaknesses may require the assessor... to think like a cyber criminal or terrorist might think." If management has not established a formal crisis management team, they say, "internal auditors... can come together as a proactive team to assist in mitigating exposures."

Although these strategies apply primarily in organizational settings, individuals and other noninstitutional users can take steps to help prevent unauthorized entry into their computer systems that could be used in DDoS attacks or other cyberattack activities. The National Cyber Security Alliance (NCSA) is a public/private partnership sponsored by computer hardware and software companies, ISPs, and others "focused on promoting cyber security and safe behavior online." The NCSA issues guidelines directed toward individuals, home users, and small businesses. It sponsors an October National Cyber Security Awareness Month (see http://www.staysafeonline.info). Their 10-point guidelines include operating systems upgrades and patches, antivirus software, password protocols, and other safeguards that most Internet users can apply. Some of these are simple enough to be applied by nontechnical users, whereas others require the guidance of information technology (IT) or other professionals.

Information Technology Professionals

Large business and government organizations usually have IT professionals that make critical decisions about safeguarding their computer systems from cyberattacks and how much information flexibility is built into their systems. Too much filtering screens out important information, whereas too little may risk penetration by intruders. Those that maintain systems connected to SCADA systems controlling vital infrastructure have a higher stake in cybersecurity.

In a journal article overview of how IT professionals can help safeguard their organizations, Hinde (2003) points out that "it may be difficult to differentiate between legitimate operations, intrusive marketing, hacker mischief, competitor attack, criminal activity and cyberterrorism," concluding that "for a truly secure computer, ban users and connectivity." He gives nine technical steps IT professionals can take to "become proactive in defending our computer systems," including IDSs and lock downs.

IT professionals install patches for viruses and worms such as "SQL Slammer" and the "W.32.Bugbear." On January 25, 2003, many of the more than 200,000 computers running Microsoft SQL Server 2000 were vulnerable to the Slammer attack that severely disrupted Internet traffic because required "patches" had not been installed (Fisher, 2003b). Dow Jones reported that Slammer was responsible for "generating a billion attacks an hour at its peak" and "is so virulent that a vulnerable machine—one that hasn't been patched for a particular flaw—is compromised within three minutes of coming online."

In December 2002, Fisher reported, "Security researchers have discovered a set of vulnerabilities in . . . the SSHv2 protocol that could give an attacker the ability to execute code on remote machines. The new flaws are especially dangerous in that they occur before authentication takes place. Attackers could, in some cases, run code on remote machines or launch denial-of-service attacks" (Fisher, 2002). IT professionals implement protective actions against such security flaws.

IT professionals also can help provide feedback to software vendors. In 2002, an average of 50 new software vulnerabilities were reported per week, and a SANS (SysAdmin, Audit, Network, Security) Institute official was quoted as saying, "What this illustrates is that a program that expects end users to patch their systems is futile," adding, "The only solutions are to make software developers, such as Microsoft, responsible for supplying safe, automatic updates or for companies to do much more aggressive filtering of traffic into their networks" (Richmond, 2003).

The Microsoft patches reportedly "were so difficult to install or so poorly publicized that some of Microsoft's own database administrators failed to install them." Database administrators "were required to manually stop each instance of the software running in their organizations, rename or remove some files, and paste the patch files into various directories in each instance." Microsoft released a self-installing patch in November 2002, shortly after the October 21, 2002, attack that swamped the Internet's 13 root servers in Japan, Europe, and the United States, "but it was given only to customers who contacted Product Support Services" (Vaas, 2003). In 2004, Microsoft released Service Pack 2 for XP that has been widely used and closes many of the potential illicit access points.

Professional IT organizations such as the ITAA helped formulate the National Strategy to Secure Cyberspace and participated in the National Cyber Security Summit. ITAA publishes newsletters and maintains an Information Sharing and Analysis Center (ISAC) to disseminate security information among its members and help organizations that do not have adequate resources to maintain their own security. It helped establish the I-ACERT security certification program (Miller, 2003).

The National Cyber Security Division of the DHS works with IT professionals in businesses, universities, and other organizations to promote the new IPv6 Internet protocol, which comes with an improved security framework promising fewer networking vulnerabilities (Fisher & Carlson, 2003). Anticipating its adoption, the updated IPv6 protocol is being implemented by many operating systems, some of which have already begun shipping.

Michael Rasmussen (2003), vice president for Standards and Public Policy for the Information Systems Security Association, says "If we can build the ideal and perfect IT security architecture—we will still have information security and privacy incidents. That is because we have people involved who are human, make mistakes, and succumb to greed and other motives." Regardless of how good technical security becomes, there will always be the chance of human error or inside complicity allowing access to secure IT resources.

Business and Industry

Some companies control vital physical infrastructure and have much to lose through cyberattacks, but there is wide variation in how they have taken protective action—and their attitudes toward the problem. Prior to 9/11, many companies were not taking effective steps to protect themselves from cyberattacks, and many were not sharing what they learned. Often, from a purely business point of view, it makes more sense for a company to deal with the issue internally than to report it to police or other investigative agencies. "Corporate leaders, in many instances, simply never tell the outside world they've been victimized, to avoid spooking investors or customers" (O'Connor, 2000).

An April 2002 CNN.com report on the seventh annual Computer Crime and Security Survey noted, "About 90 percent of the respondents detected a security breach within the last 12 months. However, only 34 percent reported the intrusions to law enforcement officials." It added, "There is much more illegal and unauthorized activity going on in cyberspace than corporations admit to their clients, stockholders and business partners or report to law enforcement." It quoted an FBI assistant director, "Now, more than ever, the government and private sector need to work together to share information and be more cognitive of information security so that our nation's critical infrastructures are protected from cyber-terrorists" (Sieberg, 2002).

Some companies have been lax in applying even modest protective measures. In February 2002, Richard Clarke, then the White House advisor on Cyberspace Security, gave the U.S. Senate a figure that has been widely quoted as short of meeting the need for security. "In the private sector," said Clarke, "the amount of money spent on IT security is roughly .0025% of total revenue. That is less than the amount of money spent on coffee in the same companies" (Wynne, 2002). New figures show that is changing.

In October 2002, the Associated Press reported on the W.32.Bugbear virus, calling it "the worst computer security outbreak in the world" (Associated Press, 2002a). Once a computer is infected, the hacker can steal and delete information. The worm lasted well into 2003 because many users did not realize that their computer was infected. Incidents such as these, although destructive in the short term, have a beneficial effect in prodding laggard businesses. "The expectation is that shareholders will eventually hold boards accountable for security breaches, and, in turn, boards will hold security officials responsible" (Carlson, 2002b).

A leading journal reported that a 2004 *CSO* magazine survey found that "online criminals…cost business an estimated $666 million in 2003." In a reversal of earlier surveys, 40% named outside hackers as the biggest cybersecurity threat, compared with 28% citing internal threats, such as disgruntled employees. The magazine concluded, "Auditing firms should include cybersecurity readiness as part of the criterion for determining whether companies have adequate internal and financial safety controls" (*The Information Management Journal*, 2004).

Many CIOs dispute Collin's or Clarke's extreme threat scenarios against physical infrastructure attacks. For example, Berinato examines safeguards in place at the Massachusetts Water Resource Authority (MWRA) and concludes that a cyberterrorist would need to penetrate firewalls and SCADA control barriers through two "very narrow access points," have insider knowledge of how the system operates, and then successfully "plant surreptitious code that would allow remote control of the chemical distribution or even the flow of water itself" and assume that the changes would go undetected long enough to have severe negative effects. An MWRA director calls them "ridiculous barriers." The article concludes, "The real threat is to critical data, not to property" (Berinato, 2002).

In recent years, companies have increased IT spending, much of it for improved security against viruses and worms (discussed elsewhere in this *Handbook*), aimed at loss of valuable data of computing systems. The 2004 "State of the CIO" survey shows that IT headcount increased in 37% of firms and decreased in only 17%. IT's budget as a percentage of organizational revenue ranged from 13.8% for financial firms down to 2.6% for manufacturers, with an average of 5.6% for all firms. The highest technology priority, after enhanced system performance, was ensuring data security and integrity (*CIO Magazine*, 2004).

Haimes (2002) and others emphasize a "holistic" approach to cyberthreats, using systems analysis that includes understanding the system's nature and improving the decision-making process. *The Information Management Journal* (2002a) reports that experts recommend educating personnel, establishing a crisis management team, and enforcing a "total risk management program."

Part of the holistic approach is to become more conscious of all types of threats. The journal points out, "A corporate Web site is a virtual gold mine for competitive intelligence gatherers." Especially when companies control SCADA devices or other physical infrastructure, cyberterrorists can use that information to help plot attacks. Preventive measures include using search engines to periodically check on who is linking to your company's site, not revealing too much information on job postings, and keeping "to a minimum the strategic information filed with government agencies" (*The Information Management Journal*, 2002c).

Companies face a balancing act in information sharing. They want to avoid the bad publicity associated with having had their systems and facilities compromised by a cyberterrorist; they want to protect proprietary information from scrutiny by agencies that would turn it into public record through the Freedom of Information Act; they are concerned that if they work too closely with competitors, they may be accused of antitrust violations; and many fear that they will be required to spend more time on assessment and managing security than on productive work.

Although America's largest buyer—the federal government—has no power to directly force business and industry into cooperation, it is using its purchasing power to force better security standards, establish configuration benchmarks, and encourage information sharing and cooperation through the National Cyber Security Summit and other initiatives (Fisher & Carlson, 2003). The National Strategy to Secure Cyberspace business sector strategy calls for a heightened awareness and responsibility within companies and promotes company-wide corporate security councils to integrate all aspects of security, including cybersecurity—a mostly voluntary emphasis. Some say it should be mandatory.

In the United States and many other economically advanced countries, 70% of the GNP is services. Although most large, information-intensive organizations have their own IT resources, many smaller entities cannot justify maintaining technical staffs, so it makes sense to outsource. In the past several years, an entire service industry has grown up around the idea of helping companies with cybersecurity.

Creating an internal security unit may be costly, require the recruitment of specialized personnel, entail substantial start-up time, and risk isolation from new developments. Service providers have highly trained people able to leverage their information and knowledge over several businesses.

Companies are investing in software, firewalls, virtual private networks (only minimally connected to the Internet), and other security components with a high services content. Global investment in e-security services were expected to total $14.5 billion in 2005, with North America accounting for 58% of the global total (McMahon, 2002). Some of these service companies have evolved as for-profit branch organizations of private interest groups that disburse information or other resources for counteracting cyberterrorism.

Government

The 9/11 attack was a "wakeup call" that helped galvanize support around the world for stronger government measures against terrorism, including cyberterrorism. In the United States, these include protection of government cyberspace activities, proactive coordination, and aggressive laws allowing an expansion of wiretapping and other surveillance.

Introspection and Protection

Compared to private business, government security has lagged. An ITAA survey in September 2002 found that 77% of respondents felt the private sector was more advanced

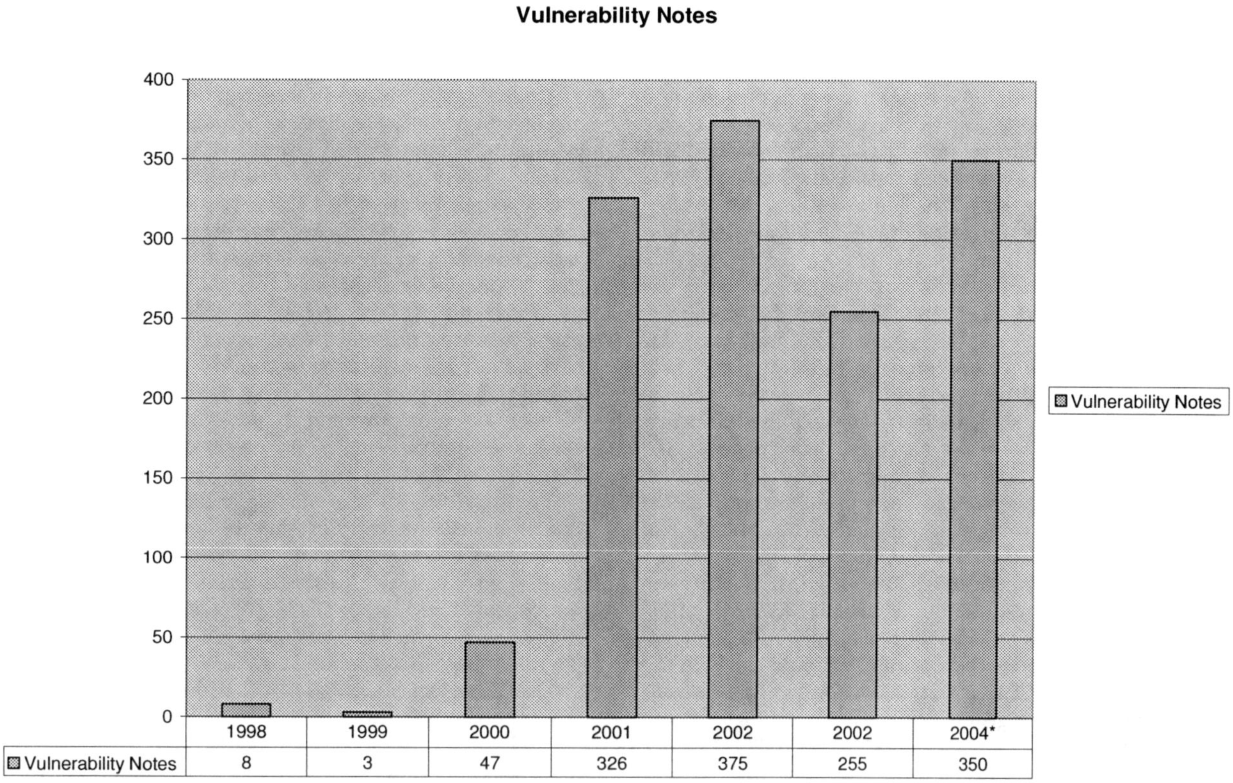

Figure 4: Vulnerability notes (from www.certs.org/stats/). Asterisk indicates the 2004 estimate is based on 175 notes reported through Q2.

in hardening information systems than the public sector (Miller, 2003). This may be explained, in part, because "Government . . . staffs are paid less and don't have access to the latest software and hardware defenses" (Weiss, 2001).

In December 2002, President Bush signed the Federal Information Security Management Act (FISMA), which mandates that government agencies develop annual reports and risk assessments, configuration guidelines, continuity plans, security policies, and inventories of systems. Graded A–F on the security state of their cybersystems, including software security, employee training, and other factors, most agencies failed.

Agencies counter that the grades are "unfair" because "the self-evaluation the agencies must perform can cost hundreds of thousands of dollars, depending on the size of the network," and they simply have had "difficulty finding money in their budgets to comply" (Fisher & Carlson, 2003).

The situation is improving. In 2003, although the government received an overall D grade, it was up from an overall F in 2002. In 2003, 14 of the 24 agencies that were evaluated improved their year-over-year scores, although the DHS still received a failing grade. The Nuclear Regulatory Commission improved to an A from a C, and the National Science Foundation improved to an A- from a D- (Greenspan, 2003a).

Successful attacks on U.S. government systems are declining, having peaked in 2001 (Greenspan, 2003a). The Cert Center publishes vulnerability notes that capture similar incidents. These increased dramatically in 2001, but have been relatively steady since then (CERT, 2004b) (see Figure 4).

Coordination

In September 2002, a draft of the President's National Strategy to Secure Cyberspace addressed ISPs, wireless networks, and other information security points of convergence for business and home Internet users. A final plan was released in February 2003. The report included 60 recommendations for government, companies, institutions, and individuals in the United States and other nations, including five priorities: (a) a national cyberspace security response system, (b) threat and vulnerability reduction, (c) security awareness and training, (d) securing government cyberspace, and (e) international cooperation (Fisher, 2003a).

Recommendations for government included improving federal cybersecurity, early warning and crisis management plans, and partnering to help develop new security technologies in science and industry. It "strives to ensure that any interruptions will be infrequent, brief, manageable, geographically isolated, and minimally detrimental to the welfare of the United States" (Porteus, 2002).

Many of these initiatives were merged into the DHS, established in November 2002. The DHS absorbed 22 federal agencies, including five cybersecurity offices and programs, and expanded the government's powers to obtain information from telephone and Internet service providers. About $3 billion was reserved for technology in the DHS 2003 and 2004 budgets, each approximately $30 billion. "One important DHS priority will be to examine the vulnerabilities found in security systems. The emphasis will be on catastrophic terrorism—threats to the security of our homeland that could result in large-scale loss of life as well as triggering major economic repercussions" (DHS, 2003).

In December 2003, the DHS and leading industry associations, including the U.S. Chamber of Commerce, the Business Software Alliance, the ITAA, and TechNet, hosted the National Cyber Security Summit. This "first forum of its kind since the release of the President's Strategy" brought together leaders from the public and private sectors to "support the National Cyber Security Division's efforts to improve the security of cyberspace, to strengthen the country's ability to prevent and respond to cyber attacks, and to cultivate and sustain a public-private partnership for cyber-security" (CERT, 2003a).

The government continues to pursue public/private cyberspace security initiatives, including ISACs such as CERT for "sharing information on cyber-attacks, vulnerabilities, countermeasures, and best practices" (ISAC, 2003). The ISACs deal with telecommunications, financial, chemical, energy, information technology, water, transportation, aviation, and food (Porteus, 2003). Other government activities include collaborating with organizations developing the more powerful and secure IPv6 Internet protocol, sponsoring simulations such as Digital Pearl Harbor, promoting ties with legitimate businesses investigating potential security risks, and improving surveillance.

Surveillance and Investigation

On October 26, 2001, the Patriot Act (Providing Appropriate Tools Required to Intercept and Obstruct Terrorism) was signed into law by President Bush. Tracking cyberterrorists and terrorists in cyberspace is a key objective of the act, which gives authorities broad powers to investigate terrorism. That same month, the President's Critical Infrastructure Protection Board was created. The Patriot Act is being reviewed by Congress in 2005, and it is likely it will be continually modified in future years.

In a broad sense, cyberspace surveillance systems are weapons that rely on prevention rather than actively destabilizing terrorist networks. The FBI was already experimenting with a controversial electronic surveillance system called Carnivore, which looked for suspicious activity in cyberspace, and had other tools under development. Through the Patriot Act, the DHS has been assigned additional powers of obtaining investigatory information from ISPs and other cyberspace service providers.

Opponents of these systems maintain that they are intrusive and do not warrant the increased invasion of privacy. The uses of commercial databases in data collection, along with many of the new surveillance tools, DHS reporting requirements for ISPs and other cyberspace service providers, and increased aggressive investigatory techniques, are being challenged by the American Civil Liberties Union (ACLU) and privacy organizations (discussed later in this chapter and in other chapters in this *Handbook*).

The government maintains that the Patriot Act of 2001 and other surveillance and investigative powers have materially improved security and prevented attacks in both government and private entities. In December 2002, FBI Director Robert Mueller reported that in the period of just over a year since the World Trade Center attack, "tens of attacks, probably close to a hundred around the world" have been detected and stopped through improved surveillance (Associated Press, 2002b).

At the end of 2003, increased cyberspace "chatter" by suspected international terrorists triggered additional security at airports and other vulnerable points. Such "data mining" from programs similar to the FBI's Carnivore project is designed to identify potential threats using cyberspace patterns—which we might call *cybermetrics* or digital forensics.

The government has been aggressive in investigating other potential security threats. In late August 2002, the Associated Press reported an FBI raid on the offices of a San Diego consulting firm, which claimed that, motivated to expose a need for better security, it had "identified 34 military sites where it said network security was easily compromised" (CNN.com, 2002d).

On December 5, 2002, federal agents raided a Quincy, Massachusetts, company "that provides critical software to major U.S. agencies and is suspected of having ties to Osama bin Laden and Al Qaeda terrorists.... Officials suspected 'back doors' may have been built into the software to enable terrorist access to federal computers." Customers included the Department of Energy, the FBI, the U.S. Air Force, the Naval Air Systems Command, the Federal Aviation Administration, the House of Representatives, and NATO (Fox News, 2002).

In 2004, inbound international airline traffic was repeatedly interrupted for additional passenger screenings, based on intelligence information. In January 2004, the United States began photographing and fingerprinting noncitizens entering the country, implementing the U.S. Visitor and Immigrant Status Indicator Technology (US-VISIT), which uses "biometrics"—technology that identifies people using digitized biological traits. That program was extended to other nations in September 2004. The proposed new Computer Assisted Passenger Pre-Screening (CAPPS-2) and Automated Commercial Environment (ACE) were designed to use digital technology to collect and analyze data. Although these programs are not specifically targeted at cyberterrorists, data from them could be cross referenced with information about individuals engaged in cyberterrorist activities.

Legal and Privacy Concerns

Privacy advocates and cyberterrorism fighters often are on a collision course. One side is for maximizing personal liberties, whereas the other wants to minimize terrorism. It is probably impossible to satisfy both sides. Other nations face similar issues.

Rowland, discussing a balance between anonymity and "strategic lawsuits against public participation" (SLAPPs), points out that U.S. and international laws in this area have only recently begun to consider the issue in cyberspace (cyberSLAPPs). She asks, "To what extent will the law protect those who use anonymity... to enable them to engage in public debate without the fear of reprisal and recrimination?" When it is relatively easy to hide an identity in cyberspace and asymmetric response is potentially devastating, "the fear of cyberterrorism... provides another rationale for intervention and regulation" (Rowland, 2003). That debate will continue.

For years, the FBI and CIA were constrained in what they could do with respect to human intelligence—actual agents on the street. In response, they developed Carnivore, Magic Lantern, and other electronic surveillance technologies to monitor worldwide telephone conversations, e-mail, and other correspondence, all of which are intrusive.

A May 2004 magazine reported that the General Accounting Office (GAO) "enumerates nearly 200 data mining initiatives in operation or in the works," and many of these "rely on data purchased from the commercial sector" (Carlson, 2004). The Pentagon's Total Information Awareness project—renamed Terrorism Information Awareness (TIA)—was blocked in Congress following privacy objections (TIA details are on the DARPA Web site, www.darpa.mil). There are critics on both sides.

The ACLU and small but vocal private interest groups argue that electronic eavesdropping and the Patriot Act and other new antiterrorism laws violate fundamental rights guaranteed by the Constitution and the Bill of Rights, especially when they purchase data from commercial firms. They contend that the resulting loss of freedom is not worth the security benefits, the ends do not justify their means, and the government has too much power over individuals.

The other side argues that the National Strategy to Secure Cyberspace is not forceful enough, and we need more laws and regulations allowing increased oversight. Mark Rosh, formerly the Justice Department's top computer crimes prosecutor said, "You need to put some teeth into some of the proposals" (CNN.com, 2002a). Many who advocate more aggressive government monitoring recommend that private-sourced data be integrated into government surveillance programs.

Former Justice Department attorney Orrin Kerr maintains, "The law is a lot more balanced than people thought. The government ended up introducing a law that didn't really take any major steps." Under the Patriot Act, noncitizens are investigated by intelligence agencies with broad powers, but citizens are handled by the FBI, which is much more restricted. They can monitor online communications, but as with wiretapping or other surveillance, agents must get judicial permission to obtain message content (Borland & Bowman, 2002).

The new strategy, new laws, and new technology increase government and companies' ability (and perhaps willingness) to collect personal data. In an interview with the *Boston Globe*, Richard Hunter discussed companies' data collection policies and excerpts from his book, *World Without Secrets*: "Information is constantly recorded and made available to almost anyone who wants it, regardless of intent.... The amount of information that's out there, and readable, is already huge" (Denison, 2002). Companies already have most of the data, and the government can get it.

Data that the government controls is subject to the Privacy Act of 1974 and other restrictions, and information brokers have generally resisted selling to federal law enforcement agencies. Although the numbers are still low, as of 2002, it was reported, "The FBI's use of commercial databases has grown 9,600 percent over the last decade" (Carlson, 2002a).

Institutions, Organizations, and Conferences

Not-for-profit and private institutions typically do not have the same security needs as commercial companies. It would be rare for them to have control over nuclear power plants, electrical grids, dams, or other vital infrastructure. However, in many cases they hold considerable financial and information resources that may be vulnerable to cybercrime and terrorism, especially with extended definitions.

Although institutions seldom have enough in-house expertise to combat potential cyberterrorism, many of the security techniques companies are using apply equally to institutions. They are good candidates for private security firms, but resource constraints make it difficult to afford the needed services. This is an area that will benefit from closer attention.

Not-for-profit and private institutions are included in government initiatives such as the National Strategy to Secure Cyberspace. Many private and semiprivate groups that combat cybercrime and cyberterrorism now are connected in some way to the DHS. In addition, many operate programs to disseminate information about potential cyberterrorist threats. For example, the Carnegie Mellon Software Engineering Institute's CERT Coordination Center, which tracks cyberspace "incidents" and "vulnerabilities," publishes a stream of security notes designed to help businesses, organizations, educational institutions, government, and technical individuals. Organizations without full-time IT staffing can access these reports on the Internet and use them as indicators for when to consider contracting for needed services. Security notes rose dramatically beginning in 2001 (CERT, 2004b).

The SANS Institute together with the FBI publishes a top 20 list of security threats. The list is "especially intended for those organizations that lack the resources to train, or those without technically advanced security administrators" (Wagner, 2002).

The Critical Infrastructure Protection Project (CIP), part of the George Mason University School of Law, is associated with the DHS and over 30 local, state, and national associations, including the Association of Metropolitan Water Agencies (AMWA), the North American Electric Reliability Council (NERC), and the ITAA. It publishes reports to Congress and a monthly newsletter, *The CIP Report*, for constituents "who have an interest in critical infrastructure protection."

The NIC publishes papers on global trends under the aegis of the National Foreign Intelligence Board and the Director of Central Intelligence, sometimes together with other government or private centers. It sponsors conferences such as the Future Threat Technologies Symposium and The Global Course of the Information Revolution: Technological Trends (NIC, 2000). The National Infrastructure Protection Center (NIPC) and the

National Association of State Chief Information Officers (NASCIO) have partnered to form an ISAC "to disseminate intelligence quickly and prevent unauthorized and destructive infiltrations" (Greenspan, 2002b).

Some of these conference organizations sell business services to commercial, nonprofit, and government entities. Many participate in, sponsor, or promote conferences that call attention to cyberterrorism issues and cybercrimes. Some have become partnered with the DHS or otherwise help in implementing the National Strategy to Secure Cyberspace and other governmental programs. In all, they are an important component in counteracting cyberterrorism.

Higher Education Institutions

Higher education institutions have many of the same resources and opportunities as other organizations. In addition, they usually have considerable in-house expertise. Colleges and universities were Internet pioneers. Long before the graphical World Wide Web existed and before business was allowed to use the Internet for commercial purposes, the academic community was file sharing and facilitating group research using the Internet.

Many higher education institutions became leaders in developing security skills and experience with the UNIX operating system and its associated Internet protocols, TCP/IP. Individuals in higher education have a tradition of working long and hard in making UNIX and Internet tools robust—often with little or no compensation. Many of them are working on cyberterrorism issues.

Today, public and private universities, community colleges, and specialized institutions such as the American Military University develop innovative technologies and popular new courses to counteract terrorism and cyberterrorism. In a letter to alumni, John Hennessy, President of Stanford University said, "Professor William Perry, former Secretary of Defense, was one of the many faculty members who made extraordinary efforts to accommodate students in oversubscribed classes. Bill's class on 'Technology in National Security' swelled from an enrollment of 145 in the fall of 2000 to 329 students this past year!" (Hennessy, 2002).

In September 2002, it was reported that Congress approved National Science Foundation (NSF) grants for 7 large projects and 240 smaller projects. Between $500,000 and $13.5 million will go to each recipient organization, many of which are higher education institutions (Legon, 2002b). Many of these support antiterrorism initiatives.

Small Business and Individuals

In the past several years, the number of individuals using cyberspace has skyrocketed, and they are included in the National Strategy to Secure Cyberspace and other cooperative initiatives. E-mail is the most common application, and many users participate in chat rooms, instant messaging, or contribute Web content through Web logs (blogs) and other forums.

Most individuals become exposed to hackers or cybercriminals—not cyberterrorists—through credit card fraud, identity theft, or property crimes. Programs such as ISpyNOW, SpyBuddy, and Cute Spy enable hackers to monitor computer keystrokes and create logs that pick up e-mail messages, passwords, and other confidential information. Some can be installed remotely, potentially through back doors. Programs such as SpyCop have been used to detect the spy, tell when it was installed, and optionally disable it.

Many small business and individuals use digital cable or DSL lines for high-speed access through an ISP, often remaining connected 24 hours per day. Hackers can gain access to connected computers that have no firewall or if the firewall is ineffective against "back door" access points. Home and small business users may lack the technical expertise to configure these access points to protect against intrusion. The "I Love You" virus caused an estimated $4 billion in damages to individuals and international systems (Information Warfare Database, 2000). Hackers also plant worms or other invasive programs to hijack the computer and use it to send spam or to carry out DDoS or other forms of cyberattacks, a potential contributor to cyberterrorism.

PC Magazine listed 10 "bad guys" of cyberspace, including DDoS attacks, worms, viruses, e-mail attachments, open network or TCP ports, and "persistent connections" (usually 24/7). The article gives often-attacked filenames, discusses strengths and weaknesses of hardware or software firewalls, offers nine safety tips, details specific information about instant messaging hazards, and names vulnerable ports hackers exploit (Karagiannis & Sarrel, 2002). These data are somewhat more detailed than the NCSA guidelines (see http://www.staysafeonline.info).

The National Strategy to Secure Cyberspace makes simple recommendations to private users to regularly update antivirus and operating systems, turn off computers at night, and install firewall software or physically disconnect when offline. In addition, the strategy recommends that users apply caution in opening e-mail attachments that may contain viruses, worms, or other invasive components. Other common preventive measures include using strong passwords that mix characters and numbers, disabling unnecessary applications and services, maintaining proper browser security settings, and relentless vigilance.

WHO WILL WIN THE BATTLE OF CYBERTERRORISM?

This chapter is about the terrorist threat as it can best be seen from today, with the benefit of no hindsight. A long struggle with cyberterrorism may be just beginning. It could be a battle of minimization, not elimination. In the days following the 9/11 attacks, Secretary of Defense Donald Rumsfeld said of the war on terrorism:

> The cold war, it took 50 years, plus or minus. It did not involve major battles. It involved continuous pressure. It involved cooperation by a host of nations. And when it ended, it ended not with a bang, but through internal collapse. It strikes me that might be a more appropriate way to think about what we are up against here. (*World Almanac and Book of Facts*, 2002)

Richard Clarke adds, "We reserve the right to respond in any way appropriate: through covert action, through military action, any one of the tools available to the president" (Holland, 2002). This could indicate the future of counteracting cyberterrorism.

IT professionals in government, business, institutions, schools and universities, and private interest groups are interconnected through cyberspace. Each will play a role in combating cyberterrorism. Many government programs have been designed to bring these groups together, help secure systems from outside attack, monitor internal usage, and detect suspicious activity. Working together, they will become more effective in counteracting cyberterrorism.

In the coming years, cyberterrorists will have more powerful tools at their disposal. At the same time, government, businesses, institutions, and individuals will work together to craft strategies to counteract it. Although that effort seems to be making progress in protecting critical infrastructure, networks, and computer systems, continued vigilance will be required as terrorists obtain new tools.

How actively should governmental intervention policies regulate vulnerabilities in cyberspace? Parks (2003) takes the aggressive position, suggesting codification and compliance. "When we were approaching Y2K, also known as 'the end of the world,' the federal government required that all public companies disclose to their shareholders what measures had been taken to prevent predicted disruptions and failures in their systems, [and we] should implement information security regulations along those same lines." Others advocate cooperative, voluntary approaches that can react quickly to flexible threats and conditions, without rigid legal requirements.

People will need to learn to live with cyberterrorism and minimize its impact. Some individuals have resigned themselves to some loss of freedoms to counteract terrorist threats. Others have remained committed to preserving individual privacy. This will be an important issue in the next several years.

One thing seems clear: as cyberterrorism becomes increasingly global, governments worldwide and international governing organizations will need to participate in what is almost certain to be a long-term commitment. Balancing control with individual rights will take on an increasingly global perspective, and what was initially perceived to be a threat may become an opportunity to establish increased overall cooperation.

The strong level of disagreement between extreme points of view, such as those of Richard Clarke, who predicts doom and gloom, and opponents who do not see great danger, is an obstacle to effective policy. At least, in our changing environment, it should make people think and debate. Hopefully, the dialectic will lead to effective solutions.

GLOSSARY

9/11 The World Trade Center and Pentagon attacks, which occurred on September 11, 2001.

24/7 An activity that can occur 24 hours per day 7 days per week, as do many broadband Internet connections.

Asymmetric Response A one-sided response and a generic explanation why cyberterrorists behave as they do. Unable to achieve their objectives through conventional means, an extremist may strike against the "enemy" with a one-sided act of terror.

Border Gateway Protocol (BGP) Tables that detail the more than 100,000 routes information can travel over the Internet. BGP routers exchange information about routes and improve data flow efficiency.

Cybercrime Activity in cyberspace usually associated with fraud, commercial espionage, or theft of intellectual property, identity, or private data that can result in loss of data or corruption of computer files.

Cyberspace/Digital World/Virtual World The world of discrete mathematical values, usually ones and zeros at its lowest level, that powers computers and networks and can be used to represent the physical world. It is generally outside time and space, unless it is applied to a physical object through an interface to the analog world.

Cyberterrorism An evolving body of activity that includes both acts *in* cyberspace and *using* cyberspace tools to create fear or panic, often done by subnational groups or clandestine agents and directed toward intimidating or coercing a government or some segment of the noncombatant civilian population, usually in furtherance of political or social objectives; differs from hacking and cybervandalism in its intent and the degree of severity of the attacks.

Denial of Service (DoS) Attack A condition under which a Web site or other Internet resource is disabled by an attack from an overwhelming number of inbound messages. A distributed denial of service (DDoS) attack has the inbound messages coming from multiple computers.

Department of Homeland Security (DHS) Signed into law in November 2002, the DHS absorbed 22 federal agencies, including five cybersecurity offices and programs.

Graphical User Interface (GUI) Typically used to describe the graphical interface between a computer's display and the internal hardware workings or the interface between a computer's display and images served up on the Web.

Hacker A person who gains unauthorized entry into computers or other digital devices through cyberspace, usually for the purpose of minor damage or annoyance, such as defacement of a Web site or observation of data.

Hardware Physical devices that process mathematical ones and zeros. Hardware has an interface to the physical world, such as a keyboard or monitor display. SCADA devices include hardware.

Information Sharing and Analysis Centers (ISACs) Formal or informal groups that share information on cyberattacks, vulnerabilities, countermeasures, and information services best practices relating to telecommunications, financial, chemical, energy, information technology, water, transportation, aviation, food, and so on.

Physical World/Analog World The world of physical objects and forces in time and space. The analog world is continuous. It can be represented in cyberspace by devices that use digital ones and zeros.

SCADA Systems Supervisory control and data acquisition systems used in networks of digital computer-controlled devices for physical infrastructure.

Software Programming code that, at its basic level, delivers ones and zeros that can be used to control the operation and function of hardware devices, including SCADA systems.

Transmission Control Protocols/Internet Protocols (TCPs/IPs) The set of rules by which the Internet operates and communicates among devices.

World Wide Web (a.k.a. Web) The graphical overlay that resides on top of the Internet and allows graphics to be served and browsed.

CROSS REFERENCES

See *Cybercrime and the U.S. Criminal Justice System; Cyberlaw: The Major Areas, Development, and Information Security Aspects; Hackers, Crackers, and Computer Criminals; Hacktivism.*

REFERENCES

Annan, K. (1999). *Report of the Secretary General on the work of the organization* (A/54/1/, para. 254). Retrieved from http://www.un.org/Docs/SG/Report99/toc.htm

Arena, K. (2003, December 5). Al Qaeda tape likely used to rally, recruit. Retrieved December 5, 2003, from http://www.cnn.com/2003/US/12/05/holiday.terror.threat/index.html

Associated Press (AP). (2002a, October 7). Stealthy e-mail worm bores into computers in a dozen countries. *Medford Mail Tribune*.

Associated Press (AP). (2002b, December 16). FBI Director: 100 terror attacks thwarted. Retrieved December 16, 2002, from http://www.foxnews.com/story/0,2933,73122,00.html

Associated Press (AP). (2003a, March 27). Al-Jazeera Web site hacking. Retrieved March 27, 2003, from http://www.foxnews.com/printer_friendly_story/0,3566,82375,00.html

Associated Press (AP). (2003b, November 10). Report: New terrorists harder to track. Retrieved November 11, 2003, from www.foxnews.com/printer_friendly_story/0,3566,102728,00.html

Associated Press (AP). (2004, September 15). FAA radio outage affects airports, flights in West. *Medford Mail Tribune*, p. A6.

BBC Worldwide Monitoring (2002, August 31). "Southeast Asian nations agree tougher measures to counter cyberterrorism," Radio Australia, Melbourne. Retrieved November 7, 2002, from http://www.lexis-nexis.com

Borland, J., & Bowman, L. (2002, August 27). *E-terrorism: Liberty vs. security*. Retrieved December 19, 2003, from http://zdnet.com.com/2100-1105-955493.html

Carlson, C. (2002a). Data search stirs concern. *eWeek, 19*(32), 22.

Carlson, C. (2002b). Feds pitch cyber-fence. *eWeek, 19*(36), 18.

Carlson, C. (2004, May 27). *GAO report reveals rampant federal data mining*. Retrieved May 28, 2004, from http://www.eweek.com/print_article/0,1761,a=128302,00.asp

Caruso, J. (2002, March 21). *On combating terrorism: Protecting the United States*. FBI Press Room, testimony to U.S. House of Representatives. Retrieved August 8, 2002, from www.fbi.gov/congress/congress02/caruso032102.htm

CCNMatthews (2004, May 17). *World's top financial institutions struggle to fend-off escalating security threats, Deloitte study finds*. Canadian Corporate Newswire. Retrieved September 24, 2004, from http://www.lexis-nexis.com

CERT. (2003a). *Homeland Security announces the National Cyber Security Summit*. Carnegie Mellon CERT Coordination Center. Retrieved December 19, 2003, from http://www.cert.gov/press_room/detail/summit.html

CERT. (2003b). *Remarks by Secretary Tom Ridge at the National Cyber Security Summit*. Retrieved December 19, 2003, from http://www.cert.gov/press_room/detail/RidgeSummitSpeech.html

CERT. (2004a). *2004 E-crime watch survey shows significant increase in electronic crimes*. Carnegie Mellon CERT Coordination Center. Retrieved September 13, 2004, from http://www.cert.org/about/ecrime.html

CERT. (2004b). *CERT/CC statistics 1988–2004*. Carnegie Mellon CERT Coordination Center. Retrieved September 13, 2004, from http://www.cert.org/stats/cert_stats.html

Chakrabarti, A., & Manimaran, G. (2002). Internet infrastructure security: A taxonomy. *IEEE Network, 16*(6), 13–21.

Christensen, J. (1999, April 6). *Bracing for guerrilla warfare in cyberspace*. Retrieved July 25, 2002, from http://www.cnn.com/TECH/specials/hackers/cyber-terror/

CIO Magazine. (2004, October 1). *State of the CIO: The survey*. Retrieved October 4, 2004, from http://www.cio.com/archive/100104/survey.html

Clinton, W. (2000, December 11). *A foreign policy for the global age*. Address at the University of Nebraska. Retrieved August 14, 2002, from http://usembassy.state.gov/islamabad/wwwh00121101.html

CNN.com. (2002a, September 18). *Cyber-security plan avoids call for new rules*. Retrieved September 18, 2002, from http://www.con.com/2002/TECH/internet/09/18/cyber-security.ap/index.html

CNN.com. (2002b, October 25). *FBI: Al Qaeda operatives may target U.S. railroads*. Retrieved October 25, 2002, from http://www.cnn.com/2002/US/10/25/railroad.warning/index.html

CNN.com. (2002c, July 5). *Yale accuses Princeton of hacking*. Retrieved July 25, 2002, from http://www.cnn.com

CNN.com. (2002d, August 23). *FBI raids firm after military hacking claim*. Retrieved August 23, 2002, from http://www.cnn.com/2002/TECH/internet/08/23/computer.security.ap/index.html

CNN.com. (2003a, March 3). *Fierce cyber war predicted*. Retrieved March 3, 2003, from http://www.cnn.com/2003/TECH/ptech/03/03/sprj.irq.infro.war.ap/index.html

CNN.com. (2003b, October 18). *NATO needs rapid-response force*. Retrieved October 19, 2003, from http://

www.cnn.com/2003/WORLD/europe/10/18/nato.defense/index.html

Collin, B. C. (1996). *The future of cyberterrorism: Where the physical and virtual worlds converge*. Paper presented at 11th Annual International Symposium on Criminal Justice Issues. Retrieved July 23, 2002, from www.afgen.com/terrorism1.html

Convention on Cyber-crime. (2001a). *30 States sign the Convention on Cyber-crime at the opening ceremony*. Retrieved December 23, 2002, from http://press.coe.int/cp/2001/875a(2001).htm

Convention on Cyber-crime. (2001b). *The Convention on Cyber-crime, a unique instrument for international co-operation*. Retrieved December 23, 2002, from http://press.coe.int/cp/2001/893a(2001).htm

Conway, M. (2002, November). Reality bytes: Cyberterrorism and terrorist "use" of the Internet. *First Monday, 7*(11). Retrieved December 20, 2002, from http://firstmonday.org/issues/issue7_11/conway

Cyberatlas. (2001, December 13). *Internet, computer security concerns Americans*. Retrieved July 23, 2002, from http://cyberatlas.internet.com/big_picture/geographics/article/0,,5911_939161,00.html

DCI Counterterrorist Center, CIA. (2002). *The war on terrorism: A call to action*. Retrieved August 14, 2002, from http://www.cia.gov/terrorism/ctc.html

Denison, D. C. (2002, May 19). "Smart" stats: business at the speed of a fastball. *The Boston Globe*.

Denning, D. (1999, December 10). *Activism, hacktivism, and cyberterrorism: The Internet as a tool for influencing foreign policy*. Retrieved September, 2004, from http://www.nautilus.org/gps/info-policy/workshop/papers/denning.html (Denning's publications are available at http://www.cs.georgetown.edu/~denning/publications.html)

Denning, D. (2001, November 1). *Is cyber terror next?* Retrieved December 20, 2002, from http://www.ssrc.org/sept11/essays/denning.htm

DHS. (2003). *Department of Homeland Security Web site*. Retrieved December 19, 2003, from http://www.dhs.gov/dhspublic/display?theme=26&content=46&print=true

eWeek. (2003, February 26). *Mitnick: Leaving the dark side*. Interview transcript. Retrieved February 28, 2003, from http://www.eweek.com/print_article/0,3668,a=37623,00.asp

FBI. (1999, November 10). News release, Tampa, FL Retrieved August 6, 2002, from http://tampa.fbi.gov/pressrel/1999/11_10_99.htm

Fisher, D. (2002, December 16). Researchers warn of serious SSH flaws. *eWeek*. Retrieved February 4, 2003, from http://www.eweek.com/article2/0,1759,1657019,00.asp

Fisher, D. (2003a, February 4). Cyber-security plan counts on private sector's input. *eWeek*. Retrieved February 4, 2003, from http://www.eweek.com/print_article/0,3668,a=36580,00.asp

Fisher, D. (2003b). New dangers exposed in the wake of Slammer. *eWeek, 20*(5), 1.

Fisher, D., & Carlson, C. (2003, December 15). Feds unite on security benchmarks. *eWeek, 20*(50), 1.

FOX News. (2002, December 6). *Feds raid software company suspected of terror ties*. Retrieved December 6, 2002, from http://www.foxnews.com/story/0,2933,72345,00.html

Gartner. (2002, August 13). *Cyber-attacks: The results of the Gartner/U.S. Naval War College Simulation*. Transcript of conference call. Retrieved December 19, 2003, from www3.gartner.com/2_events/audioconferences/dph/dph.html

Gellman, B. (2002, June 26). Cyber-attacks by Al Qaeda feared, terrorists at the threshold of using Internet as tool of bloodshed. *Washington Post*.

Gomes, L. (2002, December 16). Digital Pearl Harbor is more marketing ploy than a real threat. *Wall Street Journal*.

Gordon, S., & Ford, R. (2002). Cyberterrorism? *Computers & Security, 21*(7), 636–647.

Green, J. (2002, November). *The myth of cyberterrorism*. Retrieved September 13, 2004, from http://www.washingtonmonthly.com/features/2001/0211.green.html

Greenspan, R. (2002a, September 27). *Computers still insecure*. Retrieved September 28, 2002, from http://cyberatlas.internet.com/big_picture/applications/article/0,1323,1301_1472111,00.html

Greenspan, R. (2002b, August 31). *Cyberterrorism concerns IT pros*. Retrieved September 28, 2002, from http://cyberatlas.internet.com/big_picture/geographics/article/0,,5911_1448291,00.html

Greenspan, R. (2003a, December 11). *U.S. gov't computers get barely passing grade*. Retrieved January 9, 2004, from http://cyberatlas.internet.com/big_picture/geographics/print/0,,5911_3288101,00.html

Greenspan, R. (2003b, January 16). *2003: Year of the worm?* Retrieved January 31, 2003, from http://cyberatlas.internet.com/big_picture//applications/print/0,,1301_1577811,00.html

Haimes, Y. (2002). Risk of terrorism to cyber-physical and organizational-societal infrastructures. *Public Works Management & Policy, 6*(4), 231–240.

Hennessy, H. L. (2002). Letter to alumni, Stanford University, August 2002.

Hensgen, T., Desouza, K., Evaristo, J., & Kraft, G. (2003). Playing the "cyber terrorism game" towards a semiotic definition. *Human Systems Management, 22*(2), 51–61.

Hinde, S. (2003). Cyberterrorism in context. *Computers & Security, 22*(3), 188–192.

Holland, J. (2002, February 13). *White House expert says US may retaliate with military if terrorists try cyberterrorism*. Retrieved July 31, 2002, from http://www.lexis-nexis.com

Information Management Journal. (2002a). A megabyte of prevention. *Information Management Journal, 36*(4), 10.

Information Management Journal. (2002b). Cyber security: Key to homeland security. *Information Management Journal, 36*(4), 10.

Information Management Journal. (2002c). Virtual vulnerabilities. *Information Management Journal, 36*(4), 11.

Information Management Journal. (2003). Cyber crime code could punish online protesters. *Information Management Journal, 37*(3), 10.

Information Management Journal. (2004). Online crime costs rising. *Information Management Journal, 38*(4), 14.

Information Warfare Database. (2002). *The Terrorism Research Center, in cooperation with Georgetown University*. Retrieved October 2, 2002, from http://www.terrorism.com/iwdb/incidents.asp

ISAC. (2003). *World Wide Information Sharing and Analysis Center, v1.51*. Retrieved December 19, 2003, from www.wwisac.com/aboutus.cfm and www.wwisac.com/faq.cfm

Jaeger, C. (2003). Cyberterrorism. In *The Internet Encyclopedia* (pp. 353–371). New York: John Wiley & Sons, 2003.

Jane's Information Group Ltd. (1999, October 21). *China–Taiwan hacker wars*. Retrieved from http://www.infowar.com/hacker/99/hack_10299a_j.shtml;Internet

Johnson, M., & Radcliff, D. (2001, November 9). *Cybersecurity czar: Protect IT infrastructure.* Retrieved July 31, 2002, from http://www.cnn.com/2001/TECH/internet/11/09/infrastructure.protection.idg/index.html?related

Kaplan, F. (August 15, 2003). *The Al-Qaeda question*. Retrieved December 19, 2003, from http://slate.msn.com/id/2087037

Karagiannis, K., & Sarrel, M. (2002, November 19). Keep hackers out: Part one, personal edition. *PC Magazine.* Retrieved December 2, 2002, from http://www.pcmag.com/print_article/0,3048,a=32564,00.asp

Legon, J. (2002a, October 23). *FBI seeks to trace massive Net attack.* Retrieved October 24, 2002, from http://www.cnn.com/2002/TECH/internet/10/23/net.attack/index.html

Legon, J. (2002b, September 27). *New net project aims to avoid hacking.* Retrieved September 28, 2002, from http://edition.cnn.com/2002/TECH/internet/09/27/iris.internet/

Lemos (2002, August 26). *What are the real risks of cyberterrorism?* Retrieved August 29, 2002, from http://zdnet.com.com/2100-1009_22-955293.html

Lewis, J. A. (2002, December). *Assessing the risk of cyber terrorism, cyber war and other cyber threats.* Center for Strategic & International Studies, Washington, DC. Retrieved from http://www.csis.org/tech/0211_lewis.pdf

Lipson, H. F. (2002, November). *Tracking and tracing cyber-attacks: Technical challenges and global policy issues*. Retrieved December 23, 2002, from http://www.cert.org/archive/pdf/02sr009.pdf

Marcella, A., Jr., Roth, J., & Espersen, D. (2003). A question of preparedness. *Internal Auditor*, October, 67–69.

Mark, R. (2003, February 7). *Report: Bush considering cyber warfare*. Retrieved February 7, 2003, from http://dc.internet.com/news/article.php/1580981

McMahon, T. (2002, June 13). *Terrorist attacks mean big e-security spending.* Retrieved December 23, 2002 from http://www.europemedia.net/shownews.asp?ArticleID=10960

Meriweather, D. (1995). *Takedown*. Retrieved August 14, 2002, from http://www.takedown.com

Meyer, D. (2002). *University of Oregon route views project*. Retrieved December 23, 2002, from http://www.antc.uoregon.edu/route-views

Miller, H. (2003, November). *Information security: The long campaign*. The CIP Report, p. 4. Retrieved December 19, 2003, from http://techcenter.gmu.edu/programs/cipp/cip_report.html

Moran, J. M. (2002, February 5). Eye on cyberterrorism. *The Hartford Courant*.

Naraine, R. (2002, October 23). *Massive DDoS attack hit DNS root servers*. Retrieved October 25, 2002, from http://www.internetnews.com/ent-news/article.php/1486981

NIC. (1999, October 14). *Buck Rogers or rock throwers?* Conference report. Retrieved August 14, 2002, from http://www.cia.gov/nic/pubs/conferenece_reports/buck_rogers.htm

NIC. (2000, December). *Global Trends 2015: A dialogue about the future with nongovernment experts*. Retrieved August 14, 2002, from http://www.cia.gov/nic/pubs/2015_files/2015.htm

NIPC. (2001a, October). *CyberProtests: The threat to the U.S. information infrastructure*. National Infrastructure Protection Center. Retrieved July 25, 2002, from www.nipc.gov

NIPC. (2001b, June 15). *Cyberterrorism: An evolving concept*. National Infrastructure Protection Center. Retrieved July 25, 2002, from www.nipc.gov

O'Connor, R. (2000, November 6). Cracker jacked! Feds losing battle against cyberintruders. *Interactive Week,* 7(45), 14–16.

Overill, R. (2003). Reacting to cyber-intrusions: The technical, legal, and ethical dimensions. *Journal of Financial Crime, 11*(2), 163–167.

Parks, C. (2003). Cyber terrorism: Hype or reality? *The Journal of Corporate Accounting & Finance, 14*(5), 9–11.

Pastore, M. (2001, April 17). *Cyber-crime worries Americans, with good reason*. Retrieved July 23, 2002, from http://cyberatlas.internet.com/big_picture/hardware/article/0,1323,5921_744811,00.html

Pollitt, M. M. (2002). *Cyberterrorism—Fact or fancy?* Retrieved August 14, 2002, from http://www.cs.georgetown.edu/~denning/infosec/pollitt.html

Porteus, L. (2002, September 19). *White House releases cyber-security plan*. Retrieved September 19, 2002, from http://www.foxnews.com/story/0,2933,63452,00.html

Porteus, L. (2003, March 26). *Government creates its own private cyber network*. Retrieved March 26, 2003, from http://www.foxnews.com/printer_friendly_story/0,3566,82273,00.html

Rasmussen, M. (2003, December 5). *The cyber-security challenge*. Transcript from Live Online discussion. Retrieved December 19, 2003, from www.washingtonpost.com

Regan, T. (1999, July 1). When terrorists turn to the Internet. *Christian Science Monitor*, p. 17. Retrieved August 14, 2002, from http://csmweb2.emcweb.com/durable/1999/07/01/p17s1.htm

Reuters. (2003, November 19). *Tree root cause in U.S., Canadian blackout*. Retrieved September 24, 2004, from www.cnn.com/2003/US/11/19/blackout.report.reut

Richmond, R. (2003, January 27). *Companies continue to wrestle with Slammer computer worm*. Retrieved January 28, 2003, from www.schwab.com

Rowland, D. (2003). Privacy, freedom of epression and CyberSLAPPs: Fostering anonymity on the Internet? *International Review of Law Computers & Technology, 17*(3), 303–312.

Sargent, M. (2001). *Twisted list: Five most notorious hackers ever*. Retrieved August 14, 2002, from http://www.techtv.com/screensavers/twistedlist/story/0,24330,3321221,00.html

Sieberg, D. (2002, April 7). *Cyber-crime rising, yet fewer companies reporting incidents*. Retrieved July 31, 2002, from http://www.cnn.com/2002/TECH/internet/04/07/cyber-crime.survey/index.html?related

Snyder, J. (2002, June 28). Could the next terror target be the Internet? *Canadian Business and Current Affairs*. Retrieved July 31, 2002, from http://www.lexis-nexis.com

Springer, D. (2002). *Electronic voting worries add to booth tensions*. Retrieved October 24, 2002, from http://www.foxnews.com/story/0,2933,66562,00.html

Tang, R. (2001). *China–U.S. cyber war escalates*. Retrieved August 14, 2002, from http://www.cnn.com/2001/WORLD/asiapcf/east/04/27/china.hackers

Vaas, L. (2003). Laborious updates leave SQL databases unpatched. *eWeek, 20*(5), 12.

Van Marsh, A. (2004, January 6). *How the Army used tech to nab Saddam*. Retrieved January 6, 2004, from www.cnn.com/2004/TECH/ptech/01/06/sprj.nirq.troop.tech/index.html

Vatis, M. (2001). *Interview with Michael Vatis, chief of National Infrastructure Protection Center (NIPC)* [Television Broadcast]. New York and Washington, DC: Public Broadcasting Service. Retrieved July 25, 2002, from http://www.pbs.org/wgbh/pages/frontline/shows/hackers/interviews/vatis.html

Vickers, A. (2002, October 25). FBI hunt megahackers who blitzed Internet. *The Mirror*. Retrieved November 7, 2002, from http://www.lexis-nexis.com

Wagner, J. (2002, October 2). *SANS/FBI names top 20 network threats*. Retrieved October 2, 2002, from http://www.internetnews.com dev-news/article.php/1474281

Wald, M. (2004, September 15). Radio failure in west disrupts air traffic. *The New York Times*, p. 18A.

Watson, D. L. (2002). *The terrorist threat confronting the United States*. Retrieved August 6, 2002, from http://www.fbi.gov/congress/congress02/watson020602.htm

Weiss, T. R. (2001). *Denial-of-service warning issued by FBI*. Retrieved July 31, 2002, from http://www.cnn.com/2001/TECH/internet/05/08/dos.warning.idg/index.html

World Almanac and Book of Facts, 2002. Notable quotes in 2002, (2000) Retrieved July 31, 2002, from http://www.lexis-nexis.com

Wylie, M. (2002, November 1). No safety net—Stopping hackers is one thing, but who guards the actual networks? *The Star Ledger*, p. 45.

Wynne, J. (2002). *White House advisor Richard Clarke briefs Senate panel on cyber-security*. Retrieved December 20, 2002, from http://usinfo.state.gov/topical/global/ecom/02021401.htm

Yoran, A. (2003). *Amit Yoran, NCSD director speaks at the summit*. Retrieved December 19, 2003, from http://www.uscert.gov/events/summit/YoranSummitSpeech.html

The Legal Implications of Information Security: Regulatory Compliance and Liability

Blaze D. Waleski, *Fulbright & Jaworski LLP*

INTRODUCTION

Modern business is all but dependent upon information technology (IT), and reliance on the exchange of electronic information is rapidly becoming entrenched in our day-to-day personal lives (e.g., through the Internet, wireless devices, and other interactive means of data transfer). To an ever greater degree, business relies on technologies that connect with its customers, and with other businesses, for example, to streamline supply routes, control inventory, and minimize time to market, exchange services and products in business-to-business trade platforms, enhance distribution channels, boost sales through e-commerce, improve fulfillment operations, and enrich customer databases with valuable information concerning customer spending patterns and the like. There are, in fact, companies, such as Axciom Corporation, Abacus Direct, Equifax, Experian, and InfoUSA, that focus on compiling and aggregating consumer-related data.

The Internet has been the foremost catalyst of this business evolution, precipitating a global interconnectivity of computer systems that permits ready access by businesses and individuals to vast amounts of corporate and consumer information, which, thanks to advancements in IT, are becoming increasingly easy to access, search, and retrieve. A by-product of this evolving global electronic business model is the interdependence on the access to and sharing of data. IT—through software applications, hardware and communications equipment, networking systems, and the many related services—facilitates this access to and sharing of data.

Rethinking the Security of Data in Light of Modern IT

Modern IT, and particularly the Internet, has caused a rethinking of how corporate data and personal information should be handled. Most of that information is now in electronic form. It is quite common now for a business's key information to reside in an electronic data format, sometimes never being transformed into paper hardcopy at all. Because it can be easily accessed, copied, and widely distributed in electronic form, via the Internet for example, and often as easily as by typing a few keystrokes, concerns of security are greater than ever. With the efficiencies brought about by modern IT have come greater risks—risks that often involve undesired, or even illegal, use of, access to, and disclosure of sensitive data.

Public awareness of these risks, at least with regard to personal information, has raised the bar for information security by putting pressures on business to assure consumers of the security of their information. To allay consumer concern, many Web sites display a privacy policy aimed at reassuring consumers hesitant about uploading their personal information online and have taken steps to secure that data. Today's business also operates with an understanding that a security breach could cause echoing negative public relations. For example, *In the Matter of Eli Lilly and Co.* (2002), Eli Lilly had offered users of several drugs, including the antidepressant medication Prozac, an e-mail reminder service that would allow each user to receive personal e-mail messages to remind them to take or refill their medication. On June 27, 2001, Lilly sent an e-mail to all 669 subscribers of the e-mail service, but listed each of their e-mail addresses in the "To:" field of the e-mail, thereby unintentionally disclosing to each individual subscriber the e-mail addresses of all other subscribers. Lilly's privacy policy included statements such as "Eli Lilly and Company respects the privacy of visitors to its Web sites, and we feel it is important to maintain our guests' privacy as they take advantage of this resource." The Federal Trade Commission (FTC) alleged that Lilly's claim of privacy and confidentiality was deceptive because it "failed to maintain or implement internal measures appropriate under the circumstances to protect sensitive consumer information," as evidenced by its June 27, 2001, disclosure.

Public concern has also prompted lawmakers to enact legislation affecting how certain personal information is handled. Those laws can impact a business's implementation of IT, can create regulatory compliance obligations, and may pose the potential for liability to third parties if the data are mishandled. The new regulatory environment and its corporate compliance issues, coupled with corporate concern for negative public relations, the potential for civil liability, and the heightened risks brought about by advancements in IT, have caused businesses to pay closer attention to IT security practices and to look at how IT may be used to both satisfy compliance obligations and minimize liability.

WHAT IS AT RISK?

Corporate Data and Personal Information

Corporate data are often a valuable asset. Trade secrets, confidential business information such as customer lists, and other sensitive business information such as internal operating procedures are guarded with great care, are protected from unauthorized disclosure to outsiders, and should be secured.

Additionally, the personal information of employees and consumers (sometimes referred to in legal texts as nonpublic personal information, personally identifiable information, or simply personal data), such as contact information, financial data and transaction records, and personal health information, is generally viewed as private and confidential to the individual and therefore protected against unauthorized access by and disclosure to third parties. It is not uncommon for a business to invest in the security of human management and payroll systems to ensure adequate protection of information about employees. Nor is it unusual for a business to safeguard consumer information, not only because its unauthorized disclosure may pose a risk of regulatory noncompliance, but also because such information may be considered a valuable asset, the disclosure of which could result in a competitive loss in the marketplace.

Nature of the Data

Data of little commercial value, or that are not highly private to an individual, may pose little risk. However, data that may pose a distinct risk if subject to a security breach, and that may result in liability, could include sensitive information such as the following:

1. Company trade secrets, which may include customer lists or business methods. Rights in trade secrets are governed by state law (*Roton Barrier, Inc. v. Stanley Works*, 1996). The Restatement of Torts acknowledges that a customer list may be a trade secret (see Restatement of Torts §757, Comment b). A business must protect the secrecy of a trade secret to retain its trade secret status (see *Defiance Button Machine Co. v. C&C Metal Products Corp.*, 1985, in which rights in a customer list were forfeited because information was not kept confidential).
2. Information that may not necessarily be a trade secret, but which a business nonetheless considers to be confidential (e.g., price lists, internal policy manuals) and does not want disclosed to certain other parties (e.g., competitors) or publicly (see *Overholt Crop Insurance Service Co. v. Travis*, 1991, in which the court enforced a company's rights in its customer information that had been revealed under a confidential relationship, even if the information was "technically not a trade secret").
3. Confidential information of a business partner, of a contracting entity, or of a business customer and of which an organization is in possession and for which the organization has agreed to keep confidential (e.g., through a contract, such as a nondisclosure agreement).
4. Information collected from or about a consumer (such as contact information, demographic information, transaction records, credit report data, purchasing habits, or Web site surfing activity), which may be subject to:
   (a) Specific laws governing redisclosure and use of consumer information, such as financial information and medical records. Examples of such laws include the Financial Services Modernization Act of 1999 (more commonly known as the Gramm-Leach-Bliley Act or GLB), which governs the protection of "personally identifiable financial information," and the Health Insurance Portability and Accountability Act (HIPAA), which governs the protection of "protected health information." In Europe, the Data Protection Directive (1995) governs generally the protection of "personal data."
   (b) More general consumer protection laws governing personal information of consumers. Examples of such laws include the Federal Trade Commission Act (FTCA, 1914) and individual state consumer protection laws.
   (c) A commitment by the business to keep the consumer's information private, such as in a Web site privacy policy or in a legally required privacy notice (such as a GLB notice).

In many instances, the nature of the data will determine whether certain statutory or regulatory obligations are triggered and thus whether the data are subject to regulatory compliance requirements (e.g., HIPAA pertains only to "protected health information," a statutorily defined term). The nature of the data may affect the risk in two ways: (1) highly sensitive data, such as trade secrets, customer credit card information, and consumer financial account information, will be a target for hackers, increasing the likelihood of unauthorized disclosure by intrusion, and (2) in the event of a breach, more sensitive data may pose a greater degree of harm and perhaps result in a public relations fiasco as well.

Attendant Risks

It is important to understand how the data are used and what therefore could happen to them (or, if a breach has occurred, what has happened to the data). Key to this understanding is knowing how the data are gathered, transmitted, used, and stored and where in that process the data might be (or have been) compromised in one way or another. This exercise pinpoints where the integrity of those data may be (or was) compromised.

Why is this important? Certain regulatory obligations specifically address the handling of data (e.g., GLB prohibits an unauthorized disclosure to a nonaffiliated third party). In terms of devising an appropriate compliance program, it is necessary to understand fully how the data are to be used, and what access, use, and disclosure restrictions need to be placed on those data. Moreover, the potential for liability to others will depend to a large extent on how the data are handled (e.g., liability might attach under a negligence theory if the data were handled in an unreasonable fashion). The implementation of appropriate IT infrastructure and data security policies and procedures can often help to satisfy compliance obligations and to mitigate the potential for liability.

At the preventive stage, there are several security considerations, the evaluation of which provides a good framework for assessing and testing security controls:

Physical security. Physical security refers to the security measures in place to prevent unauthorized physical entry to the location at which computer equipment is located and may include such relatively simple measures as locked entryways and access to central computing rooms via authorized identification card only or more sophisticated measures such as biometric screening systems such as fingerprint or retinal scan recognition. Ordinarily, locked entryways and access restricted to authorized identification cards would suffice, but other measures may be considered when highly sensitive data are at issue.

Technical security. Technical security encompasses the use of logical security, which includes implementation of hardware and software designed specifically to secure data. Logical security has been defined as "security measures for controlling access to electronic information resources through logical means (e.g., via software or network controls), procedural controls related to software development and change control, security of data, communications, and reduction of risk from harmful and intrusive computer software." See "University of Central Florida" (2001). It contemplates controls within software that limit access by a secure means of authentication and authorization. Logical security includes issuance and maintenance of user identifications and corresponding passwords and other software-related protocols for identifying authenticity. Extranets, virtual private networks, and remote access typically employ varying degrees of logical security. Logical security also involves securing networks and securely integrating applications and systems by using software and hardware designed specifically to secure or otherwise prevent risk to data. Examples include software firewalls, virus and monitoring applications, and hardware firewalls and routers. Software that is implemented should be regularly updated (e.g., with current security patches). Virus scanning software should be regularly updated with current virus definitions. Technical security may also include adequate contingency plans, including routine backup and archiving of data, to minimize the risk in the event of data loss.

Personnel and administrative security (employee and consultant policies and procedures). The nature of the data may warrant that they be accessed by a limited number of personnel having higher security clearance. Moreover, personnel with access should be trained as to the business' policies and procedures with regard to the use and disclosure of such data. There should also be fail checks built into the system, or some sort of counterintelligence mechanisms, to identify individuals who may not follow procedures or who may, themselves, seek to access, copy, steal, or release data improperly. Background checks may be made on persons being considered for hire as employees or to be retained as consultants who are expected to have access to sensitive data or to the systems that store or transmit such data. Adequate training and ongoing support may minimize the risk of data being inadvertently deleted or altered by human error or ignorance. Adequately trained personnel should administer the business' security policies and procedures.

Operational security. The overall operations of the business should be guided by a security policy that takes into account the unique risks and vulnerabilities associated with the attendant business practices, which will include several of the foregoing security concerns. Certain laws (e.g., GLB) require a business to implement a security program suitable for its size, business practices, risks, and vulnerabilities.

As shown below, failures in the foregoing may lead to regulatory noncompliance and also may give rise to third-party liability. Security breaches that may trigger regulatory obligations, or generate the potential for third-party liability, include unauthorized access, use, or disclosure of data or systems and destruction, loss, or corruption of data.

Unauthorized Access, Use, and Disclosure. Information of a sensitive nature—for example, corporate trade secrets, confidential information of a business partner, or personal information of consumers—poses a distinct risk of liability if it is not properly safeguarded. Most organizations recognize that this information should be kept confidential. Not all organizations, however, appreciate how their IT infrastructure and policies impact the potential for liability.

Liability may arise when the information is accessed by an unauthorized person, such as a hacker. A common fear in the corporate sector is that an intruder will infiltrate the organization's systems and steal valuable data. The intruder, who may be an outsider, a contractor, or even an internal employee, may seek to blackmail the organization, threatening to publicly disclose the data unless the organization pays a sum of money. At times, a business may want to avoid the negative implications of a public disclosure and heed the intruder's demands. Other times, law enforcement will intervene, but the intruder is not always apprehended, and the news of the security breach may not be well received by customers or shareholders. In other instances, the hacker may, unbeknownst to the business, use or sell the stolen information for illegitimate purposes, such as identity theft.

Although the threat of an intruder is typically recognized by an organization's risk management, liability for unauthorized access, use, or disclosure of data may arise in other contexts, such as with inadvertent disclosures caused by human error or by a technology snafu. For example, data may be misdirected or transferred to the wrong destination (e.g., in e-mail) or unintentionally released or displayed (e.g., on a Web site), any of which could result from technological failure or human oversight.

Employee unawareness of legal obligations may also lead to regulatory noncompliance and third-party liability. An employee may not know that certain data should not be disclosed. For example, under GLB, a financial institution may not use or disclose nonpublic personal information except as set forth in the institution's privacy notice, and then, in certain regards, only to the extent that the consumer has not opted out of specific disclosures. If, for example, the marketing arm of a firm has access to customer information, such as via the firm's customer relations management software, but has not been informed of the regulatory restrictions, or of any consumer opt-outs, it might improperly share the data with third parties in marketing campaigns in violation of GLB. Personnel not familiar with the applicable data restrictions might unwittingly misuse the data, causing an organization to be noncompliant with regulatory requirements.

In other situations, an organization may contract to use data for certain limited purposes, such as in a data supply agreement or in a service provider relationship in which either the service provider or the customer commits contractually to limit its use and disclosure of the data it receives. Usage or disclosure of the data outside the contract parameters may result in a breach of the contract. Proper IT implementation and practices, including adequate personnel training and education, should help to avoid such problems.

There are also risks associated with unauthorized access to computer systems, even where data are not accessed or compromised. For example, a denial of service attack could render business operations ineffective, creating potential business loss and third-party liability. Unauthorized access to a network could likewise create potential losses and liability.

Corruption, Destruction, or Loss of Data. Liability may also arise from the corruption, destruction, or loss of data. Where a business has contracted with another to process certain data, implicit in which is the maintenance or preservation of those data, or where a business expressly agrees to preserve data (such as where a contract contemplates routine backup of data), the corruption or loss of those data may lead to contractual liability. Adequate procedures with respect to the handling of the data, as well as backup and disaster recovery practices, should mitigate the potential for such loss.

Data may be destroyed, lost, or corrupted due to a number of factors, including viruses, Trojan horses, worms, or other harmful software code; ill-intentioned efforts by intruders; software errors, malfunctions and bugs; failed hardware or media; telecommunications glitches and failure; noncompliance with internal procedures; or natural disaster, terrorism, an act of God, or other force majeure events. None of the foregoing may be absolutely avoidable, but the likelihood of an occurrence, or of data being destroyed, lost, or corrupted in the event of an occurrence, may be mitigated by proper precautionary measures. Many businesses employ a backup regimen, for example. The procedures vary from company to company, depending upon the nature and value of the data and the attendant risks. It is fairly common for a business to employ a nightly backup of all transactions that occurred during the day onto tapes that are stored offsite periodically. Certain data may warrant more elaborate, and costly, backup procedures involving duplicate or redundant systems that copy data daily, hourly, or at other assigned times or that mirror data immediately. Frequent backups should lessen the amount of data that could be lost and would therefore need to be restored, thus reducing the potential for liability.

When data are destroyed, lost, or corrupted, a business faces both (1) additional costs and expenses for its internal efforts, and perhaps for external services to assist, in restoring the data and (2) potential liability to third parties, such as, for example, where the security of the data was entrusted to that party and the data cannot be fully restored or cannot be restored in a timely manner, causing an interruption in the other party's business operations. Steps taken to avoid events that may compromise the data will obviously lessen a business's risk. Moreover, adequate backup and disaster recovery programs will minimize the extent of data lost, and thus the potential financial exposure, in the event that data are compromised.

Risks Incumbent With the Internet and Subcontracting

The makeup of an organization's IT infrastructure may impact the risk of a security breach and the potential for liability. It may also affect the organization's regulatory compliance. The IT upon which a business depends typically involves a mix of internal technology, such as owned or leased computer equipment and networking systems, licensed or proprietary software, and IT personnel responsible for the smooth operation of the business's IT systems and, to a varying degree, technology solutions offered by one or more IT service providers, such as managed network servicers, telecommunications providers, application service providers, hosting companies, and outsourcing providers. Many of those services are provided remotely, through the Internet, or otherwise contemplate access via the Internet. How an organization's IT infrastructure is deployed may influence whether a particular statutory or regulatory obligation is triggered and may affect the potential for third-party liability.

Web Sites and the Internet

An overriding consideration in any legal assessment is whether the data are collected from or accessible to the outside. Where an organization collects information through a Web site or stores data on a server connected to the Internet, the potential for unauthorized access and disclosure to someone outside the organization may be greater than with a closed system. Furthermore, data that are transmitted or stored unencrypted are at greater risk if intercepted or otherwise accessed by an intruder.

Consumer data collected via a Web site may also subject a business to certain obligations under consumer protection laws, or perhaps contractual liability under the business's own privacy policy if the terms in that policy are not followed.

Outsourcing and Subcontracting

Utilizing third-party service providers may be an attractive option where such providers are, given the efficiencies created by their niche expertise or their economies of scale, capable of providing a service at reduced costs when compared with supporting the service in-house. In other instances, there may be no alternative to engaging an IT service provider, as is typically the case with a telecommunications provider. Furthermore, vendors that concentrate on providing a particular service may have expertise in an area that may be difficult to replicate in-house. A hosting company is a good example. Many hosting companies maintain large server farms on which they host many Web sites for their customers. A hosting company often negotiates favorable terms with hardware and software providers, and with an Internet Service Provider (ISP) or telecommunications provider for Internet access, and can build those savings into its offering to its customers. A hosting company can also reduce costs by using shared servers and allocating personnel to multiple accounts.

When IT is handled primarily in-house, the organization has direct control over its IT operations and can usually achieve an acceptable comfort level with its risk and liability assessments by review and enforcement of its own internal policies and procedures, and through the periodic undertaking of internal compliance audits. However, when a business elects to engage a third-party vendor to provide certain of its IT services, a number of legal issues arise that are more difficult to assess. When certain aspects of the IT program are outsourced or otherwise entrusted to a third party, direct control over some or all of the IT operations, and the security of its data, is lost. The business is then dependent, to an extent, on the vendor (and its subcontractors) to ensure that adequate security policies and procedures are in place, monitored, and enforced (e.g., to meet the business's regulatory obligations and to minimize the potential for liability).

Allowing third parties access to corporate and personal data and the business's IT systems obviously poses a level of risk that should be considered when looking to engage any vendor. Some amount of due diligence should be conducted to gain a satisfactory level of comfort with the vendor (e.g., reference checks, background checks, and Dunn & Bradstreet financial checks). Moreover, the contract between the vendor and the customer should clearly spell out the expectations of the parties, including who is responsible for what (e.g., in the event of a security breach), how data are to be handled (e.g., which restrictions attach to which data), which types of security are to be implemented, and who is liable for what. In certain instances, engaging a subcontractor will trigger regulatory obligations with regard to the subcontract itself (e.g., HIPAA requires that a subcontractor sign a business associate agreement that must satisfy certain express regulatory requirements).

Service provider contracts will often attempt to disclaim liability for these types of events (e.g., in a force majeure clause, in general or specific disclaimers, in disclaimers of damages, or in limitations of liability). From the customer's perspective, such disclaimers may be acceptable so long as they are qualified as being outside the service provider's reasonable control, not reasonably avoidable with proper due diligence and foresight, and the contract elsewhere affirmatively requires the provider to undertake steps to maintain the security and integrity of the data.

STATUTORY AND REGULATORY COMPLIANCE

The Impact of the Law: Determining Regulatory Obligations and Assessing the Potential for Liability

Security breaches may pose liability under a number of different legal theories, depending upon the nature of the data and the circumstances surrounding the breach. They may also create noncompliance situations with regulatory obligations, subjecting the organization to penalties and possible enforcement actions by government regulators. This section looks at statutory and regulatory obligations and the potential for liability for failures to comply with those obligations. The remainder of this chapter looks at the potential for third-party liability under contract and tort theories.

As an introduction, it is worthy to note that there is a body of decisional law in the United States premised upon an individual's right to privacy in certain information. It has been held, for example, that an individual has a constitutional right to privacy in the very intimate aspects of his or her personal life, such as with certain medical information. It has also been held that an individual may maintain an action in tort for an invasion of his or her privacy, which could, for example, include the privacy of financial information. See *McNally v. The Pulitzer Publishing Co.* (1976), which differentiated between the constitutional right of privacy and the common law right recognized by state tort law. The failure to safeguard such information may give rise to claims of a violation of either a constitutional right or of a tort involving the invasion of privacy. Although possible claims in tort are discussed in a later section of this chapter, the concept of this right to privacy has influenced, and continues to influence, the development of statutes and regulations that impose upon organizations an obligation to safeguard certain personal information.

Damages

Certain statutes may provide for statutory remedies (e.g., a dollar figure for violations or treble damages). To the extent that a statute imposes a duty to maintain the security of data, and allows a private claim to be brought for a breach of that statutory duty, unless otherwise provided in the statute, the claimant will likely need to demonstrate that he or she suffered some actual damage to recover under the statute (*Doe v. Chao*, 2004). In the *Doe v. Chao* case, the plaintiff alleged a violation of the Privacy Act of 1974, which requires federal agencies not to disclose data, because the Department of Labor had disclosed his Social Security number on public documents. The Privacy Act states that a claimant who suffered damages as a result of a violation of the act may receive "actual damages sustained by the individual . . . but in no case shall a person entitled to recovery receive *less than* the sum of $1,000" (5 U.S.C. §552a(g)(4)(A)). In declining to award the statutory $1,000, the Court held that the plaintiff's assertions "that he was 'torn . . . all to pieces' and 'greatly concerned and worried' because of the disclosure of his Social Security number and its potentially 'devastating' consequences" was insufficient to establish that he had, in fact, suffered actual damage (2004 U.S. LEXIS at *8).

In many instances, it may be difficult for a claimant to establish any damages arising from an unauthorized disclosure of his or her personal information. This topic is further addressed in the discussion about remedies under the next section of this chapter. It would be ill-advised, however, to assume that damages may never be assessed in respect of disclosures of consumer data.

Legislative Developments

The growing concern for privacy in recent years has prompted legislative action both in the United States and abroad requiring organizations to protect the privacy of personal information. The statutory approach in the United States is often referred to as sectoral in nature because the laws are drawn along industry lines; that is, they pertain to specific information gathered by organizations in specific industries (namely financial and medical). Unlike the Data Protection Directive, for example, which has been adopted in European countries and which imposes restrictions on the collection, use, and disclosure of personal information generally, regardless of the context of the relationship in which the information was collected—whether financial, medical, or otherwise, the United States has no comparable broad stroke law that restricts generally the collection, use, or disclosure of personal information (see Data Protection Directive, 1995).

The U.S. approach, therefore, creates one anomaly in that the same information collected via different relationships could in one instance be subject to statutory and regulatory restrictions and in another instance not be regulated at all. Moreover, in some instances the information could be subject to more than one statutory scheme (e.g., information might fall under both HIPAA and GLB, raising the issue of which regulation should govern—GLB regulators have addressed this by suggesting that the applicable regulation be the one more protective to the consumer). See Privacy of Consumer Financial Information; Final Rule, 65 Fed. Reg. 35,164 (2000). Whether specific information is governed by regulation requires a thorough understanding of the statutory scheme.

U.S. Federal Law

Two U.S. federal statutes that directly address IT security are the Financial Services Modernization Act of 1999 (more commonly known as the GLB) and HIPAA (1996). These two statutes, and their accompanying regulations, focus on the privacy of certain personal information, but also specifically address the security of data. Neither statute concerns corporate data (e.g., corporate trade secrets or confidential information), unless that information includes the personal information of individuals that is protected by the statute. The following takes a close look at the regulatory obligations imposed on data security by these statutes, but by no means is an exhaustive review of all the regulations. Neither statute allows for a civil cause of action (enforcement would be brought by the applicable federal agency or state authority), but the security requirements set out in the regulations might reflect standards that a court could consider in addressing a liability claim brought by a private party.

GLB. Although it is limited to "nonpublic personal information" collected by "financial institutions," GLB is a good example of statutory and regulatory initiatives that directly impact IT operations and data security procedures. It is worthy to note that GLB applies broadly to many businesses that handle financial data in one way or another and not just banks. GLB was enacted in 1999.

What Are Financial Institutions?

GLB applies only to financial institutions, a term broadly defined by the statute. The term *financial institution* means "any institution the business of which is engaging in financial activities as described in section 1843(k) of title 12" (Financial Services Modernization Act, 1999, 15 U.S.C. §6809(3)(A)). 12 U.S.C. §1843(k) describes a long list of activities as being financial in nature. 12 U.S.C. §1843(k) includes a list of entities that includes the more traditional financial institutions, such as lending institutions, banks, insurance companies, underwriters, investment companies, financial advisors, and funds and broker-dealers. In addition to the traditional financial activities identified in 12 U.S.C. §1843(k), the term *financial activities* includes activities that the Federal Reserve Board has found, by regulation, order, or interpretation, to be either closely related to banking (12 U.S.C. §1843(k)(4)(F)) or usual in connection with the transaction of banking or other financial operations abroad (12 U.S.C. §1843(k)(4)(G)).

Activities that are "closely related to banking" are identified at 12 C.F.R. §225.28 and 12 C.F.R. §225.86(a), and include, in certain circumstances, brokering or servicing loans; leasing real or personal property (or acting as agent, broker, or adviser in such leasing) without operating, maintaining, or repairing the property; appraising real or personal property; check guaranty, collection agency, credit bureau, and real estate settlement services; providing financial or investment advisory activities including tax planning, tax preparation, and instruction on individual financial management; management consulting and counseling activities (including providing financial career counseling); courier services for banking instruments; printing and selling checks and related documents; community development or advisory activities; selling money orders, savings bonds, or traveler's checks; and providing financial data processing and transmission services, facilities (including hardware, software, documentation, or operating personnel), databases, advice, or access to these by technological means.

Activities that are "in connection with the transaction of banking or other financial operations abroad" are identified at 12 C.F.R. §211.5(d) and 12 C.F.R. §225.86(b), and include leasing real or personal property (or acting as agent, broker, or adviser in such leasing), where the lease is functionally equivalent to an extension of credit; acting as fiduciary; providing investment, financial, or economic advisory services; and operating a travel agency in connection with financial services.

Given the broad definition of financial institution, many organizations that were not traditionally thought of as financial institutions may nonetheless be subject to GLB and therefore required to comply with its security and privacy regulations.

Who Are the Regulators?

GLB provides the statutory framework but instructs the relevant federal and state agencies and authorities to promulgate regulations governing the application of the statute for those entities within their respective jurisdictions. Accordingly, the Securities and Exchange Commission (SEC) issued a Privacy Rule that incorporates its Security Rule (17 C.F.R. §248.30) and implements GLB's statutory requirements with regard to the entities governed by the SEC (investment advisers registered with the SEC, brokers, dealers (broker-dealers), and investment companies (funds); 17 C.F.R. Part 248; See Final Rule: Privacy of Consumer Financial Information (Regulation S–P) (SEC), 65 Fed. Reg. 40,334 (2000)). Similarly, the various banking agencies—the Federal Reserve System, Federal Deposit Insurance Corporation, Office of Comptroller of the Currency, Department of the Treasury, and the Office of Thrift Supervision, Department of the Treasury—issued a Joint Privacy Rule and Joint Security Guidelines (12 C.F.R. Part 40) governing the various banking institutions under their jurisdiction. The National Credit Union Administration (NCUA) issued regulations (12 C.F.R. Parts 716 and 741) governing credit unions that it regulates. For insurance companies, GLB regulations are implemented by the applicable state insurance department or authority of the state in which the person is domiciled. The National Association of Insurance Commissioners has proposed a model regulation for adoption by the states (See *What's happening with privacy*, n.d.).

For all those entities that do not otherwise fall under the jurisdiction of the federal agencies identified above, or the state insurance departments or authorities, but nevertheless are financial institutions under the broad statutory definition of that term, GLB authorizes the FTC to regulate such entities with regard to GLB compliance. The FTC issued its Privacy Rule (16 C.F.R. Part 313) and Security Rule (16 C.F.R. Part 314) in 2000.

Restrictions on Handling of Data

GLB limits the disclosure of nonpublic personal information. Nonpublic personal information is defined as "personally identifiable financial information provided by a consumer to a financial institution resulting from any transaction with the consumer or any service performed for the consumer or otherwise obtained by the financial institution" (Financial Services Modernization Act, 1999, 15 U.S.C. §6809(4)(A)). This is broadly construed to "encompass any information that 'is requested by a financial institution for the purpose of providing a financial product or service,' 65 Fed. Reg. at 33,658, inasmuch as all such information can be fairly characterized as 'relating to finance and financiers'" (*Trans Union LLC v. Federal Trade Commission*, 2002). Accordingly, information collected in connection with a financial transaction would be subject to GLB's security and privacy requirements, even if the information itself is not necessarily financial in nature (nonpublic personal information would therefore include, e.g., any name, address, telephone number, e-mail address, Social Security number, contact information, or other information supplied by a consumer in connection with an application for a financial product or service).

Precisely how GLB limits the use of nonpublic personal information can be a bit complicated under the statutory and regulatory scheme. In essence, however, GLB requires a financial institution to disclose clearly to consumers in a privacy notice its policies and procedures with regard to the collection, use, and disclosure of nonpublic personal information. The notice must clearly indicate what information is collected, how it is used, and to whom it is disclosed and, in certain instances, the consumer must be afforded an opportunity to opt out of disclosures of the information to nonaffiliated third parties. The institution must ensure that it complies with its notice and any opt-out elections made by a consumer. Failure to do so may result in a regulatory enforcement action and civil penalties.

Security Obligations

GLB requires each agency to establish appropriate standards relating to administrative, technical, and physical safeguards:

- to ensure the security and confidentiality of customer records and information;
- to protect against any anticipated threats or hazards to the security or integrity of such records; and
- to protect against unauthorized access to or use of such records or information which could result in substantial harm or inconvenience to any customer (Financial Services Modernization Act, 1999, 15 U.S.C. §6801(b)).

Each agency issued its own security guidelines or regulations. The following outlines the security guidelines promulgated by the banking agencies. The FTC's security rule is found at 16 C.F.R. §314; the Securities and Exchange Commission's security rule is included in its privacy regulations (Regulation S-P) at 17 C.F.R. §248.30.

A financial institution must develop and implement "a comprehensive written information security program that includes administrative, technical, and physical safeguards" (a) designed to protect the security and confidentiality of "customer information" and (b) to assess, manage and control risks pertaining to the institution's "customer information systems" (12 C.F.R. Part 30, Appendix B, ¶ II.A-C). Customer information is "any record containing nonpublic personal information, as defined in §40.3(n) of this chapter, about a customer, whether in paper, electronic, or other form, that is maintained by or on behalf of the bank" (12 C.F.R. Part 30, Appendix B, ¶ I.C.2.c). This includes "data, files, or other information" about the consumer. It includes records that may contain other than nonpublic personal information, even records that contain very little nonpublic personal information. Records that contain little nonpublic personal information are still customer information under the guidelines; this fact may be a factor in determining the appropriate level of protection. See Interagency Guidelines Establishing Standards for Safeguarding Customer Information (Banking Agencies), 66 Fed. Reg. 8,618 (2001). "Customer information systems" are "any methods used to access, collect, store, use, transmit, protect, or dispose of customer information." This includes "electronic or physical" methods. A "financial institution's responsibility to safeguard customer information continues through the disposal process" (12 C.F.R. Part 30, Appendix B, ¶ I.C.2.d).

The guidelines do not impose specific requirements in terms of the administrative, technical, and physical safeguards to be adopted by an organization. They are, instead, intended to be flexible, permitting an institution to develop a program "appropriate to the size and complexity of the bank and the nature and scope of its activities" (12 C.F.R. Part 30, Appendix B, ¶ II.A).

Assess Risks

The guidelines allow an organization latitude in developing an information security program appropriate for its business. The organization must assess the risks that customer information may be compromised (e.g., disclosed, misused, altered, or destroyed), taking into consideration internal and external threats, the likelihood and potential damage of these threats (including the sensitivity of the customer information), and the arrangements in place to control the risks. There is no requirement that all organizations afford the same degree of protection to all customer information. Rather, the guidelines permit the organization "the discretion to determine the levels of protection necessary for different categories of information" (Interagency Guidelines Establishing Standards for Safeguarding Customer Information (Banking Agencies), 66 Fed. Reg. 8,621 (2001)).

For example, sensitive data that are stored on or transmitted through "systems that are accessible through public telecommunications networks... may require more and different protections, such as encryption, than if it were located in a locked file drawer" (Interagency Guidelines Establishing Standards for Safeguarding Customer Information (Banking Agencies), 66 Fed. Reg. 8,621 (2001)). Such data may include customer account numbers and access codes because they are more at risk of being targeted by a hacker and their disclosure would cause the customer considerable harm.

Manage and Control Risks

The information security program must be appropriate for an organization's activities, considering the risks stated above. A number of security measures that are to be considered and, if appropriate, adopted are identified at 12 C.F.R. Part 30, Appendix B, ¶ III.C.1.a through h. They include the following:

1. Access controls (e.g., passwords for customers to access their information electronically, identification criteria to be used by employees before providing account information, procedures to guard against pretext calling).
2. Access restrictions at physical locations (to permit access by authorized personnel only to computer facilities, record storage facilities, etc.).
3. Encryption of customer information (in electronic format while in transit or while residing on electronic storage devices, in either case where access may be gained by unauthorized individuals).
4. Review of updates and upgrades to customer information systems (to ensure continued integrity of the financial institution's information security program).
5. Dual control procedures, segregation of duties, and employee background checks for employees with responsibilities for or access to customer information. Dual control procedures "refers to a security technique that uses two or more separate persons, operating together to protect sensitive information. Both persons are equally responsible for protecting the information and neither can access the information alone." (Interagency Guidelines Establishing Standards for Safeguarding Customer Information (Banking Agencies), 66 Fed. Reg. 8,622 (2001)).
6. Monitoring of customer information systems (to detect attempted and actual attacks and intrusions).
7. Response procedures (specifying actions to take when it is suspected or verified that unauthorized individuals have accessed the financial institution's customer information systems, including, when appropriate, reports to law enforcement and regulatory agencies).
8. Contingency plans and measures to protect against loss of or damage to customer information (e.g., due to fire, water damage, or technological failures).

The information security program should include training "designed to train employees to recognize, respond to, and report unauthorized attempts to obtain customer information" (12 C.F.R. Part 30, Appendix B, ¶ III.C.2). Staff should be properly informed about the organization's procedures for reporting suspicious activities (such as suspicious activity reports [SARs]) and other federal reporting requirements. An institution regulated by the FRS must file an SAR with the Financial Crimes Enforcement Network of the Department of the Treasury "when it detects a known or suspected violation of Federal law, or a suspicious transaction related to a money laundering activity or a violation of the Bank Secrecy Act" (12 C.F.R. §208.62). The NCUA also requires federally insured credit unions to file similar reports (see 12 C.F.R. §748.1(c)).

Systems Testing

An information security program should include regular testing of key controls, systems, and procedures. There is no requirement that an organization apply specific tests to evaluate the key control systems of its program; the organization must determine the frequency and nature of the testing based on its risk assessment. The tests should be conducted or reviewed by independent third parties or by staff independent of those that develop or maintain the security programs or operate the customer information systems.

Adjustments to Security Program

Adjustments should be made to the information security program "as necessary to reflect changes in both internal and external conditions" (Interagency Guidelines Establishing Standards for Safeguarding Customer Information (Banking Agencies), 66 Fed. Reg. 8,623 (2001); see 12 C.F.R. Part 30, Appendix B, ¶ III.E). An organization must adjust, as appropriate, the program "in light of any relevant changes in technology, the sensitivity of its customer information, and internal or external threats to information security" (12 C.F.R. Part 30, Appendix B, ¶ III.E). This would include analyzing the risks to customer information posed by new technology before adopting that technology to ascertain whether any adjustments to the security program are necessary. The program should also be adjusted to reflect an organization's "own changing business arrangements, such as mergers and acquisitions, alliances and joint ventures, outsourcing arrangements, and changes to customer information systems" (12 C.F.R. Part 30, Appendix B, ¶ III.E).

Service Providers and Subservicers

An organization may, in the course of its business, outsource certain business functions or otherwise engage service providers to handle certain business operations that would necessarily require or permit their access to customer information. Such activities create additional risks to the security and confidentiality of the information and, to protect against such risks, the "institution must take appropriate steps to protect information that it provides to a service provider, regardless of who the service provider is or how the service provider obtains access" (Interagency Guidelines Establishing Standards for Safeguarding Customer Information (Banking Agencies), 66 Fed. Reg. 8,618 (2001)). An organization is responsible for customer information accessed by its service providers. Service providers are broadly defined and include "any person or entity that maintains, processes, or otherwise is permitted access to customer information through its provision of services directly to the bank" (12 C.F.R. Part 30, Appendix B, ¶ I.C.2.e). A service provider does not include a person or entity, such as a subservicer, that indirectly provides services to a financial institution. A subservicer that is retained by a primary service provider would not be a service provider to the organization that engaged the primary service provider, because it has no contractual relationship with the subservicer. A subservicer is "any person who has access to an institution's customer information through its provision of services to the service provider and is not limited to mortgage subservicers" (Interagency Guidelines Establishing Standards for Safeguarding Customer Information (Banking Agencies), 66 Fed. Reg. 8,619, fn. 8 (2001)).

An organization must exercise due diligence in selecting a service provider, which would include a review of the (a) measures taken by a service provider to protect customer information and (b) controls the service provider has in place to ensure that any subservicer used by the service provider will be able to meet the objectives of the guidelines. An organization should enter into a contract with its service providers that requires the provider to implement appropriate security measures designed to meet the objectives of the guidelines.

An organization must exercise an appropriate level of oversight over each of its service providers to ensure that the provider is implementing the security measures for which it has been contracted. The oversight responsibilities should be consistent with the organization's own risk assessment procedures. Not all outsourcing arrangements need be monitored or monitored in the same fashion. Where, for example, a service provider is also a regulated financial institution or subject to other legal and professional standards that require it to safeguard customer information, it may be reasonable to rely on the fact that the provider must comply with such restrictions, and therefore it may not be necessary to provide as much oversight.

The service provider may be monitored through periodic review of audits, summaries of test results or other equivalent measures of the service provider. The contract with the service provider should call for the receipt of copies of audits and test result information adequate to confirm that the service provider is implementing security measures consistent with the provider's contractual obligations. A contract may call for the service provider to submit to periodic audits of its security measures.

Liability and Enforcement Actions

The banking rule is not intended to impose absolute liability for a financial institution that has a security breach. This is evident in the qualification in 12 C.F.R. Part 30, Appendix B, ¶ II.B that a security program is to be *designed* to accomplish the statutory objectives set out at 15 U.S.C. §6801(b).

Under certain of the guidelines, if an agency determines that an organization has failed to satisfy the security standards set forth in the guidelines, the agency may request the institution to submit a compliance plan that sets out the steps it will take to correct the deficiency and how long those steps will take. If the organization fails to submit or implement a compliance plan, the agency shall, by order, require the institution to correct the deficiency and may take further actions. If the organization fails to comply with an order, the agency may seek enforcement and a civil money penalty in court.

HIPAA. HIPAA was enacted in August 1996. In accordance with HIPAA, the United States Department of Health and Human Services (HHS) promulgated regulations titled Standards for Privacy of Individually Identifiable Health Information (the HIPAA Privacy and Security Rule), which became effective in April 2003 and established national standards for the privacy and security of health information (45 C.F.R. Parts 160 and 164. See 65 Fed. Reg. 82462; 67 Fed. Reg. 53182).

Who and What Are Regulated by HIPAA?

HIPAA applies to covered entities, which include health plans, health care clearinghouses, and certain health care providers. A health plan is an individual or group plan that provides, or pays the cost of, medical care. Health plans include group health plans, health insurance issuers, health maintenance organizations, Parts A and B of the Medicare program, a Medicaid program, Medicare supplemental insurers, and certain long-term care insurers. A health care clearinghouse is an entity that processes, or facilitates the processing of, health information into a standard format or standard data elements, receives health information in a standard format and process, or facilitates the processing of that information into a nonstandard format or nonstandard content. A health care provider is broadly defined and includes all persons and organizations who furnish, bill, or are paid for providing health care, services, or supplies related to the health of an individual, in the normal course of business. If the health care provider transmits health information electronically in connection with certain transactions, it is a covered entity under the HIPAA Privacy and Security Rule.

HIPAA pertains to protected health information (PHI), which includes medical records and other health information that identifies or could be used to identify an individual, regardless of its form (electronic, paper, or oral), that are created or received by a covered entity or its business associate. PHI includes, for example, any information about payment for health care.

Outsourcing and Vendors

The HIPAA Privacy and Security Rule imposes specific regulatory obligations on outsourcing and other vendor relationships. Where a covered entity engages a third-party contractor, HIPAA requires the covered entity to secure specific contractual commitments from the contractor, which the HIPAA Privacy and Security Rule refers to as a "business associate" (45 C.F.R. §160.103). A business associate may be a subcontractor, an outsourcer or any party that (a) performs a function or activity on behalf of the covered entity and that function or activity involves the use or disclosure of PHI (for example, claims processing, data analysis, utilization review, and billing functions) or (b) provides certain specified services to a covered entity (namely legal, actuarial, accounting, consulting, data aggregation, management, administrative, accreditation or financial services).

The HIPAA Privacy and Security Rule requires covered entities to have business associates execute a business associate agreement. Among other things, the business associate agreement may not permit the business associate to use or disclose PHI in any manner that would violate the HIPAA Privacy and Security Rule if done by the covered entity, must limit the use of PHI only for the purpose for which the business associate is engaged, and must provide assurances that the business associate will safeguard the PHI from misuse. For example, the business associate agreement must

- Require the business associate to use appropriate safeguards to prevent the unauthorized use or disclosure of PHI (the HIPAA Privacy and Security Rule does not define the appropriate safeguards; 45 C.F.R. § 164.504(e)(2)(ii)(B)).
- Report to the covered entity any unauthorized use or disclosure of PHI of which it becomes aware (45 C.F.R. § 164.504(e)(2)(ii)(C)).
- Ensure that any agents of the business associate, including any subcontractor, to whom the business associate provides PHI agree to the same conditions and restrictions that apply to the business associate with respect to the PHI (45 C.F.R. § 164.504(E)(2)(ii)(D)).
- Permit access to PHI to satisfy the covered entity's obligations to allow individuals to amend their PHI or to provide individuals with an accounting of the disclosures of their PHI (45 C.F.R. § 164.504(e)(2)(ii)(E)-(G)).
- Return or destroy all PHI received from or created or received by the business associate on behalf of the covered entity or ensure its continued protection upon the termination of the contract (45 C.F.R. § 164.504(e)(2)(ii)(I)).

The business associate agreement may permit the business associate to disclose PHI as required by law (e.g., court orders, court-ordered warrants, a civil or an authorized investigative demand, subpoenas or summonses issued by a court, a governmental or tribal inspector general or an administrative body authorized to require the production of information, Medicare conditions of participation with respect to health care providers participating in the program, and statutes or regulations that require the production of such information if payment is sought under a government program), so long as the business associate obtains certain assurances from the person to whom the PHI is disclosed.

Security

HIPAA imposes general requirements on covered entities to maintain the security of PHI. For example, the HIPAA Privacy and Security Rule requires covered entities to

- Ensure the confidentiality, integrity, and availability of all electronic PHI the covered entity creates, receives, maintains, or transmits.
- Protect against any reasonably anticipated threats or hazards to the security or integrity of such information.
- Protect against any reasonably anticipated uses or disclosures of such information that are not permitted or required under the rule (45 C.F.R. §164.306(a)).

As with GLB, HIPAA allows flexibility in determining the approach to ensuring security. The following factors must be considered in devising a security program appropriate for a particular organization:

- The size, complexity, and capabilities of the covered entity.
- The covered entity's technical infrastructure, hardware, and software security capabilities.
- The costs of security measures.
- The probability and criticality of potential risks to electronic PHI (45 C.F.R. §164.306(b)(2)).

The HIPAA Privacy and Security Rule implements these statutory requirements by setting out a fairly lengthy list of administrative, physical, technical, and organizational safeguards that a covered entity must institute (or, in certain instances, must consider instituting) to protect the integrity of PHI. Those safeguards are detailed at 45 C.F.R. §§164.308-164.314 and include the following:

Administrative Safeguards

Risk analysis. Conduct accurate and thorough assessment of the potential risks and vulnerabilities to the confidentiality, integrity, and availability of electronic PHI held by the covered entity.

Risk management. Implement security measures sufficient to reduce risks and vulnerabilities to a reasonable and appropriate level.

Information system activity review. Implement procedures to regularly review records of information system activity, such as audit logs, access reports, and security incident tracking reports.

Assigned security responsibility. Identify the security official who is responsible for the development and implementation of the policies and procedures required by the rule.

Workforce security. Implement policies and procedures to ensure that all members of the workforce have appropriate access to electronic PHI and to prevent those workforce members who do not have access from obtaining access to electronic PHI.

Security awareness and training. Implement a security awareness and training program for all members of the workforce (including management).

Protection from malicious software. Procedures for guarding against, detecting, and reporting malicious software (e.g., viruses, worms, or Trojan horses).

Log-in monitoring. Procedures for monitoring log-in attempts and reporting discrepancies.

Password management. Procedures for creating, changing, and safeguarding passwords.

Security incident procedures. Implement policies and procedures to address security incidents.

Response and reporting. Identify and respond to suspected or known security incidents; mitigate, to the extent practicable, harmful effects of security incidents that are known to the covered entity and document security incidents and their outcomes.

Contingency plan. Establish (and implement as needed) policies and procedures for responding to an emergency or other occurrence (for example, fire, vandalism, system failure, and natural disaster) that damages systems that contain electronic PHI.

Data backup plan. Establish and implement procedures to create and maintain retrievable exact copies of electronic PHI.

Disaster recovery plan. Establish (and implement as needed) procedures to restore any loss of data.

Emergency mode operation plan. Establish (and implement as needed) procedures to enable continuation of critical business processes for protection of the security of electronic PHI while operating in emergency mode.

Testing and revision procedures. Implement procedures for periodic testing and revision of contingency plans.

Applications and data criticality analysis. Assess the relative criticality of specific applications and data in support of other contingency plan components.

Physical Safeguards

Facility access controls. Implement policies and procedures to limit physical access to its electronic information systems and the facility or facilities in which they are housed, while ensuring that properly authorized access is allowed.

Facility security plan. Implement policies and procedures to safeguard the facility and the equipment therein from unauthorized physical access, tampering, and theft.

Access control and validation procedures. Implement procedures to control and validate a person's access to facilities based on their role or function, including visitor control and control of access to software programs for testing and revision.

Maintenance records. Implement policies and procedures to document repairs and modifications to the physical components of a facility that are related to security (for example, hardware, walls, doors, and locks).

Workstation use. Implement policies and procedures that specify the proper functions to be performed, the manner in which those functions are to be performed, and the physical attributes of the surroundings of a specific workstation or class of workstation that can access electronic PHI.

Workstation security. Implement physical safeguards for all workstations that access electronic PHI to restrict access to authorized users.

Device and media controls. Implement policies and procedures that govern the receipt and removal of hardware and electronic media that contain electronic PHI into and out of a facility and the movement of these items within the facility.

Technical Safeguards

Unique user identification. Assign a unique name or number for identifying and tracking user identity.

Emergency access procedure. Establish (and implement as needed) procedures for obtaining necessary electronic PHI during an emergency.

Automatic logoff. Implement electronic procedures that terminate an electronic session after a predetermined time of inactivity.

Encryption and decryption. Implement a mechanism to encrypt and decrypt electronic PHI.

Audit controls. Implement hardware, software, or procedural mechanisms that record and examine activity in information systems that contain or use electronic PHI.

Organizational Safeguards

Business associate contracts. The contract between a covered entity and a business associate must provide that the business associate will do the following:

- Implement administrative, physical, and technical safeguards that reasonably and appropriately protect the confidentiality, integrity, and availability of the electronic PHI that it creates, receives, maintains, or transmits on behalf of the covered entity.

- Ensure that any agent, including a subcontractor, to whom it provides such information agrees to implement reasonable and appropriate safeguards to protect it.
- Report to the covered entity any security incident of which it becomes aware.
- Authorize termination of the contract by the covered entity, if the covered entity determines that the business associate has violated a material term of the contract.

The HIPAA Privacy and Security Rule also requires a covered entity to designate a privacy official responsible for the development and implementation of its PHI policies and procedures. Those policies and procedures must be updated as necessary and appropriate to comply with changes in the law, including any changes in the HIPAA Privacy and Security Rule. A covered entity's workforce must be trained about its policies and procedures with respect to PHI, as necessary and appropriate for the workforce members to carry out their duties. A covered entity must have and enforce appropriate sanctions against members of its workforce who fail to comply with its privacy and security policies and procedures.

HHS may pursue violations of HIPAA and the HIPAA Privacy and Security Rule. Violations carry a civil penalty of not more than $100 for each such violation, except that the total amount imposed on the person for all violations of an identical requirement or prohibition during a calendar year may not exceed $25,000.

Other Laws. Other U.S. statutes are relevant to the discussion of IT security insofar as they may impose obligations with regard to data security or give rise to liability in the event of a security breach. Given that steps to ensure privacy of information in electronic format will depend, in large part, upon adequate information security measures, some laws may indirectly impact IT security by imposing obligations to maintain the privacy of personal information.

Consumer Protection Laws

Federal Trade Commission Act

Consumer protection law at the U.S. federal level may be found in the Federal Trade Commission Act (1914). Under Section 5 of the FTCA, the FTC is authorized to take action against businesses involved in unfair or deceptive acts or practices in or affecting commerce. The FTC is permitted a fair amount of latitude under the FTCA in determining what constitutes "unfair or deceptive acts or practices." (See *FTC v. Colgate-Palmolive Co.*, 1965: "This statutory scheme necessarily gives the Commission an influential role in interpreting §5 [of the FTCA as to what are deceptive practices] and in applying it to the facts of particular cases arising out of unprecedented situations . . . the Commission is often in a better position than are courts to determine when a practice is 'deceptive' within the meaning of the Act.")

The FTC has taken the position that a misrepresentation as to the handling of personal information is a violation of Section 5 of the FTCA. For example, in the complaint filed by the FTC in *In the Matter of Geocities* (1998), the FTC alleged, "The acts and practices of respondent as alleged in this complaint [that Geocities misrepresented its information collection practices] constitute unfair or deceptive acts or practices in or affecting commerce in violation of Section 5(a) of the Federal Trade Commission Act" (Complaint at ¶ 20). Geocities had allegedly misrepresented that the personal information it collected from its users would not be disclosed to third parties without the user's consent when Geocities actually disclosed it to third-party marketers.

The FTC may consider a promise to safeguard personal information—in a Web site privacy policy or in some other commitment made by a company—as a representation by that company that the personal information will be safeguarded in the manner promised. For example, in *In the Matter of Guess?, Inc.*, the FTC asserted that

> since at least October 2000, Guess' Web site has been vulnerable to commonly known attacks such as "Structured Query Language (SQL) injection attacks" and other web-based application attacks. Guess' online statements reassured consumers that their personal information would be secure and protected. The company's claims included "This site has security measures in place to protect the loss, misuse, and alteration of information under our control" and "All of your personal information, including your credit card information and sign-in password, are stored in an unreadable, encrypted format at all times." In fact, according to the FTC, the personal information was not stored in an unreadable, encrypted format at all times and Guess' security measures failed to protect against SQL and other commonly known attacks. In February 2002, a visitor to the Web site, using an SQL injection attack, was able to read in clear text credit card numbers stored in Guess' databases, according to the FTC.

The FTC alleged that Guess misrepresented "the extent to which it maintains and protects the security of personal information collected from or about consumers" (In the Matter of Guess?, Inc., 2003).

In *In the Matter of Microsoft Corporation* (2002), the FTC asserted that Microsoft's Passport service "collects personal information from consumers and allows them to sign in at any participating website with a single name and password." According to the FTC, "Microsoft's Passport privacy policies included statements such as, 'Passport achieves a high level of Web Security by using technologies and systems designed to prevent unauthorized access to your personal information.'" After an investigation, the FTC alleged, among other things, that "Microsoft falsely represented that [i]t employs reasonable and appropriate measures under the circumstances to maintain and protect the privacy and confidentiality of consumers' personal information." (See also Muris, 2001, who stated, "Having encouraged commercial Web sites to post these notices, the FTC needs to ensure compliance. Privacy promises made offline should be held to the same standard.")

The failure to comply with such a representation in a privacy policy may be declared a violation of the FTCA for which the FTC may take action. Under the FTCA, the FTC may seek preliminary and permanent injunctive relief to remedy "any provision of law enforced by the Federal Trade Commission" whenever the FTC has "reason to believe" that a party "is violating, or is about to violate" a provision of law enforced by the FTC (15 U.S.C. §53(b)).

If the conduct were such as "a reasonable man would have known under the circumstances was dishonest or fraudulent," the FTC may also pursue consumer redress in the form of "rescission or reformation of contracts, the refund of money or return of property, the payment of damages, and public notification respecting the rule violation or the unfair or deceptive act or practice," or such other "relief as the court finds necessary to redress injury to consumers or other persons, partnerships, and corporations resulting from the rule violation or the unfair or deceptive act or practice" (15 U.S.C. §57b). Under the FTCA, the FTC may also seek civil penalties when the violator had "actual knowledge or knowledge fairly implied on the basis of objective circumstances that such act is unfair or deceptive and is prohibited by such [unfair or deceptive acts or practices] rule" under Chapter 2 of the FTCA (15 U.S.C. §45(m)(1)). The civil penalty is capped at $10,000 per violation.

Electronic Communications Privacy Act

An amendment to the Wiretap Act, the Electronic Communications Privacy Act (ECPA, 1986) prohibits anyone from intentionally accessing, using, or disclosing stored communications, such as e-mail or stored voice messages, without authorization. Violations of the ECPA are punishable by fines, imprisonment, or both. The ECPA allows for a civil cause of action and recovery of actual damages but not less than $1,000 per violation of the statute, plus the costs and reasonable attorneys' fees in pursuing the action. If the violation were willful or intentional, the court may assess punitive damages (18 U.S.C. §2707(c)).

The ECPA also expressly prohibits providers of "electronic communication" or "remote computing services" from knowingly divulging the contents of a communication in electronic storage, except under certain enumerated circumstances (18 U.S.C. §2702(a)). The following disclosures are excepted from the statutory prohibition: (a) to intended recipients and their agents; (b) with the consent of the originator or the recipient of the communication, and in the case of remote computing services, the subscriber to the service; (c) to a person employed or authorized to forward the communication to its destination; (d) as necessarily incident to providing a service or to protecting the rights or property of the service provider; (e) to a law enforcement agency, if the communication was inadvertently obtained and appears to pertain to criminal activity; and (f) as otherwise authorized by law (18 U.S.C. §2702(b)).

Electronic communication services are defined as "any service which provides to users thereof the ability to send or receive wire or electronic communications" (e.g., an ISP) or telephone company that offers digital services (18 U.S.C. §2510(15)). Remote computing services are defined as "the provision to the public of computer storage or processing services by means of an electronic communications system" (e.g., application service providers and certain Web-based services that provide services to the public; 18 U.S.C. §2511(2)).

The ECPA does not address security of data per se; however, to the extent it prohibits certain disclosures, organizations must be cognizant that such disclosures are not intentionally or knowingly made without authorization (e.g., providers of electronic communication or remote computing services need to ensure that such disclosures are not knowingly made unless expressly permitted by the ECPA). Where, for example, an employee or agent intentionally or knowingly discloses a stored communication (e.g., because he or she did not appreciate the restrictions on disclosure of such information or otherwise failed to follow privacy or security procedures), under certain circumstances the act of the employee or agent may be imputed to the employer, in which event the employer could be liable under the ECPA.

In *Muskovich v. Crowell* (1996), the court held that a telephone company did not knowingly disclose an unlisted telephone number (which the court assumed fell within the definition of electronic communication). There, an MCI employee, in violation of MCI's employee policies, obtained a subscriber's unlisted number and made a number of harassing phone calls to her. Finding that "the term knowingly means that the Defendant was aware of the nature of the conduct, aware of or possessing a firm belief in the existence of the requisite circumstances and an awareness of or a firm belief about the substantial certainty of the result," the court held that since "MCI trained Crowell in policies requiring confidentiality of customer information and prohibiting profanity and personal use of company facilities, services or customer information" and the defendant "violated MCI's express policies by making personal use of confidential information he obtained from customer records," without MCI's actual knowledge, MCI had not violated the ECPA by knowingly disclosing such information (*Id.* at *12-14).

The Uniting and Strengthening America by Providing Appropriate Tools Required to Intercept and Obstruct Terrorism Act (USA Patriot Act) amended the ECPA to expressly allow organizations to cooperate with law enforcement as part of a legitimate investigation and to permit the voluntary disclosure of stored communications in certain instances. The ECPA also permits the disclosure of stored communications with the consent of the originator or addressee of the stored communication. Such consent may be obtained, for example, through an appropriate employee manual, workplace policy, terms of use, or other agreement with the originator of the stored communication.

Sarbanes-Oxley Act

The Sarbanes-Oxley Act (SOX) was enacted in July 2002 in response to the corporate accounting scandals in the 1990s. The law has far-reaching implications on the disclosures and accounting practices of public companies and applies generally to companies (whether organized in the United States or elsewhere) that have registered equity or debt securities with the SEC under the Securities Exchange Act (SEA). Although SOX does not directly impose security requirements, it requires, among other things, that chief executive officers (CEOs) and chief financial officers (CFOs) of public companies provide a written statement with each periodic report certifying that the report fully complies with the requirements of Section 13(a) or 15(d) of the SEA and that the information contained in the report fairly presents, in all material respects, the financial condition and results of operations of the company. A CEO or CFO who provides such certification knowing that the report does not meet those standards may be fined up to $1 million, imprisoned for up to 10 years, or both. A CEO or CFO who willfully provides the certification knowing that the report does not meet those standards may be fined up to $5 million, imprisoned for up to 20 years, or both.

SOX also requires, through SEC rules, that the principal executive officers and principal financial officers of public companies certify the following in each annual and quarterly report:

1. the certifying officer has reviewed the report;
2. based on the knowledge of the officer, the report does not contain a material misstatement or material omission and the financial statements and other financial information included in the report fairly present, in all material respects, the financial condition and results of the operations of the company; and
3. each certifying officer (a) is responsible for establishing and maintaining effective internal controls; (b) has designed such internal controls to ensure that material information relating to the company is made known to him or her; (c) has evaluated the effectiveness of those controls as of a date no more than 90 days before filing the report; (d) has presented in the report his or her conclusions about the effectiveness of those controls; (e) has disclosed to the outside auditors and to the audit committee any significant deficiencies in those controls and any fraud involving management or other employees who have a significant role in the company's internal controls; (f) has identified to the outside auditors any material weaknesses in those controls; and (g) has stated in the report whether or not there were significant changes in the internal controls that could affect those controls, including any corrective actions.

SOX therefore imposes upon the directors and officers of a public company direct responsibility for corporate accounting practices and reporting and oversight over the company's internal controls relating thereto. The requirements placed upon directors and officers by SOX have had an indirect impact on security measures as increasingly auditing firms and other entities realize that the integrity of financial data cannot be ensured without an adequate security program and periodic audits thereof. SOX should therefore indirectly impact a company's use of IT by creating incentives to deploy adequate IT security solutions, and internal control measures, that will ensure and protect the integrity of corporate data comprising the company's SEC disclosures and reporting.

Furthermore, to the extent that any business maintains records in electronic format, and the data in those records is used in preparing corporate tax filings or SEC disclosures, the business may be required to later reproduce those data to support the accounting in the tax filings or the representations made in the disclosures. Accordingly, adequate safeguards should be undertaken to protect the integrity of that data.

Uniform Computer Information Transactions Act

The Uniform Computer Information Transactions Act (UCITA, 1999) was drafted by the National Conference of Commissioners on Uniform State Laws (NCCUSL) and was originally proposed as an amendment to the Uniform Commercial Code (UCC) in the form of a new article (UCC Article 2B). Fundamental disagreement over the substance of the language caused the project to be dropped as a proposed amendment to the UCC and recast as a stand-alone model act that could be adopted by each of the states. Approved by NCCUSL on July 29, 1999, only two states—Virginia and Maryland—have adopted UCITA as state law, and each has adopted the model act with some modifications.

Although UCITA attempted to establish uniform laws governing the licensing and use of software, it has been criticized on a number of grounds. For example, UCITA essentially validates shrink-wrap or click-through licenses—the standard, take-it-or-leave-it licenses that are often tied to software. A trap for any business would be the downloading and installation by employees of software onto company computers, where the software is accompanied by click-through licensing terms. In such instances, the business could be subject to those terms, even though the terms were not formally reviewed and accepted by the legal department.

UCITA also validates stop code, or software code, mechanisms that may deactivate the functionality of the software automatically over time, switch off use of the software for other reasons (e.g., if installed on a replacement computer), or otherwise allow the vendor to shut down the software remotely through a back door (e.g., through an Internet connection). The implications of such stop code are obvious, particularly where incorporated within mission critical software.

Anyone doing business in a jurisdiction that has recognized UCITA should consider the implications of that act. Furthermore, in negotiating any licensing or IT agreement, the parties should also be aware of a contract clause that attempts to apply any or all of the provisions of UCITA to the terms of the agreement.

Computer Fraud and Abuse Act

The Computer Fraud and Abuse Act (CFAA, 1986) is intended to reduce hacking of commercial computer systems and prohibits, among other things, anyone from intentionally accessing a computer without authorization and thereby improperly obtaining information from the computer (18 U.S.C. §1030 *et seq.*). The CFAA applies to computers (a) storing certain financial information, (b) storing information from any department or agency of the United States, and (c) used in interstate or foreign commerce or communication (18 U.S.C. §1030(a)(2)).

Violation of the CFAA is punishable by imposition of a fine, imprisonment, or both (18 U.S.C. §1030(c)). The CFAA permits, under certain circumstances, a person damaged by reason of a violation of the CFAA to bring a civil cause of action for compensatory damages and injunctive or other equitable relief (18 U.S.C. §1030(g)).

Although the CFAA requires intent to access a computer without authorization, instances may arise in which, for example, overzealous employees seek, intentionally, to obtain information from competitors to obtain a competitive advantage in the marketplace or in which a software tool is used, intentionally, to crawl, mine, or extract data from Web sites and databases available online, however, in doing so circumvent authorization requirements for legitimate access to that data. Such conduct could run afoul of the CFAA and risk civil liability, in addition to fines and, in certain instances, imprisonment of the violator.

Other U.S. Federal Statutes

Other U.S. statutes that impact data security from one angle or another (some of which apply only to government agencies) and are worth mentioning include the following:

1. The Privacy Act of 1974 which, in relevant part, provides that "no [government] agency shall disclose any record which is contained in a system of records by any means of communication to any person, or to another agency" (5 U.S.C. §552a).
2. The Computer Security Act of 1987 (amended by the Clinger-Cohen Act of 1996 and the E-Government Act of 2002), which requires the government to promulgate standards for computer security, train relevant employees in computer security and establish plans for the security and privacy of computer information. In relevant part, the act requires that

> each federal agency shall provide for the mandatory periodic training in computer security awareness and accepted computer security practice of all employees who are involved with the management, use or operation of each Federal computer system within or under the supervision of that agency... [and] establish a plan for the security and privacy of each Federal computer system... that is commensurate with the risk and magnitude of the harm resulting from the loss, misuse, or unauthorized access to or modification of the information contained in such system. (40 U.S.C. §1441)

3. The Clinger-Cohen Act (1996; formerly known as the Information Technology Management Reform Act), which directs executive agencies of the government to establish the position of chief information officers (CIO) and places responsibility on the CIO for

> providing advice and other assistance to the head of the executive agency and other senior management personnel of the executive agency to ensure that information technology is acquired and information resources are managed for the executive agency...; developing, maintaining, and facilitating the implementation of a sound and integrated information technology architecture for the executive agency; and promoting the effective and efficient design and operation of all major information resources management processes for the executive agency, including improvements to work processes of the executive agency. (40 U.S.C. §1401)

4. The Trade Secrets Act (2000), which criminalizes unauthorized government disclosure of trade secrets.
5. The Uniform Trade Secrets Act (1985), which has been adopted by a majority of the states in one form or another and which protects certain confidential information receiving the status of a trade secret under the terms of the act.
6. The Fair Credit Reporting Act (1970), which limits the disclosure and use of certain credit information appearing on a consumer's credit bureau report.
7. The Children's Online Privacy Protection Act (1998), which prohibits the online collection and use of information from children under the age of 13 without parental consent.
8. The Controlling the Assault of Non-Solicited Pornography and Marketing Act of 2003, which places certain restrictions on the transmittal of commercial e-mail.

See *Cobell v. Norton* (2001).

U.S. State Laws. There is a growing trend among the states, undoubtedly prompted by increasing public concern for such things as identity theft and misuse of private information, to enact privacy laws that would supplement the protections afforded by federal law. California, for example, has enacted a number of privacy-driven statutes, among them being the California Information Practices Act.

California Information Practices Act

California passed a unique law, effective July 1, 2003, requiring notification of security breaches. An amendment to the California Information Practices Act (2003), and titled Notice of Security Breach, the law requires any business or California state agency that maintains unencrypted computerized data that include personal information to notify any California resident of a security breach involving his or her personal information (CA Civil Code §§1798.29 and 1798.82–1798.84). The purpose of the law is to give affected individuals the opportunity to take steps to protect themselves from identity theft.

Under the California Act, personal information refers to "an individual's first name or first initial and last name in combination with any one or more of the following data elements, when either the name or the data elements are not encrypted" (CA Civil Code §1798.82(e)):

- Social Security number.
- Driver's license number or California identification card number.

- Account number, credit or debit card number, in combination with any required security code, access code, or password that would permit access to an individual's financial account.

"'Breach of the security of the system' means unauthorized acquisition of computerized data that compromises the security, confidentiality, or integrity of personal information maintained by the person or business" (CA Civil Code §1798.82(d)). The law states that

> any person or business that *conducts business in California*, and that owns or licenses computerized data that includes personal information, shall disclose any breach of the security of the system following discovery or notification of the breach in the security of the data to any resident of California whose unencrypted personal information was, *or is reasonably believed to have been*, acquired by an unauthorized person. (CA Civil Code §1798.82(a); emphasis added)

Because the law applies to any business or person that *conducts business in California*, it has the potential to affect many businesses located outside the state of California (i.e., even if the business does not have a physical presence within the state), particularly companies that conduct business through a Web site via the Internet. Furthermore, because the law requires a business to notify affected individuals if a security breach is *reasonably believed* to have occurred, businesses that believe they may have been subject to a breach will need to make a prompt assessment of the situation to determine whether notification is required under the law.

To the extent applicable, the owner or licensee of the information must also be notified (CA Civil Code §1798.82(b)). For example, where a data processor or outsourcer is handling data on behalf of another organization and the data processor's systems are breached, and the other organization is deemed the owner of the data, the data processor will need to notify the organization of the security breach. The statute allows for a private cause of action, thus permitting those who have been injured by a violation of the statute to seek redress in a lawsuit (CA Civil Code §1798.84).

Because many organizations shy away from public disclosure of security breaches, largely because of the public relations fallout, the California law has caused a fair amount of commotion. The law will require, at least when the personal information of California residents is concerned, that organizations immediately notify such individuals (and perhaps the organization's business associates, if they own the data) when there is reason to believe that their personal information has been compromised due to a breach of the organization's (or its subcontractor's) IT systems. At least one lawsuit, seeking class action status, has been filed under the California law (see *Hamilton v. Microsoft Corp.*, 2003). The complaint alleged that Microsoft's response to security vulnerability, in respect of its Windows operating system and other software products, is not sufficient to protect important and vital information and data.

State Consumer Protection Laws

Given its limited resources, the FTC has not often pursued privacy violations of the sort mentioned in the foregoing section. State attorneys general may pursue claims under state consumer protection laws whether or not the FTC pursues the matter under the FTCA. For example, in the FTC Toysmart action (*Federal Trade Commission v. Toysmart.com, LLC*, 2000), the FTC proposed a settlement with Toysmart, but the attorneys general of 47 states rejected that settlement, filing an objection to the FTC's application to enter the settlement (see *In re Toysmart.com, LLC*, 2000).

There are a number of state consumer protection laws that resemble the FTCA in addressing false, misleading, or deceptive business practices. In some states, the language of the state consumer protection law parallels that of Section 5 of the FTCA. See *Vermont v. International Collection Service, Inc.* (1991), in which "fourteen states have adopted this version [of the Unfair Trade Practices and Consumer Protection Law as proposed by the FTC], commonly known as the mini-FTC act." State consumer protection laws are typically enforced by the office of the state attorney general but may allow for a private cause of action by consumers. See *Florez v. Linens 'n Things, Inc.* (2003), in which California consumer protection law permits private action regarding retailer's collection of personal information from customer.

Attorneys general have already shown an indication that they will pursue action where the security of personal information is compromised. For example, the New York State Office of the Attorney General (NYOAG) announced a multistate agreement with technology publisher Ziff Davis Media Inc. to "redress an Internet security breach that exposed the personal information of thousands of magazine subscribers online." According to the NYOAG,

> a magazine promotion Ziff Davis ran on its website in November of [2001]...allowed a computer file of approximately 12,000 subscription orders for Electronic Gaming Monthly to be accessed by anyone surfing the Internet. Personal data was exposed, including credit card information, which resulted in some subscribers becoming victims of identity theft.

The NYOAG noted that Ziff Davis's "privacy policy promised reasonable security, but it was not effective in this case" (Office of New York State Attorney General Eliot Spitzer, 2002).

In October 2003, the NYOAG settled a claim against Victoria's Secret Direct, LLC that the company's Web site allowed users to view online order information of other users, including personal information such as name, billing address, and items ordered. The NYOAG noted that

> the published privacy policy for Victoria's Secret indicated that: "Any information you provide to

us at this site when you establish or update an account, enter a contest, shop online or request information . . . is maintained in private files on our secure web server and internal systems. . . . " (Office of New York State Attorney General Eliot Spitzer, 2003)

Where a private cause of action is allowed, an aggrieved consumer may sue to recover his or her damages or, if permitted by the statute, statutory damages, treble damages, or both.

Foreign Laws. The security of data may be impacted by laws outside the United States. For example, the European Union follows a Data Protection Directive that imposes various limitations and restrictions on the access, use, and disclosure of personal information (European Parliament, 1995). The Data Protection Directive is implemented as national law by the member countries of the European Union. The directive requires certain security measures to be taken:

1. The organization having control of the personal data (the controller) must implement appropriate technical and organizational measures to protect personal data against accidental or unlawful destruction or accidental loss and against unauthorized alteration, disclosure or access, in particular where the processing involves the transmission of data over a network, and against all other unlawful forms of processing. Having regard to the state of the art and the costs of their implementation, such measures shall ensure a level of security appropriate to the risks represented by the processing and the nature of the data to be protected (European Parliament, 1995, Article 17, ¶ 1).
2. The "controller must, where processing is carried out on his behalf, choose a processor who provides sufficient guarantees in respect of the technical security measures and organizational measures governing the processing to be carried out and must ensure compliance with those measures" (European Parliament, 1995, Article 17, ¶ 2).
3. The carrying out of processing by a processor must be governed by a contract binding the processor to the controller and stipulating in particular that (i) the processor shall act only on instructions from the controller, and (ii) the obligations set out in paragraph 1 above shall also apply to the processor (European Parliament, 1995, Article 17, ¶ 3).

The Data Protection Directive also restricts the transfer of certain information outside the European Union to countries that do not provide adequate safeguards to ensure the privacy and security of the data. See European Parliament (2002). As of March 2004, the United States was not considered to be a country that provides adequate safeguards. Thus, under the directive, personal data (e.g., employee data collected by human resource departments, customer information, and prospective client lists) cannot normally be transferred from the European office of a company to its U.S. office or to any other person or entity in the United States. There are three mechanisms in place, however, to legally effectuate such a transfer:

1. Where the individual consents to the transfer of his or her data.
2. Where the parties enter into a contract incorporating model clauses approved by the European Commission in which the transferee agrees to safeguard the data in accordance with those clauses (see "Model contracts," n.d.).
3. For data transferred to the United States, where the U.S.-based business registers for and adheres to the Safe Harbor, a set of rules developed by the U.S. Department of Congress and approved by the European Commission (see "Safe harbor overview," n.d.).

Under certain local European laws, the transfer of personal data must be registered with a designated local authority. The failure to adhere to the restrictions of the Data Protection Directive could result in a violation of European law.

CONTRACTUAL LIABILITY

Liability may arise under a breach of contract claim. There are at least two distinct categories of contracts that could be impacted by a security breach:

1. Business-to-business contracts, such as vendor agreements, outsourcing agreements, facility management agreements, independent contractor agreements, application service provider agreements, service bureau agreements, transaction fulfillment agreements, hosting agreements, co-location agreements, and agreements for contingency planning, backup, and disaster-recovery services—in all of which one party is being entrusted with responsibility for, or has access to, sensitive data of the other party.
2. Consumer contracts, which may arise in varying contexts, such as through a Web site click-through agreement, privacy policy, terms of use, subscriber agreement or user agreement, or, perhaps, where statutorily mandated, such as for financial information governed by GLB and health information covered by HIPAA or in any other context in which an organization has made a representation to the consumer with respect to the privacy or security of his or her personal information.

Requirements of a Binding Contract

There must be mutual intent of the parties for there to be a binding contract, including an offer, acceptance, and consideration. See generally, Restatement (Second), Contracts, ch. 3, 4; see also *Maher v. United States* (2002). These requirements are almost always satisfied with a written agreement signed by at least two parties, particularly in a commercial setting in which the agreement is usually entered into by relatively sophisticated parties and often reviewed by attorneys. Although a contract need not necessarily be in writing to be binding, it is customary for many to be written instruments.

In the absence of an express agreement, a promise may nonetheless be enforceable under the theory of promissory estoppel or implied contract.

> The elements of promissory estoppel are: (1) a promise unambiguous in its terms; (2) reliance on such promise by the party to whom it is made; (3) this reliance is expected and foreseeable by the party making the promise; and (4) the one to whom the promise is made must rely on the promise to his injury. (*Cohabaco Cigar Co. v. United States Tobacco Co.*, 1999)

A "standardized contract, which, imposed and drafted by the party of superior bargaining strength, relegates to the subscribing party only the opportunity to adhere to the contract or reject it" is referred to as a contract of adhesion (Armendariz v. Foundation Health Psychcare Services, 2000) (citations and internal quotation omitted); see also *Farnsworth on Contracts* §4.26 (2001). ("The form may be a take-it-or-leave-it proposition, often called a contract of adhesion, under which the only alternative to complete adherence is outright rejection.") An online agreement, for example, may be a contract of adhesion since the end user may either accept or reject it, but has no power to negotiate its terms (Comb v. PayPal, Inc., 2002, for reviewing online agreement in terms of a contract of adhesion). If there were unequal bargaining power in the formation of a contract, as is true with a contract of adhesion, courts are likely to interpret any ambiguity in the contract against the drafter and in favor of the nondrafting party (*Farnsworth on Contracts* §4.26 (LEXIS 2001); *Comb*, 2002, 218 F. Supp. 2d at 1172). Furthermore, the fact that a contract is one of adhesion may sway the court that a provision of the contract is unconscionable and thus unenforceable (*Comb*, 2002, 218 F. Supp. 2d at 1172).

There is case law that supports the view that a cause of action may be maintained in contract for an unauthorized disclosure of personal information. For example, in *Peterson v. Idaho First National Bank* (1961), the Idaho Supreme Court dismissed the plaintiff's invasion of privacy claim but held open the possibility that the bank had breached an implied contractual duty of confidentiality. In that case, the plaintiff's manager had asked the bank to inform him when any of his employees did anything to discredit his company. A bank official informed the manager that the plaintiff had written several bad checks. The plaintiff brought suit against the bank for its unauthorized disclosure of his personal information. The court focused on the relationship of the parties and the nature of the information in finding that "it is implicit in the contract of the bank with its customer or depositor that no information may be disclosed by the bank or its employees concerning the customer's or depositor's account, and that, unless authorized by law or by the customer or depositor, the bank must be held liable for breach of the implied contract" (*Id.* at 290; see also *Barnett Bank of West Fla. v. Hooper*, 1986, acknowledging that a bank may have an implied contractual duty not to disclose information regarding a customer's account absent special circumstances such as fraud; and *Suburban Trust Co. v. Waller*, 1979, recognizing a bank's implied contractual duty to keep private information concerning its customer's account).

Remedies

Damages

In a breach of contract action, the normal remedy for the aggrieved party is to recover his or her actual damages attributable to the breach. Where personal information has been disclosed due to a security breach, it may, however, be difficult to quantify the damages. In fact, a consumer may have no provable damages. For example, it has been held that a person suffered no quantifiable damage when his personal information was sold to third parties for marketing purposes (*Dwyer v. American Express Co.*,1995, in which the plaintiffs did not suffer damages by credit card company's disclosure of cardholders' credit card purchases and contact information; and *Smith v. Chase Manhattan Bank, USA, N.A.*, 2002: "Thus, the 'harm' at the heart of this purported class action, is that class members were merely offered products and services which they were free to decline. This does not qualify as actual harm.").

However, if the disclosure results in identity theft, there could be some level of real damages incurred. A survey by CalPIRG and the Privacy Rights Clearinghouse in May 2000 found that the average consumer identity theft victim spends 175 hours and $800 resolving identity theft problems and that it takes 2 to 4 years for victims to resolve all the resulting problems ("Identity theft," n.d.). Thus, there could be a quantifiable amount of actual damages in which a breach results in the disclosure of personal information of many individuals. Furthermore, it would be naïve to assume that any unauthorized disclosure of personal information would result in no damage, especially in light of the changing legal climate concerning the privacy and security of such information.

Consumer harm aside, in the commercial context the disclosure or loss of corporate data could have a substantial financial impact. For example, an unauthorized disclosure of trade secrets or customer information could put a business at a significant competitive disadvantage and, in some cases, ruin the business. Most commercial contracts will contain disclaimers of certain damages and limitations of liability. Depending on which side of the contract you are on, this may or may not be reassuring. For example, many contracts disclaim liability for consequential damages. Whereas direct, or compensatory, damages usually equate to the amount of money to put the aggrieved party in as good a position had the breaching party not breached (e.g., the amount of money that a customer had agreed to pay), indirect, or consequential, damages reflect the natural and probable consequences flowing from the breach and can be significantly more than the direct damages. Examples of damages that, depending upon the nature of the contract, tend to be consequential in nature include lost profits, loss of business, and loss of goodwill.

Damages that are consequential may not be recoverable if the parties have contracted to exclude them from liability in the event of a breach. Thus, if the disclosure of a trade secret or some other confidential information causes a business to lose a competitive edge in the marketplace, results in a public relations fiasco possibly driving down the stock, or if the loss or corruption of data leads to a loss of business or loss of clients, to the extent the damages are consequential in nature, the injured party may not be able to recover. Some contracts, however, exclude from the disclaimer of damages certain breaches of the contract or conduct of a party, such as a breach of an obligation to maintain the confidentiality of confidential information, a breach of a security requirement, or for reason of a party's negligence, recklessness, willful misconduct, or intentional conduct. Such exceptions could allow for recovery for such losses under certain circumstances.

Additionally, commercial contracts often limit the amount of liability to a dollar figure or a fixed amount, such as the total fees paid or a multiple thereof. Some contracts will limit the amount to the fees paid during a particular term of the contract, such as 1 year preceding the accrual of the claim. Unless there is an express carve out from the limitation of liability, the dollar cap would typically apply to any claim under the contract, including a claim for breach of confidentiality or breach of security (unless, for example, the applicable jurisdiction recognizes a tort claim for gross negligence or willful misconduct in such instance or otherwise, for public policy reasons, would disregard the contractual limitation of liability given the reckless or intentional conduct of the breaching party). The limitation of liability and disclaimers of damages are therefore very important aspects of any IT-related contract because, depending on which side of the contract a person is on, these clauses will greatly impact his or her financial risk in the event of a security breach. Accordingly, the precise wording of these clauses should be carefully considered during the contract negotiations.

Many contracts also include some type of indemnity, which can likewise affect financial liability arising from a security breach. For example, a clause that requires Party A to indemnify Party B for third-party claims arising out of a breach of a representation or warranty, or for Party A's or its subcontractors' negligence, recklessness, or willful misconduct, could make Party A contractually obligated to defend, indemnify, and hold harmless Party B should Party B become involved in a claim based on Party A's unauthorized disclosure of Party B's confidential information. The indemnity there could be triggered where, for example, the contract contained a representation or warranty regarding the confidentiality, privacy, or security of information or a representation or warranty against viruses, Trojan horses, worms, or other malicious code. It could also be triggered if Party A were negligent in, for example, exercising adequate safeguards to protect the information (e.g., in failing to use suitable firewalls or encryption, failing to screen employees and subcontractors and to do background checks, failing to provide adequate employee training, or failing to utilize reasonable physical and logical security).

Where there is a stream of providers of technology services, it is wise to ensure that the contractual chain is not broken at some point, thereby exposing one party to unnecessary liability. It is not at all uncommon to have various contracts and subcontracts involving multiple providers of IT services. In many instances, it is desirable to have the contracts contain similar obligations—particularly concerning liability—flowing upstream. For example, a provider that assumes responsibility to its customer in a contract, and then subcontracts out some or all of its obligations to another party, should take care to ensure that the contract with its subcontractor contains obligations similar to those in its customer contract. If there are gaps in the contractual obligations, the provider may, in the event of a breach, find itself in between its customer and its subcontractor with no contractual recourse against its subcontractor. This is particularly acute when the provider has agreed to indemnify its customer, but has failed to secure the same indemnity from its subcontractor. If, for example, the subcontractor releases customer data without authorization, thereby triggering the provider's indemnity to its customer, the provider may have to indemnify its customer, but not have a reciprocal right to obtain indemnity from the subcontractor. Thus, to the extent feasible, contractual obligations, particularly those affecting liability (e.g., indemnities, warranties, and disclaimers), should flow upstream.

It is worth noting that the value of any indemnity is tied directly to the financial wherewithal of the party giving it. That is, if the indemnifying party should become insolvent, the indemnity may be worthless. The contracting parties may therefore wish to explore, in addition to an indemnity provision, specific insurance commitments in the agreement.

It is also prudent to recognize downstream liability. For example, a provider of certain data may restrict the usage of data it provides to another service provider which, in turn, may offer those data bundled with other products and services to an end user. The end user may be bound, through its contract with the service provider, to adhere to the data provider's restrictions. In the absence of such a contract, the data may be protected by copyright or other intellectual property rights. Accordingly, the end user should be aware of potential liability it faces for any misuse of the data.

Equitable Relief

Equitable relief may be available where damages will not adequately compensate the injured party. If there is a contract, a court may order that the nonbreaching party specifically perform its obligations under the contract (see *Marquardt and Roche/Meditz and Hackett, Inc. v. Riverbend Executive Center, Inc.*, 2003, in which "the specific performance remedy is a form of injunctive decree in which the court orders the defendant to perform the contract"). In the context of a promise not to disclose personal information, a court may order the business to perform its promise not to disclose the information or to cease an ongoing disclosure. The burden rests with the party seeking equitable relief to show that there is no adequate remedy at law (see *Marquardt*, 74 Conn. App. at 421, 812 A.2d at 182, in which "a party seeking injunctive relief has the burden of alleging and proving irreparable harm and lack of an adequate remedy at law").

As a practical matter, to prevent the business from disclosing the information while the merits of the case are adjudicated, the claimant would seek interim relief in the form of a preliminary injunction. To obtain a preliminary injunction, the claimant must show that he or she will be irreparably harmed if the action is not enjoined (*Chicago Research & Trading v. New York Futures Exchange, Inc.*, 1982, in which "injunctive relief will be afforded only in those extraordinary situations where the plaintiff has no adequate remedy at law and such relief is necessary to avert irreparable injury.").

Web Sites

The Internet presented a new twist to traditional contract theory. In the online context, such as with a Web site terms of use, there is a written document (albeit in electronic form) but no signatures by the parties (at least not in the traditional penmanship sense; there may be electronic signatures for purposes of logging a transaction). Nonetheless, a business that posts an online terms of use or privacy policy on its Web site may be bound to the promises made in those terms or that policy. A terms-of-use or privacy policy may be a binding contract, enforceable by the customer against the organization that posted the terms or policy on its Web site. The enforceability of an online contract depends essentially upon basic contract principles. An online contract has been held enforceable (see *Hughes v. America Online, Inc.*, 2002, in which enforcing forum selection clause in an online click-through terms-of-service agreement; see also *Comb v. PayPal, Inc.*, 2002, in which a binding online agreement may shown by the assent of the parties).

The FTC has urged businesses to clearly inform consumers of their information collection practices. See, for example, FTC's Fair Information Practice Principles (n.d.). Although posting a privacy policy on a Web site is not legally required, it has become common practice. A carefully drafted privacy policy might be considered a proper means of disclosing to consumers a business's information collection, use, and disclosure practices and thereby fend off claims by consumers that they were unaware that, by uploading their personal information to a Web site, the information would be used or disclosed in various ways. In that regard, so long as the privacy policy accurately reflects an organization's practices, and the organization follows those practices, the policy might be used as a means to head off potential consumer confusion and complaints. An organization must, however, adhere to the statements in its policy. (According to Simpson, 2001, "Amazon.com and its Alexa Internet subsidiary probably made deceptive statements about their privacy practices ... [by] surreptitiously collecting personal data on customers through its Alexa system, which is designed to assist shopping and other activities online.")

Terms of Use and Privacy Policies

As a general principle, a Web site agreement will be enforceable against the end user if there is mutuality, that is, if the end user has assented to its terms. Courts have enforced online terms of service where the end user had to view the terms and affirmatively accept them (e.g., by clicking an I Accept button). The evolving case law indicates that where a business seeks to enforce its online terms against the end user, it must demonstrate that the end user affirmatively assented to the terms. See, for example, *Hughes v. America Online, Inc.*, 2002, which upheld the forum selection clause in a click-wrap agreement governing use of an e-mail service; *Groff v. America Online, Inc.*, 1998, which enforced the click-through choice of law clause in online terms of service agreement where user clicked "I agree" not once but twice; and *Caspi v. Microsoft Network, LLC*, 1999, which enforced forum selection clause in a click-through agreement for use of Internet service. See also *Stomp, Inc. v. Neato*, 1999, which commented that "'clickwrap agreement' allows the consumer to manifest its assent to the terms of a contract by 'clicking' on an acceptance button on the website."

Conversely, it would appear evident that the terms should be enforceable against the owner of the Web site who actually posted them. Under basic contract theory, the posted terms would, in essence, be an offer of a contract. If the end user accepts, there should be a binding contract. The end user, however, must have accepted the terms for them to be binding. See, for example, *Gibson v. United States*, 2003, in which elements of a contract must be shown to be entitled to a reward; and *Otworth v. The Florida Bar*, 1999, in which an offer for a reward is contractual and a "claimant must allege 'knowledge of existence of the offer of reward' to be entitled to the benefits of such reward." It has been held that an individual need only have been aware of the terms, and not have relied upon a particular term or even have read the terms, of a contract for it to be binding upon him or her (*Reuben H. Donnelley Corp. v. American Protective Services Corp.*, 1986, in which "this court agrees and holds that APS [American Protective Services] cannot avoid the contracts on the basis that it chose not to read them"). Where a Web site has posted terms, and an end user alleges he or she was aware of the terms, the owner of the Web site will be hard pressed to argue that it is not contractually bound to those terms. If a terms-of-use or privacy policy makes overly broad claims about maintaining the privacy or ensuring the security of personal information, it is conceivable that an end user may bring a breach-of-contract claim if there is a security breach that discloses his or her personal information. Identity theft resulting from an unauthorized disclosure is one area of significant concern and may generate such claims.

Two important considerations regarding privacy policies are (1) amendments to a privacy policy and (2) the sale of assets that include information collected under an existing privacy policy. If an organization desires to amend the terms of a privacy policy, and wishes the amendment to apply retroactively to information it had collected under the earlier privacy policy, it should notify all those whose information it had already collected of the amendment. This may be done by e-mail or, perhaps, by posting notice of the amendment on its Web site, so long as the organization has reason to believe that the affected individuals will receive notice in that manner. If an individual objects to his or her information being used in the manner set forth in the amendment, the organization should respect the individual's request and take appropriate measures, such as removing his or her information from the database or otherwise tagging that information for restricted use or disclosure. In addition to raising contracting concerns (e.g., such as an unconscionable term in a contract of adhesion), a failure to follow these steps could run afoul of the FTCA or state consumer protection laws as improper use of a consumer contract or possibly a misrepresentation to the consumer.

Where assets subject to purchase in a business transaction include information collected under an existing privacy policy, the acquiring business may have difficulty obtaining the information if it were collected under a privacy policy that indicated that such information would not be disclosed to third parties. For example, in 2000 the FTC and state attorneys general attempted to block the transfer of customer information collected by failed online toy retailer Toysmart.com LLC in a bankruptcy asset sale because the company had collected the information under a privacy policy that stated that personal information "is never shared with a third party." In response to the Toysmart matter, many businesses amended their privacy policies to state that they could transfer information in event of bankruptcy or an acquisition, merger, or sale of the company's assets. The FTC has indicated that a business obtaining such personal information should continue to respect the commitments made in the privacy policy under which the information was collected, unless it seeks to amend the terms of the privacy policy.

Privacy Seal Programs

Some private companies offer, for a fee, to certify that a privacy policy and the privacy practices of a business are trustworthy. Two companies that maintain seal programs are TRUSTe and BBBonline. If the policy and practices are certified, the business is permitted to display the sponsor's privacy seal. An organization may enter into an agreement with the sponsor of a seal program to display the seal on its Web site. The agreement will likely require, in addition to compliance with the organization's own posted policies and procedures, adherence to certain other policies regarding personal information that is required by the seal sponsor. Should the organization fail to comply with the terms of its agreement with the sponsor, due to a security breach or otherwise, it may find itself in breach of its contractual obligations to the sponsor. For example, in the Toysmart bankruptcy, TRUSTe intervened to enjoin the sale of Toysmart's customer list, asserting that the sale would be in breach of its seal licensing agreement with Toysmart. See Objection of Trusted Universal Standards In Electronic Transactions (TRUSTe) To Motion To Approve Stipulation, *In re Toysmart.com, LLC*, 2000.

TORT LIABILITY

A tort is "a legal wrong committed upon the person or property independent of contract" (Garner, 1983). In certain instances, the law will impose upon a person a duty of care. If the person fails to fulfill that duty, he or she may be liable to another person who has suffered damage as a result of the failed duty. Liability under tort theory may apply where there is no contract between two parties. Negligence, gross negligence, willful misconduct, and strict liability are common tort theories of liability.

Elements of a Tort

A party may be liable under a tort theory if

- the law recognizes a duty of care (e.g., to maintain the security of data or to prevent security breaches);
- there is a breach of that duty;
- there is a proximate relationship between the breach of the duty and the injury; and
- actual loss or damage is incurred as a result of the breach.

There is presently no clearly established duty of care with regard to the security of data under tort law. A leading case discussing when a tort duty should be imposed is *United States v. Carroll Towing Co., Inc.*, 1947. That case assessed whether a duty should be imposed based upon several factors: (1) the probability that harm will occur, (2) the gravity of the resulting harm, and (3) the burden of adequate precautions (*Id.* at 173). Under that rationale, a duty should exist if the probability of harm occurring and the magnitude of that harm outweigh the burden of avoiding the harm.

A handful of cases may offer guidance as to whether there exists such a duty. For example, in the banking context, it has been held that a bank has a duty to keep certain information confidential (*DJowharzadeh v. City Nat'l Bank & Trust Co.*, 1982). In that case, a bank customer provided to the bank's loan officer certain confidential information about a proposed real estate purchase, which the loan officer then disclosed to other individuals who used the information to the customer's detriment. Stating that the "customer's cause of action is, with these special facts, properly framed in terms of tortious conduct," the court held that the "bank's relationship to a loan applicant implicitly imposes the duty to keep the contents of loan applications confidential. This duty has existed traditionally and continues to exist, if not specifically in the law books, at least in the mind of the public in general and within the banking community in particular" (*Id.* at 620).

On the other hand, in *Stevens v. First Interstate Bank of California* (2000), the court held that a bank does not have a duty to safeguard personal information. In that case, the court framed the issue as follows:

> Where a third party misappropriates personal or credit information that a depositor had provided to a bank, and that misappropriation is the result of the bank's failure to adequately protect the information from such misappropriation, is the bank liable for the depositor's resulting emotional distress? (*Id.* at 285–286)

Viewing the bank–customer relationship in that case as "more analogous to a merchant-customer relationship in which the customer, in transacting a credit card or other noncash purchase, provides certain information to the merchant," the court concluded that the relationship between the parties had no element of a trust in it (e.g., in holding money in trust for someone) and, therefore, did not give rise to a duty on the part of the bank to protect the information from misappropriation (*Id.* at 288).

At least one case has found a duty to secure sensitive records accessible via the Internet under the theory that the party responsible for trust fund records had a fiduciary duty to protect them from unauthorized disclosure (*Cobell v. Norton,* 2001). In *Cobell*, the Department of the Interior (DOI) held or created in systems managed and administered by the Bureau of Indian Affairs Office of Information Resources Management certain Indian trust funds and individual Indian trust records. The information was kept on systems that were accessible to the Internet without firewalls, encryption, or other means of reasonable security. In a scathing report, the special master criticized the DOI for failing to employ adequate safeguards and recommended that the court intervene to take control over the DOI's IT systems. The special master found that the DOI had a fiduciary duty to safeguard information relating to the trust and that the DOI had derogated that duty by failing to implement satisfactory IT security safeguards (*Id.* at *141).

The fiduciary relationship in the *Cobell* case arose because of the special nature of the data—trust fund records—the special duty for which was already well established in common law. See *Rippey v. Denver U.S. Nat. Bank* (1967), in which "it is generally agreed that a trustee owes a duty to his beneficiaries to exercise such care and skill as a man of ordinary prudence would exercise in safeguarding and preserving his own property." Absent such a relationship, however, it is not clear that a duty would exist to safeguard sensitive information such as names, addresses, telephone numbers, or Social Security numbers. The lack of clear precedent either way—whether in favor of a duty or declining to recognize any duty—renders the notion of a tort claim for data security somewhat uncertain. The issue will undoubtedly present itself, and may, for example, arise in the context of an individual whose personal information was allegedly not adequately safeguarded, for example, after he or she uploaded that information through a Web site.

What Is Reasonable?

Were a court to find that a tort duty exists, the duty of care could vary depending upon the circumstances. Generally, however, the law will apply a duty to exercise *reasonable* care. A person who fails to exercise a reasonable duty of care is said to have been negligent. In tort cases, courts routinely determine what is reasonable under the circumstances drawing upon what has been learned in past cases and evidence offered in the current case. The oft-quoted measure in assessing reasonableness is what would a reasonable person have done under the circumstances. Of course, the issue of reasonableness is often open to debate and the subject of intense disagreement during a litigation.

Perhaps one of the most significant hurdles in a claim of negligence regarding data security is ascertaining what would be reasonable. Many people—courts included—lack a good understanding of the technical nuances that comprise IT and information security. A genuine lack of familiarity with the subject makes it extraordinarily difficult to assess reasonableness because one would have to defer to others' experiences as to what may or may not be reasonable on an otherwise foreign subject. Moreover, like IT in general, security technologies are ever in flux, rapidly changing as computer technologies change. What may be reasonable one day may not be a short time later.

There is also a wide range of security needs, depending upon the nature of the data and the perceived risks. For example, sensitive personal information that a business considers a valuable asset and that represents a would-be target for thieves might require greater levels of security than similar, but less sensitive, information of little interest to hackers. Thus, there could be widely divergent security standards that are, nonetheless, reasonable under differing circumstances.

Because there are many differing approaches to security, the idea of one reasonable standard that could be applied across the board may be difficult to accept. Indeed, a single common standard for data security might even prove undesirable insofar as it could actually make hacking easier if would-be hackers knew that most security systems adhered to a similar common technical standard. However, it may be prudent to have certain general principles governing policies and procedures regarding security, but allow the technical implementation of security devices, applications, and systems to differ across individual business enterprises. Following the example in the HIPAA Privacy and Security Rule, for example, it may be acceptable to establish administrative, physical, technical, and organizational standards for safeguarding data, leaving the implementation of those standards to each organization (this, of course, would not completely solve the issue as there would still need to be some level of determination as to whether the standards were reasonably implemented within the parameters established).

For torts commonly seen by courts, there is ample case law to draw upon in assessing what would be reasonable. Where there is no well-established standard, as appears currently true for data security, a court may look to several factors in its attempt to assess what would have been reasonable under the circumstances. For example, a court may consider an argument concerning the costs to implement certain levels of security in relation to the risks involved. A plaintiff may be able to proffer a convincing argument that, where the risks substantially outweigh the costs or where the costs are relatively insignificant to a corporate budget, a business acted unreasonably in not applying more rigid, but costly, security protocols. A court may also entertain expert testimony concerning the security policies and procedures of other similarly situated organizations, the thinking being that if certain policies and procedures are being exercised by a number of a defendant's counterparts, it would be reasonable for the defendant to have followed similar policies and procedures.

A court may also consider industry standards to the extent there is some agreement within an industry as to what those standards are. In this regard, a court may look to examples in organizations that proffer security standards or otherwise audit security risks. It may also consider evidence of relevant statutory language and the requirements set out in regulatory pronouncements, such as GLB and HIPAA, that speak to the security of data.

Establishing a Standard

A judicially construed standard may be drawn from various sources. The following offers examples of sources that could be given weight in arriving at such a standard.

Statutes and Regulations

A statute that was enacted in 2002, the Federal Information Security Management Act (FISMA), may provide guidance as to what steps an organization should take in safeguarding. FISMA applies to government agencies and is therefore binding upon them. It is not binding upon private sector companies, but its principles may serve to establish standards applicable to private business. FISMA was enacted to

> (1) provide a comprehensive framework for ensuring the effectiveness of information security controls over information resources that support Federal operations and assets;
> (2) recognize the highly networked nature of the current Federal computing environment and provide effective government wide management and oversight of the related information security risks, including coordination of information security efforts throughout the civilian, national security, and law enforcement communities; (3) provide for development and maintenance of minimum controls required to protect Federal information and information systems; [and] (4) provide a mechanism for improved oversight of Federal agency information security programs. See 44 U.S.C. § 3541(1)-(4).

It is intended to provide a framework for government agencies to improve security and risk management processes by mandating reporting on security compliance with a set of standard internal controls. FISMA makes government agencies accountable for implementing defensible security measures and requires greater reporting on these security activities. The intent is to show government regulators an agency's security benchmark, how each agency is progressing against this benchmark, and how they continue to improve agency security measures on a year-over-year basis.

Among other things, FISMA focuses on (1) developing and overseeing the implementation of information security policies; (2) requiring agencies to identify and provide information security protections commensurate with the risk and magnitude of the harm resulting from the unauthorized access, use, disclosure, disruption, modification or destruction of information or information systems used by or on behalf of an agency (including systems operated by agency contractors); and (3) coordinating the development of standards and guidelines under the National Institute of Standards and Technology (NIST) Act with agencies and offices operating or exercising control of national security systems (including the National Security Agency) to ensure, to the maximum extent feasible, that such standards and guidelines are complementary with standards and guidelines developed for national security systems (see 44 U.S.C. §3543(1)-(3)). FISMA requires that each federal enterprise information security program be placed under the CIO and mandates an independent information security program audit function which is assigned to each agency's Office of Inspector General. Because the program is placed under the CIO, it can be fully and completely integrated into the budget process to ensure that information security is adequately addressed throughout the life cycle of any and all IT-related programs. This framework allows for budget integration and independent audit functions and, by way of such, is intended to result in an effective security program.

Other statutes, such as GLB and HIPAA, which outline requirements for information security, might also be considered in developing broader security standards for corporate and personal information.

Government and Industry Standards

The Bush administration outlined a plan to enhance security of IT systems known as *The National Strategy to Secure Cyberspace* (2003). In conceptual terms, it articulates five national priorities for security; identifies eight major actions and initiatives to reduce threats and related vulnerabilities; identifies four major actions and initiatives for awareness, education, and training; identifies five major actions and initiatives for the securing of governments' cyberspace; and identifies six major actions and initiatives to strengthen U.S. national security and international cooperation. Although the concepts are general in nature, and are not necessarily binding on anyone (they are set out in a strategy), they may be one of several things that factor into broad security standards.

In December 2003, the president signed Homeland Security Presidential Directive-7 (HSPD-7) titled "Critical Infrastructure Identification, Prioritization, and Protection." Based on that directive, the Department of Homeland Security has chartered the National Cyber Security Division (NCSD), and that office is responsible for implementing the national strategy. NCSD chartered the U.S. Computer Emergency Response Team (US CERT).

Guidance may also be gleaned from organizations that propose standards for IT security. For example, Statement on Auditing Standards (SAS) No. 70 is an auditing standard developed by the American Institute of Certified Public Accountants (AICPA). SAS 70 requires service organizations to disclose their control activities and processes to their customers and their customers' auditors in a uniform reporting format. The purpose of an SAS 70 examination is for a service organization to have its control objectives and control activities examined by an independent accounting and auditing firm that will issue an auditor's opinion ("About SAS 70," n.d.).

Implementation and Security Risk Analysis ISO 17799 is a detailed security standard offered by the International Organization for Standardization (ISO). ISO is a nongovernmental organization that develops standards for a variety of applications, particularly technical standards. ISO 17799 is intended to counteract interruptions to business activities and to critical business processes from the effects of major failures or disasters. It sets out a number of standards concerning business continuity planning, system access control, system development and maintenance, physical and environmental security, compliance, personnel security, security organization, computer and operations management, asset classification and control, and security policies ("ISO 17799: What Is It?" n.d.).

Another agency that promulgates guidelines relevant to IT security is the NIST. NIST "works with industry, research, and government organizations to make [information] technology more usable, more secure, more scalable, and more interoperable than it is today" (*Cobell v. Norton*, 2001, *34, fn. 21, quoting Dr. William O. Mehuron, "Information Technology Laboratory: What ITL Does," n.d.). Pursuant to the Information Technology Management Reform Act (Public Law 104-106), the secretary of commerce approves standards and guidelines that are developed by the NIST for federal computer systems. These standards and guidelines are issued by NIST as the Federal Information Processing Standards (FIPS) for government use. "NIST develops FIPS when there are compelling federal government requirements such as for security and interoperability and there are no acceptable industry standards or solutions" (*Cobell*, 2001, at *35, fn. 22, citing "General Information," n.d.). NIST standards are now mandated for federal agencies by FISMA.

The Computer Emergency Response Team Coordination Center (CERT/CC), a federally funded research and development center operated by Carnegie Mellon University, also provides a great deal of information regarding systems security and vulnerability (see http://www.cert.org). CERT/CC offers a method for evaluating security risks, security practices that an organization can implement (including evaluating security architecture to detect and respond to intrusions), and training courses for managers and technical personnel. The security practices developed by CERT/CC and other organizations may prove helpful in assessing what practices an organization should reasonably undertake to safeguard data. CERT/CC has a relationship with the US CERT.

Security Certifications

There are also organizations that offer to audit and certify IT systems from a security standpoint. For example, SysTrust is a certification program sponsored by the AICPA that is intended to audit and certify IT systems for availability, security, integrity, and maintainability (see "What is SysTrust," 2001). TruSecure is a private company that also offers a security certification program ("TruSecure Programs," n.d.). The knowledge and efforts of these organizations may help contribute to a standard.

The foregoing provides only a few possible examples from which to draw upon a legal standard for IT security. In developing a legal standard for any duty of care, a court, for example, may look to one or more of the above, or to other resources, in formulating what is reasonable and appropriate under the circumstances.

Damages

The damages typically recoverable for a tort are those that are reasonably foreseeable and are proximately caused by the act or omission of the wrongdoer. Some jurisdictions do not permit a tort plaintiff to recover economic losses in the absence of physical damage. This economic loss rule was typically applied to claims for pain and suffering or emotional distress where there was, in fact, no actual physical harm. In the case of unauthorized disclosure of information, the rule might prohibit recovery of any damages, because the loss would be essentially economic in nature without any underlying physical harm. Nonetheless, a number of courts now recognize an exception to this rule. See, for example, *People Express Airlines v. Consolidated Rail Corp.* (1985). Given the climate for data privacy and security, it would not be surprising for the exception to apply to security breaches. Whether the damages are quantifiable is another issue (as discussed above), but one not to be lightly taken.

CONCLUSION

Advancements in IT are rapidly changing the way business is done and how we conduct our personal lives. IT has, in many ways, made the world a smaller place by making information readily accessible. As a result, sensitive corporate and personal information, in electronic form, is at all times vulnerable to compromise, whether by human error, technical fault, ill-intent, or otherwise. Organizations that rely on or process such data may have legal obligations to maintain the security of the data and may face potential liability in the event of a security breach.

Given the increasing concern among businesses, consumers, and lawmakers for hackers, breaches of data systems and networks, identity theft, and the security of information generally, it is prudent to take steps to review existing security practices and to anticipate the potential for liability under current and evolving laws. Because data security is a relatively new area for the law, an organization would do well to keep advised of statutory, regulatory, judicial, and other legal developments as they arise, and to adapt its security practices accordingly. The risk of regulatory noncompliance and of potential third-party liability may be mitigated by the implementation of adequate IT infrastructure and practices based on a proper understanding of the legal framework affecting an organization.

GLOSSARY

Application Service Provider A business that offers remote access to and use of software application services, often through the Internet.

Click-wrap Agreement An agreement setting forth the terms and conditions for use of intellectual property or a service (e.g., a Web site), which must be assented to by the user by an affirmative action such as clicking an I Accept button or the equivalent.

Confidential Information Any information deemed confidential and having pecuniary value and that is protected from unauthorized disclosure to others.

Customer Relations Management Software Software designed to aggregate, compile, organize and sort data relating to a business's customers.

Equitable Relief Relief in the form of an injunction or specific performance, instead of money damages, that may be ordered by a court.

European Commission (formally the Commission of the European Communities) The executive of the European Union, whose primary roles are to propose and enact legislation and to act as guardian of the treaties that provide the legal basis for the European Union.

Federal Trade Commission (FTC) U.S. federal agency established in 1914 by the Federal Trade Commission Act to enforce, among other things, federal consumer protection laws by investigating complaints against individual companies.

Financial Services Modernization Act of 1999 (more commonly known as the Gramm-Leach-Bliley Act [GLB]) U.S. federal legislation enacted in 1999 governing the privacy and security of personally identifiable financial information.

Force Majeure An act of God or an event outside the reasonable control of a person or entity.

Health Insurance Portability and Accountability Act (HIPAA) U.S. federal legislation enacted in 1996 governing the privacy and security of heath information.

Hosting Company A business that offers services that host Web sites on computer servers and keep those Web sites available for access through the Internet.

Information Technology (IT) The technology required for processing information and the use of computers and computer software to convert, store, protect, process, transmit, and retrieve information.

Internet Service Provider (ISP) A business that offers users access to the Internet and related services.

Managed Network Servicer A business that manages and oversees an organization's computer networks.

Outsourcing The act of a business in subcontracting to a third party the responsibilities for certain services or equipment, which may include computer systems or software or the responsibilities for operating and maintaining such computer systems or software.

Privacy Policy A disclaimer placed on a Web site informing users about how the website collects, uses and shares the user's personal information.

Privacy Seal A seal of approval issued by a private company, which may be displayed on a Web site, certifying that the Web site has agreed to adhere to certain standards for the privacy and security of data transferred through the site.

Risk Management The total process of identifying, controlling, and mitigating risks.

Security Certification A certification issued by a private auditing firm certifying that an IT system adheres to certain minimum security requirements.

Terms of Use A set of rules set up by the owner of intellectual property or a service (e.g., a Web site) to govern its use and is often a contract between the owner and the user.

Tort Under common law, a civil wrong for which the law provides a remedy.

Trade Secret A confidential practice, method, process, design, or other information used by a company to compete with other businesses, which is protected from general disclosure to others.

Uniform Commercial Code (UCC) One of the uniform acts, dealing with sales and commercial transactions, that attempts to harmonize the law of the 50 U.S. states.

Web Site A collection of Web pages accessible via hypertext transfer protocol through the Internet.

CROSS REFERENCES

See *Cyberlaw: The Major Areas, Development, and Information Security Aspects; Digital Identity; Online Contracts; Privacy Law and the Internet; Risk Management for IT Security.*

REFERENCES

About SAS 70 (n.d.). Retrieved March 11, 2004, from http://www.sas70.com/about.htm

Armendariz v. Foundation Health Psychcare Services, 24 Cal. 4th 83, 113 (2000).

Barnett Bank of West Fla. v. Hooper, 498 So. 2d 923, 925 (Fla. 1986).

California Information Practices Act, CA Civil Code §1798 (1977). Retrieved March 11, 2004, from http://www.privacyprotection.ca.gov/code/cc1798.291798.82.htm

Caspi v. Microsoft Network, LLC, 323 N.J. Super. 118, 126 (1999).

Chicago Research & Trading v. New York Futures Exchange, Inc., 446 N.Y.S.2d 280, 282, 84 A.D.2d 413, 416 (N.Y. App. Div. 1982).

Children's Online Privacy Protection Act 15 U.S.C. §§6501–6506 (1998).

Clinger-Cohen Act, 40 U.S.C. §1401 (1996).

Cobell v. Norton, U.S. Dist. LEXIS 20453, *24–27 (D.C. 2001).

Cohabaco Cigar Co. v. United States Tobacco Co., 1999 U.S. Dist. LEXIS 17210, at *27 (N.D. Ill. 1999).

Comb v. PayPal, Inc., 218 F. Supp. 2d 1165, 1172 (N.D. Ca. 2002).

Computer Fraud and Abuse Act, 18 U.S.C. §1030 *et seq.* (1986).

Computer Security Act, 40 U.S.C. §1441 (1987).

Controlling the Assault of Non-Solicited Pornography and Marketing Act, Pub. L. 108–187 (2003).

Defiance Button Machine Co. v. C&C Metal Products Corp., 759 F.2d 1053, 1063 (2d Cir. 1985).

DJowharzadeh v. City Nat'l Bank & Trust Co., 646 P.2d 616 (Okla. Ct. App. 1982).

Doe v. Chao, 124 S. Ct. 1204, 2004 U.S. LEXIS 1622 (2004).

Dwyer v. American Express Co., 273 Ill. App. 3d 742, 750, 652 N.E.2d 1351, 1357 (App. 1995).

Electronic Communications Privacy Act, 18 U.S.C. § 2701 *et seq.* (1986).

European Parliament. (1995, November 23). Directive 95/46/EC of the European Parliament and of the Council of 24 October 1995 on the protection of individuals with regard to the processing of personal data and on the free movement of such data. *Official Journal of the European Communities L, 281,* 31–50. Retrieved March 11, 2004, from http://europa.eu.int/smartapi/cgi/sga_doc?smartapi!celexapi!prod!CELEXnumdoc&lg=EN&numdoc=31995L0046&model=guichett

European Parliament. (2002, July 31). Directive 2002/58/EC of the European Parliament and of the Council of 12 July 2002 concerning the processing of personal data and the protection of privacy in the electronic communications sector (directive on privacy and electronic communications). *Official Journal of the European Communities L, 201,* 37–47.

Fair Credit Reporting Act, 15 U.S.C. §§1681, 1681a–1681v (1970).

Fair information practice principles. (n.d.). Retrieved March 11, 2004, from http://www.ftc.gov/reports/privacy3/fairinfo.htm

Farnsworth on Contracts §4.26 (LEXIS 2001).

Federal Information Security Management Act, 44 U.S.C. §3541 *et seq.* (2002).

Federal Trade Commission Act, 45 U.S.C. §45 *et seq.* (1914).

Federal Trade Commission v. Toysmart.com, LLC, No. 00-11341-RGS (D. Mass., 2000).

Final Rule: Privacy of Consumer Financial Information (Regulation S–P) (SEC), 65 Fed. Reg. 40,334 (2000).

Financial Services Modernization Act (Gramm-Leach-Bliley Act), 15 U.S.C. §§6801–6809 (1999).

Florez v. Linens 'n Things, Inc., 2003 Cal. App. LEXIS 641, *6–7 (2003).

FTC v. Colgate-Palmolive Co., 380 U.S. 374, 385, 85 S. Ct. 1035, 1043 13 L. Ed. 2d 904, 914 (1965).

Garner, B. A. (Ed.). (1983). *Black's law dictionary* (5th ed.). Eagan, MN: West. General information. (n.d.). Retrieved March 11, 2004, from http://www.itl.nist.gov/fipspubs/geninfo

Gibson v. United States, 55 Fed. Appx. 938, 2003 U.S. App. LEXIS 2368, *3 (App. Fed. Cir. 2003).

Groff v. America Online, Inc., No. 90-8077, 1998 R.I. Super. LEXIS 46, at *13 (1998).

Hamilton v. Microsoft Corp., No. BC303321, Cal. Super. Ct. (October 1, 2003). Retrieved March 11, 2004, from http://www.computerbytesman.com/security/hamilton_v_microsoft_complaint.htm

Health Insurance Portability and Accountability Act, 42 U.S.C. §§1301 *et seq.* (1996).

Hughes v. America Online, Inc., 204 F. Supp. 2d 178, 181 (D. Mass. 2002).

Identity theft. (n.d.). Retrieved March 11, 2004, from http://www.privacy.ca.gov/cover/identitytheft.htm

Information Technology Laboratory: What ITL does. (n.d.). Retrieved March 11, 2004, from http://www.itl.nist.gov/itl-what_itl_does.html

Interagency Guidelines Establishing Standards for Safeguarding Customer Information (Banking Agencies), 66 Fed. Reg. 8,618 (2001).

In re Toysmart.com, LLC, No. 00-13995-CJK (Bankr. D. Mass., 2000).

In the Matter of Eli Lilly and Co., FTC File No. 0123214 (2002). Retrieved March 11, 2004, from http://www.ftc.gov/opa/2002/01/elililly.htm

In the Matter of Geocities, FTC File No. 982 3051 (1998). Retrieved March 11, 2004, from http://www.ftc.gov/os/1998/08/index.htm

In the Matter of Guess?, Inc., FTC File No. 0223260 (2003). Retrieved March 11, 2004, from http://www.ftc.gov/opa/2003/06/guess.htm

In the Matter of Microsoft Corporation, FTC File No. 0123240 (2002). Retrieved March 11, 2004, from http://www.ftc.gov/opa/2002/08/microsoft.htm

ISO 17799: What is it?" n.d.). Retrieved March 11, 2004, from http://www.iso17799software.com/what.htm *Maher v. United States*, 314 F.3d 600, 606 (Fed. Cir. 2002).

Marquardt and Roche/Meditz and Hackett, Inc. v. Riverbend Executive Center, Inc., 74 Conn. App. 412, 421, 812 A.2d 175, 182, n.2 (Ct. App. 2003).

McNally v. The Pulitzer Publishing Co., 532 F.2d 69, 76 (8th Cir. 1976).

Model contracts for the transfer of personal data to third countries. (n.d.). Retrieved March 11, 2004, from http://europa.eu.int/comm/internal_market/privacy/modelcontracts_en.htm

Muris, T. J. (2001, October 4). *Protecting consumers' privacy: 2002 and beyond.* Remarks of FTC Chairman Timothy J. Muris at The Privacy 2001 Conference, Cleveland, OH. Retrieved March 11, 2004, from http://www.ftc.gov/speeches/muris/privisp1002.htm

Muskovich v. Crowell, 1996 U.S. Dist. LEXIS 22634 (S.D. Iowa 1996).

National Institute of Standards and Technology Act, 15 U.S.C. 278g-3.

The National Strategy to Secure Cyberspace. (2003). Washington, DC: Government Printing Office. Retrieved March 11, 2004, from http://usinfo.state.gov/journals/itgic/1103/ijge/gj11.htm

Office of New York State Attorney General Eliot Spitzer. (2002, August 28). Major tech publisher reaches agreement with attorney general on e-commerce security standards [Press release]. New York: Author. Retrieved March 11, 2004, from http://www.oag.state.ny.us/press/2002/aug/aug28a_02.html

Office of New York State Attorney General Eliot Spitzer. (2003, October 21). Victoria's Secret settles privacy case [Press release]. New York: Author. Retrieved March 11, 2004, from http://www.oag.state.ny.us/press/2003/oct/oct21b_03.html

Otworth v. The Florida Bar, 71 F. Supp. 2d 1209, 1215 (M.D. Fla. 1999).

Overholt Crop Insurance Service Co. v. Travis, 941 F.2d 1361, 1368 (8th Cir. 1991).

People Express Airlines v. Consolidated Rail Corp., 495 A.2d 107, 116 (N.J. 1985).

Peterson v. Idaho First National Bank, 367 P.2d 284 (Idaho 1961).

Privacy Act of 1974, 5 U.S.C. §552a(g)(4)(A), 2004 U.S. LEXIS at *8.

Privacy of Consumer Financial Information, Final Rule, 65 Fed. Reg. 35,164 (2000).

Reuben H. Donnelley Corp. v. American Protective Services Corp., No. 85 C 9086, 1986 U.S. Dist. LEXIS 23252, at *6 (N.D. Ill. July 2, 1986).

Rippey v. Denver U.S. Nat. Bank, 273 F. Supp. 718, 735 (D.C. Colo. 1967).

Roton Barrier, Inc. v. Stanley Works, 79 F.3d 1112, 1116 (1996).

Safe harbor overview (n.d.). Retrieved March 11, 2004, from http://www.export.gov/safeharbor/sh_overview.html

Sarbanes-Oxley Act, 15 U.S.C. §78 *et seq.* (2002).

Simpson, G. (2001, May 29). FTC: Amazon "deceptive" about privacy policy. *Wall Street Journal Online.*

Smith v. Chase Manhattan Bank, USA, N.A., 2002 N.Y. App. Div. LEXIS 3790, *5 (N.Y. App. Div. 2d Dept. 2002).

Stevens v. First Interstate Bank of California, 167 Ore. App. 280 (Or. Ct. App. 2000).

Stomp, Inc. v. Neato, LLC, 61 F. Supp. 2d 1074, 1081, n.11 (C.D. Cal. 1999).
Suburban Trust Co. v. Waller, 408 A.2d 758, 763–64 (Md. Ct. Spec. App. 1979).
Trade Secrets Act, 18 U.S.C. §1905 (2000).
Trans Union LLC v. Federal Trade Commission, 353 U.S. App. D.C. 42, 51, 295 F.3d 42, 51 (Ct. App. D.C. 2002).
TruSecure programs. (n.d.). Retrieved March 11, 2004, from http://www.trusecure.com/solutions/programs/index.shtml
Uniform Computer Information Transactions Act, 17 U.S.C. §107–109 (1999).
Uniform Trade Secrets Act (1985).
United States v. Carroll Towing Co., Inc., 159 F.2d 169 (2d Cir. 1947).
University of Central Florida Administrative Data, Information, and Computer Security Guidelines. (2001, April 5). Retrieved March 11, 2004, from http://ucf.edu/ADICSG.html
Vermont v. International Collection Service, Inc., 156 Vt. 540, 547, 594 A.2d 426, 430 (Vt. 1991).
What is SysTrust. (2001). Retrieved March 11, 2004, from http://www.systrustservices.com/fs_whatis.html
What's happening with privacy at the NAIC and in the states? (n.d.). Retrieved March 11, 2004, from http://www.naic.org/privacy/

Legal, Social, and Ethical Issues of the Internet

Kenneth Einar Himma, *Seattle Pacific University*

INTRODUCTION

Use of the networked world has resulted in many social and individual benefits. The World Wide Web, for example, makes it possible for people to access a wealth of information from the comfort of their own homes. E-mail capabilities enable individuals to communicate information from one country to another at a fraction of what it would cost to do so by making an international telephone call. Bulletin boards and discussion lists provide large groups of like-minded persons with a forum in which they can exchange ideas. All of these media are fully available to the user at any time of the day.

The unique capabilities of these new technologies, however, have also given rise to novel legal, social, and ethical problems. The ability to communicate information to potentially millions of people facilitates socially desirable expression, but it also facilitates expression of questionable morality and legality. Because, for example, the harm to an individual's reputation caused by defamation is a function of how many people receive the defamatory material, the capabilities of the Web increase a user's potential for causing harm by publishing defamatory material. Similarly, because the economic loss to a copyright holder caused by the unauthorized distribution of copyrighted materials is also determined by how many people receive those materials, the capabilities of the Web also increase a user's potential for causing harm by sharing copyrighted materials.

These new information technologies, then, can be used in ways that implicate a wide variety of interests of legal, social, and ethical significance. These interests include interests in privacy, free speech, security, economic well-being, and property. This chapter discusses some of the important ways in which these technologies have unfavorably implicated these interests, although it should be emphasized that the selection of issues here, of necessity, falls well short of being complete.[1]

FREE SPEECH ON THE INTERNET

While the establishment of the World Wide Web has greatly enhanced the ability of ordinary individuals to receive and communicate information and ideas, online speech also poses ethical and social problems. Unfortunately, the Internet has been used not only to seek information and truth, but also to defame, defraud, sexually exploit, and incite other people. It is not surprising, then, that such conduct is giving rise to much controversy about the scope of the right to free speech and its application to online activity.

Legal Protection of Free Speech

There is a consensus in Western nations that citizens have a moral right to free speech that is sufficiently important to deserve legal recognition and protection. A number of nations, including Canada and the United States, have formal constitutions that explicitly create a right of free speech limiting state restrictions on the free flow of ideas. The Canadian Charter, for example, provides that "Everyone has the following fundamental freedoms: (a) freedom of conscience and religion; (b) freedom of thought, belief, opinion, and expression, including freedom of the press and other media of communication; (c) freedom of peaceful assembly; and (d) freedom of association."[2] The First Amendment to the U.S. Constitution provides that "Congress shall make no law...

[1] A number of important topics cannot be discussed here because of space limitations. Notable examples include e-commerce, the digital divide, data quality, and e-learning.

[2] Canadian Charter of Rights and Freedoms, Part I, Section 2, "Fundamental Freedoms"; available at http://laws.justice.gc.ca/en/charter/.

abridging the freedom of speech, or of the press; or the right of the people peaceably to assemble, and to petition the Government for a redress of grievances."[3]

European nations also regard the free flow of information among individuals as a fundamental value. For example, Article 5 of the German constitution (*Grundgesetz*) guarantees the right of free speech and expressly prohibits censorship of any kind.[4] Similarly, a recent draft of the proposed Charter of Fundamental Rights of the European Union includes a provision establishing a right of free speech: "Everyone has a right to freedom of expression. This right shall include freedom to hold opinions and to receive and impart information and ideas without interference by public authority and regardless of frontiers."[5] Free speech is also protected by the courts in many European nations as an "implied right."

Moral Legitimacy of Free Speech Rights

Utilitarian justifications for legal protection of speech emphasize the benefits of free speech to the common good. John Stuart Mill (1989), for example, argued that allowing people the freedom to speak their minds and express their creative abilities promotes human happiness in several ways. First, allowing speech conduces to the speaker's well-being by facilitating the development of his or her critical faculties. Second, allowing creative expression promotes the ideological and technological betterment of humanity. Third, and most important, allowing free debate increases the likelihood that the truth will be discovered—and knowing the truth always conduces, on Mill's view, to human well-being.

Deontological justifications argue that there are strict moral limits on the extent to which one person may justifiably interfere with the autonomy of another person. Nozick (1977) argues, for example, that every autonomous moral agent has a "natural" right to liberty that includes the right to express her views free of coercive interference. Since people have natural rights in virtue of their status as moral persons and not in virtue of their status as citizens of some state, the operation of natural rights is not limited to obligating other individuals; even the state must respect a person's natural rights. Indeed, so important are these rights that Nozick (1977) notes that the state's only legitimate function is to protect them.

Contractarian theorists argue that the state's legitimate lawmaking authority depends entirely on the consent of citizens and that citizens consent only to limited restrictions on free speech. Although classical contractarian theories require that citizens *actually* consent, whether expressly or tacitly, to state authority, the most influential modern approach focuses on what citizens *would* consent to under certain counterfactual circumstances. John Rawls argues that a just state is bound by those principles that rational self-interested agents would choose if they had to select principles constraining the government without having any specific information about their own particular preferences, abilities, and social circumstances.[6] On Rawls's view, citizens behind such a "veil of ignorance" would protect themselves from oppression by choosing a principle of personal liberty that defines a right to free speech.

Internet Issues

Web Pornography and Children

Pornographic material on the Web is both plentiful and easy to come by. A search of the word "sex" on any mainstream search engine will produce not only links to scientifically and medically useful information on sex, but also links to pornographic Web sites. Entering http://www.sex.com into a Web browser will take the user to a portal that provides links to various types of pornographic material, ranging from standard sexually explicit material to material that appeals to various fetishes. As is evident, the word "sex" can be used in a variety of Web-based devices to locate Web sites specializing in graphic sexual content.

This raises the worry that children who are emotionally unprepared for pornographic content may encounter it while surfing the Web. Although it is fair to say that the effects of pornography on adults remain unclear, child development experts agree that chronic exposure to pornographic materials can have long-lasting and harmful effects on children (see, e.g., Benedek & Brown, 1999). Such materials can affect the way in which children view sex, relationships, and women; they can also diminish the prospects for successful love relationships and might even raise the likelihood of sexual violence. Richard Spinello (2000, p. 57) eloquently described the concern:

> Given the power of sexuality in one's life, the need for carefully integrating sexuality into one's personality, and the unfortunate tendency to regard others as sexual objects of desire (rather than as human beings), there is a convincing reason for fostering a climate in which impressionable children can be raised and nurtured without being subjected to images of gross or violent sexual conduct that totally depersonalize sexuality, exalt deviant sexual behavior, and thereby distort the view of responsible sexual behavior.

The ease with which such materials can be accessed on the Web creates the possibility of such exposure in children—and its harmful consequences.

Legislators on both sides of the Atlantic share concerns about the potential impact of Web pornography on the emotional well-being of children. The European Parliament (1997), for example, strongly advocates legislation that would protect children from access to inappropriate sexual material on the Web. It formally resolved that "minors should be protected as soon as possible against access, via the new networks and services, to material which may harm their physical and psychological development."

It is unclear, however, what sorts of restrictions on Web pornography should be enacted by legislators. Although

[3] United States Constitution, First Amendment; available at http://caselaw.lp.findlaw.com/data/constitution/amendment01/.

[4] For an English translation of the German constitution, see http://www.psr.keele.ac.uk/docs/german.htm.

[5] Draft of the Charter of Fundamental Rights of the European Union, Chapter 2, Article 11; available from http://www.europarl.eu.int/charter/pdf/text_en.pdf.

[6] In particular, Rawls stated that citizens would choose a principle (the Liberty Principle) that grants each agent as much freedom as is compatible with like freedom for all other agents.

the legitimacy of concerns about minors is undeniably a point in favor of legal regulation of Web pornography, there are legitimate concerns militating against it. Any restriction on Web pornography is likely to impact socially desirable forms of speech and will thereby have the effect of limiting the access of adults to legitimate content and thereby violating their moral rights to free speech. As a historical matter, censors have typically tended to err on the side of restricting too much content in the name of sexual morality, frequently attempting to censor books and paintings that are now regarded as literary and artistic masterpieces. The effect on moral rights to free speech, had such efforts been successful, would have been significant.

Part of the problem here is that any restriction on sexually explicit content on the Web will have to be couched in abstract terms that admit of varying degrees of vagueness. Terms such as "obscene," "indecent," "pornography," and "sexually explicit" are all vague at the margins and admit of very different interpretations, depending on what background assumptions are incorporated into the interpretation. Some people, for example, would characterize explicit instructions about how to use a condom as "indecent" or "sexually explicit." Indeed, it is the very vagueness of these terms that makes it likely that too much, rather than too little, material will be censored.

Complicating the difficulty of trying to balance these competing interests is the issue of how much responsibility society should collectively bear to assist parents in raising children. On one view, society bears minimal responsibility; the primary responsibility for raising children rests with parents. On another, society has much at stake in how children are raised because the social costs of poorly raised children can be significant; accordingly, citizens must be prepared to make some sacrifices to increase the likelihood that children are raised in a way that ensures they become productive, well-adapted adults.

The various positions on how to balance these competing considerations are being debated not only by citizens, but also by legislative and judicial officials. Consider, for example, the controversy in the United States attending the enactment of statutes like the Communications Decency Act (CDA). The CDA prohibited the "transmission of any comment, request, suggestion, proposal, image, or other communication which is obscene or indecent, knowing that the recipient of the communication is under 18 years of age" and the "knowing [transmission] to a specific person or persons under 18 years of age ... [of] any comment, request, suggestion, proposal, image or other communication that, in context, depicts or describes, in terms patently offensive as measured by contemporary community standards, sexual or excretory activities or organs." The CDA authorized a prison sentence of up to 2 years for violations.

Although the CDA struck the balance in favor of children, the U.S. Supreme Court struck the balance in favor of speech, striking down the CDA on the ground that it would restrict the constitutionally protected speech of adults (see *Reno v. ACLU*, 1997, at 2329). Crucial to the Court's decision was the observation that the Web is entitled to greater First Amendment protection than television and radio because one must take a series of affirmative steps to view specific content online. Children are far less likely to be exposed accidentally to sexually explicit material on the Web than on television because they cannot randomly sample Web pages simply by changing channels. Although curious children can seek out such materials, it is the "ease with which children may obtain access to broadcasts" that, according to the Court, "justifie[s] special treatment of indecent broadcasting" (see *Reno v. ACLU* at 2342).

In response, critics argue that the difference between television and broadcasting is a difference in degree that does not justify treating the two media differently—and not a difference in kind. Although the likelihood that a child will accidentally encounter inappropriate content on the Web is lower than the likelihood he or she will accidentally encounter inappropriate content on television, the likelihood of the former is still morally significant; after all, a few mistaken keystrokes (e.g., inadvertently clicking on a link from a search) will expose a child to pornographic content. If the harm associated with such content is substantial enough to justify restricting it on television, then it is also substantial enough to justify restricting it on the Web, as long as there is a theoretically significant probability of accidentally encountering it there.

Perhaps persuaded by such reasoning, Congress subsequently enacted the Child Online Protection Act (COPA), which makes it illegal for commercial Web sites to allow persons under 17 to view sexually explicit materials that are "harmful to minors." Although the drafters of COPA deliberately attempted to avoid the constitutional problems of the CDA by restricting the speech of only commercial Web sites, a federal appeals court recently struck it down on the ground that it is unconstitutionally overbroad in two respects. First, the court held that "COPA's definition of 'material harmful to minors' impermissibly places at risk a wide spectrum of speech that is constitutionally protected" (*Ashcroft v. ACLU*, 2003, at 267). Second, it held that its definition of "minor" reaches material that is clearly protected for adults and is not obscene to older minors (*Ashcroft v. ACLU*, at 268).

Whether enactments such as COPA achieve a proper balance between the speech rights of adults and the social interests in the well-being of children remains hotly debated, but this much is clear: the interests in speech and the well-being of children are both legitimate and important in the sense that they both deserve some level of governmental protection. One can expect European and American nations to continue to invest considerable resources to working out the proper balance between the two interests.

Online Hate Speech

There are a growing number of racist, anti-Semitic, and heterosexist Web sites worldwide that advocate violent measures to achieve hate-inspired political agendas. White supremacist Web sites, for example, frequently call for "race wars." Extremist antiabortion Web sites feature photographs of women coming to or leaving abortion clinics. The most infamous of these sites once posted a "Wanted List" of abortion doctors and currently features an editorial advocating the arrest (which it describes as "an act of love") of all persons with a same-sex sexual preference.[7]

Online hate speech creates a host of social problems. To begin with, the anonymity of online communications has emboldened racists, anti-Semites, and homophobes to create more hate sites with increasingly egregious content. Further, the worldwide availability of such content enables bigots to find one another with unprecedented ease and to more easily reach people whose educational and economic circumstances make them susceptible to content that identifies an "Other" as scapegoat. Finally, many hate sites explicitly encourage terrorism to achieve their political agendas. These considerations point in the direction of restricting online hate speech.

Yet, as was true of pornography, there are considerations militating against regulation of such speech. Some opponents argue that restrictions on hate speech will not reduce racism, anti-Semitism, or heterosexism. On this line of analysis, such restrictions simply drive bigotry underground where it can fester until it results in serious social problems that will be far more difficult to address. Restricting hate speech, then, runs the risk of chilling legitimate speech ("hate speech" is as vague as, say, "indecency") without producing the intended desirable consequences. The best response to hate speech, as the point is sometimes put, is more speech, not less.

Reflecting the difficulties in balancing such considerations is the fact that various nations have adopted different approaches to online hate speech. (For an outstanding analysis of the social and legal issues presented by hate speech, see Stuart Biegel, 2001.) Legislation restricting hate speech is not feasible in the United States. According to prevailing interpretations of the U.S. Constitution, hate speech does not fall into the traditional categories of unprotected speech and is hence protected by the First Amendment. For this reason, laws targeting online hate sites on the basis of their content are constitutionally impermissible in the United States.

The United States is unique among Western industrial nations in this regard. Many European nations, such as Germany, have laws criminalizing certain forms of hate speech. Indeed, the Council of Europe (n.d.) is currently preparing legislation that would prohibit posting or distributing racist or xenophobic material through a computer system. For its part, Canada has already enacted extensive legislation against online hate. The Canadian Human Rights Act (n.d., Section 13) prohibits the communication over computer networks of "any matter that is likely to expose a person or persons to hatred or contempt by reason of the fact that that person or those persons are identifiable on the basis of a prohibited ground of discrimination."

Spam

Unsolicited mass e-mailings ("spam") are ethically problematic because they impose significant costs on Internet users. First, spam consumes scarce network resources (e.g., time and disk space) for which recipients must pay. Second, recipients must expend time and energy to deal with unsolicited mailings; as Spinello (2000, p. 63) points out, "If a vendor sends out 6 million messages and it takes 6 seconds to delete each one, the total cost of this one mailing is 10,000 person hours of lost time." Third, Internet service providers (ISPs) and consumers are harmed because large quantities of spam can overload networks, slowing response rates and causing downtime. Spam raises ethical issues because these costs are typically imposed on consumers without their consent.[8]

Intentionally deceptive spam raises additional issues. Many senders attempt to ensure that recipients view their mailings by concealing their commercial nature. Such practices are ethically problematic not only because they are dishonest, but also because they deliberately attempt to frustrate the intent of consumers who wish to save time online by deleting spam mailings without viewing them. When such spam is of a graphically sexual nature, the risk that children and adults are exposed to unwanted and potentially harmful pornographic images is dramatically increased.

Western nations agree on the need to restrict spam but disagree on what restrictions are legitimate. The European Union recently adopted a directive requiring spammers to obtain the consumer's consent before sending unsolicited commercial e-mail (Saunders, 2002). Although such legislation is not possible in the United States because commercial speech is protected by the First Amendment, intentionally deceptive commercial speech can be prohibited. Indeed, Congress recently enacted the CAN-SPAM Act (i.e., the Controlling the Assault of Non-Solicited Pornography and Marketing Act), which prohibits many deceptive practices that have become common among spammers. CAN-SPAM prohibits, among other things, transmitting multiple commercial e-mails with the intent to deceive and intentionally falsifying header information before transmitting multiple commercial e-mails. The act became law in the United States on January 1, 2004.[9]

Whether such restrictions are ultimately efficacious in reducing objectionable spam, however, remains to be seen. First, there are a variety of increasingly sophisticated techniques that enable spammers to conceal their ultimate location. An increasing amount of spam, for example, is sent from innocent agent machines to which spammers have surreptitiously gained access because owners have unwittingly downloaded programs allowing backdoor access to their machines. Second, spam received in one country frequently originates from a different country. These factors make it difficult to enforce legal restrictions on spam and hence reduce the deterrent effects on potential spammers.

[7] The infamous Nuremberg Files Web site can be found at http://www.christiangallery.com.

[8] The proliferation of pop-up advertisements on the Web raises some similar issues. For example, the consumer must expend time and effort to close a pop-up ad; in this respect, pop-up ads are like spam. Even so, there is one fundamental difference between the two: to receive a particular pop-up ad, one must perform a specific cyberact—namely, direct a Web browser to retrieve the contents of a particular Web site. Receipt of spam, in contrast, does not require any specific act on the part of the user (apart from having an e-mail account).

[9] CAN-SPAM supplements the preexisting efforts of many states to legislate spam. In 1998, for example, the Washington State Legislature prohibited the transmission of unsolicited commercial e-mail to Washington state residents that contains false sender addresses or deceptive subject lines. Washington's Unsolicited Commercial Electronic Mail Act was upheld by the state's highest court in 2001.

Filtering Devices

A number of products filter objectionable content online. Individual filtering programs, for example, can be installed on a user's personal computer to block access to Web sites using certain sexually explicit terms or featuring images with a disproportionate quantity of fleshtones. Additionally, an increasing number of Web sites, although still a comparatively small percentage of total Web sites, participate in the PICS (Platform for Internet Content Selection) ratings system, which suppresses Web sites that rate themselves for mature audiences, as well as Web sites that decline to be rated.

The most contentious issue regarding such products involves their use by public libraries. Although many people believe public libraries should install such devices out of respect for the values of the communities they are intended to serve, library professionals and associations frequently oppose their use on two grounds. The first is that filtering programs are imprecise at this point in time—they sometimes fail to block access to pornographic content and sometimes block access to unobjectionable scientific or health-related content. The second is that there is a concern about whether it is ever appropriate for a library to censor content. The American Library Association, for example, takes the position that "A person's right to use a library should not be denied or abridged because of origin, age, background, or views." On this view, any form of censorship is inconsistent with the duty of libraries to ensure the free flow of information to individuals of all ages.

The U.S. Congress recently entered the filtering controversy with the enactment of the Children's Internet Protection Act (CIPA) in 2002, which requires public libraries to use filtering devices as a condition for receiving certain federal funds. Although a federal appellate court struck down CIPA on the ground that filtering devices typically screen out protected content (*American Library Association v. United States,* 2002), the U.S. Supreme Court recently upheld CIPA. Because CIPA requires library personnel to disable filtering devices on the request of an adult, the Court held that it leaves open alternative channels for adults to receive blocked content (*United States v. American Library Association,* 2003).

Search Engines

Search engines are an indispensable tool for sifting through the approximately 8 billion pages now on the Web (Suzukamo, 2002).[10] If the user knows (a) which sites contain the needed information and (b) the precise URL addresses of those particular sites, he or she can simply enter the addresses into the browser and it will call up those sites. If, as is more often the case, the user does not know where to go to find the needed information, he or she must rely on a search engine to find appropriate Web sites; navigating the Web without the use of a search engine can be a time-consuming process that fails to produce appropriate sites.

A search engine imposes order on the Web by creating a large database that contains an index of each page's URL, along with a fairly substantial list of key words describing its contents. When the user submits particular key words to a search engine, the engine returns a ranked list of URLs containing those key words. Search engines structure the Web by, in effect, characterizing each indexed page in terms of its content (as indicated by the appropriate key words).

Search engines, then, determine which pages users are likely to visit in two ways. First, search engines make available only those pages they have indexed—and there is currently no engine that has indexed every page on the Web.[11] For many people, a page that is not listed on any of the search engines doesn't exist; as Introna and Nissenbaum (2000) put the matter, "to exist is to be indexed by a search engine." Second, users are more likely to visit only highly ranked pages. Anecdotal evidence suggests that users are likely to visit only the top 10 to 20 pages (or "hits") returned by a search engine (Introna and Nissenbaum). If a low-ranked page exists for users, its existence is far less substantial than that of a highly ranked Web site.

Insofar as the criteria that determine the inclusion and ranking of pages determine how frequently a Web site is visited, they have two consequences of ethical significance on speech rights. First, they determine to what extent a particular publisher's Web speech is received. Second, they determine what content is ultimately available to persons seeking information on the Web. Given these critical effects, it is reasonable to think that search engines ought to employ ranking and inclusion criteria that satisfy ethical and technical standards.

Most search engines employ criteria that do not *explicitly* favor any particular class of publishers over another for reasons unrelated to merit. Web sites are usually either manually submitted to search engine editors who decide whether they are suitable for indexing or are retrieved by "spiders" that crawl the Web automatically indexing pages. A page's rank is usually determined by either the number of times a particular key word appears in the page or the number of other pages that contain links to the page.[12]

Some search engines, however, use economic criteria that favor firms willing to pay. Some engines, for example, allow a Web site to pay for expedited indexing, a process that can otherwise take months. Some engines permit firms to buy advertising linked to key words; any search using a particular key word will turn up a screen with an advertisement from a company that sells a related product or service. Some search engines have gone so far as to allow firms to bid on their top rankings.

Although some believe that market-driven search engine criteria are no more problematic than market-driven criteria for production of any other goods, critics have objected to economic criteria on three grounds. First, economic criteria rank content on the basis of characteristics that are irrelevant with respect to the quality or utility of the information; the ability or willingness of a Web site

[10] In 1999, Lawrence and Giles estimated that there were 800 million Web sites. If these estimates are accurate, the number of sites on the Web was 10 times as large in 2002 (Suzukamo, 2002) as it was 3 years earlier.

[11] Google, one of the most comprehensive search engines, states that it has indexed approximately 3 billion Web pages. See http://www.google.com/help/features.html (retrieved November 1, 2003).

[12] Some newer search engines attempt to evaluate a page's "authority." Teoma, for example, ranks a site based on the number of same-subject pages, as opposed to general pages, that reference it. The goal is to be able to identify pages that are regarded as "expert" among a particular subject community. See www.teoma.com.

owner to pay has nothing to do with the quality of the information contained in the site. Second, as Introna and Nissenbaum (2000) put the point, economic criteria compromise the ideal of the Web as a public good insofar as the Web "fulfills some of the functions of other traditional public spaces—museums, parks, beaches, and schools" and thereby contributes to the common good. On this view, selling influence on the Web is as ethically problematic as selling influence in a museum or school; in neither case should the common good be sold to the highest bidder. Third, failure to disclose that a Web site has bought its rank may mislead search engine users to believe the site's rank was determined by characteristics having to do with the quality and utility of the site.

INTELLECTUAL PROPERTY

The Web impacts the intellectual product of content creators and publishers in a variety of ethically significant ways. The Web provides them with another legitimate means to distribute intellectual product to an appropriate class of persons, but it also makes it possible for persons to distribute intellectual product to large numbers of persons without the authorization of those who claim to have property rights in that product. Since mass distribution of content on the Web can obviously reduce the economic market for the product, such distribution raises issues concerning the extent to which persons have legitimate property interests in content.

Legal Protection of Intellectual Property

Western nations generally offer three types of legal protection for intellectual property. First, patent law protects a person's interests in his or her own inventions, which includes newly designed useful processes.[13] A patent protects an invention by granting the inventor a limited monopoly power over the invention. This allows a patent holder the right to prevent other firms and persons from making or marketing it. Similar protections ("design patents" in some nations, "designs" in others) are also available for various aspects of a product's ornamental design.

Second, trademark law protects the right of a product or company owner to use marks that distinguish its goods and services from others. Trademark infringement generally occurs when a firm or individual uses a mark that is likely to confuse a reasonably intelligent consumer about the source or sponsorship of a good or service. Many nations allow a firm to establish a trademark simply by using it, but formal registration is frequently available as well.

Third, copyright law protects the original expression of ideas and facts—the particular form, language, and structure of articulated ideas, as opposed to the facts and ideas themselves, which are never protected.[14] Originality of expression requires the introduction of something new to the world; a person who simply copies the expression of someone else has not produced anything original that can be protected by copyright. Copyright protection applies to original literary works (including computer programs), musical works, dramatic works, choreographic works, artistic works, sound recordings, and architectural works.

Copyright law typically defines two intellectual property rights. First, it grants to the author an exclusive right to reproduce, modify, distribute, perform, and display the protected work. Second, it grants to the author certain moral rights of authorship. Such entitlements may include the right to claim authorship in the protected work; the right to prevent someone from attributing a work to the author that he or she didn't create; the right to prevent someone from attributing a work to the author that diverges significantly from a protected work; the right to prevent intentional distortion, mutilation, or modification of a protected work that would detract from the author's reputation; and the right to prevent intentional or grossly negligent destruction of a protected work.

Most nations include an exception for "fair" uses.[15] Copyrighted material may be used for news, educational, and research purposes, provided that such material is not directly used for material gain. In determining whether a use of copyrighted material is fair or not, courts may look to the purpose of the use (e.g., whether it is commercial), the nature of the copyrighted material, the amount of material used relative to the copyrighted work as a whole, and the effect of the use on the market for the work. The last factor is especially important insofar as copyright is intended to protect an author's right to collect the economic value of his or her expression.

Moral Legitimacy of Intellectual Property Rights

Theorists have produced three main lines of justification for legal protection of intellectual property. The first line is grounded in the Lockean view that persons have natural moral (as opposed to merely social) property rights in their bodies and labor. Because the particular sequence of words or symbols chosen by an author to express an idea or fact is the product of his or her labor, the author acquires an exclusive property right to that particular sequence of words or symbols—as long as no one else has a prior right to that sequence. The Lockean argument can roughly be summarized as follows: he or she made it; therefore, he or she owns it.

The second line of justification for intellectual property rights is grounded in the Hegelian view that creators use symbols, words, and sounds to express their person. As an expression of personhood, an original creative work realizes and *extends* the creator's person. Because no one but the author has a protected interest in his or her person, the author acquires a protected interest in his or her expression because such expression is, in some vague but morally significant sense, an extension of his or her person. Roughly put, this line of argument can be summarized as follows: it is part of him or her; therefore, it is his or hers.

The third principal line of justification is utilitarian in character. Protection of intellectual property rights is

---

[13] The intellectual property statutes of various English-speaking nations are available at the following Web sites: Canada—http://strategis.gc.ca/sc_mrksv/cipo/welcome/welcom-e.html; United States—http://www.law.cornell.edu/topics/topic2.html; United Kingdom—http://www.intellectual-property.gov.uk/.

[14] Thus, others are free to express the same ideas and facts as long as they do not intentionally duplicate the author's original expression.

[15] See, for example, the "Fair Dealing" exception to Canadian copyright law beginning at Section 29 of the Canadian Copyright Act (R.S. 1985, c. C-42); and the "Fair Use" exception to U.S. copyright law beginning at 17 U.S.C. Section 107.

justified because such protection conduces to the common good. People will be far more likely to invest time and energy in creating the intellectual products that contribute so much to human happiness, flourishing, and well-being if they are granted an exclusive property right in their original creations. Roughly put, this line of argument is as follows: giving it to him or her benefits all of society; therefore, it is his or hers.

These justifications, however, are vulnerable to serious objections. Critics have argued, for example, that the utilitarian line of argument is problematic in a couple of important respects. First, it presupposes that the primary motivation for creation of content is material, but this presupposition is difficult to reconcile with the success of "open-source software." Open-source software is generally characterized by two features: (a) it is available either free of charge or at a purely nominal price, and (b) the source code of such software is made readily available to users who are free to improve the software by fixing bugs as they are identified. Although proponents of open-source software agree on the undesirability of strong copyright protection for software, they disagree on the reasons. Some proponents, such as Richard Stallman (e.g., 2002), argue that ownership of software is morally illegitimate, whereas others argue that such protection is undesirable because it discourages innovation and improvement: allowing users access to the source code ultimately results in superior software. In any event, the fact that there are many high-quality open-source software products available to users (e.g., Linux) seems to refute the idea that the primary motivation for content creation is material.[16]

Second, the utilitarian argument assumes that the social benefits of intellectual property protection can be achieved by no less restrictive measure than granting extended exclusive rights to intellectual property. Even if the primary incentive for content creation were material in character, there are other ways to protect it: a society could, for example, pay a salary or a fee to content creators. After all, software companies have enjoyed considerable success paying employees a salary for creating software.

Opponents of strong intellectual property protection also argue that intellectual objects are different from physical objects in two ways that diminish the force of the Lockean and Hegelian natural rights arguments. First, intellectual objects, unlike physical objects, are not scarce; one person's consumption of, say, a recipe does not reduce the supply of the recipe available for other persons. Second, intellectual objects, unlike physical objects, can be simultaneously consumed by all persons; whereas a hairbrush can be used by one person at a time, every person can simultaneously use the same recipe. Although this makes sense, on this line of reasoning, to assign exclusive rights to scarce objects that can be consumed by only one person at a time, it is problematic to assign traditional property rights to objects that can simultaneously be consumed by every person without reducing the amount of the object potentially available to others.

Some theorists also worry that the increasing willingness of online users to infringe copyright law undermines the social legitimacy of protecting intellectual property in cyberspace. On this line of analysis, which is roughly grounded in social contract theory, the legitimacy of any particular law depends on its being acceptable to those whose behavior it purports to govern. The growing tendency, however, especially among younger online users, to reproduce and distribute copyrighted works without permission calls into question whether intellectual property protection continues to enjoy widespread acceptance and support among citizens. Insofar as there is no longer a consensus on the legitimacy of such laws, the contractual basis for protecting intellectual property is arguably deteriorating.

Finally, some critics argue that advancements in information technology have made intellectual property rights morally obsolete. For example, Barlow argues that existing intellectual property laws have no proper application in cyberspace. First, Barlow (1996) believes that cyberspace is a distinct metaphysical reality that lies beyond the proper jurisdiction of any nation: "Your legal concepts of property, expression, identity, movement, and context do not apply to us. They are all based on matter, and there is no matter here." Second, Barlow (1992–1993) argues that information is itself a life form that, like any other life form, is entitled to some moral standing. On Barlow's view, information has a morally protected interest in freedom: "information," as he has notoriously put the matter, "wants to be free."

Internet Issues

Domain Names. Every computer on a network has its own Internet protocol (IP) address consisting in a unique sequence of numbers and dots (e.g., 213.57.66.938) that defines its location on the Web. When a user accesses a particular Web site, the contents of that site are sent from the host server's IP address to the IP address of the user's computer. In effect, then, IP addresses make it possible for networked computers to find each other, enabling users to access the contents of Web sites hosted at other locations on the network.

In most cases, users need not know a complicated IP address to access a Web site. Most Web sites have a natural language domain name (e.g., http://www.sportinggoods.com) assigned to their IP addresses that permits easier and more intuitive access to their contents. The user simply types in the natural language domain name, and the ISP either looks for the corresponding IP address or submits a request to a "root server" that serves as a digital directory associating IP addresses and domain names. Once the ISP has determined the corresponding IP address, the desired site is accessed.

Domain names can be valuable commodities. An intuitive domain name saves consumers time and energy; it is much easier to find a site with an intuitive domain name than with a long IP address that is difficult to find and remember. The resulting convenience to users can naturally translate into economic benefits; the easier it is to access

[16] It is worth noting that the open-source spirit is finding expression in other ways on the Internet. The free online encyclopedia, *Wikipedia*, for example, allows users to add and edit entries as they see fit. See http://www.wikipedia.com.

a commercial Web site, the more likely users are to visit and buy from that site.[17]

In consequence, there have been conflicts over the use and ownership of domain names. Early in the development of the Web, some people registered domain names featuring the trademarked names of large firms in the hope that the firms would buy those names whenever they decided to go online. Although a few such "cybersquatters" made a quick profit for their trouble, courts now treat the practice of speculating on domain names incorporating trademarks as actionable trademark infringement (see, e.g., *Panavision v. Toeppe,* 1998).

More commonly, a slightly modified version of a popular Web site's domain name is used to capture some of its traffic. One commercial pornographic Web site in the United States, for example, uses the domain name "www.whitehouse.com." Users who type "www.whitehouse.com" instead of "www.whitehouse.gov" into their browsers—a common mistake—will access sexually explicit material instead of the U.S. president's official Web site. By such means, a person can dramatically increase traffic to his or her site.

Although such practices appear deceptive, they can facilitate legitimate purposes of free expression. A user who mistakenly types "www.gwbush.com" instead of "www.georgebush.com" will access a site criticizing George Bush's views and policies instead of his personal Web site. While the commercial use of a domain name similar to a trademarked name can dilute the value of the trademark and is hence unethical, the politically motivated use of a domain name to express legitimate criticism is arguably unobjectionable—as long as users are not likely to be confused about the origin of the site.

Illicit Copying Over the Internet

No case better exemplifies the clash between the intellectual property rights of copyright holders and the increasingly libertarian spirit of online users than the proliferation of MP3 file sharing over the Web. The development of the MP3 format was the first significant step in realizing the Internet's latent potential for online dissemination of music files. Earlier technologies offered little incentive to share music files; the files were too large to be uploaded and downloaded quickly, and their sound quality was generally inconsistent. MP3 technology, however, permits the compression of nearly perfect digital reproductions of sound recordings into small files that are efficiently transmitted from one user to another.

Napster augmented MP3's capabilities by introducing true peer-to-peer (P2P) file sharing. Whereas users of earlier file-sharing technologies had to download previously uploaded files from a central Web site or file transfer protocol (FTP) site, Napster users could simply take music files directly from the computers of other users. Although a central server was needed to keep a searchable list of all the available MP3 files, its purpose was limited to helping Napster users find each other. Because users could share music files online without anyone needing to take the time to upload music files to some central server, Napster made it easier than ever before for large groups of users to share their sound recordings.

Napster's P2P networking capabilities also inhibited the efforts of recording companies to stop reproduction and distribution of their copyrighted materials. When music files had to be transmitted through a central server, recording companies could demand that the server's owner destroy copyrighted files or litigate an expensive civil suit. Because Napster eliminated the need for centralized storage of such files, however, there was no one entity that could be pressured by copyright holders. Not surprisingly, the music industry viewed Napster as a grave threat to the value of its copyrights.

The conflict came to a head when a group of music companies sued Napster for "indirect" violations of U.S. copyright law. Because Napster's role was limited to enabling users of Napster's MusicShare software to gain access to the hard drives of other users, the company could not be held liable for direct infringements. Instead, the plaintiffs sought to hold Napster liable for contributory infringement (i.e., knowingly assisting others in directly infringing a copyright) and vicarious infringement (i.e., benefiting financially from infringements when it has the ability to supervise and terminate users).

Although the litigation did not settle the legal issues, it resulted in a preliminary injunction forcing Napster off the Web temporarily. A U.S. federal court issued an injunction prohibiting Napster from assisting users in sharing copyrighted materials without the express permission of the owners (*A&M Records v. Napster,* 2000). The court based its injunction on a prediction (as opposed to a final judgment) that Napster would lose at trial because (a) users were deriving an unfair economic benefit from using Napster by saving the cost of the relevant recordings and (b) Napster use was decreasing CD sales among users (*Napster*, 2000 at 1017). Napster recently returned to the Web offering music downloads for sale after negotiating contract agreements with five major record labels and hundreds of independent labels (see http://www.napster.com/about_us.html).

Because the litigation never resulted in a final judgment on the issue of file sharing, music-sharing technologies and Web sites have continued to proliferate,[18] apparently cutting into industry profits by reducing CD sales ("Downloads Blamed," 2002). In a controversial response, the Recording Industry Association of America recently started suing individuals, instead of music-sharing Web sites, for making music files available on these sites ("Recording Industry Begins Suing," 2003; "RIAA Strikes Back," 2003). These lawsuits have targeted not only adult users, but also the parents and grandparents of children users (RIAA Leaning on Kids' Parents, 2003). Although such tactics have been passionately criticized, they seem to have succeeded, according to recent reports, in reducing illegal file sharing—at least temporarily (Borland, 2003).

[17] Compaq reportedly paid more than $3 million to purchase the domain name www.altavista.com from the former owner of Alta Vista Technology after acquiring the company. Until Compaq purchased the domain name, it was forced to use the ungainly www.altavista.digital.com (Kornblum, 1998).

[18] Indeed, http://www.afternapster.com lists 32 file-sharing Web sites, many of which improve on the P2P networking capabilities of Napster.

Plagiarism

The availability of so much information on the Web has especially benefited students. First, students have access to far more written academic materials than ever before; the availability of academic writings on the Web is a welcome supplement to the offerings of school and public libraries. Second, student research efforts are no longer tied to the operating hours of libraries; students can access a wide range of materials at any time from wherever they happen to be with their computers. A student with a cellular modem does not even need to be near land-based telephone lines.

The Web also makes student plagiarism much more tempting, however. It not only provides easy online access to an abundance of quality writings, but also produces it in a form that is easy to plagiarize. Formerly, a plagiarist had to take the time to copy a text sentence by sentence onto a medium that could be turned in as her or his own; not infrequently, this involved hours of time typing or writing the text. Now a plagiarist can take someone else's text with a few keystrokes: one need do no more than highlight the relevant text, enter the appropriate keystrokes to copy and paste it into a word processing document, and unethically claim authorship in the work.

Student plagiarism also raises third-party ethical issues, because there are a number of Web sites offering original research papers for sale. One such Web site boasts: "Our 80 full-time researchers are available 24 hours a day, 7 days a week. Order now, and we will write your term paper within your specified deadline."[19] Although students must accept moral responsibility for initiating the sequence of acts that culminates in plagiarism, Web sites offering term papers for sale are not beyond ethical reproach because the operators must be aware there is a high likelihood that students will claim the work as their own.

Indeed, these sites seem to invite student plagiarism. After all, the only writing that is appropriately characterized as a "term paper" is writing that is being turned in as coursework; thus, advertising a piece of writing as a "term paper" is not unreasonably construed as a claim that the work is suitable to be turned in for a grade. If, as seems reasonable, knowingly aiding someone in committing an ethical violation is unethical, then offering term papers for sale in such a suggestive manner is also unethical.[20]

INFORMATION PRIVACY

The networked world has had ethically significant impact on information privacy. Internet users have a variety of ways to produce communications that are anonymous in principle or in effect, thereby empowering them to engage in more legitimate speech-related activities without fear of reprisal. Such anonymity also facilitates socially undesirable behavior, however: The lower the risk of being caught for criminal activity, the less effective the social consequences will be in functioning as a deterrent.[21] It is, for example, much easier to make anonymous threats over the Internet than by, say, telephone; whereas one can find a variety of ways to conceal one's identity in cyberspace from the comfort of one's own computer, it is virtually impossible for one to fully conceal one's identity by a telephone call made from one's home or cell phone.

Legal Protection of Information Privacy

The various constitutions differ with respect to how much protection they provide to privacy. The Canadian Charter and U.S. Constitution both contain a number of provisions that can be construed as concerned with protecting privacy. Each contains clauses protecting freedom of speech, thought, conscience, and religious worship, as well as freedom from unreasonable searches and seizures.[22] Such protections are reasonably construed as being concerned to establish a zone or sphere of privacy in which a person's movements are protected against state intrusion.

Neither the Canadian Charter nor the U.S. Constitution, however, contains a provision that explicitly defines a privacy right in personal information or data. While the U.S. Supreme Court has grounded a general right of privacy in the "penumbras" of the various protections mentioned above, the constitutional right to privacy in the United States has most commonly been cited as a justification for invalidating laws that restrain reproductive freedom.[23] What protections there are in Canada and the United States for personal information are defined largely by statute and common law.

In contrast, a recent draft of the Charter of Fundamental Rights of the European Union provides explicit privacy protection for personal information. Article 8 provides that "(1) Everyone has a right to the protection of personal data concerning him or her [; and] (2) Such data must be processed fairly for specified purposes and on the basis of the consent of the person concerned or some other legitimate basis laid down by law. Everyone has the right of access to data which has been collected concerning him or her, and the right to have it rectified."

It is worth noting that European statutory law provides comprehensive protection of a person's interest in information privacy. The European Parliament and Council of October 24, 1995, have issued a general directive governing the processing of personal information.[24] Chapter 1, Article 1 provides that "Member states shall protect the

[19] Retrieved September 7, 2002, from http://www.term-paper-time.com. It should be noted that the site also states in ironically ungrammatical fashion: "We always urge them not to use the work as their own. Although the work we do is completely original and cannot be found anywhere else on the Web" (http://www.term-paper-time.com/html/aboutus).

[20] There are now a number of Web-based products that assist instructors in detecting student plagiarism. Such products can be found at www.canexus.com/eve/index3.shtml, www.plagiarism.com, and www.powerresearcher.com. Nevertheless, it should be noted that these products will assist only in detecting instances of cut-and-paste plagiarism; they will not help in detecting instances where students have purchased specially written papers.

[21] For an empirical and normative analysis of the positive and negative effects of the anonymizing capabilities of the Internet, see Kling, Lee, Teich, & Frankel, 1999; Teich, Frankel, Kling, & Lee, 1999.

[22] See the First, Third, Fourth, Fifth, and Ninth Amendments to the U.S. Constitution; see Sections 2, 7, 8, 9, 11, and 13 of the Canadian Charter of Rights and Freedoms.

[23] See, for example, *Griswold v. Connecticut*, 381 U.S. 479 (1965); and *Roe v. Wade*, 410 U.S. 113 (1973).

[24] The full text of the directive is available from http://www.privacy.org/pi/intl_orgs/ec/final_EU_Data_Protection.html.

fundamental rights and freedoms of natural persons, and in particular their right to privacy, with respect to the processing of personal data."[25] Among other things, the directive limits the purposes for which personal information on an individual may be collected to "specified, explicit and legitimate purposes" and guarantees a right of access of the individual to such data.

In contrast, the U.S. approach to protecting information privacy has been somewhat uneven. On the one hand, pursuant to the Health Insurance Portability and Accountability Act (HIPAA; 1996), the U.S. Department of Health and Human Services (2000) promulgated the first federal standards for protecting the privacy of medical records. On the otherhand, the U.S. PATRIOT Act, which was enacted in response to the terrorist attacks of September 11, 2001,[26] expands the surveillance capacities of the government in a number of ways. Section 213, for example, allows the government to conduct a search without notifying the subject that a warrant has been executed if "the court finds reasonable cause to believe that providing immediate notification of the execution of the warrant may have an adverse result." Similarly, Section 216 allows the government to monitor an individual's movements on the Web upon a showing that "the information likely to be obtained . . . is relevant to an ongoing criminal investigation." If the expansion of such investigative capacities arguably promotes citizens' security interests, it does so at some (possibly justified) cost to privacy interests.

Moral Legitimacy of Information Privacy Rights

Consequentialist theories justify privacy rights as necessary for a person's happiness and well-being. James Rachels (1975) argued, for example, that protection of privacy rights is justified by our need to control the structure of our social relationships: "If we cannot control who has access to us, sometimes including and sometimes excluding various people, then we cannot control the patterns of behavior we need to adopt . . . or the kinds of relations with other people we will have." Moreover, it is commonly believed that protection of privacy rights is justified by a concern to prevent the embarrassment or offense that would be caused to a person by disclosure of certain facts.

Deontological theories of privacy, in contrast, take the position that private facts about a person are "nobody else's business," regardless of what the consequences of disclosure might be. Privacy should be respected, on this line of reasoning, not just because it conduces to well-being, but also because persons are intrinsically valuable beings entitled to be treated as autonomous ends in themselves. The intrinsic value of each person, then, requires that certain facts be treated as private and subject to the control of that person, even if those facts turn out to be extremely useful to other people.

Some theorists, however, caution that legal protection of privacy should be narrowly crafted to avoid unnecessarily restricting the free flow of information. Singleton (1998), for example, argued that the collection and dissemination of consumer information from business to business should not be restricted by privacy protections. Business dissemination of consumer information, on her view, is not morally distinguishable from ordinary gossip. Inasmuch as a legal ban on ordinary gossip would violate the right to free speech, so, too, would a ban on the dissemination of ordinary consumer information. Thus, she concludes, "[any] country that takes the freedom of information seriously cannot properly prohibit one business from communicating information about real events and real people to other businesses."[27]

Public and Private Information

The general claim that personal information ought to be protected by law does not, by itself, tell us much about how to determine what information about a person deserves legal privacy protection. For example, the altogether plausible consequentialist claim that protection of information is justified by a personal need to control the structure of various social relationships says little as to what information about a person ought to be protected by the law. For this reason, general justifications of privacy rights, such as those discussed in the last section, represent only a starting point in determining what content privacy law ought to have.

It is reasonable to think that whether a person ought to have a protected privacy right in a piece of information depends in part on the character of that information. Some facts about a person are generally accepted as private facts in which a person has a legitimate expectation of privacy. Because, for example, I am entitled to draw my drapes to prevent people from viewing what is going on in my home, the facts about what is going on my home are private—at least when the drapes are drawn[28] and my behavior is lawful. Thus, I have a legitimate expectation of privacy in aspects of my behavior that I may rightfully prevent people from viewing; these aspects of my behavior define private facts.

Some facts, however, should be regarded as private in virtue of their intimate character. It is almost universally accepted that certain physical functions, such as those involving the sexual and excretory organs, express private facts because of their felt intimate character. Information regarding a person's physical and emotional health is also widely regarded as private information that he or she should be entitled to control; indeed, so intimately vital

[25] "Processing of personal data" includes "collection, recording, organization, storage, adaptation or alteration, retrieval, consultation, use, disclosure by transmission, dissemination or otherwise making available, alignment or combination, blocking, erasure or destruction." Chapter 1, Article 2(b).

[26] The text of the USA PATRIOT Act is available from http://www.eff.org/Privacy/Surveillance/Terrorism_militias/20011025_hr3162_usa_patriot_bill.html. For a critical evaluation of the implication of the act on information privacy, see http://www.eff.org/Privacy/Surveillance/Terrorism_militias/20011031_eff_usa_patriot_analysis.html.

[27] Nevertheless, it should be noted that the U.S. Financial Services Modernization Act (Pub. L. 106–102) requires financial institutions (a) to inform customers of their policies regarding the collection, use, and dissemination of customer information and (b) to honor customers' requests not to have their information disseminated to third-party businesses. Although this, of course, does not amount to a ban on such practices, it significantly restricts what Singleton characterizes as the privacy equivalent of gossip.

[28] I can, of course, always voluntarily make private facts public by leaving my drapes open.

are these facts that medical professionals are charged with a legal duty of confidentiality.

Although many privacy issues concern private facts, others are concerned with information of a significantly different character. Some information contained in public records concerns matters that most individuals would regard as sensitive. For example, many people are reluctant to make their debt history readily available to anyone who happens to be curious about it—and this is especially so if that history includes a bankruptcy. Likewise, many people who have paid their debt for criminal offenses are reluctant to make their criminal records easily available out of a concern that such information would be used to discriminate against them.

The issue of whether a person has a moral right to control a particular piece of information that ought to be protected by the law thus depends on a variety of considerations. It will depend not only on broad theoretical arguments regarding the general justification of information privacy, but also on the character of the particular piece of information and how that information might be used by other persons. Such determinations present difficult issues of policy and ethics.

Internet Issues

Corporate Use of Personal Information

Many commercial firms collect information from visitors to their Web sites, which is stored in small data files called "cookies" and deposited on the visitors' own computers. These files typically contain information—such as passwords, on-site searches, dates of previous visits, and site preferences—that can be used by the firm to customize the user's experience when revisiting its site. For example, a bookselling Web site might store a list of previous searches on the user's computer so it can be accessed by the site on subsequent visits to generate a list of books to recommend to the user. This enables the site to provide what it considers to be better service by tailoring the user's Web environment to his or her preferences as expressed in previous visits to the site.

Although the use of cookies thus has a plausible business rationale, it raises ethical issues. Typically, cookies are transmitted from the user's hard drive to the site and retransmitted (possibly with modifications) from the site to the user's hard drive in a way that does not interrupt the user's browsing experience. This means that, in many cases, the user's hard drive—that is, his or her physical (as opposed to intellectual) property—is being modified without his or her consent. Although the legitimacy of intellectual property rights may be controversial, the legitimacy of personal property rights in physical objects is not (at least not in mainstream theorizing). The idea that someone else can, in essence, modify the user's physical property without his or her consent raises, to begin with, ethical issues concerning the user's property rights over the contents of his or her computer.

Moreover, some theorists worry that the use of cookies to keep information on the consumer raises privacy issues. As Spinello (2000, p. 111) puts the matter, "cookie technology is analogous to having someone follow you through the mall with a video camera." In both cases, the technology keeps information on where you have gone, what you have looked at, and what you have purchased. To the extent that one has a legitimate expectation that one's movements in a public mall not be recorded, it can reasonably be argued that one also has a legitimate expectation that one's movements in cyberspace not be recorded.

Although it is possible for users to set up their browsers to refuse cookies or to alert them whenever a site attempts to store a cookie, this can cause inconvenience to the user. Refusing all cookies restricts the user's options in cyberspace because some Web sites cannot be viewed without accepting cookies. Setting a browser to ask before accepting cookies can result in frequent interruptions that radically change the quality of the browsing experience. Many users who restrict cookies find that the disutility associated with such frequent interruptions outweighs, at least in the short run, their privacy concerns and restore their browsers to the default setting that allows for unrestricted cookies.

There is thus a sense in which users who decline to configure their browsers to refuse cookies can be presumed to consent to cookies, but such consent is of questionable ethical significance. If the initial choice between A and B is not an ethically acceptable one, then the fact that a person voluntarily chooses A does not *logically imply* consent to A. For example, the fact that I voluntarily choose giving a robber my money if my only other choice is being shot does not entail that I have, in any ethically significant way, consented to give the robber my money. Consent is ethically significant only to the extent that it is rendered in an antecedent choice situation that is ethically acceptable. Thus, *if* the choice between accepting cookies and not being able to browse a Web site efficiently is not an ethically acceptable choice to impose unilaterally on a user, then the user's choice to accept cookies does not entail ethically meaningful consent. For this reason, the issue of whether accepting cookies amounts to meaningful consent depends on the issue of whether the choice to accept cookies or accept an inferior browsing experience can permissibly be imposed on users.

More troubling to privacy advocates than the data kept by any one firm, however, is the possibility that it could be combined with the information of other firms to create a comprehensive file about a user. To continue Spinello's analogy, this is analogous to having your movements in *every* store and mall recorded by a video camera and then keeping all those recordings in one central location that can be accessed by other persons. The more information about an individual that is centrally located and available for use by other persons and firms, the more likely it is to strike individuals as involving a breach of their privacy.

Notably, there are economic forces pushing in that direction. Businesses realize that consumer information is a valuable commodity and have evinced a growing willingness to sell it. Information about a consumer's buying and browsing habits can be used to tailor advertisements and mailings to his or her particular tastes and preferences, arguably serving both the consumer and the firm. It is not surprising, then, that trading in information itself is becoming an increasingly profitable venture—not only for firms specializing in information commerce, but also for ordinary firms specializing in other areas, and hence increases the likelihood that businesses will compile comprehensive files of personal information on individuals.[29]

State Databases

State databases raise a different set of issues because they contain only information that is "public" in an ethically meaningful sense. In most cases, what is at issue is the disposition of information that the public has a right to collect through its official state representatives. Thus, the information contained in state databases, if there legitimately, is information to which the public has some sort of antecedent claim. This distinguishes privacy issues involving state information from privacy issues involving corporate use of information that is not public in this sense.

Although state information is a matter of public record, privacy advocates believe that governments should take strong steps to protect the privacy of driver's license numbers, birthdates, official identification numbers (e.g., social security numbers), and other identifying information frequently used to access sensitive information about a person. This kind of information is uniquely subject to abuse: all that an identity thief in the United States, for example, needs to obtain credit cards in another person's name is her social security number and date of birth. With those two pieces of information, an identity thief can inflict long-term damage to a person's financial health and credit record.

The online dissemination of information already available to the public also raises privacy concerns. As noted earlier, privacy advocates are opposed to posting a person's public records online on the ground that such information can be used for discriminatory purposes. The availability of criminal records on the Web, for example, increases the likelihood that employers will discriminate against persons with criminal histories who have paid their debts to society.[30] Indeed, even a person's marital history can be used to discriminate against her or him. A landlord might refuse to rent to an older person who has never been married out of a suspicion that he or she might be gay. It is the possibility of such discrimination that, on this line of reasoning, requires granting a protected privacy interest in information that is admittedly public in one sense.

Such records have always been available to the public, but the risk of misuse increases with the ease with which these records can be obtained. As a general matter, most persons are not willing to incur the inconvenience of visiting a courthouse and asking for a person's criminal or marital records. Because posting such information on the Web eliminates such inconvenience, it dramatically increases the likelihood that people will seek such information and, *a fortiori*, the likelihood that people will abuse it. For this reason, privacy advocates oppose posting this sort of public information on the Web.

These concerns are exacerbated by the amount of information that might be made available online. When it comes to privacy, the qualitative difference between what is and isn't ethical is sometimes a matter of quantity. As Spinello's mall analogy suggests, many people believe it would violate a person's legitimate interests in privacy to have his or her movements in a mall recorded and publicized. In relating this analogy to the issue of whether public records should be made available on the Web, it is crucial to emphasize that information about a person's movements around a mall is, in some sense, "public" information that is freely available to whoever might happen to be there.

Such worries are further increased by the ease with which various records might be obtainable on the Web. Indeed, some companies sell software that purports to enable people to obtain, among other things, public records that include criminal history, debt history, real property acquisitions, and marital records.[31] The idea that so much sensitive information about an individual can be obtained with just a few keystrokes makes many people rightly uncomfortable because of its susceptibility to being misused. Accordingly, privacy advocates argue that the easy availability of such information poses a significant threat to an individual's legitimate interests in information privacy.

Encryption Programs and Public Policy

A user's privacy can be violated online in yet another way. Ordinary means of communicating over the Internet are surprisingly insecure. E-mail messages are typically routed through many servers en route to their final destination. This raises the possibility that such messages could be intercepted and read by persons other than the intended recipient. For example, hackers or even system administrators could breach a user's privacy rights by reading his or her confidential e-mail.

One means for preventing these violations of privacy is the use of encryption programs. The most popular encryption programs function by means of an electronic binary "key" that maps strings of linguistic symbols into unintelligible code that can be deciphered only by someone who has the key. Senders and recipients who share a viable key, then, can communicate privately by means of encrypted messages.

Although encryption programs vary in sophistication, some programs enable encryption that is impossible to decode without the appropriate key. Although programmers have enjoyed considerable success in breaking even more sophisticated encryption programs, a "strong encryption" program incorporating a 128-bit algorithm (i.e., 2^{128} possible values) is, at least at this juncture, virtually unbreakable. For all practical purposes, then, an e-mail communication encrypted with a 128-bit algorithm cannot be deciphered and understood by anyone lacking the

[29] Online privacy services, such as Trust-E and BBB Online Privacy Program, rate various Web sites according to whether they agree to disclose their policies regarding the collection and dissemination of personal information by businesses. Trust-E is located at http://www.truste.org/; BBB Online is located at http://www.bbbonline.org/.

[30] Indeed, the ready availability of such information on the Web could increase the probability of recidivism. If employers unfairly refuse to hire persons with criminal records, they are likely to reoffend.

[31] One Web site boasts of a program, which it calls "the Internet's best selling spy software," that will allow persons to find "driver's records, lawsuits, criminal records, asset identification, . . . tax liens, . . . and court documents." http://www.oddworldz.com/landoh34/learn.html?. Other Web sites offering spy software include http://www.spy-patrol.com and http://www.spectorsoft.com.

key. Such communications are, given existing technologies, perfectly secure.

Some U.S. legislators and citizens favor legislation that restricts the export of such sophisticated encryption programs employing 128-bit keys. There have been a number of proposals, ranging from outright bans to restrictions that allow the state some sort of access to the keys. For example, the so-called Clipper computer chip, which was originally intended for encrypting telephone communications, came encoded with an algorithm enabling law enforcement agencies to decode encrypted communications. One half of the decryption key was given to each of two law enforcement agencies, thus requiring that one obtain the consent of the other to decrypt communications.

Supporters of such regulations have stressed security interests. On this line of reasoning, the interest in, or right to, security is the most important interest or right in the moral hierarchy and hence trumps other interests and rights in the event of a direct conflict. Supporters argue that restrictions on strong encryption are morally legitimate because they are necessary to ensure that intelligence and law enforcement agencies have sufficient resources to protect the public's security interests against the serious threat posed by the activities of terrorists and international criminals.

Opponents have stressed both privacy and speech interests. Restrictions on encryption that allow the state access to keys chill the exercise of legitimate speech interests because, under such restrictions, citizens must worry about whether the state can eavesdrop on encrypted communications. Privacy and speech rights require, on this view, that citizens feel (and be) utterly free to communicate with selected individuals without having to worry about whether the state can listen in on their private communications. Moreover, many believe that the continuing expansion of e-commerce, and the economic growth it makes possible, also depends on consumers feeling their transactions are protected against governmental eavesdropping.

COMPUTER SECURITY

The term "security" is something of a catch-all term. In its broadest use, the term connotes nothing more specific than "freedom from danger,"[32] but "danger" itself is a broad term appropriately used to characterize *any* serious threat to a morally significant interest. On this usage, then, any law that protects life, liberty, or property is fairly characterized as attempting to ensure a person's "security."

This portion of the chapter, however, is concerned only with legal and ethical issues as they arise in connection with *computer* security, "computer security" being construed to mean "freedom from unauthorized computer intrusions." Accordingly, this section is concerned with legal protections against unauthorized computer intrusions, the justification for such protection, and the challenge posed to such justifications by hackers.

[32] See, for example, Merriam-Webster Online Dictionary; available from http://www.m-w.com/.

Legal Protection of Computer Security

Security from unauthorized computer intrusions has become a priority for lawmakers. Most, if not all, developed nations have laws prohibiting unauthorized computer intrusions. In the United States, for example, the Computer Crime and Fraud Act (18 U.S. Code Section 1030) authorizes fines and imprisonment of up to 20 years for, among other things, "knowingly caus[ing] the transmission of a program, information, code, or command, and as a result of such conduct, intentionally caus[ing at least $5,000 in] damage without authorization, to a protected computer." Similarly, Section 342.1 of the Canadian Consolidated Statutes and Regulations authorizes imprisonment for up to ten years for, among other things, the fraudulent and wrongful "intercept[ion], direct[] or indirect[], [of] any function of a computer system."

The European Union has also endorsed strong protections against unauthorized computer intrusions. Article 2 of the European Convention on Cybercrime requires member nations to "adopt such legislative and other measures as may be necessary to establish as criminal offences under its domestic law, when committed intentionally, the access to the whole or any part of a computer system without right."[33] The clear intent of Article 2 is that unauthorized intrusions be prohibited by law.

Moral Legitimacy of Computer Security Rights

At first glance, laws prohibiting unauthorized computer intrusions seem easy to justify on ethical grounds. Although the more malicious intrusions involve serious ethical transgressions because of the harm they are intended to cause, all seem morally objectionable for two reasons. First, they appear to constitute an electronic form of trespass onto the *physical* property of another person. To obtain unauthorized entry into some other person's network or computer seems, from an ethical perspective, straightforwardly analogous to uninvited entry onto the real property of another person. Even if it turns out that there are no natural moral rights to intellectual property, it seems clear that persons have property rights in their computers and networks (which are, after all, material objects and not intellectual objects). Such trespass is widely regarded as morally wrong, regardless of whether it results in damage or harm, because it violates the property right of the owner to control the uses to which his or her property is put and hence to exclude other people from its use. Similarly, hacking into someone else's computer or network is wrong, regardless of whether it results in damage, because it violates the owner's property right to exclude others from using his or her computer or network equipment.

Second, such computer intrusions seem to violate the legitimate privacy rights of the victims. If it is true that persons have a property right in their physical hardware, then it is reasonable to think that they have privacy rights in the documents and files they store on that hardware. If I know that I may legitimately exclude you from appropriating my computer, then I have a reasonable expectation

[33] See http://conventions.coe.int/Treaty/en/Reports/Html/185.htm.

that I may exclude you from the files and documents that I store on my hard drive. On this second line of reasoning, hacking into someone else's hardware is wrong because it violates the legitimate privacy expectations of the owners. This is true regardless of whether owners actually store sensitive information on those machines: breaking into my home involves a violation of my privacy even if the perpetrator acquires no private information about me.

It is worth noting here that considerations having to do with the legitimacy of intellectual property rights do not play a general role in justifying laws prohibiting unauthorized computer intrusions. The reason for this is that unauthorized intrusions need not involve infringement on those interests protected by intellectual property law; there is nothing in the nature of such an intrusion that entails, say, the infringement of interests that are protected by a patent or by trademark law. In contrast, unauthorized computer intrusions seem, by definition, to impinge on someone's property rights in their computer hardware and hence on reasonable privacy expectations.

Internet Issue: Hackers

There are a growing number of well-publicized incidents in which hackers obtain unauthorized entry into a firm's or state agency's servers. Some of these incidents involve comparatively innocuous exploration of a network's structure; in such cases, hackers look around and leave without altering the system. Others involve the commission of computer pranks; one such famous incident involved an insulting message left by hackers on the *New York Times* Web site (see, e.g., Nutall, 1998). Yet others involve the commission of cyberterrorism that threatens national security, as when a hacker breaks into a government network that stores classified material, or individual well-being, as when a hacker breaks into a corporate server and takes credit card and bank account numbers.[34]

Many hackers reject the claim that all unauthorized computer intrusions can legitimately be prohibited to protect moral interests in property and privacy, arguing that some hacking activity can be justified in terms of its social benefits, at least when it results in no damage or harm to innocent persons. These computer intrusions, they point out, contribute to increasing our technological knowledge in a number of ways. First, by gaining insight into the operations of existing networks, hackers develop a base of knowledge that can be used to improve those networks. Second, the very break-ins themselves call attention to security flaws that could be exploited by malicious hackers or, worse, terrorists. Thus, electronic trespass is distinguished, according to proponents, from other forms of trespass in that it inevitably conduces to public benefit.

Certain hacking activities have also been defended as a form of free expression in two ways. First, the permissibility of benign break-ins appears to be a consequence of the claim that "information wants to be free." If it is true, as an ethical matter, that all information should be free, then security measures designed to keep hackers out of networks are morally objectionable on the ground that they inhibit the free flow of information.[35] Second, some writers have argued that benign break-ins can be defended as a form of protest or political activism ("hacktivism"). On this line of reasoning, such incidents express legitimate outrage over the increasing commercialization of the Web. Politically motivated hacking, according to these writers, should be permitted as long as it results in neither harm nor profit (Manion & Goodrum, 2000).

E-VOTING

Central to the legitimacy of democratic governance is the right to vote. At the foundation of all democratic theories is the idea that every competent person has a right to autonomy that entitles her or him to participate actively in his or her own governance and hence has a right to participate in the political decision-making process. The right to participate protects a variety of activities other than voting; for example, it entitles competent persons to run for elected office. Its centerpiece is the right to vote in elections that determine either the content of the law or the persons who will serve as legislators or judges.

The traditional mechanism for exercising the right to vote is the paper ballot. Up until now, the vast majority of votes have been cast on paper or punch-card ballots; citizens indicate the candidate of their choice by making a physical mark of some kind on the ballot, either by writing a mark of some kind or punching a hole next to the appropriate candidate's name. Although these ballots have usually been counted by hand, a process that is highly vulnerable to abuse and error, election precincts in many countries are now using new automated technologies for counting votes.

There are a variety of new and developing technologies that fall under the rubric of e-voting. A number of companies have developed technologies enabling citizens to vote merely by touching a computer screen that is located at their precincts; votes can then be counted at the precinct by a local automated mechanism or can be transmitted via the Internet to a central location where votes from different precincts can be counted by a machine. Many proponents of e-voting envision a day when every voter can vote via his or her personal computer from the convenience of his or her own home.

These new and developing technologies implicate the right to vote in a variety of ethically significant ways. This section explores the various social and ethical issues that arise in connection with the application of these information technologies to the democratic process.

Legal Protection of Voting

Because the right to vote is the foundation of democratic governance, it is not surprising that democratic nations typically afford strong legal protection to the right to vote. Article I of the U.S. Constitution provides that federal legislators be democratically elected by citizens according to certain prescribed procedures (which may be defined in part by the states).[36] Similarly, Section 3 of the

[34] Some people distinguish "hacking" from "cracking." Cracking, unlike hacking, involves a malicious purpose; the intent is to gain entry to a network to cause harm or damage. In contrast, hacking is motivated primarily by curiosity.

[35] For a critical discussion of this claim, see Spafford (1992).

[36] The Fifteenth and Nineteenth Amendments prohibit restricting any person's right to vote on grounds having to do with race, color, gender, or previous servitude.

Canadian Charter provides that "Every citizen of Canada has the right to vote in an election of members of the House of Commons or of a legislative assembly and to be qualified for membership therein." Finally, Article 39 of the European Charter of Fundamental Rights states that "Every citizen of the Union has the right to vote and to stand as a candidate at election to the European Parliament."

The centrality of the right to vote is underscored by the fact that the justification for other fundamental rights is frequently couched in terms of the contribution they make toward democratic governance. The legal right to free speech, which is protected in North America and Europe, is frequently justified in terms of its contribution toward producing an informed and responsible electorate. Without free speech, on this line of reasoning, citizens would lack information that is essential to being able to exercise the right to vote in an ethically meaningful way.

Moral Legitimacy of E-Voting

The legitimacy of adopting e-voting technologies will largely depend on a number of factors. For starters, the legitimacy of such technologies depends on how accurate and how secure they are; the less accurate or secure a technology is, the less justified a state would be in adopting it. Further, the legitimacy of such technologies depends upon their effects on the voting behaviors of citizens. To the extent that adopting such technologies would result in a decrease in significant turnout among some important segment of the population, such technologies "chill" the exercise of the right to vote among members of the affected segment. For example, excessive polling taxes are illegitimate because they make it harder for less affluent citizens to exercise that right and thus violate their rights to vote. This section surveys some of the arguments that have been made on both sides of the issue.

Ethical Arguments for E-Voting

Accuracy of Technologies. Arguments for the adoption of the new E-voting technologies usually focus on the effects of such technologies on various aspects of the election process. For example, newer technologies make it possible to determine the results of an election more quickly than is possible using hand counting or the older automated technologies, which require the physical transportation of ballots from voting box to the counting technology. Accordingly, these newer technologies dramatically reduce the waiting period associated with traditional technologies.

Proponents of e-voting technologies also argue that fully automating the voting process will improve the accuracy of the counting process by eliminating human judgment. Proponents point to the problems that arose in connection with counting ballots cast in Florida during the 2000 U.S. presidential election. Fallible and potentially biased human beings had to sort through a large number of ambiguously marked ballots and attempt to discern the voter's intent in marking the ballot. Fully automating the process takes elections out of the hands of human beings, replacing them with a much faster and more reliable technology.

Effects on Voter Turnout

These features of the new technologies, according to proponents, will help to improve turnout for elections by restoring voter confidence in the electoral system. For example, the problems with the 2000 presidential election have led to continuing debate about the legitimacy of the Bush presidency and weakened confidence among citizens in the U.S. electoral process, which presumably operates to reduce voter turnout. Because the new technologies are more securely insulated from human judgment—and hence from human fallibility and bias—citizens are more likely to trust the results and hence to participate in elections.

Proponents argue that future Web-based technologies will boost turnout by making it easier than ever for citizens to express their political views and preferences through the voting process. Citizens who own a personal computer with an Internet connection is, other things being equal, more likely to vote if they can reliably vote using the personal computer from the privacy of their home than if they can vote only by traditional means (which, it should be noted, include absentee ballots). It is true, of course, that not every citizen owns a personal computer, but this, proponents insist, is an argument for retaining other voting technologies and not an argument against adopting Web-based voting technologies as they are developed. As long as such voters are not unfairly disadvantaged by the adoption of newer technologies, it is ethically permissible and socially desirable to adopt these technologies.

Web-based technologies, on this line of reasoning, are especially likely to boost turnout among citizens who have disabilities that severely limit their ability to travel away from home. Appropriately adapted Web-based voting technologies ensure that severely disabled citizens (who own personal computers and have an Internet connection) can exercise their right to vote with far less inconvenience than is involved for them in using the traditional voting technologies.

To appreciate fully the force of these arguments, it is important to realize that the legitimacy of an election requires that all eligible citizens be in a position to meaningfully exercise their right to vote without incurring significant costs. It is clear, for example, that an election system requiring an expensive fee to vote is illegitimate because less affluent voters will be far less likely to vote. In consequence, elected officials are considerably less likely to take their wishes and needs into account in the lawmaking process. If the point of democracy is to ensure that all constituencies are fairly represented, then voting fees (or polling taxes) defeat democracy's very point.

Putting citizens in a position to be able to participate meaningfully in elections presumably requires not only that they receive sufficient education to minimally understand the issues, positions, and candidates, but also that elections be staged in a way that enables each citizen to exercise his or her right to vote without the sort of inconvenience that is likely to deter his or her from voting. Although it may sometimes be accurate to construe a citizen's failure to vote as indifference on his or her part, this is not necessarily true: it is reasonable to hypothesize that many persons who would like to vote are not able to do so because of the costs or inconveniences associated with traditional voting technologies.

Ethical Arguments Against E-Voting

Discriminatory Effects on Poor. There are a number of arguments against the adoption of e-voting technologies. Some opponents have grounded arguments against the adoption of technologies that would allow Internet-based voting in considerations having to do with economic justice. On this line of reasoning, the adoption of such technologies discriminates against people who cannot afford a personal computer and broadband access. Although the adoption of such technologies is likely to increase turnout among wealthier (and hence technologically savvy) voters, they are also likely to have the effect of reducing turnout among less affluent persons. Even if less affluent persons can still vote by traditional means or by using computers in public schools and libraries, the use of such means could be stigmatized (in much the same way, for example, that inhabitants of public housing projects are stigmatized), thereby reducing voter turnout among less affluent voters who do not have a personal computer. As a matter of economic justice, such discrimination is unfair.

Such disproportionate effects on turnout are objectionable from the standpoint of democratic principles as well. In theory (if not in practice), full voter turnout ensures that the interests of all persons will be adequately represented in the lawmaking process and hence that the content of the law will protect and advance those interests; a lack of participation, then, by any theoretically significant constituency makes it far less likely that the content of the law will adequately protect the interests of that constituency. If the adoption of Internet-based e-voting technologies is likely to increase turnout among wealthy voters but decrease turnout among less affluent voters, then the adoption of such technologies is objectionable on democratic principles as well as on principles of economic justice. By diminishing turnout among the poor, the adoption of these technologies would operate to ensure that their interests are not fairly represented in the lawmaking process.

Unreliability of Existing E-Voting Technologies

Although e-voting proponents believe that automating voting procedures is likely to increase the accuracy of results, opponents can point to a number of instances in which existing e-voting technologies produced inaccurate results.[37] In a 2002 election primary in Clay County, Kansas, for example, an automated counting technology falsely indicated that a candidate for county commissioner had lost by a slim margin of 4 percentage points, when a hand recount showed that he had actually won by a landslide with 76% of the votes (Harris, 2004; "Mayo Won by a Landslide," 2002). A "bad chip" was apparently to blame for a mistaken win by two Republican candidates for county commissioner in Scurry County, Texas; a recount using a new chip indicated that the Democratic candidates had won by a large margin ("Ballot glitches," 1998; Harris, 2004).

Mistaken election results are ethically problematic for at least two reasons. First, undiscovered mistakes can result in a losing candidate's holding a legislative office to which he or she was not elected and hence not entitled to hold. In such instances, the official's acts are politically illegitimate and not, strictly speaking, binding as a matter of law, but are nonetheless treated as being legally binding, something that is especially problematic when the acts involve paradigmatic lawmaking activities. Second, the proliferation of such errors is likely to diminish the confidence of citizens in the voting system procedures and is hence likely to reduce voter turnout in elections.

Security Concerns

Perhaps the most significant concern with adopting Internet-based e-voting technologies has to do with the insecurity of networks on the Internet. Hackers are continually becoming more sophisticated and better able to find gaps in even the most secure Internet-based systems. Not only can the best hackers find ways to circumvent the most sophisticated security technologies, they are also becoming better at minimizing the likelihood that they will be detected during an intrusion and subsequently apprehended. It is probably true that it is not possible to break into a system without leaving some physical trace (or record) of the intrusion, but it is also true that a more sophisticated hacker can take steps to diminish the number of traces he or she leaves.

For this reason, it is reasonable to worry about the security of Internet-based e-voting technologies. One concern is, of course, the worst-case scenario in which a highly sophisticated hacker changes the results of an election without ever being detected. Another concern is that the mere possibility of such a scenario is enough to significantly diminish the electorate's confidence in election results and the integrity of the voting process. The potential consequences of such a decrease in confidence range from widespread suspicion among citizens about closely contested elections to a dramatic reduction in voter turnout.

Although many reasonable persons believe that, at this point, the security problems outweigh the potential benefits of Internet-based e-voting technologies, it is important to keep in mind that this need not always be the case. The magnitude of the relevant security risks of e-voting is a function of both the state of the security technologies intended to protect the process and the state of the technologies available to hackers. As the states of both these technologies evolve over time, we should expect that an assessment of the relevant risks and benefits will vary over time. At any given time, then, an assessment of the risks and benefits will require an empirical analysis of the states of all the relevant technologies. This leaves open the possibility that if it is true, as opponents believe, that Internet-based e-voting technologies are not yet secure enough, they might someday be.

CONCLUSION

Although the advent of the Internet age has empowered ordinary citizens in novel ways, it has also created a number of equally novel ethical and social problems. Indeed, as is generally true, the very capabilities that increase a

[37] For a detailed account of many of these incidents involving elections in the United States, see chapter 2 of Harris (2004).

person's ability to promote public and private interests also increase his or her ability to harm other people. To the extent that, for example, the Internet enables the ordinary citizen to reach a worldwide audience, it dramatically improves his or her ability to propagate unethical and dangerous ideas.

We should expect that the social and ethical issues of the Internet are no less complicated than the remarkable technology that engenders them. For every argument that invokes traditional ethical and social values in defending a position about online behavior, there is a countervailing argument that resists the application of these values to a technology that seems so radically different from what has preceded it. The debates on these fascinating issues will fill the pages of academic and popular publications for the foreseeable future.

GLOSSARY

Consequentialism The class of ethical theories that determine the moral goodness or badness of an action entirely in terms of its consequences.

Cookies Small files deposited by a Web site on a user's computer for the purpose of enabling the Web site to track the user's preferences.

Copyright Legal device that grants an exclusive right to the holder to reproduce and distribute fixed, original expression.

Cyberterrorism Hacking activity that attempts to harm innocent persons and thereby create a general sense of fear or terror among the general population for the purpose of achieving a political agenda.

Deontologism Ethical theories that take the position that the moral goodness or badness of some actions is determined, not by their consequences, but by their intrinsic features.

Domain Names Natural language phrase (e.g., www.sportinggoods.com) that is associated with a Web site's Internet protocol address.

Encryption The translation of data (including that transmitted in e-mail messages) into code that cannot be deciphered and read by unintended recipients.

File Transfer Protocol (FTP) A device that allows a user to transfer files from his or her personal computer to a central network server and conversely.

Filters Programs designed to prevent a user from accessing Web sites with content that is deemed inappropriate.

Hackers Persons who attempt to gain unauthorized entry to network servers or other computers. Hacking is usually distinguished from "cracking" in that the latter, unlike hacking activity, is intended to cause harm to innocent persons.

Hacktivism Hacking activity motivated by a desire to express a political view or agenda. For example, a hacktivist might target a corporate Web site as a means of protesting the increasingly commercial character of the Web.

Intellectual Property Mental and abstract entities considered as property. Intellectual property includes music, expression of ideas, and designs.

MP3 Files Digital files using a format that permits the compression of nearly perfect digital reproductions of sound recordings into small files that can efficiently be transmitted from one user to another.

Patent Legal device that grants an inventor monopoly power over the design of his or her invention.

Peer-to-Peer (P2P) File Sharing A file-sharing device that allows Web users to directly access files that are stored on the computers of other Web users.

Spam E-mail sent indiscriminately without the recipient's consent or against the recipient's wishes.

Trademark Legal device that grants a firm an exclusive right to use a mark that distinguishes its goods and services from those of other firms.

Utilitarianism A consequentialist moral theory that holds that the goodness or badness of an action is determined entirely by its consequences on well-being, happiness, the number of preferences satisfied, or pleasure in the community.

CROSS REFERENCES

See *Copyright Law; Electronic Speech; Internet Censorship; Privacy Law and the Internet; Secure Electronic Voting Protocols.*

REFERENCES

A & M Records v. Napster, 114 F. Supp. 2d 896 (2000).

American Library Association v. United States, 201 F.Supp.2d 401 (2002).

Ashcroft v. ACLU, 322 F.3d 240 (2003).

Ballot glitches reverse two election results. (1998, September 3). *Houston Chronicle*

Barlow, J. P. (1992–1993). A taxonomy of information. Retrieved from http://www.eff.org/~barlow/EconomyOfIdeas.html.

Barlow, J. P. (1996). A declaration of the independence of cyberspace. Retrieved from http://www.eff.org/~barlow/Declaration-Final.html.

Benedek, E., & Brown, C. (1999). No excuses: Televised pornography harms children. *Harvard Review of Psychiatry, 7,* 236–240.

Biegel, S. (2001). *Beyond our control? Confronting the limits of our legal system in the age of cyberspace.* Cambridge, MA: MIT Press.

Borland, J. (2003, July 15). File-sharing down after music industry crackdown. *Silicon.com.* Retrieved November 1, 2003, from http://www.wired.com/news/digiwood/0,1412,59756,00.html.

Canadian Human Rights Act, Section 13. Retrieved from http://laws.justice.gc.ca/en/H-6/28764.html#rid-28778.

Council of Europe. (n.d.). Retrieved from http://www.coe.int/T/E/Communication_and_Research/Press/Theme_Files/Cybercrime/Index.asp.

Department of Health and Human Services. (2000). Standards for privacy of individually identifiable health information. Retrieved from http://www.hhs.gov/ocr/combinedregtext.pdf.

Downloads Blamed for Low CD Sales. (2002, August 26). *Wired News.* Retrieved November 1, 2003, from http://www.wired.com/news/business/0,1367,54767,00.html.

European Parliament. (1997). Resolution on the Commission Green Paper on the protection of minors and human dignity in audiovisual and information services (COM(96)0483-C4-0621/96). Retrieved from http://www.gilc.org/speech/eu/ep-minors-resolution-1097.html.

Harris, B. (2004). *Black box voting.* Tallon. Retrieved from http://www.BlackBoxVoting.org.

Health Insurance Portability and Accountability Act. Pub. L. No. 104-191 (1996). Text available at http://aspe.hhs.gov/admnsimp/pl104191.htm.

Introna, L. D., & Nissenbaum, H. (2000). Shaping the Web: Why the politics of search engines matter. *Information Society, 16,* 169–186.

Kling, R., Lee, Y.-C., Teich, L., & Frankel, M. S. (1999, February). Assessing anonymous communication on the Internet: Policy deliberations. http://www.indiana.edu/~tisj/readers/full-text/15-2%20kling.pdf.

Kornblum, J. (1998, August 11). Compaq buys AltaVista domain. CNET News.com. Retrieved from http://news.com.com/2100-1023-214326.html?legacy=cnet.

Lawrence, S., & Giles, C. L. (1999). Accessibility and distribution of information on the Web. *Nature, 400,* 107–109.

Manion, M., & Goodrum, A. (2000). Terrorism or civil disobedience: Toward a hacktivist ethic. *Computers and Society, 30,* 14–19.

Mayo won by a landslide—election reversed. (2002, August 22). *Wichita Eagle.*

Mill, J. S. (1989). *On liberty.* Cambridge University Press.

Nozick, R. (1977). *Anarchy, state, and utopia.* New York: Basic Books.

Nuttall, C. (1998, September 17). Hackers Hit *New York Times*. BBC Online Network. Retrieved from: http://news.bbc.co.uk/1/hi/sci/tech/170999.stm.

Panavision v. Toeppe, 141 F.3d. 1316 (1998).

Rachels, J. (1975). Why privacy is important. *Philosophy and Public Affairs, 4,* 323–333.

Rawls, J. (1999). *A theory of justice* (rev. ed.). Cambridge, MA: Harvard University Press, 1999.

Recording industry begins suing P2P file sharers who illegally offer copyrighted music online. (2003, September 8). Retrieved November 1, 2003, from the Recording Industry Association of America Web site: http://www.riaa.com/news/newsletter/090803.asp.

Reno v. ACLU, 117 S.Ct. (1997).

RIAA Leaning on Kids' Parents. (2003, July 24). *Wired News*. Retrieved November 1, 2003, from http://www.wired.com/news/digiwood/0,1412,59756,00.html.

RIAA strikes back at music pirates in 2003. (2003, October 21). Retrieved the Recording Industry Association of America Web site: November 1, 2003, from http://www.riaa.com/news/newsletter/102103.asp.

Saunders, C. (2002, May 31). EU OKs spam ban, online privacy rules. *Internet News.* Retrieved from http://www.internetnews.com/IAR/article.php/1154391.

Singleton, S. (1998, January 22). Privacy as censorship: A skeptical view of proposals to regulate privacy in the private sector. Cato Institute Policy Analysis No. 295 Retrieved from http://www.cato.org/pubs/pas/pa-295es.html.

Spafford, E. (1992). Are computer hacker break-ins ethical? *Journal of Systems Software, 17,* 41–47.

Spinello, R. (2000). *Cyberethics: Morality and law in cyberspace.* Sudbury, MA: Jones and Bartlett.

Stallman, R. M. (2002). *Free software, free society: Selected essays.* Boston: GNU Press.

Suzukamo, L. B. (2002, September 7). Have you Googled yet? *Seattle Times,* C7.

Teich, A., Frankel, M. S., Kling, R., & Lee, Y.-C. (1999). Anonymous communications policies for the Internet: Results and recommendations from the AAAS Conference. *The Information Society* 15(2). Retrieved from http://www.indiana.edu/~tisj/readers/full-text/15-2%20teich.pdf.

United States v. American Library Association, 123 S. Ct. 2297 (2003).

FURTHER READING

Books

Johnson, D. (2001). *Computer ethics* (3rd ed.). Upper Saddle River, NJ: Prentice Hall.

Tavani, H. T. (2004). *Ethics and technology: Ethical issues in an age of information and communication technology.* New York: Wiley.

Anthologies

Baird, R. M., Ramsover, R., & Rosenbaum, S. E. (Eds.). (2000). *Cyberethics: Social and moral issues in the computer age.* New York: Promethius Books.

Hester, D. M., & Ford, P. J. (Eds.). (2001). *Computers and ethics in the cyberage.* Upper Saddle River, NJ: Prentice Hall.

Johnson, D. J., & Nissenbaum, H. (Eds.). (1995). *Computers, ethics and social values.* Upper Saddle River, NJ: Prentice Hall.

Langford, D. (Ed.). (2000). *Internet ethics.* London: MacMillan.

Spinello, R., & Tavani, H. T. (Eds.). (2001). *Readings in cyberethics.* Sudbury, MA: Jones & Bartlett.

Journals

Ethicomp Journal. Online journal available at http://www.ccsr.cse.dmu.ac.uk/journal/.

Ethics and Information Technology. Published by Kluwer Academic. Web site: http://www.kluweronline.com/issn/1388-1957.

Journal of Information, Communication, and Ethics in Society. Published by Troubador. Web site: http://www.troubador.co.uk/ices/default.asp.

International Journal of Information Ethics. Online journal available at http://ijie.zkm.de/.

Surveillance and Society. Online journal available at http://www.surveillance-and-society.org.

Combating the Cybercrime Threat: Developments in Global Law Enforcement

Roderic Broadhurst, *Queensland University of Technology*

INTRODUCTION

The rapid development of computer connectivity and the role of the Internet in the emergence of new e-commerce markets are key generators of the processes of globalization and have compelled national governments and international agencies to address the need for regulation and safety on the information superhighways. These astonishing tools have eroded the traditional barriers to communication, compressed our concepts of time and place, and changed the way a large part of the world does business. Although the process of globalization continues to accelerate, a fully global response to the problems of security in the digital age has yet to emerge and efforts to secure cyberspace have been reactive rather than proactive.

The convergence of computing and communications and the exponential growth of digital technology have brought enormous benefits, but with these new benefits come greater risks. The new opportunities created in cyberspace have also enhanced the capacity for criminal enterprises to operate more efficiently and effectively both domestically and across borders. Law enforcement agencies in many jurisdictions have been unable to respond effectively and even in the most advanced nations, 'play catch-up' with cybersavvy criminals (Sussmann, 1999). As never before and at little cost, a single offender can inflict catastrophic loss or damage on individuals, companies, and governments from the other side of the world. With these risks has come the awareness that information security is no longer a matter for the technical and computer specialist, but for millions of people who now engage these new media every day for business, communications and leisure. The basic issue of how to police this new arena, cyberspace, is the focus in this chapter (for related discussion of cybersecurity systems for military purposes or asymmetric warfare see chapters "Online Stalking," "Wireless Information Warfare," and "Information Assurance").

The role of digital and information technologies in the generation of national wealth now means that the new risks associated with these changes require continued attention on all fronts: national, regional, and international. At the international level, two new treaty instruments provide a sound basis for the essential cross-border law enforcement cooperation required to combat cybercrime and are briefly discussed. The first is the purpose-built Council of Europe's (CoE) Cybercrime Convention, which, although it was designed as a regional mechanism, has global significance. The second is the United Nations Convention against Transnational Organized Crime (TOC Convention), which is global in scope but indirectly deals with cybercrime when carried out by criminal networks in relation to serious crime. A further UN draft resolution in 2003 "Cybersecurity and the Protection of Critical Information Infrastructures," cosponsored by Argentina, Bulgaria, Canada, Ethiopia, and the United States, was presented at the 58th session of the General Assembly. If adopted, it invites member states and all relevant international organizations to take into account the need to protect critical information structures from possible misuses, including tracing attacks and, where appropriate, the disclosure of tracing information to other nations (Redo, 2004).

At the international level, the role of agencies such as the United Nations Office of Drug Control and Crime Prevention (UNDCP), Interpol, the Organization for Economic Cooperation and Development (OECD), and the G8 group of nations and regional bodies such as the European Union (EU), Organization of American States (OAS), Association of South East Asian Nations (ASEAN), and the Asia Pacific Economic Council (APEC) provide the political and technical expertise necessary to effect cross-border cooperation in policing. As digital technology becomes more pervasive and interconnected, ordinary crime scenes will contain some form of digital evidence. Crucially many cybercrimes take place across jurisdictional boundaries with offenders routing attacks through various jurisdictions that can only be countered by a cross-border and international policing response.

The digital divide between nation states is growing rapidly and the role of advanced information technology-based economies in bridging this divide is essential. Most developing countries do not have a telecommunications sector capable of supporting information and communication technologies (ICT). In 2000, the United Nations reported that only about 4.5% of the global population had network access, but that 44% of North Americans and 10% of Europeans did, whereas rates for Africa, Asia, and South America ranged from 0.3 to 1.6%. Currently, more than 98% of global Internet protocol bandwidth, at the regional level, connects to and from North America. Fifty-five countries account for 99% of worldwide spending on information technology production. A fifth of the world's people living in the highest-income countries have 86% of the world's gross domestic product (GDP) and 93% of Internet users, whereas the bottom fifth have 1% of GDP and only 0.2% of Internet users (United Nations, 2003, as cited in Redo, 2004—see also volume II, chapter 88).

The need for reliable and efficient mechanisms for international cooperation in law enforcement matters has never been more urgent. As noted, the international community has taken a number of significant steps to facilitate cross-border cooperation in criminal matters, including in the investigation and prosecution of cybercrime. This chapter considers some of the avenues for cooperation. However rapid the growth of ICT may be, it is unlikely to continue its apparently exponential trajectory unless the digital divide is broken and poorer nations and neighbors are included.

There is also growing concern about the potential for misuse of information technology (IT) by terrorists. This has made cyberterrorism a major strategic issue in the prevention of terrorism because the technologies themselves may be attacked and can also be used to support terrorism in the same way ITs are used by predatory cybercriminals. The use of computers by terrorists to plan, organize, and communicate is well documented and counterterrorism agencies have commonly identified high-tech media such as cellular and satellite telephones and Internet-based communications. Cases have also been reported in which hacking, physical thefts, or the corruption of officials have been used to gain access to sensitive law enforcement information (see International Narcotics Control Board, 2001). The global reach of terrorism prompted the UN General Assembly in its resolution 51/210, to note the risk of terrorists using electronic or wire communication systems to carry out criminal acts (Redo, 2000, 2004).

CRIMINALITY AND COMPUTER CRIME

With government, industries, markets, and consumers increasingly dependent on computer connectivity, they are prone to an array of threats. The most notable have been the widely publicized computer viruses, which have increased in both virulence and velocity since 2000. The beginning of 2004 saw the development of increasingly complex malicious code in the form of the MyDoom or Norvag worm. It combined the effects of a worm, spreading rapidly across the Internet, with that of a distributed denial of service attack in which computing power is directed at a target system with a view toward shutting it down. In other words, infected computers were remotely commandeered and directed against the target computer. The risks now posed by the release of malicious codes of increasing complexity (often specifically targeted against either a significant commercial or government site) were substantial and could threaten the viability of e-commerce (Moore, Shannon, Voelker, & Savage, 2003; Semple, 2004; Staniford, Paxson, & Weaver, 2002; see also volume III, part 1).

The U.S. Federal Bureau of Investigation (FBI) has also stressed that critical infrastructure protection is a priority in the United States. Given that most elements of critical infrastructure such as power generation, telecommunications, transport, and financial institutions are owned by the private sector, cooperation between law enforcement and the private sector is obvious. To help bridge the public–private gap, the FBI has introduced its Infraguard Program with over 4,000 members (Iden, 2003). There is also a crucial role for the communications and IT industries in designing products that are resistant to crime and that facilitate detection and investigation.

What Is Computer Crime?

The scope of criminal activities and their social consequences can be summarized by a typology of computer-related crime that comprises the following: conventional crimes in which computers are instrumental to the offense, such as child pornography and intellectual property theft; attacks on computer networks; and conventional criminal cases in which evidence exists in digital form. The kinds of criminality encompass the following list (by no means exhaustive—see Part 2 for further details):

- Interference with lawful use of a computer: cybervandalism and terrorism; denial of service; insertion of viruses, worms, and other malicious code.
- Dissemination of offensive materials: pornography or child pornography, online gaming or betting, racist content, treasonous or sacrilegious content.
- Threatening communications: extortion, cyber-stalking.
- Forgery or counterfeiting: ID theft; internet protocol (IP) offenses; software, CD, DVD piracy; copyright breaches; and so forth.
- Fraud: payment card fraud and e-funds transfer fraud; theft of Internet and telephone services; auction house and catalog fraud; consumer fraud and direct sales (e.g., virtual snake oils); online securities fraud.
- Other: Illegal interception of communications, commercial or corporate espionage, communications in

furtherance of criminal conspiracies, electronic money laundering.

Many of these risks appear to mimic traditional criminal exploitation, albeit often executed with unprecedented ease, speed, and impact across jurisdictions and thus the appropriate response is guided by new technological disciplines. The tasks of identifying cybercriminals and bringing them to justice pose challenges to law enforcement agencies across the globe and require a degree and timeliness of cooperation that has been until only recently regarded as impossible to achieve. However, computer intrusion is now more likely a predicate to a more serious offense. Forensic computing and evidence preservation protocols are essential to effective investigation and prosecution, especially given the trans-border nature of evidence collection (Pollitt, 2003; and see volume II, part 3, chapters 124–129). In most cases it is unlikely that a computer expert will be available at the crime scene and the risks of contaminating the evidence are high. Consequently, as with other types of crime, the emphasis is on following the traditional chain-of-evidence rules and ensuring that command and control assigns the relevant expertise promptly to the task at hand. Frequently this will require drawing on expertise in the private sector or academia.

Leading crime prevention scholars Newman and Clarke (2003) provide a review of crime prevention in the e-commerce context. In online situations, the theft of information and the manipulation of identity and trust are the key. In their approach, crime is an *opportunity* that occurs when the following conditions combine in time and place: the presence of motivated and tempted offenders and attractive and tempting targets in the absence of effective guardians. When this situation arises, crime will occur providing the offenders also have appropriate resources to undertake the crime. Consequently, efforts to reduce online offenses and e-commerce crime need to recognize these basic ingredients and the numerous pathways or opportunities for crime in the online rather than face-to-face environment. A crucial factor is how trust is acquired and maintained when merchants must be more intrusive about their (unseen) customers' identity and credit risk and the apparent ease in which trust is manipulated by fraudsters and others operating online. Risk-aversive systems of e-commerce therefore needed to be far more integrated than conventional environments and require more than passing attention to what the information security engineers like to call social engineering (see also volume III, part 2).

TRANSNATIONAL POLICING AND CYBERCRIME

The transnational nature of cybercrime reflects the process of globalization, which has intensified over the past two decades. The emergence of e-commerce, as well as the social dimension of the Internet and associated cybercrimes, is a striking example of the challenges to the independent capability of nation states to regulate social and economic order within their territories. Radical versions of globalization go further and suggest that the nation-state system of international relations no longer provides an effective methodology for regulating either domestic or transnational activity, especially international trade. In either version of globalization, substate actors, such as large commercial institutions, play a crucial role in the emergence of what Sheptycki (2000) terms a transnational-state system. Consequently the role of public–private police partnerships in the marketplace and the emergence of civil society on the Internet combined with public awareness are essential to contain cybercrime among ordinary users.

Although there now exist international conventions and treaties expressly designed to inhibit serious criminal networks or offenders operating across borders, the reach of these instruments is limited by the speed and scale of domestic ratification and consequential enabling laws. In dealing with IT crime, law enforcement is at a disadvantage because of the remarkable speed in which cybercrimes unfold against the typically low-speed cooperation offered by traditional forms of mutual legal assistance. The role of multinational agencies such as Interpol and the United Nations has never been more essential. Yet globally the results fall far short of creating a seamless web of bilateral or multilateral agreements and enforcement that would ensure a hostile environment for cybercriminals. The compatibility of criminal activity with these global changes is illustrated by the expansion and convergence of the profitable business of smuggling of humans, narcotics, or other illicit commodities with the development of communication infrastructure and trade.

The passage of the Council of Europe's Cybercrime Convention in December 2001 and its activation in July 2004 provides an international legal mechanism for cooperation in law enforcement and harmonization of laws (see Cross, 2003; Csonka, 2005; Esposito, 2004, Sato 2004), although 37 states have signed the convention and the "First Additional Protocol to the Convention on Cybercrime on the Criminalisation of Acts of a Racist or Xenophobic Nature Committed through Computer Systems" has been signed by 22 states but is yet to be ratified (see "Additional Protocol to the Convention on Cybercrime," 2003).

The convention, apart from enhancing mutual legal assistance (MLA), provides comprehensive powers to expedite preservation of stored computer data and partial disclosure of traffic data, to make production orders, to search computer systems, to seize stored computer data, to enable the real-time collection of traffic data, and to intercept the content of questionable electronic data. A number of countries outside the Council of Europe (United States, Mexico, Japan, Canada, and South Africa) were involved from the outset and have signed the convention, and many other countries, notably in South America, are considering similar model legislation (see OAS, n.d., for recommendations on an inter-American cybercrime instrument). The convention is also open to any non-member state wishing to join (via a request to the Committee of Ministers of the Council of Europe). Given the pressing need for a broader multilateral structure for cross-border cooperation in the computer crime area, every effort should be made to open up the convention for accession by a wide number of signatories as soon as is practicable (Bullwinkel, 2005). Indeed many jurisdictions in the Asian region, Thailand in particular, have looked at the convention for guidance in formulating national laws.

These developments are mirrored by the increasing transnational activities of corporate and private security. Indeed, given the role of (self-) regulatory approaches by corporations, especially multinational enterprises, the role for transnational private policing is already significant and widespread (Johnston, 2000). For example, private security is the major provider in the payment card industry, intellectual property investigations, and airline security. The sheer volume of potential global cybercrime activity compels police partnerships with banks, telecommunication providers, and corporations. Partnerships also raise real issues of shared intelligence in environments of trust. Thus, the mobilization of so-called private police and non-governmental organizations in partnership with public police are essential if cybercrime is to be contained. Crime exploits the gaps in the sovereign state system of international relations and unless that is recognized in communities of shared fate, coordinated forms of regulatory endeavor (free, for example, from unduly strict or pedantic definitions of dual criminality) may be the only means to curtail cybercrime and its inevitable cross-border dimension.

United Nations Convention against Transnational Organized Crime

Since the early 1990s, beginning with the Eighth UN Congress on the Prevention of Crime and the Treatment of Offenders (1990), the United Nations, with its network of institutes on crime prevention and criminal justice, has been actively involved in addressing problems of transnational crime and cybercrime. The scope of computer-related crime affects every country in the United Nations, and the UN General Assembly in 2001 promoted new international efforts to assist member states in dealing with computer-related crime. The General Assembly, in the "Plans of Action for the Implementation of the Vienna Declaration on Crime and Justice: Meeting the Challenges of the Twenty-first Century" (General Assembly resolution 56/261), devoted a special section to "Action against High-Technology and Computer-Related Crime," in which it provided action-oriented policy recommendations for the prevention and control of these crimes. In 2002, the General Assembly again addressed the Vienna Plan of Action (General Assembly resolution 57/170) and through the Commission on Crime Prevention and Criminal Justice recommended that the Eleventh United Congress on Crime Prevention and Criminal Justice consider the plan. In 2001, the UN secretary-general explored various options for further work on high-technology and computer-related crime and considered the following four questions: whether a global treaty, if any, should be normative or legally binding; what relationship, if any, this would have to the UN Convention against Transnational Organized Crime; how a treaty, once concluded, could be kept up to date; and how it may accommodate issues such as privacy, freedom of expression, and other human rights and commercial interests (Redo, 2004).

Although not specifically directed at cybercrime, the complementary role of the TOC Convention is a highly relevant global instrument for addressing some of the more nefarious aspects of cybercrime. The TOC Convention was introduced in December 2000 in Palermo, Italy. The TOC Convention has been signed by 147 states (and 82 parties) and came into force on September 23, 2003 (see "United Nations Convention," n.d.). The TOC Convention significantly extends the reach of the 1988 Vienna Convention against Illicit Traffic in Narcotics and Psychotropic Substances. The TOC Convention enables MLA between states and establishes several offense categories: participation in an organized criminal group, money laundering, corruption and obstruction of justice, as well as protocols in respect to trafficking in women and children (117 states and 64 parties with effect from December 25, 2003); illicit manufacturing and trafficking in firearms (52 states and 22 parties but not yet in force); and smuggling of migrants (112 states and 57 parties with effect January 28, 2004). Serious crime is defined broadly (conduct attracting punishment of four or more years' imprisonment). The basis of the framework is one that yields such flexibility in the definitions of both organized and transnational crime that it may serve as a generic legislative model across diverse common law and continental systems. In addition, the TOC Convention expressly refers (Article 29(2)) to methods for combating the misuse of computers and telecommunications networks; refers to provisions for training and materials, especially assistance for developing countries; and places obligations on capable states. The convention also establishes a number of principles and arrangements for international cooperation, which may be taken as an example of a potent global instrument against cybercrime, in line with Article 13.1(a) of the UN Charter emphasizing the progressive development of international law. They include regulations limiting the rule of double criminality for mutual assistance purposes and introduce enterprise responsibility.

The scope of the TOC Convention includes particular offenses signatories are obliged to criminalize (Articles 5, 6, 8, and 23) as well as serious crime (as defined in the Convention), "where the offence is transnational in nature and involves an organized criminal group" (see Article 3(1)). Importantly, the definitions of *serious crime* and *organized criminal group* reflect an understanding that organized criminal activity is no longer confined to a relatively narrow range of offenses traditionally associated with organizations such as Triads and the Cosa Nostra. The TOC Convention defines an offense as "transnational" if it is (a) committed in more than one state; (b) committed in a single state but planned, prepared, directed, or controlled in another state; (c) committed in one state but involving an organized group whose activities cross national boundaries; or (d) committed in a single state but has "substantial effects" in another state (see Article 3(2)). Many of the most common forms of cybercrime therefore qualify as serious crime because such offenses usually affect more than a single jurisdiction, often involve at least three or more actors, and are committed with the aim of achieving some financial or material benefit.

Article 27 deals with police-to-police cooperation and reflects the types of assistance routinely provided among police officials in the absence of a formal agreement and reflects international consensus on the need for close coordination between law enforcement authorities and to achieve this goal, states are encouraged to promote the exchange of personnel and other experts, including liaison officers. Additionally, signatories are required to "make full use of agreements or arrangements, including international or regional organisations, to enhance the cooperation between their law enforcement agencies" (Article 27(2)). With respect to formal MLA, Article 18 contains provisions nearly as lengthy and detailed as a comprehensive bilateral MLA treaty. States may seek assistance in connection with taking evidence or statements from persons, executing searches and seizures, obtaining business or government records, and identifying and tracing the proceeds of crime. A requested state has the discretion to decline assistance on the ground of the absence of dual criminality—a potentially significant limitation in the cybercrime context, as many countries do not have fully developed legislation in this area. The TOC Convention also provides for extradition (Article 16) even where a state party makes extradition conditional on the existence of a bilateral treaty. Article 16 represents a major step forward because its effect is to incorporate into existing bilateral treaty relationships the numerous offenses covered by the convention (Article 16(3)). Thus, where two states' parties have relied on outdated and narrow extradition agreements (such as a list-based treaty providing for extradition only in relation to a specified list of offenses), the TOC Convention will substantially expand the range of extraditable offenses between them (Bullwinkel, 2005; Cross, 2003).

THE COUNCIL OF EUROPE CYBERCRIME CONVENTION

The Council of Europe, founded in 1949, comprises 45 countries, including the members of the European Union (a distinctly separate entity), as well as countries from Central and Eastern Europe. Headquartered in Strasbourg, France, the CoE was formed as a vehicle for integration in Europe, and its aims include agreements and common actions in economic, social, cultural, legal, and administrative matters. As one of the two principal supranational organizations in Europe (the other being the European Union), the CoE is responsible for creating and implementing a wide variety of measures aimed at international crime and has adopted a number of widely used conventions on interstate cooperation in penal matters. In 1996, the CoE's European Committee on Crime Problems established a committee of experts to address cybercrime, which completed its work late in 2001.

The resulting Cybercrime Convention has three aims: to lay down common definitions of certain criminal offenses—nine are mentioned in the convention—thus enabling relevant legislation to be harmonized at national level; to define common types of investigative powers better suited to the information technology environment, thus enabling criminal procedures to be brought into line between countries; and to determine both traditional and new types of international cooperation, thus enabling cooperating countries to rapidly implement the arrangements for investigation and prosecution advocated by the convention in concert, for example by using a network of permanent contacts. The convention has received strong support from lawmakers and practitioners throughout Europe and beyond. But both the convention and its additional protocol have been criticized on various grounds by a number of associations, particularly those active in the protection of freedom of expression and also by industry elements (Csonka, 2005).

The CoE Convention on Cybercrime obligates signatories to criminalise a minimum list of specific offenses for which there was consensus and thus harmonized offenses to eliminate problems of dual criminality. The basic structure and content of the convention is outlined below.

Computer-Related Offenses

Title 1 addresses offenses against the confidentiality, integrity, and availability of computer data such as (1) illegal access of a computer system; (2) interception of nonpublic transmissions of computer data to, from, or within a computer system; (3) interference with computer data; (4) interference with computer systems, such as computer sabotage; and (5) the misuse of computer-related devices (e.g., hacker tools), including the production, sale, procurement for use, import, or distribution of such devices. Criminalizing illegal access, that is, hacking, cracking, or computer trespass, sends a clear signal that this conduct is illegal in itself and will be prosecuted: such intrusions may give access to confidential data (including passwords and information about the targeted system) and secrets or to free use of the system and might encourage hackers to commit more dangerous forms of computer-related offenses, such as computer-related fraud or forgery. The criminalization of illegal interception protects the privacy rights of data communication, seeks to deter the tapping and recording of communications between persons, and applies this principle to all forms of electronic data transfer, whether by telephone, fax, e-mail, or file transfer. The provision on data interference aims at providing computer data and computer programs with protection similar to that enjoyed by corporeal objects against intentional infliction of damage. Conduct such as damaging, deteriorating, or deleting computer data reduces the integrity or content of data and programs and also captures malicious codes and viruses (e.g., Trojan horses).

The convention criminalizes acts of computer sabotage and covers the intentional hindering of the lawful use of computer systems, including telecommunications facilities, by using or influencing computer data (system interference). The section covering misuse of devices establishes a separate criminal offense including some specific conduct (production, distribution, sale, etc.) involving access devices, which were primarily designed or adapted for misuse. Devices that are designed and used for legal purposes are not included. This offense therefore requires a particular purpose: that is, committing any of the other offenses against the confidentiality, integrity, and availability of computer systems or data.

Title 2 covers the traditional offenses of fraud and forgery when carried out through a computer system. For forgery, the intent of this provision is to protect computer data in the same manner as tangible documents, where such data may be acted upon or used for legal purposes (Esposito, 2004). Chapter 5 obliges signatories to criminalize the attempt to commit certain offenses on which the convention imposes a criminalization obligation, as well as aiding and abetting the commission of offenses, and also provides for the liability of legal persons.

Content-Related Offenses

Title 3 seeks to control the use of computer systems as a vehicle for the sexual exploitation of children and acts of a racist or xenophobic nature. This category of offenses concerns the subject or contents of computer communications and focuses on offenses related to children. The convention makes various acts (from the possession to the intentional distribution of child pornography) criminal offenses, thus covering all links in the chain. This provision criminalizes various aspects of the electronic production, possession, and distribution of child pornography. Most states already criminalize the traditional production and physical distribution of child pornography, but with increasing use of the Internet as the main method to distribute such material specific provisions were essential to combat this new form of exploitation. Other types of illegal content, such as racist propaganda, have also been included but in the form of an additional protocol criminalizing racist propaganda. Esposito (2004) notes that cybercrime is now defined as crimes committed against and through computer systems. The CoE's Cybercrime Convention was originally intended to cover only the first category, although there is a growing consensus, at least in Europe, of the need to address the second category (e.g., Article 9 of the Cybercrime Convention on cyber-pedopornography and the additional protocol on the fight against racism and xenophobia on the Internet).

Offenses Related to Copyright Infringement

Title 4 criminalizes willful infringements of copyright and related rights when such infringements have been committed by means of a computer system and on a commercial scale. This section targets the large-scale distribution of illegal copies of works protected by intellectual property rights (IPR). Infringements of IPR, in particular of copyright, are among the most commonly committed offenses on the Internet and cause concern both to copyright holders and to those who work professionally with computer networks.

Jurisdiction

Among the various important matters addressed by the convention was the question of jurisdiction in relation to information technology offenses, for example to determine the place where the offense was committed and which law should accordingly apply, including the case of multiple jurisdictions and the question of how to solve jurisdictional conflicts. This provision establishes criteria under which contracting parties are obliged to establish jurisdiction over the criminal offenses in the convention. The provision concerning jurisdiction also requires states exercising jurisdiction to coordinate when victims are located in different countries.

Procedural Powers

The procedural part of the convention, which also applies to the additional protocol, aims to enable the prosecution of computer crime by establishing common procedural rules and adapting traditional measures such as search and seizure and creating new measures, such as expedited preservation of data, to remain effective in the volatile technological environment. As data in the IT environment is dynamic, other evidence collection relevant to telecommunications (such as real-time collection of traffic data and interception of content data) has also been adapted to permit the collection of electronic data in the process of communication.

GLOBAL AND REGIONAL COOPERATION

Cybercrime creates an unprecedented need for concerted action from government and industry, but also unprecedented challenges to effective international cooperation. As noted, it is not always clear where computer-related offenses take place for the purpose of determining criminal jurisdiction. An offense may produce victims in many countries, as in cases involving virus attacks, copyright violations, and other offenses carried out globally through the Internet. This in turn may result in cross-border conflicts regarding which jurisdiction(s) should prosecute the offender and how such prosecutions can be carried out to avoid inconvenience to witnesses, duplication of effort, and unnecessary competition among law enforcement officials (Bullwinkel, 2005, and see volume II, part 2, chapters 92 and 93).

Most countries have domestic statutes relating to legal assistance and extradition and these sometimes enable extensive cross-border cooperation even in the absence of a formal treaty relationship. However, domestic legislation, while helpful for certain types of cooperation, is not a substitute for well-developed bilateral (or multilateral) agreements. For example, in the absence of a treaty establishing a direct relationship between legal authorities, requests for legal assistance must often be transmitted through the cumbersome and time-consuming diplomatic channel and this method is too slow to meet the challenges of cybercrime. Bilateral agreements such as MLA treaties and extradition treaties are more reliable means for international cooperation in criminal matters. Extradition treaties fall into two general categories: so-called list treaties and more modern dual criminality treaties.

In the case of list treaties, the contracting parties are bound to extradite only those offenses specified in the agreement. This may be a significant limitation, particularly in cases involving newer forms of crime (including many cybercrimes). The trend in modern treaty practice is to provide for extradition for offenses punished by imprisonment for more than a year under the laws of both parties. These dual criminality extradition treaties are as broad as the criminal laws of the requesting state but extradition for cyberoffences may prove difficult, because some jurisdictions have not yet criminalized the conduct. When this occurs the requested state should follow the practice, accepted in international law, of interpreting the treaty in favor of extradition. The advantages of a bilateral treaty are that they limit the requested state's discretion to refuse assistance. In bilateral MLA treaties, the parties will in most cases be required to execute the request unless the request relates to a political offense or to an offense under military law that would not be an offense under ordinary criminal law or when the request would prejudice the requested state's security or similar essential interests. Subject to limited exceptions and the overall scope of the agreement, bilateral treaties ordinarily oblige the signatories to provide a wide measure of assistance and often the requested assistance must be provided even in the absence of dual criminality (Bullwinkel, 2005).

The various measures now operating within the European Union, the Council of Europe's convention, the establishment of Europol, and a European Judicial Network provide examples of greater law harmonization and fewer opportunities for transnational criminals to exploit jurisdictional and legal loopholes between nations. Thus international law enforcement has shifted from a peripheral to a central role within otherwise domestically focused law enforcement agencies. In addition, the lines between the policing function and national security appear less distinct, and considerable overlap now routinely occurs between the agencies countering threats such as cybercrime, low-intensity warfare, and terrorism.

Regional efforts outside of Europe are also underway via OAS, ASEAN and the APEC forum. Such developments have yet to evolve into fully institutionalized forms of cross-border legal cooperation or to determine the response of states within the region. There are now significant regional forums for police and other law enforcement officials and there is routine exchange of consular police liaison officers (Aiziwa, 2001). The leading organizations, apart from the United Nations and the Council of Europe, involved in developing international and regional efforts against cybercrime are briefly described in the following sections.

G8 Senior Experts Group on Transnational Organized Crime

The Group of Eight (comprising Canada, Germany, France, Italy, Japan, the United Kingdom, the United States and, since 1995, Russia), although originally established to coordinate economic policy, has also developed initiatives to combat international crime. At the Halifax Summit in 1995, G8 heads of state established a cross-disciplinary group of senior government experts (the Lyon Group) to address methods of combating transnational organized crime. In 1996, the Lyon Group devised 40 recommendations aimed at increasing the efficiency of collective action against transnational organized crime via two interrelated goals: strengthened capacity in the investigation and prosecution of high-tech crime and more effective regimes for cross-border cooperation in criminal matters.

The 40 recommendations cover a range of issues and emphasized the need to eliminate delay in respect to traditional forms of cross-border assistance (such as informal police cooperation, mutual legal assistance, and extradition) and a coordinated approach in tackling high-tech crime. As a consequence of these recommendations, the Lyon Group's High-Tech Crime Subgroup was established and quickly thereafter the 24/7 computer security network, which has now expanded to countries outside the G8. As of 2004, 39 countries participated in the global 24/7 cybercrime response network. Later, G8 ministers endorsed a set of principles and an action plan to respond to transnational cybercrime cases that included provision of adequate personnel and training to fight high-tech crime; domestic laws that criminalized cybercrime and ensure that relevant evidence, including traffic data, could be preserved and obtained expeditiously; and coordination with industry to ensure that new technologies are developed in a way that will facilitate law enforcement action against cybercriminals. The 1999 Moscow meeting later endorsed principles on transborder access to stored computer data and called for a comprehensive response to Internet fraud and more industry coordination. Most recently, a joint communiqué of the G8 home affairs ministers meeting in Washington on May 10, 2004, noted, given the activation of the Council of Europe's Convention on Cybercrime, that action was required "to encourage the adoption of the legal standards it contains on a broad basis" and "all countries must continue to improve laws that criminalize misuses of computer networks and that allow for faster cooperation on Internet-related investigations" (G8 Justice and Home Affairs Communiqué 2004).

ASEAN

ASEAN comprises 10 nations: Brunei Darussalam, Cambodia, Indonesia, Laos, Malaysia, Myanmar, Philippines, Singapore, Thailand, and Vietnam. Although ASEAN has provided a limited pan-Asian approach, it does form a basis for developing a wider regional forum for considering matters of MLA. Its approach, even given the developing nature of the region, mirrors the methodology of the European Union, but the cultural and economic diversity of Asia makes the process of multilateralism fraught with difficulty (Khoo, 2003). Yet understanding the different capacities and perspectives of how each state could contribute was an essential first step. The endorsement in October 2000 of the action plan of the ASEAN and China Cooperative Operations in Response to Dangerous Drugs in partnership with the UNDCP illustrates the quickening of MLA responses to transnational crime such as cybercrime. ASEAN has conducted four ministerial meetings on problems of transnational crime (Manila 1997, Yangon 1999, Singapore 2001, and Bangkok 2003). These meetings oversee the work of the Annual Senior Officials Meeting on Transnational Crime and consider the deliberations of meetings of the ASEAN National Chiefs of Police (ASEANAPOL) and their cooperative efforts to combat transnational crime. At the Second ASEAN Ministerial Meeting on Transnational Crime (held in Myanmar in 1999), ASEAN ministers issued another ambitious communiqué outlining a broad plan of action to enhance collective efforts against the many forms of organized criminality in the region. A group of senior government officials (referred to as the Senior Officials Meeting on Transnational Crime, or SOMTC) has been tasked to assist in the execution of ministerial initiatives and directives.

The theme of greater cooperation carried over to the Third and Fourth ASEAN Ministerial Meetings on Transnational Crime, at which ASEAN ministers reiterated their commitment to collaborate further in the battle against computer-related crime and called for a stronger partnership between ASEAN and other partners and agencies, including Interpol and the United Nations ("Joint Communique of the Third ASEAN Ministerial Meeting," 2001). As noted, the ASEAN anticrime institutions, particularly SOMTC, mimics the G8's Lyon Group, indicating the relevance of such frameworks for collective government action. Particularly significant is that ASEAN's law enforcement experts group reports directly to ministers and thus, like the G8's Lyon Group, has the capacity to develop policies with support at the highest levels.

The European Union and Europol

The 1957 Treaty of Rome established the European Economic Community, which in turn evolved into the European Union, established under the Treaty of Maastricht in 1992. The European Union has 28 member states and recently completed the accession of 13 countries in eastern and southern Europe (with some new members joining on May 1, 2004). It includes supranational institutions that address international crime by adopting joint positions, directives, and other instruments addressing a wide variety of criminal activities. Among the most important in respect to the coordination of law enforcement are the adoption of a common position on negotiations relating to the CoE Cybercrime Convention and EU conventions on mutual assistance in criminal matters and extradition (see European Union, Judicial Cooperation in Criminal Matters, 1998 and see generally http://europa.eu.int/scadplus/leg/en/s22004.htm visited May 9, 2005), the establishment of a European Judicial Network consisting of liaison magistrates and representatives responsible for international judicial cooperation, and tasked with facilitating cross-border cooperation (Decision establishing Eurojust, 2002). Further strengthening of MLA is contained in the April 19, 2002, "Proposal for a Council Framework Decision on Attacks against Information Systems", adopted in June 2003 (European Union, 2003)

Included within the EU is the European Police Office or Europol, dedicated to increasing the efficiency of cooperation among the police agencies of EU member states, with an emphasis on targeting organized crime. Based in Brussels, Europol is accountable to the EU's Council of Ministers for Justice and Home Affairs. The organization is comprised of European liaison officers (who represent national law enforcement agencies across the European Union, including police, customs, and immigration officials) and Europol staff officers. Like Interpol, Europol's primary function is to support the operational activities of national law enforcement officials and was recently extended to include the fight against cybercrime. In furtherance of this, its representatives facilitate the exchange of information, provide analyses of criminal intelligence, generate strategic reports on trends and patterns of criminal activity, and provide technical expertise for ongoing investigations within the European Union. In addition, it is likely Europol will eventually assume a greater investigative and operational role.

The Organization for Economic Cooperation and Development

Established in Paris in 1960 by 20 countries (now 30 members), the OECD aims to promote economic and social welfare throughout the OECD by helping member states to coordinate their efforts to aid less developed nations. The OECD has established a presence in law enforcement, for example, by establishing the Bribery Working Group, whose efforts ultimately led to the adoption of a convention against commercial bribery. The OECD has been active in the area of cybercrime and online security, especially in regard to encryption technology, evaluating the balance between law enforcement and privacy concerns, and the means by which member states can coordinate encryption policy and in 1997 issued a series of guidelines addressing these issues. More recently, in the wake of the terrorist attacks of September 11, 2001, OECD governments developed a series of guidelines designed to counter cyber-terrorism, computer viruses, hacking, and related threats ("OECD Governments Launch Drive," 2002). Although the recommendations are not legally binding, they reflect consensus among key jurisdictions on issues affecting the security of the online environment.

A highly effective approach to intergovernmental law enforcement coordination that offers a template for transnational cooperation against cybercrime is the Financial Action Task Force (FATF) established at the G7 Paris Summit in 1989 and based in the OECD. FATF is a policy-making body whose aim is the implementation of legislative and regulatory reforms needed to combat money laundering. In 1990, FATF issued a series of 40 recommendations addressing ways to combat and deter money laundering. The recommendations are grouped into three broad categories (criminal law, banking law, and international cooperation) and serve as the basis for its activities. As a result of awareness-raising activities undertaken by FATF, a number of FATF-style organizations have also developed at the regional level including, in the Asian-Pacific region, the Asia/Pacific Group on Money Laundering, established in 1997, which operates in a manner similar to FATF and, in 2000, began to undertake a FATF-style mutual evaluation. A novel feature of FATF is that members are subject to peer review, a two-part process by which the group assesses implementation of the 40 recommendations. First, each FATF member conducts an annual self-assessment using a standard questionnaire. Second, periodically members are subject to a process of mutual evaluation, involving a site visit by three or four experts from other member governments. Mutual evaluation has proved effective in persuading governments to take steps to fill gaps in anti-money laundering (see generally http://www.oecd.org/fatf/AboutFATF_en.htm).

Interpol

The International Criminal Police Organization, or Interpol, consists of 181 member states. Headquartered in Lyon, France, Interpol coordinates its activities through national central bureaus in individual countries. Its mission is to support law enforcement organizations throughout the world, in particular by facilitating the exchange of information, coordinating joint operational activities of member states, and developing and sharing expertise and best practices covering a wide range of criminal offences (see generally http://www.interpol.int/Public/icpo/Guide). Nearly half of Interpol's member countries lack the infrastructure for online communication (Noble, 2003) and thus in respect to IT crime, Interpol has recognized the need for law enforcement officials to acquire specialized knowledge and has developed international training courses and manuals providing useful guidance for investigators working on computer-related crime (see http://www.interpol.int/Public/TechnologyCrime/WorkingParties/Default.asp#steeringCom).

Interpol's General Secretariat has also supported the formation of regionally organized working groups comprising local experts in computer-related crime who meet periodically to share experiences and develop best practices (Noble, 2003). An example is the Asia-South Pacific Working Party on Information Technology Crime that currently meets annually and has undertaken projects relating to the handling of digital evidence, forensic tools, and training. Interpol has also endeavored to build close ties to existing regional structures in Asia, including ASEANAPOL, in an effort to build on regional cooperation by facilitating the development of regional intelligence databases and the wide dissemination of data through Interpol's extensive telecommunications network. Interpol has also stressed financial and high-technology crime as two of Interpol's top five priorities (along with drugs, terrorism, people smuggling, and organized crime). In addition, Interpol has increased its focus on intellectual property-related crime, because sophisticated and well-financed organized criminal groups increasingly carry out these offenses on a global scale. Interpol hosted an initial meeting of its Intellectual Property Crime Action Group in July 2002 (see generally http://www.interpol.int/Public/FinancialCrime/IntellectualProperty/Default/.asp).

Generic problems of forgery and counterfeiting were the focus of Interpol's exemplary efforts in establishing a Universal Classification System for Counterfeit Payment Cards secure Web site. This secure site provides up-to-date information on trends and techniques with respect to the forgery of payment cards and fraud and enables law enforcement officials around the world to retrieve forensic data as well as general intelligence. Payment card industry representatives working in the anti-fraud area will also have access to the otherwise closed system. Apart from illustrating how Interpol's unique clearing-house function can be adapted to meet new problems, it showed that with support from the payment card industry the law enforcement community can be better trained and equipped. This cooperation strengthens police capacity to respond to the theft of payment cards and other computer-related crimes that reduce the integrity of the market and limit the social benefits of Internet communications. As well as serving as an example of how international agencies can assist with essential tasks such as secure shared intelligence, it also exemplifies the role of private non-state actors in the prevention of crime (Newton, 2004).

APEC

Founded in 1989 in Canberra, Australia, for the purpose of promoting economic growth among member states, APEC now consists of 21 member economies. APEC is a consensus body that meets annually at the ministerial level and historically has focused on trade, but increasingly its members look to it as a vehicle for cross-border police cooperation. APEC's work over the past several years has also evolved (as with the G8 and OECD) into a number of areas relevant to cybercrime enforcement, including an Intellectual Property Rights Working Group, an Electronic Commerce Steering Group (ECSG; see generally http://www.apecsec.org.sg/workgroup/e-commerce. html) and the work of the Council for Security Cooperation Asia and Pacific (2004). The objective of the ECSG, established in 1999, is to coordinate APEC-related activities in the area of e-commerce. Thus far, the ECSG has not directly addressed law enforcement issues in an e-commerce environment, but enforcement also connects to APEC's general interest in improving consumer trust and confidence in e-commerce.Further, the ECSG's increasingly detailed work in the areas of privacy and security in the online environment implicates law enforcement concerns.

At their meeting in Los Cabos, Mexico, in October 2002, APEC leaders noted the threat of global terrorism and the importance of increasing the protection of global infrastructures and that global communications are only as secure as its weakest link, and collectively committed to enact comprehensive cybersecurity laws, on a par with existing international standards, particularly the CoE Cybercrime Convention and UN General Assembly Resolution 55/63 of 2000; identify or create national cybercrime units and international high-technology assistance contact points; and establish computer emergency response teams that exchange threat and vulnerability assessments and information. They also called for closer cooperation between law enforcement officials and businesses in the field of information security and fighting computer crime by endorsing the APEC Cyber-security Strategy. The elements of the strategy cover legal developments, information sharing and cooperation, security and technical guidelines, public awareness, training and education, and wireless security. APEC's Telecommunications and Infrastructure Working Group has been most active in sponsoring projects to increase the ability of APEC member economies to more effectively address cybercrime, including through greater intergovernmental and public–private sector cooperation (see http://www.apectelwg.org/apecdata/telwg/28tel/estg/telwg28-ESTG-09.htm).

Urbas (2005) observed, in concluding an overview of legislation in Asia, that the development of legislation designed to counter intellectual property offenses and cybercrime showed that although some states had enacted new laws, many remained ill-equipped to deal with the cross-border nature of these offenses. Orlowski (2004) also reported an APEC cybercrime legislation survey involving 14 nations that found all had some legislative provisions to address cybercrime and to support law enforcement (see http://www.apectel28.com.tw/document/webword/estg/telwg28-ESTG-07.doc). However, mutual legal assistance, extradition arrangements, and provision of cross-border information in respect of computer offenses were found in only half the countries surveyed. The survey noted that the main concerns related to the difficulties in requesting the collection and preservation of evidence in real time, issues relating to jurisdiction for offenses and offenders, and lack of, or limitations in, mutual assistance and extradition arrangements. APEC has called for further work to develop laws and procedures that facilitate the investigation and prosecution of cross-jurisdictional cybercrime. As noted above, it is essential to continually monitor progress and where necessary provide assistance and encouragement to ensure that MLA is not impeded.

Summary of Measures for Regional Cooperation

Given the diversity of the above activities aimed at improving regional and international cooperation, the basic ingredients for a global approach can be deduced. Grabosky and Broadhurst (2005) outlined the basic elements of an effective regime for regional cooperation in combating cybercrime that include the following:

- Improve security awareness by providing adequate resources to secure transactions and equip system operators and administrators
- Improve coordination and collaboration by enabling systematic exchanges between the private sector and law enforcement including joint operations
- Take steps to ensure that technology does not outpace the ability of law enforcement to investigate and enact substantive and procedural laws adequate to cope with current and anticipated manifestations of cybercrime
- Broadly criminalize the conduct (including juvenile offenders) and focus on all violators big and small
- Strengthen international initiatives by updating existing treaties and agreements to recognize the existence, threats, and transnational nature of high-tech computer-related crimes and strive for legal harmonization
- The development of forensic computing skills by law enforcement and investigative personnel and mechanisms for operational cooperation between law enforcement agencies from different countries, that is, 24/7 points of contact for investigators.

In the future, organized crime may be expected to recruit IT specialists, intimidate corporate insiders to obtain access to IT systems, and use anonymizers and encryption in furtherance of cybercrime. In addition, there is evidence of the deployment of intelligent malicious software designed to elude detection by antivirus software. Automated intelligent computer and network attack capabilities allow remote initiation of attacks to be directed at any computer or network on the Internet while making it more difficult to identify the actual source of the attack. These advanced forms of intrusion code enable users to gain competitive advantage by extracting sensitive economic data from competitors and provide data (such as customers' records) for extortion and denial-of-service offenses. Most significant, attacks are instantaneous and often remote, disregarding national sovereignty. Whether they are the work of a 14-year-old, a terrorist, a foreign intelligence service, or an organized criminal may not be immediately apparent; all must be investigated. However, digital technology also affords new opportunities for individual citizens to communicate efficiently with police. An example is the Internet Fraud Complaint Center, which operates in the United States and receives online information from members of the public relating to questionable online activities that are evaluated and referred to the appropriate agency or jurisdiction.

Digital footprints are fragile or ephemeral, so swift action is often required. This becomes very difficult when an attack transits multiple jurisdictions with different regimes for preserving evidence. Traditional methods of law enforcement are therefore no longer adequate. A slow formal process risks losing evidence, and multiple countries may be implicated. Following and preserving a chain of evidence is a great challenge. Among the challenges faced by investigators is the enormous increase in storage capacity in today's computers and the challenge to effective and efficient searches that this entails. Almost every case will soon require computer forensics, and evidence will be located in multiple places. The challenge faced by investigators will be one of *information management* (Pollitt, 2003). Even local crimes may have an international dimension, and assistance may be required from all countries through which an attack was routed.

Many nations and regional bodies such as the Council of Europe have addressed the problem of cybercrime and laws exist that criminalize the unauthorized access and unlawful use of computers, but such laws are neither universal nor uniform. Concerns remain focused on the weakest links in the supposedly seamless security chain necessary to prevent cybercrime by predatory criminal groups. Comity thus can only be ensured if wealthy states and affected industries are prepared to extend aid to those less capable states or agencies. Consensus is the best strategy, for the suppression of computer-related crime entails a mixture of law enforcement, technological, and market-based solutions. It can be argued, however, that a strict enforcement agenda is usually not feasible because of the limited capacity of the state. It is also feared that overregulation could stifle commercial and technological development. Those skeptical of a heavily interventionist approach also argue that the marketplace may at times be able to provide more efficient solutions than the state to the problems of computer-related crime.

Although there is consensus about the risks of computer-related crime, apart from criminalizing the conduct at a global level, there is much less consensus about what might be done to prevent it. There is concern that the technological solution to information security is a mirage, more hope than reality, and that dependence on the promise of a technology fix is an approach fated to fail. So also is the faith in a deterrence-based approach in which the criminal law is deployed as the principal instrument of prevention. Deterrence is unlikely to succeed in all or even some circumstances, and experience with conventional crime suggests that over reliance on the law, as a deterrent or moral educator alone, is unlikely to help substantially even if legitimately supported by the community.

Fundamentally systems can be designed to lessen their vulnerability to criminal exploitation. Cybercrime is often facilitated by vulnerable software, much of which is designed with user-friendliness and convenience in mind rather than security. The common industry response is for manufacturers to structure their licence conditions to avoid potential liability and then to make patches available as vulnerabilities become apparent later on. Whether market forces will eventually drive the widespread development of truly secure software remains to be seen. Commercial enterprises may be in a position to achieve more protection than poorly resourced law enforcement agencies could deliver. Microsoft Corporation has now, it seems, reflected on its failure to lead the market in respect to consumer safety and to recognize that the market demands a secure and trusted environment if computers and information technology are to realize their full potential.

In conclusion, controlling crime involving digital technology and computer networks will require a variety of new networks: networks between police and other agencies within government, networks between police and private institutions, and networks of police across national borders. Over the past five years, considerable progress has been made within and between nations to develop the capacity of police to respond to cybercrime. But the pace of technological change will continue unabated and the adaptability of cybercriminals will continue to pose challenges for law enforcement. The extent of transnational law enforcement cooperation achieved thus far, promising though it may be, can only be regarded as a beginning.

GLOSSARY

Comity An association of civility and mutual benefit among nations, especially in regard to the recognition of the laws and customs of other nations.

Dual Criminality A rule governing or limiting the reach of a bilateral or multilateral treaty or convention, or a cross-border law enforcement that authorizes assistance only if the offense is criminalized in the law of both states.

Extradition The formal arrangements between nations that allow fugitives, suspects, or witnesses in one country to be transported to the country in which the crime was committed.

List Treaty A bilateral or multilateral treaty providing extradition or other legal assistance such as the seizure and preservation of evidence that is limited to the list of offenses.

Mutual Legal Assistance The general term for all informal and official forms of police, legal, and criminal justice cooperation between states usually provided on a reciprocal basis.

Social Engineering The manipulation of human behavior for the purposes of revealing passwords, source code, and other confidential information without recourse to unauthorized access to a computer system by means of exploiting or intrusion software.

CROSS REFERENCES

See *Cyberterroism and information Security; Global Aspects of Cyberlaw; Law Enforcement and Computer Security Threats and Measures; Law Enforcement and Digital Evidence; Privacy Law and the Internet.*

REFERENCES

Aizawa, K. (2001). Current mechanisms for international cooperation in criminal matters: Mutual legal assistance and extradition, 24/7 points of contact network, and training in the field of computer crime. In R. Broadhurst (Ed.), *Proceedings of the Asia Cyber Crime Summit*. Hong Kong: Centre for Criminology, University of Hong Kong, pp. 133–140.

Bullwinkel, J. (2005). International cooperation in combating cyber-crime in Asia: Existing mechanisms and new approaches. In R. Broadhurst & P. Grabosky (Eds.), *Cyber-crime: The challenge in Asia*, pp. 269–302. Hong Kong: University of Hong Press.

Council of Europe. (2003, January 28). *Additional Protocol to the Convention on cybercrime on the criminalisation of acts of a racist or xenophobic nature committed through computer systems*. Retrieved August 9, 2004, from http://conventions.coe.int/Treaty/en/Treaties/Html/189.htm

Council for Security Cooperation Asia and Pacific. (2004). *Cybercrime and its effects on the Asia Pacific region: Report of the Transnational Crime Working Group*. Retrieved August 4, 2004, from http://www.police.govt.nz/events/2001/e-crime-forum/cybercrime_and_its_effects.html

Cross, I. (2003). Enforcement and prosecution strategies in the 21st century: Combating multi-jurisdictional crime. In R. Broadhurst (Ed.), *Bridging the GAP: A global alliance on transnational organised crime*, pp. 25–36. Hong Kong: Hong Kong Police Printing Department HKSAR.

Csonka, P. (2005). The Council of Europe Convention on Cybercrime: A response to the challenge of the New Age? In R. Broadhurst & P. Grabosky (Eds.), *Cyber-crime: The challenge in Asia*, pp. 303–326. Hong Kong: University of Hong Press.

Decision establishing Eurojust (2002, 28 February). Retrieved May 9, 2005, from http://europa.eu.int/scadplus/leg/en/lvb/l33188.htm

Esposito, G. (2004). The Council of Europe Convention on Cyber-crime: A Revolutionary Instrument? In R. Broadhurst (Ed.), *Proceedings of the 2nd Asia Cyber Crime Summit*. Hong Kong: Centre for Criminology, University of Hong Kong, pp. 54–64.

European Union, (2003). Framework Decision. Retrieved May 9, 2005, from http://europa.eu.int/information_society/eeurope/2005/all_about/mid_term_review/security/index_en.htm

European Union (1998 June, 29) Judicial Cooperation in Criminal Matters. Retrieved May 9, 2005 from http://europa.eu.int/scadplus/leg/en/lvb/l33055.htm

G8 (2004, May 11), Justice and Home Affairs Communiqué, Washington. Retrieved December 11, 2004 from www.g7.utoronto.ca/justice/justice040511_comm.htm

Grabosky, P., & Broadhurst, R. (2005). The future of cyber-crime in Asia. In R. Broadhurst & P. Grabosky *(Eds.), *Cyber-crime: The challenge in Asia*, pp. 347–360. Hong Kong: University of Hong Kong Press.

Iden, R. L. (2003). Cyber crime: What's the threat, the challenge, and the policing response. In R. Broadhurst (Ed.), *Bridging the GAP: A global alliance on transnational organised crime*, pp. 69–73. Hong Kong: Hong Kong Police, Printing Department HKSAR.

International Narcotic Control Board. (2001). *Report of the International Narcotic Control Board 2001* (UN E/INCB/2001/1). Vienna, Austria: Author.

Johnston, L. (2000). Transnational private policing: The impact of global commercial security. In J. W. E. Sheptycki (Ed.), *Issues in transnational policing*, pp. 21–42. London: Routledge.

Joint Communique of the Third ASEAN Ministerial Meeting on Transnational Crime. (2001, October 11). Retrieved November 21, 2003, from http://www.aseansec.org/5621.htm

Khoo, B. H. (2003). Police cooperation in fighting transnational organised crime: An Asian perspective. In R. Broadhurst (Ed.), *Bridging the GAP: A global alliance on transnational organised crime*, pp. 44–50. Hong Kong: Hong Kong Police, Printing Department HKSAR.

Moore, D., Shannon, C., Voelker, G. M., & Savage, S. (2003). *Internet quarantine: requirements for containing self-propagating code*. Paper presented at the meeting of the IEEE INFOCOM, San Francisco, CA.

Newman, G., & Clarke, R. (2003). *Superhighway robbery: Preventing E-commerce crime*. Devon, UK: Willan.

Newton, J. (2004). Interpol and the cards industry: Global partnerships to deliver local solutions. In R. Broadhurst (Ed.), *Proceedings of the 2nd Asia Cyber Crime Summit*. Hong Kong: Centre for Criminology, University of Hong Kong, pp. 124–127.

Noble, R. (2003). Interpol's new approach: A return to basics. In R. Broadhurst (Ed.), *Bridging the GAP: A global alliance on transnational organised crime*, pp. 37–43. Hong Kong: Hong Kong Police, Printing Department HKSAR.

OECD *governments launch drive to improve security of online networks*. (2002, August 7). Retrieved from http://www.oecd.org/document/53/0,2340,en_2649_201185_1946997_1_1_1_1,00.html

Organization of American States. (n.d.). *Group of experts and cyber crime*. Retrieved October 11, 2004, from http://www.oas.org/juridico/english/cyber.htm

Orlowski, S. (2004). APEC activities to address cybercrime through public/private cooperation. In R. Broadhurst (Ed.), *Proceedings of the 2nd Asia Cyber Crime Summit*. Hong Kong: Centre for Criminology, University of Hong Kong, pp. 37–45.

Pollitt, M. (2003). Digital evidence in Internet time. In R. Broadhurst (Ed.), *Bridging the GAP: A global alliance on transnational organised crime*, pp. 82–85. Hong Kong: Hong Kong Police, Printing Department HKSAR.

Redo, S. (2000). Crime as the growing international security threat: The United Nations and effective countermeasures against transnational economic and computer crime. UNAFEI Resource Material Series No. 55, Tokyo, Fuchu, Japan, pp. 117–139.

Redo, S. (2004). The UN. In R. Broadhurst (Ed.), *Proceedings of the 2nd Asia Cyber Crime Summit*. Hong Kong: Centre for Criminology, University of Hong Kong, pp. 18–29.

Sato, T. (2004). Countermeasures against cyber-crime in Japan. In R. Broadhurst (Ed.), *Proceedings of the 2nd Asia Cyber Crime Summit*. Hong Kong: Centre for Criminology, University of Hong Kong, pp. 139–145.

Semple, K. (2004, January 27). E-mail worm snarls computers around globe. *New York Times*. Retrieved January 28, 2004, from http://www.nytimes.com/2004/01/27/technology/27CND-VIRU.html

Sheptycki, J. W. E. (Ed.). (2000). *Issues in transnational policing*. London: Routledge.

Staniford, S., Paxson, V., & Weaver, N. (2002). How to own the Internet in your spare time. In *Proceedings of the 11th USENIX Security Symposium (Security '02)*. Retrieved December 9, 2003, http//www.icir.org/vern/papers/cdc-usenix-sec02/

Sussmann, M. A. (1999). The critical challenges from international high-tech and computer-related crime at the millennium. *Duke Journal of Comparative and International Law*, 9, 451–473.

United Nations. (2003). *World public sector report 2003: E-government at the Crossroads, Sales No. E.03.II.H.3*. New York: Author.

United Nations convention against transnational organized crime. (n.d.). Retrieved August 9, 2004, from http://

www.undcp.org/crime_cicp_signatures_convention.html, visited August 9, 2004.

Urbas, G. (2005). Cyber-crime legislation in the Asia-Pacific region. In R. Broadhurst & P. Grabosky (Eds.), *Cyber-crime: The challenge in Asia*, pp. 207–242. Hong Kong: University of Hong Press.

European Union, http://www.europa.eu.int/scadplus/leg/en/lvb/114015b.htm; visited December 11, 2003.

European Union, http://www.europa.eu.int/scadplus/leg/en/lvb/133055.htm; visited December 11, 2003

Interpol, http://www.interpol.int/Public/FinancialCrime/IntellectualProperty/Default/.asp

E-Government Security Issues and Measures

William C. Barker, *National Institute of Standards and Technology*

E-GOVERNMENT INITIATIVES

Definitions of E-Government

E-government, a contraction of "electronic government," refers to the use by government agencies of information technologies (such as the Internet) to conduct interactions with citizens, with businesses, and with other arms of the government. E-government initiatives seek to improve delivery of government services to citizens, improve interactions with business and industry, empower citizens through access to information, and improve government management efficiency. E-government can potentially result in less corruption, more transparency, greater convenience, revenue growth, and cost reductions (World Bank Group, n.d.).

General

Traditionally, the interaction between a citizen or business and a government agency took place in a government office. With emerging information and communication technologies, it is possible to locate service centers closer to the clients. Such centers may consist of an unattended kiosk in the government agency, a service kiosk located close to the client, or the use of a personal computer in the home or office.

E-government is analogous to e-commerce, which allows businesses to transact with each other more efficiently and brings customers closer to businesses. E-government aims to make the interaction between government and citizens, government and business enterprises, and interagency relationships more friendly, convenient, transparent, and inexpensive.

U.S. Government–Specific

Within the United States, under the "e-gov" initiatives, e-government is to use improved Internet-based technology to make it easy for citizens and businesses to interact with the government, save taxpayer dollars, and streamline citizen-to-government communications. A major motivator for e-government within the U.S. government was the Government Paperwork Elimination Act (GPEA) of October 21, 1998, which required federal agencies, by October 21, 2003, to provide for the options of (a) electronic maintenance, submission, or disclosure of information, when practicable as a substitute for paper, and (b) use and acceptance of electronic signatures, when practicable. Implementation of the GPEA provides the management framework for electronic government. Office of Management and Budget (OMB) Memorandum M-00-10, dated April 25, 2000, provides procedures and guidance on implementing the GPEA. OMB's guidance, in addition to procedural guidance for Paperwork Reduction Act reporting, requires that an agency's implementation plan relate to strategic information technology planning in the budget process. If an agency needs additional resources to implement the plan, its budget request under OMB Circular A-11 should reflect that need, and agency GPEA reports should address progress in implementing the act and e-government initiatives. The E-Government Act of 2002 builds on the U.S. government's expanding e-government initiative with a comprehensive framework for information security standards and programs and uniform safeguards to protect the confidentiality of information provided by the public for statistical purposes. The act also assists in expanding the use of the Internet and computer resources to deliver government services, consistent with the principles of a citizen-centered, results-oriented, and market-based government.

The goal of these initiatives is to eliminate redundant systems and improve the government's quality of customer service for citizens and businesses. E-government does not just mean putting scores of government forms on the Internet. It aims to use technology to its fullest to provide services and information that are centered around citizen groups (E-Gov Web Site: http://www.whitehouse.gov/omb/egov/about_backgrnd.htm).

Examples of E-Government Program Types

There are a number of taxonomies of e-government service types. Some are based on functional relationships (e.g., government to citizen, government to business, government to government, and internal effectiveness and efficiency). Others focus on functional processes content and degree of interaction inherent in the services provided. For purposes of this security discussion, the services provided by e-government program are categorized with respect to functional processes as (a) publishing, (b) interactive processing, (c) transaction processing, and (d) service delivery.

Publishing

Publishing involves simply posting information on a publicly accessible Web site. The primary automated interaction of the public with e-government publishing services is limited to navigation around the Web site. The public should have no ability to modify government Web content.

The major challenge associated with e-government publishing is content management: the process of creating, updating, distributing, and publishing information on a Web site. Content management involves creating a central storage area for files, templates, images, and other material used to build a Web site. Content management templates support conformance of government Web pages to government standards. Content management systems also support review and approval of Web page content being published. Content management processes are also vehicles for periodic review and update of agencies' online information. Content work flow includes the following elements:

- Contribution—Content is written and placed in the Web page.
- Approval—Content is reviewed and approved or rejected.
- Publishing—Content is sent to the live site.

At each step in the work flow, someone must sign off. These sign-offs help to ensure accountability for content. No unauthorized modification of Web site content should be permitted.

To date, most e-government activity has centered on publishing.

Interactive Processing

E-government interactive processing involves private citizens or other user entities reading instructions published on agency Web sites and following those instructions to submit reports, applications, or other service requests (e.g., submit tax returns, apply for licenses or other services, renew licenses, order products or services, or provide notification of address or other status changes). Here, citizens or other private entities need to be able to write and modify some data files with which they are associated on the government Web site. No user entity, however, should be able to read or modify data files associated with another user entity, be able to read or modify data files restricted to agency use, or modify any Web page content (other than that entity's own data) or underlying program. In addition to dealing with content management issues associated with Web-based publication, agencies that host interactive Web sites need to be able to provide citizens and other customers with assurance that privacy, integrity, and binding to the originator will be preserved for information that is submitted to interactive government Web sites. Furthermore, the effective management of an interactive Web site also requires some mechanism for identifying the originator of Web-based reports, applications, and other requests with the information provided by the originator. Inputs to interactive e-government sites should not be permitted without prior completion of the following process:

- Application—The user identifies himself to the agency and requests an interactive account.
- Approval—The application is approved or rejected.
- Credentialing—The agency provides the user with an electronic credential (e.g., personal identification number, password, public key certificate) that can be used to associate information with the possessor of the credential.

Once in possession of the appropriate access credential, a user is able to access an e-government Web site, navigate to the appropriate form, enter the requested information, and submit the form. The Web site should be capable of invoking processes that receipt for the submission, including notification that the submission complied with rules regarding information format and completeness.

Interactive government Web sites are less numerous than sites limited to publication but are becoming more common.

Transaction Processing

Transaction processing includes processing of information submitted via interactive e-government Web sites, providing notification of approval for actions to be taken on the basis of that information, and activation of implementation processes (e.g., billing, payment, licensing, permit issuance, contract awards, invoice approvals, etc.). Transaction processing generally involves distributing data received from users to multiple databases and multiple processes and includes interactions with third parties. This characteristic multiplies the distribution of privacy and integrity mechanisms. It also requires a process for dissemination of the decision notification and any associated authorization information in a manner that binds the content of the notification to identity credentials associated with both the e-government originator and the user recipient. Government-issued interactive access credentials need to include some information that can be used to verify the origin and content integrity of information allegedly received from an e-government source. Cryptographic mechanisms are usually employed for this purpose.

Service Delivery

Service delivery goes beyond the transaction approval component to transaction processing, including the actual execution of actions approved on the basis of e-government interactions. Examples of such actions include acceptance of credit card payments or electronic funds transfers, execution of government payments (e.g., benefits, grants, refunds, or payments for services or products) by electronic fund transfers, and delivery of licenses or permits. Because service delivery can be difficult, expensive, or even impossible to repudiate, assured invocation and effectiveness of source authentication, destination authentication, authentication of any third-party authorization, and verification of the integrity and correctness of the information contained in the service delivery communication are essential.

SECURITY ISSUES ASSOCIATED WITH E-GOVERNMENT

Taxonomies of security issues associated with e-government usually include three to five major elements. Examples of major security categories include confidentiality, privacy, integrity, authentication, authorization, and nonrepudiation. For purposes of this discussion, the taxonomy employed by the E-Government Act of 2002 will be used. The E-Government Act of 2002, Section 3542(B), defines integrity, confidentiality, and availability attributes of security.

Threats to the security of information in an e-government environment can include natural and accidental events (e.g., flooding, fire, storms, human error, environmental problems) and deliberate threats (e.g., sabotage, fraud, information theft, Trojan horses, hacking, viruses, logic bombs). Deliberate attacks may come from criminals, hackers, terrorists, disenchanted employees, curious or mischievous users, journalists, state-sponsored or industrial spies, or state-sponsored or industrial saboteurs. The primary focus of this chapter is on threats and countermeasures affecting remote connections to e-government resources rather than on insider and other threats involving physical access to servers and other storage and processing facilities. It focuses also on the potential for denial, unauthorized alteration, and unauthorized disclosure of information rather than on some of the purposes for which successful compromise of information security can be employed. For example, the focus might be on *potential* for unauthorized access to information regarding an individual (e.g., Social Security numbers and mother's maiden name) rather than the use of that information to commit a crime such as identity fraud.

Availability

The E-Government Act of 2002 defines availability as "ensuring timely and reliable access to and use of information." Availability concerns affect publishing, interactive processing, transaction processing, and service delivery e-government activities. Availability concerns include those resulting from system faults, those intrinsic to the technologies employed to provide e-government services, and malicious activities intended to prevent access to or use of information (denial of service attacks). Although fault-related availability and intrinsic availability concerns are not usually treated as security issues, they can significantly affect access to and use of e-government services, and countermeasures that are employed against denial of service and integrity threats can often mitigate system fault and intrinsic availability concerns.

Fault-Related Availability Concerns

System faults that can affect availability of services include hardware faults, changes in program or data structures due to transients or design errors, and failures in other system facilities that are not computer based. An extensive literature addresses fault concerns (e.g., National Institute of Standards and Technology's [NIST, 1995] *A Conceptual Framework for Systems Fault Tolerance*, references listed in the *Selected Bibliography of Fault-Tolerant Computing at Hopkins* [Sullivan, 1996], and references listed in the *Bibliography on Byzantine Fault Independence* [Martin, 2004]).

Intrinsic Availability Concerns

Intrinsic availability concerns include obsolescence of storage and recovery mechanisms, deterioration of magnetic media, ephemeral continuity of access channels such as addresses and protocols, and loss of facilities due to physical damage or support infrastructure problems. Continued availability may require not only maintenance of backups and archives, but also migration to new media and formats for the backups and archives. Service availability concerns include reduced responsiveness of processes where provision is not made for, e-approval by alternate authorities (e.g., deputies, acting managers or functionaries) in the temporary actual or virtual (non-functioning automation component) absence of an approving authority resultant processing delays cannot be mitigated by "hand carrying" or other expediting mechanisms available for paper-based processes.

Obsolescence of storage and recovery mechanisms is a concern that is likely to become more acute as paperless records and transactions begin to predominate. The media (e.g., punched cards, magnetic tapes, floppy disks, CDs, DVDs, memory sticks) and formats (e.g., CP/M-, DOS-, Unix-, and Windows-) on which and in which information and information retrieval programs are stored are constantly evolving. New generations of data retrieval hardware and software tend to be incompatible with those of only a few years before. Organizations that stored volumes of information on 5¼-inch floppy disks often have failed to copy the information onto 3½-inch disks or more modern media and no longer possess either the hardware or software applications necessary to read or interpret the stored information. Where large databases are concerned, the recurring need to copy the data onto current storage media in currently accessible formats can be expensive and time-consuming. Failure to copy the information can result in loss of availability of the information.

Magnetic storage media can deteriorate over time due to oxidation, compression of plastic or metal housing components, or other causes. Again, copying the information may be necessary to maintain availability.[1]

E-government information access often involves links to related sites. Web sites are constantly changing, coming into existence, and being disestablished. If the links are not adequately maintained (e.g., maintaining currency and awareness of the status of linked sites and databases), information on which advertised e-government services are dependent may become unavailable.

In the case of cryptographically protected databases, the loss or corruption of keying material can result in loss of availability of information on which e-government services are dependent.

[1] For further information, see National Archives of Australia, Archives Advice 5, "Protecting and handling magnetic media," revised June 2002. Retrieved from http://www.aa.gov.au/recordkeeping/rkpubs/advices/advice5.html

Denial of Service Concerns

Government sites are attractive targets for malicious activities intended to prevent access to, or use of, information (denial of service attacks). These can range from relatively unsophisticated assaults that result in temporary degradation of service response times to crippling attacks that corrupt or destroy system resources. Denial of service attacks can be launched from a variety of sources and can take a number of forms.

Sources

The source of a denial of service attack can affect (a) the scale of the attack (available resources); (b) the efficiency with which large-scale attacking resources are employed; (c) timing of attacks in the context of maximizing impact on system resources and maximizing the number of e-government clients affected or criticality of services affected; (d) the intelligence information available to facilitate an attack and focus it on specific e-government services, the denial of which will cause maximum harm; (e) the degree to which the source of the attack can be obscured or otherwise shielded from countermeasures and retaliation; and (f) scale of compensation that can be extracted from or retaliation that can be invoked against an attacker.

Individual or Informally Organized Hackers

Most denial of service attacks against e-government services have been launched by individuals or informally organized groups of hackers. Some of these have resulted in significant disruption and expense to the taxpayer. Individuals have penetrated and "captured" large numbers of computers, without the knowledge or consent of their owners and used these captured computers to launch Internet-based attacks against government sites or against service providers on which e-government services are dependent. The "captured" computers employed by some individuals number in the thousands, or even tens of thousands. The computers employed often are not even in the same country as the individuals who launch the attacks.

In some cases, groups of individuals who share a common cause (e.g., religiously or politically motivated grievances against the government) cooperatively launch attacks against resources on which e-government resources are dependent. The degree to which the attacks can be coordinated tends to be limited when such groups are informally organized and their constituent individuals employ clandestine methods to avoid being identified and arrested.

Individual hackers do tend to share information. Whether they operate independently or cooperatively, they may share information regarding techniques, successes, and failures. Some of the hackers are extremely sophisticated and often are more technically capable than the government and government-sponsored personnel who are charged with defending against them. The most sophisticated designers of attacks are often not the individuals who launch them. They often simply share the attacks with other, much less sophisticated and less prudent individuals, who then launch the attacks. Historically, there is a delay between the posting of a potential attack by a designer and its launching by an attacker. This delay has often permitted detection by defenders and deployment of countermeasures in time to mitigate the effects of attacks (e.g., through distribution and implementation of software patches). However, the delays experienced between posting of potential attacks and launching of attacks has been decreasing.

Efficient allocation of defensive and law enforcement assets is relatively difficult in the case of individuals and informally organized groups. The target environment is excessively diffuse.

Nonstate Organizations

Attacks by formally organized groups can pose a much more serious threat than attacks by individuals and informally organized groups. This can result in increased efficiency with which large-scale attacking resources are employed and improved timing of attacks to maximize impact on system resources and the number of e-government clients or criticality of services affected; likewise, it can lead to improved availability and efficiency in exploiting intelligence information available to facilitate an attack and focus it on e-government services, the denial of which will cause maximum harm. On the other hand, many of the brightest hackers are individualists who have, so far, not tended to become subordinate to institutional management. Also, concentration of hacking resources into a formal organization permits more efficient employment of law enforcement and other resources charged with defending e-government systems. Although an organization may have resources to shield perpetrators of denial of service attacks, it presents an identifiable and resource-rich target against which defensive, law enforcement, and compensation assets may be employed.

State-Sponsored Attacks

State-sponsored denial of service attacks have long been a major concern for e-government activities. Very large sets of resources can be brought to bear on design and execution of attacks, and the state can (to some extent) shield the actual perpetrators from individual identification, capture, and retaliation. On the other hand, so far, many of the most effective hackers are individualists who have not tended to subordinate themselves voluntarily to government oversight. Also, if an attack can be demonstrated to be state sponsored, a range of remedies is available to discourage future attacks and extract compensation (e.g., economic sanctions, retaliation in kind, military action). State-sponsored denial of service attacks remains a largely unrealized concern.

Classes of Attacks

Denial of service attacks against e-government resources has been extensively defined and discussed in security literature. Examples include *Distributed Denial of Service (DDoS) Attacks/Tools* (Dittrich, 2004), *Denial of Service Attacks* (CERT Coordination Center, n.d.), and the Denial of Service Database. Denial of service attacks can take physical or logical forms.

Physical

Although physical attacks on e-government resources can have catastrophic and relatively enduring consequences, they usually involve significant risk exposure for the perpetrators and have a relatively uncertain prognosis. For example, the 2001 attack on the World Trade Center affected some e-government services, but some potentially catastrophic outages were avoided by chance. Some important service provider hardware remained in service in a heavily damaged building. In most cases to date, impacts on e-government services have been by-products rather than primary objectives of physical attacks.

It is possible for an individual or small organization to carry out significant attacks on e-government resources. The bombing of the Murrah Federal Building in Oklahoma City is an example of a large-scale attack on federal assets. However, the larger physical threat may still be posed by nation-states, state-sponsored organizations, and large nonstate organizations.

Logical

The simplest and so far most common denial of service attacks, logical attacks keep e-government servers so busy with fake data traffic that they can't employ their resources to provide services to their legitimate users. Most of the more common attacks take advantage of network protocol characteristics and are termed "flooding" attacks. Some flooding attack scenarios follow:

- An Internet control message protocol (ICMP) message to a server (also known as a "ping" on a server) produces an echo response to confirm the server's presence. When enough pings are sent, the target server can do nothing but respond to the requests.
- User datagram protocol (UDP) diagnostic services generate characters that are echoed back from the receiving end to the host, swamping the network with useless data.
- Multiple spoofed requests for transmission control protocol (TCP) connections force the server to keep ports open, waiting for responses.
- Some attacks (i.e., "Smurf" attacks) appear to originate from the target server's own Internet protocol address or somewhere else on the target's network. Targeted correctly, the attack can flood the network with pings and multiple responses.

Distributed denial-of-service attacks employ multiple computers across the Internet against a single target server. Most serious attacks today orchestrate the use of hundreds of machines and take the target server out of commission for the duration of the attack.

Integrity

The E-Government Act of 2002 states that the term integrity "means guarding against improper information modification or destruction, and includes ensuring information nonrepudiation and authenticity." Integrity concerns affect publishing, interactive processing, transaction processing, and service delivery of e-government activities. If published information, requests for information received from users, or authorizations or payments issued to users are improperly modified or destroyed, routed, or ascribed, then damage to confidence in the government, to user or customers, or to government assets can result.

Data Content Integrity Issues

Data content integrity issues are associated with unauthorized modification or destruction of e-government information content. This can involve modification or destruction of

- information electronically published by the government;
- information associated with reports, applications, or other service requests provided by private citizens or other user entities (e.g., submit tax returns, apply for licenses or other services, renew licenses, order products or services, or provide notification of address change or other status changes);
- notification to private citizens or other user entities of approval actions or activation of implementation processes (e.g., billing, payment, licensing, permit issuance, contract awards, invoice approvals, etc.); and
- information executing actions approved on the basis of e-government interactions (e.g., credit card payment information or electronic funds transfer information, electronic fund transfer information, and licenses or permits).

Loss of data content integrity can result from error-based integrity faults or from intentional modification or destruction of data. The consequences of loss of integrity from either cause can range from inconvenience or financial loss to users to unintentional violation of public laws or regulations by users. Impaired confidence in e-government systems is a likely consequence in any case.

Error-Based Integrity Faults

Although most error-based integrity faults (i.e., accidental losses of integrity) are not, strictly speaking, security concerns, they can have consequences similar to those of maliciously induced faults, and a number of the countermeasures to intentional modification of data are effective in mitigating the consequences of error-based faults. Note also that many fault-tolerance measures are also effective in mitigating the consequences of error-based integrity faults.

Intentional Modification of Data

Data may be modified or destroyed within e-government processors (e.g., Web servers) or in transit. In the case of the former, an attacker must gain write-access to the processor and to the desired data file or process within the processor. Penetration may be accomplished by defeating identification and authentication mechanisms or by inserting malicious code into a legitimate transaction. In some cases, information transits more than one government processor in the course of interactive or transaction processing or service delivery processes. In such cases, it may be sufficient to penetrate only one processor in the path between the originating process or database and the connection to external communications. Information transiting an intermediate processor can be modified or destroyed in that processor. In some systems, Web servers outside the security perimeter (e.g., outside the firewall) make attractive penetration targets. If the configuration of their access control mechanisms is inadequate, it may be possible for attackers to destroy, forge, or modify e-government information in these external processors (e.g., maliciously modifying Web pages).

Modification of information in transit can mean dynamic modification of information on a communications path, but it can also mean modification of information in an intermediate processor (e.g., a server belonging to an Internet service provider). It may be possible using either approach to forge or intercept and change legitimate e-government publications or transactions.

Connection Integrity Issues

Successful implementation of e-government services requires some degree of confidence on the part of private citizens or other user entities that information being read originated only with the assumed government source and that information being provided goes only to the appropriate government destination(s). Similarly, it is important to government electronic service providers that reports, service requests, and applications actually originate with the user entity claiming to make the submission and that service delivery transmissions and private or proprietary information go only to authorized destinations. Modification of header or routing information (see previous section, Intentional Modification of Data) can potentially result in distribution of information or service delivery instruments to unauthorized parties. The consequences can include simple violation of laws and regulations regarding privacy or proprietary information, identity theft with financial or legal consequences, erroneous or fraudulent issuance of permits or licenses, and diversion of services or funds.

Nonrepudiation Issues

Nonrepudiation involves proof of the origin and content integrity of data (including the property of not having been forged) in a form that can be verified at any time by a third party. Nonrepudiation most commonly applies to requests and reports from private citizens and other user entities, but there are cases in which user entities expect protection from repudiation of government-originated information or responses to requests. The following properties need to be satisfied to support nonrepudiation of e-government services:

- Publications and transaction information must be tightly bound to their claimed sources.
- Transactions must be difficult to forge without the forgery being detected.
- Transactions must be difficult to alter without the alteration being detected.
- Transactions must be verifiable.

Particularly in the case of reports required by law or regulation, it is important to the government that there be nonrepudiation with respect to both originator and content. Particularly with respect to approval actions and publication of regulations and requirements, it is important to user entities that there be nonrepudiation with respect to both originator and content. Neither the originator nor the recipient of information or a transaction request must be able to claim falsely and convincingly that the information or transaction request actually originated from a different source, was posted at a time different from when it was actually posted, or had different total content from that which was received. Particularly in the case of service delivery, the recipient must not be able to claim falsely and convincingly that information or transactions received were misdirected or not received for other reasons.

As the level of e-government service progresses from publication through interactivity and transaction processing to service delivery, the importance of nonrepudiation increases.

Confidentiality and Privacy

The E-Government Act of 2002 states that the term *confidentiality* "means preserving authorized restrictions on access and disclosure, including means for protecting personal privacy and proprietary information." E-government publication services involve primarily dissemination of information authorized to be in the public domain. Interactive e-government services may include communication to government facilities of information that is subject to laws or regulations restricting dissemination of private or proprietary information. The volume and frequency of occurrence of privacy and proprietary information increase in the cases of e-government transaction services and services delivery. In all cases, it is necessary to protect against use of e-government portals for unauthorized access to government information that has not been released into the public domain.

Distinguishing Confidentiality and Privacy Issues

The terms *privacy* and *confidentiality* are often used interchangeably. The U.S. Congress Office of Technology Assessment (OTA) has observed that "neither term possesses a single clear definition, and theorists argue variously that privacy and confidentiality (and the counterpart to confidentiality, secrecy) may be concepts that are the same, completely distinct, or in some cases overlapping" (U.S. Congress, Office of Technology Assessment, 1993). For purposes of this e-government discussion, confidentiality protection is protection against disclosure of information without the implicit or explicit consent of an entity that legitimately possesses the information, whereas privacy protection also includes protection against dissemination of information by an entity that legitimately possesses the information in violation of laws and regulations restricting the dissemination of that information.

Threats to Confidentiality and E-Government Vulnerabilities

Although intercept of transmissions between e-government facilities and user entities can be employed to achieve unauthorized disclosure of information, adversaries more commonly employ legitimate access facilities to gain unauthorized access to information (e.g., Internet connections, electronic mail, self-service kiosks and terminals, simputers[2] and other wireless devices). The adversaries can employ a variety of means to defeat system identification, authentication, filtering, and authorization mechanisms (e.g., legitimate messages that contain malicious code enclosures, password dictionary attacks, transmission of protocol messages or other control function sequences) to access information stored in government devices or alter (change or add to) address information and misdirect information transfers. The more flexible and user-friendly the e-government service, the more opportunities are usually presented to adversaries. For example, use of connectionless protocols (e.g., UDP) eliminates most effective firewall configuration options. Penetration of an e-government security perimeter often gives adversaries extensive opportunities to browse confidential, private, or proprietary files.

Impacts or Consequences of Unauthorized Exposure

The consequences of unauthorized exposure of information via e-government resources depend in large part on the specific information that is exposed.

Loss of Confidence in Institutions and Service Delivery Mechanisms

Public disclosure of e-government confidentiality breaches can result in loss of public confidence in e-government mechanisms and in the institutions that they serve. The future of e-government will be determined in large part by public acceptance of e-government mechanisms as a dependable approach to doing business with governments.

Impacts on Operations

Impacts of confidentiality breaches on government operations can include disruption of ongoing plans and operations, legal actions against government organizations, financial impacts on the public, or even public safety consequences. The U.S. National Institute for Standards and Technology's *Guide for Mapping Types of Information and Information Systems to Security Categories* (Barker & Lee, 2004) describes the impacts or consequences of unauthorized disclosure of 145 types of U.S. government information. It also identifies Executive Orders, Executive Directives, and federal laws mandating protection for various confidential, private, and proprietary information types. Probably the most damaging breach of confidentiality is unauthorized access to cryptographic variable information that would permit an adversary to pose as a legitimate user who is authorized access to sensitive or critical information (including transaction data).

Legal Issues

Government institutions are bound by law to protect confidential, private, and proprietary information from unauthorized disclosure. Consequences for government personnel can range from reprimand to fine and imprisonment, depending on the nature of the information that is disclosed and the degree to which the compromise is willful or negligent. Particularly, in the case of e-government transactions and service delivery, the legal consequences for government institutions can include breaches of contract and other bases for recovery from the government of compensatory and punitive damages.

[2] The simputer is a low-cost personal computer with multiple connectivity options; see dmoz.org/Computers/Systems/Handhelds/Open_Source/Simputer/

SECURITY MEASURES FOR E-GOVERNMENT

Mechanisms and Techniques

Security mechanisms and techniques for countering availability, integrity, and confidentiality threats are described in detail in Parts 2 and 3 of this volume. The countermeasures information provided in this chapter focuses on e-government-specific considerations for application of security mechanisms and techniques.

Availability

Availability assurance features can include design characteristics (e.g., component or path redundancy, survivable design, isolation of resources), policy and procedural characteristics (e.g., access control policies, system certification and acceptance plans and procedures, recovery and continuity plans, data and program back-ups), and access mechanisms (e.g., reliable communications protocols, identification and authentication mechanisms). E-government mission requirements limit the application of some of these assurance features. For example, because public access is central to the purpose of e-government systems, physical isolation (e.g., of kiosk or terminal devices) and logical isolation of e-government assets must necessarily be limited. Use of surveillance devices and physical hardening and alarming of terminal logic components may be possible to raise the levels of difficulty and risk associated with unauthorized installation of mechanisms to capture key strokes or information in electromagnetic form within the terminal. However, significant residual risk is probably unavoidable. Terminal penetration can permit an adversary to bring down a system to which it connects and even use that system's interfaces to launch denial of service attacks against other systems. Similarly, ease of use is a major consideration for e-government applications. This includes ease of sign-on, user-friendly interfaces (graphical user interfaces), and support for a broad range of Web page development and support and mission-support applications. In the world of Web-based network services, the same properties that support user-friendly interfaces and a multiplicity of applications tend to offer more opportunities for penetration of the system and complicate security analysis beyond the point at which reasonable assurance can be achieved. As an example, network protocols necessary to support some widely used database management applications must be connectionless, thus preventing secure configuration of firewalls (see earlier section, Protocol and Operating System Mechanisms).

Integrity

Integrity mechanisms can include operating system-based (see chapter of this *Handbook*, "Operating System Security"), protocol based (see chapter of this *Handbook*, "Firewall Basics"), or cryptographically based mechanisms.

Protocol and Operating System Mechanisms

Firewalls are front-end processors that employ primarily protocol-based screening mechanisms to protect internal systems and networks that may contain sensitive or critical information from exploitation from external sources (e.g., from Web servers accessible by the public). A primer on firewalls is provided by chapter of this *Handbook*, "Firewall Basics."

Operating system–based access control mechanisms are employed to protect e-government components outside the firewall(s) from modifications that alter either their content or their functionality. They are also used to protect the firewalls themselves from exploitation and components on internal networks from insider threats (including from unauthorized "back-end" connections to external networks or the public switched telephone network). Too often, security configuration of components outside the firewall is given insufficient attention. A number of highly embarrassing, and even damaging, unauthorized modifications to e-government publications and processes have resulted.

Ideally, processors employed to provide e-government services should have been evaluated as conforming to at least the EAL-4 level of the *Common Criteria* (CC).[3] However, most government agencies are required to employ commercial off-the-shelf (COTS) computer and communications components. It is commercial practice to modify systems regularly and replace current systems with new "improved" versions. Patches to software are constantly being made available to correct flaws or enhance capabilities. In this COTS environment, it is proving extremely difficult to maintain security configuration control. An initial CC rating (e.g., EAL-4) can mean little once the system has been patched or upgraded. Regression testing to ensure that critical security properties of systems have not been impaired can mitigate this problem.

Cryptographic Mechanisms

Digital signature (see chapter of this *Handbook*, "Digital Signatures and Electronic Signatures") and message authentication are the most commonly employed cryptographic integrity protection mechanisms. Time stamping and establishing a reliable chain of trust for the public key certificates used in digital signatures are also critical elements for providing nonrepudiation services. Public key systems rely on a chain of trust for source authentication of PKI (public key infrastructure) certificates that are used to distribute public keys (Federal Public Key Infrastructure Steering Committee, 2000). Although a PKI[4] has been developed by and is becoming standardized within the federal government, many government agencies currently contract public key management for nonnational security systems from the private sector. In this case, federal certificates that are used to transport the public keys employed to check the validity of digital signatures are generated and signed by a certification authority that is a private company. In addition, the private keys that are used to sign information (to provide source authentication and data content integrity) are also generated by, known by, and distributed by the private sector. In some cases, agencies generate the private keys and public key certificates employed within their own agencies. There is currently no common public key management system in use within the Federal government and no common chain of trust for e-government.

A complicating factor for e-government is maintenance and use of certificate revocation lists (CRLs). A CRL is a list of revoked public key certificates created and digitally signed by a certification authority. Policies and procedures regarding high-integrity distribution of notices listing revoked certificates in e-government applications are needed to achieve the level of assurance necessary to support high-value and mission-critical transactions and services delivery functions.

Currently, quantum computing (West, 2000) is in the early stages of research and development. However, if large-scale quantum computing becomes available, public key methods in current use are likely to become obsolete. Message authentication encoding based on symmetric key (secret key) cryptography will remain viable. However, distribution and management of secret keys for authenticating information is problematic, and message authentication alone does not provide the full range of digital signature services. Furthermore, there is no current infrastructure to support key notarization and other measures that would be necessary to replace public key cryptography-based digital signature. Also, there is no symmetric key infrastructure for unclassified government operations. Integrity of e-government transactions is likely to remain dependent on the security of PKI for the foreseeable future.

A final issue affecting employment of cryptographic integrity mechanisms in U.S. E-government is availability, use, and interoperability of mechanisms that meet federal standards. Federal agencies are legally bound to employ only government-approved cryptography. In the cases of unclassified systems, approved algorithms are the digital signature algorithm (DSA), the Rivest, Shamir, and Adelman (RSA) algorithm (American National Standards Institute [ANSI], 1998a), and elliptic curve DSA (ECDSA; ANSI, 1998b) as specified in the *Digital Signature Standard (DSS)*.[5] Minimum key sizes approved through the year 2010 are 1024-bit DSA, 1024-bit RSA, and 160-bit ECDSA. After 2010, 2048-bit RSA and DSA and 224-bit ECDSA will be the minima. Hash functions used in e-government digital signature processes must conform to the NIST *Secure Hash Standard* (NIST, 2002). After 2010, the 160-bit secure hash algorithm 1 (SHA-1) hash function may no longer be used in digital signatures to protect U.S. government information. It is incumbent on e-government service providers to ensure that digital signature mechanisms conform to these standards and that plans accommodate transition to the higher assurance requirements that will be in force after 2010.[6] In the case of message authentication encoding, either the triple data encryption algorithm (TDEA; Barker 2004) or the advanced encryption standard (AES) may be used, and encoding schemes employed in U.S. e-government

[3] *Common Criteria for IT Security Evaluation (CC).* Retrieved from http://csrc.nist.gov/cc/

[4] See chapter of this handbook, "PKI (Public Key Infrastructure)."

[5] Soon to be superceded by FIPS 186-3, same title.

[6] Note that SP 800-57 will require still larger key sizes after the year 2030.

operations must conform to NIST's *Recommendation for Block Cipher Modes of Operation* (Gasser, 2004).

Confidentiality and Privacy

Access to e-government information and processes is dependent primarily on the identification and authentication processes that support e-government access control mechanisms (see Availability earlier in this section). If e-government information is intercepted in transit, or accessed in storage (e.g., following penetration of system access control mechanisms), it can still be protected by encryption. (See Volume II, Part 3: "Foundations of Information, Computer, and Network Security.")

Encryption is necessary to protect confidential information that is subject to intercept or access while stored or being processed in e-government systems.

Protocol and Operating System Mechanisms

Because e-government facilities generally need to be accessible by the general public to fulfill their missions, they are subject to a broad range of hacking and other penetration attacks. Front-end security processors (e.g., firewalls, screening routers as described in chapters "Digital Signatures and Electronic Signatures", "E-mail Security", "Security for ATM Networks", and "VPN Basics", of this *Handbook*) can be used to isolate those elements of e-government facilities that are publicly accessible from those that contain confidential, private, or proprietary information. These mechanisms separate internal government networks from publicly accessible e-government facilities. They can provide identification and authentication functions, access control functions, limit the protocols that are accepted (thus limiting adversaries' opportunities to tunnel into system compartments that contain confidential information). As noted in earlier, (see Availability), there tends to be an inverse relationship between flexibility and ease of use on one hand and strength of security mechanism on the other. U.S. e-government systems should conform to *Guidelines on Firewalls and Firewall Policy* (Wack, Cutler, & Pole, 2002).

Operating system-based access control mechanisms are employed to protect e-government components outside the firewall(s) from disclosure of configuration information or other information that can assist an adversary in making modifications that alter either the content or functionality of these components. Similarly, operating system–based access control mechanisms are employed to protect the confidentiality of government systems inside the firewall (as discussed earlier; see Protocol and Operating System Mechanisms).

Cryptographic Mechanisms

Several factors complicate encryption of e-government information. First, public key (asymmetric) cryptography is sufficiently computation-intensive that encryption of large volumes of data, or of data where high throughput is required, is undesirable. Second, because of threats of exposure over time and limitations on the volume of data that should be encrypted under a single key, encrypted information needs to be decrypted, then reencrypted under a different key. This is excessively expensive for large databases. Third, protection of secret keying material in a publicly accessible system is technically challenging. Finally, there is no common government symmetric key management infrastructure for unclassified systems.

As in the case of digital signatures, the encryption algorithms employed in e-government must be government-approved. Currently, only TDEA and AES are approved for encryption of U.S. government information. Encryption schemes employed in U.S. e-government operations must conform to NIST's *Recommendation for Block Cipher Modes of Operation*.[23] Through the year 2010, either two-key TDEA or three-key TDEA may be used (see NIST's *Recommendation for the Triple Data Encryption Algorithm (TDEA) Block Cipher*, Special Publication 800-67). After 2010, only three-key TDEA may be used; and after 2030, TDEA may no longer be used for protection of U.S. e-government information.[18] To avoid transition problems, use of AES rather than TDEA may be prudent.

Database Design

Some e-government services include provision of data that are derived from aggregation or analysis of information that is subject by law to privacy protection, are proprietary, or for which confidentiality must otherwise be maintained (e.g., provision of statistical information based on Privacy Act–protected data). A number of database design and management approaches have been developed to address this problem (e.g., *A Near-Term Design for the SeaView Multilevel Database System* (Lunt, 1998). This continues to be an active research topic.[7]

Implementation and Management

Interdependency of Measures/Mechanisms

Significant interdependency exists among the various countermeasures that may be employed to mitigate e-government security concerns. At the level of individual security mechanisms, computer security mechanisms (e.g., firewall and operating system[8] access control mechanisms) may play a role in protecting secret or private keys. At the same time, cryptographic processes used by authentication elements of access control mechanisms may employ one or more of the secret or private keys. At a "system of systems" level, source and data content integrity may depend on the aggregate performance and security of a private sector PKI certificate authority, an Internet service provider, the configuration of the e-government server that manages interactions with the public, the design and configuration of the firewall between the e-government server and the government processors inside the security perimeter, and the design and configuration of those internal government processors that process confidential or private information. Security of e-government systems is a total systems problem, and managers responsible for system security must address the adequacy of security

[7] See archive.infopeace.de/msg02567.html

[8] See the discussions of operating system security found in chapters "The Common Criteria", "Internal Security Threats", "Physical Security Threats", "Fixed-Line Telephone System Vulnerabilities", "E-Mail Threats and Vulnerabilities", "E-Commerce Vulnerabilities", "Hacking Techniques in Wired Networks", and "Hacking Techniques in Wireless Networks".

features and assurances associated with each subsystem and component mechanism.

Program Requirements

The Federal Information Security Management Act of 2002, the Paperwork Reduction Act of 1995, and the Information Technology Management Reform Act of 1996 (Clinger–Cohen Act), explicitly emphasize a risk-based policy for cost-effective security. In support of and reinforcing this legislation, the OMB through Circular A-130, Appendix III, *Security of Federal Automated Information Resources*, requires executive agencies[9] within the federal government to

- *plan* for security;
- *ensure* that appropriate officials are assigned security responsibility;
- *review* the security controls in their information systems; and
- *authorize* system processing prior to operations and periodically thereafter.

These management responsibilities presume that responsible government officials understand the risks and other factors that could adversely affect their missions. Moreover, these officials must understand the current status of their security programs and the security controls planned or in place to protect their information and information systems to make informed judgments and investments that appropriately mitigate risk to an acceptable level. The ultimate objective is to conduct the day-to-day operations of the agency and to accomplish the agency's stated missions with what OMB Circular A-130, Appendix III, defines as *adequate security*, or security commensurate with risk, including the magnitude of harm resulting from the unauthorized access, use, disclosure, disruption, modification, or destruction of information.

Policies, Procedures, and Infrastructures

E-government systems must establish security policies and procedures that address the access rights of the public, requirements for protection of the privacy of its users, requirements for protection of the confidentiality of government information contained in e-government systems and government systems connected to those systems, necessary service assurances, integrity and nonrepudiation requirements, and the laws and federal regulations on which these requirements are based. Systems managers must also establish operating procedures that permit compliance with these policies while satisfying e-government mission requirements. Finally, e-government managers must identify or establish the necessary processing, communications, and security (e.g., key management) infrastructures necessary to implement system policies and procedures.

Certification and Accreditation

As stated in the *Guide for the Security Certification and Accreditation of Federal Information Systems* (Johnson, Katzke, Ross, Stoneburner, & Swanson, 2004), the E-Government Act requires each federal agency to develop, document, and implement an agencywide information security program to provide information security for the information and information systems that support the operations and assets of the agency. An e-government information security program must include

- periodic assessments of risk, including the magnitude of harm that could result from the unauthorized access, use, disclosure, disruption, modification, or destruction of information and information systems that support the operations and assets of the agency;
- policies and procedures that are based on risk assessments, cost-effectively reduce information security risks to an acceptable level, and ensure that information security is addressed throughout the life cycle of each agency information system;
- subordinate plans for providing adequate information security for networks, facilities, information systems, or groups of information systems, as appropriate;
- security awareness training to inform personnel (including contractors and other users of information systems that support the operations and assets of the agency) of the information security risks associated with their activities and their responsibilities in complying with agency policies and procedures designed to reduce these risks;
- periodic testing and evaluation of the effectiveness of information security policies, procedures, practices, and security controls[10] to be performed with a frequency depending on risk, but no less than annually;
- a process for planning, implementing, evaluating, and documenting remedial actions to address any deficiencies in the information security policies, procedures, and practices of the agency;
- procedures for detecting, reporting, and responding to security incidents; and
- plans and procedures to ensure continuity of operations for information systems that support the operations and assets of the agency.

It is essential that e-government officials have the most complete, accurate, and trustworthy information possible on the security status of their information systems to make timely, credible, risk-based decisions on whether to authorize operation of those systems. The information and supporting evidence needed for security accreditation is developed during a detailed security review of an information system, typically referred to as security *certification*. The results of a security certification are used to reassess the risks and update the system security plan, thus providing the factual basis for an authorizing official

[9] An executive agency is (a) an Executive Department specified in 5 U.S.C., Section 101; (b) a Military Department specified in 5 U.S.C., Section 102; (c) an independent establishment as defined in 5 U.S.C., Section 104(1); and (d) a wholly owned government corporation fully subject to the provisions of 31 U.S.C., Chapter 91.

[10] Security controls are the management, operational, and technical controls (i.e., safeguards or countermeasures) prescribed for an information system to protect the confidentiality, integrity, and availability of the system and its information.

to render a security accreditation decision. Security accreditation is the official management decision given by a senior agency official to authorize operation of an information system and to accept explicitly the risk to agency operations, agency assets, or individuals based on the implementation of an agreed-on set of security controls.[29]

SUMMARY

E-government shows great promise for use of improved Internet-based technology to make it easier for citizens and businesses to interact with the government, save taxpayer dollars, and streamline citizen-to-government communications. With these potential benefits come real risks to the privacy of information provided by citizens and businesses, to the confidentiality of government information contained in e-government systems and systems connected to e-government systems, to the long-term availability of records stored only in electronic form by the government, and to the integrity of citizen-to-government transactions and government-to-citizen delivery of services. These risks are based on intrinsic technical characteristics of storage and processing systems, on the potential for accidents or system faults, and on the attractiveness of e-government systems as a target for malicious activity. A variety of countermeasures are available to mitigate these risks (e.g., fault-tolerant design, disaster recovery procedures, information backups, access control logic in front-end processors and e-government service systems, digital signature for transactions, encryption of sensitive information, and database design and management that permit use of privacy-protected data without divulging the privacy-protected elements to unauthorized sources. Law requires that the security mechanisms conform to federal standards and be evaluated in accordance with a federally mandated certification and accreditation process prior to the e-government systems being placed into operation. These policy requirements, together with the projected consequences of loss of public confidence in both e-government and government institutions in general, suggest that the process of converting paper-based services to e-government services cannot be accomplished without careful planning and systems-based oversight.

GLOSSARY

Asymmetric In the context of cryptography, a type of cryptographic system in which a participant publishes an encryption key and keeps private a separate decryption key. These keys are respectively referred to as public and private. RSA and D–H are examples of asymmetric systems. *Asymmetric* is synonymous with *public key*.

Authentication A process that establishes the origin of information or determines an entity's identity.

Availability The property of ensuring timely and reliable access to and use of information.

Confidentiality Preservation of authorized restrictions on access and disclosure, including means for protecting personal privacy and proprietary information.

Cryptography The discipline that embodies principles, means, and methods for the transformation of data to hide its information content, prevent its undetected modification, or prevent its unauthorized use.

Digital Signature The results of a cryptographic transformation of data that, when properly implemented, provides the services of origin, authentication, data integrity, and signer nonrepudiation.

Encryption The process of rendering a message (a *plaintext*) into a data string (a *ciphertext*) with the aim of transmitting it privately in a potentially hostile environment.

Integrity Guarding against improper information modification or destruction, which includes ensuring information nonrepudiation and authenticity.

Interactive Processing Service that permits private citizens or other user entities to read instructions published on agency Web sites and to follow those instructions to submit reports, applications, or other service requests.

Nonrepudiation A service that is used to provide assurance of the integrity and origin of data in such a way that the integrity and origin can be verified by a third party as having originated from a specific entity in possession of the private key of the claimed signatory.

Privacy Protection against disclosure of personal information in violation of laws and regulations restricting the dissemination of information.

Private Key In an asymmetric or public-key cryptosystem, the key that a communicating party holds privately and uses for decryption or completion of a key exchange.

Public Key In an asymmetric or public-key cryptosystem, the key that a communicating party disseminates publicly.

Publishing As used in this chapter, posting information on a publicly accessible Web site.

Secret Key A cryptographic key that is used with a symmetric cryptographic algorithm that is uniquely associated with one or more entities and is not made public.

Service Delivery Actual execution of actions approved on the basis of e-government interactions (e.g., acceptance of credit card payments or electronic funds transfers, execution of government payments by electronic fund transfers, and delivery of licenses or permits).

Symmetric In the context of cryptography, a cryptographic algorithm that uses one shared key, a secret key.

Transaction Processing Processing of information submitted via interactive e-government Web sites, providing notification of approval for actions to be taken on the basis of that information and activation of implementation processes. Transaction processing generally involves distributing data received from users to multiple databases and multiple processes and includes interactions with third parties.

CROSS REFERENCES

See *Computer and Network Authentication; Digital Signatures and Electronic Signatures; E-Government; Encryption Basics; International Security Issues of E-Government; Internet Basics; Legal, Social, and Ethical Issues of the*

Internet; Password Authentication; Privacy Law and the Internet.

REFERENCES

American National Standards Institute. (1998a). *Digital signatures using reversible public key cryptography for the financial services industry* (ANSI X9.31-1998).

American National Standards Institute. (1998b). *Public key cryptography for the financial services industry: The elliptic curve digital signature algorithm (ECDSA)* (ANSI X9.62-1998).

Barker, E., Barker, W., Burr, W., Polk, W., Smid, M., & Zeigler, L. (2004). *Recommendation for key management* [draft] (Special Publication 800-57). National Institute of Standards and Technology. Retrieved from http://csrc.nist.gov/CryptoToolkit/tkkeymgmt.html July 2004.

Barker, W. (2004). *Recommendation for the triple data encryption algorithm (TDEA) block cipher*. National Institute of Standards and Technology. Retrieved from http://csrc.nist.gov/publications/nistpubs/800-67/SP800-67.pdf July 2004.

Barker, W., & Lee, A. (2004). *Guide for mapping types of information and information systems to security categories* (Special Publication 800-60). National Institute of Standards and Technology.

CERT Coordination Center. (n.d.). *Denial of service attacks*. Retrieved from http://www.cert.org/tech_tips/denial_of_service.html July 2004.

Common Criteria Project. (2004). *Common criteria for information technology security evaluation*, version 2.2. Retrieved from http://www.commoncriteriaportal.org/public/files/ccpart1v2.2.pdf July 2004.

Denial of Service Database. Retrieved from http://www.attrition.org/security/denial/ July 2004.

Dittrich, D. (2004). *Distributed denial of service (DDoS) attacks/tools*. University of Washington. Retrieved from http://staff.washington.edu/dittrich/misc/ddos/ July 2004.

E-Government Act of 2002. Title III, Federal Information Security Management Act (FISMA), Pub. L. No. 107-347 (2002). Retrieved from http://thomas.loc.gov/bss/d107/d107laws.html July 2004.

Federal Public Key Infrastructure Steering Committee, Federal Chief Information Officers Council. (2000). *The evolving federal public key infrastructure*. Retrieved from http://www.cio.gov/fpkisc/library/pkireport053100.doc July 2004.

Gasser, M. (2004). *Recommendation for block cipher modes of operation* (Special Publication 800-38). National Institute of Standards and Technology. Retrieved from http://csrc.nist.gov/publications/ August 2004.

Government Paperwork Elimination Act. Title XVII, Pub. L. No. 105-277 (1998).

Information Technology Management Reform Act (Clinger–Cohen), Title LI. Pub. L. No. 104-106 (1996).

Johnson, A., Katzke, S., Ross, R., Stoneburner, G., & Swanson, M. (2004, May). *Guide for the security certification and accreditation of federal information systems* (Special Publication 800-37). National Institute of Standards and Technology. Retrieved from http://csrc.nist.gov/publications/nistpubs/800-37/SP800-37-final.pdf July 2004.

Lunt, T. (1988, May). *A near-term design for the SeaView multilevel database system*. Presented at the Institute for Electrical and Electronic Engineers Symposium on Security and Privacy, Oakland, CA.

Martin, J.-P. (2004). *Bibliography on Byzantine fault independence*. Austin: University of Texas. Retrieved from http://www.cs.utexas.edu/users/jpmartin/bib/bibReliability.html July 2004.

National Institute of Standards and Technology, Center for High Integrity Software systems Assurance. (1995). *A conceptual framework for systems fault tolerance*. Retrieved from http://hissa.ncsl.nist.gov/chissa/SEI_Framework/framework_1.html July 2004.

National Institute of Standards and Technology. (2000, January 27). *Digital signature standard (DSS)* (FIPS 186-2). Retrieved from http://csrc.nist.gov/publications/fips/fips186-2/fips186-2-change1.pdf July 2004.

National Institute of Standards and Technology. (2001, November 26). *The advanced encryption standard* (FIPS 197). Retrieved from http://csrc.nist.gov/publications/fips/fips197/fips-197.pdf July 2004.

National Institute of Standards and Technology. (2002, August). *Secure hash standard* (FIPS 180-2). Retrieved from http://csrc.nist.gov/publications/fips/fips180-2/fips180-2withchangenotice.pdf July 2004.

Sullivan, G. F. (1996). *Selected bibliography of fault-tolerant computing at Hopkins*. Baltimore, MD: Johns Hopkins University. Retrieved from http://www.cs.jhu.edu/~sullivan/ftbiblio.html September 2004.

U.S. Congress, Office of Technology Assessment. (1993). *Protecting privacy in computerized medical information* (OTA-TCT-576). Washington, DC: U.S. Government Printing Office.

Wack, J., Cutler, K., & Pole, J. (2002, January). *Guidelines on firewalls and firewall policy* (Special Publication 800-41). National Institute of Standards and Technology. Retrieved from http://csrc.nist.gov/publications/nistpubs/ 800-41/sp800-41.pdf July 2004.

West, J. (2000). *The quantum computer.* Pasadena: Computer Sciences at California Institute of Technology. Retrieved from http://www.cs.caltech.edu/~westside/quantum-intro.html September 2004.

World Bank Group. (n.d.). A definition of e*government. Retrieved from http://www1.worldbank.org/publicsector/egov/definition.htm July 2004.

International Security Issues of E-Government

Karin Geiselhart, *University of Canberra* and *Australian National University Canberra, Australia*

INTRODUCTION

The previous chapter in this *Handbook* documents the rise of e-government and its transformative effects. The digital representation of government activities leads to a wider spread of information and decision making, both vertically and laterally. This challenges hierarchical bureaucratic procedures and established agency roles. Responses include requirements to make key documents available electronically and the development of standards for electronic consultation, or e-rule making. This effect is apparent at every level of government, from the smallest local council to the largest nation state. At the same time, the issues governments deal with are also outgrowing traditional boundaries. Sometimes the issue expands outward, as when a regional government builds a dam that decreases the water flow to neighbors. Other times issues are imposed inward, for example if decisions made in another country affect the price of a local product.

E-government is evolving to deal with transborder issues. Government responses to these supranational issues become an element in emerging forms of global governance, but it cannot be assumed that the emerging systems will serve democratic goals. It is not even clear what global forms of democracy might mean or what they might 'look like' for citizens. It is, however, certain that patterns of digital representation and decision making will impact on the overall security of peoples in today's very insecure climate. Increasingly, the security and accuracy of the information being shared globally underpins the effectiveness of governmental response, and thus affects citizen safety. This applies to a myriad of socio-political-scientific issues, from climate change to terrorism to new disease vectors.

This chapter considers the overall context in which e-government is evolving and the importance of both administrative and democratic accountabilities. It then considers some issues for which information management and security cannot be contained within national borders. These include the global information infrastructure itself, which may be thought of as a global information "commons." Global e-governance is the complex of administrative, technical, and policy arrangements that collectively form a default pattern of governance on a particular international issue. The electronic representation is embedded in the human systems that give rise to them. Transborder issues are generally subject to different constraints than are localized issues and information. The role of nongovernment players in international information arenas is outlined, along with their influence on both physical and informational security with illustrative examples from particular areas of concern. Lastly, suggestions are offered for research and modeling global e-governance as a complex adaptive system. This issue is inherently transdisciplinary and is informed by a large body of work on complex adaptive systems in human behavior.

E-GOVERNMENT EVOLUTION

From local councils through state legislatures and national programs, electronic efficiencies are altering the pace and processes of government. Typically, electronic government addresses services, administrative procedures, and transactions. A current analysis of digital government (Pavlichev & Garson, 2004) documents the issues and current state of play of digital government at the national level and some of the aspects that overflow into international dimensions. The previous chapter in this *Handbook* describes the stages of digital government from information presentation through seamless access across agencies. Much of the literature on e-government focuses on the United States or may only consider local, state, and national governments. Writers on international relations, technology, and global governance, on the other hand, may not concern themselves with the digital representation of these issues. The extension of e-government to the international sphere is, however, the subject of much speculation, and the focus of this chapter. Both the administrative and democratic dimensions of emerging forms of international e-government are relevant to global information management and security.

Technology and the State

It is common to view information technology in government as an advanced expression of technocratic efficiency. However, information system design, management, and funding are also an expression of their socio-political-economic context. In a study of U.S. government information policies, Hernon and McClure (1993) found there was inadequate public involvement in this area, although it often involved fundamental issues about how society operates and the role of government. Not surprisingly, they found overlapping impacts, fragmentation, and difficulties of categorization in complex areas. There is a gulf between the theory of wide public involvement as a democratic ideal and the practice of e-government development.

Inevitably, information systems serve the political, economic, and social systems that fund them. Beniger (1986) showed the importance of information in all forms of evolution and control, including biological evolution. Feenberg (1991) provided a critical theory of technology and revealed how the democratizing potential of information technology makes it a site for ongoing power struggles. Sclove (1995) considered the need to embed democratic assumptions in technology design. Zuboff's (1988) concept of "informating" within organizations provided an adaptive learning element, which leads to complexity theory and the developmental role of democracy and policy. A key assertion of this chapter is that information and communication systems need to be considered as manifestations of governance. The implications compound when comparing information systems across national boundaries.

Current Dimensions and Limitations of E-Government

This section considers the dominant focus of digital government at the national level as a basis for extrapolation to the international level. From local councils to national agencies, governments have focused their technology efforts on service delivery and information provision. There has been less emphasis on citizen communications with government, input into policy making, or citizen-to-citizen communications. This trend has been identified in a survey of member nations of the Organisation of Economic Cooperation and Development (OECD; Gualtieri, 1998), at local government level in the United States (Musso, Weare, & Hale, 2000), and within agencies of the Australian government (Geiselhart, 1999). Because these patterns are observable at different scales, they may be seen as fractal. If supported by data and modeling, this insight from the field of complex adaptive systems could assist in the analysis of global technology systems and patterns. The possibility of modeling governance from a normative democratic perspective suggests how the linkages between local and global activities might be integrated. While commonplace for physical data such as climate, this has not yet been fully explored in the human sciences.

The study of information technology in government has tended to focus on developed democratic states, partly because they have been the trend setters that other nations emulate as they implement digital procedures. The United Nations provides a statistical index of e-government for member states based on infrastructure and access (see http://www.unpan.org/egovernment2.asp) but does not go into qualitative detail of information on governance in relation to transparency or online citizen engagement. Most analyses have an implicit understanding that electronic applications will support democracy as the more privileged nations understand that term. This assumption is questionable, however, as specific examples throughout this chapter illustrate. The World Bank, among others, is exploring the potential of new communication technologies to assist in democratic reform. One hypothesis of this chapter is that global information and physical security will be supported most effectively by emerging forms of global e-governance that facilitate digital equity and minimize democratic deficits within and between nations. A second hypothesis is that the patterns of technology use are determined by the values of the stakeholders, and these may not always favor wider social stability or equity. In a system driven by the values of the actors and the rules for their interaction, the patterns will reflect the overall democratic information 'value chain,' and highlight the weak links as gaps in transparency and accountability. The value chain, as in business applications, consists of the linkages and transferrals of goods and data between intermediaries. For democratic information purposes, this chain contains data but not goods, although it might also consist of services, such as monitoring and evaluation. It is truly a value chain, as every link gives actors options for passing along or withholding information. The degree to which all stakeholders are included also forms part of the pattern. For example, Clover (2004) argues that in most nations fishing policy caters to a relatively small industry, without mechanisms for including the public interest.

Branscomb (1994) identified at least four types of information needed by governments and their citizens: to fulfill voting obligations; to comply with legislative and judicial decisions; to be informed about environmental, welfare, medical, and other developments; and to manage government tasks effectively, for example, census and economic data. She noted that in meeting these requirements, governments must juggle their accountabilities to operate cost-effectively, maintain maximum access, and also encourage private sector development. A report by Accenture (2004) identifies five trends in e-government, including tangible savings, improved take-up by citizens, a continuing challenge of integration, and gradual personalization of online services. Neither of these catalogues adequately capture the need for democratic accountabilities in information management.

Information technology has been an important focus for public sector reform, both for the instrumental collection and processing of information and for the government's developmental obligations to promote participation by an informed citizenry. A client focus together with web technologies have vastly increased the amount of information available to the public. The pursuit of cost-effectiveness has also encouraged electronic access. Pressures for the cost recovery of information create inevitable trade-offs between equity and efficiency. At every stage of the policy process—agenda setting, planning, implementation, and evaluation—information is a key ingredient. International standards for electronic data interchange have, with some struggle, gradually evolved for greater interoperability. But similar standards for democratic transparency of data and information access remain a battleground both within and across jurisdictions. Political globalization increases the pressures for harmonization of data flows on matters of democratic interest and public concern.

Localized Accountabilities of E-Government

Not all aspects of e-government have international ramifications. Some issues for governments can be understood and managed with reference primarily to their own jurisdiction. At the most local level, this includes rates, services such as schools and garbage collection, planning, and development. Fully responsive local governments also promote cultural activities, heritage awareness and protection, responsible business growth, and environmental sustainability. When local e-government works well, these matters are represented transparently on a web site, with provision for citizens to engage with each other and their government. This helps to complete the loop by providing ongoing feedback. It can also provide a higher level accountability by ensuring that policies are effective. Early steam engines had a "governor" that kept the engine from exploding by keeping its function within the norms needed to run efficiently. E-rule making can avoid the worst of bad policy decisions by offering a normative and iterative "governor" to stabilize government activities. A carefully planned approach to citizen consultation, supported by appropriate use of digital communications, can help manage the democratic obligations of government. This pluralistic alternative to hierarchical decision making is described by Richard (2000). She elaborates on the ways a network model, actively enabled through appropriate digital techniques, can help achieve the transformative promise of e-government.

At a local or even regional level, achieving awareness and engagement is facilitated by geographic proximity to the issues. The site for a proposed toxic dump may be visited, and community discussion can take place casually. Corruption or nepotism may be difficult to conceal. These direct and analog sources of evidence provide a form of accountability for the information that is publicly presented. If people are getting sick or the roads are in bad repair, then those who provide data to the contrary can be questioned. The checks and balances can be immediate and provide a level of information security that is probably unsurpassable.

Problems of Scale for Information Accuracy and Security

Once the systems for information collection and display exceed what can be verified by the senses, a level of abstraction is necessary. Zuboff (1988) provided a powerful description of the changes technology brings to tasks that were previously capable of being physically monitored. Workers in a factory who could once go directly to a vat to see, hear, and smell its processes become dependent on gauges and displays to tell them what is happening. The abstractions of analog gauges are compounded by even purer digital representations.

For e-government, distance from both the sources of information and decisions about how it is represented become concerns for its verification. As the scope of government covers more territory, either encompassing more issues or over a wider area, the accuracy and integrity of the information can become attenuated, and therefore less secure.

Because government process is, virtually everywhere, underpinned by information, these issues of information security and integrity grow apace with the size of the government jurisdiction. The problems that scale poses for democracy as a particular form of government were raised by Dahl (1989), along with the possibilies of telecommunications in addressing these problems. The importance of democratic protocols to drive fractal patterns of technology governance was discussed in Geiselhart (1999). Figure 1 illustrates how fractal patterns can provide alternative systems of behavior. In the case of the famous Lorenz attractor, it is the weather system, but similar analyses have been provided for human systems of government (for example, Kiel, 1994).

For a complex adaptive system such as the weather, an attractor is a pattern that recurs with minor variations, such as wet winters. In human systems, all kinds of behaviours can settle into attractor patterns. From individual investment choices to mass movements of stock dumping, human behaviour can also display fractal patterns that repeat at several scales. Democratic attractors may be thought of as those that use negative or normative feedback loops to keep the system from spinning out of control, like a runaway thermostat. Sensitivity to the direction of change is a critical monitoring activity. A reasonable assumption for democratic process is that a dynamic of increasing inequality indicates a system moving further from democratic norms. This is because, given a level playing field of information and a fair voting process, most people would presumably not vote for benefits to flow from themselves. Managed and relatively stable inequality is assumed to be the "basin of attraction" for democratic systems.

Information management, in a broad sense that encompasses verification and communication, is analogous to the problem of infrastructure in a very large building. Bigger buildings, particularly very tall ones, require increasing amounts of resources and space devoted to

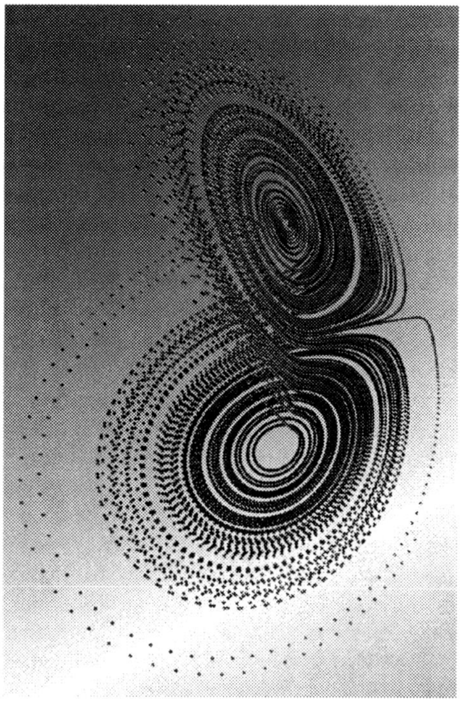

Figure 1: Lorenz Attractor, courtesy Paul Bourke, Centre for Astrophysics and Supercomputing, Swinburne University.

moving water, waste, energy, and people efficiently around the building. Likewise, as the size, scope, and scale of government expands, a proportionately large amount of resources are needed to ensure that the information necessary for good government is secure, accurate, useful, available, and democratically accountable. Of course, a dictatorship or a corrupt regime will not need to verify its information in the same way. For the purposes of this chapter, however, it is assumed that, at least theoretically, the goals of e-government aim to support democratic process. The next section outlines some of the factors affecting the management of the global information commons.

E-GOVERNMENT BEYOND NATIONAL BORDERS

Whether it involves buildings or information, efficient management has implications for both infrastructure and administration, which we may think of as a superstructure. For the global information infrastructure, it might be preferable for these to be determined on a practical basis, independent of political concerns. The realities of our globalized world mean, however, that inevitably, there will always be friction between the practical and the political. This leads to considerations of governance as a broad system of management, rather than government as a process of political control. This broader perspective also allows comparison and possibly modeling between government, nonprofit, and corporate systems.

The processes, possibilities, and problems accompanying e-government, as outlined in the previous section, do not recognize borders. Information has become central to exchanges between governments, as well as the currency of international commerce and communications. Global dynamics influence both the development of information technology and the evolution of e-government. Security in the broadest sense is now a key issue for all governments and is intimately entwined with the ways information is created, presented, distributed, and evaluated. It has become commonplace to think of the global information and communications infrastructure as a virtual neural system. This metaphor encourages consideration of the locus of control for this system. Unlike human neural networks, the networks of e-government do not access a centralized "brain."

Current manifestations of the overlap between international forms of governance and information security and management are the systems for protecting the information infrastructure. Groups such as the Communications-Electronics Security Group (http://www.cesg.gov.uk) in the United Kingdom, AusCERT in Australia, and the OECD Working Party on Information Security and Privacy (WPISP) represent high-level networks that bring together governments for collaboration and information sharing on key infrastructure security issues. Each national level group links to subnational groups and non-government players who communicate, negotiate, liaise, diffuse, and take responsibility for various aspects of information infrastructure security.

In Australia, the subnetwork is the Trusted Information Sharing Network for Critical Infrastructure Protection (TISN is at http://www.tisn.gov.au). TISN is a forum in which the owners and operators of critical infrastructure work together to share information on security issues which affect critical infrastructure. There are advisory groups for key industry sectors, such as banking, communications, emergency services, food chain, water services, etc. They share information on shared threats and vulnerabilities and appropriate measures and strategies to mitigate risk.

It is, in effect, a diffuse form of governance and management of the critical infrastructure. This infrastructure includes, but is not limited to, information. There is implicit acknowledgment that the wide range of security threats listed are linked through the information infrastructure and that defense of these assets and supplies is dependent on the quality of the information exchanges that monitor them.

Futher on this chapter outlines other international issues that are subject to similarly diffuse forms of management. In each case, their effective management is dependent on the governance arrangements for their information networks. Thus, management and security of information necessary for global citizenship is emerging as a form of governance in its own right, but without a unified or democratically accountable locus of control.

Taxation and Representation

One of the triggers of the American Revolution was colonists protesting against taxation without representation. In the 21st century, the protests come from both former colonies and nations who feel that their interests are not represented in international decision making and revenue gathering. Much consumer, citizen, and corporate activism is spurred by the lack of adequate participatory mechanisms. This presents an enormous challenge for all aspect of global e-governance. Clearly, the ability to amass revenue underpins the legitimacy and therefore also the sovereignty of governments everywhere. Perhaps less widely acknowledged is the way profit aggregation functions as a de facto form of taxation, particularly in trans-national contexts. Systems that allow information relevant to revenue collection to operate securely are as essential for international forms of governance as for existing governments. Corporations that amass and move enormous resources and revenues are increasingly subject to challenges to their legitimacy and calls for greater participation by those subject to their actions. Other dimensions of these twin issues of taxation and representation are discussed later in relation to information equity and the democratic deficit. The requirement for both resources and legitimacy is a key issue for all forms of information management, but particularly for those information security measures that are necessarily global in scope. Challenges of information governance are critical at all scales but are relatively uncharted waters for global issues.

E-Governance of Global Information Commons

At a global level, the telephone system and the Internet can only be managed through collaborative international effort. Short of a global empire or dictatorship, all nations are dependent on each other's good will to enable global communications. Global governance has been defined as "political management at the global level of a given area of human existence in the absence of global government" (Meyer & Stefanova, 2001).

This *Handbook* discusses the security aspects of these issues in depth. The routers and switches of the Internet are linked through an elaborate system of physical and administrative infrastructure. The human networks that manage the Internet include the Internet Engineering Task Force (IETF), but that is just the tip of the iceberg of organizations and agencies that develop and support the protocols that allow information to be transmitted securely. The domain name system of Internet addresses is managed by an international nonprofit corporation with appointed and elected members, the Internet Corporation for Assigned Names and Numbers (http://www.icann.org). Attempts to manage the global information commons multilaterally, for the good of all peoples, can be seen in the process for the World Summit for the Information Society, the WSIS (http://www.itu.int/wsis/).

In each of these examples, a set of players maps out agendas and actions. Even highly technical areas, such as mobile devices and protocols, have advocates of alternative approaches, standards, reporting mechanisms, and so on. The totality of infrastructure and networks for the establishment, maintenance, and accountability of a particular area constitute its governance. These may overlap, intersect, interfere, or conflict. Ultimately, however, all the pieces form a system, and it may be possible to map the overall patterns as an attractor. It may be functional in some ways and erratic in others, but the system altogether, changing and amorphous, makes up the global information commons. For democratic governance systems, the direction of change is as critical as the current state of the system. Identifying the patterns or attractors could aid predictability. It might be possible to see the outcomes of information systems with greater or less transparency and participation, by adjusting the number of nodes and rules for interaction between nodes.

The mutable networks that govern the global information commons have some resemblance to biological actors. For example, lawyers arguing about piracy may not be concerned about TCP, and the IETF may have little interest in intellectual property issues when they are developing wireless transmission protocols. Nonetheless, these separate groups might find themselves suddenly involved in negotiation over a common issue that involves all their expertise, such as identify theft. In such a case, a new network can appear, have a role, and fade away again. Although only some of the agencies or individuals might have a formal role, the cluster of actors becomes, at least for a time, an element in the global governance of the Internet. A recurrent theme is that governments are not always the key players in these patterns of global information management. As has been done for biological agents (see Kauffman, 2000), it should be possible to step back from these specifics to model the wider patterns through a normative democratic lens, and determine what outcomes result from existing rules and players.

Management of the collective set of infrastructure, resources and rules that comprises the global information systems is subject to the "tragedy of the commons." First described in relation to overgrazing of herding lands, this term refers to any resource in danger of being destroyed by undisciplined overuse and exploitation. Clover (2004) describes the impending collapse in many areas of fish stocks due to overfishing and the role of actors and governance structures (or rules) at many levels and globally. This issue dramatically illustrates how the failure of governance safeguards for the accuracy of the information, the integrity of the reporting systems and their transparency and accountability are major factors in tilting the system into unsustainability. The pattern formed by the not particularly democratic information value chain for this issue shows a sad but predictable tragedy of the commons in the making. Clover's solution includes the ultimate information-driven transparency: satellite monitoring over the Internet, live and public, of fishing boats. Transparency is a sine qua non of accountability, but cannot ensure it without other elements in the democratic information value chain.

Spam is a another example of a failure to manage part of the global information commons. The uncontrolled use of this marketing tool, most of it originating from the United States, illustrates the danger when information resources are not managed in the best interest of the widest group. This imposes costs on everyone, but particularly in a country such as Australia, which has volume-based Internet pricing. Intergovernmental arrangements for controlling this abuse are clearly inadequate, and individual businesses and consumers have little direct ability to influence their governments to enact stronger laws or interventions. Rather, a wide array of antispam activists, organizations, software solutions and networks at various levels and with varying degrees of formality have been set up to place control in the hands of users. Responses to spam show how power can seep into the gaps to create forms of management, action, and de facto governance where governments have proved inadequate.

Many information security issues are caught up in similar internationalized governance concerns. Legal matters such as identify theft, money laundering, and digital rights management (DRM) are dependent on the wide support of governments. Other aspects, such as standards and protocols for security architecture and products, require the cooperation of corporate players at least as much as governments. In the case of DRM, strong corporate lobbying on governments is countered by assertive activism by individuals and groups. Some elements, such as password protection and antivirus technology, cannot achieve widespread effectiveness unless individuals are adequately informed and motivated to take necessary precautions. The roles of nongovernment players in information security and management is expanded below.

Responsiveness, Monitoring, and Adaptation of Global Information

In addition to the difficulties of authenticating information, timeliness and quality of response also give rise to risk in a globalized world. These inadequacies have the potential to provide dysfunctional feedback patterns because power structures "circle the wagons" to deny or undermine attempts to learn from error. This deliberate political blindness to scientific information is a recurring theme in Clover's book on overfishing. A recent report from a coalition of nonprofit groups revealed that the U.S. government spent $6.5 billion in 2003 on preventing new documents from reaching the public domain. The report found that government secrecy is increasing and that secrecy between security agencies is stovepiping information, hindering the war on terrorism (Epstein, 2004).

A dynamic of diminishing access to information also makes it more difficult for the public to get the information people need to make their families safe from environmental hazards, such as the impact of toxic chemicals in the food chain. This is a direct example of information as security. Over the longer term, governance of information affects the capacity for reflectiveness and learning. If the ability to adapt is dampened, information can become not just less reliable, but dangerous. Governments that disguise risk from citizens soon find their legitimacy called into question, and these calls can come from both within and outside jurisdictional borders.

Skolnikoff (2001) outlined some of the pressures accompanying globalization that relate to technology and governance. He noted that domestic and international affairs are two parts of a whole. Governments have become ever more dependent on technology for their information, while the time for response has shrunk. Officials suffer from time scarcity, while the issues they must deal with have grown in scope and complexity. In this framework, they must make decisions which require urgent action, but whose consequences will be felt far into the future. Often the risks are high, and there may be multiple and perhaps disastrous unintended outcomes. Technical complexity of issues makes officials more dependent on specialists and experts and less able to communicate with their publics. Domestic agencies are drawn into international arenas, often inadequately prepared. Responses are caught up in bureaucratic entanglements with diplomatic offices, and cooperation with other states must be filtered through similar constraints within those nations. Skolnikoff predicted that greater autonomy may eventually be conceded to international organizations, driven by crises and system breakdowns.

Some of those who have been most successful in bypassing or undermining global security systems are the groups that are most able to mutate quickly and adapt to changed circumstances. These survival skills are as essential for legitimate regimes and industries as they are for biological viruses. For governments to survive, they need to adopt principles for information structuring, sharing, and security that mimic the most adept life forms. These approaches have been outlined in some detail for the corporate sector in relation to innovation (Tuomi, 2003) and also governmental and organizational adaptation (Kiel, 1994; Pascale, Millemann, & Gioja, 2000). These sources draw strongly on complex adaptive systems and nonlinearity as a new paradigm.

Consistency and Coordination of Global Information

The lack of uniform systems is one of the key features of information flows for international issues. Governments vary so greatly in their capacity to implement secure systems that consistency across nations is difficult to achieve. Coordination of systems suffers from not just technical discrepancies but human resource differences. Coordination is not easily outsourced to an international agency, for both practical and political reasons. A few high level institutions such as the World Bank, International Monetary Fund, and the United Nations have coordination roles, defined by their charter. Such institutions are limited by their bureaucratic distance from the individuals affected by the issues. Only a small subset of international agreements are truly enforceable, and these tend to be those relating to trade. Enforcement of the Kyoto Agreement on greenhouse emissions is limited, whereas the World Trade Organization and the World Intellectual Property Organization seem to have more potent enforcement mechanisms because strong stakeholders support them. As a result, WTO and WIPO agreements are more likely to have procedures for secure information documentation and storage and retrieval.

For most issues, there is no single global authority to direct or manage global information flows. Moreover, there is no direct representation of individuals' interests. Instead a plethora of amorphous and mutable institutions representing governments, corporations, clusters of organizations, and international entities all act on particular issues, often without coordination between them. Their lack of formal legitimacy and resources hampers their effectiveness. An example of great concern worldwide is cyber crime. Although many groups and levels of government have a strong interest in both defining and addressing cyber crime, a fully effective coordinated response is inhibited by the wide range of jurisdictions involved and the reticent cooperation of companies such as banks and Internet service providers (ISPs) to divulge commercial information or voluntarily bear associated costs. Furthermore, a government or jurisdiction that secures cooperation from its relevant industry sectors cannot guarantee that local solutions will be effective, as cyber crime, in its many manifestations described in this *Handbook*, is clearly an internationalized issue. As well as being a fundamental issue for information security and management, this problem overlaps with related areas, such as privacy, copyright protection, and electronic commerce. The tangle of approaches to this hydra-headed problem becomes, in effect, another imperfect governance system.

Citizens as well as governments incur blockages when dealing with issues that may affect them profoundly but lie beyond their legal entitlements. Hypothetically, how might a Malaysian obtain information about Indonesian plans to dump nuclear waste in common waters? There is no international provision for freedom of information, for example, to other countries. Citizens often have very limited rights to find out what is being planned, either by corporations or sometimes their own governments. This is one of many information black holes for issues that transcend national boundaries. Professor Alasdair Roberts's Web pages offer a starting point for international freedom of information issues, but there is a long way to go before freedom of information becomes a secure aspect of human rights in cyberspace. Pursuit of information generally has to go through often weaker international bodies with little enforcement capacity. There is little redress for nations, much less individual citizens. Nations can opt out of international agreements and treaties or simply not honor them. Enforcement depends on the cooperation of individual states, whereas within one country, standards for information, services, and reporting can be legislated on a national basis. Digital representation and interactivity also vary enormously among nations, reflecting an international digital divide based on another suite of infrastructure, skills, and attitudinal differences.

Under current arrangements for representation, the institutions for global governance are several links removed from citizen participation. Many countries also lack the democratic institutions and practices that foster effective participation. This has been observed in Asia, where lack of civil society structures delimits participation in the organization that manages the global Internet addressing system (Kang, 2003). However, even countries that rank well on Transparency International's assessments of corruption are subject to a democratic deficit, often in the form of more subtle undermining of democratic process. This is discussed in relation to Australia by Hindess (2004).

At a local or even a national level, it is possible to set priorities that lead to programs and systems to collect and manage the information that underpins government performance. These typically include policing and defense, health and education, but also social and economic goals. The accepted role for government leads to the services and transactions that are the bread and butter of e-government. Roads and hospitals, schools, and resource management all form part of the commons that governments exist to develop and protect. On an international level, the public goods are not so easy to reach agreement on or to quantify. One country may see its strategic goals in exactly the areas of resource development that may lead to environmental and social upheaval in another country. Even when there is accord on a universal right or a standard, there is contention over the who and how of enforcement. The involvement of non-government agents further complicates the ability of governments to negotiate equitable outcomes. World Bank studies have shown the link between good governance and economic development (Kaufman, Kraay, & Zoido-Lobaton, 1999, 2000). A corollary of this is that when government mechanisms for accountability shrivel, economic implosion may not be far behind.

Many international issues do not have clearly defined stakeholders. By their nature, they lack both geographic grounding and structures for distributed representation. Therefore, questions about the type and presentation of information, services, transactions, forms of communication, and so on tend to be answered according to importance placed on them by those with influence or resources. In the absence of uniform protocols for participation, transparency, and accountability, the establishment and monitoring of best practice in digital representation is difficult to determine and is often more driven by the relevant community of practice and influence than either public need or information technology enthusiasts.

Deterrents to Global E-Governance

The digital and democratic divides that separate nations and organizations present a huge hurdle for both global governance and managing the information commons. Highly developed countries will have organizations that are capable of advanced communications and information management. Countries and regions with few resources or minimal infrastructure will be unable to match these standards. Both their citizenry and their public institutions will be at a disadvantage in negotiating or implementing good information systems. To the extent that monitoring or evaluating a range of agreements or situations depends on information handling, these countries will be unable to exercise effective responses. If non-government players become the primary determiners of information security and control, national sovereignty is correspondingly compromised.

The gap between the "info rich" and "info poor" has long been a concern for many observers of the information society (Lyon, 1988). On a global level, this may be thought of as a scaling up of the digital divide that exists within communities. Areas at greatest disadvantage are likely to be Africa and remote areas of Asia and Latin America. Countries without adequate information infrastructure will not be able to compete economically, and this will further inhibit their ability to participate in shaping the information infrastructure to their advantage. This is also true of rural and remote areas of developed countries. In Australia, the ongoing drive to privatize fully the telecommunications carrier is being held up by the continuing inadequacy of rural infrastructure. This could become an information-as-security issue, given the vast and vulnerable northern coastline and repeated attempts at illegal landings by people smugglers. Research by the author found that remote electronic points of presence already provide a valuable service in providing information essential for the preparedness, management, response, and evaluation of natural disasters in outback Australia (Geiselhart, 2004b).

In keeping with the concept of a global information commons, the less developed countries may also be the ones whose information is critical for the well-being of the rest of the world. The challenge is to provide them with both the incentives and the ability to participate fully in information management and sharing. Countries are unlikely to be receptive to plans for globalized control of information or its infrastructure while they remain economically disadvantaged. Muslim nations might not be enthusiastic about systems for biometric identification of travelers, for example, if they thought this would place their citizens at risk of intrusive searches and delays. Some organizations claim that a global registration and surveillance infrastructure is being assembled to assist the US in anti-terrorism activities, but with profound implications for privacy and individual security (ICAMS, 2005). This could have implications for cooperation on other information issues, such as health and environment, discussed below.

The democratic deficit that exists even in the most highly developed nations offers a substantial obstacle to effective management of both the local and the global information commons. This, too, may be seen as a pattern that can be modelled and that repeats at several scales. Failures of democratic information process have much greater potential to undermine global security than inadequacies of technical standards and protocols. The democratic deficit embraces at least three interrelated aspects of governance: low voter turnout that reflects public disengagement in and cynicism about the political process; a lack of accountability in government; and the need for international governance in a globalized economy (Axworthy, 2003, 2004).

These problems with democracy that Axworthy described with reference to Canada can directly affect the security of information, as with the U.S. example on increasing government secrecy cited earlier. The democratic deficit can take many forms. A recent report indicates Australian politics is not free from corruption (McLennan, 2004). Sins of both omission and commission via information manipulation, together with the politicization of the public service, have led to debate but not much action. Endorsement of overseas intelligence claims about weapons of mass destruction, leading to commitment of Australian troops against popular opinion, and the subsequent re-election of the government that made those claims, indicates that democratic process is a complex beast indeed. Of course, the public is also part of the value chain of democratic accountability.

The democratic deficit highlights the relationship between security of information and the processes for its verification and transparency. This is particularly pertinent to global aspects of scientific decision making. Thousands of scientists in the United States, including 48 Nobel Prize winners, have signed a letter claiming political interference in scientific issues. These claims, even if only partly true, indicate how fragile knowledge can be, and the importance of checks and balances for its verification. There may not be much point in sharing information if the authentication and interpretation of that information is compromised. As with electronic financial data exchanges, scientific information needs to be free from both political and technical tampering en route, as it proceeds through policy channels. Climate scientists claim that vital information about global warming is not finding its way into government documents. This indicates the population's right to know is compromised, further weakening the entire chain of decision making. The governance dimensions of information can overtake scientific bias or error as sources of insecurity.

Another dimension to the democratic accountability of public information is the role of the media. It is only possible here to refer to the extensive literature on the role of the mass media in managing public opinion and determining what information is publicly available. A starting point for this research is McChesney (1999). This somewhat vague relationship to information security comes into sharper focus when linked to government procedures for freedom of information. Neither the "free" media nor interested individuals and organizations can easily leap the hurdles that accessing information can pose in even the most open societies. This encourages the informal networks that bypass government channels. The next section expands on the types and roles of nongovernment actors in relation to managing the information infrastructure and networks.

NONGOVERNMENT ACTORS AND GOVERNMENT INFORMATION

Actors outside governments are important influences on the overall flow of information. They are also critical players in the management of the information infrastructure and in the emerging forms of e-governance on specific issues. Networks of varying density and intensity connect nongovernment actors and stakeholders with each other and with governments. Like governments, these actors are also subject to the globalizing pressures of complexity, urgency, unquantifiable risk, time scarcity, and dependence on technological sources of information described by Skolnikoff (2001).

Each of the following sets of actors has the capacity to act and interact with the others and with governments, to form new and unexpected alliances, networks, and patterns of behavior. These can become the seeds of new regimes that support or undermine existing governments. They can also provide de facto forms of transnational e-governance through communities of practice and affiliation. The following perspective draws on Rosenau's "spheres of authority" analysis (including Rosenau, 1997) and Earnest's (2001) discussion of international relations and the changing role of the nation state. The underlying theory is a complex adaptive systems approach applied to governance, described in titles listed in the Further Reading section at the end of this chapter and in Geiselhart (1999, 2004a).

Corporate Sector

The global corporate sector has a double influence on both national and international aspects of e-governance. As systems and software contractors, they are both the subjects and the providers of digital information. They are strong lobbyists for information policy—for example, stronger IP and patent laws in areas such as biotechnology, entertainment, pharmaceuticals, and genetics. Consistent with the view presented earlier that technology design reflects its sociopolitical context, the systems design and architecture available for e-government are likely to support corporate interests and limitations.

The larger groups are relatively well resourced and often linked to global media systems. As a result, their voices tend to be clearly heard. Their role is to maximize profits, and this can lead to negative externalities. Good governance helps to manage their externalities and avoid tragedies of the commons. Their voice, like that of the public, is not homogeneous, but varies depending on the issue and where their interest lies. Some companies may be less than forthcoming when dealing with privacy invasion, pornography, software security issues, and so on if they are profiting from it. Others will be lobbyists for stronger protections and government intervention on issues that negatively affect them. All stakeholders (except perhaps cyber terrorists) seek stability, consistency, and appropriate forms of coordination.

On many issues, global corporations may band together to solve common problems of e-governance. For example, the development of electronic commerce is taking place through representation by industry bodies as well as intergovernmental panels. The International Telecommunications Union (http://www.itu.int), founded on the principle of cooperation between governments and the private sector, is active as part of a set of organizations involved with electronic commerce standards through a number of working groups, memoranda or understanding, and subprojects. Membership across the broad field of telecommunications generally includes policymakers and regulators, network operators, equipment manufacturers, hardware and software developers, regional standards-making organizations, and financing institutions. The ITU overtly states that its "activities, policies and strategic direction are determined and shaped by the industry it serves." (http://www.itu.int/aboutitu/overview/rolework.html, accessed May 13, 2005). Thus, although not formally structured to provide democratic accountabilities of representation or public good provision, the overall direction is nonetheless part of a sphere of authority that includes governments and their regulatory agencies as partners. It is a mutable, fast-evolving area, and like many organizations, the ITU aims for responsiveness and adaptation as their norm. The ITU has also been running the World Summit on the Information Society, as yet another aspect of their role that overlaps with many other dimensions of e-governance, digital divide and equitable development, and the engagement of civil society.

Another cooperative corporate project relating to e-governance is the Global Reporting Initiative (GRI). Although not directly related to information infrastructure or security, the GRI, like many global projects, makes good use of the Web's universal interface for its activities. The GRI (http://www.globalreporting.org/) is a set of consistent accounting standards used to track social, economic, and environmental outcomes. This is known as triple bottom-line accountability and illustrates how global information management of a particular form of data can occur without formal government or legal obligation. As compliance with these standards spreads, the GRI may become a valuable resource for nations as well as corporations. The impact may flow into the government sector, rather than governments attempting to impose it on the private sector. Accountabilities of the corporate sector extend beyond the nations where they have headquarters or pay taxes. Even small companies can have global reach, with global responsibilities that are often incompletely defined or enforceable.

Local Nongovernment Agencies

Many local government issues are informed by events elsewhere. Water management, urban design, drugs and crime as social concerns, best practice in early childhood development—the list is extensive. Local government authorities often need assistance in keeping up with this information. Community interest groups are often the best placed to capture and interpret additional information needed by governments. When suitably informed, they can lobby more effectively. Sometimes they can enlist the assistance of wider groups to their cause. A visiting expert with pertinent insights can cause a local welfare group to change direction abruptly in its approaches to a local government. Both success and failure can now be instantly conveyed, leading to reverberations in other localities.

This is not to underestimate the difficulties of transmitting information and gaining the benefits of local experience from around the globe, or even across the district. This is why many projects aim to facilitate networks for learning and sharing across geographic areas or communities of interest. The information networks and patterns of distribution are structural elements along with the actors that access and feed them.

International Nongovernment Agencies

These are an increasingly influential aspect of de facto global e-governance. The number of nongovernment agencies has mushroomed in recent decades. These organizations have the potential to achieve levels of trust that are often no longer available to the nation state, and thus they can speak quasi-independently to the media and over the Internet.

The larger international agencies, such as the Red Cross, Greenpeace, Human Rights Watch, Amnesty International, and Transparency International become respected players on the global relations circuit. Their reports, actions, and spokespersons often have high status at international conferences. They are supported by dispersed publics, their allegiances all the more valuable for being voluntarily given (Ernest, 2001). As part of their activities, they often contribute to, comment on, and distribute government information and reports. For example, groups such as those involved in antispam activism are players and stakeholders on issues with a direct input to information security. Thus, RIPE (http://www.ripe.net) is the regional internet registry for Europe. This independent, not-for-profit membership organisation supports the infrastructure of the Internet through technical coordination in its service region. It looks at issues of wide area IP networks but has formed an antispam working group to assist Europeans and others in combating this Internet plague. Its members, mainly Internet Service Providers (ISPs), telecommunication organisations and large corporations located in Europe and the Middle East, are part of the invisible web of cooperation that helps manage the Internet as a network of networks.

Some groups do not have a formal Web presence. For example, Al Qaeda's information is presented via other fundamentalist Web sites, including video footage of beheadings that has reverberated around the globe. The Chechen resistance is represented through the Web site http://www.kavkazcenter.com, which offers news and information about this Islamic uprising in three languages. They have designed the site so that media and others can easily keep up-to-date on their activities and relay this information to wider audiences.

Actors of all persuasions use networked strategies to assert their values and gain dominance. These include social activists as well as criminal and tax evasion syndicates. Extensive networks of information exchange and planning have underpinned, for example, the antiglobalization rallies that have become a feature at high-level international meetings. Indymedia (http://www.indymedia.org/) is just one prominent site for alternative news. Another activist group has been involved in the Civil Society gatherings of the WSIS process (http://www.wsis-cs.org/).

Political groups that embrace violence will have no compunctions about attacking information resources online to meet their ends. As a form of warfare, their skills are sophisticated and highly committed (Ronfeldt & Arquilla, 2001). Again, these tactics can be difficult for formal government processes to address, partly because they are more flexible, decentralized, and adaptive than bureaucratic structures. Even though they may be part of terrorism and be linked to cyber crime, money laundering, and attacks on infrastructure, their activities can be inadvertently protected by measures to protect identity and privacy online. Their very unaccountability to formal governance processes leaves them free to act and undermine information security globally.

Citizens Without Borders

Less ominously, citizens have responded to globalization with their own transborder activities. One of the best known features of electronic commerce is the ability to reach out to markets internationally. Likewise, activism now is more possible and more effective beyond national limits. Not all of this is mediated through organizations. Some is simple consumer choice that operates on the marketplace, often without political intent. Other dimensions, however, are overtly about creating a voice or change as diverse members of a diffuse public. One example is birdwatchers flocking together to count birds and incidentally become part of a global scientific project (Garreau, 2001).

Another area of individual (and group) activism concerns the maintenance of predigital rights. As noted earlier, digital rights management, or DRM, has become polarized between strong, almost coercive intellectual property protection versus those who want to protect "fair use" and the open exchange of ideas, information, and artistic expression. The Creative Commons project (http://creativecommons.org/) offers an alternative approach to the intense and expensive legalism of copyright law. Piracy and appropriate free use of digital material is one of the most contested areas of global e-governance.

On a formal political level, groups reach out to find the likeminded, regardless of where they might be. Parties set up convenient Web sites so expatriates can enroll to vote. The diaspora of many communities use electronic communications to inform and seek support. When disaster hits (such as a cyclone) or victory arrives (such as being awarded the privilege of staging the next Olympics) the international phone and Web links run hot for days, with congratulations, enquiries, and, if necessary, financial support. Some resource flows become semipermanent, as those in more economically advanced countries feed the organizations and movements of their choice. Inside repressive regimes dissidents continually change Web hosts and utilize all the tricks of online anonymity to get information and stories out.

Individuals need the protection of their identity, money, information, privacy, and so on when dealing within their own borders. This is usually provided by governments through legislation, policing, and so on. These protections are much less available for citizens roaming internationally, either as activists or consumers. This is where globalization gets personal, not just for nuisances such as spam and the notorious Nigerian e-mail fraud, but also for extensions of criminal behavior that endanger lives and livelihoods. Emerging forms of e-governance will need to respond to these concerns.

In enterprises such as Amazon.com, eBay, and myriad others, the inputs from many participants provide the data to shape the system. In advanced forms, the participants actually patrol and regulate the system. For example "eBay vigilantes" help flush out dishonest traders (Cronaca, 2004). Central to this approach is the ability for leaderless action, driven by intent and individual initiative. In human systems, the rules of interaction are generated by the values of the actors (Kiel, 1994; Pascale et al., 2000; Theys, 1998). Conflict between the values of various sets of actors inhibits harmonization of the global democratic information value chain and systems.

The outline just provided highlights the nature of today's globalized information interdependence. It is dispersed, mutable, and often uncontrollable and unpredictable. The following section of this chapter discusses some specific areas of high information security risk where governments are trending toward greater integration of global information systems. These reinforce earlier claims in the chapter about the critical role of information systems and their governance in wider security and sustainability concerns. In nearly all of the areas where

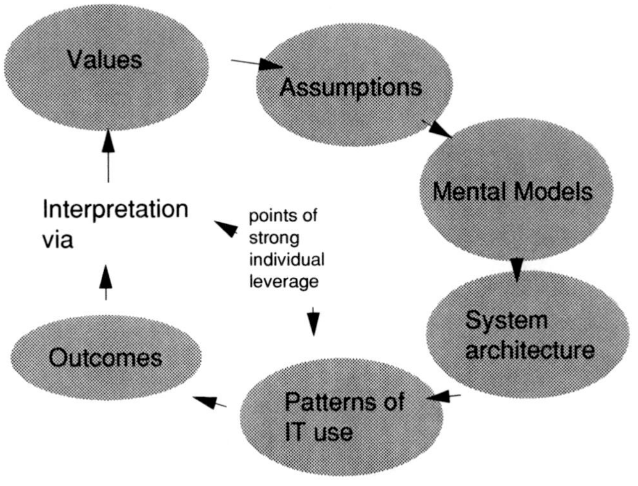

Figure 2: The IT system design value chain (Geiselhart, 1999).

formal governments operate, the processes that manage and integrate transnational information flows have a direct impact on personal, public, and national security. Figure 2 illustrates the cycle of information systems development and the role played by values in shaping these systems. At no point are patterns of governance independent of the values and mental models of the actors who shape them. This highlights the need to articulate and embed democratic values in systems of e-governance.

GLOBAL INFORMATION—AREAS OF HIGH RISK

These areas are indicative of the overlap between national and international information systems and the links between these and global security. For each of these, a long list of actors contribute to the information creating a dynamic sphere of authority, with smaller similar (fractal) patterns at national and local levels, frequently with implications for individuals. Each sphere also overlaps and is interdependent on the others, as illustrated in this section. For each, the key to information as a dimension of security lies in the patterns being created at all levels and how they interact, along with the information flows and their checks and balances. Each sphere of authority contributes to global e-governance on that issue.

International Information: Economic and Financial

The world economy is perhaps the most obvious manifestation of globalization, and the area where global e-governance is most highly coordinated. It consists of industries, flows of goods and services, resource manipulation, advertising and marketing, and consumption by governments, organizations, and individuals. Trade laws and sanctions of various kinds, unilateral, multilateral, and global, enforce and reinforce alliances or enmities. The largest industries, such as energy and agriculture, are subject to fluctuations and crises. These issues affect the ability of less well-developed nations, regions, and individuals to participate in the global economy because knowledge about innovation is also manipulated through legal and administrative controls, pricing regimes, and so on.

Where representation issues have been resolved, e-governance can be effective. For example, SWIFT (Society for Worldwide Interbank Financial Telecommunication, http://www.swift.com) is an industry-owned cooperative that provides the information infrastructure for much of global banking and finance. The banking industry is a "virtual community," with the capacity to design and manage their information systems to the mutual advantage of stakeholders. As a cooperative, its governance structures have commonalities with democratic representation. International financial and commercial transactions have rigorous requirements for digital documentation. The forms of information security include nonrepudiation, verification, and authentication. The governance role of many hybrid government and industry organizations in setting standards and norms is a theme of this paper. Similar patterns or attractors of representation, negotiation, and collaboration are repeated for many other aspects of the information superstructure.

For many forms of communication between sovereign nations, clarity about information structure, content, transparency, and security is much more elusive. Diplomatic communications, for example, are not likely to travel on public networks without strong encryption. Likewise, documents relating to the negotiation of treaties cannot be entrusted to public systems. Many reports and much research commissioned with public money will be provided to other governments for purposes of negotiation without being made available to citizens of either country. Further, the procedures by which such information might be made public are continually subject to contestability by relevant stakeholders, often on a subject by subject basis. The potential for a unified framework for disclosure, even within one country or jurisdiction, is restricted by political pressures and the bureaucratic artifacts of fragmentation and compartmentalization.

Legal and Administrative Information

Legal matters include taxation, treaties, and intellectual property, along with judicial and criminal issues relating to extremes of behavior from innovation to terrorism. Collecting tax becomes more difficult when individual and corporate actors can move and conceal their money and transactions. Some nations actively provide tax havens, and others seek global sanctions to eliminate them. Some corporate players position themselves to aid and abet tax avoidance as a market opportunity. Individuals as well as companies seek gaps in taxation monitoring and take advantage of the limited cooperation on reporting to shield their income from governments (Geiselhart & Singh, 2001). Addressing these taxation issues is a major concern for nations and relates closely to information security issues relating to support for terrorism. Transparency is the other side of the representation coin for e-governance. As global integration increases, questions of who will guard the guardians of information will intensify.

Again, there are national and nonstate actors, public organizations, and underground groups that seek influence in each of these spheres. The issues are notoriously entwined. One legal–economic example is the superannuation industry. Individual citizens have accounts and accumulate funds from various employers, in addition to their own contributions. This has a government element because the government agency sets the rules by which citizens can enter or withdraw as well as taxation limits and a whole range of administrative and legal issues. There is also a powerful corporate element because there are companies, both for profit and not for profit, that manage and administer the investments of these funds. Finally, there is also a substantial international dimension because the funds regularly invest both on- and offshore, thus bringing the superannuation fund into communication and perhaps negotiation with international governments, other legal systems, concerns about possible human rights or environmental practices, corruption, and so on.

A random sampler of other legal aspects of global e-governance includes the use of biometrics at national borders; the regulation of radio frequency identification tags on consumer goods; and spim, or the next generation of spam, which is unwanted text messages sent over mobile phones. In addition to their legal and regulatory aspects, each of these has a consumer dimension and a set of privacy concerns, in addition to the purely technical dimensions of standards and transmission. It is not clear where the representation of global citizens' interests falls in each of these. This is one function of modelling, to develop maps of how the parameters interact and identify their sources.

Environmental Information

A growing area is disaster planning, response, recovery, and evaluation. Natural and human events can disrupt the global communication system, precisely when and where coordination of information and response is most needed.

The broader field of secure information relating to environmental communications encompasses details of climate variation and communications about short-term events and medium and longer term dynamics, along with species identification, documentation and preservation, water resource allotment and management, air quality monitoring, and many other issues. Information on these matters is important not only for the ability to preview and model scenarios, but also to adopt precautions and preventive strategies where possible. Information sharing in response to catastrophe, both human and natural, as well as recovery and evaluation to promote learning, are other dimensions of global environmental management. There is an increasing risk of rogue states endangering the planet with chemical or nuclear weapons. One approach to minimizing these risks is international standards for reporting, documentation, and information sharing and enforcement on the total life cycle of materials with the potential to become weapons of mass murder. Many current systems for reporting do not include the full value chain of information to include democratic stakeholders.

The outstanding global example of the environmental dimensions of information as security is climate change. Information on this topic is highly debated. The overlaps with economic, legal, and also health and transport are self-evident. Alliances are forged along interest lines, and each faction produces copious information to support its stand. The level of risk is extreme, and potential for harmonization is limited by the relative power of key actors. This information cascades to every level of global structure because there is virtually no place on earth that is outside this sphere. Here, too, individual actors have to make risk assessment decisions based on the information available to them locally and their level of confidence in wider sources of information. Many writers are documenting the potential for a global form of 'open source politics' (Sifry, 2004) that compels the kinds of ultimate transparency and citizen monitoring that Clover (2004) has described for fisheries and that he sees on a smaller scale in Iceland.

Other aspects of environmental information reveal why some writers suggest environmental degradation will be the main security risk in this century (Kaplan, 1994). These issues are intimately entwined with the other spheres of authority. Thus concerns about security and quality of water are coupled with globalizing pressures to privatize supply, and increasing dependence on fossil fuels is coupled with uncertainty about reserves. According to Thomas (2001), the greatest undermining factor to security in a globalized system of trade, finance, and ecology is poverty. This may be seen as the weakest link in the democratic information value chain, creating vulnerabilities where disease or terror can fester.

Health Information

Health is a critical integrating area, where forms of information are inextricably caught up in their political context. Health crises are by nature complex and often defy state-centric approaches (Lee & Dodgson, 2000). Nations seeking to go it alone during an outbreak of a new disease, for example, can endanger multiple other populations beyond their borders.

Clearly, this is closely related to environment, but health issues are associated with additional information components that require global information sharing: epidemiological patterns and patterns of antibiotic resistance, new disease vectors, promulgation of best practice, and economically viable approaches.

Lee and Dodgson (2000) have documented the ways in which the patterns of cholera have reflected those of globalization. They maintain that the systemic ills of globalization itself are reflected in health challenges. They observe an erosion of spatial, temporal, and cognitive boundaries. They also note a failure of the rationalist thinking that says these problems can be solved by simply adding more information, when it is the patterns of interconnection that need to be addressed. This is another way of stating the importance of management and governance procedures for existing information.

Health and administrative–legal matters are closely related because the intellectual property arrangements for pharmaceuticals are a key focus for trade liberalization. Bilateralism can dampen plurality and transparency and result in essentially "a covert form of private governance" (Drahos & Henry, 2004). In such cases the information systems are likely to reflect the degree of covertness.

Consider a situation of a biological infestation in an exporting country's wheat crop. This can diminish food supply in one country and national income in another, as well as create hunger and stress at both end points. These large-scale dynamics are mediated at both ends by relevant national bureaus, industry groups, farmer organizations, welfare agencies, and unions. Every point of possible action is a node in a complex array of actors and rules for information transmission. There may be little or no direct communication between the end points of producer and consumer in the two countries. These groups will be more or less dependent on the quantity, quality, and timing of the information made available to them. The security of their livelihood or sustenance may, in the extreme case of famine, be as tenuous as the weakest link in these global flows. Equally important is the chain of accountability for the information that determines whether they will know that information has been withheld or distorted. This chain is only as strong as the civil and political institutions and values that generate the democratic information value chain.

This scenario of interdependence is repeated for other spheres of the global economy. The steel industry would have parallel sets of government, industry, and local worker and consumer groups. These spheres intersect through groups that have an overall role of coordinating economic development, or trade, or occupational health and safety, or biological safety, in the case of wheat. The information systems servicing these diverse actors and agencies can be secure, but closed to scrutiny, or they may be porous and open to review to a greater or lesser extent to those with an interest in holding them accountable. The urgency of each economic strand will depend on its role in the national and global economy and the current dynamics of its production. There is probably little current interest in, for example, the international paper clip industry, except as a very minor product in global steel production and exports.

Transport Information

Our last issue is transport, again connected with the others. The carriage and smuggling of dangerous materials is one aspect, including radioactive substances, chemicals, machines, and equipment of warfare and weapons of mass destruction. Legal and administrative matters overlap, for example, in the insurance arrangements that affect oil tankers and the consequences for spills.

The transport of people is also now a large international trade, both legal and illegal. These people bring not just disease vectors, but challenges to cultural, welfare, political, religious, and legal situations. Tourism is not an unmixed blessing for the host nations, particularly if it encourages terrorist attacks, as in Bali when Australians and Balinese met a common fate. There were claims that the Australian government had knowledge of the impending threat but did not provide warnings. Around the world, more travelers are paying closer attention to whatever information sources they think can provide a margin of safety through information about such matters.

CONCLUSIONS

This chapter has argued that democratic governance processes sit at the centre of information security issues, rather than on the periphery as a desirable but distant goal. It has shown that e-government is now more diffuse, particularly for the many issues that overlap national boundaries. In examining the drivers of e-government that flow beyond the nation state, many examples have demonstrated the other side of the information security coin: information as security. The author suggests that a democratic information value chain enhances transparency and participation and therefore accountability. In this scenario, government information becomes a tool to identify, manage, and defuse risk. The alternative is information as weapon and control, ultimately destabilizing when governments are unable to harness the new integrating dynamic. Yet another possibility is information out of control, where lies, misinformation, and hatred can infect both computers and minds. More optimistically, new forms of organization are emerging that provide "citizens sans frontiers" with the information tools to help shape and manage the global information commons. All these scenarios are the subject of intense debate and speculation. Figure 3 illustrates how actors at various levels or scales of influence might combine to determine the processes of information exchange. This figure is part of important work now being done on the role of open standards and social networks in developing trust relationships for Internet governance (see Reed, Le Maitre, Barnhill, David, & Labalme, 2004).

Given the paradigm shift toward a complex adaptive systems approach in recent years, it is likely that this perspective will inform modeling the protocols for a democratic management of the global commons. It is hoped

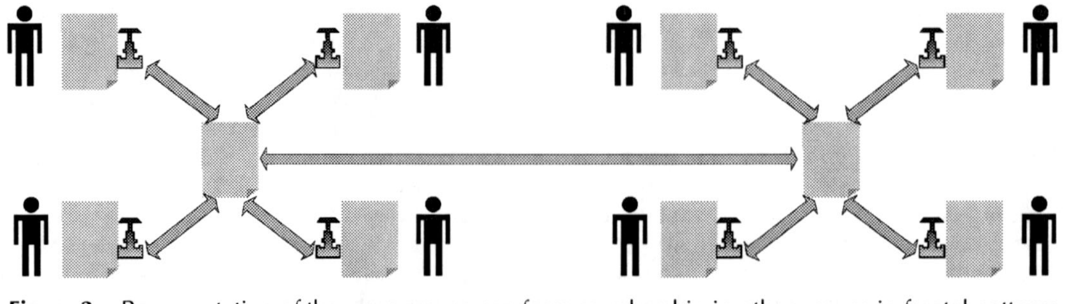

Figure 3: Representation of the ways groups can form membership in other groups in fractal patterns at many levels of complexity (from Reed et al., 2004).

that international e-governance and democratic information systems may eventually converge as part of a triple bottom line to address current environmental and political crises.

For all the issues discussed in this global context, the security of information is only as good as its distribution, management and governance. This chapter has provided a brief overview of the international dimensions of government information, and the implications for security. Information security and measures for transparency and accountability are an integral part of the risks associated with each issue. Issues with greatest acceleration are subject to the greatest risk, as these have the potential for sudden bifurcations. The compression of time makes pattern recognition more urgent, as does the interaction between issues and regimes to manage them. Government collection, creation, and dissemination of information is always and intensely a matter of national security. It is likely that modeling and simulations of governance, based on patterns for information creation, verification, transmission and access will become as common as economic and climate modeling is today.

Future research on international dimensions of e-government is needed to determine the forms of information sharing and management that will be most productive of protecting the global information commons. These may eventually take the form of protocols, growing out of such processes as the WSIS. There have been many attempts to codify the design features of democratic information systems, including Sclove (1995) and Geiselhart (1999). These principles for electronic democracy are based on a report from the OECD (2003) and may suggest the following avenues for research into specific information projects with global dimensions:

- create new public spaces for political interaction and deliberation
- provide for multidirectional, interactive communication flow
- integrate e-democratic processes within broader constitutional structures and developments
- facilitate and summarize public inputs
- ensure information is of high quality and trustworthy
- recruit the widest range of public voices
- provide equal access to the democratic process.

Another possibility is the development of an international charter of rights relating to the global information commons. Preliminary work on this has been done by Cameron and Geiselhart (1997). Work on the effects of information transparency and availability should help to establish which patterns are most productive of both information security and democratic process.

GLOSSARY

Attractor A state, condition or pattern that a system tends to stabilise in

Complex Adaptive System A system based on agents and rules for interaction, typified by evolution and unpredictability.

Democratic Deficit The gaps between formal democratic processes and government functioning and accountability.

Digital Divide The gap in communications technology knowledge, skills, and use between different groups.

Global E-Governance The electronic dimensions of emerging mechanisms for managing transnational issues and resources.

Global Information Commons The total human and physical infrastructure that supports the flow of information globally.

Globalization The process of increasing interdependency among countries, accompanied by convergent patterns of economic development and technology use.

Fractal Patterns that repeat at different scales, such as a coastline, or behaviors and institutions.

Triple Bottom Line Accounting procedures that include economic, environmental, and social elements.

CROSS REFERENCES

See *E-Government; E-government Security Issues and Measures*.

REFERENCES

Accenture. (2004). EGovernment leadership: High performance, maximum value. Fifth Annual Accenture eGovernment Study. Retrieved May 2005 from http://www.accenture.com/xd/xd.asp?it=enweb&xd=industries\government\gove_egov_value.xml

Axworthy, T. (2003–2004, December–January). The democratic deficit: Should this be Paul Martin's next Big Idea? *Policy Options*, pp. 15–19.

Beniger, J. R. (1986). *The control revolution—Technological and economic origins of the information society.* Cambridge, MA: Harvard University Press.

Branscomb, A. W. (1994). Who owns information? New York: Basic Books.

Cameron, J., & Geiselhart, K. (1998). A charter for citizens of the global information society. In J. Berleur & D. Whitehouse (Eds.), *The ethical global information society*, London: Chapman and Hall. Retrieved September 2004 from http://doctordemocracy.net/html/charter.htm

Clover, C. (2004). *The End of the Line: how overfishing is changing the world and what we eat.* Ebury Press: London.

Cronaca. eBay Vigilantes. (2004, March 22). No author provided. Retrieved June 2004 from http://www.cronaca.com/archives/002201.html

Dahl, R. A. (1989). Democracy and its critics. New Haven and London: Yale University Press.

Drahos, P., & Henry, D. (2004, May 29). The free trade agreement between Australia and the United States [Editorial]. *British Journal of Medicine, 328,* 1271–1272. Retrieved July 2004 from http://bmj.bmjjournals.com/cgi/content/full/328/7451/1271?etoc

Earnest, D. (2001, February). Will no one rid me of this meddlesome state? Social inequality and the new social contract. Author's draft of paper prepared for delivery at the 42nd Annual Convention of the International Studies Association, Chicago.

Epstein, E. (2004, August 27). White House takes secrecy to new levels, coalition reports. *San Francisco Chronicle,* August 27, 2004. Retrieved September 2004 from http://www.fas.org/sgp/news/2004/08/sfc082704.html

Feenberg, A. (1991). *Critical theory of technology.* New York and Oxford: Oxford University Press.

Garreau, J. (2001, May 9). Flocking together through the Web: Bird watchers may be a harbinger of a true global consciousness. *The Washington Post*. Pg C01 Retrieved May 2005 from http://www.changemakers.net/library/temp/wpost050901.cfm

Geiselhart, K. (1999). Does democracy scale? A fractal model for the role of interactive technologies in democratic policy processes. Doctoral dissertation, University of Canberra. Retrieved September 2004 from http://www.doctordemocracy.net/thesis

Geiselhart, K., & Singh, M. (2001). Tax issues for e-commerce, in e-commerce diffusion: Strategies and challenges (edited by M. Singh & T. Teo). Melbourne: Heidelberg.

Geiselhart, K. (2004a). Digital government and citizen participation in international context. In A. Pavlichev & D. Garson (Eds.), *Digital government: Principles and best practices*. Hershey: Idea Books.

Geiselhart, K. (2004b). The electronic canary: Sustainability solutions for Australian teleservice centres. Community TeleServices Australia, Inc. A report commissioned by the Networking the Nation Board, Department of Communications, Information Technology and the Arts, March 2004. Retrieved May 2005 from http://www.teleservices.net.au/

Global Reporting Initiative. Retrieved April 2004 from http://www.globalreporting.org/

Gualtieri, R. (1998). *Impact of the emerging information society on the policy development process and democratic quality.* OECD Public Management Service. (No longer available online).

Hernon, P., & McClure, C. R. (1993). Electronic US government information: Policy issues and directions. *Annual Review of Information Science and Technology (ARIST)*, 28, 45–110.

Hindess, B. (2004). Corruption and Democracy in Australia. Part of the Democratic Audit of Australia. Retrieved May 2005 from http://democratic.audit.anu.edu.au/focussedaudits.htm

ICAMS (International Campaign Against Mass Surveillance). (2005). The Emergence of a Global Infrastructure For Mass Registration and Surveillance: 10 Signposts. Retrieved May 2005 from http://www.i-cams.org/Surveillance_intro.html

International Telecommunications Union. http://www.itu.int. Accessed May 13, 2005.

Kang, M. (2001). Beyond underdevelopment of the public sphere: democratizing Internet governance in Asia. *Info—The Journal of Policy, Regulation and Strategy for Telecommunications, 3,* 348–358.

Kaplan, R. (1994, February). The coming anarchy. *Atlantic Monthly*. Retrieved May 2004 from http://www.theatlantic.com/politics/foreign/anarchy.htm (Now requires subscription). Also retrieved May 2005 from http://dieoff.org/page67.htm

Kauffman, S. (2000). Investigations. Oxford: New York.

Kaufman, D., Kraay, A., & Zoido-Lobaton, P. (1999). Aggregating governance indicators. World Bank Policy Research Working Papers (no. 2195). Retrieved July 2004 from http://www.worldbank.org/wbi/gac

Kaufman, D., Kraay, A., & Zoido-Lobaton, P. (2000). Governance matters. World Bank Policy Research Working Papers (no. 2196). Retrieved July 2004 from http://www.worldbank.org/wbi/gac

Kiel, D. (1994). *Managing chaos and complexity in government*. San Francisco: Jossey-Bass.

Lee, K., & Dodgson, R. (2000). Globalization and cholera: Implications for global governance. *Global Governance, 6*, 213–236.

Lyon, D. (1988). *The Information Society - Issues and Illusions.* Cambridge, England: Polity Press.

McChesney, R. (1999). Rich media, poor democracy: Communication politics in dubious times. Champaign: University of Illinois Press.

McLennan, D. (2004, August 17). Corruption rife in politics: Study. *Canberra Times*, p. 2.

Musso, J., Weare, C., & Hale, M. (2000). Designing Web technologies for local governance reform: Good management or good democracy? *Political Communication, 17,* 1–19.

Meyer, W. H., & Stefanova, B. (2001). Human rights, the UN Global Compact, and global governance. *International Law Journal, 34,* 501–522.

Organisation for Economic Co-operation and Development. (2003). *Promise and Problems of E-Democracy: Challenges of online citizen engagement.* Paris: Author.

Pascale, R., Millemann, M., & Gioja, L. (2000). *Surfing the edge of chaos: The laws of nature and the new laws of business.* New York: Crown Business.

Pavlichev, A., & Garson, D. (2004). *Digital government: Principles and best practices*. Hershey: Idea Books.

Reed, D., Le Maitre, M., Barnhill, B., Davis, O., & Labalme, F. The social Web: Creating an open social network with XDI. *Planetwork Journal.* Retrieved September 2004 from http://journal.planetwork.net/article.php?lab=reed0704&page=1

Richard, E. (2000). Lessons from the network model of Online Engagement of Citizens. Paper presented to LENTIC colloquium, Brussels. Retrieved August 2004 from the Canadian Policy Research Networks Web site: http://www.cprn.org

Roberts, A. (n.d.). Freedom of information resources. Retrieved September 2004 from http://www.foi.net

Ronfeldt, D., & Arquilla, J. (2001). Networks, netwars, and the fight for the future. *First Monday, 6.* Retrieved May 2004 from http://www.firstmonday.dk/issues/issue6_10/ronfeldt/index.html

Rosenau, J. (1997). *Along the domestic-foreign frontier: Exploring governance in a turbulent world.* Cambridge, England: Cambridge University Press.

Sclove, R. E. (1995). *Democracy and Technology.* New York: Guilford Press.

Sifry, M. (2004). The rise of open source politics. *The Nation*. Retrieved May 2005 from http://www.thenation.com/doc.mhtml?i=20041122&s=sifry

Skolnikoff, E. (2001). International governance in a technological age, in knowledge, politics and governance. In De la Mothe, J. (Ed.), *Science, 9*. London: Continuum.

Theys, M. (1998). The new challenges of management in a wired world. *European Journal of Operational Research, 109*, 248–263.

Thomas, C. (2001). Global governance, development and human security: Exploring the links. *Third World Quarterly, 22*, 159–175.

Trusted Information Sharing Network for Critical Infrastructure Protection (TISN). Retrieved May 2005 from http://www.tisn.gov.au/

Tuomi, I. (2003). *Networks of innovation: Change and meaning in the age of the Internet*. London: Oxford.

Zuboff, S. (1988). *In the age of the smart machine—the future of work and power.* Oxford: Heinemann Professional.

FURTHER READING

Bossomaier, T., & Green, D. (1998). *Patterns in the Sand: Computers, Complexity and Life.* Sydney: Allen Unwin.

Bourke, P. Web pages on fractals. Retrieved July 2004 from http://astronomy.swin.edu.au/~pbourke/fractals/ (Accessed September 2004.)

CALResCo Complexity Writings. Retrieved May 2005 from http://www.calresco.org/themes.htm

Holland. J. (1997). *Emergence: From chaos to order*. Boston: Addison-Wesley.

Organisation for Economic Co-operation and Development. (2003). http://hermia.sourceoecd.org/vl=12883288/cl=86/nw=1/rpsv/~6674/v2003n4/s1/p1l

Suarez, P. (n.d.) Urbanization, climate change and flood risk: Addressing the fractal nature of differential vulnerability. Retrieved July 2004 from http://www.iiasa.ac.at/Research/RMS/dpri2002/Papers/suarez.pdf

Privacy Law and the Internet

Ray Everett-Church, *PrivacyClue LLC*

INTRODUCTION

Understanding privacy is a true challenge, in no small part due the difficulty in defining the concept of privacy itself. The textbook definition of privacy only begins to scratch the surface of a deeply complex issue, made all the more complex because of the strong personal feelings evoked by privacy breaches. Accounting for privacy concerns can be a daunting task, especially when one is building Internet-based services and technologies whose success can depend on not offending consumers' mercurial sensibilities about the value of their privacy versus the value of those services that depend on free-flowing personal data.

This chapter discusses the roots of privacy law, including the different ways privacy matters are dealt with under constitutional law, statutes, and common law. With the fundamentals established, the rest of this chapter will discuss how many of those principles have come to be applied in today's Internet-oriented privacy terrain, and how businesses must prepare for doing business in this new environment.

PRIVACY LAW BASICS

Privacy Defined

The Merriam-Webster Dictionary of Law defines **privacy** as "freedom from unauthorized intrusion: state of being let alone and able to keep certain especially personal matters to oneself." Within this broad "state of being let alone," particular types of privacy intrusion have been recognized under law. How one defends themselves against intrusions differs, however, based on who it is doing the intruding.

Constitutional Privacy

Even though you will find no trace of the word "privacy" in the U.S. Constitution, a series of Supreme Court decisions beginning in the 1920s began to identify the modern concept of privacy. As the Court refined its views on privacy, it found the idea of privacy within the spirit of the Constitution's protections, if not in the plain language of the document. In 1928, in a landmark wiretapping case *Olmstead v. United States*, 277 U.S. 438 (1928), Supreme Court Justice Louis Brandeis articulated these ideas in some of the most important words ever written about privacy:

"The makers of our Constitution undertook to secure conditions favorable to the pursuit of happiness. They recognized the significance of man's spiritual nature, of his feelings and of his intellect. They knew that only a part of the pain, pleasure and satisfactions of life are to be found in material things. They sought to protect Americans in their beliefs, their thoughts, their emotions, and their sensations. They conferred, as against the Government, the right to be let alone—the most comprehensive of rights and the right most valued by civilized men" (Brandeis dissenting, *Olmstead* at 478).

Brandeis's phrase, "the right to be let alone," is one of the most often-repeated ideas in privacy and has influenced the court's inquiry beyond the plain words of the Bill of Rights to find other privacy rights that are logical extensions of the meaning contained in the original words, including

- The First Amendment right of free speech has been read to include the right to speak anonymously. Free speech has also been interpreted in reverse: you have the right to not be forced to say certain things.

- The First Amendment right of free association means that you can join clubs and affiliate yourself with anyone you choose. Inherent in that right, according to the court, is the right not to say whom you're associating with.
- The Fourth Amendment prohibits the government from searching your home and property and from seizing your papers or possessions, except under very specific circumstances. The Fourth Amendment has also been read to give certain rights against government wiretaps and surveillance.
- The Fifth Amendment includes various rights of due process, which means that if the government is interested in depriving you of any of your rights—throwing you in jail, for example—it must first follow strict procedures designed to protect your rights. Among those is the right against being forced to incriminate yourself.
- The equal protection clause of the Fourteenth Amendment requires that both sexes, all races, and all religions be given equal protection under all the laws of the United States and all the laws of every state. This protection comes despite other amendments that can be read to permit some types of discrimination.

But these rights aren't absolute, for example:

- The government can set up wiretaps, perform surveillance, and perform searches and seizures if they have the reasonable belief ("probable cause") that a crime has been committed and if given permission (a "warrant") by a judge;
- The government can establish secret wiretaps and surreptitiously search your home or car, without a normal warrant, if you are suspected of being a terrorist or an "agent of a foreign power;"
- It can be illegal to keep certain materials in your home, such as drugs or child pornography;
- Certain public organizations (like the Jaycees, which was the subject of a lawsuit that established this precedent) cannot use the First Amendment right of free association to exclude protected classes of people, such as women or certain minorities. On the other hand, at the time this book was written, the Boy Scouts could discriminate against gay people.

But the Constitution only affects privacy issues involving the government. What are your rights against people who are not part of the government, such as individuals and corporations? That's where a patchwork of common law privacy protections and several statutes comes into play.

Common Law Privacy

The common law is a set of rights and obligations first recognized by courts rather than by legislatures. Just because it is "judge-made" law, though, one cannot discount the common law as being less forceful. In fact, many common-law rights have been enforced for centuries and are some of the most powerful precedents in our legal system. They are rarely overturned by legislatures, and many state and federal laws are simply codifications of common-law ideas that have been around for hundreds of years.

In a groundbreaking law review article in 1960, William Prosser set out four broad categories of common law that underlie privacy-related torts:

- Intrusion into one's seclusion;
- Disclosure of private facts;
- Publicizing information that unreasonably places one in a false light; and,
- Appropriation of one's name or likeness. (Prosser, 1960)

Intrusion. The tort of intrusion recognizes the value of having your own private space, and provides relief from those who would seek to violate it. Eavesdroppers and "peeping toms" are two examples of activities considered intrusion.

Disclosure. The tort of disclosure recognizes that making public certain private facts can cause harm to an individual. For example, disclosures about someone's health status, financial records, personal correspondence, and other kinds of sensitive personal information can cause harm if made public.

False Light. The tort of false light is similar to libel in that it involves publicizing falsehoods about someone, but it is subtly different. One famous case of false light, *Cantrell v. Forest City Publishing Co.*, 419 U.S. 245 (1974), involved a family who was inaccurately portrayed in a news article in a humiliating fashion that brought shame and embarrassment. Another, *Douglass v. Hustler Magazine*, 769 F.2d 1128 (1985), involved a model who posed nude for a popular pornographic magazine, which were instead published with embarrassing captions by a notoriously vulgar magazine instead.

Appropriation. This tort involves using the name or likeness of someone for an unauthorized purpose, such as claiming a commercial endorsement by publishing someone's image (or even that of a look-alike impersonator) in an advertisement.

In this age of modern technology, there appear to be many new ways of violating these centuries-old privacy torts. The prevalence of miniature "Web-cams," highly sophisticated digital photo editing applications, and the vigorous online trade in pornographic imagery, have each added to the ways in which individual privacy can be violated.

PRIVACY LAWS IN THE UNITED STATES AND ABROAD

In a 1973 report to Congress, the U.S. Department of Health, Education and Welfare (HEW) outlined four tenets of fair information practices. These guidelines were groundbreaking in that they set forth four characteristics that any fair policy regarding the collection and use of personal information had to take into account. The four tenets were

Notice. Details of information practices and policies should be disclosed to data subjects.

Choice. Data subjects should be given the ability to exercise choices about how data may be used or disclosed.

Access. Data subjects should be permitted access to data gathered and stored about them.

Security. Holders of personal data should be responsible for providing reasonable levels of security protection for data in their possession (HEW, 1973).

Since then, there have been a number of laws enacted in the United States dealing with individual privacy. The standard U.S. approach is, however, to focus on particular types of information used by or about specific sectors:

Banking Records. Your personal banking information is protected by law, up to a point, including under provisions of a new law called the Financial Services Modernization Act (also known by its authors as the Gramm-Leach-Bliley Act).

Credit Reports. The Fair Credit Reporting Act (FCRA) requires that credit bureaus handle your data in certain ways.

Medical and Health Insurance Records. Laws and regulations governing how medical records can be used have been in place for several decades, and provisions of a new law called the Health Insurance Portability and Accountability Act (HIPAA) are creating new rights for patients to protect and access their own health information (HHS 2002).

Government Records. The Privacy Act of 1974, which included the original tenets outlined in the HEW report, sets limits on how government agencies can collect and use personal information, while laws like the Freedom of Information Act of 1966 require government to give all citizens access to certain government records, provided that the government also take precautions not to breach privacy when making that information public.

Children's Privacy. While not limited to one business sector, a law called the Children's Online Privacy Protection Act (COPPA) places restrictions on online organizations that seek to collect data from one sector of the public: children under the age of 13. COPPA requires the publication of a privacy policy to explain data practices relating to children's information, requires verifiable parental consent before any personally identifiable information may be collected from children over the Internet, and limits companies ability to share children's information with third parties.

International Privacy Law

The recognition of privacy rights in international law goes back to December 10, 1948, when the United Nations adopted the Universal Declaration of Human Rights. Article 12 of that document says: "No one shall be subjected to arbitrary interference with his privacy, family, home or correspondence, nor to attacks upon his honour and reputation. Everyone has the right to the protection of the law against such interference or attacks" (UN, 1948).

Building on that foundation, and applying the four tenets articulated in 1973 by the U.S. government, in 1980 the multinational Organization for Economic Cooperation and Development (OECD), of which the United States is a member, issued its eight Principles of Fair Information Practices. These principles consisted of:

Collection Limitation. There should be limits to the collection of personal data, and any such data should be obtained by lawful and fair means and, where appropriate, with the knowledge or consent of the data subject.

Data Quality. Collection of personal data should be relevant to the purposes for which they are to be used, and, to the extent necessary for those purposes, should be accurate, complete and kept up to date.

Purpose Specification. The purposes for which personal data are collected should be specified not later than at the time of data collection and the subsequent use limited to the fulfillment of those purposes or such others as are not incompatible with those purposes and as are specified on each occasion of change of purpose.

Use Limitation. Personal data should not be disclosed made available or otherwise used for purposes other than those specified in accordance with principle of purpose specification, unless done with the consent of the data subject or by authority of law.

Security Safeguards. Personal data should be protected by reasonable security safeguards against such risks as loss or unauthorized access, destruction, use, modification, or disclosure of data.

Openness. There should be a general policy of openness about developments, practices and policies with respect to personal data. Means should be readily available of establishing the existence and nature of personal data, and the main purposes of their use, as well as the identity and usual residence of the data controller.

Individual Participation. An individual should have the right to obtain from a data controller confirmation of whether data are held about the individual, to be given access to the data in an intelligible form, and to have the data erased, rectified, completed, or amended.

Accountability

A data controller should be accountable for complying with measures which give effect to the principles (OECD, 1980).

The European Union has taken the OECD principles and incorporated them into a sweeping Data Privacy Directive that establishes these principles in law. The directive mandates the following minimum standards in all countries that are members of the European Union:

- Companies can only collect information needed to complete the transaction, and must delete it after the transaction is over, unless they have explicit permission.
- Consumer's personal information must be kept up to date, or deleted.
- The purpose for collecting data must be given at the time that data are collected.
- An individual's personal information cannot be used for any other purpose (e.g., mailing catalogs or coupons) unless they have explicit permission.
- Companies must have appropriate security safeguards in place to guarantee privacy of any data in their possession.
- Companies must keep consumers advised in a clear and open manner about their data practices and how consumer's privacy will be impacted by any changes.
- Consumers must be permitted to see any information a company has on file about them, must be permitted to correct any errors, and must be allowed to delete data unless there's a legally mandated reason for keeping it.
- Companies who keep consumer information must have someone in the company accountable for assuring that the privacy laws are being adhered to.
- Companies may not transfer data outside the E.U. unless the country to which the data is being transferred has privacy laws as strict as those in the E.U. (EC, 1995)

It should also be noted that these restrictions apply to all data in a company's possession, whether customer data or employee data. And these are minimum standards; individual member countries can—and have—enacted laws that are even stricter.

To enforce their privacy laws, many E.U. member countries have established data protection authorities—government agencies whose mandate is the policing of data practices within, and crossing, national borders. These authorities often require corporations who possess personally identifiable information about any citizen of their nation to register with the agency and file detailed statements of what data are collected and how it is utilized.

In addition, while U.S. law focuses on certain categories of information, such as financial or healthcare data, holders of the data such as credit bureaus, or categories of data subjects such as children, the E.U. law gives special consideration to data about:

- Race
- Religious Affiliation
- Membership in Political Parties and Trade Unions
- Criminal Records

These topics are of particular concern to Europeans, in part because of how records containing information about race, religion, and trade union memberships were gathered and used by the Nazi regime in Germany and in their occupied countries to decide who should be shipped off to concentration camps. For Europeans, the threat of private information being misused is more than a test of wills between marketers and consumers, but meant the difference between life and death for the parents and grandparents of today's European lawmakers.

Cross-Border Data Flow

The issue of cross-border data flow has been particularly vexing for U.S. corporations, especially given the number of Internet-based firms with operations in the E.U. that depend upon data flows from the E.U. back to the United States Because the United States does not have broad privacy-protecting statutes on par with the E.U., U.S. corporations face the prospect of being unable to communicate customer data, or even personnel records, back to U.S.-based facilities.

Recognizing the potential for numerous disputes, the United States and E.U. entered into a series of negotiations in the late 1999 and 2000, culminating in an agreement to create a **Safe Harbor** program. This program permits U.S. corporations to assert their adherence to an array of basic privacy requirements, with the assumption that those who certify compliance and bind themselves to enforcement measures in the event of misbehavior will be permitted to continue transferring data from the E.U. into the United States (DOC, 2000).

BALANCING PRIVACY AND LAW ENFORCEMENT

In post-"September 11" America, a great deal of public concern centers around the extent to which new anti-terrorism intelligence gathering will negatively impact the privacy of average citizens. While few individuals will ever believe they merit the kind of surveillance activities implemented for mafia dons, drug kingpins, or terrorists, many are concerned that ubiquitous surveillance capabilities will result in less privacy for everyone, average citizens and mafia dons alike. Therefore, it is appropriate to briefly discuss the kinds of issues raised by increasing surveillance capabilities, and to discuss a number of programs and laws that are adding to the pressures on personal privacy. More significantly, given the extent to which American business is increasingly becoming the repository of detailed information about the lives and business transactions of individuals, it is also appropriate to discuss how businesses are increasingly being called on to aid law enforcement in their investigatory efforts, and why businesses need to exercise some judgment in deciding when and how to comply with law enforcement requests.

Surveillance, searches, and wiretaps raise extremely complex legal and technical issues that are impossible to cover in this brief space. Should these issues arise in your personal or professional activities, it will not be possible for you to deal with them without the assistance of qualified legal counsel. There are, however, some things to keep in mind that will help you to understand how an organization may be affected.

Most domestic wiretapping is governed by the Electronic Communications Privacy Act of 1986 (ECPA). In addition, the Foreign Intelligence Surveillance Act of 1978 (FISA) governs wiretaps and surveillance of those considered "agents of a foreign power." Both the ECPA and the FISA were modified, clarified, and in some cases expanded significantly, by the Uniting and Strengthening America by Providing Appropriate Tools Required to Intercept and Obstruct Terrorism Act of 2001, or "USA PATRIOT Act" for short. While some provisions of the USA PATRIOT Act were due to expire in 2004, some portions have been further expanded upon by more recent acts of Congress and remain an issue of much contentious debate.

ECPA

The ECPA generally prohibits providers of communications services (e.g., Internet service providers) from disclosing the contents of an electronic communication, whether it is in transmission or in storage, to any person other than the intended recipient. However, the ECPA also contains a number of exceptions, some of which include:

- Service providers may make disclosures to law enforcement, if proper warrants are presented. The ECPA explains those procedures in some detail.
- The ECPA's limitations only apply to services offered to the public, not to operators of, for example, an internal corporate system.
- The ECPA does not restrict the collection, use, or disclosure to non-governmental entities, of transactional information such as email addressing and billing information.
- Disclosures to private parties pursuant to subpoenas issued by civil courts may also be permitted.

In addition, the ECPA permits the government to request "dialing and signaling" information from telephone companies. Under these so-called "trap and trace" orders, law enforcement can use devices known as "pen registers" to capture the numbers being called and other information about the communications, short of the actual contents of the calls themselves. The contents of the calls can also be gathered, but only under a separate warrant that requires much more rigorous procedures and additional judicial review.

FISA

In cases where information is sought about the activities of agents of foreign powers, such as terrorists or spies, law enforcement may seek disclosure of information relevant to an investigation through a special warrant procedure. There are two noteworthy differences between standard warrants and FISA warrants: First, the FISA creates a system of special "FISA courts" in which judges meet, hear evidence, and issue warrants in total secrecy. Second, FISA warrants are much more sweeping than normal warrants and are not required to meet the same evidentiary standards as normal warrants. These differences raise significant Constitutional questions that have been raised in recent challenges to the activities of the FISA courts. Ironically, the FISA courts themselves have not been oblivious to the questions their seemingly unchecked powers have raised: a recently released decision of the FISA appeals court—the first document ever released publicly by the body—cited dozens of cases in which law enforcement provided deceptive or outright false information to the court in support of wiretap applications. Appealing to the US Supreme Court, the Bush Administration successfully overrode the FISA appeals court's objections to expanded wiretap procedures (EPIC FISA Archive, 2003).

Concerns about state-sponsored collection of data about individuals are nothing new. Privacy watchdogs and investigative journalists have widely publicized programs like the FBI's "Carnivore" (a device for intercepting and recording Internet-based communications) (EPIC Carnivore Archive, 2001), "Magic Lantern" (a piece of software that can be surreptitiously installed on a targeted computer, allowing law enforcement to capture every keystroke) (Sullivan, 2001), and the rumored international wiretapping consortium called "Echelon" (EU Parliament, 2001).

In 2002, the U.S. Department of Defense sought funding of an anti-terrorism program called "Total Information Awareness" which would have compiled electronic records on nearly every business, commercial and financial transaction of every U.S. citizen. The massive database would then be analyzed in an effort to uncover transactions and patterns of behavior that could be deemed suspicious. While the Total Information Awareness program was stripped of most of its funding by Congress in early 2003, the Department of Defense has vowed to keep researching the issues and technologies needed to undertake such a program (EPIC TIA Archive, 2003). In a September 10, 2003, op-ed piece for the *New York Times*, Department of Defense official (and controversial figure from the Reagan Administration's Iran-Contra affair) Admiral John Poindexter defended the rechristened "Terrorism Information Awareness" program (Poindexter, 2003). However, as of this writing, the program has not regained support, or funding, in Congress.

Business Issues Under Wiretap Laws

The wiretap activities under the ECPA and the FISA have until recently been relatively limited in their effects on businesses. Aside from telephone companies and some Internet service providers, few businesses were affected by these procedures. But under recent changes to the FISA made by the USA PATRIOT Act, law enforcement is now permitted to request business records from nearly any business to assist it in foreign intelligence and international terrorism investigations.

Previously, the FISA only allowed law enforcement to request business records from certain categories of businesses, such as common carriers, hotels, and car rental facilities. But under the new rules, subpoenas can be issued without limit to particular categories, including banks, retailers, and any other entity within the government's reach. The USA PATRIOT Act also expanded the search and seizure from merely "records" to "any tangible things," such as computer servers.

The pen register and trap/trace provisions of the ECPA have been expanded under the USA PATRIOT Act to add "routing" and "addressing" to the phrase "dialing and signaling," making it clear that these activities now include Internet traffic, not just telephone calls. The act does specify that the information retrieved through this process "shall not include the contents of any communication." There will undoubtedly be significant litigation in coming years to define where the dividing line falls between "content" and "addressing." For example, entering a search term or phrase into a search engine may cause the content of that search to be embedded in the address of the Web page on which the results are displayed.

PRIVACY ISSUES FOR BUSINESSES

Similarly, the Society for Human Resource Management (SHRM) reported in January 2004 that 57 percent of HR professionals are somewhat or very concerned about workplace violence in part as a result of the terror incidents of September 11, 2001. Eighty percent of human resources professionals now say they conduct background checks on employees, up 29 percent from a similar survey in 1996, and 35 percent conduct credit checks to screen potential employees, an increase of 16 percent from 1996. Eighty-two percent of human resources professionals report their organizations investigate the background of potential employees, up from 66 percent in 1996 (SHRM, 2004).

Workplace privacy concerns do, however, predate the September 11 security concerns. For example, in a widely published 2000 survey of over 2,000 U.S. corporations, the American Management Association (AMA) discovered that 54 percent of companies monitor their employees' use of the Internet, and 38 percent monitor their employees' e-mail. In a follow-up survey in 2001, the percentage of companies doing Internet monitoring rose to 63, with 47 percent monitoring e-mail (AMA, 2001). The rise in monitoring tracks with the rise in potential problems that can flow from providing access to the Internet. Along with the ability to work more efficiently, companies are now finding themselves held responsible when bad things find their ways into employees' desktops. In the same AMA study, 15 percent of the companies surveyed have been involved in some kind of legal action concerning employee use of e-mail and/or Internet connections. In several noteworthy cases, companies have been held liable for sexual harassment-related claims from

- harassment occurring over employer-operated message boards;
- employees leaving pornographic images on computer monitors; and,
- employees distributing sexually explicit jokes through office e-mail.

In response to these concerns, many companies have installed filtering mechanisms on their e-mail traffic looking for unacceptable language. Other companies have implemented software that blocks pornographic Web sites. Still others have opted for the low-tech approach of implementing zero-tolerance policies regarding the use of office computers for anything inappropriate.

Unfortunately in some instances, these measures have resulted in confusion and in some cases have wound up creating problems for both innocent and not-so-innocent people. For example, it was widely reported in 1999 that 23 employees of the *New York Times* were fired for trading dirty jokes over the office e-mail system (Oakes, 1999). Yet, in other cases, recipients of unsolicited e-mail have opened the fraudulently labeled mail and been subjected to a barrage of pornographic images and salacious Web pop-up ads (Levine et al., 2002).

Because Web monitoring logs and filtering systems may not be able to differentiate between Web pages viewed accidentally and those viewed purposefully, innocent workers can (and have) been left fearing for their jobs. For these reasons, companies are beginning to adopt internal privacy policies that help set better guidelines and establish reliable procedures for dealing with trouble when it arises.

Employee Privacy Policies

In most circumstances, there are very few legal restrictions on what employers can do with their own computers and networks, up to and including monitoring of employee's communications. While some firms quietly implement employee monitoring policies and wait to catch unsuspecting employees in unauthorized activities, many firms give notice to their employees that they may be monitored. Still others require employees to relinquish any claims of privacy as a condition of employment.

Increasingly, however, companies are recognizing the negative impact of paternalistic monitoring practices on employee morale. So to engender trust, rather than inspire fear, increasing numbers of firms have begun providing their employees with privacy statements in their corporate employee handbooks, or by publishing policy statements on company-internal Web sites. According to the AMA's 2001 survey, four out of five respondent firms have a written policy for e-mail use, and 77 percent for Internet use; 24 percent have training programs to teach these policies to employees, and an additional 10 percent plan one (AMA, 2001).

As noted earlier with regard to the European Union's Data Privacy Directive, companies with operations in the E.U. are already familiar with the mandate to provide data subjects—in these cases, employees—with information about the company's data gathering and usage policies. While there is currently no U.S. equivalent to these requirements, a growing number of firms are proactively recognizing that a well-defined set of privacy policies and practices can avoid misunderstandings and can even provide the basis of a legal defense in cases where companies are accused of failing to act on claims of Internet-based sexual harassment.

Developing an Employee Privacy Policy

The creation of a privacy policy for internal use in an organization can be as simple or as complex as the organization itself. Most companies collect information from their employees in the form of personnel records. Firms may also collect personal information from customers or clients. An internal privacy policy should address acceptable practices with regard to each type of information maintained by the company.

A good internal privacy policy should define what standards of behavior are expected of those who have responsibility over the data held by the company—including both employee data and the personal data of a company's customers—and should inform employees about the consequences of noncompliance. Additional topics that can be covered in a privacy policy include procedures for reporting breaches, procedures for allowing employees to access and correct their own personnel records, procedures regarding access to proprietary records such as customer lists, and procedures for auditing compliance and for training employees how to comply with the company's guidelines.

CONSUMER INTERNET PRIVACY

Before the Web existed, companies gathered whatever information they could get about their customers from a variety of sources, such as real estate transaction records, credit bureaus, court documents, and motor vehicle records. But for many companies, among the most elusive, and hence the most valuable information—what you are interested in buying and exactly when you are ready to buy—was largely unavailable. Occasionally, a clever marketer could devise an algorithm or a statistical model that might be used to infer some purchase preference from the tidbits of information that might be gathered about a customer from scattered sources. But the Internet has made such information gathering much more commonplace.

Browser Privacy Issues

Much of the average computer user's online activities revolve around the two most popular Web browsers, Internet Explorer and Netscape. Browsers continue to evolve and improve, especially where privacy and security issues are involved. However, even the most recent versions have some fundamental privacy problems that arise not by accident but by design. In many cases, there are default settings that permit the collection and storage of usage data. These include

- Browsers regularly tell Web sites what kind of browser it is, what version, what operating system it running on, and even what Web site "referred" you to the current page you are visiting.
- Some browsers have settings that permit users to automatically capture and enter user IDs and passwords for Web sites, as well as other personal information such as credit card numbers. These "wallet" features provide convenience, but also present a privacy risk should anyone gain access to that machine and use it to log into sites or access your personal information.
- Browsers can be instructed by Web sites to store little text files, called **cookies**, on your local hard drive. Cookies can be used to store personal information or to assign unique identifiers that allow sites to identify you individually on future visits.
- Browsers can keep a log of every Web site you visit and may even keep copies of the pages and images you have viewed. The "history" function can log this data for days, weeks, or even months. Depending on the size of the hard drive and the default settings for a browser, it may also store days or weeks of Web page files and images in a "cache" folder.

Internet Explorer and Netscape have their own built-in privacy settings and controls. However they do vary in the level of control they allow over elements like cookies. The Help file that comes with each browser explains the browser's privacy settings and describes how to control them.

IP Addresses and Browser Data

In 1990, an engineer at a Swiss physics laboratory, Tim Berners-Lee, invented a new data exchange standard in an effort to speed the sharing of information between researchers at widely dispersed locations. His creation was the hypertext transport protocol, or http, and it made data sharing across the Internet literally as easy as point-and-click (Cailliau, 1995).

But when the first Web servers and Web browsers were developed, not much attention was paid to subjects like security and privacy. Because Berners-Lee and other engineers needed to troubleshoot their fledgling Internet connections, they built many automatic reporting features, that would let them easily get to the root of the problem when something went haywire. This need for information such as browser type, version, operating system, and referring page, was built into the earliest browsers and persists there today.

While not a tremendous privacy concern, the collection of this browser data is a standard function of most web server software. Most sites collect this data for troubleshooting purposes and then delete it after some period of time, mostly because it can become very voluminous very quickly, and its usefulness diminishes over time.

One element of the data that is also captured in the process of requesting and serving Web pages is the **IP address** of the user's computer. An IP, or Internet Protocol, address is a formatted string of numbers that uniquely identifies your computer out of all of the other computers connected to the Internet. IP addresses, which look something like 192.168.134.25, are assigned in blocks to Internet service providers, who in turn dole them out to their customers. With most dial-up Internet access accounts, users are assigned a "dynamic" IP address, meaning that the IP address assigned to your computer changes every time you log onto your ISP, and gets tossed back into the ISP's pool of addresses when you disconnect. By contrast, dedicated servers and some desktop computers in corporate or academic settings may have a "static" IP address, which is unique to that machine and may persist for the life of the equipment.

But in this age of always-on Internet connections, such as those provided by DSL or cable modem services, it is possible for an average user's computer to have the same IP address for days, weeks, or months on end. From a privacy perspective, a static IP address can compromise one's privacy because an unchanging IP address make it easier for the truly determined to track an individual's Internet usage. For example, a site that collects IP addresses in their server logs may be able to correlate with other transactional records (e.g., purchase history or search parameters) to associate a unique IP address with a unique user and their online activities.

Given that most consumers use Internet service providers that regularly use dynamic IP addressing (as most of the DSL and cable modem providers claim), IP addresses are not considered a very reliable means of allowing Web sites or online advertisers to track users uniquely. However, this lack of reliability should not be confused with anonymity. As a routine bookkeeping matter, many service providers log which IP address was allocated to which user's account at a given period of time. These connection records are frequently sought by prosecutors investigating criminal activities perpetrated via the Internet and by parties in private lawsuits over online activities. In recent years, dozens of companies have successfully uncovered the identities of "anonymous" critics by obtaining court orders for the release of user identities. Not every Internet service provider has willingly provided that information; in 2002, Verizon Internet fought attempts by the Recording Industry Association of America to release records identifying users accused of illegally trading music files. As of this writing, the federal district court in Washington, DC, held that Verizon was required to reveal the user's identity, however Verizon has appealed (McCullagh, 2003). Ultimately courts ruled that the recording industry needed court approval for subpoenas seeking the identity of alleged music pirates (Borland, 2003).

Cookies

Connections made using http are called "stateless," which means that after your computer receives the content of a requested page, the connection between your computer and the far-away Web server is closed. Rather than maintain a constant open connection "state," each file that makes up the page (e.g., each of the graphics on a page) creates a new and separate connection. This is why, for example, it is sometimes possible to receive all the text of a Web page, but not the images; if the Web browser breaks the connection, or the distant server is too busy, it will not be able to open additional connection to receive the additional data.

The benefit to a stateless connection is simple: it enables one machine to serve a much higher volume of data. However, the downside to a stateless connection is that on occasion it might be helpful for a server to remember who you are. For example, when someone logs onto their stock portfolio, privacy and security dictate that the server not reveal your account information to anyone else, however, efficiency demands that every time you load a page, you should not have to reenter your user ID and password for every new connection your browser makes to the remote computer. So how do you make a server remember who you are? You do so by creating a constant state in an otherwise stateless series of connections. And the method for doing this is the cookie.

Cookies contain a piece of data that allows the remote Web server to recognize a unique connection as having a relationship to another unique connection. In short, the cookie makes sure that the server can remember a visitor through many steps in a visit or even when time has passed between visits. As a basic security measure, it should be noted that cookies are designed to be read only by a server within the same domain that created it. So, for example, only a server in the yahoo.com domain can read cookies set by a server in the yahoo.com domain.

Cookies enable a myriad of helpful features, such as the ability to personalize a Web site with your choice of colors, or language, or stock symbols on a stock ticker. It also enables features such as shopping carts on e-commerce Web sites, permitting you to select multiple items over the course of a long visit and have them queued for purchase at the end of your visit.

Not all cookies are used for collecting or retaining information over a long period of time, such as those used by advertisers. For example, many Web sites contain a great deal of frequently changing content and generate their Web pages from large databases of text. In some of these cases, the Web servers require cookies to help determine, for example, what page it should serve up to you based upon the search terms that you entered into a search engine.

A special type of cookie, called a **session cookie**, is set to be automatically deleted after a relatively short period of time, usually within about 10 minutes after you leave a site. This type of cookie is typically used for remembering information over a short duration, such as what you may have stored in a shopping cart. Because session cookies are so short lived, they do not have quite the same privacy implications as their longer-lived cousin, the **persistent cookie**. Persistent cookies often have expiration dates set many years in the future.

Most web browsers have settings that allow a user to accept or reject certain cookies. For example, an alternative brand of Web browser called Opera, favored among the privacy community, allows users to accept or reject cookies based on whether it is a **first-party cookie** being set by the site the user is actively visiting, or whether it is a **third-party cookie**, being set by some other entity, such as an advertising service via an ad banner appearing on the site.

Web Bugs

Another popular technology for tracking users' activities online is the **Web bug**, also called "Web beacons," "1-by-1 pixels," or "clear GIFs." (GIF, which stands for Graphics Interchange Format, is a particular type of file format for images.)

Web bugs are special links embedded in Web pages, or other HTML-coded documents such as some types of email, that allow the link's creator to track every instance in which the document is viewed (Smith, 2001). As discussed earlier, every time a Web page is loaded, images on the page are loaded in a separate transaction with the Web server. When a Web bug is programmed into a Web page, its code looks similar to the code for just about any graphic image appearing on that page. In reality, though, it has three differences:

- The Web bug graphic can be called from any site, most often from a third-party site, allowing that site to record deals about your visit.
- The Web address used to call in the Web bug graphic is often encoded with specific data relating to the page being visited, or in the case of HTML email, it

may be encoded with information about your e-mail address.

- The graphic image associated with the Web bug is deliberately made to be so tiny that it is invisible to the naked eye.

Most Web bugs are the size of a single screen pixel. What is a pixel? Every image on a computer screen is comprised of very tiny dots. The smallest unit of dot on your computer screen is the pixel. But even a single pixel can still be visible, so Web bug images are often made of a graphic image called a clear GIF, or a transparent GIF, which allows the background color or image to show through it, rendering it effectively invisible.

Because Web bugs can be embedded in any Web page or HTML document, they can also be included in e-mail, allowing sites to track details about when a message is read, and to whom the message might be sent. This versatility is why Web bugs have become so widely used. It is also why an industry group called the Network Advertising Initiative, which represents a growing category of online advertising firm called **ad networks**, responded to pressure from privacy advocates and legislators by agreeing to a set of guidelines for notice and choice when Web bugs are in use.

Ad Networks

Some sites rent out space on their Web pages to third parties, often for placement of advertisements. Along with those ad banners, many third-party advertising companies also try to set their own cookie on your browser. These cookies can be used for things like managing ad frequency (the number of times an advertisement is shown to a particular individual), and to track users movements between the many sites on which the advertising companies place their cookies. These ad networks are a type of advertising agency that rents space on dozens or hundreds of websites, and frequently uses cookies placed on all of the sites in their network to build a profile about the kinds of Web sites a particular user likes to visit.

What is increasingly a marketer's paradise is becoming a consumer's nightmare: the deluge of commercial messages in e-mail inboxes, parades of pop-up advertisements, and even solicitations arriving by cellular phone and pager are making consumers leery of the alleged benefits of this ubiquitously wired world. In response to growing consumer concerns, companies have sought to develop privacy polices that help consumers better understand how their information is gathered and used.

PRIVACY POLICY FUNDAMENTALS

According to the Federal Trade Commission (FTC), if a company makes a promise that it does not deliver on, that is considered an unfair or deceptive trade practice, for which the offender can be fined up to $11,000 per violation, in addition to other legal remedies (FTC OGC, 2002). Central to the FTC's advocacy of greater consumer privacy protections has been the call for companies to adopt privacy policies that provide consumers with useful information about how their personal information is gathered and used. While there are no federal laws that require the publication of a privacy policy, except where data collection from children is involved, it is widely considered an industry "best practice" to publish a privacy policy on any public Web site.

Considering the liability created by writing a privacy policy that a company cannot deliver on, the drafting of a privacy policy is not something to be undertaken lightly or without advice of legal counsel. However, good privacy policies tend, at minimum, to address those elements contained in the widely accepted fair information principles, which have also been endorsed by the FTC: notice, choice, access, and security. We will discuss the FTC's role in policing privacy matters later in this section, but it should also be noted that legal actions by state Attorneys General, as well as private lawsuits, are also driving companies toward some level of uniformity in privacy disclosures.

Those privacy policies cited by privacy advocates as being "best of class" also include the elements of the OECD's principles of fair information practices. There are also a number of online privacy policy generators that allow you to create policies by picking and choosing from predefined language based on the applicable situation. According to the privacy organization, TRUSTe, their recommended Model Privacy Statement has several key elements that echo the OECD principles:

- What personally identifiable information the company collects.
- What personally identifiable information third parties collect through the Web site.
- What organization collects the information.
- How the company uses the information.
- With whom the company may share user information.
- What choices are available to users regarding collection, use and distribution of the information.
- What types of security procedures are in place to protect the loss, misuse or alteration of information under the company's control.
- How users can correct any inaccuracies in the information. (TRUSTe, 2004)

Once a company has surveyed their data practices and articulated them clearly in a privacy policy document, the next most important task is to assure that the company lives up to its promises. There are three ways to do this: manage privacy matters internally, look to industry-sponsored groups for guidance on compliance, or wait for law enforcement to come after you.

Chief Privacy Officers

As the importance of privacy has grown in the corporate setting, and as the risks from privacy problems have increased, companies have begun to create a new management position, the Chief Privacy Officer (CPO), as the designated point-person for managing privacy policies and practices.

Since the first CPO position was created in 1999 at the start-up Internet advertising firm AllAdvantage.com, the CPO job description (if not always the title) has been rapidly adopted across corporate America; by the end of 2000, a significant number of Fortune 100 firms had a CPO-type position, often reporting to the seniormost levels of the organization. According to the Privacy Working Group of the advocacy group Computer Professionals for Social Responsibility, there are many benefits to appointing a CPO:

> A talented and properly-positioned CPO will add value across corporate divisions from development to customer relations, from liability mitigation and risk management to increased market share and valuation. Perhaps most importantly, the Chief Privacy Officer promotes an essential element of new economy corporate citizenship—Trust. (Enright & McCullough, 2000)

The CPO has both an internal and an external role at his or her company. The internal role includes participation in companywide strategy planning, operations, product development and implementation, compliance monitoring and auditing, and employee training and awareness. The external role of the CPO involves enhancing the company's image as a privacy sensitive organization, through fostering positive relationships with consumers and consumer groups, privacy advocates, industry peers, and regulators.

In many respect, the CPO becomes the focal point for a company's privacy activities, and in turn can become the company's public face on the privacy issue. The position is most effective if it is perceived as objective, with ombudsman-like qualities, serving as a protector of consumer interests while seeking balance between those interests and the interests of the company. Yet there are other organizations offering assistance in the ombudsman role: trustmark organizations.

Trustmarks

There are several independent, industry-sponsored organizations that will certify a company's privacy policy in order to improve consumer perceptions. Upon certification, they permit sites to use their "seal of approval," sometimes referred to as a **trustmark**, to demonstrate to the public their commitment to privacy concerns. The most popular privacy seal programs—BBBOnline, CPA WebTrust, and TRUSTe—certify the validity of the policies on many thousands of Web sites. And the growing use of these trustmarks does seem to be having an effect: an August 1999 study found that 69 percent of Internet users said that they recognize the TRUSTe seal, the most widely adopted of the privacy seal programs.

Seal programs verify that a Web site's privacy policy covers certain privacy topics (e.g., the use of cookies and sharing data with third-party marketers). However, the seals do not set any specific quality standards, benchmarks, or specific data handling practices. As such, a site could, theoretically, earn a seal for making the required disclosures, even if in the course of the disclosure it reserves for itself the right to make whatever use of personal information it sees fit. This has been one of the criticisms leveled at the seal programs, as has their dependence on licensing fees from those entities they are asked to police.

Federal Trade Commission

Under their broad legislative mandate to proscribe deceptive and unfair trade practices, the FTC began reviewing online marketing practices back in 1996. Soon the FTC's investigators were uncovering evidence of what they felt was egregious behavior by a few online marketers. Major corporations quickly distanced themselves from the alleged "bad actors," but acknowledged that privacy was a growing concern for online consumers, and promised the FTC that the industry would do better at policing itself.

After numerous public controversies over well-known corporations continuing to abuse consumer privacy, and despite repeated pledges to adhere to standards promulgated and policed by the industry itself, surveys have continued to show that consumer perceptions of the potential for privacy abuses (whether perceived or actual) by online marketers continues to be a factor in consumer hesitance to fully embrace Internet commerce. In response, the FTC has sought on numerous occasions to assist companies in adopting practices that are more conducive to consumer confidence. These efforts have focused on the well-worn mantra: notice, choice, access, and security.

In December 1999, the FTC convened an Advisory Committee on Online Access and Security to provide advice and recommendations to the agency regarding implementation of these basic fair information practices. The committee, consisting of representatives from the online industry, trade groups, academia, and privacy advocates, sought to provide guidance on how to solve the last two elements of fair information practices: access and security. Their report outlines many of the problems with setting universal standards for access and security, and in the end came to few conclusions (FTC ACOAS, 2000).

Some six years after first looking into online privacy issues, the FTC is still warning online companies that if they do not clean up their act, stricter measures might be required. During the intervening years, however, the FTC has not been completely idle:

- In 1998, the FTC reached a settlement with GeoCities, a personal Web site hosting service, over charges that it misrepresented how user information would be used and engaged in deceptive practices relating to its collection of information from children. Part of the settlement required GeoCities (now owned by Yahoo!) to post, "a clear and prominent Privacy Notice, telling consumers what information is being collected and for what purpose, to whom it will be disclosed, and how consumers can access and remove the information." The notice, or a link to it, was required on the Web site's home page and on every page where information was collected (FTC, 1998).
- In 1999, the FTC issued regulations implementing the Children's Online Privacy Protection Act, which requires online businesses to seek permission from parents before gathering personally identifiable information from children under age 13. It has since brought several enforcement actions to punish Web sites that have ignored those regulations (FTC "Kidz Privacy," 2003).

- In recent years, the FTC has filed numerous actions against Internet-based fraudulent schemes, get-rich-quick scams, and quack medical remedies promoted via e-mail and on the Web.
- In 2000, the FTC intervened in the bankruptcy sale of a customer list belonging to defunct online toy retailer Toysmart.com. The basis of the action was to prevent the list from being used in any way inconsistent with the privacy policy under which it was gathered (FTC, 2000).
- In 2001, the FTC settled with pharmaceutical firm Eli Lilly and Company over an e-mail that improperly disclosed the e-mail addresses of hundreds of users of a prescription reminder service at the Web site Prozac.com, in violation of the site's privacy policy (FTC, 2002).
- In 2003, the FTC settled with clothing manufacturer Guess? Jeans, Inc., over security breaches in the database associated with their online sales Web site. The FTC claimed that Guess? Jeans had failed to use reasonable measures to protect the privacy of consumers' credit card and other personal information when they failed to implement a security patch to remedy a well-known security vulnerability in their database software (FTC, 2003).

The FTC has steadfastly refused to seek greater legislative authority than its already broad mandate under the Federal Trade Act to police unfair or deceptive trade practices. However the agency has threatened the industry that it will indeed seek more specific privacy-oriented enforcement authority if companies do not improve their self-regulatory efforts. It must also be noted that the FTC is just one governmental authority with the ability to prosecute privacy violations: most state Attorneys General have state versions of the Federal Trade Act that enable them to seek remedies similar to those available to the FTC. Indeed, Attorneys General in Michigan, Washington, California, and Massachusetts, have all been active in undertaking privacy-related enforcement actions, and the National Association of Attorneys General has held many seminars on investigating and prosecuting Internet privacy matters (NAAG, 2001).

CONCLUSION

Consumers and businesses alike are grappling with the complex privacy concerns that the Internet era has brought to the fore. This chapter is a necessarily brief overview of the privacy landscape. Indeed, entire books can—and have—been written about the ways Internet technologies have created new challenges to the average person's desire to "be let alone." But as this chapter has shown, there are a number of concepts that find their way into privacy-related policies and practices. Among them, the fundamental principles of notice, choice, access, and security, are driving both consumer expectations and business planning. Keeping these principles in mind, many who are called on to seek privacy solutions in their own particular business or personal context have a conceptual framework within which to arrive at their own conclusion.

GLOSSARY

Ad Network A consortium of Web sites linked together by an advertising agency for purposes of aggregating advertising placements and tracking consumers movements among and between member sites.

Cookies A small file saved by your Web browser, at the direction of a Web site, containing data that may be later retrieved by that Web site. See also persistent cookies, session cookies, third-party cookies.

COPPA Children's Online Privacy Protection Act of 1998. Legislation that limits operators of commercial Web sites and online services from collecting personal information from children under age 13.

ECPA Electronic Communications Privacy Act of 1986. Legislation governing the use of wiretaps for domestic law enforcement activities.

FISA Foreign Intelligence Surveillance Act of 1978. Legislation governing the use of wiretapping and physical searches in investigations involving terrorists and agents of foreign powers.

GLB Gramm-Leach-Bliley Act, also known as the Financial Services Modernization Act. Legislation that instituted major changes to the U.S. banking system. In pertinent part, GLB requires that organizations providing financial services disclose their data collection practices to customers, and to provide the ability to opt-out of those practices.

HIPAA Health Insurance Portability and Accountability Act of 1996. Legislation that instituted a number of changes to health insurance practices. In pertinent part, HIPAA included privacy-related provisions applicable to health information created or maintained by health care providers, health plans, and health care clearinghouses.

Internet Protocol (IP) Address The unique numerical address assigned to each computer connected to the Internet. An address may be assigned temporarily (called a dynamic IP address) or may be assigned for long periods (called a static IP address).

OECD Organization for Economic Cooperation and Development. A group of 30 democratic, market economy countries working collaboratively on economic, social, and trade issues.

Persistent Cookies Cookie files designated to be stored for long periods, sometimes as long as 10 years.

Privacy Freedom from unauthorized intrusion. A state of being let alone and able to keep certain especially personal matters to oneself.

Safe Harbor A legal concept which permits an entity to reduce and/or avoid legal liability by agreeing to adhere to certain standards or procedures. In the context of Internet privacy, Safe Harbor refers to an agreement between the United States and the European Union that permits U.S. companies to certify that they adhere to the stricter privacy standards required by European law, thereby avoiding a more burdensome set of country-by-country registration procedures.

Session Cookies Cookie files designated to be stored for only the duration of a visit to a Web site; usually ten minutes or less.

Third-Party Cookies A cookie file set by some entity other than the operator of the Web site being visited by the user. Third-party cookies are often used by advertising services to track user movements between multiple Web sites over periods of times.

Trustmark A symbol used to identify those Web sites who have subjected their privacy policy to review by a third-party watchdog organization.

Web Bugs (also called Web Beacons, 1-by-1 Pixels, or Clear GIFs) Special links embedded in Web pages, or other HTML-coded documents such as some types of email, that allow the link's creator to track every instance in which the document is viewed.

CROSS REFERENCES

See *Copyright Law; Cryptographic Privacy Protection Techniques; Legal, Social and Ethical Issues of the Internet; The Legal Implications of Information Security: Regulatory Compliance and Liability.*

REFERENCES

American Management Association (AMA) (2001). 2001 Workplace Monitoring and Surveillance: Policies and Practices. Available at: http://www.amanet.org/research/pdf/ems_short2001.pdf (Date of access: August 21, 2005).

Borland, J. (2003). Court: RIAA Lawsuit Strategy Illegal. News.com. Available at: http://news.com.com/2100-1027-5129687.html (Date of access: February 8, 2004)

Cailliau, R. (1995). A Little History of the World Wide Web. Available at: http://www.w3c.org/History.html (Date of access: February 8, 2004)

Cantrell v. Forest City Publishing Co., 419 U.S. 245 (1974). Available at: http://laws.findlaw.com/us/419/245.html (Date of access: February 8, 2004)

Children's Online Privacy Protection Act. (15 U.S.C. §§ 6501–6506) Available at: http://www.ftc.gov/ogc/coppa1.htm (Date of access: February 8, 2004)

Douglass v. Hustler Magazine, 769 F.2d 1128 (1985)

Electronic Communications Privacy Act of 1986. (18 U.S.C. § 2701) Available at: http://www4.law.cornell.edu/uscode/18/2701.html (Date of access: February 8, 2004)

Electronic Privacy Information Center (EPIC) Carnivore Archive. (2002) Available at: http://www.epic.org/privacy/carnivore/ (Date of access: February 8, 2004)

Electronic Privacy Information Center (EPIC) Foreign Intelligence Surveillance Act (FISA) Archive. (2003) Available at: http://www.epic.org/privacy/terrorism/fisa/ (Date of access: February 8, 2004)

Electronic Privacy Information Center (EPIC) "Terrorism" Information Awareness (TIA) Archive. (2003) Available at: http://www.epic.org/privacy/profiling/tia/ (Date of access: February 8, 2004) (Editing note: the strikethrough text is on the original Website title)

Enright, K. P. and McCullough, M. R. (2000). Computer Professionals for Social Responsibility Privacy Working Group: CPO Guidelines. Available at: http://www.privacylaw.net/CPO_Guidelines.pdf (Date of access: December 3, 2002)

European Commission (EC). (1995). Directive 95/46/EC of the European Parliament and of the Council of 24 October 1995 on the protection of individuals with regard to the processing of personal data and on the free movement of such data. *Official Journal L., 281*, 31. Available at: http://europa.eu.int/comm/internal_market/privacy/index_en.htm (Date of access: February 8, 2004)

European Union (EU) Parliament. Temporary Committee on the ECHELON Interception System Report. (2001) Available at: http://www.europarl.eu.int/tempcom/echelon/pdf/prechelon_en.pdf (Date of access: February 8, 2004)

Fair Credit Reporting Act. (15 U.S.C. §§ 1681–1681(u), as amended) Available at: http://www.ftc.gov/os/statutes/fcra.htm (Date of access: February 8, 2004)

Federal Trade Commission (FTC). (1998). In the Matter of GeoCities, File No. 982 3051. Available at: http://www.ftc.gov/os/1998/08/geo-ord.htm (Date of access: February 8, 2004)

Federal Trade Commission (FTC). (2000). FTC v. Toysmart.com, LLC, and Toysmart.com, Inc. (District of Massachusetts) (Civil Action No. 00-11341-RGS). Available at: http://www.ftc.gov/opa/2000/07/toysmart.htm (Date of access: February 8, 2004)

Federal Trade Commission (FTC). (2002). In the Matter of Eli Lilly and Company, File No. 012 3214. Available at: http://www.ftc.gov/opa/2002/01/elililly.htm (Date of access: February 8, 2004)

Federal Trade Commission (FTC). (2003). In the Matter of Guess?, Inc., and Guess.com, Inc., File No. 022 3260. Available at: http://www.ftc.gov/opa/2003/06/guess.htm (Date of access: February 8, 2004)

Federal Trade Commission (FTC) Advisory Committee on Online Access and Security (ACOAS). (2000). Final Report. Available at: http://www.ftc.gov/acoas (Date of access: February 8, 2004)

Federal Trade Commission (FTC) "Kidz Privacy" Education Campaign Site. (2003) Available at: http://www.ftc.gov/bcp/conline/edcams/kidzprivacy/news.htm (Date of access: February 8, 2004)

Federal Trade Commission (FTC) Office of the General Counsel (OGC). (2002). "A Brief Overview of the Federal Trade Commission's Investigative and Law Enforcement Authority." Available at: http://www.ftc.gov/ogc/brfovrvw.htm (Date of access: February 8, 2004)

Foreign Intelligence Surveillance Act of 1978. (codified at 50 U.S.C. §§ 1801–1811, 1821–1829, 1841–1846, 1861–62, as amended) Available at: http://www4.law.cornell.edu/uscode/50/1801.html (Date of access: February 8, 2004)

Freedom of Information Act of 1966. (5 U.S.C. § 552) Available at: http://www.usdoj.gov/oip/foia_updates/Vol_XVII_4/page2.htm (Date of access: February 8, 2004)

Gramm-Leach-Bliley Act. (Codified in relevant part at 15 U.S.C. §§ 6801–6809) Available at: http://www.ftc.gov/privacy/glbact/glbsub1.htm (Date of access: February 8, 2004)

Levine, J. R., Everett-Church, R., & Stebben, G. (2002). Internet Privacy for Dummies. New York: Wiley Publishing, Inc.

McCullagh, D. (2003). Labels, Verizon DMCA Battle Rages. ZDNet News. Available at: http://zdnet.com.com/2100-1104-983896.html (Date of access: February 8, 2004)

National Association of Attorneys General (NAAG). (2001). 39 Attorneys General, the District of Columbia Corporation Counsel, and the Georgia Governors Office of Consumer Affairs Submit Comments to FCC Urging Better Privacy Protections For Consumers. Available at: http://www.naag.org/issues/pdf/20011228-signon-fcc.pdf (Date of access: February 8, 2004)

Network Advertising Initiative (NAI). (2001). Web Beacons: Guidelines for Notice and Choice. Available at: http://www.networkadvertising.org/Statement.pdf (Date of access: February 8, 2004)

Oakes, C. (1999). 23 Fired for Email Violations. Wired News. Available at: http://www.wired.com/news/politics/0,1283,32820,00.html (Date of access: February 8, 2004)

Olmstead v. United States, 277 U.S. 438 (1928) Available at: http://laws.findlaw.com/us/277/438.html (Date of access: February 8, 2004)

Organization for Economic Cooperation and Development (OECD). (1980). Guidelines on the Protection of Privacy and Transborder Flows of Personal Data. Available at: http://www.oecd.org/document/25/0,2340,en_2649_34255_1888153_1_1_1_1,00.html (Date of access: February 8, 2004)

Poindexter, J. M. (2003) Finding the Face of Terror in Data. *New York Times*. Available at: http://www.nytimes.com/2003/09/10/opinion/10POIN.html (Date of access: February 8, 2004)

Privacy Act of 1974. (5 U.S.C. § 552A) Available at: http://www.usdoj.gov/foia/privstat.htm (Date of access: February 8, 2004)

Prosser, W. L. (1960). Privacy. *California Law Review, 48*, 383

Smith, R. M. (2001) FAQ: Web Bugs. Available at: http://www.eff.org/Privacy/Marketing/web_bug.html (Date of access: February 8, 2004)

Society for Human Resource Management. (2004). SHRM Finds Employers Are Increasingly Conducting Background Checks To Ensure Workplace Safety. Available at: http://www.shrm.org/press_published/CMS_007126.asp#P-5_0 (Date of access: February 8, 2004)

Sullivan, B. (2001). FBI Software Cracks Encryption Wall. MSNBC News. Available at: http://www.msnbc.com/news/660096.asp (Date of access: February 8, 2004)

TRUSTe. (2004). Model Privacy Statement. Available at http://www.truste.org/webpublishers/pub_modelprivacystatement.html (Date of access: February 8, 2004)

United Nations. (1948). Universal Declaration of Human Rights. Available at: http://www.un.org/Overview/rights.html (Date of access: February 8, 2004)

Uniting and Strengthening America by Providing Appropriate Tools Required to Intercept and Obstruct Terrorism (USA PATRIOT) Act of 2001. (Pub. L. No. 107-56) Available at: http://www.epic.org/privacy/terrorism/hr3162.html (Date of access: February 8, 2004)

U.S. Department of Commerce. (2000) Safe Harbor. Available at: http://www.export.gov/safeharbor (Date of access: February 8, 2004)

U.S. Department of Health and Human Services (HHS). (2002). Medical Privacy—National Standards to Protect the Privacy of Personal Health Information, Office for Civil Rights. Available at: http://www.hhs.gov/ocr/hipaa/ (Date of access: February 8, 2004)

U.S. Department of Health, Education and Welfare (HEW). (1973). Records, Computers and the Rights of Citizens. Available at: http://aspe.hhs.gov/datacncl/1973privacy/tocprefacemembers.htm (Date of access: February 8, 2004)

Hackers, Crackers, and Computer Criminals

David Dittrich, *University of Washington*
Kenneth Einar Himma, *Seattle Pacific University*

INTRODUCTION

Early on, the threat posed by hackers, crackers, and computer criminals was comparatively minor. For starters, most people lacked sufficient access to the new information technologies to be affected in any significant way by computer crime. Equally important, most computer intruders lacked the skills and expertise to do significant damage to affected individuals.

Much has changed in the past 20 to 25 years. An ever-increasing number of people are coming to rely on e-mail, Web access, and other digital information technologies for social, personal, and commercial purposes, and those who lack direct access to these technologies frequently depend on commercial and governmental institutions that incorporate these technologies into key operations. In consequence, the increasing number of computer intrusions implicates, at least indirectly, the interests of the vast majority of people in the industrial world and a growing number of people in the developing world.

Moreover, computer criminals have been developing a more sophisticated (and dangerous) palate of tools for committing intrusions. Partly because computer technologies are so sophisticated, computer criminals tend to be more intelligent and more focused than other criminals. Not surprisingly, they have worked hard to hone their skills at breaking into computer systems and concealing their presence in those systems.

These efforts have paid off. Over time, scripts and programs have been improved to automate more and more of the various processes involved in staging a digital attack or intrusion. These new technologies can employ multiple attack vectors, install backdoors, disable antivirus and firewall software, disable and wipe log files, alter the operating system to run them at every reboot, and do all of this in a matter of seconds.[i]

The result is that hackers, crackers, and computer criminals now pose a serious threat to individuals, commercial firms, and state institutions. Because sophisticated intruders can command hundreds of thousands of computers to stage attacks against innocent persons and institutions, they can cause catastrophic harm. A sustained attack taking down a commercial Web site, for example, can result in the loss of millions of dollars in revenue—and potentially the loss of jobs. It is not overstating matters to characterize computer crime as one of the most important problems facing law enforcement today.

DEFINITIONS AND EXAMPLES

Defining the Terms: Hacking and Cracking

The words "hacker" and "cracker" are contentious terms, meaning different things to different people. Many people in the programming community, especially those who were programming in the seventies and eighties, view the word "hacker" as a term of approbation. Indeed, the original *Hacker's Dictionary*[ii], maintained for years by students at the Massachusetts Institute of Technology (MIT), defines "hacker" in terms that naturally lend themselves to such an interpretation:

[i] To get a sense for how much the computer criminal's tools and tactics have improved, consider this: ten years ago, it would take an expert hacker weeks, and even months, to break into several hundred systems; today, an expert hacker can compromise many more computers in a matter of days. For an example of the former, see Mann and Freedman (1998).

[ii] http://www.dourish.com/goodies/jargon.html

> HACKER n. 1. A person who enjoys learning the details of programming systems and how to stretch their capabilities, as opposed to most users who prefer to learn only the minimum necessary. 2. One who programs enthusiastically, or who enjoys programming rather than just theorizing about programming. 3. A person capable of appreciating hack value (q.v.). 4. A person who is good at programming quickly. Not everything a hacker produces is a hack. 5. An expert at a particular program, or one who frequently does work using it or on it; example: "A SAIL hacker". (Definitions 1 to 5 are correlated, and people who fit them congregate.) 6. A malicious or inquisitive meddler who tries to discover information by poking around. Hence "password hacker", "network hacker".

According to the first five clauses of this early definition, the term "hacker" is used to pick out a class of people with a variety of intellectual virtues, including special expertise in computer and network systems. On this usage, the term applies only to persons of distinction—whether in virtue of their special skills or in virtue of their passion for intellectual pursuits. Indeed, as defined here, the term's connotation is sufficiently positive that it was bestowed as an honor: to be a hacker was to possess extraordinary programming ability and intellectually virtuous character traits.

Definition 6 comes closest to expressing the current use of the term "hacker" that is now irrevocably associated with computer crime. A hacker, on this usage, is a malicious or inquisitive meddler who pokes around to discover information. The use of "malicious," "meddler," and "poking around," at the very least, evokes the contemporary idea that a hacker is someone who intrudes upon the computer systems and networks of other people.

The different definitions reflect the history of hacking and the associated terms, which arguably extend as far back as the mainframe computer. Taken together, the various historical treatments of hacking distinguish a number of different classes or generations of persons who have been characterized as hackers. These classes include (1) the original MIT hackers who worked with mainframe computers in the 1950s and 1960s; (2) the hardware hackers of the so-called personal computer revolution of the 1970s; (3) the software hackers of the 1980s who developed new architectures for computer games; (4) so-called microserfs who have abandoned the original hacking culture to join large corporate firms as programmers and developers; (5) open source programmers; (6) hacktivists who commit computer intrusions for the purpose of advancing social and political causes; and (7) the hackers and crackers who commit computer intrusions for other malicious and nonmalicious purposes.[iii]

But, for better or worse, Definition 6 comes closest to capturing the meaning of the word as currently used in the community at large. Although many persons in the computer industry continue to use the term "hacker" to pick out programmers of distinction, the term "hacker" is now used by most persons only to pick out persons who intrude upon systems and machines belonging to other people without any meaningful authorization (whether through the consent of the owners or through the legal process). Anyone who trespasses upon someone else's system or network qualifies under this definition as a hacker according to this common usage.

In consequence, the term has lost its normative connotations (at least outside the computer industry). To the general population, it no longer connotes either expertise in programming or intellectual virtue of any kind. The media, for example, typically use the term, to the chagrin of many who lament these changes in conventional usage, to refer to the most unskilled intruders, including so-called script kiddies who simply take the most primitive hacking tools off the Web and use them without any understanding or creativity.

Even so, many persons attempt to distinguish intrusions motivated by malicious purposes (e.g., to destroy someone else's files) from intrusions motivated by benign purposes (e.g., to investigate security flaws in some operating system). Hacking that is motivated by a malicious intent to cause damage or harm is called "cracking" (or "black-hat hacking").[iv] Persons who distinguish hacking from cracking reserve the term "hacking" (or "white-hat hacking") for intrusions not associated with destructive or malicious purposes.

Motivations and Examples

Given the problems associated with hacking and cracking, it is important to understand the motivations of those who engage in such behaviors. Hacking and cracking, by definition, involve unauthorized intrusions upon the computers (and hence property) of other persons; as such, these behaviors are fairly characterized as antisocial. As is true of other antisocial behaviors, the problems associated with computer misconduct cannot be successfully addressed without some understanding of what motivates it.

Fame

It is not surprising that one very common motivation for hacking and other forms of computer misconduct is a desire for fame and notoriety. Fame and notoriety, after all, are common motivations in many other walks of life. Given the amount of media attention devoted to successful large-scale computer attacks and to such hacker celebrities as Kevin Mitnick, it is clear that hacking, cracking, and computer crimes are all viable paths to fame.

Hackers motivated by such considerations are primarily concerned with achieving recognition within the hacker community and have publicized their exploits among fellow hackers in a variety of ways. Early hackers, for example, discussed their exploits on special bulletin boards or print publications devoted to hacking, such

[iii] These classifications owe to several different historical treatments of hacking. See Levy (1984), Taylor (1999), and Taylor and Jordan (2004). I am indebted to an anonymous reviewer for drawing my attention to the importance of this point.

[iv] The term *cracking* is sometimes used to refer to people who produced high-quality programs for circumventing copywrite-protection technologies. See, for example, *Interview with Mike Hudack* (n.d.)

as *2600*. Contemporary hackers can discuss their exploits on Web logs (blogs) and in Internet chat rooms. In both cases, the idea was to find a comparatively private forum in which hacker exploits could be shared among a sympathetic community without incurring a risk of prosecution.

Even so, a hacker's desire for fame sometimes proves to be his or her undoing.[v] As former Justice Department Internet crimes prosecutor Marc Zwillenger put it, "[For t]he kind of people who do this, fame and notoriety are the primary motivation. They don't derive financial benefit from releasing a worm. If they can't claim credit, what's the point?"[vi] Indeed, many hackers who would otherwise have gotten away with their attacks have been caught because they claimed credit for an attack on a bulletin board or in a chat room.

Curiosity

Some intrusions are motivated by nothing more sophisticated than curiosity. Robert Tappan Morris wrote and released the first Internet worm in 1998 simply to satisfy curiosity. Morris did not intend the damage the worm eventually caused and did not anticipate that many sites would choose to shut off their Internet connections entirely because of the ensuing disruption to affected systems.[vii] Indeed, he had no developed sense of what the worm would do or how people might respond: he released the worm, in essence, just to see what would transpire.

Boredom

A desire to relieve boredom is another common motivation. Adrian Lamo wandered through the networks of WorldCom, Microsoft, Excite@Home, Yahoo!, and the *New York Times* partly out of boredom. Lamo entered a variety of networks, sometimes gaining access to sensitive information. After entering the *New York Times* network, he viewed employee records and Social Security numbers, as well as accessed the contact information for the newspaper's sources and columnists, including former U.S. president Jimmy Carter, former Marine colonel Oliver North, and hip-hop artist Queen Latifah. Somewhat sheepishly, Lamo attributed his behavior to boredom: "I was looking for something to do."[viii]

Intellectual Challenge

One of the most widely cited motivations, and the one most typically associated with the stereotype of the hacker as a social nerd, is the intellectual challenge involved in finding a way into a system. For example, Kevin Mitnick stole the source codes for Sun Microsystems' operating system, Nokia's cell phones, and Motorola's cell phones. In testimony before the U.S. Senate Committee on Governmental Affairs, Mitnick explained his motivations as follows:

> My motivation was the quest for knowledge, the intellectual challenge, the thrill and also the escape from reality—kind of like somebody who chooses to gamble to block out things that they would rather not think about. My hacking involved pretty much exploring computer systems and obtaining access to the source code of telecommunication systems and computer operating systems, because my goal was to learn all I can about security vulnerabilities within these systems.[ix]

Such motivations presumably echo the intentions of many younger hackers who are eager to learn more about the relevant technologies, as well as to improve their own skills.

To Help Secure Systems

Hackers are sometimes motivated by a desire to improve the security of affected systems. For example, when the MSBlaster worm infected millions of computers in 2001, an unknown hacker wrote and released a counterworm that attempted to install a patch disabling MSBlaster. Although this counterworm was christened the Good Samaritan Worm for the salutary motivations of its creator, many experts feared that it might have more undesirable than desirable effects.

Indeed, computer intruders frequently lament that their victims do not seem to welcome their assistance. For example, an anonymous intruder to the National Aeronautics and Space Administration (NASA) expressed disappointment when his help was not accepted:

> I would email the system administrators sometimes and tell them that their computers were vulnerable. I would tell them how to break in, and how to fix the problems. I'd give them advice, and they would never follow it. Three weeks later I would go in and I *still* had access to their computers.[x]

These hackers believe that their efforts are legitimate because they are motivated by the best of intentions—the desire to help secure systems.

Financial Gain

Not surprisingly, some intrusions are motivated by financial gain. In 1994, Russian Vladimir Levin used stolen passwords to transfer an estimated $10 million out of Citibank into accounts around the world. Levin reportedly used stolen account names and passwords to make the transfers. All but $400,000 was recovered.[xi]

Russian hackers Vasily Gorshkov and Alexey Ivanov broke into a number of corporate networks and Internet

[v] It is worth noting, despite the use of "his or her" in this context, that the world of computing technology has been largely dominated by males. This is no less true of the hacking community: hackers are nearly always male.

[vi] See "Few Clues in Web Worm Whodunit" (2003).

[vii] See ftp://coast.cs.purdue.edu/pub/doc/morris_worm/

[viii] Lemos (2001).

[ix] http://www.pbs.org/wgph/pages/frontline/shows/hackers/whoare/testimony.html Mitnick turned out to be a master at using information to trick employees at these companies into giving him full access to the systems that contained the source code he sought (see the Social Engineering section for a discussion of such tactics). Mitnick went on to say, "The human side of computer security is easily exploited and constantly overlooked. Companies spend millions of dollars on firewalls, encryption, and secure access devices and it's money wasted because none of these measures address the weakest link in the security chain: the people who use, administer, operate and account for computer systems that contain protected information." *Id.*

[x] *Id.*

[xi] See http://www.pbs.org/wgbh/pages/frontline/shows/hackers/whoare/notable.html

service providers, looking for credit card numbers.[xii] If they were unsuccessful in finding credit card numbers, they would extort money from the victims to "fix" the holes. But if they were successful, they would use the numbers to purchase nonexistent items they sold on eBay, subsequently laundering the purchases through PayPal and fake e-mail accounts. The two reportedly caused an aggregate loss of more than $25 million.[xiii]

The U.S. Federal Trade Commission reported that, in 2003, $437 million was lost in online fraud.[xiv] These losses resulted from identity theft involving stolen credit cards and attacks aimed at inducing individuals, by fraudulent means, into giving out personal and financial information.[xv]

Financially motivated distributed denial of service attacks (DDoS) have also increased.[xvi] These attacks, which frequently involve a large number of innocent agent machines, threaten to deny customers access (or deny service) to online materials and services unless victims pay a substantial sum. Many attacks have affected online transaction-processing services[xvii]; the British Association of Real-time Gambling Operators (ARGO) reported, for example, that their members had paid over $73 million to extortionists between January and June 2004.[xviii] There is even a case (the first of its kind) in the United States involving someone allegedly hired to attack business competitors.[xix] This trend is growing at an alarming rate worldwide and is becoming a major focus of international law enforcement resources.

Political Activism (Hacktivism)

Some unauthorized intrusions are motivated by political and expressive purposes. In 1999, political activists sought to buttress the protests against the World Trade Organization (WTO) by striking at the WTO Web site. U.K.-based E-hippies, an activist group, attempted to shut down a WTO Web site hosted by Conxion by overwhelming it with requests for information. Similarly, in early 2000, a number of activists launched similar attacks against a variety of commercial Web sites, including Amazon.com and eBay.com, as a means of protesting the increasing commercialization of the Web. These self-styled activists viewed their attacks as a form of civil disobedience justified by the justice of the causes they sought to advance. These politically motivated attacks have come to be known as hacktivism.

Revenge

Some unauthorized intrusions are motivated as revenge for some sort of perceived slight.[xx] Convinced that he was not being fairly compensated, Roger Duronio resigned from his position at Paine Webber as a system administrator. He planted a logic bomb (i.e., a program designed to take malicious action at a particular point in time) on 1,000 of PaineWebber's approximately 1,500 networked computers around the country, attempting to profit from the resulting damage.[xxi] Duronio purchased $21,000 of put options on stock in UBS, the parent company of PaineWebber, in the hope that the logic bomb would cause the value of UBS stock to drop, thereby increasing the value of his options. Although the logic bomb was successfully activated on March 4, 2002, causing an estimated $3 million in damages to PaineWebber, the anticipated drop in the price of UBS's stock did not occur.[xxii]

TACTICS, TECHNOLOGIES, AND TECHNIQUES

Hackers, crackers, and computer criminals have a growing palate of tactics and technologies that can be used to achieve their purposes. Common tactics include sniffers that harvest passwords from unsuspecting computer users connecting over the network; stepping stones that conceal the ultimate source of an intrusion; and stolen disk space to serve as caches for, among other things, attack programs, password files, or stolen credit card numbers. Attackers often use more than one of these tactics depending on their skill sets, timelines, and available bandwidths for targeting hosts. These and other tactics are discussed below.

Sniffers

Sniffers are the digital analog to wiretap devices in the telecommunications context. Whereas a wiretap is a physical device that records the analog transmissions of voice communications over a telephone line, a sniffer is a program that allows one to "see" and record the packets of data that contain the communication between people using computers. Just as a wiretap must be placed on one of the lines being monitored, sniffing can occur only on local area network segments (which include aggregator switches and backbone networks).[xxiii] It is not possible either to sniff traffic from multiple network hops (i.e., network interconnections) away from the target network or to tap a phone line physically located inside a building that the would-be wiretapper cannot enter.

Computer criminals frequently use sniffers to harvest passwords from unsuspecting computer users connecting over the network. These passwords can subsequently be used to gain access to valuable information that is stored on the user's network in e-mail and other files. Passwords can be obtained by sniffing the traffic associated with login authentication or by looking for passwords transmitted as part of text messages, such as e-mail, chat, or instant messages. (For this reason, users should be wary of transmitting very sensitive information on any channel that does not encrypt the transmissions.)

[xii] http://www.usdoj.gov/criminal/cybercrime/gorshkovconvict.htm

[xiii] http://www.usdoj.gov/criminal/cybercrime/ivanovSent.htm

[xiv] Naraine (2004).

[xv] These attacks have become known as phishing attacks. See the Social Engineering section for more detailed discussion of such attacks.

[xvi] See the Denial of Service section for a more detailed description and discussion of such attacks.

[xvii] Sullivan (2004).

[xviii] See Bullough (2004). The ARGO submission to the UK All Party Internet Group can be found at http://www.apig.org.uk/ARGO%20Evidence.doc

[xix] See Poulson (2004). See also the indictment against the suspects: http://www.reverse.net/operationcyberslam.pdf

[xx] These most frequently occur in the context of an employer–employee relationship that has gone bad. See http://abcnews.go.com/sections/business/TechTV/techtv employee revenge 020604.html

[xxi] See http://www.cybercrime.gov/duronioIndict.htm

[xxii] As of the date of this writing, there has been no resolution to this case. See http://www.usdoj.gov/criminal/cybercrime/cccases.html

[xxiii] For a more detailed description of network sniffers, see Dittrich (1998).

Internet Protocol Spoofing

The exchange of data between computers on the Internet is made possible through the use of various protocols. These protocols are layered in what is known as a stack, with lower level protocols handling transmission over physical media or wireless transmission and higher level protocols responsible for routing packets between networks. The latter eventually leads up to application-level protocols or higher.

For example, applications that use the Internet for communication rely on either the unreliable datagram protocol (UDP), which is used for quick but unreliable transmissions, or the transmission control protocol (TCP), which is used for more reliable transmissions. Applications using UDP typically send simple request/reply packets (somewhat like electronic versions of postcards) without the overhead associated with ensuring that packets actually make it from one computer to the intended destination. Applications that must ensure the integrity of the data being transferred can use TCP, which manages the process of establishing connections by tracking the number of bytes sent and received through use of sequence numbers and by checking to ensure they are transmitted without error through the use of checksums. This is part of the state information about transmissions maintained by the TCP portion of the TCP/Internet protocol (IP) stack.

Both TCP and UDP rely on a lower level routing protocol to get packets from one Internet host to another (sometimes through a dozen or more intermediary routers) known as the IP. Communication at the IP layer is handled by transmitting individual packets of data (known as datagrams) from sender to receiver and back again. Packets in transit are identified by several attributes, specified by fields in the packet's header, including their source and destination IP addresses. IP addresses are 4-byte values that are represented by dotted quads that consist of four decimal values between 0 and 255 separated by periods; these addresses specify the locations, so to speak, of the various computers and networks making up the Internet (an example of a dotted quad IP address is 192.168.0.1).

As may be evident, the exclusive use of numeric IP addresses for users to identify computers on the Internet is impractical in one important respect: sequences of up to 12 digits separated by three decimal points are very difficult for people to remember. To circumvent the need for people to remember these source addresses, methods of mapping names to IP addresses were developed. The Internet relies today on the domain name system (DNS) to map these decimal sequences to more easily remembered names. For example, the MIT computer housing the GNU Open Source software repository in California is named "prep.ai.mit.edu" in DNS and has the IP address 199.232.41.9. (The trailing period is just there to make that a valid English sentence. IP addresses do not end in periods.)

Unfortunately, the most widely used version of the Internet protocol (IPv4)[xxiv] is vulnerable to being exploited because IPv4 lacks any mechanism for guaranteeing the reliability of source addresses. It is possible for someone to generate a series of bytes forming a valid IP packet, inject it into the network, and route it to some unknowing receiving host. For example, a computer that tries to communicate with prep.ai.mit.edu might wind up exchanging information with a computer pretending to be 199.232.41.9.[xxv]

The problem is that it is quite difficult for a user to ascertain whether he or she is connecting to the intended source or to an imposter. File transfer protocol (FTP), Telnet,[xxvi] and hypertext transfer protocol (HTTP) browsers provide no way for the user to determine that he or she is not connecting to some imposter site. With some basic protocols (UDP services, for example, or the Berkeley "r" utilities), especially on TCP/IP stacks using predictable sequence numbers, someone can forge an entire series of packets and, as long as they reach the victim host before replies reach the host being faked, the victim will respond to them.

This unreliability in the validity of IP source addresses leads to several types of spoofing attacks. Blind spoofing attacks generally target stateless protocols, such as UDP, that do not employ any mechanism for authenticating clients or servers.[xxvii] These attacks are typically staged from one or more network hops from the targeted network and proceed by forging packets that make it appear that the targeted network is communicating with some acceptable host network; they are characterized as blind because they do not require that the attacker have visibility of the packets being sent back and forth to trick the target host.[xxviii]

Another common use of IP spoofing is in connection with denial of service (DoS) attacks. As will be discussed in more detail in the Denial of Service section, a DoS attack attempts to shut down a targeted network by overwhelming it with more traffic than it can handle. Perpetrators of such an attack frequently spoof a source address on the packets to either make it more difficult for the victim to identify the flooding hosts or make it more difficult for network operators to find and clean up the affected host.

Session Hijacking

Intruders can take over a user's session by deflecting traffic from its intended destination and interjecting their own

[xxiv] The newest version of the Internet Protocol, Version 6 (IPv6), includes features for cryptographic authentication and encapsulation that are intended to make address forgery and sniffing attacks impossible. As of this writing, IPv6 is still not in widespread use in the United States, although it is becoming very popular in some Asian and European countries.

[xxv] There are various types of attacks that involve IP spoofing, some more difficult than others, depending on where the attacker is located—in network terms—in relation to the victim. For more on IP spoofing attacks, see http://www.securityfocus.com/infocus/1674.

[xxvi] Even though clear-text password vulnerabilities have existed in programs such as FTP and Telnet for decades, some vendors still distribute these programs in their operating systems, and some people still continue to use them. This is most common behind firewalls or in home local area network environments, where users believe they are secure. Many sites ban these programs by policy and instead try to provide users with cryptographically secure services that do not expose passwords on the network, such as SSH or SSL.

[xxvii] Some protocols don't keep any state whatsoever and, in consequence, may respond to a reply that is received by a system that never even initiated a request. One such attack on the address resolution protocol compromises the mapping of IP addresses to the physical (e.g., Ethernet or MAC) addresses of network cards.

[xxviii] A more complex nonblind spoofing attack is described below in the Session Hijacking section.

traffic into the user's stream of communication. For example, someone making a connection to an FTP server or using Telnet will likely have an account on the server that would not exist if someone was simply impersonating the server. To circumvent this obstacle, intruder tools have been developed that act as a man in the middle and relay all traffic to and from the real server until the victim has logged in. The attacker can then interject packets into the stream with the client's forged source address and effectively take over the session.

This tactic has come to be known as *session hijacking*. By displacing the victim's traffic with his or her own, the attacker hijacks the victim's session. The victim will notice that the session has hung or died and may simply kill the session and start again, thinking that some relevant application has malfunctioned.

Simple forms of session hijacking can be defeated by using more secure communication methods, such as Secure Socket Layer (SSL) or SSH, which employ cryptographic certificate or key pair mechanisms to verify the authenticity of one or both ends of the connection and which encrypt the content of the communication. This effectively defeats the simple forms of session hijacking because, in ordinary cases, the attacker will not have access to the proper keys to get past the encryption used.

Certain man-in-the-middle attacks on SSL and SSH remain possible, but these can succeed only if users ignore warnings that encryption keys have changed since their last use or that certificates either do not match expectations or are not signed by proper certificate authorities. The weakest point is the first time a user connects to a site using a new SSL certificate or uses a new client to connect to an SSH server; at this point, the user must verify that a fingerprint matches to determine whether he or she is connecting to the real server or whether he or she is being tricked by a man-in-the-middle attack. Many users are not trained to do this fingerprint verification, and many sites do not provide users with a secure means to verify the fingerprint in the first place. Thus, even though strong encryption is available, it may be used improperly and only provide a false sense of security and be easily defeated by an intruder.

Buffer Overflows

Buffer overflows take advantage of a decades-old class of programming errors involving low-level languages such as C that use pointers to data structures in memory and do not take into consideration the size of those data structures. Programmers frequently make themselves vulnerable by defining a buffer to be of some small, fixed size—say 32 bytes—and then calling a function to read an arbitrary amount of data from a network socket. This programming error enables an intruder to attack by feeding a much larger amount of data into the socket, say 4,096 bytes, which effectively overwrites the 32 bytes (typically located on the stack, surrounded by other variables such as function call return addresses, frame pointers, etc.). This makes it possible for the intruder to inject binary machine language code and manipulate return addresses on the stack, tricking the computer into executing code that the intruder has injected.

Buffer overflow conditions can be identified by examining source code, by writing programs to generate large strings and examining their effect on a program using a debugger or by reverse-engineering the program using a disassembler. When, for example, Microsoft confirmed that source code to parts of its Windows NT and 2000 operating systems had been leaked on the Internet, the immediate fear of many security experts was that this would result in a slew of new exploits.

John the Ripper and Password-Cracking Techniques

A variety of techniques have been used to store passwords on systems for the purpose of authenticating users. For example, the UNIX operating system formerly combined the user's password and a two character "salt" to produce a scrambled string, which was stored on the system in a file visible to all applications and users.[xxix] The system would authenticate the user by combining the same two salt characters with the password provided by the user; if the result was the same as the stored string, then the same password was given.[xxx] If not, access was denied. The encrypted passwords were deemed to be safe in visible form, since computers at the time were not sufficiently powerful to attack the encryption mechanism or to use brute-force methods to try to determine the passwords (an attack known as password cracking). More recently, systems use hashing algorithms[xxxi], such as Message Digest 5 (MD5), that produce output with a much larger number of bits, making brute-force comparisons against longer pass phrases much more difficult.

John the Ripper is one of the most commonly used password cracking programs. Its popularity derives from its flexibility in handling many types of password hashing or encrypting mechanisms, its dictionary-attack techniques, and its functions for restarting interrupted sessions. It operates by detecting weak UNIX passwords and is compatible with a variety of different platforms, including DOS, Win32, BeOS, and Open VMS.

John the Ripper's core strength rests in using predefined dictionaries of words that are algorithmically permuted in ways commonly used by people choosing passwords, such as replacing letters such as "O," "A," and "S" with the digits "0," "4," and "5"; adding digits or punctuation as a prefix or suffix to words, and so forth. By allowing the selection of targeted dictionaries, an attacker

[xxix] For a discussion of how Unix passwords are encrypted, the role of a salt value in password encryption, weaknesses in the original crypt algorithm, password cracking attacks, and some proposed ways to harden Unix passwords, see "The Ambitious Amateur vs. crypt(3) or Pondering the Lifespan of Visible Passwords against Brute Force Attack," http://personal.stevens.edu/~khockenb/crypt3.html

[xxx] At the time, programmers believed that the algorithm was sufficiently complex that no risk would result from allowing all users to see the encrypted password.

[xxxi] Hash functions take a variable length input and convert it to a fixed length output. The kinds of hash functions used for passwords are known as cryptographic hash functions. Properly used, such functions should make it difficult for an attacker to find the same input (i.e., the user's password or pass-phrase) that resulted in the hash value stored in the password hash file. For more details, see http://en.wikipedia.org/wiki/Cryptographic_hash_function

can increase the likelihood of cracking weak user passwords. For example, if an attacker knows the password file comes from a system used by chemists, he or she can increase the chances of cracking the system's passwords by using a dictionary that includes chemical terms, names of famous chemists, and chemical companies (over one, say, that includes European poets or figures in African history). Dictionaries exist for all common fields of study and professions–hence the common admonishment to refrain from using words or names found in dictionaries or encyclopedias, even if they are foreign words or names.

There are a number of defenses against password cracking. Systems can defend against such attacks by securing the password hash file, requiring that users select hard-to-guess passwords and change them frequently, or using some form of *second-factor authentication* mechanisms (i.e., adding to the username or password another authentication challenge, such as a one-time password or key fob or card that generates random numbers).

In any event, intruders can obtain passwords without attempting to decrypt them or reverse hashing functions (assuming this is even theoretically possible). In many cases, they can simply attack the password authentication mechanism itself (i.e., the login/password challenge presented by the system) by attempting to predict a person's choice of password (people are not very good at generating randomness in passwords) or by taking advantage of weaknesses in the hashing algorithms themselves. The simple dictionary attack similar to the one used by John the Ripper, if targeted and sorted according to the frequency of occurrence of commonly used terms, can often break passwords in seconds.[xxxii]

These kinds of attacks (which do not require access to the stored password file) are becoming very popular against Windows computers running Windows remote access services, file-sharing services, as well as against SSH servers on non-Windows platforms. Programs such as Phatbot[xxxiii] implement remote dictionary-based attacks against Windows computers using over 100 popularly chosen passwords.[xxxiv] It is very successful in identifying hosts using these weak passwords. Informing users how to form strong passwords can prevent Phatbot from entering systems using this method.

Up to this point, this portion of the chapter has discussed only tools and techniques for gaining entry to a computer system. In addition to gaining entry, it should come as no surprise that attackers typically wish to maintain access to the system they have compromised by avoiding detection over time as well as minimizing the chances they will be caught if and when they are detected. To accomplish these goals, the attackers must destroy evidence of the intrusion, conceal their presence in the system, and hide their true locations and identities. The next section discusses some of these techniques.

Postintrusion Concealment Using Rootkits

Rootkits are programs designed to conceal an intruder and his or her files, directories, or programs by making an operating system lie to its owner. The term *root* relates to the system administrator account, but also serves as a verb in the hacker vernacular referring to the act of gaining system administrator rights on a system ("Betty rooted that Unix system"). The term *kit* refers to the programs that are bundled by an attacker into a neat and easy-to-distribute and install package form (often a *tar* archive file).

Rootkits come in a few distinct types:

1. Straight replacements of, or modifications to, basic operating system programs that are designed to filter out strings based on rules or configuration;
2. Kernel modules that are loaded into the running operating system kernel that perform filtering and privilege escalation at a level below the operating system commands; and
3. Modifications to the kernel's run-time memory that alter system call tables, execution paths within system calls, or the return values of security checks to bypass intended access control mechanisms.

Rootkits elevate privileges on demand, provide continual unfettered (and nonlogged) access, and conceal the intruder's presence in a computer system. Although these methods generally leave some kind of trace in the system's file system,[xxxv] they all make the job of intrusion response

[xxxii] Sadly, many people do not try to choose passwords that either have the appearance of randomness or are hard-to-guess words or phrases. One recent study showed that the most frequently used password is "password." See, e.g., bCentral (2005) http://www.bcentral.co.uk/issues/technology/networks/securityconsiderations.mspx

[xxxiii] LurHQ (2005) http://www.lurhq.com/phatbot.html

[xxxiv] One version of Phatbot uses the following list of passwords: admin, Admin, password, Password, 1, 12, 123, 1234, beer, !@#$, asdfgh, !@#$%, !@#$%^, !@#$%^&, !@#$%^&*, WindowsXP, windows2k, windowsME, windows98, windoze, hax, dude, owned, lol, ADMINISTRATOR, rooted, noob, TEMP, share, r00t, freak, ROOT, TEST, SYSTEM, LOCAL, SERVER, ACCESS, BACKUP, computer, fucked, gay, idiot, Internet, test, 2003, 2004, backdoor, whore, wh0re, CNN, pwned, own, crash, passwd, PASSWD, iraq, devil, linux, UNIX, feds, fish, changeme, ASP, PHP, 666, BOX, Box, box, 12345, 123456, 1234567, 12345678, 123456789, 654321, 54321, 111, 000000, 00000000, 11111111, 88888888, fanny, pass, passwd, database, abcd, oracle, sybase, 123qwe, fool, server, computer, Internet, super, 123asd, ihavenopass, West, godblessyou, enable, xp, 23, 2002, 2600, 0, 110, 2525, newfy, 111111, 121212, 123123, 1234qwer, 123abc, 007, alpha, 1776, newfie, patrick, pat, root, sex, god, foobar, 1778, a, aaa, abc, test, temp, win, pc, asdf, secret, drugs, qwer, yxcv, zxcv, home, xxx, owner, login, Login, west, Coordinatore, Administrador, Verwalter, Ospite, administrator, Default, administrador, admins, teacher, student, superman, wmd, supersecret, kids, penis, wwwadmin, database, changeme, dope, test123, user, private, 69, root, 654321, xxyyzz, asdfghjkl, mybaby, vagina, pussy, leet, metal, work, school, mybox, box, werty, baby, porn, homework, secrets, x, z, bong, qwertyuiop, secret, Administrateur, abc123, password123, red123, qwerty, admin123, zxcvbnm, poiuytrewq, pwd, pass, love, mypc, texas, Texas, Washington, washington, Tennessee, tennessee, jackdaniels, whisky, whiskey, azerty, poiut, mouse, ordinateur, souris, imprimeur, cederom, cédérom, bière, biere, moonshine, athlon, oil, opteron, écran, ecran, reseau, carte, merde, mince, ami, amie, copin, copine, 42, harry, dumbledore, hagrid, potter, hermione, hermine, gryffindor, azkaban, askaban, cauldron, buckbeak, hogwarts, dementor, quidditch, madre, switch, mypass, pw. It also attempts to use an empty password, which also is a surprisingly popular choice of passwords, even for the administrator account.

[xxxv] Nevertheless, it is important to note that modifications of kernel memory space are considerably less likely to leave detectable traces than the other methods.

more difficult because the system appears completely normal to the unwitting system owner or administrator. In many cases, the presence of a rootkit can be confirmed only by monitoring and analyzing network traffic from outside the system, as the intruder must get packets over the network to remotely control the computer.

Log Alteration

Once inside a computer system, attackers will often begin by disabling, deleting, or modifying logs to eliminate traces of their break-in and subsequent access to the system. A computer system contains two basic types of logs that intruders can alter to eliminate evidence of their presence in the system:

1. Binary logs that require a program or special application programming interface (API) to process and convert the logs to human readable text form. Examples of binary log files are Windows Event logs and Unix *wtmp/utmp/lastlog* files.
2. Text logs from services and applications that have already been converted to human readable form and simply need to be viewed. Examples of text log files are Apache Web server *access_log* and Unix *syslog* log files.

Use of Stepping Stones

The concept of a stepping stone is helpfully explained in terms of a physical analogy. If someone wishes to move from a point on one side of, say, a placid Japanese water garden to a point on the other side, he or she must find a series of solid and dry stones that can be used to step or hop from one side to the other. These *stepping stones* provide a safe path from one point to another point. If the number and proximity of these stepping stones is great enough, a person can make repeated trips across the water using different combinations of stones such that the path is not predictable and is possibly never repeated in the exact same sequence. Like physical stepping stones, digital stepping stones make it possible for a user to move from one machine location on the Internet to another.

The analogy, however, breaks down in one crucial respect. Digital stepping stones are used for the purpose of concealing the starting point of an intruder's path—and not for the purpose of moving from one location to another. Unlike physical stepping stones, digital stepping stones are not bound by physical constraints of movement; an attacker can conceivably move from any stone to any other stone—including from starting stone to destination stone; this means that intermediate stones are not necessary to enable the user to travel from a starting location to the final destination.

Digital stepping stones conceal the starting point of an attack from the ultimate victim.

To compromise a machine or network for use as a stepping stone, the attacker must gather intelligence about it.[xxxvi] A sophisticated attacker will typically spend considerable time reconnoitering a network to identify its structure, the trust relationships[xxxvii] between hosts, the points of vulnerability, and the alarms and access controls in place. These efforts aim at identifying weaknesses that can be exploited to use the machine or network as a stepping stone.

Intruders sometimes exploit trust relationships between systems by gaining access (frequently through firewalls) to a host within the network perimeter and then masquerading as a trusted insider to hop from this system to other systems. If an attacker can install the SucKIT rootkit on a Linux server, for example, he or she can do two things: (1) harvest passwords by sniffing terminal sessions after they have been decrypted (i.e., even SSH sessions will be sniffed and passwords logged) and (2) use the back doors provided by SucKIT and bundled intruder tools to bounce from this system to others on the network.

Unfortunately, most networks have neither flow-level monitoring capabilities that detect new services showing up on a compromised host (e.g., the back doors) nor mechanisms for detecting and correlating connections involving the stepping stone (i.e., coming in from and bouncing to other systems). This typically means the operators or network administrators at a site have no idea when, how, or from where they are being attacked.

It is worth noting that stepping stones are frequently located in countries other than the ultimate target of the attack. For example, an attacker might start in the United States, bounce through a system in South Korea or Germany (both in different time zones and with different native languages), and then come back into the United States to a stepping stone within another network, moving finally into the targeted system. These stepping stones can literally be anywhere in the world, making it nearly impossible to tell where the attack originates. Four, five, or even more hops are feasible if the network latency is sufficiently low that keystroke delay does not become an issue. As network bandwidth increases worldwide, the attacker's ability to maintain anonymity and untraceability over the Internet also improves.

Antiforensics

As a general matter, forensic science is concerned with identifying and classifying information that will assist in investigating crimes. *Computer forensics* is concerned with gathering information about computers that will provide or lead to information about computer crimes. One of the first published white papers on computer forensics, "Basic Steps in Forensic Analysis of Unix Systems," explains the term "computer forensics" as follows:

[xxxvi] The same, of course, is true about the ultimate target of an attack.

[xxxvii] A trust relationship is formed between two systems when there is a shared authentication mechanism, like the same login name and password, or some other means of getting from one system to another. Trust is also found in external access control mechanisms, such as hardware or software firewalls. When trust relationships exist, an attacker who gains access to a single account on a single host may have actually gained access to hundreds or even thousands of other systems that trust the initially compromised host. In addition to the added reach of the intrusion, these trust relationships make great stepping stones to make it harder to detect or trace the attacker, and to make it easier to extend the attacker's reach into the network as if he or she were now an insider (which, for all intents and purposes, he or she now is.)

> The science [of computer forensics involves] methodical, premeditated actions to gather and analyze evidence. The technology, in the case of computers, are programs that suite particular roles in the gathering and analysis of evidence. The crime scene is the computer and the network (and other network devices) to which it is connected.[xxxviii]

Accordingly, computer forensics is concerned with the preservation and analysis of the available data for the purpose of allowing a victim of computer attack to determine the extent of damage or intrusion and to take actions to remediate and bring back under the victim's control all computer and network resources compromised by the attacker. Computer forensics can either be employed by official law-enforcement agencies or by the victim in gathering information about a computer attack. In every case, however, it is concerned with determining the facts about the attack.

Antiforensics measures, in contrast, seek to alter evidence on a computer system to defeat defensive incident-response and law-enforcement investigations; such measures may include destroying existing evidence or planting false evidence. Although it is very difficult to go entirely undetected on a computer system,[xxxix] an attacker with full control of a computer and its operating system kernel can affect all time stamps, attributes, and memory contents. This can make it significantly more difficult for victims and law enforcement to detect intrusions and determine their ultimate sources.

Some techniques that have been discussed publicly and implemented include the following:

1. Deletion of all *i-node* attributes (including file name). I-nodes are data structures in Unix file systems that articulate the attributes of files, such as the file's owner, permissions, time stamps, location of blocks on a disk holding the file contents, and so forth. Directory entries then associate file names, and implicitly the path to the file within the file system (e.g., */home/users/bob/foo.tar.gz*), to the blocks on the disk where the contents of that file are stored. File systems, such as the Linux EXT3 file system, destroy the information that links the I-node to the blocks on the disk holding the file contents, but leave the file name, ownerships, time stamps, and so forth intact. Antiforensics tools wipe out these data to eliminate as much information as possible about the files that have been deleted.[xl]
2. Encryption provides a means of concealing the true contents of a file. Most computer users are familiar with encryption as a means of hiding a password or an e-mail message from unintended eyes. But programs can also be encrypted, a feature that enables an attacker to defeat analysis of surface features (e.g., embedded strings, command prompts) and of the program while it runs using debuggers. Encryption can also effectively lock the program so that it can be run only by someone who knows a password. By encrypting portions of the program on disk, only to decrypt them at run time, and by exploiting other weaknesses in debugging APIs (e.g., the ptrace system call) and debugging applications (such as GNU, gdb, or objdump), attackers can make it more difficult to analyze or control the execution of malicious programs.[xli]
3. Kernel-system call-table modification can be used to conceal running programs, stored files, and network connections and to disable logging. By affecting the operating system's functioning at the level of the kernel's own memory image, rather than through replacement of programs that implement external commands, these measures make possible more comprehensive concealment. Taking over the exec system call, for example, can allow an attacker to control which programs are run, thereby providing one behavior for normal accounts and giving elevated privileges for special accounts. The SucKIT rootkit, described earlier, implements these features.

Covert Channels

The use of *covert channels* is intended to conceal the attacker's use of a compromised computer. Although an attacker can hide his or her presence within a computer system without much trouble, the act of communicating with the compromised system requires transmission of packets to and from that compromised system. In cases where these transmissions pass through other network devices not under the attacker's control, the attacker's use of the compromised computer can, in principle, be detected (by, e.g., a network operator, a security operator, an investigator, or even another attacker) while communications are in transit on the network. A covert channel is a mechanism for concealing the attacker's traffic by either hiding it or making it appear legitimate to third parties.

The Department of Defense's Trusted Computer System Evaluation Criteria defines a "*covert channel* as "any communications channel that can be exploited by a process to transfer information in a manner that violates the system's security policy."[xlii] In practical terms, covert channels involve the use of some communication method that avoids the standard methods supported by the system

[xxxviii] See http://staff.washington.edu/dittrich/misc/forensics/. The authors go on to describe the job of the computer forensic scientist as follows: "Your job, as a forensic investigator, is to do your best to comb through the sources of evidence—disc drives, log files, boxes of removable media, whatever—and do two things: make sure you preserve as much of this data in its original form, and to try to re-construct the events that occurred during a criminal act and produce a meaningful starting point for police and prosecutors to do their jobs."

[xxxix] The reason for such difficulties is that computer intrusions necessarily involve changes to the system that leave traces, and the operating system must have some visibility of these changes to continue running the attacker's programs while functioning in a stable manner. To eliminate every single change to the system is nearly impossible, but it is certainly possible to hide from all but the most skilled system administrators and incident responders.

[xl] The grugq's *The Defiler's Toolkit* implements these techniques. See http://www.phrack.org/phrack/59/p59-0x06.txt

[xli] Programs like TESO's *burneye* encryption engine and Neel Mehta's and Shaun Clowes's *shiva* (see http://www.securiteam.com/tools/5XP041FA0U.html) implement these techniques.

[xlii] See Department of Defense (1985) http://www.radium.ncsc.mil/tpep/library/rainbow/5200.28-STD.html

and does so in a way that avoids logging or detection. For example, files may be transferred out of a system by encoding them in packets using the TCP sequence number or ID fields.[xliii]

These techniques make it difficult for victims and law enforcement to detect malicious software. The operation of malicious software blends in with normal traffic, getting lost in the massive volume of traffic on large networks. If network operators have little understanding of what normally flows over their networks, these techniques can be highly effective. (For example, there are 255 possible IP protocol values, only about half of which are even defined at this time, yet most networks route all of them. Some network monitoring tools will only look for TCP, UDP, ICMP (Internet Control Message Protocol), and Multicast, and lump everything else into one bucket called "other.")

Covert channels pose unique difficulties for anti-intrusion efforts. First, they are quite easy to use. Second, they can be implemented in many ways that use a forged source address together with directly routed traffic between sender and receiver to bounce packets off a third-party computer as a means of concealing the true source of network traffic (such as implemented by Simple Nomad's ncovert tool, released at BlackHat 2003).

Viruses, Trojan Horses, and Worms

Viruses, Trojan horses, and worms are malicious programs that pose a growing problem for computer users.[xliv] A *virus* is a program that infects computers by attaching itself to programs accessed by the affected computer (from its own file storage system or from remotely mounted file systems on a file server or network storage device).[xlv] Viruses are usually contrived to inflict damage on the victim while distributing themselves to as many other victims as possible through one or more available *infection vectors*, such as e-mail attachments or the boot block on removable media.

As the name suggests, a *Trojan horse* is an innocent-looking program that performs malicious functions that alter the victim's system without his or her knowledge. For example, an attachment to an e-mail message that purports to be a screen saver but actually creates a back door on the system through which it installs malicious software is a Trojan horse. Unlike viruses, Trojan horses generally attempt to deceive the user into running the attachment and hence rely on a form of social engineering (described in the next section).

[xliii] See, for example, Rowland (1996).

[xliv] Not every such program is motivated by a malicious purpose. Some viruses, Trojan horses, and worms have been developed to serve some legitimate purposes. For example, system administrators at the Xerox Palo Alto Research Center (PARC) developed a worm that would, among other things, clean up the Altos computers on their network. Unfortunately, such salutary intentions can have very bad results, as the users of PARC's network found out one morning in 1978 when a worm written by two PARC administrators rendered all 100 workstations useless due to a bug in the worm. See Lemos (2001) http://ecoustics-cnet. com.com/Year+of+the+Worm/2009-1001_3-254061.html and Hiltzik (1999).

[xlv] Viruses can also infect documents that support macro languages (which effectively incorporate programs into those documents).

A *worm* is a program that compromises a system by way of a remotely accessible vulnerability and then uses the infected host to distribute the worm to other hosts with the same vulnerability. Worms are usually malicious, but there have been worms, like the so-called Good Samaritan Worm, that attempted to close some existing vulnerability in compromised machines.

Attackers will sometimes use combinations of these programs to compromise a site. In cases where a direct attack against a firewall is not possible but e-mail is allowed into the site, an attacker can, for example, send e-mail messages to victims inside the network with an attachment containing a program that makes a connection to the attacker's Web site. If the victim opens the attachment, the connection is treated by the firewall as a legitimate connection initiated by the victim inside the network; in this way, attackers can circumvent the network's firewall protection to achieve a connection to the computer inside the firewall.

Another way to combine these tools begins with the release of a worm that opens a back door in infected machines. The attacker can then use a scanner or other malicious software to find and use these systems at a later date. An example of this is the program Phatbot, which looks for and takes control of systems infected by Bagle or MyDoom viruses.

Social Engineering

Although the term *social engineering* has a number of meanings,[xlvi] crackers use it to refer to social mechanisms (e.g., threats or fraudulent misrepresentations) that deceive a victim into doing what the attacker wants him or her to do. One especially effective form of social engineering is a *phishing scam*.[xlvii] Phishing involves the transmission of a message reporting to be from a security department of a popular bank, online auction site (such as eBay), or other online financial service (such as PayPal). The message claims that hackers have broken into the victim's account and that the victim must connect to the site to verify his or her personal information. The Web site is designed to appear legitimate to induce the victim to disclose information that can be used to steal his or her identity. In some cases, the attacker's site will even link back to the legitimate site for any number of subpages other than the authentication page, which is redirected to a Web server under the control of the attacker.

Denial of Service

A *denial of service attack* is a digital attack calculated to crash or shut down a Web site, server, or network either by exploiting a vulnerability in the system or by overwhelming it with more traffic than it can handle (e.g., in the form of sham requests for information).[xlviii] DoS attacks are distinguished from many of the attacks described previously in that they are directed not at the confidentiality or

[xlvi] It is sometimes used, for example, to refer to the use of the law to encourage socially desirable practices and attitudes among citizens.

[xlvii] US-CERT (2004) http://www.us-cert.gov/cas/tips/ST04-014.html

[xlviii] For a more complete description of denial of service, see Mirkovic, Dietrich, Dittrich, and Reiher (2005).

integrity of information systems, but rather at the availability of information systems. The point is not to gather confidential information, but instead to shut down the target and render its contents unavailable to its legitimate users.

The most potent form of a DoS attack is a *distributed denial of service* (DDoS) attack. DDoS attacks are usually staged from a large number of innocent machines that have been compromised without the owners' knowledge. Attackers install on these machines special attack software designed to overwhelm the target Web site, network, or server with requests for information; the attack is launched from these machines when the programs are simultaneously activated.

The use of compromised agent machines in DDoS attacks not only allows the attacker to direct more force at the target than could be deployed through a simple DoS attack, but also makes the identity of the culpable attacker much more difficult to ascertain. The use of innocent agent machines interposes, as it were, a layer of insulation between the target and the culpable attacking party, making it more difficult for the victim or law enforcement agencies to trace the attack path back to the originating source.

It is worth noting that DDoS attacks frequently employ a form of IP spoofing. Some DDoS programs forge a large number of random addresses, thereby making the attack appear to the user as if it came from everywhere on the Internet. Sites that do not filter packets, leaving their network with addresses that do not exist within the network (*egress filtering*), or do not filter packets entering their network with addresses from inside the network (*ingress filtering*) are particularly vulnerable and can make an attacker's job much easier by making it harder for a victim to trace the ultimate sources of the attack.

Unfortunately, the intensity of DDoS attacks has increased dramatically since they first appeared on the Internet landscape in 1999. Although the first DDoS attacks involved no more than 2,000 to 5,000 compromised attacking computers[xlix], more recent DDoS attacks have involved as many as just under half a million hosts.[l] The increasing number of attacking machines makes these latter DDoS attacks particularly effective in making unavailable the contents of target sites.

THE COMMON MORALITY ON HACKING AND CRACKING

This section considers whether and to what extent various types of computer intrusions by private persons[li] are ethically permissible according to what Bernard Gert, in an influential article on computer ethics, calls the "common morality."[lii] The common morality, as Gert defines it, is "the [shared] *moral system* that people use . . . in deciding how to act when confronting moral problems and in making their moral judgments" (Gert, 1999, p. 58). As Gert points out, there is much more agreement among persons in any given culture on moral issues than there is disagreement; though it is quite natural to focus energy on what we disagree upon, "such controversial matters form only a very small part of those matters about which people make moral decisions and judgments" (Gert, 1999, p. 57).

This section attempts to identify those principles of the common morality that are relevant with respect to evaluating the various computer intrusions. Such principles include general norms protecting moral rights to property, privacy, intellectual property, autonomy, and free speech as well as certain norms encouraging the promotion of such social benefits as knowledge. Accordingly, the analysis in this section purports, following Gert, to be grounded in principles that are widely accepted in cultures such as this one—though some of these principles, such as those protecting intellectual property, have themselves come under increasing scrutiny within the past few years.

This is, of course, not the only worthwhile framework for evaluating ethical issues. There is a wide variety of general theoretical approaches to ethics, which include deontological ethical theories such as Kantian theories, virtue theories, theories of care, and an array of utilitarian theories (including hedonistic, preference, and welfare versions of act and rule utilitarianism). There is also a wide variety of more specific approaches to computer ethics—including Deborah Johnson's *global information ethics*, James Moor's *just consequentialism*, and Luciano Floridi's *conception of information as having moral standing*. But none of these frameworks, as is evident from the sheer number of them, commands general assent among either theorists or informed laypersons.

Fortunately, these theoretical approaches tend to agree on most moral principles. All mainstream theoretical approaches, deontological and consequentialist, afford substantial moral protection to our interests in life, liberty, property, physical security, and privacy. Indeed, the vast majority of these are fairly characterized as defining moral rights to life, liberty, property, physical security, and privacy that can be justifiably infringed only by reference to some other right that is at least as important. Accordingly, insofar as these theories all agree on these widely accepted principles of the common morality, hacking and cracking can be fruitfully evaluated by appealing to principles of the common morality.[liii]

Two final preliminary observations are in order. First, as articulated here, the common morality may presuppose a deontological (or duty-based) framework. Many theorists think that act utilitarianism is inconsistent with the existence of rights as this notion is commonly understood. On this line of reasoning, any act that maximizes utility

---

[xlix] The first public analyses of DDoS attack tools were published by David Dittrich in December 1999. See http://staff.washington.edu/dittrich/misc/trinoo.analysis.txt; http://staff.washington.edu/dittrich/misc/tfn.analysis.txt; and http://staff.washington.edu/dittrich/misc/stacheldraht.analysis.txt.

[l] See http://www.securityfocus.com/news/8573.

[li] Public acts (i.e., those performed by state agencies) raise radically different issues. States are frequently permitted to do things that private individuals are not—such as incarcerating persons.

[lii] See Gert (1999).

[liii] The arguments in this section parallel those made by Spafford in his classic article "Are Computer Hacker Break-ins Ethical?" (2001). Though Spafford does not explicitly characterize his analysis as grounded in the common morality (not surprising given that Spafford's article was written long before Gert's), he relies on principles that he takes to be largely uncontroversial among all but act-utilitarian theories.

is morally required by utilitarianism regardless of what kind of interest it might infringe. Critics of act utilitarianism have, for example, charged that killing an innocent person would wrongly be required by act utilitarianism if doing so were, all things considered, to maximize utility in a particular situation.

It is not entirely clear whether this criticism succeeds, as some act utilitarians deny these counterexamples, but the following analysis presupposes in any event that morality affords strong protection to our interests in life, liberty, property, physical security, and privacy. To the extent that act utilitarianism is inconsistent with the existence of moral rights and, as seems clear, the common morality presupposes the existence of moral rights (such as rights to life and liberty), the analysis of the common morality is deontological in character in the sense that it presupposes that our ethical principles are grounded in general rules that establish at least some duties that cannot justifiably be infringed to secure some set of desirable consequences.[liv]

Second, many of the principles of the common morality are directly challenged by hackers through their activities; hackers, for example, reject traditional views regarding the protection of property[lv] and privacy rights that ground many of the arguments that will be described further. Even so, it is important to realize that the burden rests on dissenters to make some sort of articulate case for rejecting these principles precisely because the various moral theories all tend to agree on these ordinary views.[lvi] Because there is so much agreement on the basic principles, it is not enough simply to deny them.

In any event, the analysis in this section should be understood as a plausible attempt to identify the implications of these common commitments. Because the analysis here does not seek to defend these common commitments or the moral theories that validate them, it cannot provide the final word. It is safe to say that the debate will continue.

The Case against Cracking

The moral case against cracking is straightforward according to the common morality.[lvii] Cracking involves unauthorized computer intrusions that are intended to cause harm or damage to the victims. According to the common morality, it is wrong for one person to deliberately cause harm to another person. Indeed, as Gert (1999) points out, many of our more specific moral commitments (as well as those commitments identified by most general theories) could be summed up in the rule "Do not cause harm."

Of course, the rule "Do not cause harm" is not absolute.[lviii] Although there are certain principles that can rebut the presumption of impermissibility, these principles do not apply to cracking in ordinary cases. For example, principles allowing punishment of wrongdoing do not apply because they justify only the state in carrying out a punishment; punitive measures by private individuals are almost universally condemned in Western cultures as wrongful vigilantism. Likewise, the principles that allow use of force in self-defense are clearly inapplicable in ordinary cases of cracking because those cases are not responses to attacks on others.

Nevertheless, principles of common morality allow for the possibility that cracking might be morally justified in highly exceptional cases if done without malicious purpose to bring about a great moral good. For example, someone who knows that stolen sensitive information about persons is about to be wrongfully published on a known terrorist Web site might, according to the common morality, be justified in attempting to destroy that information as a means of preventing the great harm that would result—provided that there is no other way to prevent the harm.

But it is doubtful that any cracking case has involved circumstances like the highly unusual ones described here. Indeed, such cases are sufficiently exceptional that it is reasonable to conclude that ordinary cracking is always wrong under the common morality—and the extent of the wrong is determined in part by the extent of the harm that is actually caused and in part by the extent of the harm that is intended by the cracker. The more malicious the intent, the worse the moral transgression involved in cracking. The garden-variety cracker, then, is guilty of committing a serious moral wrong under the common morality.

The Case against Hacking

The case against hacking seems no less straightforward under the common morality. Although the more malicious

[liv] It is worth noting that this does not imply that all moral rules are absolute. Some deontologists, like Kant, have taken this position; Kant, for example, believed that it is always wrong to lie—even when necessary to save someone's life. See, for example, Immanuel Kant, *Groundwork for the Metaphysics of Morals*; available at http://www.swan.ac.uk/poli/texts/kant/kantcon.htm. Most deontologists, however, have taken the position that less important duties are qualified by more important duties when they conflict. Thus, for example, if the duty to respect property comes into conflict with the duty to refrain from deliberately killing innocent persons, the former is qualified by the latter. The rule defining the duty to respect property is limited by the rule defining the duty not to kill innocent persons. See, for example, Ross (1930). As the latter view seems more in line with the common morality, I will presuppose it.

[lv] The term *property* here should not be construed as including intellectual property. It is meant here to pick out only concrete entities, such as land and computers, that are traditionally thought to receive moral protection.

[lvi] There have been various attempts to describe a hacker ethic, but these attempts have not really engaged the basic assumptions about property and privacy. Some of these efforts, as discussed further, are intended to justify certain intrusions by describing their benefits and motivations. But these arguments generally assume that such considerations win out over any moral interests people might have in their property and privacy. What is needed, however, is a sustained defense of this assumption.

Indeed, it is worth noting that much that has been written about the hacker ethic has been concerned to describe a work ethic that involves a profound commitment of time and energy to understanding hard and soft computing technologies. See, for example, chapter 1 in Himanen (2001). These efforts, however, do not even purport to engage these assumptions, which have nothing to do with describing a work ethic.

[lvii] Two preliminary observations about usage should be made at the outset. First, this entry uses *hacker* and related terms to refer to persons who commit unauthorized intrusions and the intrusions themselves. Second, as used here, the terms *hacker* and *hacking* encompass only unauthorized computer intrusions *not* intended to cause damage, whereas *cracker* and *cracking* encompass only unauthorized computer intrusions intended to cause damage.

[lviii] See Note 52, above.

intrusions involve serious transgressions because of the harm they are intended to cause, all unauthorized intrusions are morally objectionable because they wrongfully impinge upon the morally protected interests of their victims.

First, unauthorized intrusions impinge upon property interests that are clearly legitimate under the common morality. Someone who gains access to my computer without my permission has gained access to a physical entity in which I have a legitimate property interest; it is, after all, my computer—and I have, at the very least, a presumptive moral right, under the common morality, to exclude other people from appropriating my computer.[lix] Indeed, an unauthorized entry into some other person's network seems straightforwardly analogous to a trespass onto the real property of another person. According to the common morality, such trespass is morally wrong regardless of whether it results in damage because it violates the owner's property right to exclude other people from the use of his or her belongings.[lx]

Second, unauthorized intrusions can result in harm even when they are not intended to do so. Even skillful hackers who intend no damage can inadvertently cause significant damage to files and programs in which the victim has legitimate property interests under the common morality. The likelihood of causing such accidental damage is an additional factor that supports thinking that hacking is morally wrong.

Third, unauthorized intrusions impinge upon privacy interests that are clearly legitimate under the common morality.[lxi] Someone who gains access to my computer without permission is gaining access to space in which I have a legitimate privacy interest. If it is true that I may legitimately exclude others from use of an access to my computer, then it is not unreasonable to regard my computer as a private space in which I can store sensitive information. Even benign intrusions impinge, then, upon these legitimate privacy interests.

Accordingly, the common morality seems straightforwardly to condemn even benign intrusions because they impinge upon legitimate privacy and (physical) property interests—and this is true regardless of whether any actual damage is caused to the victim or the victim's property.

Hacker Attempts to Justify Hacking

Not everyone is convinced that hacking is wrong. Many hackers believe that, at the very least, nonmalicious intrusions are morally permissible and have offered a number of arguments purporting to justify such intrusions (and hence to qualify or limit the rules governing property and privacy rights). Some argue, for example, these intrusions are justified because they result in an increase in humanity's stock of knowledge about the relevant technologies. Others argue that any barriers to information are morally illegitimate and hence deserve no respect. This section explains and critically evaluates these arguments under the common morality.

The Social Benefits of Benign Intrusions

Hackers argue that benign intrusions increase our technological knowledge in a couple of ways. First, by gaining insight into the operations of existing networks, hackers develop a base of knowledge that can be used to improve those networks. Second, the break-ins themselves call attention to security flaws that could be exploited by crackers or, worse, cyberterrorists. Thus, electronic trespass is distinguished from other forms of trespass in that it inevitably conduces to the public's benefit.

Neither consideration, however, justifies benign intrusions under the common morality. Even if the privacy and property interests of computer owners might sometimes yield to such considerations, these arguments are problematic because these social benefits can be achieved in other ways that do not infringe upon any legitimate interests.

Hackers can, for example, develop the techniques that enable them to break into other systems in settings where the consent of all parties has been obtained. In cases where hackers seek entry to the machines of ordinary users, they can solicit the consent of other like-minded users to allow them to attempt to circumvent the relevant security measures. In cases where hackers seek entry to the machines of large commercial users, they can seek employment at those firms or provide advice to employees of those firms.[lxii] It seems impermissible to infringe privacy and property interests to achieve benefits that can be achieved without infringing those interests.

Moreover, the social benefits arguments fail to take into account the social costs of hacking. The continuing threat of hacker attacks force companies to invest capital into security that they would otherwise invest in more productive areas. Hacker attacks may contribute to improving security technologies, but these technologies could arguably be developed at a much lower cost if hackers would cooperate with companies in developing these technologies—instead of forcing companies to develop them in an ongoing process of having to defend against such attacks.

There is, however, a deeper problem with these arguments. According to the common morality, the privacy and property interests of computer owners rise to the level of moral rights.[lxiii] But it is part of the very concept of a right that the infringement (as opposed to violation) cannot be justified by an appeal to the resulting good. The mere fact that someone could do a lot of social good by stealing, say, a billion dollars from Bill Gates cannot justify stealing that sum if Gates has a property right in that money. As Ronald Dworkin famously puts the point, rights trump consequences.[lxiv]

[lix] It should be noted that a computer is physical property and not intellectual property; for this reason, the argument does not rely on any contested claims about intellectual property.

[lx] Eugene Spafford, for example, characterizes hackers as "trespassers" and "burglars," which presupposes that hackers are violating property rights of some kind. See Spafford (1992, pp. 335, 340).

[lxi] See, e.g., Spafford (1992, p. 336).

[lxii] As Spafford (1992, p. 337) puts this point, "People wishing to report a problem with the security of a system need not exploit it to report it. . . . [O]ne does not set fire to the neighborhood shopping center to bring attention to a fire hazard in one of the stores."

[lxiii] It should be noted that this argument will not satisfy an act utilitarian who takes the position that there are no moral rights.

[lxiv] See, for example, Dworkin (1978).

The social benefits arguments, then, fail because they are the wrong kind of arguments under the common morality. The property and privacy rights that computer owners have in their machines can justifiably be infringed by an unauthorized intrusion only if required to secure some more important right that outweighs those privacy and property rights. If rights trump consequences, then hackers must identify some stronger right that justifies an intrusion: the appeal to social benefits, by itself, is insufficient to do so. Such an argument is considered in the next section.

Benign Intrusions as Free Expression

Hackers have also attempted to defend benign intrusions as free expression. On this line of reasoning, hacking is sometimes justifiable as an exercise of the moral right to free expression; in certain circumstances, hackers are morally entitled to intrude upon the computers of others—as long as they do nothing reasonably calculated to cause harm. The assumption here is that the hacker's right to free speech is more important than and hence qualifies (or limits) the victim's privacy and property rights.

The Free Flow of Information

This line of argument is grounded in the idea that the moral right to free expression is such that there should be no restrictions on the free flow of information; as this latter idea is sometimes put, information *wants* to be—or, better, *ought* to be—free.[lxv] If, on this reasoning, it is true that any restrictions on the free flow of information are morally wrong in virtue of violating the right to free expression, then security measures designed to keep hackers out of networks violate their rights to free expression because they inhibit the free flow of information.[lxvi] As long as hackers do no harm, it is morally permissible for them to intrude into networks to gain information.[lxvii]

The claim that there are no morally legitimate restrictions on the free flow of information is inconsistent with two widely accepted principles of the common morality. First, it is inconsistent with there being a right to informational privacy that entitles persons to exclude others from information in which they have a reasonable expectation of privacy; efforts that exclude others from information, by definition, impede the free flow of information.[lxviii]

Second, it is inconsistent with the claim that people have at least some moral right to control the disposition of their intellectual creations.[lxix] On this line of analysis, people have some intellectual property interest in their creations because such creations are the result of their labor and express their personality.[lxx] If, as most people believe, at least one of these commonly held judgments is correct,[lxxi] then it is false that the right of free expression entails that there are no legitimate restrictions on the flow of information.

But even if it were true that there are no legitimate restrictions on the free flow of information, it doesn't follow that, as an ethical matter, people have carte blanche to get information. For example, it would clearly be wrong, under the common morality, for someone to break into my house to gain information about what books I buy. Similarly, if hacking violates the legitimate property interests of a person in his or her computer, then it is wrong regardless of whether the hacker is otherwise entitled to information on the victim's computer.

Hacking as Political Activism

Mark Manion and Abby Goodrum argue that politically motivated hacking is morally justifiable as civil disobedience as long as it results in neither harm to the victims nor profit to the hackers.[lxxii] If civil disobedience is morally justifiable to protest against injustice, it is sometimes justifiable to commit benign intrusions to protest injustice.[lxxiii] Insofar as it is permissible to stage a sit-in in a commercial or governmental building to protest, say, laws that violate human rights, Manion and Goodrum argue that it is sometimes permissible to benignly intrude upon commercial or government networks to protest such laws.

The problem with this argument is that hacking is not like ordinary civil disobedience in one very important respect under the common morality. Benign and malicious digital intrusions tend to inflict significantly greater harm than sit-ins or other ordinary forms of civil disobedience. For example, a DDoS attack that shuts down a large commercial Web site can result in millions of dollars in losses to that site and potentially in losses of livelihoods and it seems clear, under the common morality, that the infliction of such harms on ordinary people cannot be justified as a form of political activism or expression.

Here it is important to note that civil disobedience is typically motivated by a moral view that is deeply contested in the culture; in many cases, the view motivating civil disobedience is one that is held by a small percentage of people in the culture. Because there is no reliable way to determine which side of the view is correct, there are moral limits on what sorts of harm or inconvenience can justifiably be inflicted on persons who are not morally responsible for the policy being protested. Hacking that can result in the loss of jobs is always problematic, but is especially so when grounded in views that have not been adequately defended—as is all-too-frequently the case.

---

lxv See, for example, Barlow (n.d.). For a detailed analysis and criticism of this idea, see Himma (in press).

lxvi For a critical discussion of this claim, see Spafford (1992, pp. 41–47).

lxvii Accordingly, this argument does not even address, much less justify, cracking.

lxviii See Spafford (1992, p. 336).

lxix It is important to note, however, that the idea that people have intellectual property rights in various kinds of content has become increasingly controversial in recent years. For this reason, it is not entirely clear whether there is something fairly characterized as a *common morality* on this issue. Nonetheless, I include the argument here for the sake of completeness.

lxx For a discussion of these views, see, for example, Hughes (1988).

lxxi There is, of course, much controversy about whether and to what extent intellectual property rights are morally legitimate. See, for example, Hettinger (1989)

lxxii See Manion and Goodrum (2000). Though Manion and Goodrum do not explicitly refer to the common morality, their argument purports to be grounded in widely shared moral judgments about certain kinds of cases and is also fairly characterized as an argument that appeals to the common morality.

lxxiii Civil disobedience is typically justified as a form of political expression, a means of expressing one's political conscience and of bringing unpopular political ideas to the attention of an unsympathetic populace and government. See, for example, Dworkin (1978, chap. 9).

Thus, hacktivism will generally be unjustified under the common morality because there are no widely accepted principles that allow persons to inflict great harm on ordinary innocent parties as a means of expressing a political view or protesting injustice.

Benign Intrusions as Avoiding Waste

Hackers have also defended benign intrusions on the grounds that they make use of computing resources that would otherwise go to waste. On this line of reasoning, it is morally permissible to do what is needed to prevent valuable resources from going to waste; benign hacking activity is justified on the strength of a moral principle that condemns squandering valuable resources in a world of scarcity in which there are far more human wants than resources to satisfy them.

This argument also fails under the common morality. According to ordinary judgments, if one person has a property right in some object X, it is wrong for other persons to appropriate X without permission to prevent X from being wasted. As Spafford aptly puts this point:

> I am unable to think of any other item that someone may buy and maintain, only to have others claim a right to use it when it is idle. For instance, the thought of someone walking up to my expensive car and driving off in it simply because it is not currently being used is ludicrous. Likewise, because I am away at work, it is not proper to hold a party at my house because it is otherwise not being used. The related positions that unused computing capacity is a shared resource, and that my privately developed software belongs to everyone, are equally silly (and unethical) positions.[lxxiv]

If such reasoning is correct, hacking cannot be justified under the common morality to prevent waste.

THE LEGALITY OF HACKING

Whatever doubts one might have about whether some intrusions are ethically permissible, most are unambiguously prohibited by the law in most Western industrialized nations. This section discusses the law of the United States, Canada, and the European Union.

The United States

The primary federal law in the United States that covers unauthorized access and damage to computer systems is the Computer Fraud and Abuse Act (CFAA; i.e., 18 U.S.C. §1030.)[lxxv] The CFAA defines a number of crimes. Of particular relevance is Section 1030(a)(5), which provides as follows:

> Whoever... (A)(i) knowingly causes the transmission of a program, information, code, or command, and as a result of such conduct, intentionally causes damage without authorization, to a protected computer; (ii) intentionally accesses a protected computer without authorization, and as a result of such conduct, recklessly causes damage; or (iii) intentionally accesses a protected computer without authorization, and as a result of such conduct, causes damage; and (B) by conduct described in clauses (i), (ii), or (iii) of subparagraph (A), caused (or in the case of an attempted offense, would, if completed, have caused)—(i) loss to 1 or more persons during any 1-year period... aggregating at least $5,000 in value; (ii) the modification or impairment, or potential modification or impairment, of the examination, diagnosis, treatment, or care of 1 or more individuals; (iii) physical injury to any person; (iv) a threat to public health or safety; or (v) damage affecting a computer system used by or for a government entity in furtherance of the administration of justice, national defense, or national security ... shall be punished as provided in subsection (c) of this section.

Subsection (c) authorizes fines and imprisonment of up to 20 years for specified violations of the quoted provision.

Although the relevant provisions apply only to protected computers, the definition of protected computers is potentially quite broad. In particular, the category of protected computers includes government computers and computers used by financial institutions, but also includes any "computer... used in interstate or foreign commerce or communication." Construed literally, this latter provision would include any computer used to send an e-mail from a person in one state to a person in another state or used to access any Web page published on a server physically located in a different state from the user. If so, this would include the vast majority of computers capable of being hacked because they are connected to a network; it is hard to imagine that any person who is connected to a network long enough to be hacked has not used his or her computer in one of these ways.

Although this subsection clearly applies to intrusions that cause or are intended to cause significant damage, it also potentially applies to benign intrusions. All that is required for liability is that the user gain unauthorized access to a machine that causes specified kinds or levels of damage. As long as the intrusion is deliberate and unauthorized, the damage need not be intended. Since even

---

[lxxiv] Spafford (1992, p. 340). Nevertheless, it is worth noting that the law sometimes permits a person to take possession of property through a wrongful act of trespass. According to the law of adverse possession, a person may come into possession of land by openly and notoriously occupying the land in a way that is clearly adverse to the owner's interests for an extended period of time; if the owner takes no action to halt the adverse possession, the land becomes the trespasser's after the end of the prescribed period (which may vary from one jurisdiction to the next). The justification for this rather counterintuitive law is that the community has an interest in ensuring that a scarce resource like land does not lie fallow. See, for example, http://www.propertylawuk.net/adversepossessionsquatters.html for a discussion of these interesting issues.

[lxxv] The Department of Justice maintains a Web page that lists recent computer crime cases. This site is primarily concerned with violations of the CFAA (18 U.S.C. §1030). But there is some information at the bottom of the page on other laws that were cited in various cases. See http://www.cybercrime.gov/cccases.html

benign intrusions run an obviously foreseeable risk of causing significant damage to protected machines, hackers can be held liable under this act for recklessly causing damage during a putatively benign intrusion.

In addition, benign intrusions may also violate legal rights to privacy—though such violations are perhaps more likely to give rise to civil, rather than criminal, liability—or state laws that criminalize unauthorized computer intrusions. Indeed, a growing number of states are enacting statutes that criminalize various forms of computer misuse which include, but are not limited to, unauthorized computer intrusions.

The relevant federal privacy statutes in the United States are collectively known as the Electronic Communications Privacy Act (or ECPA, for short). The ECPA is made up of the Wiretap Statute (18 U.S.C. §§2510-22), the Pen Register/Trap and Trace Statute (18 U.S.C. §3121) and the Stored Communications Statute (18 U.S.C. §2701). These statutes were further amended in 2001 by the Uniting and Strengthening America by Providing Appropriate Tools Required to Intercept and Obstruct Terrorism (USA PATRIOT) Act. The most likely to be used for prosecuting computer intrusions involving sniffers or keystroke monitors would be the Wiretap Statute.

As described earlier, a recent trend in computer crime is the use of very large (using perhaps as many as half a million compromised computers[lxxvi]) DDoS networks to cause disruption of online gambling sites in the United Kingdom to extort money from these sites. A total of $73 million were lost to extortion by these online gambling sites in the first part of 2004.[lxxvii] Three suspects were arrested by the British National High Tech Crime Unit in June 2004 for these attacks.[lxxviii] Had the victims been in the United States, such attacks could violate several other federal statutes, such as the following:

- 18 U.S.C. §1951—Extortion that affects commerce
- 18 U.S.C. §875—Threats transmitted in interstate commerce
- 18 U.S.C. §876—Mailing threatening communications
- 18 U.S.C. §877—Mailing threatening communication from a foreign country
- 18 U.S.C. §880—Receipt of the proceeds of extortion

Other possible violations of law include the following acts. Using a sniffer to steal account and password combinations for the purpose of using these stolen accounts can be prosecuted under the Fraud and Related Activity in Connection with Access Devices Statute (18 U.S.C. §1029). The willful and malicious destruction of data or systems used for communications can be prosecuted under the Communication Lines, Stations, or Systems Statute (18 U.S.C. §1362).[lxxix]

Canada

Section 342.1 of the Canadian Consolidated Statutes and Regulations defines the general framework that applies to hacker attacks. In particular, Subsection (1) provides the following:

> Every one who, fraudulently and without colour of right (*a*) obtains, directly or indirectly, any computer service, (*b*) by means of an electro-magnetic, acoustic, mechanical or other device, intercepts or causes to be intercepted, directly or indirectly, any function of a computer system, (*c*) uses or causes to be used, directly or indirectly, a computer system with intent to commit an offence under paragraph (*a*) or (*b*) or an offence under section 430 in relation to data or a computer system, or (*d*) uses, possesses, traffics in or permits another person to have access to a computer password that would enable a person to commit an offence under paragraph (*a*), (*b*) or (*c*) is guilty of an indictable offence and liable to imprisonment for a term not exceeding ten years, or is guilty of an offence punishable on summary conviction.

On its face at least, Section 342.1 seems to create a more stringent standard protecting against unwanted computer intrusions. In contrast to the U.S. Computer Crime and Fraud Act, Section 342.1 lacks a damage requirement and hence appears to prohibit both malicious and benign computer intrusions.

In addition, Section 430 of the Canadian criminal law prescribes penalties for the crime of mischief, which occurs when one party, without authorization, intentionally damages, destroys, or renders less valuable the property of another person. Subsection 1.1 specifically defines damage to data as criminal mischief subject to specified penalties:

> Every one commits mischief who willfully (*a*) destroys or alters data; (*b*) renders data meaningless, useless or ineffective; (*c*) obstructs, interrupts or interferes with the lawful use of data; or (*d*) obstructs, interrupts or interferes with any person in the lawful use of data or denies access to data to any person who is entitled to access thereto.

Section 430 (1.1), then, creates additional liability for malicious intrusions (i.e., cracking) that result in damage.

The European Union

The Council of Europe has demonstrated a firm commitment to adopting a unified approach to dealing with computer misuse. On November 8, 2001, the Committee of Ministers of the Council formerly adopted the Convention on Cybercrime, which states guidelines for the various members of the European Union in formulating laws

[lxxvi] According to ARGO, 518,000 IP addresses were implicated in DDoS attacks associated with extortion demands. See http://www.apig.org.uk/ARGO%20Evidence.doc

[lxxvii] See Bullough (2004) http://www.usatoday.com/tech/news/internetprivacy/2004-07-28-russian-hackers_x.htm

[lxxviii] See http://zdnet.com.com/2100-1105_2-5278046.html

[lxxix] For a list of current and recent computer crime prosecutions under these federal statutes in the United States, see the Computer Crimes and Intellectual Property Section Web page of the Department of Justice at http://www.cybercrime.gov

regarding computer misuse.[lxxx] The council observes the following in an explanatory note:

> The fast developments in the field of information technology have a direct bearing on all sections of modern society. The integration of telecommunication and information systems, enabling the storage and transmission, regardless of distance, of all kinds of communication opens a whole range of new possibilities.... By connecting to communication and information services users create a kind of common space, called "cyber-space", which is used for legitimate purposes but may also be the subject of misuse. These "cyber-space offences" are either committed against the integrity, availability, and confidentiality of computer systems and telecommunication networks or they consist of the use of such networks or their services to commit traditional offences.... The criminal law must therefore keep abreast of these technological developments which offer highly sophisticated opportunities for misusing facilities of the cyber-space and causing damage to legitimate interests.[lxxxi]

Section 1 of Chapter II of the convention states guidelines for formulating substantive criminal law as it pertains to unauthorized access of computers, unauthorized interception of data, data interference, system interference, misuse of computing devices, computer fraud, child pornography, and copyright infractions. Article 2 of the convention is of particular relevance for this entry as it defines the relevant guidelines for criminalizing unauthorized access to computers and associated technologies. Article 2 provides as follows:

> Each Party shall adopt such legislative and other measures as may be necessary to establish as criminal offences under its domestic law, when committed intentionally, the access to the whole or any part of a computer system without right. A Party may require that the offence be committed by infringing security measures, with the intent of obtaining computer data or other dishonest intent, or in relation to a computer system that is connected to another computer system.[lxxxii]

Insofar as the defining characteristic of a hacker attack is the attempt to gain unauthorized access, Article 2 purports to guide the adoption of criminal laws regarding hacker attacks. The clear intent, of course, is that unauthorized intrusions be prohibited by law.

Presumably, every member nation of the European Union already has laws on the books prohibiting hacking activities. Although these laws probably differ in particulars, it is reasonable to think that they satisfy the spirit of Article 2's general call to prohibit unauthorized intrusions.

[lxxx] Council of Europe (2001).
[lxxxi] Council of Europe (2001).
[lxxxii] See Council of Europe (2001)

CONCLUSIONS

It is reasonable to hypothesize that incidents of computer misconduct will continue to increase as hackers, crackers, and computer criminals progress in developing more sophisticated and destructive techniques and technologies for intruding upon and attacking the computers and networks of innocent persons. These new techniques will, in turn, give rise to new ethical issues and policy challenges as lawmakers struggle to keep abreast with the latest technologies. Unfortunately, at this time, legislators, policy makers, and law enforcement agencies have not been able to keep pace with the increasing incidence of hacking, cracking, and computer crimes. This chapter has attempted to provide an overview of the relevant technological, ethical, and legal challenges posed by the problem of computer crime.

GLOSSARY

Agent Machines Machines belonging to innocent parties that are compromised by an attacker and used to stage a digital attack or intrusion of some kind.

Antiforensics Measures that seek to alter evidence on a computer system to defeat defensive incident-response and law-enforcement investigations; such measures may include destroying existing evidence or planting false evidence.

Cracker Someone who trespasses onto the computers or networks of other persons without authorization and with an intent to harm.

Cybercrime Criminal activity that involves unauthorized use of computer technology in an essential way.

Cyberterrorism Hacking activity that attempts to harm innocent persons and thereby create a general sense of fear or terror among the general population for the purpose of achieving a political agenda.

Denial of Service A digital attack that is calculated to shut down a Web site, server, or network, usually by overwhelming it with sham requests for information.

Digital Intrusion An act intended to gain unauthorized access to the digital contents (e.g., files or programs) of another person. Such access can be for comparatively benign purposes (e.g., merely to look at files) or for malicious purposes (e.g., to destroy files).

Hackers Persons who attempt to gain unauthorized entry to network servers or other computers. Hacking is usually distinguished from cracking in that the latter, unlike hacking activity, is intended to cause harm to innocent persons.

Intrusion Response Measures adopted by the victim of a digital intrusion intended to investigate, repel, or punish the intrusion.

Internet Protocol (IP) Spoofing The use of a false IP address for the purpose of deceiving the user about the source of incoming packets.

Logic Bomb A program designed to take malicious action at a particular point in time.

Rootkits Programs designed to conceal an intruder and his or her files, directories, or programs by making an operating system lie to its owner.

Session Hijacking Hijacking that occurs when an intruder deflects traffic from the user's intended destination and interjects its own traffic into the user's stream of communication.

Sniffers Programs that are designed to monitor network traffic on local area network segments.

Stepping Stones Chains of login sessions across multiple computers, often in different countries and time zones.

Trojan Horse A program that appears innocuous, but actually performs malicious functions that alter the victim's system without his or her knowledge.

Virus A malicious program (i.e., one intended to cause damage) that infects computers by attaching itself to programs accessed by the affected computer and attempts to distribute itself to as many other victims as possible through one or more available infection vectors, such as e-mail attachments.

Worms Programs that compromise a system by way of a remotely accessible vulnerability and then use the infected host to distribute the worm to other hosts with the same vulnerability.

CROSS REFERENCES

See *Computer Viruses and Worms; Cybercrime and the U.S. Criminal Justice System; Cyberterrorism and Information Security; Denial of Service Attacks; Electronic Attacks.*

REFERENCES

Barlow, J. P. (n.d.). *The economy of ideas.* Retrieved May 24, 2005, from http://www.eff.org/~barlow/EconomyOfIdeas.html

Bullough, O. (2004, July 28). Police say Russian hackers are increasing threat. Retrieved May 24, 2005, from http://www.usatoday.com/tech/news/internetprivacy/2004-07-28-russian-hackers_x.htm

Council of Europe. (2001). *Convention on cybercrime.* Retrieved May 24, 2005, from http://conventions.coe.int/Treaty/en/Reports/Html/185.htm

Dittrich, D. (1998). One sniff and your password is stolen. *Windows on Computing, 21.* Retrieved May 24, 2005, from http://www.washington.edu/tech_home/windows/issue21/password.html

Dreyfus, S. (1997). *Underground: Tales of hacking, madness and obsession on the electronic frontier.* Sydney: Random House Australia.

Dworkin, R. (1978). *Taking rights seriously.* Cambridge, MA: Harvard University Press.

Few Clues in Web Worm Whodunit. (2003, January 29). WiredNews.com. Retrieved May 24, 2005, from http://www.wired.com/news/infostructure/0,1377,57462,00.html

Gert, B. (1999). Common morality and computing. *Ethics and Information Technology, 1,* 57–64.

Hettinger, E. C. (1989). Justifying intellectual property. *Philosophy and Public Affairs, 18,* 31–52.

Hiltzik, M. (1999). The worm that ate the Internet. In *Dealers of lightning: Xerox PARC and the dawn of the computer age.* New York: Harper Collins.

Himanen, P. (2001). *The hacker ethic.* New York: Random House.

Himma, K. E. (in press). Information and intellectual property protection: Evaluating the claim that information should be free. *APA Newsletters on Philosophy and Computing.*

Hughes, J. (1988). The philosophy of intellectual property. *Georgetown Law Review, 77,* 287.

Interview with Mike Hudack. (n.d.). Retrieved May 24, 2005, from http://uit.no/breifilm/4276/7

Lemos, R. (2001, December 6). *Hacker had WorldCom in his hands.* Retrieved December 6, 2001, from http://news.com.com/Hacker+had+WorldCom+in+his+hands/2100-1001_3-276711.html

Levy, S. (1984). *Hackers: Heroes of the computer revolution.* New York: Penguin-Putnam.

Manion, M., & Goodrum, A. (2000). Terrorism or civil disobedience: Toward a hacktivist ethic. *Computers and Society, 30,* 14–19.

Mann, C. C., & Freedman, D. H. (1998). *At large: The strange case of the world's biggest Internet invasion.* New York: Simon & Schuster.

Mirkovic, J., Dietrich, S., Dittrich, D., & Reiher, P. (2005). *Internet denial of service: Attacks and defense mechanisms.* Englewood Cliffs, NJ: Prentice Hall.

Naraine, R. (2004, January 23). FTC: Online fraud losses hit $437M. Retrieved May 24, 2005, from http://www.clickz.com/stats/sectors/finance/article.php/5961_3303041

Poulson, K. (2004). FBI busts alleged DDoS mafia. Retrieved May 24, 2005, from http://www. securityfocus.com/news/9411

Ross, W. D. (1930). *The right and the good.* Oxford: Oxford University Press.

Rowland, C. H. (1996). Covert channels in the TCP/IP Protocol suite. Retrieved May 24, 2005, from http://www.firstmonday.dk/issues/issue2_5/rowland/

Slatella, M. (1996). *Masters of deception: The gang that ruled cyberspace.* New York: Perennial.

Spafford, E. (1992). Are computer hacker break-ins ethical? *Journal of Systems Software 17,* 41–48.

Stoll, C. (2000). *The cuckoo's egg.* New York: Pocket Books.

Sullivan, B. (2003, August 20). *Sobig variant floods inbox.* Retrieved May 24, 2005 from http://msnbc.msn.com/id/3078590/

Sullivan, B. (2004). Experts fret over online extortion attempts. Retrieved May 24, 2005, from http://www.msnbc.msn.com/id/6436834/

Taylor, P. (1999). *Hackers: Crime in the digital sublime.* New York: Routledge.

Taylor, P., & Jordan, T. (2004). *Hacktivism and cyberware: Rebels with a cause?* New York: Routledge.

Hacktivism

Paul A. Taylor, *University of Leeds, United Kingdom*
Jan Ll. Harris, *University of Salford, United Kingdom*

INTRODUCTION

Elsewhere (Jordan & Taylor, 2004; Taylor, 1999; Taylor, 2001), we have provided detailed accounts of both hacking and the attendant phenomenon of hacktivism. The purpose of this chapter is to provide a more succinct account of the way in which the key attributes of hacking have been adopted by new social movements that have pressed them into the service of the burgeoning antiglobalization movement. In carrying out this task, we will explore the points of contact and divergence that exist between traditional hacking and the recent emergence of hacktivism, the latter defined as the deployment of hacking tactics within the context of an explicit political agenda. Although hackers tend to be much more politically motivated than their hacker predecessors, their innovative acts are in fact very much in keeping with the original hacker ethic of using technology in the most ingenious manner possible. Hacking has, almost from its first emergence, been marked by a certain politics. However, this politics has revolved around the problem of the freedom of information and access to technology. The innovative feature of hacktivism is the way it takes this preexisting hacker ethic and applies it to the field of specific social protest movements whose concerns are not solely technological. Because hacktivism attempts to wrest control of the technologies of globalization from the hands of the state and corporations and to turn them against the very order that developed and deployed them, it can be said, to continue a trend in computer culture which, from the 1960s onward, hacktivists have sought to challenge the assumption that technology is intrinsically the tool of capitalism and the state.

This chapter begins with an introduction to the key ethical aspects of hacking and offers a schema that traces the evolution of hacking as a concept and practice through various generations. Although a more traditional and apparently politically neutral hacking culture is still extant, we will show how hacktivism, under the impetus of the antiglobalization movement, has emerged as a separate and distinct practice. Despite the common perception of hacking as a computer-related act, the term in its earliest use described a particular, playfully innovative, and irreverent attitude toward any technology or associated system. The gradual reduction of the term solely to the field of computing is, it will be argued, commensurate with apparent erosion of the hacker ethic as reflected in Microsoft's corporate co-optation of gifted programmers and their culture, a takeover whose stakes are encapsulated in the term *microserfs*. From a radical political perspective, the microserf generation is shown to represent a particularly low point, and the political nature of hacktivism, as described through the notion of electronic civil disobedience and examples of specific hacktivist groups, is presented as a revival of hacking's early political promise. The uses to which these groups put the hacker ethic is then contrasted with the open-source (OS) movement, which despite lacking hacktivism's clear agenda, nevertheless retains a strong fidelity to the original aims of hacking. The chapter concludes with an analysis of the global trends that hacktivism and the OS movement simultaneously challenge and utilize.

THE CULTURE AND FOUNDING ETHICS OF HACKING

> Access to computers—and anything which might teach you something about the way the world works—should be unlimited and total. Always yield to the Hands-On Imperative!
>
> All information should be free
> Mistrust Authority—Promote Decentralisation
> Hackers should be judged by their hacking,
> not bogus criteria such as
> degrees, age, race, or position.
> You can create art and beauty on a computer.
> Computers can change your life for the better.
> (Levy, 1984, pp. 40–45)

So runs Levy's (1984) summary of the hacker ethic. Firsthand research among various groups of hackers (Taylor, 1999) suggests that central beliefs in the overarching value of technological ingenuity and a fascination with the innate complexity of systems should be added to Levy's ethical commandments. It is important to emphasize that it is only in relatively recent years that hacking became associated just with computers. When carrying out firsthand empirical research, hackers provided examples of their favorite hacks that included a number of different artifacts ranging from coffee machines to parking meters and a diverse range of systems encompassing the abstractions of the legal establishment (from a hacker who worked on his own legal defense in jail) and the labyrinthine practicalities of phone networks. Perhaps at its most basic level the term invokes a sense of *bricolage*, that is, a sort of creative or Puckish tinkering with technologies and systems so that they exhibit proprieties and display functions beyond those intended by the designers.

Himanen (2001) offers another perspective on the hacker ethic, arguing that hackers can be distinguished from their ambient culture by their overdeveloped work ethic. They have broken with the Protestant work ethic, in which regulated labor as the cornerstone of a virtuous life finds its reward in material remuneration and a clear conscience. Hackers, although by no means adverse to work, labor in a nonalienated fashion; their hours are irregular and determined by the waxing and waning of their own interest rather than by external dictates. Hackers do not value labor in itself, but rather their specific labor; their enthusiasm is not for the material rewards of work, but for the task itself. In this light, hacking at its most basic level is a joyous, playful, or creative activity. In this respect, the work ethic of the hacker is close to that of the creative artist or the academic, both of whom (ideally) work for the sake of the work (Moody, 2002, p. 154). But in the case of the latter there is a tendency toward individualism, an autonomous even solipsistic aspect that is absent in hacking. Such a formulation may appear paradoxical, given the popular image of the hacker as a socially maladroit loner, happier with code than people. Yet, although this stereotype is not without a grain of truth, it nonetheless fails to recognize the deeply social nature of hacking. To quote Marvin Minsky, "Contrary to popular belief, hackers are more social than other people" (as cited in Himanen, 2001, p. 52). Hackers, although perhaps solitary as individuals, are as a group or collective highly social. Peer recognition, and a desire to produce tools that are socially useful, is the lifeblood of their endeavor. Thus, hackers harness the traits of creativity and enthusiasm associated with highly individualized forms of production toward communal or collaborative projects. This social aspect is perhaps most clear in the activities of the open-source/free software communities but can be observed even in the more questionable activities of hackers.

All these ethical values emerged in the earliest days of computing and are perhaps most readily associated with Levy's further classification of the first three generations of hackers:

"True" hackers: these pioneers made their name experimenting with the large mainframe computers at such U.S. universities as the Massachusetts Institute of Technology during the 1950s and 1960s.

Hardware hackers: these were the entrepreneurial innovators of the 1970s who played a key role in making computing accessible to the masses by both facilitating and promoting the personal computing revolution and its much smaller, decentralized computing hardware.

Game hackers: in the 1980s, building upon the hardware successes of the personal computer (PC) revolution, the game hackers were responsible for the development of popular gaming software applications.

In view of the development of computer culture since Levy's analysis, four additional categories should be added to these earlier generations:

Hacker/cracker: from the mid-1980s to the present day, these terms are used (frequently interchangeably) to describe a person who illicitly breaks into other peoples' computer systems. The choice of term tends to vary depending upon the moral interpretation used by a commentator for acts that tend to be essentially the same. *Hacker*, for example, tends to be used by those sympathetic to the values of the computer underground, whereas *cracker* tends to be used by those who have a much sterner interpretation, such as the computer security industry that has grown up over time in response to such unsolicited intrusions.

Microserfs: this is the phrase used in Douglas Coupland's novel (1995) of the same name to describe those computer programmers, who, while exhibiting various obsessive and independent-minded traits of the hacker subculture, nevertheless became sucked into the corporate world of bonds and the desire to vest them.

Open source/free software hackers: A breed of hacker who self-consciously differentiates themselves from the both the corporate microserf and the deviant cracker. Based primarily around the open source GNU/Linux operating system, they can be seen as a return to the original spirit of the 1960s and 1970s. Indeed, there is a direct link in the form of Richard Stallman, whom Levy described in his 1984 volume as *the last hacker*. Stallman, in particular through the concept of *copyleft* and its adoption by Linus Torvalds, has operated as an intergenerational bridge, perpetuating the original hacker ethic. Unlike hacktivists, the open-source community are political by circumstance rather than by choice, that is, to the degree that their working methodology proves a challenge to the monopolistic agenda of Microsoft and the like.

Hacktivists: the mid-1990s marked a pivotal point at which previous, largely apolitical hacking activity was incorporated into a much more overtly political form. The political activity of the previous generations tended to be limited to securing freer access to computing facilities rather than questioning too deeply the political purposes for which the equipment could be used. The rise of hacktivism fundamentally changed this political blind spot and continues to integrate global networks of information technologies to object against the perceived excesses of global capitalism.

It should be noted that these generations represent a conceptual schema and that the real history of hacking and hacktivism is inevitably more complex, offering overlaps and concurrencies that problematize a simple subdivision of hacking into the previous generations. Notwithstanding these limitations, the schema nevertheless provide a useful overview of the way in which there has been a move away from, and then a return (in the form of open source and free software) to, key aspects of the original hacker ethic:

engagement with systems
hands-on curiosity applied to *any* technology
a desire to reverse the original purposes of an artifact or system.

Before looking at the sophisticated and self-reflexive politics of hacktivism that has sought to revisit and reapply these values, it is necessary to trace the decline in the political potential of early hacker groups and their subsumption within the corporate takeover of the information revolution.

FROM HACKING TO MICROSERFDOM

> These were the radical or guerrilla hackers, who were destined to give the computer a dramatically new image and a political orientation it could never have gained from Big Blue [IBM] or any of its vassals in the mainstream of the industry. At their hands, information technology would make its closest approach to becoming an instrument of democratic politics. (Roszak, 1986, p. 138)

In support of the above claim from Roszak, it is possible to trace a line of influence from the radicalized student population of the 1960s to the computer culture of the 1970s, for instance at the University of California Berkeley, famous as a breeding ground for both hackers and radical politics. This impression is reinforced by a number of influential texts, for instance Ivan Illich's *Tools for Convivality* (1973) and Ted Nelson's *Computer Lib/Dream Machines* (1974). Both books made an explicit connection between an emancipatory politics and an emancipated technology. Nelson's text, in appearance a sort of smazidat publication resembling the *Whole Earth Catalog*, was particularly prophetic. It offered the neboulous but inspiring vision of a *hypertextual* (this term's first appearance) system called Xanadu that would connect every document with every other document in a universal database. Perhaps more important was the fact that Nelson's vision was couched in a revolutionary rhetoric that argued that computing should be accessible to all and not the preserve of corporations or academics. Nelson's text thus assigned the hobbyist and the underground hacker "a noble role in the battle for humanity's future and recruited them for the rebellion they were witnessing on their college campuses" (Wolf, 1995, p. 8). Similarly, Illich argued for the liberation of the design of technology so that the principles were accessible to all, the *convivial* tool aimed to dissolve the distinction between user and producer. His thesis inspired members of the Homebrew Computer Club, such as Lee Felstein, whose "TV Typewriter or Tom Swift Terminal" was an early attempt to hack a monitor/interface using a keyboard and television and produce a "convival cybernetic device" inspired by Illich's vision of a convival technology (Levy, 1984, p. 210; see also Felsentein, 1995) and in this manner Illich's ideas were part of the matrix that spawned the PC revolution.

Thus, on the one hand, a hacker's belief in the ingenious use of technology offered an immediate potential for countercultural activity. If you see subversion in every object placed before you, it is likely that you will develop tendencies that can easily be viewed as subversive by those in authority. On the other hand, however, any radicality within the early generations tended to be mostly confined to issues of access. In other words, hackers could be radical but only tended to be so to gain time for hands-on experimentation with the artifacts and systems that they loved so much. The early radical wing of the hacking ethos was reflected in the advent of the *Youth International Party Line* an underground newsletter run by Abbie Hoffman established in 1971 and which changed its name in September 1973 to the *Technological American Party* (TAP). Newsletters were produced that vividly manifested the ubiquity of the pure hacker hands-on imperative with their raft of detailed technical information on such issues as how to phone-phreak (obtain free phonecalls through the technical manipulation of the phone system) and reengineer a large range of artifacts and techniques including burglar alarms, lock picking, pirate radio, and gas and electric meters.

TAP ceased publication in 1984, but its mantle was quickly assumed with the launch of the phone-phreak/hacker magazine *2600* whose anti-Big Brother government bent was immediately indicated by the editor's choice of the nom de plume Emmanuel Goldstein (the oppressed protagonist of George Orwell's *1984*). Meanwhile, in 1981 in Europe, a German hacker group established the Chaos Computer Club. It directly expressed the digitally correct implications of the original hacker ethic, "All information wants to be free," in the following declaration:

> A development into an "information society" requires a new Human Right of worldwide free communication. The Chaos Club... claims a border-ignoring freedom of information which deals with the effects of technologies on human society and individuals. It supports the creation of knowledge and information in this respect. (As cited in Bowcott and Hamilton, 1990, p. 53.)

We shall see in our subsequent discussion of hacktivism how this emphasis upon the primacy of informational flows lies behind the major schism between human rights and digital rights-orientated hacktivists (see Jordan & Taylor, 2004, for more details). Notwithstanding this perennial tension with the computer counterculture between radical politics and pragmatic issues of access, the first and second generations both exhibited a form of electronic populism. Their subversive desire to hack and the attempt to make technology more universally available were complementary facets of the same hacker agenda.

The earliest hackers had noncorporatist values to the extent that they inhabited cloistered university environments and were motivated by pure intellectual curiosity rather than business applications. With the more outward-looking second generation of hackers, a certain explicit anticorporate ethos, as evinced in the names of some of the early start-up companies such as the *Itty-Bitty Machine Company* (a parody of IBM) and *Kentucky Fried Computers* (Jordan & Taylor, 2004, p. 142). Likewise, the Apple computer company chose its symbol because of its "whole earth" connotations. This countercultural spirit was not to last, however, and the initial socially liberating potential of such computers increasingly became subordinated to their status as mere commodities: "all the bright possibilities seem so disturbingly compatible with corporate control and commercial exploitation" (Jordan & Taylor, p. 155). This corporate appropriation of the original hacker ethic was most dramatically illustrated by Apple's famous 1984 television commercial (directed by Ridley Scott) that culminated with the anti-Orwellian image of a woman sprinting across the screen to launch a huge hammer at a menacingly glowering Big Brother.

As computing technology developed within the ever-widening circles of commercially sponsored dissemination, the commodity view of information gained pace over the countercultural desire for a more politically engaged democracy fueled by the exponential increase in the accessibility of information. Thus the perennial tension between hacking's potential radicalism and the affinity of its code-loving tendencies to economic libertarianism was increasingly resolved in favor of the latter: the countercultural hopes pinned upon the computer as vehicle for antiestablishment values floundered as the *wunderkinds* of the 1970s became the software giants of the 1980s. Given the intrinsically commercial dimension of their activity, the second generation of game hackers was naturally primed to take advantage of the subsequent dot-com boom, whereas the third generation of crackers/hackers increasingly found an outlet for their idiosyncratic skills in the deliberately collegiate atmosphere of Microsoft's headquarters. The early hackers' desire to promote free access to computers and information as a means of facilitating an informed, and thereby empowered, demos had quickly retreated to a self-serving concern with access to computing for its own sake.

Thus the youthful, antiauthoritarian attitudes within the early generations of hacking were soon sublimated into a frustrated desire to consume computing resources (see Taylor, 1999, pp. 53–56) such that teenage hackers came to "resemble an alienated shopping culture deprived of purchasing opportunities more than a terrorist network" (Ross, 1991, p. 90). The nadir of this process was vividly portrayed in Douglas Coupland's (1995) geist-busting "factional" account of the lifestyles of the young programmers working at Microsoft's Seattle headquarters in *Microserfs*. The hacker/cyberpunks' willingness to immerse themselves in the labyrinthine matrices of code was easily co-opted to the creation of a particularly extreme form of *homo economicus*:

> In the 1980s corporate integration punctured the next realm of corporate life invasion at "campuses" like Microsoft and Apple—with the next level of intrusion being that borderline between work and life blurred to the point of unrecognizability. *Give us your entire life or we won't allow you to work on cool projects*. In the 1990s, corporations don't even hire people anymore. People become their own corporations. It was inevitable. (Coupland, p. 211 [emphasis in the original].)

Microsoft's subsumption of hacker culture has been so successful because traits such as "high productivity, maverick forms of creative work, energy, and an obsessive identification with on-line endurance (and endorphin highs)" (Ross, 1991, p. 90) from the outset blurred the boundaries between work and play, labor and creativity. Thus it engineered an environment in which these qualities, which might have proved problematic in a traditional structure, served solely to valorize "the entrepreneurial codes of silicon futurism" (Ross, p. 90). In this manner, hacking's apparent political potential was diffused and business as usual had restabilized its hegemony. This was arguably because an essential part of the specific act of hacking is its love of the technical means rather than the political or philosophical end. Thus, although the hacking mentality could theoretically be applied to a multitude of artifacts, in practice it was limited to the joy of the hack and the technological means by which it is effected. In other words, an appreciation of the relation of the hacked artifact to the overarching technological system and the possibility of hacking as a subversive intervention in this system tends to be an underdeveloped dimension of hacking.

Similarly, from a political point of view, such a close attachment to the technological system results in a necessary convergence with the aims of the wider social systems that sustain it; to quote the Critical Art Ensemble (CAE),

> The hacker is generally obsessed with efficiency and order. In producing decentralized technology, a fetish for the algorithmic is understandable and even laudable; however, when it approaches a totalising aesthetic, it has the potential to become damaging to the point of complicity with the state (1994, p. 137).

This was demonstrated in one of the authors' (Taylor, 1999) early research into the original hacking communities where, in addition to the moral judgments about hacking made by external groups such as the computer security industry and law enforcement officers, hackers themselves readily expressed their ethical disapproval of those who engaged in destructive acts of electronic trespass. This was because it drew attention to, and thereby endangered, their otherwise harmless engagement with both artifacts and systems. Put another way, hackers did not want to alienate themselves unnecessarily from the society upon which they were dependent for their technological sandpits. Thus, in confirmation of the manner in which many hacker traits appear fundamentally ambiguous with respect to the wider political questions, the peculiar mixture of individuality and communality that characterized hacking culture proved a limitation on its political possibilities. Thus, while hacking produced novel forms of collective endeavor (e.g., live-in mini-gangs, conferences, chat room groups), the narrow activity itself remained fundamentally solitary, even solipsistic.

This is reflected in some of the cultural aspects of the early hacker communities. For example, the Electronic Frontier Foundation (EFF) was an interest group that although not specifically devoted to hacking per se, was, as its name suggests, closely akin to the hacker demand for unfettered access to the digital plains. This appeal to imagery of the Wild West tapped into a deep stratum of the American psyche and finds its echo in the influential fictional genre of cyberpunk that gave us the epochal term *cyberspace*, wherein suitably glamorized hacker protagonists are referred to as *console cowboys*. These tropes of rugged individualism in both cyberpunk depictions and organizations such as the EFF indicate how readily the original hacker ethic was elided with a libertarian, laissez-faire economic ideology. Rather than the socially inclusive dream of an informatically enabled populace that motivated some of those involved in the first wave of the PC revolution, computer networks were increasingly seen as an unprecedented, technologically facilitated opportunity to create virtual social conditions unencumbered by the regulatory weight of real-world government interference. Thus, the key significance of hacktivism and elements of the free software movement is the way in which they, by virtue of a reassertion of a revised set of countercultural values, challenge this apparently total surrender of every aspect of social life to the values of the market. Moreover, this challenge does not occur outside of the market, but rather within the context of the technologies that have played no small role in creating this situation.

HACKTIVISM, TACTICAL MEDIA, AND THE VIRTUAL SIT-IN

> As hackers become politicized and as activists become computerized, we are going to see an increase in the number of cyber-activists who engage in what will become more widely known as Electronic Civil Disobedience. The same principles of traditional civil disobedience, like tresspass and blockage, will still be applied, but more and more these acts will take place in electronic or digital form. The primary site for Electronic Civil Disobedience will be in cyberspace (Wray 1998: 3).

As with the hackers before them, there are competing definitions of which activities and people deserve the terms *hacktivism* and *hacktivists*. The conceptual categories offered in this chapter thus inevitably involve simplification of blurred, if not contested, terminological boundaries. Thus, there may be examples of online individuals or groups who use hacking techniques for destructive activities while claiming a political motivation and as a consequence various interpretations can be made as to whether such people should be classed as hacktivists, hackers, or even the pejorative term *crackers*. Denning's comprehensive analysis of hacktivism provides a useful distinction between it, an online activism that simply uses new technologies, and the more sinister cyberterrorism: "Activism refers to normal, non-disruptive use of the Internet in support of an agenda or cause... hacktivism refers to the marriage of hacking and activism... cyberterrorism refers to the convergence of cyberspace and terrorism" (Denning, 1999, p. 2). Recently, within the post-9/11 context, the Uniting and Strengthening America by Providing Appropriate Tools Required to Intercept and Obstruct Terrorism (USA PATRIOT) Act has collapsed hacktivism, cyberterrorism, and the more traditional activities of crackers. All, in the eyes of U.S. law at least, can constitute cyberterrorism, and because that act allows for the extradition of cyberterrorists thus defined, it is has implications for any group considering adopting hacktivist strategies.

Out of these definitions this chapter focuses on the fusion of hacking and activism and its points of contact with the free software movement, which in concert offer the most theoretically interesting and legitimate direct challenge to the commercial paradigms that have dominated the Internet in recent years. In view of this terminological uncertainty, *tactical media* is a useful generic phrase that can be used largely synonymously with hacktivism, the following definition of which is offered by the Critical Art Ensemble:

> The term "tactical media" refers to a critical usage and theorization of media practices that draw on all forms of old and new, both lucid and sophisticated media, for achieving a variety of specific noncommercial goals and pushing all kinds of potentially subversive political issues. (The organizers of the 1993 Amsterdam event Next Five Minutes, as cited in CAE, 1994, p. 5.)

The definition by some of its practitioners (one of whose number has been recently detained under the USA PATRIOT Act, see www.caedefensefund.org) demonstrates its fidelity to the original hacking ethic's emphasis upon the ingenious reappropriation of *any* technological artifact or system. The other key feature of this definition is the inclusive phrase of "a variety of specific noncommercial goals." This is the main unifying feature of hacktivists: their self-reflexive political perspective. Again, in keeping with the original hacking ethic, they seek imaginative methods to reengineer the purpose of a system: in this case the global capitalist system of communication and commodity flows. They also reengineer concepts of protest so that conventional notions of civil disobedience are redesigned for the digital age. Most prominent among these techniques is that of the *virtual sit-in*:

> A virtual sit-in is little more than a collective, simultaneous requesting of a Web site. If one requests a Web site faster than it can be transferred and built up on the end user's screen, the server receives, on the one hand, a message telling it that the first request is no longer valid, and on the other hand, the new request. Scripts running on one's own computer or on go-between servers automate this process, and after a certain number of requests, the server under attack begins to suffer under the strain. One has to differentiate very specifically between knocking out a server

> for private motives and a political action openly disrupting a Web site for clearly formulated reasons and for a limited time. That's when it becomes comparable to a warning strike during wage negotiations, a means of civil disobedience signalling that one side has the willingness and courage to fight (Grether, 2000, p. 5).

A practical example of this theory of electronic civil disobedience was provided in 1998 when a group known as the Electronic Disturbance Theater (EDT) coordinated a series of Web sit-ins in support of the Zapatistas, a Mexican antigovernment group largely made up of indigenous people from the Chiapas region. The sit-ins used an automated piece of software called Flood Net. The idea behind this program is that once downloaded onto a computer, it helps users to automatically connect their computer to constantly request access to a preselected Web site and renew the request every 7 seconds. If thousands of people use Flood Net on the same day, the combined effect of such a large number of activists will severely disrupt the operations of a particular site. The particular way in which Flood Net was used illustrates the important distinction to be made between pure hacktivism and the early hacking mentality that arguably lives on in the form of digitally correct hacktivism (see Jordan & Taylor, 2004). The overriding concern of digitally correct hacktivism is the maintenance of bandwidth functionality and the technical elegance of a hack. In contrast, the political success and strength of the Flood Net action was the very fact that it was not a highly sophisticated and largely automated program. It was relatively simple from a technological point of view and this meant that it required the mass participation of willing volunteers. This gave it a political credibility it would not otherwise have had. Before moving on to analyze further the political motivations and implications of hacktivism, it is helpful at this point to review some brief examples of hacktivist groups and their actions.

FURTHER EXAMPLES OF HACKTIVIST ACTIONS

Electronic Pressure Group Actions: The Etoy Campaign

> Despite all the naysaying, the Net is offering individuals new opportunities to take action and giving ideas a better shot at taking hold. It allows and even encourages cooperation in virtual groups, and in the best of situations, a self-organizing countermatrix as well that can make short work of a highly organized and powerful corporation (Grether, 2000, para. 2).

Grether (2000) provides a full account of the 1999 Etoy campaign by activists created in response to the court action initiated by a commercial company in an attempt to remove an art collective's Web site domain name (*etoy*) because it was too close to their own (*etoys*). The company's action was implemented despite the fact the art collective had been operating under its name first and generated enough online ill will to generate a highly coordinated campaign that incorporated various hacktivist (e.g., the Flood Net program) and public relations initiatives (e.g., mass mailings, countercourt actions, satirical mirror Web sites). The campaign was successful and the company was forced to retreat from its aggressively litigious stance. The incident illustrated the extent to which online actions can produce an unprecedentedly effective degree and speed of coordination constituting an important, new countervailing power to corporate influence.

Culture Jamming

> One two-dollar can of spray can reverse a hundred-thousand-dollar media campaign (Rushkoff, 1994, p. 281).

Although usually considered separately, culture jamming fits enough of this chapter's schematic requirements to be considered a form of hacktivism. Its basic purpose is to hack the symbolic codes of what its practitioners perceive to be an excessively commodified culture. It can be considered as a semiotic form of aikido, in so far as it seeks to use a minimum of effort to turn the strength of commercial culture back on itself (see also Klein, 2001, pp. 279–309). The Adbusters group, for example, uses techniques known as billboard banditry and subvertising to make small, but hugely significant, changes to hugely expensive advertising campaigns. One vivid example of this technique was the use of cheap spray cans on the giant billboard figures of gamine Calvin Klein models. In this case culture jammers used the hacker technique of reverse engineering to give the models on the posters "zipper mouths" and blacked out eyeballs and a consequently skeletal appearance. As the above quote demonstrates, this practice is not intrinsically technological; nevertheless, the new media and the algorithmic manipulability that underwrites them provide a range of novel possibilities for culture jamming. Thus, common hacktivist tactics such as *Web redirects*, in which Web sites are hijacked and their users redirected to politically significant sites (for instance Nike.com redirected to a site concerned with worker's rights), and *Web site defacements,* such as those that proliferated at the start of the Iraq war and around the long-running Palestinian–Israel conflict, which were directed at a range of targets (Al Jazeera, the U.S. military, etc.) by a range of interest groups (both for and against the action and its various participants) (Allen & Demchack, 2003), can be seen as examples of technologically driven forms of culture jamming.

To this cultural jamming we might also add forms of intervention at the level of both software and hardware. In the case of hardware, this can take the form of a reverse engineering of artifacts that deliberately shut out or artificially delimit the options of their users. For instance, Microsoft's entry in the game console market, the X-Box, contained a fairly decent Windows-only computer. Users, through the addition of a mod chip, were able to release this computer, install an alternative operating system, and use it in a manner of their choosing. Such hacking is political only to the extent that it asserts a freedom to modify over a proprietorial vision of technology, in the case of a joint project carried out by CAE and the

Carbon Defense League, a similar technological detournement of the Nintendo Game Boy was implemented for explicitly political purposes, in this case to draw attention to the ideological programming inherent in game design (http://www.carbondefense.org/writing_4.html).

Perhaps of greater significance than this reverse engineering are attempts to develop forms of software that challenge or embody political positions, examples of which might include programs such as *Freenet*—an entirely decentered and encrypted person-to-person network whose raison d'etre is the prevention of any form of control or censorship, which attempts to enshrine at the level of code the values of free speech—and a range of software developed to override attempts by various governments and other organizations to delimit access to the Internet on the behalf of their populations. On a more general level, the proliferation of hacks to evade state and commercial control over the flow and ownership of data, software, and hardware can be seen as a form of cultural jamming in that they attempt to preserve the decentralized free flow of information that for many is the Net's most important dimension (Deibert, 2003).

Precision Targeted Satire: RTMark and the Yes Men

> To restate a situationist expression, rather than "fighting alienation with alienated methods" (bureaucracy, political parties, militancy, deferment of pleasure), one uses derision, irony, laughter—all underground strategies which undermine the process of normalization and domestication which are the goals of the guarantors of the external and hence abstract order. (Maffesoli, 1996, p. 50)

The emphasis upon performance has been given a sustainedly satirical treatment by such groups as RTMark and The Yes Men. RTMark's name stems from the phrase *registered trademark* and its distinctive mode of operation rests upon its pastiche of corporate organizational forms. For example, in an imitation of the conventional stock market, it offers investments in imaginative stocks. The investments are made in the form of such countercultural stunts as the switching of the voice boxes in GI Joes and Barbie dolls by a group calling themselves the Barbie Liberation Organisation. The Yes Men have recently released an independent film of their stunts and have particularly focused their attentions upon the global economic policies of the World Trade Organization by misleadingly carrying out satirical presentations at various high-profile public events while pretending to be World Trade Organization representatives. Another example of this precision-directed satire was offered by re-code.com, which aimed at exposing the fallacy of the empowered consumer (perpetrated by sites such as priceline.com). It lets consumers dictate the price of purchase by providing users of the online site with the ability to access and manipulate the barcodes of popular products sold. Users were able to modify, download, and print barcodes that could then be attached to their item of choice. Although the creators of this site stressed that its purpose is solely satirical, a number of companies, including Wal-Mart, took a less charitable view of its activities and currently re-code.com is the subject of a legal action.

OPEN SOURCE AND FREE SOFTWARE: THE REBIRTH OF THE HACKING ETHIC?

Within the context of the issues under discussion, the emergence in the 1990s of the free software/open-source movement both confirms and consolidates many of the trends displayed by hacktivism, while also highlighting the perennial problems that plague the politicization of hacking. As stated above, the free software movement serves as a bridge between the ideals of the early generation of hackers and a new movement that has emerged in direct response to the increasing commodification of software and the Internet. We have spoken of tactical media as a synonym for hacktivism, and in this light, hacktivism can be seen as operating at the level of the message rather than the medium. In contrast, free software offers the possibility of an intervention in the structure of the medium because it renders the medium's design political. However, the politics of free software are a fraught matter, not least because the movement contains within itself a number of conflicting tendencies. Unlike hacktivism, which is irreducibly political, the politics of free software are in some respects extrinsic, that is to say the result of its context rather than a product of an explicit agenda. This resembles the problems faced by the first generations of hackers, with their predominant concern over the question of access, and like that generation the resolution of its immediate arena of conflict would possibly neutralize any wider political charge that the movement might possess. Certainly there are hackers among this community who see their work in political terms, not only as a challenge to the proprietorial model and monopolistic ethos of Microsoft and the like but also as a defense and assertion of fundamental freedom. But equally many of those who contribute to the project regard it simply in terms of an effective means for software design.

As a result, in 1998 the movement fractured into two factions when the Open Source Initiative, led by Eric Raymond, split from Richard Stallman's Free Software Foundation. The former claims to offer open-source software without "ideological tub-thumping" and a "losing attitude and symbolism" (http://www.opensource.org/advocacy/faq.html), arguing that OS is primarily a successful methodology for the development of software and as such is entirely compatible with the aims of big business. It has deliberately sought to meliorate those aspects of the movement that prove objectionable to corporate clients (not least a propensity toward long hair, beards, woolly hats, and comic T-shirts). In contrast, the free software faction has upheld the original hacker ethic and remains firm in the belief that free software partakes of a fundamental intellectual freedom. It argues that software should evolve in the way that science evolves, through the free exchange of information, for free software information should always be free (although as Stallman repeatedly points out the freedom he talks of is that of "free speech rather than free beer"). Despite these differences, their common methodology is in direct conflict with that practiced by Microsoft. Indeed, the color of the rhetoric the latter has used to describe OS indicates the threat this model represents; thus, Steve Ballmer of Microsoft has described it as "un-American" and a "cancer." Such pathological metaphors reveal the magnitude of the stakes involved, as do the infamous Halloween documents, a series of internal reports produced by Microsoft that describe free software as "long term credible" and a direct threat to Microsoft's revenues (http://www.opensource.org/halloween/links.php). The crux of the contention is the question of source code. Microsoft and a range of other software developers uphold a proprietorial model in which the codes that underpin their software are unavailable to its users or rivals.

The core principles to which both factions of the free software movement subscribe and that have provoked such strong reactions can be summarized as follows (see Cramer, 2000):

Free Software may be freely copied.

Not only the executable binary code, but also the program source code, are freely available.

The source code may be modified and used for other programs by anyone.

There are no restrictions on the use of Free Software. Even if Free Software is used for commercial purposes, no license fees have to be paid.

There are no restrictions on the distribution of Free Software. Free Software may be sold for money even without paying the programmers.

Free software is not freeware or shareware; that is to say, it can be sold. However, even if this is the case, the source code remains available and open to modification by the user or other programmers. These principles, known collectively as copyleft, have rapidly evolved within the context of the Internet and accommodate its open architecture into the very process of software design. Indeed, much of this architecture was written as free software, not for ideological reasons but because it predates the commodification of code that took place in the 1980s. Free software emerged as a response to this process, and attempted to preserve within a legislative framework (the GNU License) the freedoms threatened by this model. In this manner the open architecture of the Internet, constructed in part from nonproprietorial code, created an environment that facilitated the collaborative production of software. Thus the GNU/Linux system has been developed entirely online through the medium of e-mail and bulletin boards. In Microsoft's words "the ability of the OSS [open-source software] process to collect and harness the collective IQ of thousands of individuals across the Internet is simply amazing." In OS development, a multitude of unpaid console cowboys participate in a vast collaborative project, a system of cybernetic feedback in which the divisions between work and play and between user and consumer are continually transgressed for the sake of the product. This collectivism challenges both the self-serving mythos of the free market and the lone hacker, as well as the dictatorial hierarchy of conventional project development. Moreover, as Cramer (2000) notes, it constitutes an archive that cannot be erased: the code, once written, is in the public realm and can be drawn upon by anyone. In this respect it offers an intimation of collective intelligence or, in Microsoft's phrase, a "mindshare."

The relation of open source to wider political questions is complex. Terranova (2000) argues that its breakdown of the distinction between consumer and producer reflects an extension of the market into every aspect of contemporary existence. DeLanda (2001) argues that despite its insistence on freedom, "the very fact that the [GNU] license acts as an 'enforcement mechanism' for openness shows how far its function is from one of just promoting 'freedom' (that is, Stallman's original intention)" (para. 7). Eric Raymond (n.d.) argues for open source as gift economy, but as Richard Barbrook notes this economy exists within an inescapable relation to a commodity economy: "money commodity and gift relations are not just in conflict with each other, but also co-exist in symbiosis" (Barbrook, 1997, p. 137). Similarly, Stefan Merten, one of the organizers of the Wizards of OS conferences that have been held on a yearly basis in Berlin since the late 1990s, argues for the emergence of a General Public License society in which "immaterial," intellectual, or "affective" labor would be exchanged along an open-source model (Merten, 2001). This immateriality and free software's association with it has been the source of critique regarding the ultimate significance of open source. According to Matteo Pasquinelli,

> Softwares are immaterial machines.... Free Software... [in] its immateriality... often fails to clash with the real world. Even if we know that it is a good and right thing, we ask polemically: what will change when all the computers in the world will run free software? The most interesting aspect of the free software model is the immense cooperative network that was created by programmers on a global scale, but which other concrete examples can we refer to in proposing new forms of action in the real world and not only in the digital realm? (Pasquinelli, 2004, p. 3)

The supposed immateriality of contemporary labor is the product of a Western myopia that fails to see that material labor, rather than having disappeared, has merely been outsourced to number of developing countries. In these regions, the division between producer and consumer remains firmly entrenched, because many of the goods manufactured by the coolies of global economy remain beyond the economic reach of their producers. However, it is worth pointing out that free software (for sound economic reasons) has found a welcome in developing countries, for instance India, where a large number of skilled programmers are contributing to a range of OS projects (Moody, 2002, p. 317).

Such contradictions might suggest that open source, like the politicized hacking of the 1970s, is too mired in the contradictions of its milieu to constitute a viable challenge to the values of late capitalism. But, to the extent that it exists and produces a technically superior product using methods that implicitly challenge the dominant values of contemporary economic thought, it stands as an index of possibilities. It demonstrates that the Internet can indeed support new productive relations and thus offers a positive model for movements such as hacktivism.

ALL THAT IS SOLID MELTS INTO AIR

Marx and Engels famously declared in the *Communist Manifesto* that under capitalism:

> All fixed, fast-frozen relations, with their train of ancient and venerable prejudices and opinions, are swept away, all new-formed ones become antiquated before they can ossify. All that is solid melts into air, all that is holy is profaned, and men at last are forced to face . . . the real conditions of their lives and their relations with their fellow men (Marx & Engels, 1977, p. 46).

This prophetic articulation of the dematerializing qualities of commodity culture has recently found its echo in the titles of a spate of pro-business books that celebrate the putative weightlessness of the digital economy. For example, business books such as *Living on Thin Air, The Weightless World*, and *The Empty Rain Coat* are all premised upon an acceptance of, if not excitement about, the spatial disorientation created by globalization, and the new information technologies that have brought about these conditions. As stated previously, radical protest movements have sometimes been suspicious of too close an involvement with the technologies of their perceived enemies. The hacktivist groups and activities highlighted in this chapter represent a much more positive engagement with the realities of an increasingly networked world. Rather than rail against the enframing and circumscribing qualities of global systems, these movements have recognized, in Lash's words, that "there is no escaping from the information order, [and] thus the critique of information will have to come from inside the information itself" (Lash, 2002, p. vii). There is thus a growing recognition among new social movements that any desire for change to the social order will have to make use of, but also change the nature of, its present communication channels. They have chosen to concentrate upon the concluding part of Marx and Engel's pellucid assertion, that is, a recognition with "sober senses" of the "real conditions of their lives and their relations with their fellow men."

From the critical antiglobalization perspective, the increased efficiency of communication flows enabled by the new information technologies is part of both the problem and the solution. The same trends that result in the phenomenon of the *maquiladoras* (swallow factories—named after the way the fast-moving bird touches down momentarily before swooping off again) also provide such opportunities for global cooperation as that practiced by the EDT and their high-tech support for otherwise fragmented and globally disparate groups of people. What is important here is the to-and-fro movement of co-optation and counterresponse that takes place between corporate and anticorporate philosophies. Just as the hacker ethic became co-opted for the corporate requirements of Microsoft, so those wishing to oppose commercial forces do so in an adopt-and-adapt element of a system they oppose: free software is at once outside capitalism and within, where hacktivists in detourning the tools of economic globalization both challenge and acknowledge the reality of the system. In this light, Pasqunielli's (2004) dichotomy between the immateriality of cyberspace and the harsher conditions of the material world is too bald; it is a question not of testing one against the other, but of discovering the shifting and unstable alliances and the sudden conversions and adaptations that take place between the two.

CONCLUSION

This chapter has provided a brief overview of the main features, protagonists, and underlying philosophy of a number of emergent technologically orientated challenges to the current informational hegemony. Perhaps it was only a matter of time before anticorporate protestors saw globalization as an opportunity as well as a threat, but as much as its techniques involve new high-tech means they are essentially in keeping with both the original hacker ethic and conventional Marxist analysis of capitalism in which it is asserted that commercial power contains the seeds of its own downfall. In less polemical terms, more mainstream economic analysis also recognizes some of the inherent tensions created in the increasingly immaterial new economy that has spawned hacktivism. The fact that commodities are becoming increasingly immaterial means that it can be difficult to assert proprietary rights over them. This is a problem that both the music and the film industries are presently grappling with as they attempt to deal with the implications of the growth of online file sharing. Yet the sublimation of fixed values described by Marx and Engels a century and a half ago has still not resulted in capital's downfall: the market's powers of recuperation are robust. The basic situation faced by commercial and radical groups alike is that the online world creates conditions of flux. The "space of flows" of the information society (Castells, 2000) creates opportunities and challenges for resistance and capital alike, and in the case of open source these two vectors meet in a single praxis. This chapter has shown that, in contrast, hacktivism's most striking feature is not so much its imaginative reappropriation of technological methods and infrastructures, but its determination to apply such techniques for a social, rather than merely a technical, end. In the past, protest movements have been ill-equipped to do little more than reactively berate the worst aspects of changing social conditions whereas their corporate opponents have surfed the wave of change. The various generations of hackers have produced resources for different beasts; new sharks may now be in the water.

GLOSSARY

Antiglobalization/Anticapitalism Movements A new generation of protest movements that challenge the current neoliberal hegemony and attempt to draw attention to the intrinsically exploitative reality of free trade. They are distinguished by their decentralization, a lack of coherent ideology beyond what they oppose, and a willingness to engage in new methods of political protest.

Culture Jamming An attempt to overturn or expose the hidden agenda of cultural products by subverting their messages through low-tech means; rather than an external critique, it operates immanently at the level of specific cultural artifacts.

Free Software Software that includes its source code, which is available to all users who in principle can modify or contribute to its development. It is free as in "free speech" and not "free beer." This freedom is ensured by the use of licenses, which preserve the freedom of the code.

Hacker Ethic The belief that information sharing and technical innovation is in itself a positive act and that it should not be constrained or artificially delimited.

Hacking The ingenuity-driven activity of manipulating or modifying technologies without respect to their original functions, which should be distinguished from *cracking*, a more destructive or transgressive form of hacking.

Hacktivism The adoption of various procedures drawn from hacking for explicitly political ends; more generally, a recognition that political struggle in the 21st century necessarily includes information technologies.

Microserfs Term adopted from Douglas Coupland's eponymous novel, which describes the lives and frustrations of Microsoft employees in the mid-1990s.

Open-Source Movement A faction of the free software movement, that embraces the distribution of source code, but that views this freedom in terms of market choice and a rejection of centralized state control in favor of a free-market model. The most vocal proponent of this vision is Eric S. Raymond.

Source Code Source code is written in the higher programming languages that allow programmers to manipulate and assemble binary codes. This source code is not necessary for computers to run programs.

Virtual Sit-in A virtual sit in, like its physical counterpart, aims to immobilize a target by obstructing its services. The coordinated deployment by numerous users to bring down Web sites by accessing them several times a minute until the site collapses is an example of a virtual sit-in.

CROSS REFERENCES

See *Cyberterrorism and Information Security; Hackers, Crackers and Computer Criminals; Legal, Social and Ethical Issues of the Internet.*

REFERENCES

Allen, D. P., & Demchack, C. (2003, March–April). The Palestinian-Israel cyberwar. *Military Review*. Retrieved May 14, 2005, from http://www.findarticles.com/p/articles/mi_m0PBZ/is_2_83/ai_106732244

Barbrook, R. (1997). The digital economy. Retrieved from www.nettime.org

Bowcott, O., & Hamilton, S. (1990). *Beating the system: Hackers, phreakers & electronic spies*. London: Bloomsbury.

Castells, M. (2000). *The rise of the network society*. Oxford, UK: Blackwell.

Coupland, D. (1995). *Microserfs*. London: Flamingo.

Cramer, F. (2000). *Free software as collaborative text*. Retrieved May 14, 2005, from http://www.netzliteratur.net/cramer/free_software_as_text.html

Critical Art Ensemble. (1994). *The electronic disturbance*. New York: Autonomedia.

Deibert, R. J. (2003). Black code: Censorship, surveillance, and militarization of cyberspace. *Millennium: Journal of International Studies, 32*(3).

DeLanda, M. (2001). *Open-source: A movement in search of a philosophy*. Retrieved May 14, 2005, from http://www.cddc.vt.edu/host/delanda/pages/opensource.htm

Denning, D. (1999). Activism, hacktivism, and cyberterrorism: The Internet as a tool for influencing foreign policy. Retrieved May 14, 2005, from http://www.nautilus.org/gps/info-policy/workshop/papers/denning.html

Felsenstein, L. (1995). Convivial cybernetic devices: From vacuum tube flip-flops to the singing Altair: An interview with Lee Felsentein. *The Analytical Engine: Newsletter of the Computer History Association of California, 3*, 3–14.

Grether, R. (2000, January). How the Etoy campaign was won. *Telepolis*. Retrieved May 14, 2005, from http://www.heise.de/tp/english/inhalt/te/5843/1.html

Himanen, P. (2001). *The hacker ethic and the spirit of the information age*. London: Secker and Warburg.

Illich, I. (1973). *Tools for conviviality*. New York: Harper & Row.

Jordan, T., & Taylor, P. (2004). *Hacktivism & cyberwars: Rebels with a cause?* London: Routledge.

Klein, N. (2001). *No logo*. London: Flamingo.

Lash, S. (2002). *Critique of information*. London: Sage.

Latour, B. (1988). *The prince* for machines as well as for machinations. In B. Eliot (Ed.), *Technology and social process* (pp. 20–43). Edinburgh: Edinburgh University Press.

Levy, S. (1984). *Hackers: Heroes of the computer revolution*. New York: Bantam Doubleday Dell.

Maffesoli, M. (1996). *The time of the tribes: The decline of individualism in mass society*. Sage: London.

Marx, K., & Engels, F. (1977). *Manifesto of the Communist Party*. Moscow: Progress.

Merten, S. (2001). Free software & GPL society: Stefan Merten of Oekonux interviewed by Joanne Richardson. Retrieved May 14, 2005, from http://subsol.c3.hu/subsol_2/contributors0/mertentext.html

Moody, G. (2002). *Rebel code: Linux and the open source revolution*. London: Penguin Books.

Nelson, T. (1974). *Computer lib/dream machines*. Sausalito, CA: Mindful Press.

Pasquinelli, M. (2004). *Radical machines against the techno-empire: From Utopia to network*. Retrieved May 14, 2005, from http://www.republicart.net/disc/empire/pasquinelli01_en.pdf

Raymond, E. S. (n.d.). *Open source F.A.Q.* Retrieved May 14, 2005, from http://www.opensource.org/advocacy/faq.html

Ross, A. (1991). *Strange weather*. London: Verso.
Roszak, T. (1986). *The cult of information: The folklore of computers and the true art of thinking*. New York: Pantheon.
Taylor, P. A. (1999). *Hackers: Crime in the digital sublime*. London: Routledge.
Taylor, P. A. (2001). Hacktivists: In search of lost ethics? In D. Wall (Ed.), *Crime and the Internet*. London: Routledge.
Terranova, T. (2000). Free labour: Producing culture for the digital economy. *Social Text 63, 18*(2), 33–57.
Wolf, G. (1995). The curse of Xanadu. *Wired, 3*(6), 158–202.
Wray, S. (1998a). Transforming Luddite resistance into virtual Luddite resistance: Weaving a World Wide Web of electronic civil disobedience. Retrieved May 14, 2005, from http://www.thing.net/~rdom/ecd/luddite.html
Wray, S. (1998b). *On electronic civil disobedience*. Paper presented to the Socialist Scholars Conference. Retrieved from http://www.nyu.edu/projects/wray/oecd.html

The Digital Millennium Copyright Act

Seth Finkelstein, *SethF.com*

INTRODUCTION

In 1998, citing the United States' obligations under World Intellectual Property Organization (WIPO) copyright treaties, Congress passed the Digital Millennium Copyright Act (DMCA). The DMCA is a wide-ranging addition to copyright-related law, encompassing such topics as take-down procedures in copyright infringement disputes and safe-harbor defenses for Internet service providers (ISPs). This chapter focuses on the aspects of the DMCA that have particular relevance to research by academics and professionals: the portions that define offenses such as "circumvention" or "trafficking."

BASICS AND CRITICAL PROVISIONS

The DMCA is structured as a set of prohibitions, followed by various qualifications and exemptions to those prohibitions. The initial provisions are very broad and far reaching. It is a matter of much controversy whether subsequent interpretations and legal holdings will sufficiently constrain the scope of what constitutes a violation. The law in this area is very unsettled, with new cases being argued regularly. Significant judicial opinions are expected for years to come, and in response to those rulings, various legislative modifications and amendments will be proposed. Although it is always good practice to check for the most recent work, the subject matter in this instance is evolving particularly rapidly.

Circumvention

The first provision of this type is §1201(a)(1), defining circumvention violations. It reads:

> (a) Violations Regarding Circumvention of Technological Measures.—(1)(A) No person shall circumvent a technological measure that effectively controls access to a work protected under this title.

Circumvention is a new offense, one created by the DMCA. It is not copyright infringement, which is an infraction against a different set of rights, most commonly the making of copies in violation of copyright law. Rather, the §1201(a)(1) circumvention offense itself is obtaining unauthorized access to copyrighted material ("work protected under this title"). This new offense can be confusing to those who have formed their idea of copyright law from earlier incarnations. One common reaction is to repeat the defenses to infringement, such as fair use. However, circumvention is not infringement so the defenses that apply to infringement do not apply to circumvention. Indeed, this difference in defenses is one of the most significant aspects of the DMCA.

It should be stressed that *access* is not necessarily *copying*. Obtaining unauthorized access may involve nothing more than viewing encrypted video on an operating system that does not have a licensed (authorized) decryption player. Inversely, copying is not necessarily access. Encrypted copyrighted material can be reproduced while still encrypted. However, often these two actions are necessarily intertwined.

Technological Measure and "Effectively Controls Access"

The DMCA goes on to define the terms used in the circumvention offense as follows:

> (A) to "circumvent a technological measure" means to descramble a scrambled work, to decrypt an encrypted work, or otherwise to avoid, bypass, remove, deactivate, or impair a technological measure, without the authority of the copyright owner; and
>
> (B) a technological measure "effectively controls access to a work" if the measure, in the ordinary course of its operation, requires the application of information, or a process or a treatment, with the authority of the copyright owner, to gain access to the work.

It is important to take note of the phrase, "effectively controls access." This is often misunderstood by scientists or engineers as meaning that a measure successfully controls access, implying perhaps a necessity to use strong cryptography. No such requirement is present. In fact, the access control can be very weak in technological terms. Possibly the best analogy is the phrase used to characterize the criminal offense, "breaking and entering." This offense does not require anything to be damaged physically, which is one ordinary sense of the word "breaking." Even opening a closed door would qualify. That the open door is not a broken object, in the English sense of the word, is irrelevant. The argument that "effectively controls access" has a paradoxical meaning has been both attempted repeatedly in court and strongly ruled incorrect by judges.

The judicial failure of "effectively" as a limiting argument cannot be overemphasized. Technologists often reinvent and propose that interpretation. To give one important rejection, in *Universal City Studios Inc. v. Reimerdes* (2000), the trial court wrote at length regarding how the definition cannot be viewed as self-defeating:

> Finally, the interpretation of the phrase "effectively controls access" offered by defendants at trial—viz., that the use of the word "effectively" means that the statute protects only successful or efficacious technological means of controlling access—would gut the statute if it were adopted. If a technological means of access control is circumvented, it is, in common parlance, ineffective. Yet defendants' construction, if adopted, would limit the application of the statute to access control measures that thwart circumvention, but withhold protection for those measures that can be circumvented. In other words, defendants would have the Court construe the statute to offer protection where none is needed but to withhold protection precisely where protection is essential. The Court declines to do so. Accordingly, the Court holds that CSS effectively controls access to plaintiffs' copyrighted works.

When the case was appealed, *Universal City Studios Inc v. Corley* (2001), the appeals court accepted the above reasoning regarding what constitutes effectiveness. In *321 Studios v. Metro Goldwyn Mayer et al.* (2004), the trial court rejected a challenge to the concept of effective control stemming from widespread availability:

> 321, in a footnote, questions whether CSS is an effective control or protection of DVDs, since the CSS access keys are widely available on the internet. However, this is equivalent to a claim that, since it is easy to find skeleton keys on the black market, a deadbolt is not an effective lock to a door.

Further, in the case *RealNetworks, Inc. v. Streambox, Inc.* (2000), merely setting a bit flag (called there a "Copy Switch") was held by the district court to qualify as effective protection when combined with an authentication scheme:

> 8. In conjunction with the Secret Handshake, the Copy Switch is a "technological measure" that effectively protects the right of a copyright owner to control the unauthorized copying of its work. See 17 U.S.C. §1201(b)(2)(B) (measure "effectively protects" right of copyright holder if it "prevents, restricts or otherwise limits the exercise of a right of a copyright owner"); . . . To access a RealMedia file distributed by a RealServer, a user must use a RealPlayer. The RealPlayer reads the Copy Switch in the file. If the Copy Switch in the file is turned off, the RealPlayer will not permit the user to record a copy as the file is streamed. Thus, the Copy Switch may restrict others from exercising a copyright holder's exclusive right to copy its work.

A password has been also been ruled to meet the standard of an effective technological measure. However, the unauthorized use of a password has been held *not* to be circumvention within the meaning of the DMCA, in a district court case, *I.M.S. Information Management Systems, LTD. v. Berkshire Information Systems, Inc.* (2004):

> Defendant is alleged to have accessed plaintiff's [password] protected website without plaintiff's authorization. Defendant did not surmount or puncture or evade any technological measure to do so; instead, it used a password intentionally issued by plaintiff to another entity. As an analogy to Universal Studios, the password defendant used to enter plaintiff's webservice was the DVD player, not the DeCSS decryption code, or some alternate avenue of access not sponsored by the copyright owner (like a skeleton key, or neutralizing device). Plaintiff, however, did not authorize defendant to utilize the DVD player. Plaintiff authorized someone else to use the DVD player, and defendant borrowed it without plaintiff's permission. Whatever the impropriety of defendant's conduct, the DMCA and the anti-circumvention provision at issue do not target this sort of activity.

In sum, the standard is legal, not cryptographic. The key element is not the computational strength of a cipher or any type of certification to an industry standard or best practices procedure. Rather, only a minimal effort is needed. Just meeting a simple test concerning the procedure by which access to the work is obtained will trigger the application of the law.

Trafficking

Building on the prohibition of circumvention itself, a second provision, §1201(a)(2), forbids various types of trafficking:

(2) No person shall manufacture, import, offer to the public, provide, or otherwise traffic in any technology, product, service, device, component, or part thereof, that—

And then the law sets out a qualifying test, which is important to understand in terms of implications:

(A) is primarily designed or produced for the purpose of circumventing a technological measure that effectively controls access to a work protected under this title;
(B) has only limited commercially significant purpose or use other than to circumvent a technological measure that effectively controls access to a work protected under this title; or
(C) is marketed by that person or another acting in concert with that person with that person's knowledge for use in circumventing a technological measure that effectively controls access to a work protected under this title.

As circumvention is different from infringement, trafficking is different from circumvention. One need not do any circumvention oneself in order to violate the trafficking provision, and no infringement need be done in either case. Trafficking provisions concern tools and are sometimes analogized to laws against burglary tools. This analogy has problems though, as many burglary tools are often legal in and of themselves, with related offenses requiring an intent to commit burglary.

Although trafficking is often discussed in terms of devices, the text of the law specifically forbids "any technology." This has been held to encompass the source code of computer programs (*Universal v. Reimerdes*, 2000, footnote 135). A very controversial question is whether it also extends to academic research papers (Liu, 2003).

The test to qualify as a circumvention tool addresses certain frequent objections to the concept of prohibited devices. For example, a general-purpose debugging program would not qualify because it is not "primarily designed" for circumvention, nor does it have "only limited commercially significant purpose or use" except for circumvention.

Closely related to §1201(a)(2) is another trafficking provision, §1201(b)(1). Although §1201(a)(2) is concerned with a technological measure that effectively protects *"access,"* §1201(b)(1) addresses trafficking regarding *"a right of a copyright owner."* Except for this change, the language of §1201(b)(1) is otherwise parallel to that of §1201(a)(2).

Fair Use Implications

As has been discussed above, the offenses defined by the DMCA are distinct from the concept of copyright infringement. These differences, particularly fair use rights, are mentioned in a provision of the DMCA, §1201(c), which begins:

(c) Other Rights, Etc., Not Affected.
(1) Nothing in this section shall affect rights, remedies, limitations, or defenses to copyright infringement, including fair use, under this title.

This is an especially subtle statement, going to the heart of the debates over the meaning of fair use. The logical problem is an interpretation that, as a legal matter, because the DMCA offenses are not copyright infringement, by definition defenses to copyright infringement such as fair use are not affected. This view holds that if a prohibition against circumvention of access controls makes impossible any unauthorized use at all, that does not affect the ability to argue fair use as a defense to copyright infringement. More simply, if a copy could be made, fair use could be argued as a defense to copyright infringement. However, the fact that the copy might not be able to be made in the first place, without violating access controls, is deemed irrelevant.

One way to think of this problem is as a conflict about whether fair use is a reflection of a substantive right, grounded in the First Amendment, or merely one particular defense to one specific part of copyright law having to do with infringement. The legal results so far have supported the latter viewpoint. In the case *Universal v. Corley* (2001), the court stated:

> We know of no authority for the proposition that fair use, as protected by the Copyright Act, much less the Constitution, guarantees copying by the optimum method or in the identical format of the original. Although the Appellants insisted at oral argument that they should not be relegated to a "horse and buggy" technique in making fair use of DVD movies, [Footnote 36] the DMCA does not impose even an arguable limitation on the opportunity to make a variety of traditional fair uses of DVD movies, such as commenting on their content, quoting excerpts from their screenplays, and even recording portions of the video images and sounds on film or tape by pointing a camera, a camcorder, or a microphone at a monitor as it displays the DVD movie. The fact that the resulting copy will not be as perfect or as manipulable as a digital copy obtained by having direct access to the DVD movie in its digital form, provides no basis for a claim of unconstitutional limitation of fair use.

The court concluded: "Fair use has never been held to be a guarantee of access to copyrighted material in order to copy it by the fair user's preferred technique or in the format of the original."

The footnote 36 in the passage above is notable in itself:

> 36. In their supplemental papers, the Appellants contend, rather hyperbolically, that a prohibition on using copying machines to assist in making fair use of texts could not validly be upheld by the availability of "monks to scribe the relevant passages."

These interpretations are another instance where the legal reasoning strikes many technologists as paradoxical if not incomprehensible. One might ask, in what sense can a right be said to exist, if the means to exercise it are heavily constrained? The judicial resolution of this quandary, via strict theoretical partitioning of the concepts, invites repeated challenges because of the practical connections. Yet, so far, all rulings on this issue have been consistently along the above lines. For example, in *321 Studios v. MGM* (2004),

> This Court agrees with this analysis in Corley: ["optimum method" conclusions repeated]
> The fact that the resulting copy will not be as perfect or as manipulable as a digital copy obtained by having direct access to the DVD movie in its digital form, provides no basis for a claim of unconstitutional limitation of fair use.

These rulings all demonstrate how complex and counterintuitive are the fair use issues in view of the DMCA's constraints on access and copying tools.

MAJOR EXEMPTIONS

Despite not having a general defense for fair use, the DMCA does exempt various activities. These exemptions are notably restrictive and narrow, but some are worthy of discussion for academic or scientific applications.

Reverse Engineering

The §1201(f) provision contains a limited right to engage in circumvention (§1201(a)(1)) for the purpose of reverse engineering, specifying the qualifications as follows:

> (f) Reverse Engineering.—(1) Notwithstanding the provisions of subsection (a)(1)(A), a person who has lawfully obtained the right to use a copy of a computer program may circumvent a technological measure that effectively controls access to a particular portion of that program for the sole purpose of identifying and analyzing those elements of the program that are necessary to achieve interoperability of an independently created computer program with other programs, and that have not previously been readily available to the person engaging in the circumvention, to the extent any such acts of identification and analysis do not constitute infringement under this title.

The most important portions of this provision are the "sole purpose" aspect and the clause "to the extent... not constitute infringement." These narrow the range of the defense considerably in practice. It is critical to keep in mind that these determinations may be affected by the court's view of the overall value of the activity and of the character of the defendants. In *Universal v. Reimerdes* (2000), the court ruled very unfavorably on the "sole purpose" aspect of this provision, with notable comments:

> Finally, it is important to recognize that even the creators of DeCSS cannot credibly maintain that the "sole" purpose of DeCSS was to create a Linux DVD player. DeCSS concededly was developed on and runs under Windows—a far more widely used operating system. The developers of DeCSS therefore knew that DeCSS could be used to decrypt and play DVD movies on Windows as well as Linux machines. They knew also that the decrypted files could be copied like any other unprotected computer file. Moreover, the Court does not credit Mr. Johansen's testimony that he created DeCSS solely for the purpose of building a Linux player. Mr. Johansen is a very talented young man and a member of a well known hacker group who viewed "cracking" CSS as an end in itself and a means of demonstrating his talent and who fully expected that the use of DeCSS would not be confined to Linux machines. Hence, the Court finds that Mr. Johansen and the others who actually did develop DeCSS did not do so solely for the purpose of making a Linux DVD player if, indeed, developing a Linux-based DVD player was among their purposes.
>
> Accordingly, the reverse engineering exception to the DMCA has no application here.

Yet, the ability to conduct reverse engineering is deeply affected by the development of tools to aid in the process. The exemption addresses that trafficking prohibitions by providing a limited ability to make and communicate such tools. As §1201(f) goes on to state,

> (2) Not withstanding the provisions of subsections (a)(2) and (b), a person may develop and employ technological means to circumvent a technological measure, or to circumvent protection afforded by a technological measure, in order to enable the identification and analysis under paragraph (1), or for the purpose of enabling interoperability of an independently created computer program with other programs, if such means are necessary to achieve such interoperability, to the extent that doing so does not constitute infringement under this title.
>
> (3) The information acquired through the acts permitted under paragraph (1), and the means permitted under paragraph (2), may be made available to others if the person referred to in paragraph (1) or (2), as the case may be, provides such information or means solely for the purpose of enabling interoperability of an independently created computer program with other programs, and to the extent that doing so does not constitute infringement under this title or violate applicable law other than this section.

Note though, that the permissions are again constrained by the qualifiers as to "solely for the purpose" and "not constitute infringement." It is especially important to observe that although §1201(f)(1) permits a person to circumvent, and §1201(f)(2) allows them to develop tools, §1201(f)(3) restricts distribution of the fruits of these efforts to apply only to the person who has done them in the first place. Therefore, against what would be a prevailing conception, third-party republication is not within this exemption. Again, in *Universal v. Reimerdes* (2000), Judge Kaplan said: "First, Section 1201(f)(3) permits information acquired through reverse engineering to be made available to others only by the person who acquired the information. But these defendants did not do any reverse engineering. They simply took DeCSS off someone else's web site and posted it on their own."

Judge Kaplan went on to say, "Defendants would be in no stronger position even if they had authored DeCSS. The right to make the information available extends only to dissemination "solely for the purpose" of achieving interoperability as defined in the statute. It does not apply to public dissemination of means of circumvention, as the legislative history confirms. [footnote 151] These defendants, however, did not post DeCSS 'solely' to achieve interoperability with Linux or anything else."

In a different case, (*Lexmark International Inc. v. Static Control Components, Inc.*, 2003) the district court said quite bluntly: "Sections 1201(f)(2) and (3) of the DMCA are not broad exceptions that can be employed to excuse any behavior that makes some device "interoperable" with some other device." However, a successful appeal resulted in a more robust view, where the appeals court opinion stated "the statue is silent about the degree to which the "technological means" must be necessary, if indeed they must be necessary at all, for interoperability."

Encryption Research

The exemption of most interest to the academic reader is certainly the §1201(g) provision, which provides a DMCA framework for "permissible acts of encryption research." It lays out a complex series of definitions and tests that must be met to qualify for the exemptions. The term "encryption research" is defined as

o (1) Definitions.—For purposes of this subsection—

(A) the term "encryption research" means activities necessary to identify and analyze flaws and vulnerabilities of encryption technologies applied to copyrighted works, if these activities are conducted to advance the state of knowledge in the field of encryption technology or to assist in the development of encryption products; and

(B) the term "encryption technology" means the scrambling and descrambling of information using mathematical formulas or algorithms.

Note the clause requiring activities to be "conducted to advance the state of knowledge." It provides fertile ground for argument over what qualifies as proper research. Although much security research is conducted within an unquestioned academic context, not all such activity is necessarily sympathetic to the courts or public opinion.

The text of the exemption specifies further conditions—that one must have "lawfully obtained the encrypted copy," have "made a good faith effort to obtain authorization before the circumvention," and not otherwise have violated any laws. Then it enumerates complicated qualifying conditions. These conditions warrant detailed study, as they are most relevant to avoiding being the target of litigation:

o (3) Factors in determining exemption.—In determining whether a person qualifies for the exemption under paragraph (2), the factors to be considered shall include—

+ (A) whether the information derived from the encryption research was disseminated, and if so, whether it was disseminated in a manner reasonably calculated to advance the state of knowledge or development of encryption technology, versus whether it was disseminated in a manner that facilitates infringement under this title or a violation of applicable law other than this section, including a violation of privacy or breach of security;

+ (B) whether the person is engaged in a legitimate course of study, is employed, or is appropriately trained or experienced, in the field of encryption technology; and

(C) whether the person provides the copyright owner of the work to which the technological measure is applied with notice of the findings and documentation of the research, and the time when such notice is provided.

This might be seen as an attempt to codify a distinction between "black hats" and "white hats" (crackers versus scientists) in terms of research. Yet, given the arguments over practices and methods of disclosure of security vulnerabilities, there is certain to be ample room for debate over who will be protected under the above criteria.

CRIMINAL PROVISIONS

Although copyright law is commonly thought of in terms of monetary damages and civil lawsuits, there has always been a criminal law component. The DMCA criminal offenses are at §1204:

> Sec. 1204.—Criminal offenses and penalties
>
> (a) In General.—
>
> Any person who violates section 1201 or 1202 willfully and for purposes of commercial advantage or private financial gain—
>
> (1) shall be fined not more than $500,000 or imprisoned for not more than 5 years, or both, for the first offense; and
>
> (2) shall be fined not more than $1,000,000 or imprisoned for not more than 10 years, or both, for any subsequent offense.

Note all violations of section 1201 are included, encompassing §1201(a)(1) circumvention offenses and §1201(a)(2) and §1201(b)(1) trafficking offenses.

The critical element in the above provisions is *"for purposes of commercial advantage or private financial gain."* Satisfying this provision turns out to be much easier than one might think. In particular, it does not require any money to be exchanged, contrary to intuitive expectations. In a comparable copyright law provision (No Electronic

Theft Act, 1997), the US Department of Justice sample language for jury instructions regarding this element is that "the Government need not prove that the defendant actually received a profit from the infringement. The Government need only show that the defendant acted with the hope or expectation of some commercial advantage or financial gain."

The Department Of Justice Criminal Resource Manual (1997a, b) states clearly, "Emphasis should be placed on the word 'purpose,' because it is not necessary to prove that any profit was realized." Later in the document, the manual stresses with emphasis that the key word in the requirement is *"purpose"* (emphasis in original): "Evidence of discrete monetary transactions (i.e., the selling of infringing goods for a particular price) provides the clearest evidence of financial gain, but such direct evidence should not be a prerequisite to prosecution. Such a stringent requirement would ignore the plain wording of the statute, which requires only the showing of commercial or financial *purpose*."

The overall requirement seems to be construed broadly (bartering, being an employee, etc.), encompassing "expressed or implied intent of the parties." This aspect of being an employee was seen very specifically in the *United States v. Elcom Ltd.* (2002) "Sklyarov" case, discussed below.

EXEMPTION PROCESS—ANTICIRCUMVENTION RULEMAKING

Section 1201(a)(1)(C) of the DMCA provides a process by which users of a "class of works" can apply for an exemption from the §1201(a)(1) circumvention prohibitions. These exemptions specifically do not apply to any trafficking prohibitions. This process takes places every 3 years, starting from 2000. All exemptions last for only one 3-year cycle and must be reargued from the start at every rulemaking.

Note these exemptions do not affect any other laws that might be used against a researcher. In particular, copyright infringement, trade secret law, and shrinkwrap license prohibitions against reverse engineering are all potential legal problems (Copyright Office, 2003).

Although this process does have an effect, it also has notable limitations. As outlined in the "Statement of the Librarian of Congress Relating to Section 1201 Rulemaking" (Billington, 2003; see Library of Congress, 2003)

> It is important to understand the purposes of this rulemaking, as stated in the law, and the role I have in it. The rulemaking is not a broad evaluation of the successes or failures of the DMCA. The purpose of the proceeding is to determine whether current technologies that control access to copyrighted works are diminishing the ability of individuals to use works in lawful, noninfringing ways. The DMCA does not forbid the act of circumventing copy controls, and therefore this rulemaking proceeding is not about technologies that control copying. Some of the people who participated in the rulemaking did not understand that and made proposals based on their dissatisfaction with copy controls. Other participants sought exemptions that would permit them to circumvent access controls on all works when they are engaging in particular noninfringing uses of those works. The law does not give me that power....

Despite these restrictions, the anticircumvention rulemaking is one of the few avenues where researchers can attempt to ameliorate the effects of the DMCA in even the smallest way. Participation does not require a law degree, being part of a lobbyist organization, or access to Congressional legislative staff. As stated in the "Recommendation of the Register of Copyrights" (Peters, 2003) regarding one particular exemption (censorware): "The Register's recommendation in favor of this exemption is based primarily on the evidence introduced in the comments and testimony by one person, Seth Finkelstein, a nonlawyer participating on his own behalf."

It is possible for a researcher to be heard (Finkelstein, 2002, 2003).

Classes of Works Exempted (2003)

At the time of the writing of this chapter, the 2003 rulemaking process had recently been completed. The following exemptions were granted:

(1) Compilations consisting of lists of Internet locations blocked by commercially marketed filtering software applications that are intended to prevent access to domains, websites or portions of websites, but not including lists of [spam or viruses].
(2) Computer programs protected by dongles that prevent access due to malfunction or damage and which are obsolete.
(3) Computer programs and video games distributed in formats that have become obsolete and which require the original media or hardware as a condition of access.
(4) Literary works distributed in ebook format when all existing ebook editions of the work... contain access controls that prevent the enabling of the ebook's read-aloud function and that prevent the enabling of screen readers to render the text into a specialized format.

However, these exemptions did not come close to covering all the various areas of research that have been affected by the DMCA.

MAJOR CASES

Much of the meaning of the DMCA is being shaped by judicial interpretation. This is an ongoing process, as various questions are considered and ruled on. The law may change, and the reader must keep that in mind. The material below is accurate as of mid-2004.

Universal City Studios, Inc. v. Reimerdes (DeCSS)

The most significant case of litigation under the DMCA is arguably *Universal City Studios, Inc. v. Reimerdes*, aka the DeCSS case. Many movie and TV shows available on DVD format disks are encrypted with a process known as content scramble system (CSS). This encryption restricts the material to access only on authorized DVD players, which are licensed to decrypt the content. Notably, commercial-grade bit-for-bit copying of the DVD disks can proceed whether or not the content is encrypted with CSS. However, it is of little use to exchange the encrypted data over file-sharing networks. Moreover, tying viewing the DVD video to licensed players enforces a geographical market segmentation scheme known as "region coding." Each DVD can have a region assigned to it, which makes it viewable only on players that are coded to the corresponding region.

DeCSS is a program that decrypts the CSS encryption. The unencrypted files can then be viewed on unlicensed players and exchanged over networks, and region coding becomes irrelevant. Making the DeCSS program available quickly led to lawsuits. One lawsuit branch involved trade secret law (*DVD-CCA v. Bunner* and *DVD-CCA v. Pavlovich*, California DeCSS cases), and is not discussed here. The *Universal v. Reimerdes* case (New York DeCSS case, later appealed as *Universal v. Corley*, has become the leading law on the DMCA. These are two different phases of the same case. At the trial level, in district court, Reimerdes was the main defendant. Later, after an adverse decision, Corley appealed to the U.S. Court of Appeals for the Second Circuit, which decided that case.

Contrary to many newspaper reports, it is not accurate that a 15-year-old Norwegian teenager (Jon Johansen) broke the encryption code. Perhaps the best account of the origin of DeCSS can be found in the testimony of Jon Johansen during the trial (Johansen, 2000, p. 619).

> Q. Who wrote DeCSS?
>
> A. I and two other people wrote DeCSS.
>
> ...
>
> Q. Mr. Johansen, what did you do next towards making DeCSS?
>
> A. We agreed that the person who I met would reverse engineer a DVD player in order to obtain the CSS algorithm and keys.
>
> ....
>
> Q. Thank you very much. Now, you testified on direct that a German person, I think, had reverse-engineered the Xing DVD player, is that correct?
>
> A. Yes, that is correct.
>
> Q. And that person goes by the nick Ham?
>
> A. Yes, that's correct.
>
> Q. And it's Ham who wrote the source code that performed the authentication function in DeCSS, is that correct?
>
> A. No, that is not correct. He did not write the authentication code. He wrote the decryption code.
>
> ...
>
> Q. And it was Ham's reverse engineering of the Xing DVD player that revealed the CSS encryption algorithm, am I right?
>
> A. Yes, that's correct.
>
> Q. Reverse engineering by Ham took place in or about September 1999?
>
> A. Yes, I believe it was late in September of 1999.
>
> Q. And you testified that it was this revelation of the CSS encryption algorithm and not any weakness in the CSS cipher that allowed MORE to create DeCSS, is that correct?
>
> A. Yes, that's correct.
>
> Q. You obtained the decryption portions of the DeCSS source code from Ham, correct?
>
> A. Yes, that's correct.
>
> Q. You then compiled the source code and created the executable?
>
> A. Well, in the form I received it, it was not compatible.

The actual writer of the DeCSS decryption code remains anonymous to this day. Given that Jon Johansen was criminally prosecuted in Norway for his role in the creation of the DeCSS code, the consequences for the programmer behind the decryption would certainly be severe.

Johansen was tried on charges related to a Norwegian law concerning data security and was acquitted. However, Norwegian law allowed the prosecutor to appeal the case. Johanson was then retried and reacquitted.

However, the litigation in the U.S. case was not concerned with creation of a program, but rather with its distribution. At issue was the right to publish the decrypting programs, not liability for their production. As software involves speech issues, several constitutional principles were at stake. However, the eventual court ruling went completely against publication rights (*Universal v. Reimerdes*, 2000).

> The District Court, Kaplan, J., held that [sic]: (1) posting decryption software violated DMCA provision prohibiting trafficking in technology that circumvented measures controlling access to copyrighted works; (2) posting hyperlinks to other web-sites offering decryption software violated DMCA; (3) DMCA anti-trafficking provision was content-neutral as applied to computer program; (4) DMCA did not violate First Amendment as applied to defendants and decryption software; (5) defendants failed to establish anti-trafficking provision was overly broad on grounds that it prevented noninfringing fair use of movies; (6) application of anti-trafficking provision to enjoin defendants from hyper-linking to other web-sites offering decryption software did not violate First Amendment; and (7) plaintiffs were entitled to injunction enjoining defendants from posting decryption software or hyperlinking to other web-sites that made software available.

As the leading case authority on the DMCA, this decision has been cited repeatedly for the manner is which it interprets the various controversies.

United States v. Elcom (Dmitry Sklyarov, eBooks)

Many people believe that DMCA criminal sanctions will be applied only to large-scale commercial copyright infringers. The case of Dmitry Sklyarov, the first programmer to be arrested and face criminal charges under the DMCA, shows that the reach of the law is much further than assumed. Dmitry Sklyarov was a Ph.D. student at the Bauman Moscow State Technical University. Working for the Russian company ElcomSoft, he developed software (Advanced eBook Processor; AEBPR) to decrypt the encrypted eBook format developed and marketed by the document technology platform company, Adobe Systems.

While attending a conference in the United States, Skylyarow was arrested for violating DMCA provision §1201(b)(1), under a theory of trafficking in copy-control circumvention tools. Contrary to the popular conception, he was not arrested for anything he said at the conference itself. Rather, his appearance there presented an opportunity for the United States to exercise jurisdiction. The facts that the AEBPR program itself was sold commercially and he had been listed at one time as the copyright owner were taken to be sufficient for criminal liability (*U.S. v. Sklyarov Criminal Complaint*, 2001).

Notably, it was not necessary for any actual infringement to have taken place. A ban on merely selling a circumvention tool itself (which fell under the DMCA's standards) was ruled to be a reasonable prohibition (*U.S. v. Elcom*, 2002, aka *Elcomsoft*):

> Pirates and other infringers require tools in order to bypass the technological measures that protect against unlawful copying. Thus, targeting the tool sellers is a reasoned, and reasonably tailored, approach to "remedying the evil" targeted by Congress. In addition, because tools that circumvent copyright protection measures for the purpose of allowing fair use can also be used to enable infringement, it is reasonably necessary to ban the sale of all circumvention tools in order to achieve the objectives of preventing widespread copyright infringement and electronic piracy in digital media.

The arrest of a programmer at a conference caused widespread public concern, especially within the security and cryptography communities. Protest rallies were held, and the case attracted interest that publicized problematic aspects of the DMCA. Eventually the charges were dropped against Sklyarov in return for his testimony against his employer. Finally, ElcomSoft was acquitted in a jury trial (Bowman, 2002). There has been extensive argument regarding what implications should be drawn from both the initial prosecution and the subsequent acquittal (Liu, 2003).

321 Studios v. MGM

321 Studios makes and sells programs called DVD Copy Plus and DVD-X COPY. These programs are marketed for the purpose of making a personal, archival backup copy of content on a DVD, even of CSS-encrypted content, such as a commercial movie. 321 Studios sought a declaratory judgment that, in distributing these programs, it was not in violation of the DMCA. It was opposed by members of the Motion Picture Association of America (MPAA).

The eventual ruling thoroughly rejected the claims of 321, on summary judgment (i.e., ruling that simply as a matter of a law, 321 was in violation of the DMCA). The court found prior cases—*Universal v. Reimerdes* (2000), *Universal v. Corley* (2001), *United States v. Elcom* (2002)—"dispositive on many of the same issues" of fair use and application of the DMCA: "This Court finds, as did both the Corley and Elcom courts, that legal downstream use of the copyrighted material by customers is not a defense to the software manufacturer's violation of the provisions of §1201 (b)(1)."

Though the case was appealed, 321 Studios was driven out of business by legal costs from being the target of many lawsuits (Cowley, 2004).

Felten et al. v. RIAA

Princeton University Computer Science professor Edward Felten is a researcher in the field of information security. His research group participated in a challenge by the Secure Digital Music Initiative (SDMI) to evaluate vulnerabilities in digital watermarking systems for music files. When the group (Felten, Scott Craver, Bede Liu, Min Wu, Dan Wallach, Ben Swartzlander, Drew Dean, and Adam Stubblefield) planned to present a paper detailing its research results showing weaknesses in the various technologies, Professor Felten was threatened with legal liability by the Recording Industry Association of America and the SDMI, on the grounds of violating a "click-through agreement" and the DMCA (Oppenheim, 2001):

> In addition, because the public disclosure of your research would be outside the limited authorization of the Agreement, you could be subject to enforcement actions under federal law, including the DMCA. The Agreement specifically preserves any rights that proponents of the technology being attacked may have "under any applicable law including, without limitation, the U.S. Digital Millennium Copyright Act, for any acts not expressly authorized by this Agreement." The Agreement simply does not "expressly authorize" participants to disclose information and research developed through participating in the Public Challenge and thus such disclosure could be the subject of a DMCA action.

Although later statements from the RIAA and SDMI denied there was a legal threat, a "declaratory judgment" suit was brought against them to establish that such scientific research would not be chilled by the fear of litigation. However, the court was not convinced that there was an actual case or controversy qualifying for a legal opinion. The paper in question had been published after the issue was publicized widely, and further judicial action was ruled premature.

This case is notable for the implication that the reach of the DMCA extends to "information and research," at least to the extent of generating a formal letter regarding legal action from organizations that object to the dissemination of the material.

EXAMPLE CONTROVERSY—MEDIAMAX CD3

Although not a legal case, this widely publicized conflict between a company and a graduate student is additionally instructive regarding what academic researchers may face and how the issues can be phrased.

SunnComm is a company that manufactures a copy-restriction system for CD music, MediaMax CD3. John Alex Halderman was a Princeton Ph.D. student studying computer security with, interestingly enough, Edward Felten as his advisor. Halderman published a report, "Analysis of the MediaMax CD3 Copy-Prevention System," detailing vulnerabilities of SunnComm's technology. SunnComm reacted with nationally publicized threats to sue on various grounds, including the DMCA (SunnComm, 2003a; Vance, 2003).

Although SunnComm was widely reported to be angered that its copy-control technology could be disabled by the use of the shift key (Borland, 2003), deeper examination indicates that the most contentious issue was publishing details of its MediaMax drivers (Halderman, 2003):

> Next, follow these additional steps to disable MediaMax:
>
> 1. Select the SbcpHid driver from the Device Manager list and click "Properties" from the Action Menu.
> 2. Click the Driver tab and click the Stop button to disable the driver.
> 3. Set the Startup Type to "Disabled" using the dropdown list.

A little-noted part of the SunnComm press release explained the basis under which SunnComm considered it had grounds for a lawsuit under the DMCA (SunnComm, 2003a):

> In addition, SunnComm believes that Mr. Halderman has violated the Digital Millennium Copyright Act (DMCA) by disclosing unpublished MediaMax management files placed on a users computer after user approval is granted. Once the file is found and deleted according to the instructions given in the Princeton grad students report, the MediaMax copy management system can be bypassed resulting in the copyrighted protected music being converted or misappropriated for potentially unauthorized and/or illegal use. SunnComm intends to refer this possible felony to authorities having jurisdiction over these matters because: 1. The author admits that he disabled the driver in order to make an unprotected copy of the discs contents, and 2. SunnComm believes that the authors report was disseminated in a manner which facilitates infringement in violation of the DMCA or other applicable law.

One commentator in a discussion forum, who claimed to be a SunnComm employee, put the issue as follows (AfterDawn.com, 2003):

> Just out of complete curiosity, do you guys *really* think that the shift key/autorun issue was what the problem was about?
>
> ...do you guys *really* believe..and i mean **really** believe that the shift key 'escaped' notice, going thru the various dev cycles, testing 3rd party testing etc etc??? *especially* if the autorun feature was going to be used???
>
> Just a little FYI for all..the issue was about disclosing file names, locations and circumvention directions, which, if i read the DMCA correctly could be construed as a possible violation..
>
> ...
>
> were we *ever* gonna sue over the shift key? jeez..are you guys serious? that makes us laugh every time we see it, in big bold headline stories, such as at the top of this one..
>
> btw, he didn't get sued, we decided not to go after him, and not because of the shift key, but because ultimately, the media's 'spin' would eventually become bigger (and badder) than the actual inital problem....

Translated from the informal phrasing, the commentator argues that SunnComm considered charging Halderman with violating the §1201(a)(2) trafficking provisions, under the theory that the details in his paper constituted *technology* for circumvention (not that the shift key was a circumvention device). Likely a §1201(a)(1) circumvention access violation was intended as well.

Although these theories are expansive, it is notable how the language of the press release is directed toward countering the §1201(g) research exemption. The "disseminated in a manner which facilitates infringement" phrasing is a direct reference to the §1201(g)(3)(A) factor "in determining if a person qualifies for the exemption" for performing "permissible acts of encryption research." Further, other parts of the press release seem aimed to delegitimatize Halderman with regard to the §1201(g)(3)(B) "legitimate course of study" factor. It is possible to see an attack on the §1201(g)(3)(C) "notice" factor too. If this construction was intended, SunnComm had designed its press release to set the terms of public debate in a way that would nullify Halderman's obvious defenses.

SunnComm (2003b) quickly retracted its legal threats in the wake of an enormous amount of bad publicity. However, all researchers cannot count on having such favorable publicity.

CODE AS SPEECH

Consider the following text (Winstein & Horowitz, 2001)

```
s"$/=\2048;while(<>){G=29;R=142;if((@a=unqT="C*",_)
[20]&48){D=89;_=unqb24,qT, @ b=map{ord qB8,unqb8,
qT,_^$a[--D]} @INC;s/...$/1$&/;Q=unqV,qb25,_;H=73;O=$b[4]<<9
|256|$b[3];Q=Q>>8^(P=(E=255)&(Q>>12^Q>>4^Q/8^Q))<<17,
O=O>>8^(E&(F=(S=O>>14&7^O)^S*8^S<<6))<<9,_=
(map{U=_%16orE^=R^=110&(S=(unqT,"\xb\ntd\xbz\x14d")
[_/16%8]);E^=(72,@z=(64,72,G^=12*(U-2?0:S&17)),
H^=_%64?12:0,@z)[_%8]}(16..271))[_]^((D>>=8)+=P+(~F&E))
for@a[128..$#a]}print+qT,@a}';s/[D-HO-U_]/\$$&/g;s/q/
pack+/g;eval
```

Above is a series of symbols that form a program in the computer language Perl. In this sentence, the words are a series of symbols that convey meaning in the language English. Though more people are familiar with the latter than the former, can there be said to be an intrinsic, or practically sustainable, distinction? As noted in one legal brief (Tyre, 2001): "If '$plain_text = $file_key ^ $xor_block' seems unapproachable, consider what those not trained in the language of legal citation would make of '111 F.Supp.2d 294, 326 (S.D.N.Y. 2000).' Each is meaningless to those unfamiliar with the language; but each is more precise and compact for those who do understand than would be an English narrative equivalent."

As a further example, consider the following different explanations of a simple cipher:

> The ROT13 algorithm explained ("Caesar Cipher"):
>
> 1) The decryption algorithm for ROT13 is to take the range of letters from a-z, and for those twenty-six letters, replace the first thirteen of them with the range of letters from n-z and the second thirteen of them with the range of letters from a-m
>
> 2) To un-ROT13, do a tr/a-z/n-za-m/ over each character in the file
>
> 3) perl -pe 'tr/a-z/n-za-m/;' < infile > outfile
>
> Where was the line crossed, from "speech" to "code"?

The potential narrative equivalence between English and computer language will undoubtedly be a subject of much contentious litigation over the boundaries of permissible expression (Touretzky, 2000). Possible disputes are foreshadowed in *Universal v. Reimerdes* (2000) where the court remarked

> During the trial, Professor Touretzky of Carnegie Mellon University, as noted above, convincingly demonstrated that computer source and object code convey the same ideas as various other modes of expression, including spoken language descriptions of the algorithm embodied in the code.... He drew from this the conclusion that the preliminary injunction irrationally distinguished between the code, which was enjoined, and other modes of expression that convey the same idea, which were not, id., although of course he had no reason to be aware that the injunction drew that line only because that was the limit of the relief plaintiffs sought. With commendable candor, he readily admitted that the implication of his view that the spoken language and computer code versions were substantially similar was not necessarily that the preliminary injunction was too broad; rather, the logic of his position was that it was either too broad or too narrow.... Once again, the question of a substantially broader injunction need not be addressed here, as plaintiffs have not sought broader relief.

Arguably, that "broader relief" would have been requested by SunnComm versus Halderman had the controversy proceeded to a lawsuit as threatened. Strategic considerations on this matter may have been one reason for the withdrawal by SunnComm.

However, because new languages and ways of expressing computational concepts are continually being invented, the exact reach of the DMCA will remain unclear for the foreseeable future. The DeCSS algorithm has even been expressed in Haiku format poetry (Schoen, 2004).

HOW NOT TO GET SUED UNDER THE DMCA

Given the potential for the DMCA to chill cryptography and security research, many professionals are concerned with what they can do to reduce their risk of prosecution. Dmitry Sklyarov's arrest and criminal charges show that the problem is not in the realm of fantasy.

Surveying the behavior of plaintiffs in many DMCA cases, the critical variable seems to be the perception of the character of the defendant. Although a corporation might have the legal ability to bring DMCA charges against a university professor, any prospect of setting an unfavorable legal precedent with a sympathetic defendant results in the withdrawal of threats. Conversely, an unsympathetic defendant appears not to do well in the judicial process (Bowman, 2001): "As soon as the judge says 'hacker,' you know you've lost," University of Minnesota law Professor Dan Burk said. "There is an attempt to paint defendants as unsympathetic, low-priority, on the fringe—to make it seem like nobody respectable is going to be harmed except for weird hacker types."

In view of this, the best practice is arguably to have as much professional and institutional backing as is possible. Consulting staff counsel, if available, can help with specific situations.

Keeping in mind the text of the §1201(g) exemption, preliminary notification of parties adversely affected by the research should not be done casually or without prior legal consultation. The fact that such notification is an element of a DMCA defense means it will affect how a court views any potential case. Pragmatically, it presents an opportunity for one to be the target of a legal threat aimed at chilling the presentation of results. This topic is extensively covered in Liu's 'The DMCA and the Regulation of Scientific Research" (2003), and the interested reader should consult that paper for further discussion.

CONCLUSION

The DMCA has profoundly unsettled the delicate balance that existed earlier in copyright law. Advances in technology, which have vastly increased the ability to make copies, have been in direct conflict with the imperative of copyright-concerning controls on content. The compromises of fair use and ability to produce and market technology if the technology has substantial noninfringing use may be irreconcilable in practice with the offenses of circumvention itself and the broad prohibitions against trafficking in circumvention technology. Moreover, the interpretation of contraband technology to encompass computer programs (even source code), and hence perhaps technical speech itself, greatly extends the reach of copyright-related regulation. Potentially the effects could lead to a chilling effect on academic research.

Various proposals have been made to ameliorate the negative effects of the DMCA. However, there is a fundamental clash between the needs of copyright owners to suppress information regarding copy-controlling encryption algorithms and the needs of the free exchange of methodology and validation of results for any research. This clash may ultimately be unsolvable.

GLOSSARY

1201(a)(1) The DMCA provision prohibiting the act of *circumvention* of a *technological protection measure* that effectively controls *access* to a copyrighted work.

1201(a)(2) The DMCA provision prohibiting trafficking in "any technology, product, service, device, component" for *circumvention* of a *technological protection measure* that effectively controls *access* to a copyrighted work.

1201(b)(2) The DMCA provision prohibiting trafficking in "any technology, product, service, device, component" for *circumvention* of a *technological protection measure* that effectively protects a right of a copyright owner (usage controls).

Circumvention To "descramble... decrypt..., or otherwise to avoid, bypass, remove, deactivate, or impair a technological measure, without the authority of the copyright owner." This is legally and conceptually distinct from *infringement*. Note that circumvention encompasses much more than decryption.

CSS Content scramble system, an encryption algorithm used to control access to content on DVD format disks. Although CSS does not affect commercial-grade duplication of a DVD, it prevents meaningful consumer copying and peer-to-peer file sharing.

DeCSS A program that decrypts the CSS encryption created by a team of three programmers (not, as commonly believed, the work of one teenager). Lawsuits concerning DeCSS have been the most prominent DMCA litigation.

Effectively A legal standard for content restriction. A technological protection measure "effectively controls access" if it, "in the ordinary course of its operation, requires the application of information, or a process or a treatment, with the authority of the copyright owner, to gain access to the work." A technological protection measure "effectively protects a right of a copyright owner" if it "in the ordinary course of its operation, prevents, restricts, or otherwise limits the exercise of a right of a copyright owner."

Fair Use In law, a defense against copyright infringement, allowing legal use of copyrighted material for such purposes as criticism, comment, news reporting, teaching, scholarship, or research. More philosophically, a safety valve for resolving the conflicts between copyright's restrictions on the use of speech and the U.S. Constitution's First Amendment provision concerning freedom of speech.

Infringement A violation of any of certain exclusive rights granted by copyright law. Some examples of these rights are reproduction, making of derivative works, performance, and display. This is legally and conceptually distinct from *circumvention*. Fair use is one defense against infringement.

Reverse Engineering In legal terms, "to study or analyze (a device, as a microchip for computers) in order to learn details of design, construction, and operation, perhaps to produce a copy or an improved version." (see *Bowers v. Baystate Technologies Inc.*, 2002)

Trafficking To "manufacture, import, offer to the public, or otherwise traffic in any technology, product, service, device, component, or part thereof" that violates the relevant DMCA provision. It is important to note that devices are just one part of this term, as it also encompasses the very broad idea of technology (which is extended to computer program source code).

CROSS REFERENCES

See *Copyright Law; Cybercrime and the U.S. Criminal Justice System; Encryption Basics; Legal, Social and Ethical Issues of the Internet.*

REFERENCES

321 Studios v. Metro Goldwyn Mayer et al., No. C 02-1955 SI (N.D. Cal. Feb. 19, 2004). Retrieved June 21, 2004, from http://www.eff.org/IP/DMCA/MGM_v_321Studios/20040219_Order.pdf

AfterDawn.com (2003, October 9). *Student uses Shift key, gets sued (discussion)*. Retrieved June 21, 2004, from http://www.afterdawn.com/news/archive/4569.cfm

Billington, J. H. (2003, October 28). *Statement of the Librarian of Congress relating to Section 1201 rulemaking*. Retrieved June 21, 2004, from http://www.copyright.gov/1201/docs/librarian_statement_01.html

Borland, John (2003, October 7). Shift key breaks CD copy locks. *CNET News.com*. Retrieved June 21, 2004, from http://news.com.com/2100-1025-5087875.html

Bowers v. Baystate Technologies Inc., 64 USPQ2d 1065 (CA FC 2002).

Bowman, L. M. (2001, May 2). Putting a kind face on copyright battles. *CNET News.com*. Retrieved June 21, 2004, from http://news.com.com/2100-1023-256912.html

Bowman, L. M. (2002, December 17). ElcomSoft verdict: Not guilty. *CNET News.com*. Retrieved June 21, 2004, from http://news.com.com/2100-1023-978176.html

Copyright Office (2003). *Rulemaking on Anticircumvention web page*. Retrieved June 21, 2004, from http://www.copyright.gov/1201/

Cowley, S (2004, August 10). 321 Studios reaches post-mortem deal with MPAA. *The Industry Standard*. Retrieved June 14, 2005 from http://www.thestandard.com/article.php/20040810194622938

Department of Justice. (1997a, August 20). *Federal prosecution of violations of intellectual property rights, sample language for jury instructions, 18 U.S.C.S., §2319*. Retrieved June 21, 2004, from http://www.usdoj.gov/criminal/cybercrime/intell_prop_rts/app_h.htm

Department of Justice. (1997b, October). *United States Attorneys' Manual Title 9, §1851*. Retrieved June 21, 2004, from http://www.usdoj.gov/usao/eousa/foia_reading_room/usam/title9/crm01851.htm

Digital Millennium Copyright Act (DMCA) of 1998, Pub. L. 105-304, 17 U.S.C.S. §1201 (2004). Retrieved June 21, 2004, from http://www4.law.cornell.edu/uscode/17/1201.html

Digital Millennium Copyright Act (DMCA) of 1998, Pub. L., 17 U.S.C.S. §1204 (2004). Retrieved June 21, 2004, from http://www4.law.cornell.edu/uscode/17/1204.html

DVD-CCA v. Bunner and *DVD-CCA v. Pavlovich* archives. Retrieved June 21, 2004, from: http://www.eff.org/IP/Video/DVDCCA_case/

Finkelstein, S. (2002). *How to win (DMCA) exemptions and influence policy*. Retrieved June 14, 2005, from http://www.eff.org/IP/DMCA/finkelstein_on_dmca.html

Finkelstein, S. (2003, April 11). *DMCA anticircumvention hearing testimony*. Retrieved June 21, 2004, from http://sethf.com/anticensorware/hearing_dc.php

Halderman, J. A. (2003). Analysis of the MediaMax CD3 copy-prevention system. *Princeton University Computer Science Technical Report* (TR-679-03). Retrieved June 21, 2004, from http://www.cs.princeton.edu/~jhalderm/cd3/

I.M.S. Inquiry Management Systems, LTD. v. Berkshire Information Systems, Inc, 307 F.Supp. 2d 541 (S.D.N.Y. 2004).

Johansen, J. (2000). *Testimony in Universal City Studios Inc. v. Reimerdes*. Retrieved June 21, 2004, from http://www.eff.org/IP/Video/MPAA_DVD_cases/20000720_ny_trial_transcript.html

Lexmark International Inc. v. Static Control Components, Inc. 253 F.Supp. 2d 943 (E. D. Ky. 2003), reversed, 387 F.3d 522 (6th Cir. 2004). Retrieved June 14, 2005, from http://www.eff.org/legal/cases/Lexmark_v_Static_Control/

Library of Congress. (2003, October 21). *Copyright Office exemption to prohibition on circumvention of copyright protection systems for access control technologies* 68 Fed. Reg. 62,011 (to be codified at 37 C.F.R. pt. 201). Retrieved June 21, 2004, from http://www.copyright.gov/fedreg/2003/68fr2011.html

Liu, J. (2003). The DMCA and the regulation of scientific research. *Berkeley Technology Law Journal, 17,* 501. Retrieved June 21, 2004, from http://papers.ssrn.com/sol3/papers.cfm?abstract_id=457742

No Electronic Theft Act of 1997, PL 105-147 (HR 2265), codified at 17 U.S.C.S. §506 (2004).

Oppenheim, M. (2001, April 9). *RIAA/SDMI legal threat letter*. Retrieved June 21, 2004, from http://www.eff.org/IP/DMCA/Felten_v_RIAA/20010409_riaa_sdmi_letter.html

Peters, M. (2003, October 27). *Recommendation of the Register of Copyrights in RM 2002-4; Rulemaking on exemptions from prohibition on circumvention of copyright protection systems for access control technologies*. Retrieved June 21, 2004, from http://www.copyright.gov/1201/docs/registers-recommendation.pdf

RealNetworks, Inc. v. Streambox, Inc., No. 2:99CV02070, 2000 WL 127311 (W. D. Wash. 2000). Retrieved June 21, 2004, from http://www.law.uh.edu/faculty/cjoyce/copyright/release10/Real.html

Schoen, S. (2004). *The history of the DeCSS haiku*. Retrieved June 21, 2004, from http://www.loyalty.org/~schoen/haiku.html

SunnComm. (2003, October 9). *SunnComm CEO says Princeton report critical of its MediaMax CD copy management technology contains erroneous assumptions and conclusions*. Retrieved June 21, 2004, from http://www.sunncomm.com/press/pressrelease.asp?prid=200310091000

SunnComm. (2003, October 10). *SunnComm Technologies reverses decision to bring legal action against Princeton researcher*. Retrieved June 21, 2004, from http://www.sunncomm.com/press/pressrelease.asp?prid=200310101150

Touretzky, D. S. (2000). *Gallery of CSS descramblers*. Retrieved June 21, 2004, from http://www-2.cs.cmu.edu/~dst/DeCSS/Gallery/

Tyre, J. S. (2001, January 23). *Programmers' & Academics' Amici Brief in "MPAA v. 2600" Case, Brief of Amici Curiae in Support of Appellants and Reversal of the Judgment Below (Jan. 26, 2001); Universal v. Reimerdes (Jan. 26, 2001) 00-9185*. Retrieved June 21, 2004, from http://www.eff.org/IP/Video/MPAA_DVD_cases/20010126_ny_progacad_amicus.html

U.S. v. ElcomSoft & Sklyarov Archive. Retrieved June 21, 2004, from http://www.eff.org/IP/DMCA/US_v_Elcomsoft/

United States v. Elcom LTD., 203 F. Supp.2d 1111 (ND Cal. 2002). Retrieved June 14, 2005, from http://digital-law-online.info/cases/62PQ2D1736.htm

United States v. Sklyarov Criminal Complaint (2001, 2001). United States District Court, Northern District Of California. Retrieved June 21, 2004, from http://www.eff.org/IP/DMCA/US_v_Elcomsoft/20010707_complaint.html

Universal City Studios Inc. v. Reimerdes, 2000 Copr.L.Dec. P 28,122, 55 U.S.P.Q.2d 1873 111 F.Supp.2d 294, United States District Court, S.D. New York. affirmed, Universal City Studios, Inc. v. Corley, 273 F.3d 429 (2nd Cir. 2001), amended January 29, 2002. Retrieved June 14, 2005, from http://cyber.law.harvard.edu/openlaw/DVD/NY/trial/op.html

Universal City Studios Inc. v. Corley, No. 00-9185 November 28, 2001, 273 F.3d 429, 60 USPQ2d 1953, U.S. Court of Appeals, Second Circuit, amended January 29, 2002. Retrieved June 14, 2005, from http://www.eff.org/IP/Video/MPAA_DVD_cases/20011128_ny_appeal_decision.html

Vance, A. (2003, October 16). SunnComm CEO demands to be called a "laughing stock." *The Register*. Retrieved June 21, 2004, from http://www.theregister.co.uk/2003/10/16/sunncomm_ceo_demands/

Winstein, K., & Horowitz, M. (2001). *qrpff (see Touretzky, 2000, Gallery of CSS descramblers)*. Retrieved June 21, 2004, from http://www-2.cs.cmu.edu/~dst/DeCSS/Gallery/qrpff.pl

CHAPTER 42

PROTECTING DIGITAL RIGHTS: TECHNICAL APPROACHES

Robert Guess, Jennifer Hadley, Steven Lovaas, and Diane E. Levine

42.1 INTRODUCTION. Ever since publishing and commerce were introduced to the digital world, the risks to intellectual property and to personal privacy in cyberspace have steadily escalated on comparable but separate paths. These paths have now converged. Unfortunately, many times, antipiracy efforts lead to possible breaches in personal privacy.

Efforts to stem the flow of pirated software worldwide remain mediocre in efficacy; piracy is still proving to be big business in the new millennium. According to the Business Software Alliance (BSA), a 2006 study shows that "thirty-five percent of the packaged software installed on personal computers (PC) worldwide in 2005 was illegal, amounting to $34 billion in global losses due to software piracy."[1] This single-year loss equals 57 percent of the total for years 1995 to 2000 combined. Although the methods the BSA used to make this estimate have been criticized,[2] the problem is nevertheless significant for the software industry. Continuing piracy means lost jobs, wages, tax revenues, and a potential barrier to success for software start-ups around the globe.

At the same time, freedoms inherent in the Internet have made maintaining privacy of personal information a true challenge. Identity theft keeps rising, as more and more companies actively engage in the accumulation of customer data through e-commerce. By paying bills, checking medical insurance accounts, or completing taxes online, people are making their personal information available to be stockpiled, shared, and regurgitated to the point that simply "Googling" one's identity can be a real eye opener. Technologies that aim to prevent piracy have the potential to use this wealth of available personal information in a way that significantly erodes personal privacy. In particular, some of these technologies send personally identifiable information to servers on a routine basis (see, e.g., Section 42.4.2). The idea that a corporation—or a government—could be scanning what a specific person reads, listens to, or views is grounds for concern to civil libertarians.

42.1.1 Digital Rights. In this environment of rapid change in both piracy and privacy, even the term "digital rights" is ambiguous. When software companies and music producers talk about digital rights, they mean the kinds of rights long protected by copyright, trademark, and patent law. When privacy advocates argue about digital rights, however, they may be talking about a completely different thing: that an individual does not forfeit personal rights, including the right to privacy, merely by turning on a computer. This chapter's primary focus is on technologies designed to protect traditional rights of content producers, but it also enumerates areas where those technologies threaten personal privacy.

42.1.2 Patent, Copyright, and Trademark Laws. There are differences among the applicable laws and the materials they protect.

Patents give owners exclusive rights to use and license their ideas and materials; patents generally protect nonobvious inventions in mechanical and electrical fields, as well as those that can be embodied in computer software and hardware.

Copyrights give owners the exclusive rights to create derivative works, to reproduce original works, and to display, distribute, and conduct their works. Copyrights apply to original works of authorship including paintings, photographs, drawings, writings, music, videos, computer software, and any other works that are fixed in a tangible medium. Copyrights, their infringement, and remedies are described in the Copyright Act of 1976.

Trademarks give owners the right to restrict the use of distinctive marks in certain contexts. These rights may apply to words, sounds, distinctive colors, symbols, and designs.

For an extensive discussion of intellectual property law, see Chapter 11 in this *Handbook*.

42.1.3 Piracy. Once thought of as a mere copyright infringement of printed matter or production of a counterfeit audiotape, piracy has grown with technology and has expanded to encompass intellectual property, digital data, DVDs, CDs, VHS, analog and high-definition TV, and streaming media.

There are several types of piracy. End user piracy occurs when end users use a single copy of software to run on several different systems, or when they distribute copies of software to others without permission of the software manufacturer. Reseller piracy occurs when unscrupulous resellers distribute multiple copies of a single software package to multiple customers, preload the same software on multiple systems, or knowingly sell counterfeit software to customers. Internet and bulletin board (BBS) piracy occurs when users download and upload copyrighted materials and use it or make it available for use by others without proper licenses.

To understand why and how piracy occurs and the enormous impact on society worldwide, we need to have a clear understanding of what we mean by the word "piracy." Whenever information is created and published in print, on the Internet, or incorporated into software, that information may be protected by copyright, patent, or trademark law. This principle applies to a broad spectrum of material that includes, for example, the Wright Brothers' specifications for their "Flying Machine"; Microsoft Windows software; the icon Mickey Mouse and all related materials; television shows, plays, movies, and music created and performed live and on recordings. Making unauthorized copies of such material in any medium is referred to as piracy.

In 2000, the Software & Information Industry Association (www.siia.net) found that 91 percent of software for sale on Internet auction sites like Yahoo!, eBay, Excite, and ZDNet is pirated. SIIA initiated action against a total of 1,016 companies during that year. Enforcement efforts have grown more effective recently; in 2006, two major data pirates were given record jail terms and fines. One was given 7 years 3 months in jail and was ordered to pay $5.4 million in restitution for illegally selling over $20 million in copyrighted software via text ads on Google.[3]

42.1.4 Privacy. As in many aspects of security, end users are now being called on to protect their online (and off-line) identities through diligent monitoring of financial activities and through awareness programs focused on personal rights, laws, and obligations of Internet use. The average Web user today can create and publish a blog or personal video to the Web faster than that same user can apply software patches to a desktop PC. So widespread is this new facility that the law has yet to catch up with the needs and expectations of the users in online society. It is difficult to keep data private when—with a mouse click—it is easy to share personal information with the whole world.

Beyond bad personal habits that reduce privacy, however, a whole new class of applications termed "Digital Rights Management" (DRM) collects more personal information than ever before in an effort to reduce improper use of copyrighted material. DRM products may record and report on an individual's Web-browsing habits, types of files created and accessed by a particular program, number of uses of a particular file or program, source IP address of the user's system, and presence (or absence) of a license for a program. In the name of protecting digital rights for content producers, the consumers of this content are being cataloged and tracked in a way that the framers of copyright laws would have been hard-pressed to imagine.

For extensive coverage of privacy issues on the Internet, see Chapter 69 in this *Handbook*.

For a glossary of terminology used in discussing digital rights management, see Section 42.8.

42.2 SOFTWARE-BASED ANTIPIRACY TECHNIQUES.

A variety of software-based technical approaches are used to prevent inappropriate use of copyrighted and otherwise protected material in an organization's networks and on the public Internet. Current methods include ensuring proper configuration of operating systems, monitoring of installed software, encryption of content, and insertion of some sort of key or identifier in the digital product itself.

42.2.1 Organizational Policy. Controls in free-standing commercial applications represent only one of the technical means to protect digital content. Existing system controls are also useful in this regard. Operating system access controls can specify who can access particular content, while encryption supported by the OS and other applications can limit access to users who possess the appropriate key. More generally, organizational policy should specify good practices in configuring operating systems and applications in order to help protect content. Such policy includes:

- Allow users to install only software that is necessary.
- Encrypt information that should not be publicly viewable.
- Install software with the lowest possible privilege consistent with the ability to do its job.
- Disable active content (Java, JavaScript, ActiveX, cookies, etc.) wherever feasible.
- Use network operating system access controls to limit access to shared, copyrighted media to members of the organization for whom licenses are purchased.

42.2.2 Software Usage Counters. Software metering has been popular for several years. Special software monitors system usage and inventories the software on the system or network. This type of software also can be used to block or limit the use of specific software, such as browsers and games. In addition to fighting piracy, it can reduce the load on IT personnel by reducing complications due to use of unauthorized software.

42.2.2.1 Controlling Concurrent Installations. Software metering products can monitor concurrent installations even on networks used by people in different geographic areas who have different requirements and different software installed. The metering software permits an administrator to maintain a live and updated inventory of the software installed at different locations on the network. The logs show where installation has taken place, when the licenses expire, and when updates are necessary. Alerts can be set to notify system administrators when a license is about to expire or when an update has been accomplished.

42.2.2.2 Controlling Concurrent Usage. Software metering allows network administrators to identify and resolve cases of illegal installation of unauthorized copies of authorized software and also to catch people who install unauthorized software on the organization's computers. Metering software also allows a company to report and analyze logon and logout times, track software usage, and meter software licenses to keep those in the company legal. In addition to avoiding legal entanglements, monitoring can reduce the demand on system resources, network bandwidth, and technical support staff.

42.2.2.3 Examples and Implementation. Microsoft announced in 2000 that to combat piracy, new releases of the Office 2000 program would include a counting feature making the programs malfunction if the owner had not registered the software after launching it 50 times.[4] Prior to this announcement, Microsoft published antipiracy literature and provided a great deal of consumer education regarding the effects of software piracy on society; it established, as well, a piracy hotline (1-800-RU-LEGIT). Novell (1-800-PIRATES), Adobe, and Xerox are other companies that have vigorous antipiracy programs in place, although they have not yet announced that they are building metering into their products.

Metering software requires a bona fide license in order for it to be implemented. Typically, companies establish CD-ROM keys that are printed on legitimate copies of their product installation discs or jewel cases. The keys include checksums or message authentication codes that can be checked by the installation routines. The algorithms for the checksums are intended to cause difficulty for people trying to create counterfeit keys. The security of such measures depends on the cryptographic strength of the validation keys.

Software counters for controlling concurrent usage need to store information securely so that each load operation increments a counter and each unload operation decrements it. However, the security problem is to store this information in such a way that unauthorized people cannot modify it easily. Encrypting the data in a complex sequence of operations can stop most abuses of the system by making the effort required for circumventing the mechanisms more costly than buying a license.

More recently, copies of the Windows Vista operating system must be registered (Microsoft calls this "activating" a copy) soon after installation, or they will go into "reduced functionality mode," in which basic functions are available for only an hour of operation before logging on again.[5] For single-copy home use, Vista relies on a license key encoded on the installation medium. For enterprise deployments of Vista, an organization needs to run key servers to allow the registration to occur.[6]

42.3 HARDWARE-BASED ANTIPIRACY TECHNIQUES.

Working on the theory that software is prone to misconfiguration and compromise, antipiracy groups and researchers have experimented with a variety of hardware-based approaches to preventing inappropriate use of protected content. These techniques include dongles and specialized readers attached to the reading hardware, evanescent media designed for viewing or playing only a limited number of times, and software keys incorporated into the media and the reading hardware.

42.3.1 Dongles.

Dongles are hardware lock devices or modules that connect to a computer and communicate with software running on the computer. Without a dongle in place, the external device or regulated software does not work fully, or at all.

Initially, dongles controlled printing. With a dongle installed on the computer, no one could print data from the computer without authorization. However, there is now a necessity for protecting all types of devices. Now dongles are used to protect scanners; external drives (e.g., ZIP drives); CD-ROMs and rewritable CD-ROMs; DVDs and DVD-Rs; VHS recorders; Playstation, Nintendo, and Sega video gaming systems; and even personal digital assistants (PDAs).

The most common type of dongle provides a pass-through port to connect a device cable. Generally a dongle incorporates some type of algorithmic encryption in its onboard microelectronic circuitry. The sophistication of the encryption varies depending on the manufacturer and the device. Many dongles provide additional onboard nonvolatile memory for the software to access. Some models even have real-time checks that keep track of date and time information, including when an application's license (temporary or leased) is set to expire.

Dongles provide some definite advantages:

- Because a dongle is an external device, it is fairly simple to install and uninstall. Early dongles used serial or parallel ports, but USB has become the norm in recent years. In most cases, since manufacturers support their devices, an ordinary user can install and use a dongle without help from an IT department.
- Dongles also require registration, which provides adequate control over the use of the dongle and thus provides legitimacy to both the device and the users. Registration (dependent on the contract in place) may provide support for both the software and the hardware.
- Dongles that support encryption provide an extra layer of protection by making transmitted data indecipherable until it reaches its destination, unless the hardware is in place.

There are also disadvantages to using dongles:

- Consumers resist the requirement for installation, maintenance, and additional cost. Most large corporations do not use dongles for their products.
- Dongles can be lost or stolen, and they also may fail.
- Sometimes a dongle will work well with a slow computer but cause errors when installed on a faster computer.
- Since not every manufacturer automatically replaces lost or stolen dongles without charge, there may be additional costs involved in getting replacements.
- Dongles can present a serious risk-management problem for critical applications where delays in obtaining replacements or registering them may be unacceptable.
- As with any device, there can be a serious problem if the dongle manufacturer ceases to support the model of dongle a company has installed or if the manufacturer goes out of business entirely.
- Laws regarding encryption usage differ in various countries. Specialized dongles that may be legal to use in the United States may be illegal in another country.

42.3.2 Specialized Readers. One of the impediments to illegal copying used to be the difficulty and cost of obtaining specialized hardware and software for reading and copying proprietary materials with fidelity. However, today such copying equipment is inexpensive and easy to find. In addition, the media for distributing illegal copies are less expensive than ever.

42.3.2.1 Audio. According to the Recording Industry Association of America (RIAA), the global audio industry loses in excess of $4 billion every year to piracy worldwide.[7] RIAA says that $1 million a day, in just physical product, is lost in the United States alone. The loss of ancillary revenues drives the figures higher. But the RIAA claims that these figures are low, since it estimates that in some countries up to 98 percent of the music in use comes from illegal copies.

As part of an industry-wide, organized approach to highlighting and reducing the music piracy problem, the RIAA has taken a very active role in pursuing legal action against suspected pirates. Through the 1990s and continuing into the current decade, the biggest problem with audio piracy was illegally copied CDs. In 1998, for example, the RIAA confiscated 23,858 illegal CDs in the first half of the year. In that same year,

Operation Copycat—a joint investigation by RIAA, the Motion Picture Association of America (MPAA), and the New York Police Department—saw the arrest of 43 CD pirates and the shutdown of 15 illegal manufacturing locations. Many of the CDs seized in these types of operations apparently came from Asia and Eastern Europe, financed by organized crime operations with ties to drugs and prostitution.[8] By 2002, even corner convenience stores were contributing to the problem, providing coin-operated CD copying machines akin to photocopiers, along with the familiar posted warning transferring liability to the user.[9] Given the enormous profits involved, the problem has been simply too large and widespread for law enforcement to control. In 2005, the RIAA seized approximately 5 million illegal CDs.[10]

More recently, the RIAA has focused on the problem of music files illegally shared across the Internet. Using free software, sometimes already bundled into commercial operating systems, anyone can download music tracks and burn CDs. The MP3 music file format has become a ubiquitous way to share music with others. The RIAA originally protested against MP3 players, but the phenomenal success of personal digital music players, particularly the Apple iPod, has rendered such efforts futile. Some musicians and independent record labels have adopted the MP3 format to promote their records, showing that the technology itself has no inherent ties to piracy. These musicians and recording studios claim that they are happy with consumers downloading the music, and they are at odds with the RIAA.

Some musical groups have even experimented with severing ties with the traditional music industry altogether, using Web sites and social networking services to advertise and distribute digital music files directly to their listeners.[11] As more musicians begin to use the Internet either in addition to or in lieu of traditional distribution models, the very model of music distribution is in flux.

Meanwhile, the music industry continues to face serious financial loss due to illegal downloading. The industry, through the RIAA, has been pursuing legal remedies. Some major lawsuits have achieved significant press coverage and have been instrumental in enforcing or changing existing laws or in helping develop new laws. For instance, deliberate copyright violations resulted in an award of $50 million in statutory damages and $3.4 million in legal fees to Universal Studios in a suit against the MyMP3.com music service. MyMP3 created a database of over 80,000 albums, which, when combined with the MyMP3 software, let users access and store music digitally, without paying a fee.

Perhaps the most recognizable name in the music field in regard to piracy at one time was Napster, a site that enabled individuals to share tracks of music via the Internet. The site provided free downloadable software for downloading and playing MP3 files. Essentially, Napster software turned a user's PC into part of a distributed server network that published available music files. It did not take long for the site to acquire a user group of millions of people who after "sampling" the music might then go to a store and buy the entire CD.

However, since the Napster site did not limit the length of the download, many users simply downloaded the entire track. Most never bought the commercial version of the music. Adding to successful piracy attempts was the development and ready availability of rewritable CD drives. More and more Napster users decided to download the music tracks they wanted and then burn their own CDs without ever purchasing the CDs made by the recording artists and music companies.

Creating a stir in the industry and ultimately a landmark judicial case, Napster was forced to radically alter operations in March 2000 after protracted court proceedings. Upon the verdict, Jack Valenti, president and chief executive officer of MPAA, commented that the consumer would benefit most from the court's decision because "You cannot take for free what belongs to someone else."[12] But the subject of Napster and audio piracy remains highly controversial. Although some people argued that little-known artists received exposure that they may never have gotten without the free file-sharing service, others, especially large music companies and recording artists, argue that they were being denied the royalties they deserve.

Napster attempted to re-create itself as a pay-for-subscription music download service but found record labels unwilling to work with it. In 2002, Napster folded; the name was eventually purchased by Roxio, Inc. to rebrand its own subscription service. In the meantime, other peer-to-peer (P2P) file-sharing protocols and applications appeared to fill the void left by Napster. By the time the iTunes Music Store emerged as a powerful contender with music company backing and with copyright protection, the world of free file sharing was reinvigorated by names such as Gnutella, FastTrack, Grokster, Limewire, and Kazaa.

Over the last few years, the music industry has identified universities as fertile ground for pursuing illegal downloading activities. In 2007, the RIAA launched a new round of attempts to bring music pirates to justice, sending letters offering to settle with students identified as probably sharing copyrighted files, in advance of any trial.[13] The RIAA's tactics have been raising hackles in the higher education community, with opponents criticizing the letters as bordering on extortion. Some universities are refusing to forward the letters to students; one university agreed to forward the letters, but promised to bill the RIAA $11 for every letter to pay for its staff time.[14]

42.3.2.2 Video. On the video side, Scour, Inc., provided free downloads of digital movies as well as software allowing users to share the downloaded files among themselves without the use of a central server. With an easy-to-use interface and quick response time, Scour.com became quite popular in a short period of time. Launched in 1997, with a Web search feature added in 1998 and a subsequent P2P tool, Scour eventually attracted negative attention from the movie and music industries. In July 2000, MPAA, RIAA, and the National Music Publishers Association (NMPA) sued Scour, accusing it of large-scale theft of copyrighted material and of trafficking in stolen works. By November 2000, the company was out of business.[15]

This case did not stop the counterfeiting of video media. Despite increasingly steep fines, judicial rulings, and even raids by various law enforcement agencies, counterfeit video is readily available. Along Fifth Avenue in New York City, for $5 to $10 anyone can buy the latest films and DVDs; in markets in Hong Kong, Southeast Asia, and India, the copies are even cheaper. It is true that some of the copies available may have been "legally produced," but it is more than likely that the counterfeit or bootleg copies were made illegally from a master copy that was either borrowed or stolen.

Advances in consumer electronics help the trend, as many PCs now come with a recordable/rewritable DVD player as a standard component. Arguments about legality of time-shifting and space-shifting that once defended the practice of making personal mixes on audiocassette have now moved to the realm of digital video.

42.3.2.3 Television (Analog). Broadcast television has been one of the most successful technologies in history, and financial interests are still huge, despite the growth of cable and satellite services. In January 2000, major television companies, the National Football League, and the National Basketball League all filed complaints against iCraveTV, a Canadian company that had been in existence for only a year.

According to the complaints, iCraveTV was illegally using broadcast television signals without authorization or payment and streaming the signals to the iCrave Internet site for viewing free of charge. Although this practice apparently did not violate Canadian copyright laws at the time, U.S. judges ruled in February 2000 that the unauthorized transmissions of broadcast signals into the United States via the Internet were a direct violation of U.S. copyright law, and iCraveTV was ordered to stop the practice. Shortly after iCraveTV agreed to an out-of-court settlement, the Web site was shut down and iCraveTV went out of business.[16]

Hacking cable decoders is another technique for obtaining services without paying for them. Although it is not illegal to buy, install, or modify equipment for converting encoded cable TV signals from pay-per-view or other commercial suppliers, it is illegal to use such set-top decoders to obtain services without paying for them.

In the United States, Congress has mandated that after February 17th 2008 all TV stations must transmit in digital format (DTV) only.

42.3.2.4 Television (HDTV). The first television image was created in 1884 when Paul Nipkow created a mechanical scanning disk. With only 18 lines of resolution, the picture was poor. Current National Television System Committee (NTSC) standard TV transmissions are done with bandwidth that does not exceed 6 MHz. The current analog system broadcasts 30 frames per second and 525 lines per frame.

High-definition television (HDTV) is a digital television system that offers twice the horizontal and vertical resolution of the current TV system. HDTV has the ability to deliver a video composed of approximately 1,125 lines per frames and 60 frames per second. Viewers then see a picture quality close to that of 35mm film. Obviously, transmitting images containing that large amount of audio and video information requires wide bandwidth, actually about 18 MHz. Such bandwidth would permit the transmission of 1,050 lines of 600 pixels per line. However, the Federal Communications Commission (FCC) decided to limit HDTV to a 6-MHz maximum bandwidth. In order to meet that requirement, MPEG compression would be used.

MPEG compression applies algorithms to pixel groups and records information that changes within a frame, rather than all of the information in all of the frames. Audio is synchronized to the video. Using MPEG saves storage space and transmission requirements while retaining high image and sound quality. According to the Advanced Television Committee Standard (ASTC), the FCC will require that audio and video compression as well as the transmission of HDTV terrestrial signals follow this standard.

As with all other transmissions and media, there are serious concerns about piracy of HDTV transmissions and programs. At the present time, even though many TV transmissions are scrambled in order to thwart reception, it is fairly simple, although illegal, to purchase a descrambler and unscramble the transmissions. It is, however, legal for home viewers to record programs for their own personal use.

The HDTV market space has been evolving, and consumer demand for HD-capable devices has exploded over the past several years. Attempts by U.S. television producers to protect themselves and their content using a variety of scrambling and encryption schemes, including content scrambling systems (CSSs), have been made difficult by the frequent changes in hardware and signal formatting that have accompanied this rapid market expansion.

Encrypting terrestrial broadcast television programming would secure the transmissions, but according to the Home Recording Rights Coalition (HRRC), such encryption will threaten established home recording rights. The HRRC contends that Section 1202

(k) of the Digital Millennium Copyright Act provides a carefully balanced approach to analog home recording rights and stipulates that mandated technology may not be applied to interfere with consumer recording of free, over-the-air terrestrial broadcasts.

Furthermore, the HRRC contends that encrypting the free television broadcast content will create very little incentive for consumers to switch from regular analog to digital television. Instead of thwarting digital pirates, the HRRC contends that strong encryption will impose unfair and even illegal restrictions on consumers.

42.3.2.5 *Consumer Acceptance of Specialized Readers.* Illegal sharing of copyrighted content is common across the Internet. When the Software Publishing Association (SPA) was first formed, the group, together with law enforcement agencies, raided the physical premises of companies believed to be using pirated software. As a result of finding quantities of the pirated software, SPA won many legal actions and related settlements.

Some people see encryption as a challenge and work at breaking the algorithms so they can pirate the data—digital, video, or audio. In addition, the lack of standardization of laws throughout industries and countries has led to controversy and ongoing piracy.

Although average consumers do not think of themselves as intellectual property pirates, many otherwise honest citizens do get and use illegal programs, applications, games, audio tracks, CDs, DVDs VHS, and television signals. This situation might be attributed to a lack of ethical education, but many people like to save money and simply do not believe they will be caught and punished for such pilfering. A 2001 study by the Pew Internet & American Life Project, based on phone interviews with 4,205 adults 18 and over, some 2,299 of whom were Internet users, suggested that around 30 million U.S. residents had downloaded music from the Internet.[17] At that time, the phrase "had downloaded music from the Internet" was basically equivalent to "had *illegally* downloaded music from the Internet," since legal means of doing so had yet to evolve.

Since that report, Apple's 2001 announcement of its iTunes and iPod products, and the 2003 launch of the iTunes Music Store, began a movement to provide consumer-friendly ways of downloading music that also give compensation to copyright owners. iTunes uses device authentication and proprietary encoding formats to limit redistribution of downloaded songs and videos. Despite—or perhaps because of—Apple's attempts to comply with copyright laws, it is clear that Apple filled a perceived need in the market, as it has generated both a host of competitors and substantial sales. Consumers downloaded the first million songs from the iTunes Store in five days, and the overall market for digital music has grown to at least $790 million per year. At $0.99 per song, downloads from the iTunes Music Store passed the $1 billion mark on January 23, 2006.[18]

42.3.3 Evanescent Media. There are many interpretations of the term "evanescent media." The broad interpretation includes digital imaging, optics, multimedia and other electronic art, and data that are short-lived or transitory. When such media are original, creative works, society has an interest in protecting them against piracy.

Since most evanescent media involve some visual aspects as well as text, antipiracy techniques now being used or considered for other types of data may be applicable. Such techniques include previously discussed dongles, software keys, watermarks, encryption, and digital rights management. Part of the problem in electing and implementing a solution is the lack of existing standards that specifically deal with this new area of art and science.

42.3.4 Software Keys. Software keys of various kinds are used to secure data and equipment. A software key is generally a string of numbers that is used for identification purposes, either to allow access to the use of equipment or to permit authorized printing, processing, or copying of data. As described earlier in the discussion of dongles, most anticopying hardware devices are accompanied by software that works in tandem with the hardware. A software key activates or deactivates the hardware lock. When the software is working perfectly, there are generally no difficulties. However, all software can malfunction, and when that happens, there can be serious problems in getting equipment to work. Additional problems occur when the computer containing the software key malfunctions, and the software key cannot be made to work on a replacement machine.

42.3.4.1 Videocassettes versus Copy Machines. Watermarking is one of the techniques being seriously considered for protecting videocassettes and DVDs. In 1995, the ASTC formed a Copyright Protection Technical Working Group, which spun off a special Watermarking and Embedded Data Encoding subgroup. The group has broad representation including representatives from the PC market, the Macintosh market, the MPAA, the Consumer Electronics Manufacturers Association (CEMA) and related manufacturers, technicians, and users. Their task is to look for technologies and services that might use hidden data clues as a means of inhibiting or barring digital piracy. Using a hidden watermark that can be embedded in the content would then prevent machines from making copies or would alert the operator that the videocassette is marked and that unauthorized copies would be considered pirated.

42.3.4.2 DVD Area Encoding. Digital video requires very large storage space—too large for a single CD to hold. However, by applying compression techniques, the digital video can be compressed to fit into the digital videodisc's maximum capacity of 17 gigabytes. Two different types of compression are used for encoding audio and video content for DVD: constant bit rate (CBR) and variable bit rate (VBR) compression.

In order to prevent piracy of the content of the DVD, many companies are turning to encryption. The compressed data are encapsulated through a mathematical algorithm that can be decrypted only through the use of a decryption key.

42.3.4.3 Implementation. For shorter programs, CBR is ideal. Based on MPEG-2 encoding, CBR compresses each frame of audio and video by a user-selected amount. This degree of compression is then applied to the entire program. Using VBR, it is possible to create a database of video content based on the amount of change in each frame or scene. This is particularly useful in programs with a long format. To construct the database, the encoding software does several analytical passes of the master footage and then makes a final digitizing pass. From the created database, the computer can encode the video with a variable data rate allowing a higher bit rate for scenes with pans, zooms, and fast motion and giving scenes with little or no motion low data rates. By greatly compressing the areas of lower detail, areas of higher details can be allocated more space and use less compression.

42.3.4.4 Watermarks. Watermarking involves embedding one set of data inside a larger set of data. The embedded set of data identifies the origins or ownership of a specific work, just as a watermark does on paper.

Using digital watermarks can help copyright owners track the use of anything digital, including music, movies, photographs, and clip art. Digital watermarking is widely used for protecting images. For instance, photographers often post low-resolution (low-res) versions of their photos on public Web sites and use visible digital watermarks to clearly label the low-res images as copyrighted. Upon payment of the appropriate fee, the customer receives the high-resolution version of the photo, presumably with at least any visible watermarks removed. The use of invisible watermarks to prevent undetected sharing after purchase of digital content is more controversial and more prone to questions about reliability of detection; for instance, how many false positives and false negatives will occur? Additionally, there is the question of survivability of the mark itself as it is run through various transformations.

The music industry flirted with digital watermarking to protect music files beginning in 1998 with the formation of the Secure Digital Media Initiative (SDMI), a consortium of technology, security, and music organizations. The SDMI developed several watermarking schemes, and in 2000, it offered a reward to anyone who could crack the code and remove the watermark from a song protected by SDMI's technologies. The Electronic Frontier Foundation asked the Internet community to boycott the contest, stressing that the use of DMAT (Digital Music Access Technology) would mean that manufacturers and users would be forced to adopt the DMAT format in equipment and would create additional costs for manufacturers and consumers. A team of researchers, led by Princeton professor Ed Felten, was able to remove the invisible watermarks. When Felten attempted to publish the results of his process, attorneys for SDMI threatened to sue him under the Digital Millennium Copyright Act (DMCA). SDMI never filed suit, but Felten himself sued for a declaratory judgment to clarify the matter. Felten's suit was dismissed by a federal judge, but not before the government and the RIAA agreed that researchers should not be punished under the DMCA for testing technologies to protect copyright.[19] The SDMI has been inactive since 2001.[20]

42.3.4.5 *Resistance to Reverse Engineering.* Reverse engineering allows a programmer to work backward from the finished program or product. Encryption keys can be extracted by reverse engineering playback software. Reverse engineering can circumvent most antipiracy solutions. As a result, manufacturers of antipiracy software and hardware are strongly opposed to permitting reverse engineering. The DMCA does allow reverse engineering, but the provisions of DMCA were not intended to enable the circumvention of technical protection measures (TMPs) in order to gain unauthorized access to or to make unauthorized copies of copyrighted works.

42.3.4.6 *Published Attacks.* The most notable attack on a software key took place when a licensee of CSS neglected to encrypt a decryption key. Obtaining a key by reverse engineering the XingDVD from Xing Technologies, the hackers were then able to guess many other keys. This left the hackers with a collection of decryption keys; even if the XingDVD key was removed, they could still copy DVDs by using the other keys. Using the results of this compromise, a group of people including the Norwegian teenager Jon Lech Johansen developed a program called DeCSS to decrypt CSS-encrypted DVDs and play them on Linux machines.

A variety of groups, including the DVD CCA, sued Johansen for publishing tools to subvert copyright protection. Johansen was acquitted twice in Norwegian courts. As of 2007, all remaining lawsuits against him have been dropped,[21] and a number of programs like DeCSS are freely available across the Internet.

42.4 DIGITAL RIGHTS MANAGEMENT. Recognizing that piracy is a huge moral and financial problem, software developers have adopted and modified another type of system that can be applied to print, audio, video, and streaming media. Called Digital Rights Management (DRM), the system was originally devised to protect proprietary information and military information. The idea behind the system is to protect all types of intellectual digital content from anyone who would take it without the consent of the developer(s) or owners. Major companies like Microsoft, Adobe, and IBM are developing and marketing DRM systems, and dozens of smaller companies are springing up.

42.4.1 Purpose. The purpose of DRM is to protect all digital content that originators or owners want protected. DRM permits distributors of electronic content to control viewing access to that content. The content can be text, print, music, or images. Basically, DRM systems use a form of customized encryption. When an end user purchases viewing, listening, or printing rights, an individual "key" is provided. The system works on rules, meaning that although a key is provided, it generally comes with limitations regarding the copying, printing, and redistribution.

Unfortunately, there is no agreement on a DRM solution. Lack of standards is hampering businesses from moving forward with online business initiatives. Because there are so many companies promoting their own incompatible forms of DRM, customers will have to download megabytes of code for each version. Maintaining, upgrading, and managing all of those different versions are major headaches for customers. There does not appear to be a simple solution; rather than being a technology issue, it is really a matter of business and politics.

42.4.2 Application. Typically, when users become prospective owners of digital rights, they download a content file. The DRM software does an identity check of users, contacts a financial clearinghouse to arrange for the payment to be made, and then decrypts the requested file and assigns users a key. The key is used for future access to the content.

Because the system works on rules, it is possible to impose restrictions. One user might pay just to view material, while another user might want to have printing privileges. A third user might want to download the content to his or her own machine, and, finally, a fourth user might want to have viewing privileges for a specified time. The four different authorized users would thus use the same content, and each would pay according to a rate scale established by the content distributor. Throughout all of the transactions, each user would need a mechanism that allows secure transmissions and identifies that user and the associated level of access privileges.

Although this approach to publishing may sound fairly simple, it is really quite complex. In addition to arranging for different users to access material according to the set rules and to pay according to a rate schedule, it is also necessary for content distributors to handle the back end of the application. Everyone involved in the creation, production, and distribution of the content has to be paid fairly for the use of the content.

Payment is especially important as more and more content providers digitize materials that they can show or print on demand. Many users will read books online, but some physical printing on paper will continue. However, publishers will be able to print precisely those volumes that are requested. This approach will provide customized printing (e.g., large-print editions) as well as saving paper and physical warehouse storage space.

42.4.3 Examples. Several different types of DRM systems exist. Experts agree that the best DRM systems combine both hardware and software access mechanisms. With the advent of the eBook, the digital pad, PDA modems, Internet access devices, and increasingly smaller laptop computers, tying access rights directly to storage media gives publishers and distributors control of where the content is being used as well as by whom.

With the passage of the Electronic Signatures in Global and National Commerce Act, referred to as the E-Sign Bill and the increasing use of digital signatures, original documents (e.g., legal, medical, or financial) will be stored digitally. President Clinton signed the E-Sign Bill on June 30, 2000, in Philadelphia's Congress Hall using a ceremonial pen and a digital smart card. The bill went into effect on October 1, 2000. The E-Sign Bill gives an online signature (a John Hancock) the same legal status as a signature etched on paper and makes the digital document the original. Any printout will be considered a copy so the ability to view documents and videos (e.g., living wills) digitally will actually give the viewer access to the original. Eventually, records for medical treatment and documents for trials may be totally digital and may require submission and viewing digitally. When this becomes the norm rather than the exception, strict adherence to DRM in order to maintain privacy, as well as to provide restitution, will be paramount. In addition, such content-protection schemes will prevent unauthorized modifications of the digital data that would otherwise contribute to fraud.

For example, IBM has released antipiracy technology called the Electronic Media Management System that allows for downloading music tracks but puts controls on how many copies can be made or allows for a copy length limitation to be inserted. Thus, a minute of music could be downloaded to give a listener a taste, but not a chance to pirate the entire music track. To obtain the entire track, the user would be required to pay a fee.

Microsoft distributes free software that embeds metatags in each audio file. The metatags refer back to a central server in which the business rules are stored. This approach requires that material be tagged as it is created; otherwise, if it is released without the embedded tags, it can be illegally copied.

Major companies like Xerox, Microsoft, IBM, and Adobe got heavily involved producing and using this software in the 1990s, and many smaller firms opened shop. As with other new technology launches, eventually many of the small entrants went out of business or were bought by larger firms. Some of the small companies, such as ContentGuard (www.contentguard.com) and Pay2See (www.pay2see.com), continue to exist independently, as of this writing.

42.5 PRIVACY-ENHANCING TECHNOLOGIES.

Although DRM may seem to be a valid solution for the piracy problem, dissenters feel that DRM and other antipiracy measures give producers and distributors too much control. The rationale is that excessively restrictive rights management may undermine the fair use rights of consumers and academics. Partly as a result of these conflicting viewpoints, many consumers are making increasing use of privacy-enhancing technologies (PET), a broad term for a range of technologies designed to hide the identity and activities of individual users and computers as their traffic traverses the Internet.

42.5.1 Network Proxy. One broad class of tactics and tools used to enhance privacy is based on the concept of a network proxy. In its most general form, a proxy takes a network connection request from a client and redirects it to the ultimate destination, changing the address headers to make it look like the original request came from the proxy itself. When the destination server responds, the proxy returns the results to the requesting client. Proxies have long been used within organizations, both to protect internal users as they make requests to untrusted networks and to track and sometimes block access to undesirable content. For more details on the use of proxies in Web content filtering and monitoring, see Chapter 31 in this *Handbook*.

More recently, proxies have been employed outside the bounds of corporate networks to allow anonymous connections across the Internet. These so-called anonymizing proxies sometimes use encryption to hide the traffic in transit and so also provide protection from traffic analysis. Anonymizing proxies are a serious threat to organizations that desire (or are required by law) to monitor and block users from accessing certain kinds of information. More advanced versions of this concept use multiple routers to hide the path that a request takes through the public network. As a general class, these are known as mixing networks. One example described as early as 1981 is the Chaum Mix.[22] Recently, a concept known as onion routing has become popular in its incarnation as TOR (The Onion Router), which uses nested layers of traffic encryption as a session travels from one router to the next.[23] See Chapter 70 in this *Handbook* for further information about anonymity on the Internet.

42.5.2 Hidden Operating Systems.

Rather than relying on network technologies, some users are choosing to make their actions on the network private by using hidden operating systems. Two basic approaches are common: the virtual machine and the bootable system.

A virtual machine is a system that runs within another operating system. Long used for cross-platform compatibility and the ability to run multiple systems on a single hardware platform, virtual machines, such as Java Virtual Machine, VirtualPC, and VMware, are also used to hide activity from those who would disapprove of it (system administrators, parents, law enforcement, etc.), since the activities of the virtual machine can be made invisible to the host machine.

The bootable system approach, however, stores an entire operating system on some sort of bootable medium, such as a CD or USB device. If a computer can boot from such media and store downloaded content to a peripheral device rather than the host operating system's hard drive, then no record of the usage will remain when the host is next booted up.[24]

42.6 FUNDAMENTAL PROBLEMS.

A number of experts have pointed out that there are fundamental flaws in all the methods for preventing illegal copying of digital materials as described in this chapter. Bruce Schneier, a respected cryptographer, has repeatedly explained that all digital information must be converted to a cleartext (unencrypted) form before it is displayed or otherwise used. Schneier calls this "the Achilles' heel of all content protection schemes based on encryption."[25] Because the cleartext version has to reside somewhere in volatile or nonvolatile memory for at least some period of time to be usable, it is theoretically possible to obtain a copy of the cleartext version regardless of the complexity of the methods that originally concealed or otherwise limited access to the data. For example, if a DVD movie using complex regional encoding is to be seen on a monitor, at some point the hardware and software that decoded the DVD have to send that data stream to a monitor driver. The decoded data stream is vulnerable to interception. By modifying the low-level routines in the monitor driver, it is possible to divert a copy of the raw data stream to a storage device for unauthorized replay or reconstitution. Similarly, a system may be devised to prevent more than one copy of a document from being printed directly on a printer; however, unless the system prevents screen snapshots, a user can circumvent the restrictions by copying the screen as a bit image and storing that image for later, unauthorized use. Although hardware devices such as dedicated DVD or CD players may successfully interfere with piracy for some time, the problem is exacerbated under the current popular operating systems that have no security kernel and thus allow any processes to access any region of memory without regard to security levels.

42.7 SUMMARY.

Piracy is a rapidly growing societal problem affecting a multitude of people and industries. Although producers may suffer the greatest financial losses, there is a substantial impact on consumers. Pirated copies are generally inferior in quality and are sometimes defective. If anything goes wrong, pirated copies, being illegal, are unsupported. Additionally, producers' financial losses due to pirated copies may push the cost of legitimate copies up. Retailers and distributors also suffer due to the loss of sales to pirates. Illegal copies generally are sold more inexpensively than legitimate copies, so retailers and distributors cannot compete on price.

Creative talent, whether software developers, writers, musicians, artists, or performers, plus all the people who helped create the book, magazine, record, performance, painting, concert, or other media, are cheated out of their royalties by pirates. Frequently, because of the amount of time and effort needed to create the end product, the creators depend on the royalties for their livelihood. In addition, poor quality of stolen concepts can irreparably damage the reputation of the creative talent.

Publishers, record companies, art dealers, and other individuals and companies that invest artistic and technical skill along with money and effort to create an original work also lose revenues when that work is pirated. Because of the expenses already laid out to create the original product, companies frequently have to recoup their losses by raising prices for the consumer.

Due to the sophistication of systems and the increased use of the Internet, piracy has become more widespread and has an even greater financial impact worldwide. Many different types of antipiracy systems and techniques have been developed and implemented in an effort to cut down on the ever-increasing instances of piracy. One drawback to all of the systems is the lack of standards applied to software, audio, video, and other media. One of the most promising antipiracy systems is digital rights management. However, even DRM systems are not yet standardized, thus creating even more confusion regarding which is best and what to use.

The media industry is still working out which DRM solution it likes best, or whether it likes DRM at all. As this book was going to print, Apple's Steve Jobs was announcing that a large portion of EMI's song catalog will be available for DRM-free download from the iTunes Music Store, at a price per song just $0.30 higher than the standard $0.99. Previously downloaded songs, with DRM, will be upgradeable to a DRM-free version for the difference in the two prices.[26] This move echoes Jobs's recent comments encouraging the music industry to move away from DRM. Apple's actions notwithstanding, some consumers and privacy organizations continue fighting what they see as serious threats to individual privacy in nascent DRM efforts. The use of network proxies and hidden operating systems is adding to the difficulty of discovering inappropriate use of content, much less preventing or prosecuting it. As the balance between content producers and consumers works itself out, it seems likely that many more technologies will come and go, and DRM may be the harbinger of things to come or an unfortunate choice on the way to a bold, new business model for the media industry.

42.8 GLOSSARY.

Discussions of piracy and privacy often are riddled with a confusing array of terms and acronyms. Some of the most commonly used terms, organizations, and acronyms are listed in this glossary.

AAC—Advanced Audio Coding. A standardized, lossy compression and encoding scheme for digital audio. Most commonly used format for compressing audio CDs for Apple's iPod and iTunes.

ACATS. Advisory Committee on Advanced Television Service.

Anti-Bootleg Statute (Section 2319A). A U.S. federal statute that criminalizes the unauthorized manufacture, distribution, or trafficking in sound recordings and music videos of "live" musical performances.

ATSC. Advanced Television Systems Committee.

ATV. Advanced Television.

Bootleg recordings. The unauthorized recording of a musical broadcast on radio or television, or at a live concert or performance. These recordings are also known as underground recordings.

BSA—Business Software Alliance. A consortium of major software developers, including IBM, Microsoft, Novell, Apple, Dell, and Sun Microsystems, that is attempting to stem lost revenues from pirated computer software. BSA educates computer users on software copyrights and fights software piracy. Individual members, such as Microsoft and Adobe, have their own antipiracy programs in addition to belonging to the BSA.

CEA. Consumer Electronics Association.

CEMA. Consumer Electronics Manufacturers Association.

CSS—Content Scrambling System. A form of data encryption used to discourage reading media files directly from the disc, without a decryption key. Descrambling the video and audio requires a 5-byte, 40-bit key.

DeCSS—Descrambling Content Scrambling System. A utility developed by Norwegian programmers via reverse engineering and posted on the Web. This utility decrypts CSS and allows individuals to make illegal copies of DVD movies.

DFAST. Dynamic Feedback Arrangement Scrambling Technique.

DMAT. Digital Music Access Technology.

DMCA. The Digital Millennium Copyright Act signed into law October 28, 1998. Designed to implement World Intellectual Property Organization (WIPO) treaties (signed in Geneva in December 1996); the DMCA strengthens the protection of copyrighted materials in digital formats.

DivX. A brand name of products created by DivX, Inc. (formerly DivXNetworks, Inc.), including the DivX Codec. Known for its ability to compress lengthy video segments into small sizes, it has been the center of controversy because of its use in the replication and distribution of copyrighted DVDs. Many newer DVD players are able to play DivX movies.

DRM—Digital Rights Management. Refers to any of several technologies used by publishers or copyright owners to control access to, and usage of, digital data or hardware and to restrictions associated with a specific instance of a digital work or device.

DVD CCA—DVD Copy Control Association. A not-for-profit corporation that owns and licenses CSS. DVD CCA has filed numerous lawsuits against companies and individuals that make pirated copies of films.

EFF—Electronic Frontier Foundation. A nonprofit organization working in the public interest to protect fundamental civil liberties, including privacy where computers and the Internet are concerned. The organization frequently disagrees with the steps that other organizations and corporations want to take to protect copyrighted materials.

EPIC—Electronic Privacy Information Center. A public interest research group established in 1994 to focus public attention on emerging civil liberties issues and to protect privacy, the First Amendment, and constitutional values.

FairPlay. A digital rights management (DRM) technology created by Apple Inc. (formerly known as Apple Computer), built in to the QuickTime multimedia technology, and used by the iPod, iTunes, and the iTunes Store. Every file bought from the iTunes Store with iTunes is encoded with FairPlay. It digitally encrypts AAC audio files and prevents users from playing these files on unauthorized computers.

FAST—Federation Against Software Theft. A group headquartered in Great Britain represents software manufacturers and works with law enforcement agencies in finding and stopping software pirates in Europe.

FCC. Federal Communications Commission.

grpff. A 7-line, 526-character program of Perl code developed by two students at the Massachusetts Institute of Technology. More compact than DeCSS, the program descrambles DVDs but does not contain a decryption key. The code is readily available on the MIT campus via hats, T-shirts, business cards, and bumper stickers.

Hard disk loading. PCs with unlicensed software preinstalled. Use of a single copy of a software program but installed illegally on many machines. The original disks and the documents that should come with the PC are often missing or incomplete.

HDTV—High-Definition Television. Digital television transmissions are mandated in the U.S. to be the standard.

HRRC—Home Recording Rights Coalition. A coalition representing consumers, retailers, and manufacturers of audio and audiovisual recording products and media. The HRRC dedicates itself to keeping products free of government-imposed charges or restraints on the products' distribution or operation.

IFPI—International Federation of the Phonographic Industry. An organization that promotes the interests of the international recording industry worldwide. Its mission is to fight music piracy; promote fair market access and good copyright laws; help develop the legal conditions and the technologies for the recording industry to prosper in the digital era; and promote the value of music.

IIPA—International Intellectual Property Alliance. A private-sector coalition formed in 1984. The organization represents the U.S. copyright–based industries in efforts to improve international protection of copyrighted materials.

MP3. A technology for downloading music files using the MPEG format via the Internet.

MPAA—Motion Picture Association of America. Composed of member companies that produce and distribute legitimate films and videos. This organization serves as the official voice and advocate of the American motion picture industry. MPAA also assists law enforcement in raids and seizure of pirated videocassettes and DVDs.

MPEG—Moving Pictures Experts Group. A generic means of compactly representing digital video and audio signals for consumer distribution. MPEG video syntax provides an efficient way to represent image sequences in the form of more compact coded data.

NMPA—National Music Publishers Association. A trade association that represents 700 U.S. businesses that own, protect, and administer copyrights in musical works.

NTSC. National Television System Committee.

PET—Privacy-Enhancing Technologies. The general term for a variety of new technologies and Internet protocols designed to enhance online privacy; includes anonymizing proxies, mixing networks, and onion routing.

Pirated recordings. Unauthorized duplicates of the sounds of one or more legitimate recordings.

RIAA—Recording Industry Association of America. The group has an antipiracy unit that handles initial examination of product on behalf of the recording industry. Pirates can be turned in by calling RIAA at 1-800-BAD-BEAT.

SAG—Screen Actors Guild. The union for screen actors. Members do not get residuals from pirated films, as they do from authorized copies.

SDMI—Secure Digital Music Initiative. A forum of 200 companies from the electronics, music, telecommunications, and information technology industries and the RIAA. The group was active from 1998 to 2001.

SIIA—Software & Information Industry Association. A trade organization of the software and information content industries representing over 800 high-tech companies that develop and market software and electronic content. The organization provides policies and procedures for dealing with software and Internet use within businesses. SIIA also provides guidelines for telling if software is pirated or counterfeited. The SIIA Anti-Piracy Hotline is 1-800-388-7478.

SPA—Software Publishers Association. This association, a division of SIIA, assists in enforcement in dealing with software piracy and also provides education about software piracy. SPAudit Software is one of the first software audit and inventory tools made available for use by companies (in the 1980s). Improved versions of the software are now available.

Trademark Counterfeiting—Title 18 U.S.C. Section 2320. A federal statute that deals with sound recordings that contain the counterfeit trademark of the legitimate manufacturer or artists.

Trafficking in Counterfeit Labels—Title 18 U.S.C., Section 2318. A federal statute that covers counterfeit labels printed for use on a sound recording.

U.S. Copyright Law (Title 17 U.S.C.). A federal law that protects copyright owners from the unauthorized reproduction or distribution of their work.

WGA—Writers Guild of America. The union for writers of television, video, and film scripts.

WMA—Windows Media Audio. A proprietary compressed audio file format developed by Microsoft Corporation.

42.9 FURTHER READING

Business Software Alliance-USA Homepage. *Anti-Piracy Information*, 2007, www.bsa.org/usa/.

Cohen, Julie E. "DRM and Privacy." *Berkeley Technology Law Journal*, 2003, www.law.berkeley.edu/institutes/bclt/drm/papers/cohen-drmandprivacy-btlj2003.html.

Copyright Act of 1976 (Public Law 94-553); Title 17 U.S.C. Sections 101–120, www4.law.cornell.edu/uscode/html/uscode17/usc_sec_17_00000101—000-.html.

Electronic Freedom Foundation home page: www.eff.org.

Electronic Privacy Information Center (EPIC) home page: www.epic.org.

Gross, T. "The Music Industry, Adapting to a Digital Future: Terry Gross interviews Eliot Van Buskirk." *Fresh Air* podcast, March 13, 2008, www.npr.org/templates/story/story.php?storyId=88145070.

Harte, L. *Introduction to Digital Rights Management (DRM); Identifying, Tracking, Authorizing and Restricting Access to Digital Media*. Fuquay Varina, NC: Althos, 2006.

May, C. *Digital Rights Management: The Problem of Expanding Ownership Rights*. Oxford, UK: Chandos Publishing, 2006.

Recording Industry Association of America: www.riaa.com/default.asp.

Schneier.com: www.schneier.com/index.html.

Zeng, W., H. Yu, and C-Y. Lin, eds. *Multimedia Security Technologies for Digital Rights Managemen*t. New York: Academic Press, 2006.

42.10 NOTES

1. BSA/IDC Global Piracy Study, 2006, www.bsa.org/globalstudy/upload/2005%20Piracy%20Study%20-%20Official%20Version.pdf.
2. J. Schultz, "The Economist Rails on Flawed BSA Piracy Study," May 5, 2005, http://copyfight.corante.com/archives/2005/05/25/the_economist_rails_on_flawed_bsa_piracy_study.php.
3. S. Musil, "Man Gets 7 Years for Software Piracy," CNET News.com, September 10, 2006, http://news.com.com/Man+gets+7+years+for+software+piracy/2100-1014_3-6114012.html (retrieved April 1, 2007).
4. Microsoft, "Microsoft Incorporates New Anti-Piracy Technologies in Windows 2000, Office 2000," www.microsoft.com/Presspass/press/2000/fcb00/apfeaturespr.mspx (retrieved March 15, 2008).
5. Microsoft, "The Behavior of Reduced Functionality Mode in Windows Vista," http://support.microsoft.com/kb/925582 (retrieved March 15, 2008).
6. Microsoft, "Microsoft Product Activation," www.microsoft.com/licensing/resources/vol/default.mspx (retrieved March 16, 2008).
7. RIAA, "Anti-Piracy," www.riaa.com/issues/piracy/default.asp (retrieved April 1, 2007).
8. GrayZone Digest, "Worldwide Update," October 1997, www.grayzone.com/1097.htm (retrieved March 15, 2008).

9. P. Mercer, "Copycat CDs in an Instant," BBC News, April 16, 2002, http://news.bbc.co.uk/2/hi/entertainment/1930923.stm (retrieved March 15, 2008).
10. Recording Industry Association of America, "2005 Commercial Piracy Report," http://76.74.24.142/6BE200AF-5DDA-1C2B-D8BA-4174680FCE66.pdf (retrieved March 16, 2008).
11. E. VanBuskirk, "Fans Pay Whatever They Want for Radiohead's Upcoming Album," Underwire Blog from Wired.com, October 1, 2007, http://blog.wired.com/underwire/2007/10/fans-to-determi.html (retrieved March 15, 2008).
12. J. Valenti, Napster Statement, February 12, 2001, www.mpaa.org/Napster_2-12-2001.asp.
13. S. Butler, "RIAA Sends Another Wave of Settlement Letters," Billboard.biz, September 20, 2007, www.billboard.biz/bbbiz/content_display/industry/e3i39f76c017d89e0747eaafd53d458f14b (retrieved March 15, 2008).
14. University of Nebraska—Lincoln, "The Recording Industry and UNL," ASUN Student Government, http://asun.unl.edu/index.php?option=com_content&task=view&id=85&Itemid=78 (retrieved March 15, 2008).
15. S. Musil, "Scour to End File-Swapping Service," CNET News.com, November 14, 2000, http://news.com.com/2100-1023-248631.html (retrieved April 1, 2007).
16. J. Borland, "Broadcasters Win Battle Against iCraveTV.com," CNET News.com, January 28, 2000, http://news.com.com/2100-1033-236255.html (retrieved April 1, 2007).
17. M. Graziano and Lee Rainie, "The Music Downloading Deluge: 37 million American adults and youths have retrieved music files on the Internet," www.pewinternet.org/reports/toc.asp?Report=33.
18. J. Silverstein, "iTunes: 1 Billion Served," http://abcnews.go.com/Technology/story?id=1653881 (retrieved April 1, 2007).
19. C. Cohn, "Security Researchers Drop Scientific Censorship Case," www.eff.org/IP/DMCA/Felten_v_RIAA/20020206_eff_felten_pr.html.
20. www.sdmi.org/whats_new.htm.
21. C. Cohn, "DVD Descrambling Code Not a Trade Secret," http://www.eff.org/IP/Video/DVDCCA_case/20040122_eff_pr.php (retrieved April 1, 2007).
22. D. Chaum, "Untraceable Electronic Mail, Return Addresses, and Digital Pseudonyms," *Communications of the ACM* 24, No. 2 (February 1981); available online at http://freehaven.net/anonbib/cache/chaum-mix.pdf (retrieved April 1, 2007).
23. Tor: Anonymity Online, http://tor.eff.org/.
24. B. Schneier, "Anonym.OS," www.schneier.com/blog/archives/2006/01/anonymos.html (retrieved April 1, 2007).
25. B. Schneier, "The Futility of Digital Copy Prevention," www.schneier.com/crypto-gram-0105.html (retrieved March 15, 2008).
26. American Public Radio, *Marketplace,* April 2, 2007, http://marketplace.publicradio.org/shows/2007/04/02/PM200704024.html.

Patent Law

Gerald Bluhm, *Tyco Fire & Security*

INTRODUCTION

This chapter introduces the fundamental concepts of patent law, both in the United States and internationally, with some focus on software and Internet-related issues. Patents are exclusionary monopolies for a limited term, granted in exchange for inventors disclosing how to make or use their inventions. With the promise of such monopolies, inventors are encouraged to invent and thus reap the rewards made possible by the rights accorded. Competitors must either obtain a license to make or use a patented invention or discover new ways that circumvent a patented invention as defined by the patent claims.

Some have rejected the use of the word "monopoly" to describe patents. Regardless of whether one uses that term, certain rights are granted to the owner of a patent. For example, in the United States, the owner of a patent has the right to *exclude* others from making, using, selling, or offering for sale the invention in the United States, importing the invention into the United States, or importing into the United States something made by a patented process. Other countries convey similar rights for patents issued in those countries. What may not be obvious is that a patent does not grant its owner the right to make, use, sell, offer for sale, or import the patented invention. In fact, many patented inventions are improvements to existing patented work and, if made, used, or sold, would constitute infringement of the earlier patent.

GENERAL CONSIDERATIONS

Why Get a Patent?

There are many reasons why obtaining patent protection is beneficial, and the brief discussion presented here is not intended to be all inclusive. One reason for obtaining a patent is to protect one's intellectual property. That is, the holder of the patent may be able to prevent competition by preventing others from taking advantage of the invention. Because of the patent, others may decide not to compete at all in the particular area or may decide to spend significant amounts of time and money developing processes or products that do not infringe on it. Alternatively, if both sides are willing, the patent holder may license all or part of the patent to another party for a fixed fee, a royalty, or some combination of the two. A license is basically an agreement between a licensor (patent holder) and licensee that the licensor will not sue the licensee for what would otherwise constitute infringement of some or all of the patent claims.

Another reason for obtaining a patent is more defensive. For example, company B may be reluctant to sue company A for infringement of company B's patent, if company B thinks that company A may countersue for infringement of company A's patents. Such a situation may result in cross-licensing between the two parties, in which each agrees not to sue the other for infringement of all or part of each other's patents.

Yet another reason for obtaining a patent, especially for start-up companies, is to attract investment. Investors like to know that intellectual property has been protected and exclusive rights are controlled, providing value in their investment. The existence of one or more patents (or even pending patent applications) may be an indication of a company's viability.

Patent Term—How Long Does a Patent Last?

Patent protection begins on the day a patent is issued. Because of a change in law in 1994 to conform to the Uruguay Round of the General Agreement on Tariffs and Trade (GATT), when a U.S. patent expires depends on when the application was filed. Before the change in law, the term of a U.S. utility patent was 17 years from the issue date. Now, however, any U.S. utility patents issuing from an application filed on or after June 8, 1995 are valid for 20 years from the priority date; that is, the date of the earliest application to which the application claims priority (the earliest filing date in a chain of continuation and divisional applications). Utility patents that were still in force on June 8, 1995, and applications filed before that date but still pending receive the best of both worlds (with regard to patent terms): either 17 years from the issue date or 20 years from the priority date, whichever is later. Various adjustments and extensions may be available under certain conditions, although a discussion of these conditions is beyond the scope of this chapter. The patent terms discussed above pertain to U.S utility and plant patents. U.S. design patents expire after 14 years from the issue date.

In most other countries, a utility patent expires 20 years from the priority date.

Types of Patents

In the United States, there are three types of patents: utility patents, design patents, and plant patents. Utility patents are the most familiar type. They may be obtained for "any new and *useful* process, machine, manufacture, or composition of matter, or any new and useful improvement thereof" (35 U.S.C. §101).

Design patents may be obtained for new, original, and ornamental designs for manufactured articles. A design patent protects the way an article looks, as depicted in the drawings. Design patents have a term of 14 years from the issue date. They may be obtained for computer-generated icons, including full-screen displays and individual icons. The U.S. Patent and Trademark Office's (USPTO) *Manual of Patent Examining Procedure* (MPEP), section 1504.01(a) provides "Guidelines for Examination of Design Patent Applications for Computer-generated Icons" (see U.S. Design Patent D453,769 for an example of a design patent for a computer-generated icon). According to MPEP section 1504.01(a).1.A, to satisfy the manufactured article requirement, such an icon may be claimed as "a computer-generated icon shown on a computer screen, monitor, other display panel, or a portion thereof" or with similar language. The icon must also be fundamentally ornamental, rather than functional. Fonts may also be patented with design patents (for an example, see U.S. Design Patent D454,582).

The Plant Patent Act of 1930, now codified as 35 U.S.C. § 161, allows "plant patents" for plants that are reproduced asexually. Tubers, such as potatoes, are excluded (i.e., they are not patentable). To be patentable, a plant must have been found in an uncultivated state (e.g., *not* in a garden). A plant patent includes the right to exclude others from causing the plant to reproduce asexually or using, offering for sale, or selling the plant (or parts of the plant) in the United States, or importing the plant into the United States if it was asexually reproduced (see 35 U.S.C. §§ 161–164).

Despite the availability of plant patents, utility patents may also be obtained for both sexually and asexually reproduced plants (see *J.E.M. AG Supply Inc, dba Farm Advantage, Inc., et al. v. Pioneer Hi-Bred International, Inc.*, 1996). The requirements for obtaining a plant patent are more relaxed than those for obtaining a utility patent, however.

Outside the United States, many countries provide for patents that are not given full-blown examinations and that do not receive full-blown benefits. Germany, Spain, and France, for example, have "petty" (or "utility model") patents. Australia has an "innovation" patent, and Indonesia has a "simple" patent. These patents are typically for shorter terms and may not be required to satisfy the nonobviousness standard.

PATENT LAW IN THE UNITED STATES

Constitutional Basis

The U.S. Constitution grants to Congress the power "to promote the Progress of... useful Arts, by securing for limited Times to... Inventors the exclusive Right to their respective... Discoveries" (Article I, Section 8, Clause 8). In accordance with this power, Congress has over time enacted several patent statutes. In particular, in 1952, the present patent law, codified under Title 35 of the United States Code (35 U.S.C.; available on the Web at http://uscode.house.gov/title_35.htm), was enacted, although it has been amended many times over the years.

U.S. Patent & Trademark Office

Almost every country has a patent or intellectual property or industrial property office. In the United States, the USPTO (http://www.uspto.gov) processes patent applications and ultimately issues or grants patents. During the processing of an application (a process known as *patent prosecution*), the application is reviewed by an examiner who is familiar with the specific technology field of the invention described in the application. The examiner will reject one or more of the claims of the application if he or she feels that, when compared with prior art (existing knowledge possessed and/or information accessible by those in the subject technology field), there is nothing novel or nonobvious about the invention as claimed. The examiner may also object to the written description of the application if he or she feels that it does not satisfy the disclosure requirements of the statutes. Patent prosecution typically involves communications back and forth between the examiner and the inventor (or the inventor's patent attorney or agent) in which the inventor or attorney clarifies how the invention is in fact novel and nonobvious in relation to the prior art and is disclosed adequately by the application.

Inventors can represent themselves before the USPTO. Alternatively, an inventor or the assignee to whom the inventor assigns ownership of an invention may use an attorney or agent registered to practice before the USPTO. Both patent attorneys and patent agents must have technical backgrounds in a science or engineering field and have taken and passed a registration examination administered by the USPTO. In addition, patent attorneys must have graduated from law school and be admitted to practice law in at least one jurisdiction, whereas patent agents are not attorneys.

What Is Patentable?

An inventor may obtain a patent for "any new and useful process, machine, manufacture, or composition of matter, or any new and useful improvement thereof" (35 U.S.C. §101). In a landmark U.S. Supreme Court case in which whether a live, human-made microorganism could be patented was at issue, the Supreme Court unequivocally stated that "anything under the sun that is made by man" is patentable (*Diamond v. Chakrabarty*, 1980).

What is not patentable? Generally speaking, laws of nature, physical phenomena, and abstract ideas per se are not patentable. For example, the Supreme Court stated,

> "a new mineral discovered in the earth or a new plant found in the wild is not patentable.... Likewise, Einstein could not patent his celebrated law that $E = mc^2$; nor could Newton have patented the law of gravity." (*Diamond v. Chakrabarty*, 1980)

Of course, a practical application of some physical phenomena may be patentable. For example, although a new plant found in the wild is not patentable, its medicinal use may be. In *Diamond v. Chakrabarty* (1980), the Supreme Court clearly stated that even living things, in this case microorganisms produced by genetic engineering, are patentable. In fact, all that matters is whether the living matter is the result of human intervention.

In particular, Internet-related inventions are patentable and can be protected with method claims, apparatus claims, so-called Beauregard claims, embedded signal claims, and the like, all of which are discussed later in the chapter. Many Internet-related inventions are protected by "business method" patents.

Business Methods

Prior to the *State Street Bank & Trust Co. v. Signature Financial Group, Inc.* (1998) decision by the Court of Appeals for the Federal Circuit (CAFC), there was some uncertainty as to whether methods of doing business were patentable. Although the invention claimed was technically a "machine" that implemented business methods, this decision is cited for confirming that indeed business methods themselves are patentable.

In the *State Street Bank* case, Signature was the assignee (owner) of U.S. Patent No. 5,193,056. The claimed invention was a system in which mutual funds pool their assets into an investment portfolio to take advantage of economies of scale in administering investments. State Street Bank had been negotiating a license with Signature Financial to use that invention. When negotiations broke down, State Street Bank sought a declaratory judgment that the patent was invalid because it described a business method. The court, however, concluded that business methods are patentable subject matter.

When is a method a business method? This is not always clear. For example, Amazon.com received a patent (U.S. Patent No. 5,960,411) for its one-click process. Although the invention has been labeled a method of doing business by some, Amazon itself has asserted that its one-click patent is not a business method patent.

The USPTO has established a classification system made up of more than 400 classes that are further divided into subclasses. Every application is assigned to a class and subclass according to the technology of the invention. In general, methods that fall into the USPTO's Class 705 ("Data processing: financial, business practice, management, or cost/price determination") are considered to be business methods. The first few subcategories of Class 705 include health care management; insurance; reservation, check-in, or booking display for reserved space; staff scheduling or task assignment; market analysis, demand forecasting or surveying; and so on; see http://www.uspto.gov/web/patents/classification/USPC705/def5705.htm for a complete list of Class 705 categories.

For those inventions that are considered to be business methods, some special rules apply both during prosecution of a business method patent application and with respect to infringement. Whereas most patent applications undergo examination by a single examiner, business method applications may be subjected to multiple reviews. Extra reviews were added in part as a response to numerous complaints made in the popular press and elsewhere that many business method patents were being issued on inventions that were not patentable.

Furthermore, accused infringers of issued business method patents have at their disposal an extra defense against the accusation that infringers of other types of patents do not have. For example, for most patents, if party A receives a patent for an invention and party B has been practicing the invention prior to issuance of the patent, party B must stop its practice or obtain a license once the patent is issued. After the *State Street* decision, however, Congress added Clause § 273 to Title 35 of the U.S. Code as part of the American Inventor's Protection Act of 1999; this clause provides for "intervening rights" to protect parties who may not have applied for a business method patent based on the misconception that such patents were unobtainable. The details of § 273 are beyond the scope of this article, but basically it provides, in certain situations, a defense to an infringement claim for a party that was using the patented business method before the patent was issued.

Requirements for Patentability

An invention must meet four basic requirements before it can be patented in the United States: the invention must be (1) patentable subject matter; (2) novel; (3) nonobvious in view of the current state of the art and with respect to a person knowledgeable or "of ordinary skill" in the art; and (4) useful.

Novelty is statutorily provided for in 35 U.S.C. § 102, which describes several conditions in which a patent may not be obtained: if the invention was known or used by others in the United States prior to the patent applicant's date of invention (this could happen, for example, when two people separately invent the same invention, each unaware of the other's activity or accomplishment) or if the invention has been patented or described in a printed publication anywhere in the world. "Printed publications" may include any information that is freely accessible via the Web, even though a Web page is not technically printed in hard copy. It is not necessary that the publication be in English.

Even an inventor's own actions or writings can be held against him or her in rejecting the novelty claim. An inventor has 1 year in which to file a patent application in the United States if the invention was patented by the inventor or described by the inventor in a printed publication anywhere in the world or if the invention was in public use or on sale in the United States.

The prohibition against obviousness is statutorily provided for in 35 U.S.C. § 103(a), which states in essence that even if the invention is not disclosed in a single prior art document or is in use or on sale, if the difference between the invention and prior the art, (including use, or sale) is obvious, a patent cannot be obtained. Examiners often reject applications based on their sense that it would be obvious to combine two or more published patents or other publications that complement each other. Of course, such a combination must be obvious to a person having ordinary skill in the art, and it must have been obvious at the time the invention was made.

Often, by the time a patent is issued, which may be 2 or 3 years after the application was filed, or even at the time when the application is filed, it may seem to be obvious in light of the prior art. However, the critical time to examine obviousness is when the invention was made. As many court decisions show, it is not always easy to cast away current knowledge and place oneself back to the time the invention was made to determine whether it was obvious. Thus, assertions as to whether an invention is obvious or not in view of the cited art can be highly subjective.

Section 35 U.S.C. § 101 requires that an invention be useful, concrete, and tangible. At least three categories of subject matter have been identified by the Supreme Court as not, by themselves, patentable: laws of nature, natural phenomena, and abstract ideas. For example, the CAFC stated in the State Street Bank ruling that mathematical algorithms by themselves are unpatentable because "they are merely abstract ideas constituting disembodied concepts or truths that are not 'useful.'"

Generally speaking, the requirement that an invention be useful is an extremely low bar to patentability. Nonetheless, an invention can fail the usefulness test if an applicant fails to explain adequately why the invention is useful or if an assertion of utility is not credible. For example, the invention considered in *Newman v. Quigg* (1989) was considered to be a perpetual motion machine and thus found to be inoperative (as going against the laws of thermodynamics). It therefore did not meet the usefulness standard.

In addition to these requirements, a specification is required in the patent application that includes a written description and at least one claim. The written description must describe the invention and teach enough about it in sufficient detail so as to enable "any person skilled in the art" to make or use the invention without undue experimentation. The written description must also describe the "best mode" (i.e., the best way to carry out the invention) known to the inventor, although there is no requirement to point out a specific embodiment of the invention as the best mode. The first paragraph of 35 U.S.C. § 112 discusses the requirements of the written description.

The specification must conclude with at least one claim, which is the legal statement defining the subject matter over which the patent will confer the right to exclude. Courts look to the claims when determining whether an accused party is infringing a patent. Claims are discussed in more detail later in the chapter. Finally, 35 U.S.C. § 113 sets forth the particular requirements for drawings, which must be supplied as needed to provide an understanding of the invention.

Patent Prosecution

The process of obtaining a patent—from filing a patent application, to responding to office actions from the USPTO, to paying the issue fee—is referred to as *patent prosecution*. The first step in the patent prosecution process, other than the invention itself, is often a "prior art" search. There is no obligation on the part of an applicant to do a search, although there is an obligation to report known material information to the USPTO. Nonetheless, performing a search is often a good idea. If search results show that the invention is not novel, one can avoid a long, costly, and ultimately unsuccessful prosecution process. If the invention appears to be novel in view of the search results, often the search—by exposing those aspects that are well known or that have been described in the references uncovered in the search—will then enable the person who ultimately drafts the patent application to focus on those parts that are novel.

For example, a cursory search for U.S., Japanese, and European patents and published patent applications can be performed using, respectively, the online search facilities of the USPTO, the Japanese Patent Office (in English at http://www.ipdl.jpo.go.jp/homepg_e.ipdl), and the European Patent Office (EPO), which also enables Japanese patent searches (http://ep.espacenet.com). Most patent offices in other countries have their own Web sites that can be searched. A list of these sites can be found at either the USPTO's or the EPO's Web sites. In addition, many useful documents and news items may be found on the Web using standard Web searching facilities. More extensive (and expensive) searches may be conducted using proprietary databases that may contain articles from hundreds or thousands of trade journals, professional publications, newspapers, magazines, and so on. An online search may be quite limited in scope, and when possible one should use an experienced searcher to conduct an accurate and comprehensive search.

The next step is preparing or drafting the patent application. A patent attorney or agent ordinarily prepares the application, although inventors can represent themselves before the USPTO. The application is then filed with the USPTO. Once received by the USPTO, an application is assigned an application number, and if it is not a provisional application, it will eventually be assigned to an art group consisting of examiners who are familiar with the particular field to which the application/invention pertains. Finally, the application is assigned to a specific examiner in the art group.

That examiner reviews the application in light of both the results of his or her own prior art search and any material information submitted by the applicant. Typically, the examiner objects to one or more aspects of the application and, in an *office action*, rejects one or more of the claims based on the prior art. Or the examiner may object to unclear language in the specification or an informality in the submitted drawings. An office action is mailed to the applicant (or his or her attorney), and the applicant must reply within a certain time frame or the application will be considered abandoned.

The applicant can reply to the office action in several ways. He or she can point out the differences between the invention as claimed and the prior art cited by the examiner in the office action, emphasizing that the invention is not taught or even suggested by knowledge of the prior art. The applicant can cancel claims, amend claims for clarity, narrow claims to overcome the examiner's rejections, or even broaden claims. New claims may also be added (at least in response to a first office action). Corrections to the specification or drawings may also be made, but in any case, the applicant is never allowed to introduce new matter into the application.

The examiner often makes a subsequent office action *final*. Certain rules apply when the applicant replies to a final office action—for example, new claims cannot normally be added, and only certain amendments of a limited nature are permitted—but a final office action is not as "final" as it sounds.

If some claims are allowed in an office action, an applicant can, in the reply, cancel the rejected claims, permitting a patent to be issued with the allowed claims. A new application, called a *continuation*, can then be filed with the rejected claims. (Note that this continuation application must be filed while the parent application is pending; that is, before the parent application is issued as a patent with the allowed claims.)

Alternatively, if no claims are allowed, the applicant, in response to a final office action, may file a *Request for Continued Examination* (RCE). For the equivalent cost of filing a new application, the applicant is allowed to continue prosecution without the finality of the final office action. In older cases, those filed before May 29, 2000, the applicant may, while the first application is pending, file a continuation-type application, called a *Continued Prosecution Application* (CPA), and allow the first application to become abandoned.

During the course of prosecution, it may be desirable to file a new set of claims while allowing the original application to proceed. For example, the applicant may determine that aspects of the original application not previously claimed may be worth pursuing and may file the same specification with a different set of claims, claiming priority to the first application. This continuation application has its own filing date, but because it claims priority to the first application, it will expire (under the current statute) 20 years from the filing date of the first application (or the filing date of the earliest application in the priority chain). If new matter is added to the specification of a continuation—for example, an improvement or a new configuration—the new application is called a *continuation-in-part* (CIP). A patent issuing on a CIP application, like other utility patents, expires 20 years from the filing date of the first application to which the CIP claims priority.

In some cases, an examiner may determine that the claims of an application define two or more different inventions, each requiring its own prior art search. In this case, the examiner may issue a *restriction requirement* in which the various claims are divided into different groups, each pertaining to a different invention. The applicant is then required to select one of the groups and to cancel or amend the remaining claims. The canceled claims can be filed (while the original application is still pending) in one or more applications known as *divisional* applications. As with continuations, each divisional application has its own filing date, but each must claim priority to the parent and therefore has a term of 20 years from the filing date of the parent (or the earliest filed application in the priority chain).

Eventually, the applicant hopes, each application (including parent, continuations, CIPs, and divisionals) is allowed. For a given allowed patent application, the applicant must pay an issue fee; soon thereafter the patent is issued and is then in force. Although the term of a patent is currently 20 years from the priority date, maintenance fees must be paid at specific intervals from the date of issue or the patent will expire. These intervals are 3 years and 6 months; 7 years and 6 months; and 11 years and 6 months from the date of issue. A 6-month grace period is available for a surcharge.

Appealing an Examiner's Decision

If the applicant is dissatisfied with the examiner's conclusions as to unpatentability, the applicant can appeal to the Board of Patent Appeals and Interferences within the USPTO. Each appeal is heard by at least three members of the board. An applicant who is unhappy with the board's decision may make a further appeal to the U.S. Court of Appeals for the Federal Circuit (CAFC). The CAFC makes a decision based only on the record from the appeal to the board. Alternatively, an unhappy applicant may file a civil suit against the Director of the USPTO in the U.S. District Court for the District of Columbia. Unlike appeals to the CAFC, new evidence may be presented in these civil suits in addition to the record from the appeal to the board.

Publication and Provisional Rights

Applications filed on or after November 29, 2000 are published roughly 18 months from the priority date, unless the applicant specifically requests that they not be published, certifying at the same time that the invention has not been and will not be the subject of an application filed in another country. Early publication can be requested. Applications filed before November 29, 2000 but still pending as of that date are not typically published, but publication may be requested.

If a published application eventually issues as a patent, with a claim that is "substantially identical" to a claim published in the application publication, the owner of the patent may be entitled to a reasonable royalty, from the time of the publication date up to the issue date, from someone who makes, uses, offers for sale, or sells an infringing device as against that claim in the United States or who imports an infringing device into the United States and who has "actual notice" (currently a matter of some dispute) of the published patent application. The rights to these royalties are known as *provisional rights*.

How to Read a Patent

A patent is organized into four sections: a cover sheet, drawings, a specification, and claims. The cover sheet includes bibliographical information, a short abstract that describes the invention briefly, and usually a copy of one of the drawings considered to be representative of the invention. Drawings must be provided when necessary for understanding the invention.

The specification includes a background, a summary, a brief description of the drawings, and a detailed description of the invention. The background section describes prior art or the state of the art prior to the patented invention. The summary provides a short synopsis of the invention and often is a regurgitation of the claims in plainer language. A brief description of the drawings typically follows. Next comes a written description of one or more embodiments of the invention. As previously mentioned, the written description must enable any person skilled in the art to make and use the invention. It must also set forth the "best mode" contemplated by the inventor, although this best mode need not be pointed out as such.

In the final section, a set of claims are provided that point out and distinctly claim the protected subject matter. Each claim is written as a single sentence and typically includes a preamble, a transitional phrase, and a set of limitations. For example, claim 1 of U.S. Patent No. 6,004,596 ("Sealed crustless sandwich") appears as follows:

I claim:

1. A sealed crustless sandwich, comprising:
   a first bread layer having a first perimeter surface coplanar to a contact surface;
   at least one filling of an edible food juxtaposed to said contact surface;
   a second bread layer juxtaposed to said at least one filling opposite of said first bread layer, wherein said second bread layer includes a second perimeter surface similar to said first perimeter surface;
   a crimped edge directly between said first perimeter surface and said second perimeter surface for sealing said at least one filling between said first bread layer and said second bread layer;
   wherein a crust portion of said first bread layer and said second bread layer has been removed.

In this example, the *preamble* is the phrase: "A sealed crustless sandwich." The transitional phrase is "comprising." These elements are followed by five limitations: "a first bread layer," "at least one filling," "a second bread layer," "a crimped edge," and the condition "wherein a crust portion... has been removed." For this claim to be infringed, an unauthorized party must make, use, sell or offer to sell, or import into the United States a sandwich product that satisfies every one of these limitations. It is irrelevant that another crustless sandwich may have other components not described in the claim; for example, a cherry on top. As long as some food product meets every one of the limitations listed in claim 1, that product is said to infringe claim 1. On the other hand, if a sandwich is lacking some element, such as the crimped edge, it cannot literally infringe (but see below regarding the doctrine of equivalents).

A first claim is typically written broadly, to cover a wide range of variations. Narrower claims often follow that include the limitations of the broad claim, plus additional limitations that limit the scope of the invention recited by these narrower claims. Narrower claims are often written as dependent claims.

For example, claim 1 above is an independent claim. Claim 2 in the same patent reads as follows:

2. The sealed crustless sandwich of claim 1, wherein said crimped edge includes a plurality of spaced apart depressions for increasing a bond of said crimped edge.

Claim 2 is called a dependent claim because it *depends from* claim 1. That is, it includes all of the five limitations of claim 1, plus the further limitation that the crimped edge includes "spaced apart depressions." For a sandwich to infringe this claim, it must meet all of the limitations of claim 1 *and* claim 2. One reason for providing additional narrower claims is that often, during litigation of a patent suit, some claims may be found to be invalid. Even though a claim may be invalidated in a court of law (for example, if a publication is presented that predates the patent's priority date and that teaches or suggests one or more of the claims), a narrower claim with additional limitations may still be valid, even if it depends from the invalidated claim.

Another reason for providing additional narrower claims is the so-called doctrine of claim differentiation, under which "two claims of a patent are presumptively of different scope" (*Kraft Foods, Inc. v. Int'l Trading Co.*, 2000). According to this doctrine, if a dependent claim includes a narrowing definition of some limitation of a base claim, then the base claim is presumed to encompass not only the narrow definition but other embodiments as well. For example, claim 2 above may help support the proposition that claim 1 covers crustless sandwiches that do not have depressions that are spaced apart as well as crustless sandwiches that have other kinds of bonding mechanisms.

First-time readers of claims are often puzzled by their seemingly bizarre language and grammar. Sometimes this language results from the statutory requirement that claims particularly point out and distinctly claim the subject matter that the inventor or applicant regards as his or her invention. Thus, use of a definite article such as "the" is typically not allowed unless it refers to something already defined in the claim (i.e., there is an "antecedent basis" for the thing being referred to). For this reason, one often sees "*a* number of (things)," whereas in normal usage one would say "*the* number of (things)."

In addition, use of the word "or" is generally frowned upon as it leaves options open and is therefore not considered to distinctly claim an invention. Thus, one often sees in claims the following wording—"at least one of [Choice A], [Choice B], *and* [Choice C]" or "any of

[Choice A], [Choice B], *and* [Choice C]"—whereas in normal speech, one might say "either [Choice A], [Choice B], *or* [Choice C]." Similarly, instead of stating "one or more of," claims will more often state "a plurality of" or "at least one of," leading to even more confusing language later in the claims, such as "the at least one of." Although such language may at first be confusing, an understanding of why these terms are used may help in reading and interpreting a claim.

Another aspect of claims that can be confusing to the layperson is that often very similar language is used in two different claims. For example, a patent typically will have a method claim and an apparatus (or system) claim that use parallel language. Remember, however, that the scope of the right to exclude may be different between a method and an apparatus or composition of matter.

A limitation in an apparatus claim may also be expressed as a means or step for performing a specified function without the recital of any specific structure. Although such a limitation is not always triggered by "means for" (also called "means-plus-function") language and may even be triggered in the absence of such language, such claims are often added to a patent. A "means for" limitation is construed to cover the corresponding structure, material, or acts described in the specification and their equivalents (see 35 U.S.C. § 112, sixth paragraph).

In addition to the more or less standard apparatus, method, and "means-for" claims, computer- and software-related inventions are often additionally recited in so-called Beauregard claims and signal claims. As the USPTO states, a computer program is merely a set of instructions, capable of being executed but is not itself a process (see section 2106(a) of the *Manual of Patent Examining Procedure*). To be patentable, a computer-readable medium or an "article of manufacture" comprising a computer-readable or useable medium is claimed, having therein a computer program that performs some steps of a process. These types of claims have been called Beauregard claims after the inventor of one of the first patent applications to use such claims (see U.S. Patent No. 4,962,468).

Another type of claim one might encounter is the so-called propagated signal claim. Such a claim might appear as follows:

1. A computer data signal embodied in a carrier wave for [doing something], the computer data signal comprising:
   program code for [performing a first action];
   program code for [performing a second action]; etc.

Such claims are thought to protect against the unlicensed transmission of a computer program over a network such as the Internet or through modems. Of special concern with claims directed to client/server applications is the fact that a single party may not be performing or using all of the limitations of a claim. In other words, if a claim states actions taken by both the server and the client, which are controlled by two independent parties, then neither party can be an infringer. Therefore, it may be desirable in a patent to have one set of claims directed to the overall invention, another set of claims directed to actions taken at the server (possibly in response to messages received from a client), and yet another set of claims directed to actions taken by a client (possibly in response to messages received from a server).

Protecting Patent Rights

What Rights Are Conferred on a Patentee?

A patent confers specific "exclusive" rights on the owner of a patent. That is, the owner of a patent is granted the right to exclude other parties from various acts, including making, using, offering to sell, or selling the patented invention (as set forth in the claims) within the United States or importing the patented invention into the United States. When a process is patented as opposed to an apparatus or composition of matter, the patentee is similarly granted the right to exclude others from using, offering to sell, or selling in the United States or importing into the United States any product made by the claimed process. Note that a patent does not give an owner the right to practice the invention recited in the patent; another (broader) patent may exclude the owner from practicing the invention. These rights begin when the patent is granted—that is, when the patent is issued—and last until the patent expires.

Infringement

When someone performs one of the restricted acts described above without permission of the patent owner, the claims of the patent are said to be infringed. There are three types of infringement: direct infringement, active inducement to infringe, and contributory infringement. *Direct infringement* occurs when someone performs one of the restricted acts; that is, makes, uses, sells the invention (as set forth in at least one claim of the patent), or offers it for sale in the United States or imports it into the United States. Note that direct infringement does not require knowledge by the infringer that the invention is prohibited, nor does it require that the infringer intentionally perform the act. All that is required for direct infringement is the act.

Active inducement to infringe occurs when someone induces another to infringe. If there is no direct infringement, there cannot be an active inducement to infringe, no matter how hard someone tries to induce infringement. Of course, there could be other legal issues in this case.

Contributory infringement occurs when a component of a patented invention is sold or offered for sale in the United States or imported into the United States by a party who is aware that the component is especially made or adapted for an infringing use. As with active inducement to infringe, there cannot be any contributory infringement unless there is direct infringement by some party. Note that because use must occur within the United States, in an Internet-related patent, there may be no infringement where either a server or a client outside the United States performs some of the elements of a patent claim.

Doctrine of Equivalents

Under the *doctrine of equivalents*, a patent claim may be infringed even if the accused device does not literally infringe the claim, but the differences between the claims of the patent and the accused device are insubstantial. This means that the accused product can infringe a patent's claims if it performs the same function to achieve the same result in substantially the same way as the patent claim.

Prosecution history estoppel, however, may limit the scope of equivalents of a patent. Prosecution history estoppel applies when an applicant amends the patent claims to overcome an examiner's rejection or makes arguments during patent prosecution that help interpret the claims. After amending the claims, the applicant cannot recapture that which was given up or surrendered by narrowing the scope of the patent claim, and the applicant is estopped from claiming that he or she could not have reasonably been expected to have drafted a claim that would have literally encompassed the alleged equivalent (see *Festo Corporation v. Shoketsu Kinzoku Kogyo Kabushiki Co., Ltd*, 2002).

Remedies

When the owner of a patent believes another party is infringing on it, the owner typically seeks one of two things: (1) to have the accused party cease from engaging in the infringing acts and collect damages for past infringement and/or (2) to license the invention to the accused party in order to collect future royalties. An owner typically files a lawsuit seeking one or more remedies if he or she does not wish to license the invention, or if license negotiations break down, or to "persuade" the accused party to obtain a license. The patent owner can seek an injunction against the accused party, wherein the court can order a cessation of the infringing act. A court can also award monetary damages to compensate the owner for the infringement. These damages can be the patentee's lost profits due to lost sales or can be a reasonable royalty for the use of the invention and may include interest and other costs, if the court so decides. A court may increase these monetary damages up to three times where willful infringement is found. In exceptional cases, a court may award attorney fees for either party, whichever prevails.

Defending Against an Accusation of Infringement

There are two main ways a party accused of infringement can avoid liability: the party can assert that (1) its product does not infringe the patent(s) in question or that (2) the patent in question is invalid of when forceable, based on any one of a number of reasons (i.e., lack of novelty, obviousness, incorrect inventorship, inequiteble conduct, etc.). Issuance of a patent by the USPTO creates a presumption of validity of the patent. Nonetheless, a court may rule, based on the patent itself, the prosecution history of the patent application, and/or new evidence, that the patent is not valid. Generally speaking, damages cannot be obtained for infringements that occurred more than 6 years before the filing of the suit.

Independent of the statutory time frame, an infringement suit may be barred by *laches*; for example, if the patent owner deliberately delayed bringing the suit for an unreasonable time, knowing that the delay would work to the detriment of the accused infringer. In 2002, the CAFC confirmed the existence of *prosecution laches*, in which an unreasonable delay during prosecution of the application, together with harm to the other party caused by the delay, can result in unenforceability of a patent (*Symbol Technologies, Inc. al. v. Lemelson Medical, Education & Research Foundation, Limited Partnership*, 2002).

Court Jurisdiction in Patent Cases

Because patent law is federal law (as opposed to state law), federal courts have jurisdiction over all patent-related cases. Furthermore, although there are many federal courts of appeal, Congress, in seeking to establish a single interpretation of the patent laws, established the Court of Appeals for the Federal Circuit (CAFC) to hear all patent-related appeals (but see the discussion below of *Holmes Group, Inc.*).

Typically, a three-judge panel hears and decides an appealed case. On occasion, that decision may be appealed. One of the parties may ask for an *en banc* rehearing in which all or most of the judges from the CAFC rehear the case. If a party is not satisfied with the final ruling, it may appeal to the U.S. Supreme Court. However, very few patent cases are ever heard by the Supreme Court, typically 1 or 2 a year, if that.

One case that was heard by the Supreme Court recently was *Holmes Group, Inc. v. Vornado Air Circulation Systems, Inc.* (2002). In this case, Holmes filed a complaint seeking a declaratory judgment that its products did not infringe Vornado's *trade dress*. Trade dress is another form of protection that does not involve patents. Although the original complaint did not involve patents, Vornado filed a counterclaim alleging patent infringement. After an appeal to and decision by the CAFC, the Supreme Court heard the case.

The Supreme Court ruled that the CAFC does not have jurisdiction over a case that involves questions of patent law where the party bringing the suit did not, in its complaint, assert any patent law issues. Thus, although the CAFC was created in part to form a uniform interpretation of patent law across the country, where the original complaint does not assert any patent law issues, the CAFC may not have jurisdiction, even where patent issues are later asserted in a counterclaim.

Provisional Applications

A provisional application must have a written description and drawings sufficient to teach the invention to one skilled in the art. However, a provisional application is not examined and thus will never issue into a patent. No claims are required, although it may be preferable to include some claims for reasons beyond the scope of this article. A provisional application is relatively inexpensive to file and provides a priority date for any application filed within a year claiming the benefit of the provisional application, as to the matter disclosed in the provisional application. Note, however, that a provisional application is automatically abandoned 1 year from its filing date, unless it is converted into a nonprovisional application within that time. To receive the benefit of the filing date, within a year either a provisional application must be converted to a nonprovisional application, or more commonly a nonprovisional application must be filed. Although a provisional application establishes a priority date, the 20-year term of an issued patent claiming the benefit of the provisional application begins on the filing date of the first nonprovisional application in the priority chain.

NON-U.S. PATENTS

General Information

Patents are, of course, available outside the United States. One may file a first application almost anywhere in the world and follow up with applications in other countries within 1 year of filing the first application, maintaining the first application's filing date as a priority date.

As the USPTO's *Manual of Patent Examining Procedure* (MPEP) states, the right to rely on a foreign application is known as the *right of priority* in international patent law. The right of priority originated in a multilateral treaty of 1883, known as the Paris Convention for the Protection of Industrial Property, or more simply as the Paris Convention. The treaty is administered by the World Intellectual Property Organization (WIPO) at Geneva, Switzerland.

In addition to filing in individual countries, applications can be made in several regional areas, including the European Patent Convention (EPC; http://www.european-patent-office.org/index.en.php), the African Intellectual Property Organization (OAPI; http://www.oapi.wipo.net) made up of French-speaking African countries, the African Regional Industrial Property Organization (ARIPO; http://www.aripo.wipo.net) comprising English-speaking African countries, and the Eurasian Patent Organization (EAPO), (http://www.eapo.org/) which includes former republics of the Union of Soviet Socialist Republics.

For protection in EPC member countries, an application is filed at the European Patent Office (EPO) in Munich, Germany, designating some or all EPC member countries. Only one application needs to be filed and prosecuted to obtain coverage for any or all of the member countries. The application can be filed and prosecuted in English up to the point of issuance. A separate national patent is issued for each selected country, and each patent is subject to the patent laws of the country in which it is issued (and could ultimately be invalidated in some countries but not others). A separate European Community Patent may become available in the next few years, wherein an application filed under this regime would issue as a single community-wide patent, subject to a single jurisdiction with regard to various legal claims.

Patent Cooperation Treaty

Yet another alternative is to file an application according to the Patent Cooperation Treaty (PCT; see http://www.wipo.int/pct/en/). A PCT application serves as an application in each country that is designated. The process begins when an applicant from a member country files a PCT application in a designated receiving office (such as the USPTO). This begins the "international stage." The application is published approximately 18 months after the priority date. A search is performed and a search report sent to the applicant.

PCT procedures have undergone significant changes as recently as January 2004. For applications filed before January 1, 2004, at the request (i.e., a "Chapter II Demand") of the applicant, a preliminary examination may be performed and a written opinion is issued. This is similar to patent prosecution in the United States. However, the applicant typically has only one opportunity to respond to the written opinion and to amend the claims. Ultimately, an International Preliminary Examination Report is issued. Thirty months (31 months for some countries) from the priority date, or 20 months for some countries if the preliminary examination has not been requested, the application must enter the "national stage" in those countries or regions in which protection is sought. Prosecution of the application then continues independently in each country or region until the patent is granted.

For applications filed on or after January 1, 2004, the search authority issues, in addition to the search report, a written opinion, whether or not requested by the application in a Chapter II demand. Except in a very few countries, the national stage may be entered at 30 months regardless of whether a Chapter II Demand was made. If a Chapter II Demand is not made, the written opinion is transformed into a Chapter I "international preliminary report on patentability." For these applications, a Chapter II Demand must be made by the later of 22 months from the priority date or 3 months from the international search report.

Applications filed prior to January 1, 2004 had to designate, at filing, those countries or regions from which the applicant might later elect to enter into the national stage. Although many applicants often designated all countries just to be safe (after paying for a certain number of designated countries, the rest were free), for applications filed on or after January 1, 2004, all countries and regions are designated automatically unless expressly excluded.

Filing patent applications in multiple jurisdictions can be very expensive. To keep costs down, applicants typically file only in those jurisdictions where the invention is likely to be used most frequently and where meaningful enforcement can be achieved. A PCT application enables an applicant, for a relatively low cost, to delay for up to 30 months (31 months in some cases) both the designation of particular countries or regional jurisdictions and the costs of entering in those countries and regions.

Other Considerations

Although many procedures and rights are similar in various countries and regions, there are differences, some of which may be somewhat significant. It is not the intent of this chapter to cover the particulars of the patent laws and procedures of every nation. The number of countries is too numerous, and laws and procedures are always changing. Nevertheless, it is instructive to discuss some details to give an idea of the subtle and not-so-subtle differences among countries or regional organizations. Thus, although this section does not provide a comprehensive comparison of patent procedures and rights throughout the world, it offers an instructive examination of several different aspects employed around the world.

Although novelty, nonobviousness, and usefulness form the cornerstone in obtaining a U.S. patent for an invention, in most of the rest of the world, the requirements are stated differently. For example, a claim in a PCT application must be novel, involve an "inventive step," and be "industrially applicable."

A few countries, such as Australia, Canada, Colombia, and the United States, provide a 1-year grace period after publication of a document describing an invention during which an application for the invention may be filed. In most other countries, such a disclosure before the filing of an application is an absolute bar to obtaining a patent.

Another difference is that in the United States, when two inventors claim to have invented the invention independently, the patent is awarded to the first to invent (with some caveats). Of course, the precise instance of invention may be difficult to discern and to prove, leading to a complicated procedure known as an interference proceedings. The rest of the world follows a "first-to-file" policy, in which a patent for an invention is awarded to the first applicant to file, regardless of who invented it first.

In the United States, a computer program is patentable if it produces a "useful, concrete, and tangible result," as specified in the State Street ruling. However, in many foreign countries, software per se is explicitly barred from being patentable. Nonetheless, "thousands of patents for computer-implemented inventions have been granted by the European Patent Office (EPO) and by national patent offices," according to the Commission of the European Communities (2002).

Another notable difference is that in the United States the applicants must be the inventors (though they can assign their rights), whereas in other countries, applicants may be either the inventor or the assignee, which can be an individual or a corporation.

In the United States, examination of a patent application by an examiner is automatic. However, in many other countries, examination must be requested within some time period from the filing date. For example, in Japan, the examination must be requested within 3 years for patent applications filed on or after October 1, 2001. For applications filed before October 1, 2001, the request must be made within 7 years. In Canada, a request for examination must be filed within 5 years.

Before filing a foreign application, a foreign filing license is required for any invention *invented* in the United States, even by a non-U.S. citizen. Filing a "foreign" application without a foreign filing license could lead to invalidation or unenforceability of a patent. Italy similar requirements, although many other countries do not.

Patent prosecution procedures for the EPO are governed by the European Patent Convention (EPC; see http://www.european-patent-office.org/legal/epc/index.html). There are currently 31 member countries of the EPO and 5 "extension" countries that are expected to become members. About 18 months after the priority date, an application is published or "laid open" to public inspection. A prior art search is performed and a search report is generated, in which an examiner may cite references that show that certain claims are either not novel or do not have an inventive step (i.e., the claims are obvious in view of the prior art). The search report is typically published along with the application. (If the application was originally filed as a PCT application and the search report was performed by the EPO, then a second search is not performed.) Within 6 months of the search report, the applicant must file a request for examination.

In the United States, during patent prosecution, claims can usually be broadened or new broader claims added in an amendment. It is usually sufficient that the narrower (prebroadening) claims are supported in the specification. In the EPO, in contrast, claims typically cannot be broadened unless the claimed (broader) invention is specifically described in the specification.

EPO applications can be very expensive as the number of claims exceeds 10. Typically only one of each type of independent claim (e.g., apparatus, method) is allowed.

Types of Patent Applications

In foreign countries, the term "divisional" application covers both divisional applications and continuations. If the parent application is an innovation patent, a divisional application can be filed as either an innovation patent or as a standard patent. Australia provides for "patents of addition" for improvements and modifications to an invention (somewhat akin to U.S. CIPs) and for divisionals.

Some countries have equivalents to U.S. provisional applications. For example, in Great Britain and Canada, one can file an "informal" application without claims. Such an informal application acts, as does a U.S. provisional application, to preserve the priority date. However, the informal application is not provisional in that claims must be added within 1 year to formalize the application. Australia, in contrast, provides for a "provisional" application that must be followed within 12 months by either a "complete" or international (PCT) application. New Zealand also provides for a provisional application, with 12 months to file a regular application or up to 15 months with a 3-month extension.

Time Limits in Patent Prosecution

In both the EPO and USPTO, there is no time limit to the prosecution process, and prosecution can theoretically last for a very long time. Certain countries, however, do impose limits. For example, Great Britain requires that an application be put in order within 4-1/2 years of the priority date. At most, a 1-month extension is available. This process includes the PCT international stage and the EPO prosecution if any.

Employed Inventor Laws and Shoprights

In the United States, absent agreement otherwise, an employer has a nonexclusive, nontransferable right to use an employee's patented invention for its own use if the employee used the employer's materials or facility to develop the invention. Such rights are known as *shoprights*. Conversely, some countries, such as Germany and Japan, have "employed inventor laws." Under such laws, if an employer fails to file an application for an invention within a certain time frame, the employee can file an application in his or her own name. To protect themselves in such cases, employers may file petty patents.

Provisional Rights

Though not necessarily called by that term, many countries provide the equivalent of U.S. provisional rights. For example, in Canada, after the granting of a patent, a patentee may be entitled to reasonable compensation for infringement occurring in Canada as of the date the application was laid open.

Compulsory Licenses and U.S. March-in Rights

According to 35 U.S.C. § 203 (*march-in rights*), a federal agency that has funded development of an invention to which a small business or nonprofit organization has acquired patent rights has the right to require a contractor, an assignee, or exclusive licensee of the invention to grant a license in any field of use.

In the United States, state and federal governments and their agencies are immune from certain types of suits for infringement under the doctrine of sovereign immunity. Essentially, states may be enjoined, but not sued for damages. The federal government may be sued for a "reasonable royalty" before the U.S. Court of Federal Claims pursuant to its limited waiver of sovereignty embodied in 28 U.S.C. § 1498. Most other countries apply at least some form of sovereign immunity.

In many foreign countries, a patented invention must be manufactured or otherwise worked or exploited in that country within a certain period, typically 3 years, or the patent could be invalidated; alternatively, a compulsory license may be granted. In Canada, a compulsory license may be granted to remedy certain abuses of patent rights. Such abuses, which are beyond the scope of this article, cannot be considered until 3 years after the grant.

CONCLUSION

Patents can be valuable assets for any business, large or small, or they can be a waste of money. In return for disclosing the invention, the patentee is granted a limited term (typically 20 years from filing) in which the competition cannot use the patented device or method. The competition therefore must research and develop noninfringing alternatives, a process that could be costly, timely, and in some cases, even futile, therein giving the patentee a substantial advantage. Alternatively, the patentee may choose to license the patented technology in return for a royalty or some other consideration. A patent does not give the owner the right to practice the invention.

GLOSSARY

Claim The part of a patent that defines the actual intellectual property protected by the patent; that is, the inventive subject matter protected by the patent.

Dependent Claim A patent claim that incorporates by reference the limitations of another patent claim. Such a claim typically begins with language such as, "The device of Claim X, further comprising . . . ," which has the effect of incorporating by reference the limitations of Claim X.

Doctrine of Claim Differentiation A doctrine under which claims of a patent are presumptively of different scope, so that if a dependent claim includes a narrowing definition of some limitation of a base claim, then the base claim is presumed to encompass not only the narrow definition but other embodiments as well.

Doctrine of Equivalents A doctrine by which, even if a device or process does not exactly match every limitation of a patent's claim, the device may still infringe the patent if the differences are, to a "person of ordinary skill in the art," insubstantial (as determined by a judge or jury during an infringement hearing).

Element Although "element" and "limitation" are sometimes used interchangeably, the term "element" is used more frequently by the courts to refer to aspects of an allegedly infringing device or method. In an infringement case, the elements of the alleged infringing device or method are compared with the claim limitations of the patent allegedly being infringed. Note, however, that the U.S. statute (35 U.S.C. § 112) refers to both an "element in a claim" (sixth paragraph) and "limitations of [a] claim" (fourth and fifth paragraphs).

Independent claim A patent claim that does not incorporate any other patent claim by reference.

Infringement When a device or method has all of the limitations of a claim (which may be interpreted differently under the patent laws of individual countries), the device or method is said to infringe the claim. Various remedies may be available to the owner of the infringed patent.

Laches An equitable principle whereby a party is estopped (not allowed) from bringing a lawsuit after an unreasonable or unexplained delay that has had a detrimental effect on the party being sued.

Limitation A claim limitation is a part of a claim that defines a particular aspect of the invention (i.e., an aspect of the invention that must be practiced if the invention is to be infringed). Every claim has at least one limitation, and most claims have two or more limitations.

Means plus function A particular claim limitation may be written in "means plus function" language, wherein the limitation is recited as a means or a step for performing a specified function, without reciting the particular structure, material, or acts, which are thus construed to be those described in the specification (and equivalents). "Means plus function" claim limitations are specifically authorized by U.S. statute. In some countries, "omnibus" claims serve a similar purpose.

Nonobvious One of the basic requirements in obtaining a patent is that the invention be nonobvious to one of ordinary skill in the particular art concerned, in view of the known (prior) art.

Novelty One of the basic requirements in obtaining a patent is that the invention be novel. Legally, in the United States, this means that a claim may be barred if any of the conditions stated in 35 U.S.C. § 102 hold true; that is, a description has been published anywhere in the world, the invention has been sold or offered for sale or otherwise placed in the public domain,etc. Similar conditions apply in other countries; however, certain grace periods apply in some countries for certain types of prior disclosure.

Patent A grant that gives the holder of a patent certain rights to exclude others from practicing, (i.e., making), using, selling, offering for sale, importing, etc., a claimed invention, in the country in which the patent has been granted and for the term during which the patent is valid.

PCT The Patent Cooperation Treaty under which an applicant of a member country can file a single international patent application that may designate one, many, or all of the member countries. The PCT does not provide for the granting of patents; that occurs at the "national stage."

Prior art The accumulated knowledge of those skilled in the particular art concerned, which can bar issuance of a patent if the claims are not novel or nonobvious in view of the prior art.

Prosecution The process of obtaining a patent, from the filing of an application to the issuance of the patent (or abandonment of the application).

Prosecution laches An equitable principle in which unreasonable delay during prosecution of a patent application, together with harm to another party caused by the delay, can result in unenforceability of the issued patent.

Provisional application A particular type of patent application that is never examined but serves to provide a priority date for a future, nonprovisional application, subject to the requirement that the provisional application describes the invention fully.

Provisional rights The rights of a patent owner to a reasonable royalty for an infringing device or method, covering the period between publication of a patent application and the granting of the patent with substantially identical claims as those in the published application.

Right of priority The right to rely on another application.

U.S. Patent and Trademark Office (USPTO) The U.S. governmental agency authorized to issue patents, as well as to register trademarks (see Trademark Law in this handbook).

CROSS REFERENCES

See *Copyright Law; Legal, Social and Ethical Issues of the Internet; The Legal Implications of Information Security: Regulatory Compliance and Liability; Trademark Law and the Internet.*

REFERENCES

Commission of the European Communities (2002). *Proposal for a directive of the European Parliament and of the Council on the Patentability of Computer-implemented Inventions*. Retrieved from http://europa.eu.int/comm/internal_market/en/indprop/comp/com02-92en.pdf

Diamond v. Chakrabarty, 1980

Festo Corporation v. Shoketsu Kinzoku Kogyo Kabushiki Co., Ltd., 535 U.S. 722 (2002).

Holmes Group, Inc. v. Vornado Air Circulation Systems, Inc., 535 U.S. 826 (2002).

J.E.M. AG Supply Inc, dba Farm Advantage, Inc., et al. v. Pioneer Hi-Bred International, Inc., 1996

Kraft Foods, Inc. v. Int'l Trading Co., 2000

Newman v. Quigg (1989)

State Street Bank & Trust Co. v. Signature Financial Group, Inc. (1998). Retrieved from http://www.ll.georgetown.edu/Fed-Ct/Circuit/fed/opinions/97-1327.html

Symbol Technologies, Inc. al. v. Lemelson Medical, Education & Research Foundation, Limited Partnership, 2002

U.S. Patent and Trademark Office. (2000, June 30). *U.S. Patent Classification System—Classification definitions*. Retrieved from http://www.uspto.gov/web/offices/ac/ido/oeip/taf/def/705.htm

FURTHER READING

Albert, G. P., Jr. et al. (1999). *Intellectual property law in cyberspace*. Washington, DC: BNA Books.

Chisum, D. (2002). *Chisum on patents, a treatise on the law of patentability, validity and infringement*. New York: M. Bender. Available at LexisNexis.com

Chisum, D., Nard, C., Schwartz, H., Newman, P., & Kieff, F. S. (2004). *Principles of patent law* (3rd ed.). New York: Foundation Press.

Donner, I. H. (1999). *Patent prosecution, practice & procedure before the U.S. Patent Office* (2nd ed.). Washington, DC: BNA Books.

Faber, R. C. *Landis on mechanics of patent claim drafting* (4th ed.). New York: Practicing Law Institute.

Harmon, R. L. (2001). *Patents and the Federal Circuit* (5th ed.). Washington, DC: BNA Books.

Miller, A. R., & Davis, M. H. (1990). *Intellectual property—Patents, trademarks and copyright in a nutshell*. St. Paul, MN: West Publishing Co.

Stobbs, G. A. (1995). *Software patents*. New York: John Wiley & Sons.

Web sites

American Bar Association: http://www.abanet.org/intelprop/comm106/106general.html

American Intellectual Property Law Association: http://www.aipla.org/

CAFC opinions may be found at:

http://www.law.emory.edu/fedcircuit/ (Emory University)

http://www.ll.georgetown.edu/federal/judicial/cafed.cfm (Georgetown University)

http://www.fedcir.gov/ (CAFC)

Cornell University: http://www.law.cornell.edu/topics/patent.html

Findlaw: http://www.findlaw.com/

Intellectual Property Owners Association http://www.ipo.org

Intellectual Property Today: http://www.iptoday.com/

IPWatchdog.com: http://www.ipwatchdog.com/patent.html

Nolo: http://www.nolo.com/

PatentLawLinks.com: http://www.patentlawlinks.com/

U.S. Patent and Trademark Office: http://www.uspto.gov/

WIPO Collection of Laws For Electronic Access (CLEA): http://www.wipo.int/clea/en/index_netscape.jsp

U.S. Supreme Court: http://www.supremecourtus.gov/

Copyright Law

Randy Canis, *Greensfelder, Hemker & Gale, P.C.*

COPYRIGHT FUNDAMENTALS

Introduction

This chapter is meant to provide readers with a fundamental understanding of the core concepts of U.S. copyright law as they apply to the digital realm; these concepts are expanded further in the chapter in this handbook, The Digital Millennium Copyright Act. As copyright law is complex and ever changing, this chapter should be used for informational purposes only. It should not be relied upon as a source of legal advice; instead the reader should contact a lawyer who practices in the field of copyright law to determine whether the particular issues of concern are lawful and/or appropriate given the current state of the law.

Copyright as Intellectual Property

Intellectual property rights include trademarks, copyrights, patents, and trade secrets. These intellectual property rights share a common characteristic in that the rights granted are intangible; there is no physical embodiment of such rights that can be provided to another to transfer ownership of these rights. For example, a plastic chair is a physical asset and is personal property, whereas the method of manufacturing and assembling the chair is intellectual property. Rights in intellectual property are secured by adherence to various legal mechanisms that have been adopted and used nationwide since the ratification of the Constitution. However, the United States was not the first country to recognize intellectual property rights, and at present the vast majority of foreign countries provide similar and complementary protection schemes.

The desire for intellectual property protection in the United States originated during the Constitutional Conventions. The Founding Fathers debated to what extent various types of monopolies should be permitted in their new nation. They decided to distance themselves from some of the practices of England, one of which was the monarchy's practice of granting valuable monopolies to produce certain well-known items throughout the British Empire. Such monopolies did not encourage the development of new technologies or provide enhanced rights to the citizenry; instead, they provided certain select citizens who were friends of the monarchy with financial windfalls by giving them protection from competition. England altered some of its long-standing monopolistic practices in 1710 when Parliament enacted the Statute of Anne. This statute was intended to limit the perpetual rights of publishers to a fixed number of years, after which other publishers could produce the work.

The Founding Fathers ultimately agreed that Congress should have the authority to promulgate legislation to protect works and inventions. Article I, Section 8, Clause 8 of the U.S. Constitution provides that "Congress shall have Power . . . [t]o promote the Progress of Science and useful Arts, by securing for limited Times to Authors and Inventors the exclusive Right to their respective Writings and Discoveries." This clause provided Congress with a constitutional basis for the development of federal copyright and patent law. The Founding Fathers intended these rights to spur development of new ideas and creations by providing creators with a financial incentive to make such developments. However, these rights are not without limitation in that ultimately consumers must benefit from the provision of the additional rights to the authors and inventors. The balance between the right of authors and inventors to profit and the consumers to receive a benefit as a result of the right is a key element that Congress considers when altering the scope of protection for creations and inventions.

Copyright law fits in the scheme of intellectual property rights by enabling authors to protect their particular manner of expressing an idea. Examples of works in the digital realm that are subject to copyright protection include digital photos, Web sites, and e-books. Patent law, the intellectual property scheme most similar to copyright law, protects the underlying applied idea irrespective of its expression in a particular embodiment. Examples of various inventions that are subject to patent protection include Internet shopping carts, methods of processing digital images, and microprocessor improvements.

Trademark law enables consumers to identify and distinguish the products and services offered from one source to that offered by another and protects against consumer confusion by use of a device, such as a mark. Examples of marks that are subject to trademark protection include COCA-COLA® soft drink, YAHOO!® Internet services, and EXPRESS PERSONNEL SERVICES® employment and personnel services. Trade secret law enables persons to protect information from being taken without authorization so long as access to the information is limited. Examples of information that is subject to trade secret protection include customer lists, the names of key employees, and new product development information that has not yet been made public.

Copyright law has significantly evolved since the passage of the first Congressional set of copyright laws in 1790. Congress passed substantial revisions to the Copyright Act in 1831, 1870, 1909, 1976, and 1998 to reflect technological advances and changes in the scope of protection. Copyright law continues to adapt to the changing environment of computers and the Internet and is likely to undergo further development over the coming years as a result. Nonetheless, this chapter should provide a strong basis for understanding the basic concepts of copyright law, as well as the current state of the law.

Subject Matter of Copyright

Before the Copyright Act of 1976, copyright protection for a particular work was based on when the author first made his or her work available to the public by publishing it. Prior to publishing, the work was subject to a so-called common law copyright under the Copyright Act of 1909. By refusing to publish, the author had unlimited rights at common law to control the work so as to prevent others from utilizing it without permission. After publishing, the common law copyright was extinguished, and the statutory copyright (i.e., under the 1909 Act) governed the copyright rights in the work to which the author was entitled. However, under the 1976 Act copyright protection begins upon fixation in a tangible form as opposed to publishing. Despite the change in law, the 1909 Act is still relevant because works that entered the public domain name before the effective date of the 1976 Act (i.e., January 1, 1978) may not be protected thereunder.

COPYRIGHT REQUIREMENTS

Introduction

For an author to have a valid copyright in a particular work, the work must (1) be original, (2) remain fixed in a tangible medium of expression, and (3) have involved a minimum degree of creativity. For example, if the students in a classroom each drew a representation of the St. Louis Arch on a piece of paper, each would have a copyright in their respective drawings regardless of their artistic abilities. The aforementioned requirements for having a valid copyright are explained in greater detail in the sections below.

Originality

Copyright protection under the 1976 Act extends to original works of authorship that are fixed in a tangible medium of expression. To be protected, the creation must be an original work of the author, originating from the author claiming copyright, and not copied from another source.

There are several significant aspects of the originality requirement. Artistic merit is irrelevant to the ability to copyright the work. Without such a limitation, only works that were judged to have merit (by the Register of Copyrights) would be imbued with protection, and other such works deemed unworthy would leave the author with no such rights. This limitation would thereby encourage various types of works while discouraging others that could be unrecognized masterpieces or otherwise significant to a smaller class of people. Ultimately, appointing a person or an agency to distinguish "good works" from "bad works" is unnecessary because the public buys or supports what it likes and ignores that which it does not. As the Supreme Court stated in *Bleistein v. Donaldson Lithographing Co.* (1903),

> It would be a dangerous undertaking for persons trained only to the law to constitute themselves final judges of the worth of pictorial illustrations, outside of the narrowest and most obvious limits. At the one extreme some works of genius would be sure to miss appreciation. Their very novelty would make them repulsive until the public had learned the new language in which their author spoke. It may be more than doubted, for instance, whether the etchings of Goya or the paintings of Manet would have been sure of protection when

> seen for the first time. At the other end, copyright would be denied to pictures which appealed to a public less educated than the judge. Yet if they command the interest of any public, they have a commercial value—it would be bold to say that they have not an aesthetic and educational value—and the taste of any public is not to be treated with contempt. It is an ultimate fact for the moment, whatever may be our hopes for a change. That these pictures had their worth and their success is sufficiently shown by the desire to reproduce them without regard to the plaintiffs' rights.

In addition, the underlying idea of the work is not subject to copyright protection. Copyright law does not provide a monopoly on an idea (e.g., the process of formatting a digital image), but rather on the expression of that idea by a particular author (e.g., the way a programmer implements his or her process of formatting a digital image). Accordingly, two different authors could write stories about the friendship and similarities between a computer scientist who becomes a patent attorney and his friend who is an ambitious and famous rock drummer, and each author would be entitled separately to copyright protection for his or her stories.

Works must have some minimal degree of creativity to be original, such that the author must contribute something to the work for it to be entitled to a copyright. The author must demonstrate substantial creative input or variation; the work must be more than a trivial (i.e., insubstantial) variation or a mere reproduction of prior works. Thus, a painter who makes a hand-painted reproduction of a prior painter's work would not be entitled to copyright protection; however, a second painter's drawing of the same subject matter using different lighting, different materials, and a different view would be entitled to copyright protection. Works that fail to have the minimal degree of creativity are denied copyright protection.

Originality is not equivalent to the novelty requirement of patent law, as it is a lower standard in which the author must only create the work independently. The ideas and themes contained in a particular work may have appeared in earlier works, but so long as the work originates with the author, copyright protection is still available. For example, consider how many movies include police officers performing the good cop/bad cop scenario. None of these movies can claim the exclusive rights to such a scenario and limit the others' expression of the same. In contrast, a first entity can infringe a second entity's patent even if the first entity was not aware of the second entity's patent and had created invention independently. The comparison of the two standards frequently arises, because computer software was generally not considered patentable until the State Street Bank case as discussed in the chapter, Patent Law, found elsewhere in this handbook.

With respect to computer software and other works that may use both copyright and patent law for protection, a copyright is more likely to be found valid in a court case than a patent because of the types of challenges available to third parties. With copyright law, copying another's work is needed to demonstrate copyright infringement, whereas such information is not needed in patent law. However, the scope of protection with copyright is less in that it only protects against copying and not the underlying idea. Accordingly, companies typically seek both patent and copyright protection on their computer software.

Works of Authorship

Works of authorship define the type of "writings," as used in the Constitution, for which copyright protection is available. Congress has broadly interpreted "writings" to define these categories for works of authorship: (1) literary works; (2) musical works, including any accompanying words; (3) dramatic works, including any accompanying music; (4) pantomimes and choreographic works; (5) pictorial, graphic, and sculptural works; (6) motion pictures and other audiovisual works; (7) sound recordings; and (8) architectural works. These categories were meant by Congress to be nonexclusive so as to encompass new technologies, which include computer software and the "look and feel" of a Web site.

Unprotectible Works

Certain types of work are not subject to copyright protection because protection of those works would prevent others from using the underlying idea. To the extent that the expression cannot be delivered in another author's form, the expression is unprotectible because the underlying idea has merged with the expression. Accordingly, if there was only one way to implement an online shopping cart system, no one could claim exclusive copyright rights to such an implementation of the system, but yet the same system could be subject to patent rights. In addition, copyright protection does not extend to ideas, procedures, processes, systems, operational methods, concepts, principles, or discoveries, but rather is limited to the manner in which the creation is expressed by the author.

Works consisting of words and short phrases, such as names, titles, and slogans; familiar symbols or designs, mere variations of typographic ornamentation, lettering or coloring; and the mere listing of ingredients or contents are not subject to copyright law. For example, a list of ingredients for chocolate chip cookie mix is unprotectible. However, a book of recipes for various kinds of chocolate chip cookies may be entitled to protection as a compilation, and a particular recipe could also be subject to trade secret protection. Certain words and short phrases may still be subject to trademark protection. For example, LET'S GET READY TO RUMBLE® is a registered service mark used by Michael Buffer to promote various boxing matches.

Works that consist entirely of public domain information are also not protectible, including standard calendars, height and weight charts, tape measures and rulers, schedules of sporting events, and lists or tables taken from public documents or other common sources. Such works fail to demonstrate the more than trivial level of creativity that is necessary for copyright protection. However, even though a map consists of public information, the generation of such a map involves substantial selection and arrangement and is therefore eligible for copyright protection. For example, Internet users cannot utilize a map generated from Yahoo! or Mapquest.com in their Web site without properly obtaining a license from these companies by following the terms and conditions posted on their respective Web sites.

Other works that are not subject to copyright include typefaces, ideas, plans, methods, systems, or devices, as distinguished from the particular manner in which they are expressed or described in a writing. Thus, a translation of an existing work to another format or another language is ineligible for copyright protection as a work of a new author, whereas copying the underlying idea but utilizing new expression is eligible for such protection. However, the utilitarian aspects of such creations are protectible under patent law, such as a system for communicating digital information over a network.

Blank forms, such as time cards, graph paper, account books, diaries, bank checks, scorecards, address books, report forms, order forms, and the like, which are designed for recording information and do not in themselves convey information, are also not subject to copyright protection. The underlying facts and the methods of recording information are not protectible, but the textual information that accompanies the blank forms if significant enough may have enough originality and creativity to make the work subject to copyright protection.

Fixation

Works must be fixed in a tangible medium of expression to be protected under the Copyright Act. Without the fixation requirement, it would be difficult to determine what a particular author considered to be his or her work. In addition, the Copyright Office would be unable to review and consider whether a work should be entitled to a copyright registration. Material objects that qualify as media of expression include canvas, paper, audio and video cassettes, DVDs, CDs, and computer disk drives.

Works must be embodied in a tangible form that is "sufficiently permanent or stable to permit it to be perceived, reproduced, or otherwise communicated for a period of more than transitory duration." Accordingly, a digital image that is electronically transmitted over a computer network and is never retained in a storage medium is not subject to copyright protection. The requirement for fixation is met when the work can either be perceived directly or with the aid of a machine or other device. Unfixed works, such as extemporaneous utterances, unchoreographed dance performances, and unwritten jazz and musical performances, are all subject to common law copyright and are not covered under the federal Copyright Act because they do not meet the fixation requirement. However, when these works are recorded they may then be eligible for copyright.

TERM OF COPYRIGHT

Background of Term

The author and the author's heirs enjoy a period of exclusivity in which they can reap the financial rewards from the author's creation of the work. However, the length of the copyright per the Constitution is only for a "limited" time. Upon expiration of the term of the copyright, the work is dedicated to the public, which is then free to use it without authorization from or compensation to the author.

Term Under the 1909 Act

Under the 1909 Act, the duration of the copyright for published works was 28 years, with a single 28-year renewal term, for a maximum of 56 years. The duration under the 1909 Act was set with the intention that the author would be able to have exclusive rights to the work during his or her lifetime. Works that were not published were subject to common law copyright, and the authors (and the author's heirs) could indefinitely protect the work from copying by refusing to publish the work. If the work was ultimately published, its limited period of protection was the aforementioned two terms.

Term Under the 1976 Act

Since the adoption of the 1976 Act, works that are fixed in a medium of expression are protectible under statutory copyright, regardless of whether the work is published or unpublished. The term for such works under the 1976 Act was for the life of the author plus 50 years; for anonymous and pseudonymous works and for works made for hire the term was for 75 years from publication or 100 years from creation, whichever expired first. Accordingly, the term under the 1976 Act was meant to enable the author to have exclusive rights during his or her lifetime and for the next generation. However, the term was extended by Congress in 1988, as described below.

Sonny Bono Copyright Term Extension Act of 1998

The passage of the Sonny Bono Copyright Term Extension Act of 1998 (the Sonny Bono Amendment) extended the terms in the 1976 Act by 20 years, not only for newly created works but also for works already subject to the previous terms. Upon passage, critics complained that the Sonny Bono Amendment's retroactive effect would effectively prevent a plethora of works from entering the public domain name for an additional 20 years.

The Sonny Bono Amendment was challenged in a series of court decisions resulting in the 2003 Supreme Court case of *Eldred v. Ashcroft*. In this case, the petitioner asserted that the Sonny Bono Amendment was unconstitutional under the Copyright Clause because it extended the duration of the copyright for preexisting works, as opposed to only newly created works. The Court ruled that the amendment was constitutional because (1) the precise duration of a federal copyright has never been fixed at the time of the initial grant, (2) Congress has routinely applied new definitions or adjustments of the copyright term to both future works and existing works not yet in the public domain, and (3) the amendment did not create a perpetual copyright.

The effect on consumers of this ruling is that few works will enter into the public domain for the next 20 years, thereby preventing people such as Eldred from making such works available over the Internet for free. Copyright owners assert that consumers will receive additional benefits because copyright owners are able to reap financial rewards over a longer time period. Despite the courts' allowance of the Sonny Bono Amendment to stand, unlimited extensions for preexisting works still would appear to violate the Constitutional mandate that protection for works only be awarded for a limited time.

FORMALITIES

Copyright Notice

The accession by the United States to the Berne Convention in 1989 removed the requirement that works must contain a notice of copyright. Works protected by copyright may now optionally contain a notice of the copyright on publicly distributed copies. When used, the Copyright Act dictates that the form of the notice comprise three elements: (1) the symbol © (the letter C in a circle), or the word "Copyright" or the abbreviation "Copr."; (2) the year of first publication of the work; and (3) the name of the owner of the copyright in the work. For example, the copyright notice used with the DVD movie, "The Usual Suspects," is © 1996 Polygram Video.

The copyright notice, if affixed, must be done so in a manner and location to provide a person with reasonable notice of the copyright. Although notice of the copyright is optional on works after the accession to the Berne Convention, its inclusion in a copyright infringement case where the defendant had access to the work effectively eliminates the defendant's innocent infringement defense as described in greater detail below. For works prior to the accession to the Berne Convention, the copyright can be lost if the notice was omitted and the omission was not properly cured. Accordingly, it behooves most authors to include copyright notices on their works. For example, the author of a particular Web site can place a suitable copyright notice at the bottom of each of the Web pages by using footers on every page.

Registration with the Copyright Office

To have a copyright in a work, it is not a prerequisite to register the copyright with the Copyright Office. Rather, copyright is established upon fixation in a tangible medium of expression so long as the underlying work is original. Registration of a copyright for a work may occur at any time. However, registration is a perquisite to obtaining statutory damages, putting third parties on constructive notice of the copyright registration, and having a *prima facie* presumption of validity of the copyright. Because damages are often difficult to prove in copyright infringement suit, the ability to recover statutory damages not only greatly benefits the plaintiff's case but also increases the likelihood of a favorable settlement.

The Copyright Office provides various forms to enable copyright owners to register their copyrights: form TM for nondramatic literary works, form PA for works of performing art, form SR for sound recording works, form VA for works of visual arts, and form SE for serial works, including newspapers, magazines, newsletters, annuals, and journals. All these forms are available for free download at the Copyright Office Web site at http://www.copyright.gov. Each form generally is a double-sided page and often includes the option of providing instructions on additional pages. Despite the apparently simplicity of the documents, issues including authorship and ownership of the work can often confuse a layperson and cause him or her to complete these forms incorrectly. The author urges that persons seeking to register their works first consult an attorney who practices in the field of copyright law prior to filling.

OWNERSHIP

General Ownership

Copyright ownership provides its owner with various exclusive rights as described in greater detail below. Ownership differs from a license, as a license may only provide its user with a limited right to use a particular copy in possession of the user; for example, the usage may be for a limited time, within a set geographical area, or in a certain manner. Ownership traditionally vests with the author or jointly among a group of authors, and assignment of copyright is possible.

Work Made for Hire

One of the fundamental issues in copyright law for companies is whether a worker is the author of a particular work that was created. Unlike patent law in which inventorship cannot be altered based on employment or agreements, authorship of a particular work may vest with another, depending on the nature of the relationship between the worker and the employer and whether an agreement governs the creation of the work. If a work is considered a *work made for hire*, the employer will be considered the actual author of the work instead of the employee who created the work. For example, the work made for hire issue frequently arises when companies hire outside developers to create a Web site or write code for a computer program on behalf of the company. When the company wants to modify the Web site or distribute the software program and the developer objects without the payment of additional fees, the company frequently learns that it did not have all rights that it had anticipated in the particular work. Companies often rely on the faulty logic that if they paid a lot of money for the work, then they must own all rights to it. However, that is not a legitimate basis for determining whether a work qualifies as a work made for hire.

A work made for hire is defined differently for employees and nonemployees (i.e., contractors). For an employee's work to be considered to be a work for hire, the work must be prepared within the scope of the employee's employment. For a nonemployee, the work must be (1) specially ordered or commissioned; (2) for use as a contribution to a collective work, a part of a motion picture or other audiovisual work, a translation, a supplementary work, a compilation, an instructional text, a test, answer material for a test, or an atlas; and (3) in a written instrument signed by the parties that states the work shall be considered a work made for hire.

With employees, the key question is whether the work is within the scope of employment. If so, the work is deemed authored by the employer, and the employer will have all exclusive rights associated with the work. If the work falls outside the scope of employment, the work is deemed authored by the employee, and the employer will simply have a license to use the particular embodiment of the work without the exclusive rights associated with the work. Under the 1909 Act, whether a worker was considered an employee was based on the traditional employment relationship. However, under the 1976 Act, the determination as to whether a worker is an employee was modified as discussed in *Cmty. for Creative Non-Violence v. Reid* (1989) below.

With nonemployees, the first issue is whether the work is specially ordered or commissioned. Thus, purchasing an "off the shelf" object at a store cannot be considered a work made for hire. The second issue is whether the work falls within the defined statutory classes, which include contributions to collective works, parts of a motion picture or other audiovisual work, translations, supplementary works, compilations, instructional texts, tests, answer material for tests, and atlases. If the work falls outside these defined classes, such as is the case with computer software, it cannot be considered a work made for hire. The third issue is whether there is a properly written agreement between the parties that the work shall be considered a work made for hire. Without such a written agreement, the work will fail to qualify as a work made for hire.

In *Cmty. for Creative Non-Violence v. Reid* (1989), the Supreme Court considered whether James Earl Reid, an artist, or the Community for Creative Non-Violence (CCNV), an organization that hired Reid to produce a sculpture, owned the copyright in a sculpture. Reid agreed to donate his services to create the sculpture, and CCNV paid for the materials. However, there was no written agreement between the parties, and copyright ownership was not discussed. When the parties disagreed on how the work should be preserved and presented, communication between the parties broke down, and a lawsuit ensued.

In this case, the Supreme Court acknowledged that the copyright in a work initially vests in the author or authors of a work, subject to the important work made for hire exception. This exception provides that "'the employer or other person for whom the work was prepared is considered the author' and owns the copyright, unless there is a written agreement to the contrary." Because a sculpture is not specifically listed within the class of specially commissioned works included in the definition of work made for hire, the Court first considered whether an employee within the scope of employment made the sculpture.

The Court held that the author is an employee under the common law understanding of agency law. The factors that the Court considered to support this ruling include "the hiring party's right to control the manner and means by which the product is accomplished[,]... the skill required; the source of the instrumentalities and tools; the location of the work; the duration of the relationship between the parties; whether the hiring party has the right to assign additional projects to the hired party; the extent of the hired party's discretion over when and how long to work; the method of payment; the hired party's role in hiring and paying assistants; whether the work is part of the regular business of the hiring party; whether the hiring party is in business; the provision of employee benefits; and the tax treatment of the hired party."

Despite the apparent definiteness that work made for hire may seem to provide, circumstances with workers change that could affect whether a particular worker is still considered an employee. In addition, there may be questions as to whether a particular work is within the scope of the employee's employment. Therefore, it is always a best practice to create an employment agreement that clearly defines the scope of the employee's employment and a fallback assignment clause that provides that works will be assigned to the employer if they fail to qualify as a work made for hire.

RIGHTS GRANTED

Exclusive Rights

The copyright laws of the United States grant the author of a copyrighted work certain exclusive rights in the work, including the right to (1) reproduce the copyrighted work in copies or phonorecords; (2) prepare derivative works based upon the copyright work; (3) distribute copies or phonorecords of the copyrighted work to the public; (4) publicly perform literary, musical, dramatic, and choreographic works, pantomimes, and motion pictures and other audiovisual works; (5) publicly display literary, musical, dramatic, and choreographic works, pantomimes, and pictorial, graphic and sculptural works, including individual images from a motion picture or other audiovisual work; and (6) publicly perform sound recordings by means of a digital audio transmission. Of the six rights, the first two are infringed by an act performed publicly or privately, whereas the remaining four are infringed only when occurring publicly.

The copyright owner can transfer or license these rights in full or in part to others. The language used to provide these rights to another should be unambiguous so that there is no dispute as to what rights are being transferred or licensed, and a transfer of copyright rights must be in writing to be valid. For example, a court found that a transfer of "all right, title and interest" to computer programs and software was not merely a license to use the software, but rather a transfer of the copyright embodied in the computer programs and software.

Public Performance

Under the Copyright Act, performing a work publicly means either to (1) perform or display it at a place open to the public or at any place where a substantial number of persons outside a normal circle of a family and its social acquaintances are gathered or (2) to transmit or otherwise communicate a performance or display of the work to a place previously specified or to the public, by means of any device or process, regardless of the place and time it is received by the public. Thus, the presentation of a movie at a movie theater and a performance of a song at a music club are both considered public performances. With respect to the Internet, a Web conference between two parties would not be considered a public performance, but a worldwide WEBEX presentation to clientele would be considered a public performance.

For-profit performances of works require a license from the copyright owner. Such performances include those for which an admission fee is charged or performances that enhance the related profit-making activity of the entity. Nonprofit performances also require a license unless the performance is exempted by the fair use doctrine or the public performance is exempted under the Copyright Act. The exempted performances include some teaching activities and religious assemblies when no admission is charged or when the profit is used for educational, religious, or charitable purposes, unless the public performance is objected to by prior written notice. Public performances occur in places that are open to the public or where a substantial number of persons outside the normal circle of family and social acquaintances are gathered.

The Copyright Act does, however, provide some limitations for certain types of performances that are not infringements of copyright. These performance include performance or display of a work by instructors or pupils in face-to-face meetings and in certain proscribed circumstances: such performances include digital transmissions between such persons, performance of a nondramatic literary or musical work or of a dramatico-musical work of a religious nature or display of a work in the course of services at a place of worship or other religious assembly, and performance of a nondramatic literary or musical work otherwise than in a transmission to the public without any purpose of direct or indirect commercial advantage and without payment of any fee in certain proscribed circumstances.

Public Display

Public display is the copyright owner's exclusive right to show other people the copyrighted work. The receipt of a fee is irrelevant to whether a party displaying the work constitutes a public display. An example of when the copyright owner's exclusive right to display a copyrighted work publicly is violated includes when Internet users are allowed to view copyrighted images from a Web site upon the payment of a fee without a license from the owner of the copyrighted image and when preview clips consisting exclusively of scenes taken from full-length copyrighted feature films are presented on a Web site.

Reproduction

Phonorecords are defined as material objects in which sounds, other than those accompanying a motion picture or other audiovisual work, are fixed by any method now known or later developed, and from which the sounds can be perceived, reproduced, or otherwise communicated, either directly or with the aid of a machine or device.

The exclusive right of reproduction allows the copyright owner to prevent others from reproducing the work in the form of a copy or phonorecord. Copies are defined broadly under the Copyright Act and include all material objects, excluding phonorecords, in which a work is fixed by any method now known or later developed and from which the work can be perceived, reproduced or otherwise communicated, either directly or with the aid of a machine or device. Copies include downloading reproduced thumbnail and full-sized images taken from an Internet newsgroup to a user's hard drive.

Distribution and the First Sale Doctrine

Copyright owners are provided with the exclusive right to distribute copies of phonorecords of their works, which includes posting a work on a Web site for download by Internet users. The distribution right is limited to the first transfer of ownership, because under the Copyright Act the ownership of the copyright is distinct from ownership of a material object in which the copyright is embodied per the First Sale Doctrine as described in greater detail below.

Under the *First Sale Doctrine*, the copyright owner's right to control distribution is exhausted by the first sale of each lawfully made copy. The owner of such a copy has the right of resale or transfer, and the copyright owner has no control over resale or transfer of a particular copy. Mere possession of the copyright object by rental, lease, loan, or otherwise is insufficient to trigger first sale rights. For example, as discussed in *Adobe Sys. v. One Stop Micro, Inc* (2000), a copyright owner does not forfeit the right of distribution by entering into a distribution agreement by which it licenses off-the-shelf software; the owner can therefore prevent an educational version of a software program from being resold as a full retail version.

TYPE OF WORK

Derivative Work

A copyright owner has the exclusive right to create or authorize the creation of a work based in part on his or her underlying work. A *derivative work* is a work based upon one or more preexisting works in which the original work is recast, transformed, or adapted. The derivative work copyright protects only new materials contributed by the author and does not affect or enlarge the scope, duration, ownership, or subsistence of any copyright protection in the preexisting material. Examples of various types of derivative works include translations, musical arrangements, dramatizations, fictionalizations, motion picture versions, sound recordings, art reproductions, abridgments, and condensations. Cases involving derivative works include copying and using specific functions from a preexisting computer software in a new software program, creating a descrambler to obtain access to otherwise protected video programming content by copying portions of the original access program, and utilizing portions of source code in a computer game to create a new computer game. In addition, a work consisting of editorial revisions, annotations, elaborations, or other modifications, which, as a whole, represent an original work of authorship, is a derivative work.

Joint Work

A *joint work* is a work prepared by two or more authors with the intention that their contributions be merged into inseparable or interdependent parts of a unitary whole and for which the intent to merge the work into a unitary whole must exist at the time of creation. The second author must contribute more than the suggestions of ideas and minor bits of expression, as each author's components must be independently copyrightable. The joint owners can independently exploit the work without consent of the other joint owners, but must account to the other joint owners for such exploitation. The duration of the copyright is the life of the last author to die plus 70 years.

Composite Work

A *composite work* is a work prepared by two or more authors without the intent to merge their contributions into a unitary whole. Each part of the composite work must be licensed and terminated separately, and each part has its own copyright duration.

Compilation

A *compilation* is a work formed by the collection and assembling of preexisting materials or of data that are selected, coordinated, or arranged in such a way that the resulting work as a whole constitutes an original work of authorship. Therefore, it is not the underlying materials or data that are protected by copyright, but rather the selection, coordination, or arrangement of the work that is entitled to a copyright. Thus, although a standard program call or database read is not subject to copyright protection, the series of such calls and reads in the context of a computer program may be subject to copyright protection for the work as a compilation.

In *Feist Publications, Inc. v. Rural Telephone Service Co., Inc.* (1991), the Supreme Court addressed whether a telephone directory was subject to copyright protection. Rural Telephone Service Company issues an annually updated telephone directory comprising both white pages and yellow pages for northwest Kansas. Feist Publications publishes telephone directories that cover a wider area. Both companies distribute their directories free of charge and compete vigorously for yellow page advertisements. Of further significance is that Rural Telephone had access to subscriber information pursuant to its monopoly and was required to issue a directory as part of its monopoly agreement; however, it refused to license the directory information to Feist Publications so that it could maintain a monopoly on yellow pages listings. Feist Publications then copied the listings without authorization from Rural Telephone and a lawsuit ensued.

In its decision, the Supreme Court balanced the tensions between the two established propositions of the law that "facts are not copyrightable [and that] ... that compilations of facts generally are." The Court found that the facts did not meet the requisite level of originality because the "first person to find and report a particular fact has not created the fact; he or she has merely discovered its existence." The Court considered that the author of a compilation "chooses which facts to include, in what order to place them, and how to arrange the collected data so that they may be used effectively by readers." The Court then held that the copyright protection of the compilation only extended to the components of the work that are original to the author and that others were free to copy the facts so long as any expression used to express the facts was not copied. Accordingly, regardless of the effort expended, copyright does not protect generic selection, order, or arrangement such as is used with telephone white pages.

COPYRIGHT INFRINGEMENT

Civil Infringement

When someone violates any one of the author's exclusive rights, the person commits *copyright infringement*. Infringement may be found for both intentional and unintentional (i.e., innocent) acts, such as subconsciously copying a song written by another. The owner of the copyright is entitled to various remedies including an injunction to stop the infringing behavior and actual or statutory damages. The statute of limitations for bringing a civil action is 3 years.

To establish infringement, a party must establish ownership of a copyright and that there was impermissible copying. Ownership of the copyright is established by presenting the registration certificate received from the Copyright Office. As for copying, infringement is proven easily when actual portions of the work are copied. However, usually infringement is shown through circumstantial evidence, such as by the combination of a substantial similarity of the copied work to the original work and access by the author to the original work.

Willful Infringement

In *Playboy Enters. v. Webbworld Inc.* (1997), defendant Webbworld had implemented software that scoured Internet newsgroups for adult-oriented images and posted them on its Web site for viewing by paying customers. Playboy filed suit over images that had been taken from its magazines and posted on Webbworld's Web site. The district court found in favor of Playboy on the grounds of copyright infringement, as the posted images were found to violate Playboy's exclusive rights for reproducing, distributing, and displaying the copyrighted images. In addition, the court found that Webbworld had acted willfully despite its implementation of a "compliance program" because it copied the images from a newsgroup whose title "centerfolds" suggested that it might have copyrighted works in it. In addition, after receiving notice of infringement from Playboy, it continued to obtain infringing images from the same newsgroup. Accordingly, Internet users who receive notice of an accusation of copyright infringement should take the notice seriously and consult their attorney to determine what, if any, remedial actions should be taken.

Criminal Infringement

Any person who infringes a copyright willfully may be punished criminally for up to 10 years in prison and fined. Conduct that does not give rise to civil copyright infringement (i.e., money damages) cannot give rise to criminal infringement. The statute of limitations for the government to bring such a criminal action is 5 years.

Historically, there has been an additional requirement for criminal infringement. For an infringement to rise to a criminal level, it must be (1) for purposes of commercial advantage or private financial gain, or (2) the reproduction or distribution during any 180-day period of one or more copies or phonorecords of one or more copyrighted works must have a total retail value of more than $1,000. However, the 1997 NET Act amended the Copyright Act to make the showing of intent to create a profit to be irrelevant.

Compensatory and Statutory Damages

The copyright owner is entitled to recover the actual damages suffered as a result of the infringement, as well as any additional profits of the infringer. As an alternative to seeking actual damages and profits, the copyright owner can seek statutory damages in a lawsuit at any time before a final judgment is rendered. Statutory damages are awarded per work and range from $750 to $30,000 as the court considers just, unless there is innocent infringement or if the infringer is a nonprofit in which case the amount is reduced to $250. Finally, statutory damages may be increased to $150,000 if the infringement is willful.

Vicarious Infringement

Vicarious infringement occurs when a defendant has the legal right and physical ability to supervise the infringing activity and has a direct financial interest in those activities. Accordingly, if vicarious infringement is found, the defendant can be liable as though he or she were the party actually committing the infringement. In a typical case involving vicarious infringement, a music club owner is found liable when he or she hires a band that performs various works and the right holders to the works are not compensated.

Contributory Infringement

Contributory infringement is found when a party with knowledge of the infringing activity induces, causes, or materially contributes to the infringing conduct of another. The contribution must be more than the mere passive providing of premises, the supply of staple items of commerce, or the supply of material that can also be used for lawful activities. When contributory infringement is found, the defendant can be liable as though he or she were the party actually committing the infringement. For example, the storage on a defendant's system of infringing copies of copyrighted image files and retransmission to other servers do not constitute a direct infringement by a bulletin board system (BBS) operator of the exclusive right to reproduce the images where such copies are uploaded by an infringing user; however, those actions may be considered contributory infringement, notwithstanding defenses available to the BBS operator under the Digital Millennium Copyright Act (DMCA). The chapter in this *Handbook* on the DMCA describes more fully Congress's response to the problems associated with transmitting digital information over global networks.

LIMITATIONS ON EXCLUSIVE RIGHTS

Fair Use

The exclusive rights of a copyright owner are subject to certain limitations and exceptions under which some acts that would otherwise be considered an infringement are exempted under the doctrine of *fair use*. Whether a particular use of a work is fair depends on a balancing of four factors: (1) the purpose and character of the use, including whether such use is of a commercial nature or is for nonprofit educational purposes; (2) the nature of the copyrighted work; (3) the amount and substantiality of the portion used in relation to the copyrighted work as a whole; and (4) the effect of the use upon the potential market for or value of the copyrighted work. Whether a use qualifies as fair is determined by balancing the exclusive rights of the copyright owner against the rights of another to use the copyright material in a reasonable manner without the owner's consent. For example, the copying by a professor of an article from a newspaper for in-class distribution is much more likely to be found a fair use than the commercial copying and reselling of copyrighted music.

The balancing test for fair use is fact specific and requires a case-by-case analysis. Because the finding of whether a use is fair turns on the facts of each particular case, no bright line test is available to determine whether such use will be considered fair.

The fair use doctrine thereby permits courts in limited circumstances to prevent the stifling of creativity brought about by rigid interpretation of the Copyright Act. Ultimately, this means that cases will test the bounds of whether a certain use qualifies for a fair use or whether it is an infringement. Such decisions can have a significant impact on the markets available to a certain product, such as portable digital music players.

Fair use allows certain uses of copyrighted works for such purposes as criticism, commentary, news reporting, teaching, scholarship, and research.

With respect to the first factor of the fair use test—the purpose and character of the use—courts typically are less willing to deem a use fair when it is commercial and profit seeking in nature. Yet, uses involving nonprofit educational purposes, such as copying textbooks for students, can still be found to be infringing as such use would destroy the market for the textbooks and eliminate the incentive for authors and publishers to update their works.

Courts often favorably consider the first factor of the fair use test when the use of a work is transformative, such that the use of the work adds something new; alters the original work with new expression, meaning, or message; or is otherwise for a different or further purpose than the original work.

With regard to the second factor—the nature of the copyrighted work—the law generally recognizes a greater need to disseminate factual works than creative works, and therefore a finding of fair use is more likely with a factual work. In addition, the use of published works is more likely to qualify as a fair use because the first appearance of the artist's expression has already occurred.

For the third factor—the amount and substantiality of the portion used—it inherently makes sense that the more portions of a work that are used, whether qualitatively or quantitatively, the less likely it is that the use of such portions will be considered fair. However, taking essential parts of the original work, even when they are only a small portion of the original work, can still be found to be substantial when they are at the heart of the work. In contrast, in some cases, wholesale copying can still be considered fair use, such as copying digital images in their entirety in a reduced format for an online image search engine.

With respect to the fourth factor—the effect of the use on the market or value of the work—when the use is a commercial use, market harm is presumed and must be rebutted by the defendant. When market harm cannot be presumed, the copyright holder has the burden of proof to demonstrate the market effect. Market harm would occur when the new use of the work would become widespread, adversely affecting the market for the copyrighted work, such that it would substitute for the original. The court may also consider possible adverse affects on the potential market for derivative works.

In *Sony Corp. of America v. Universal City Studios, Inc.* (1984), the Supreme Court addressed whether the manufacture and sale of video tape recorders (VTRs) by Sony violated any copyright rights of Universal City Studios, the owner of a number of copyrights on broadcast television shows. Universal City Studios sought to find Sony liable for vicarious and contributory infringement in that Sony "sold equipment with constructive knowledge of the fact that its customers may use that equipment to make unauthorized copies of copyrighted material." The Court applied the staple article of commerce doctrine, by which the sales of copying equipment "does not does not constitute contributory infringement if the product is widely used for legitimate, unobjectionable purposes ... [or if] ... it [is] ... capable of substantial noninfringing uses." The Court also considered whether unauthorized time-shifting was fair use.

The Court found that the predominant use of the VTRs was to time-shift programming, such that a viewer could watch a televised program at a later and more convenient time because he or she was unable to view the program when broadcast. The Court ultimately ruled that VTRs were capable of a substantial noninfringing use and that home time shifting is fair use, thereby enabling many companies to sell video tape records without concern of facing massive damages for copyright infringement.

The Ninth Circuit Court addressed whether reverse engineering was a fair use in *Sony Computer Entertainment, Inc. v. Connectix Corp.* (2000). Sony produces and markets Sony Playstation gaming units on which users play Sony PlayStation games. Connectix makes and sells a software emulator program called Virtual Game Station that enables computer owners to play Sony PlayStation games on their computers. Although the Virtual Game Station does not contain any of Sony's copyright material, in the process of producing Virtual Game Station Connectix repeatedly copied Sony's copyrighted BIOS so as to determine how the Sony Playstations gaming units operated.

The Ninth Circuit found that "the methods by which Connectix reverse-engineered the Sony BIOS were necessary to gain access to the unprotected functional elements within the program." The court ruled that the "copies made and used by Connectix during the course of its reverse engineering of the Sony BIOS were protected fair use, necessary to permit Connectix to make its non-infringing Virtual Game Station function with PlayStation games." However, decisions by courts have held that such reverse engineering may still be a violation of an applicable license agreement such as where the right to reverse engineer was waived.

Audio Home Recording Act of 1992

The Audio Home Recording Act of 1992 amended the Copyright Act to prevent the importation, manufacture, or distribution of digital audio recording devices and digital audio interface devices that did not conform to the serial copy management system (SCMS). The purpose of this Act was to prevent the making of digital copies of already copied works by most consumers and provided some recourse to copyright owners by providing them with royalty payments from the sale of digital audio records and digital audio media. Although the Act's provisions for digital audio tape recorders and associated media were not controversial, the Recording Industry Association of America's attempt to prohibit the distribution of MP3 players that did not read the SCMS code resulted in a lawsuit that ultimately decided the future availability and desirability of MP3 players in the United States.

In *Recording Indus. Ass'n of Am. v. Diamond Multimedia Sys.* (1999), the Ninth Circuit considered whether the Rio portable music player was a digital audio recording device subject to the restrictions of the Audio Home Recording Act of 1992. The court considered that with the Rio player the digital audio files had to be created on a hard drive of a personal computer, and not on the player itself. Ultimately the court found that both the Rio player and computers were not digital audio recording devices within the meaning of the act and that, even when used in combination, neither where required to recognize the SCMS code.

File Sharing

In *A&M Records v. Napster, Inc.* (2001), the Ninth Circuit addressed, among other issues described in the DMCA chapter, whether persons who transmitted and received copyrighted digital music files over a computer network without authorization from the copyright owner were making a fair use of copyrighted music. With respect to the first factor in the fair use doctrine, the court found that the use was commercial, as the plaintiff demonstrated by showing that repeated and exploitative unauthorized copies of copyrighted works were being made to save the expense of purchasing authorized copies. The court determined that the copyrighted music was creative in nature, which cuts against a finding of fair use under the second factor. The court found that the third factor weighed against a finding of fair use because Napster users transmitted and downloaded copyrighted music in its entirely as opposed to portions thereof. Finally, with regard to the fourth factor, the court concluded that Napster harmed the market in at least two ways: it reduced audio CD sales among college students and raised the barriers to plaintiffs' entry into the market for the digital downloading of music. Therefore, the court ruled that the users who transmitted and received copyrighted digital music files over the computer network were not making a fair use of the copyrighted music. Additional issues involving the foregoing case are discussed at length in the DMCA chapter with respect to Napster's contributory and vicarious infringement in light of the DMCA.

In addition, a Supreme Court case issued after the drafting of this chapter held that companies that were created for the purpose of facilitating copyright infringement cannot avoid being liable for infringement themselves.

Quotations

Quotations from works can be made without consent of the author under the fair use doctrine, such as for new stories and historical analysis. However, the amount of the quotations cannot be unreasonably large and cannot destroy the marketability of the source by the copyright owner.

Innocent Infringement

The innocent infringement defense, when invoked successfully by a defendant in a copyright infringement suit, reduces the amount of damages for which the defendant could otherwise be liable. To be successful, the defendant has the burden to prove that he or she was unaware of the copyright owner's copyright and had no reason to believe that the acts constituted copyright infringement. The copyright owner can eliminate the innocent infringer defense by marking copies or phonorecords of the copyrighted work with a copyright notice.

CONCLUSION

Copyright law attempts to strike a balance between allowing authors to control and profit from their work while still providing the public with certain rights. Ultimately, the public benefits from copyright law because it encourages further creations and allows the public to enjoy the fruits of these creations. Copyright law will continue to face challenges with respect to computers and the Internet, and further significant changes to the law should be expected.

GLOSSARY

BBS An electronic bulletin board system.

Common law Law that has not been enacted by a legislature, but rather has been derived and developed from judicial decisions.

Compilation A work formed by the collection and assembling of preexisting materials or of data that are selected, coordinated, or arranged in such a way that the resulting work as a whole constitutes an original work of authorship.

Contributory Infringement The knowing contribution to another's infringing activity.

Derivative Work A work based on one or more preexisting works where the original work is recast, transformed, or adapted.

DMCA The Digital Millennium Copyright Act.

Fair Use A use that would ordinarily violate an exclusive right, but is nonetheless found to be noninfringing and permissible.

Infringement Violating any of the exclusive rights of the copyright owner.

Joint Work A work prepared by two or more authors with the intention that their contributions be merged into inseparable or interdependent parts of a unitary whole.

License An authorization from the copyright owner to use one or more exclusive rights of a work; licenses are normally negotiated and recorded in a written document that includes a variety of other terms.

Phonorecords LPs, CDs, and cassette tapes.

Public Performance A performance or display at a place open to the public or at any place where there are a substantial number of persons outside a normal circle of a family and its social acquaintances, whether in person or by means of a digital transmission.

Reverse Engineering Determining the functional aspects of a software program by monitoring the input and output of the software program.

RIAA The Recording Industry Association for America (www.riaa.org).

Statutory Law Law that has been enacted by the legislature.

VTR Video tape recorders are Betamax video recorders as discussed in the Sony case, but also include standard video cassette records (VCRs).

Work Made for Hire A work that, despite being created by one author, is considered to be authored by another.

CROSS REFERENCES

See *Legal, Social and Ethical Issues of the Internet; Patent Law; The Digital Millennium Copyright Act; The Legal Implications of Information Security: Regulatory Compliance and Liability; Trademark Law and the Internet.*

REFERENCES

A&M Records v. Napster, Inc., 239 F.3d 1004 (9th Cir. 2001).

Adobe Sys. v. One Stop Micro, Inc., 84 F. Supp. 2d 1086 (N.D.CA 2000).

Bleistein v. Donaldson Lithographing Co., 188 U.S. 239 (1903).

Cmty. for Creative Non-Violence v. Reid, 490 U.S. 730 (1989).

Eldred v. Ashcroft, 537 U.S. 186 (2003).

Feist Publications, Inc. v. Rural Telephone Service Co., Inc., 499 U.S. 340 (1991).

Playboy Enters. v. Webbworld Inc., 991 F. Supp. 543 (N.D.TX 1997).

Recording Indus. Ass'n of Am. v. Diamond Multimedia Sys., 180 F.3d 1072 (9th Cir. 1999).
Sonny Bono Copyright Term Extension Act of 1998. (1998). Retrieved from http://www.copyright.gov/legislation/s505.pdf
Sony Computer Entertainment, Inc. v. Connectix Corp., 203 F.3d 596 (9th Cir. 2000); cert denied 531 U.S. 871 (2000).
Sony Corp. of America v. Universal City Studios, Inc., 464 U.S. 417 (1984).

FURTHER READING

Aalmuhammed v. Lee, 202 F.3d 1227 (9th Cir. 1999).
Baltimore Orioles, Inc. v. Major League Baseball Players Asso., 805 F.2d 663 (7th Cir. 1986).
Bitlaw. (n.d.). *International copyright*. Retrieved from http://www.bitlaw.com/copyright/international.html
Black, J. (2002, September 27). *A case to define the digital age: A Supreme Court ruling on a 20-year extension of copyright protection could decide much of what Web surfers get to see, hear, and share*. Retrieved from http://www.businessweek.com/technology/content/sep2002/tc20020927_7367.htm
Bridgeport Music, Inc. v. Rhyme Syndicate Music, 376 F.3d 615 (6th Cir. 2004).
Campbell v. Acuff-Rose Music, 510 U.S. 569 (1994).
Central Point Software v. Nugent, 903 F. Supp. 1057 (E.D.TX 1995).
Dogan, S. (n.d.). *Copyright in cyberspace: Requirements for copyrightability*. Retrieved from http://www.cyberspacelaw.org/dogan/dogan2.html
Ebay, Inc. v. Bidder's Edge, 100 F. Supp. 2d 1058 (N.D.CA 2000).
Engineering Dynamics v. Structural Software, 26 F.3d 1335 (5th Cir. 1994).
F.E.L. Publications, Ltd. v. Catholic Bishop of Chicago, 214 U.S.P.Q. (BNA) 409 (7th Cir. 1982).
Home Recording Rights Coalition. (n.d.). *Betamax: The inside story*. Retrieved from http://www.ari.net/hrrc/html/inside_betamax.html
MacMillan, R. (2003, January 15). *Eldred v. Ashcroft: A primer*. Retrieved from http://www.washingtonpost.com/wp-srv/technology/articleseldredprimer_100902.htm
MGM Studios, Inc. v. Grokster Ltd., 380 F.3d 1154 (9th Cir. 2004).
National Football League v. McBee & Bruno's, Inc., 792 F.2d 726 (8th Cir. 1986).
NFL v. Primetime 24 Joint Venture, 131 F. Supp. 2d 458 (S.D.NY 2001).
Quality King Distributors, Inc. v. L'anza Research Int'l, Inc., 523 U.S. 135 (1998).
Sega Enters. v. Accolade, Inc, 1993 U.S. App. LEXIS 78; 93 Daily Journal DAR 304 (9th Cir. 1993).
Shaul v. Cherry Valley-Springfield Cent. Sch. Dist., 363 F.3d 177 (2d Cir. 2004).
Smith, T. (2001, March 15). *Sony buys PlayStation emulator*. Retrieved from http://www.theregister.co.uk/2001/03/15/sony_buys_playstation_emulator/
Sprenger, P. (1999, June 15). *Rio rolls Over RIAA*. Retrieved from http://www.wired.com/news/politics/0%2C1283% 2C20235%2C00.html
Three Boys Music Corp. v. Bolton, 212 F.3d 477 (9th Cir. 2000).
Ty, Inc. v. Publ'ns Int'l, 292 F.3d 512 (7th Cir. 2002).
U.S. Copyright Law. (n.d.). Retrieved from http://www.copyright.gov/title17/
Xoom, Inc. v. Imageline, Inc., 323 F.3d 279 (4th Cir. 2002).

Trademark Law and the Internet

Ray Everett-Church, *PrivacyClue LLC*

INTRODUCTION

Trademark law is a fascinating subject for many people, in part because most everybody in our society understands and appreciates the power of popular trademarks, such as Lexus, Pokemon, Yahoo!, and Safeway. Trademarks are such an integral part of our language and culture that we all have a vested interest in their protection. Because trademarks are all about meaning, trademark disputes are a kind of spectator sport: they involve popular cultural icons and turn on questions such as whether the average person is likely to be confused if a trademark is used improperly. So in many respects, everybody gets to have an opinion on trademark issues, and that opinion more often than not counts for something in the final calculus of trademark disputes.

In this chapter, we will look at the fundamental ideas that underlie the protection of trademarks and we will look at ways in which trademarks can be infringed and protected. Once that groundwork has been laid, we will then look at how these fundamentals have been applied to the unique and significant disputes that have arisen in the Internet context. In many respects, trademark law has been turned upside down by the Internet, so we will look at how the principles of trademark law are being applied in today's Internet-oriented business environment.

TRADEMARK DEFINED

Merriam-Webster's Dictionary of Law defines **trademark** as "a mark that is used by a manufacturer or merchant to identify the origin or ownership of goods and to distinguish them from others and the use of which is protected by law."

In practice, a trademark is any word (Sun), name (Calvin Klein), symbol (golden arches), device (the Energizer Bunny), slogan ("Fly the Friendly Skies"), package design (Coca-Cola bottle), colors (FedEx purple and orange), sounds (the five tone Intel Corporation sound) or any combination thereof that identifies and distinguishes a specific product or service from others in the marketplace.

As trademark law has evolved, the field has become an important subset of the larger category known as **intellectual property** law. As the name implies, intellectual property law (which also includes patent, copyright, and trade secret law) treats these rights as a kind of property right, protecting the rights of owners to exploit the property for their own benefit while prohibiting unauthorized use by others. But unlike real estate or personal property law, intellectual property law concerns ownership of intangible things such as ideas, words, and meanings, rather than physical things.

The legal protections afforded by trademark law also extend to the related concepts of **service marks** and **trade dress**. Service marks differ from trademarks in that they are marks used to identify a particular service, or to distinguish the provider of a service, rather than a tangible product. For example, the name of a consulting firm, or the name of a proprietary analytical process used by that consulting firm, might be more properly identified as a service mark. Trade dress is the overall image of a product, composed of the nonfunctional elements of its design, packaging, or labeling. This could include specific colors or color combinations, a distinctive package shape, or specific symbols or design elements.

Many people confuse trademark with copyright. Copyright is a person's exclusive right to benefit from the reproduction or adaptation of an original work of authorship, such as a literary, artistic, or musical work. Trademark differs from copyright in that trademark law does not prohibit the reproduction or adaptation of the creative products of an author. Rather trademark law seeks to prevent confusion over words or other characteristics used to uniquely identify the source or quality of a product or service. For example, Paul Simon's 1973 song "Kodachrome" refers to a trademark owned by Eastman Kodak Company even though Simon holds the copyright on his work.

The relative strength of a particular trademark depends upon where it falls within a range of five categories: fanciful, arbitrary, suggestive, descriptive, or generic. The greatest protection comes for fanciful marks consisting of invented words like Xerox, Kodak, or TiVo. The next strongest protection comes for arbitrary marks, which are commonplace words used in a manner that is unrelated to their dictionary meaning, such as Apple for computers or Shell for gasoline. Suggestive marks are familiar words or phrases that are used in an inventive way to "suggest" what their product or service really consists of, such as Home Box Office for a movie channel or Mail Boxes Etc. for a postal services franchise. The least protection comes for descriptive marks which do little more than describe the characteristics or contents of the product, such as the publication Automotive Industry News, or Cellphone Center for a cellular telephone retailer. Finally, generic names, which merely state what the product or service is, cannot function as trademarks. Some marks, such as aspirin, linoleum, escalator, or nylon, were once trademarks but became generic because the trademark holder failed to police unauthorized use.

FEDERAL TRADEMARK LAW

For trademarks used in interstate commerce, U.S. law provides protection under the Trademark Act of 1946, known more commonly as the **Lanham Act**. The Lanham Act also created a registration process for trademarks, and legal and procedural incentives for trademarks to be registered with the U.S. Patent and Trademark Office (USPTO). Many States within the U.S. also afford trademarks protections under their State's laws.

The Lanham Act provides a functional definition of what is eligible to be registered as a trademark. Potentially anything can be registered as a trademark if it functions among consumers to distinguish a specific product from other products in the marketplace. The Lanham Act does, however, prohibit certain marks, including anything immoral, deceptive, scandalous, disparaging towards an institution or national symbol, falsely suggests a connection to a person, consisting of a flag other governmental insignia, using a name or portrait of a deceased President of the United States during the life of his widow without her consent, and numerous other limitations. Once registered, a mark may also be cancelled if it has become generic, has been abandoned, was obtained through fraud, or is otherwise prohibited by the aforementioned conditions.

One important limitation on registration comes when the mark is part of the product's functionality. An aspect of the product may meet the definition of a trademark and may even be recognized as a trademark by consumers, but it cannot be registered if it is essentially a functional aspect of the product. For example, a company might sell a computer monitor that has a unique shape that is immediately recognizable to the public and distinguishes the monitor from the products of competitors. Under the functional definition of a trademark, the unique shape may be registered. However, if the shape is actually a functional aspect of the product, for example the shape is responsible for improved resolution, the shape cannot be registered as a trademark. (In such a case, though, the manufacturer may be able to seek patent protection for the unique design.)

The USPTO registers trademarks and service marks that are used in interstate commerce. Trademarks need not be registered for an owner to enforce his or her rights in court, however federal registration provides numerous legal benefits to a trademark owner at a reasonable expense. For example, once a mark is registered, the registration establishes the validity of the registrant's claims of ownership and places the world on constructive notice that the owner has exclusive rights to use the mark in commerce. If the holder of a registered trademark establishes infringement under the Lanham Act, they can not only enjoin any misuse of a mark, but they may also be able to recover statutory damages and in some cases, attorneys' fees.

Federal registration on the principal register gives nationwide protection from infringement, while common law protects the mark only in the specific geographical area in which the mark is used in commerce; and state law protects the mark only within the state where the mark is registered. Thus, another benefit of federal registration is the establishment of rights across a larger geographical area than under common law and state law.

In fact, the scope of protection for a federally registered mark is usually broader than under common law or state law. For example, under common law and many state trademark registration statutes, trademark protections may be restricted to those specific products or services for which the mark has explicitly been used, while federal law allows a mark to be protected even when used in conjunction with a wider array of related products or services, such as a family of services offered under an umbrella trademark. Finally, the Lanham Act provides legal remedies that go beyond those available at common law including, for example, treble damages against a "willful" infringer, as well as reimbursement of attorney fees in exceptional cases. It is important to note, however, that unlike many areas in which federal law supercedes state law, state and federal trademark law often co-exist well and aggrieved parties can frequently bring legal actions using both state and federal law to equal effect.

The Lanham Act's protections flow equally to trademarks and service marks. Trade dress is also protected by the Lanham Act, provided it is not a functional part of the product and is distinctive, has acquired secondary meaning as being uniquely associated with the product, and there is a likelihood of confusion on the part of the consumer if a competing product were to possess similar trade dress.

Trademark Registration

First, it is important to note that there are legal protections under trademark law for marks that have not been registered with the USPTO. Section 43(a) of the Lanham Act permits legal action against anyone who falsely makes use of a trademark word, name, or symbol in a manner that is likely to cause confusion or misrepresents the nature or origins of the product or service. This protection is not predicated on the registration of a mark with the USPTO. In addition, as noted elsewhere in this article, state laws may also provide protections as well. However, the Lanham Act, and many state laws, provide significant incentives for registration, giving additional remedies and rights to those who have availed themselves of the registration process.

For those who do choose the registration route, the USPTO maintains two types of trademark registries, the Principal Register and the Supplemental Register. The Principal Register is where a "registered trademark" is registered. There are three ways a trademark or service mark may be registered with the USPTO. The first method, called an "in use" application, is for an applicant who is already using a mark in commerce. The second method is an "intent to use" application, for marks that are not yet in use, but which the applicant is preparing to use. The third method is based upon certain international agreements, by which applicants outside the United States can file an application based upon applications or registrations in another country.

The Supplemental Register is where marks that are descriptive in nature but have not yet established secondary meaning are maintained. Marks on the Supplemental Register can use the ® symbol, and if the mark is continuously used and unchallenged for five years, the holder may file another application and claim such use presumptively establishes secondary meaning under Section 2(f) of the Lanham Act, and thereby move the mark onto the Principal Register.

The registration process itself is relatively straightforward. The application documents must be filed by the owner of the mark, usually through the services of an attorney concentrating in trademark law. (For brevity we will focus only on an "in use" application and will not further discuss the "intent to use" application.) The application contains information about the individual or corporation who owns the mark, an exact representation of the mark (in text or in image form) as well as several specimens of the mark in actual use, information about the date of first use and date of first use in commerce of the mark, a description of the goods or services used in conjunction with the mark, and the "classification" of the goods or services according to a standardized list of 42 pre-defined classifications. Some goods and services may be registered in multiple classes, with the application fees increasing accordingly.

Once received, the USPTO makes an initial review of the application to determine if the application contains all the information necessary to be considered "filed." If the application is complete, a "filing date" is issued along with a serial number and sent to the applicant. Several months after filing, an examiner at the USPTO reviews the application in more detail, researches the information provided, and makes a determination as to whether the mark should be registered. If it cannot be registered, the examiner will issue a notice called an "office action" which explains the grounds for refusal, including any deficiencies in the application itself. In some cases, only minor adjustments might be necessary in order to permit registration and sometimes the application can be corrected over the phone. Applicants have six months to respond to an office action or else the application will be considered abandoned. If the applicant cannot overcome the examiner's objections, a final office action is issued, at which point the applicant may appeal to the Trademark Trial and Appeal Board. Should the applicant be unsuccessful there, they may appeal that decision to federal court.

If there are no objections to the application, or the applicant overcomes the objections, the examiner will approve the mark for publication in the Official Gazette, a weekly publication of the USPTO. The applicant is notified of the date of publication through an official Notice of Publication.

Anyone who believes the registration harms them or is otherwise in violation of the Lanham Act has 30 days from publication to file an opposition to the registration or seek an extension of time to do so. At this point the administrative proceeding is *inter partes* (meaning between two parties, in contrast to an *ex parte* proceeding before the examiner only) and is known as an "opposition." The opposition proceeding determines the validity of the objections. If no objection is received, the mark will be registered. After the registration is issued, anyone who believes they have been harmed by the registration may begin a "cancellation proceeding," which is similar to an opposition proceeding except that it takes place after registration. In an opposition, the applicant bears the ultimate burden of establishing registerability; in a cancellation, the party seeking the cancellation bears the burden of proving the registration was improvidently issued. Opposition and cancellation proceedings are held in a formal, trial-like hearing before the Trademark Trial and Appeal Board, a division of the USPTO.

A mark will be registered only after it has been published and the opposition period has expired. Once registered, federal trademark registrations run for ten years, with renewal terms lasting ten years. Between the fifth and sixth year, however, the registrant must file an affidavit to confirm the mark is still in use. If that affidavit is not filed, the registration is cancelled. Thus, a trademark must remain in use or its registration may be cancelled, but if a mark is in continual use and that use is properly demonstrated as required by law, the registration could remain effective forever.

After five years, the owner of a registered mark may request that the mark be deemed "incontestable." Under the Lanham Act, incontestability means that certain legal avenues of challenging the mark—such as a claim that the mark is not distinctive, lacks secondary meaning, is confusingly similar to another mark, or the mark is purely functional—are no longer available. The term "incontestable" is somewhat misleading in that there remain certain circumstances in which the mark may be challenged and have the registration cancelled, such as an assertion that the mark was improperly registered in the first instance.

The Differences Between ®, ™ and ℠

Once registered, the registration symbol, ®, may be used. It is considered trademark misuse to display the registration symbol at any point before the USPTO issues the final registration notice to the applicant. In contrast, anyone who wishes to claim rights in a mark may use the TM (trademark) or SM (service mark) designation along side the mark. Use of TM or SM alerts the public to the claim of ownership and exclusive use. It is not necessary to have a registration, or even a pending application, to make use of these designations, and consequently the claim may or may not have any validity. In short, use of TM or SM tells the world that you are prepared to put up a fight.

STATE STATUTES AND COMMON LAW

Many states also have trademark registration statutes that allow registration of marks used in intrastate commerce, using procedures that function similarly to the USPTO process defined by the Lanham Act. In addition, all states protect unregistered trademarks under some combination of state statute and common law. For the sake of brevity, this section will not detail trademark protections in all fifty US states.

In most states, the common law recognizes ownership of a trademark. Ownership under common law is most often established by demonstrating when the mark was first used in commerce, but unlike federal law, common law protections extend only to those areas or markets in which the mark is actually used. In contrast, federal registration of a trademark gives a basis under federal law for a suit for infringement, in addition to any common law claims that might be available. While it is possible to protect one's rights using only common law or state statutory protections, the benefits that flow from federal registration make it highly desirable.

INFRINGEMENT AND DILUTION

There are two main rights that trademark owners will assert: **infringement** and **dilution**. Infringement of a trademark usually involves the use of the mark in a way that is so similar to the owner's usage that the average purchaser will likely be deceived, will mistake the infringing goods for the original, or will likely experience confusion. Dilution is a lessening of the value of a trademark caused by an unauthorized use of the mark, regardless of whether any actual confusion, deception, or mistake occurred.

Infringement

Under the Lanham Act the standard for determining whether a mark is infringing is whether there is a "likelihood of confusion" over the mark in a particular usage context. More specifically, infringement comes when a consumer is likely to be confused over the source, sponsorship, or approval of the goods bearing the mark.

In deciding whether consumers are likely to be confused, courts have previously looked at a number of factors, including:

- Similarity between the two marks (such as any visual, phonetic, or contextual similarities);
- Similarity of the goods or services being offered;
- Proximity of the goods in a typical retail setting;
- Strength of the plaintiff's mark as exemplified by how well known the mark is to the public at large;
- Evidence of any actual confusion by consumers;
- Evidence of the defendant's intent in using the mark;
- Likely level of care employed by consumer in the purchase of that type of product; and,
- Likely growth or expansion of the product lines.

Of these eight factors, the first two are arguably the most important. For example, using an identical mark on an identical product is a clear case of infringement, such as a company other than Ford manufacturing a midsized automobile and calling it a Taurus. Similarly, calling the vehicle a Taurius would run into problems. (This use of similarly spelled names is of particular concern in the Internet domain name context, which will be discussed in a later section.)

But mere similarity is not always determinative of infringement. For example, it is possible to find Delta Faucets just a few aisles away from Delta power tools at your local home improvement store. While made by different companies, the similarity in trademark does not constitute infringement because consumers are not very likely to mistake a belt sander for a shower head.

Dilution

To further clarify the distinction between normal trademark infringement and dilution, in 1995 Congress amended the Lanham Act by passing the Federal Trademark Dilution Act (FTDA). This legislation expanded protections granted to famous and distinctive trademarks under the Lanham Act. Unlike infringement, dilution does not require evidence of a likelihood of confusion. Instead, the plaintiff must demonstrate that their mark is "famous," that it is being used in commerce by another party, and that the use causes the dilution of the "distinctive quality" of the mark.

The FTDA says that in determining whether a mark is "famous," a court may look at factors including the length of time a mark has been used, how widely and in what geographic areas it as been advertised, how recognizable the mark is to the public, and other factors. Highly distinctive long-used and well known marks, such as Coca-Cola or Kodak are examples of famous marks. Once a plaintiff establishes the fame of a mark, the owner can seek an injunction against further use of the mark in a manner that dilutes the distinctive qualities of that mark.

There are two types of dilution of a mark: **blurring** and **tarnishment**.

Blurring. Blurring is the weakening of a mark through its identification with dissimilar goods. For example, marketing Kleenex brand refrigerators would not likely confuse someone looking for bathroom tissue to accidentally purchase a refrigerator, however the use of the trademark would dilute the marks distinctiveness as representing personal care paper products.

Tarnishment. Tarnishment is the use of a mark in an unflattering light, through associating it with either inferior or distasteful products. For example, in the case *Toys 'R' Us v. Akkaoui*, 40 USPQ.2d 1836 (N.D. Cal. 1996), the toy retailer brought a successful tarnishment claim against a pornographic web site "adultsrus.com."

Other Trademark Claims

Although dilution claims and infringement claims based upon likelihood of confusion are the two most common trademark-related causes of action, there are a number of other bases for bringing suits. Many states have enacted unfair competition laws that prohibit a range of activities known as **passing off**, **contributory passing off**, **reverse passing off**, and **misappropriation**.

Passing off. Passing off occurs when a defendant attempts to "pass off" their product as if it were the mark owner's product. For example, affixing a Dell nameplate to computers actually made in someone's basement would constitute passing off.

Contributory passing off. Contributory passing off occurs when a defendant induces a retailer to pass off a product. For example, bribing a computer store to sell computers with a fake Dell nameplate would be contributory passing off.

Reverse passing off. Reverse passing off takes place when someone tries to market someone else's product as their own. If a computer store purchased Dell computers, replaced the nameplate with its own store brand nameplate, and attempted to sell the computers, they would have engaged in reverse passing off.

Misappropriation. Misappropriation, a privacy-related tort, is traditionally defined as using the name or likeness of someone for an unauthorized purpose, such as claiming a commercial endorsement by publishing someone's image (or even that of a look-alike impersonator) in an advertisement. In the trademark context, using a mark without authorization can violate federal and state law prohibitions on certain unfair trade practices, including the unauthorized use of marks in inappropriate ways.

Parody and Fair Use

Aside from challenging the validity of a trademark claim or attacking the elements of the infringement claim, defendants in trademark infringement or dilution cases can also claim two affirmative defenses: parody and fair use.

Parody. Certain uses of a trademark for purposes of humor, satire, or social commentary, may be permissible if they are not very closely tied to commercial use. The theory underlying the protection of parody is that artistic and social commentary are valuable contributions to the society, therefore some deference to the First Amendment's protection of these types of speech is in order, even when balance against the detriment to a trademark owner. The protections vary, however. For example, in the highly amusing case of *Hormel Foods Corp. v. Jim Henson Productions*, 73 F.3d 497 (2d Cir. 1996), the use of a pig-like character named "Spa'am" in a Muppet movie was found not to violate Hormel's rights in the trademark "SPAM." However, in *Coca-Cola Co. v. Gemini Rising, Inc.*, 346 F. Supp. 1183 (E.D.N.Y. 1972), the printing of posters with a stylized slogan and logo reading "Enjoy Cocaine" were found to violate the rights of Coca-Cola in the stylized slogan and logo "Enjoy Coca-Cola."

Fair Use. Fair use occurs when the public benefit of allowing the use is perceived to override any perceived harm to the trademark owner. For example, in the case *Zatarains, Inc. v. Oak Grove Smokehouse, Inc.*, 698 F.2d 786 (5th Cir. 1983), the defendant's use of "fish fry" to describe a batter coating for fish was not an infringement of the plaintiff's mark "Fish-Fri." The court held that fair use prevents a trademark owner from monopolizing a descriptive word or phrase to the exclusion of anyone else who seeks merely to accurately describe their goods. The defense of fair use is only available, however, when the mark at issue is descriptive, and then, only where the descriptive term is used descriptively. Federal trademark statute also contains a right to fair use limited to usage in comparative advertising.

POLICING TRADEMARK ON THE INTERNET

Along with the tremendous growth in the usage of the Internet for both commercial and personal use, there has been a similar expansion in the number of trademark-related disputes involving the Internet. In a later section we will discuss the complex legal issues arising from trademark disputes over Internet domain names. But first there are a number of trademark issues that arise just from the very nature of the Internet as a facilitator of ubiquitous information sharing and access.

Perhaps the most important reason behind the growing amount of trademark-related litigation is that uncovering instances of trademark violations can be as simple as typing your trademark into an Internet search engine. Just a decade ago, a trademark owner in Maine might have no idea that his trademark might be in use by someone in Oregon. But with the ability to quickly and cheaply search the Internet, trademark owners are quickly able to perform searches that might have been impossible—or just impossibly costly—a few years ago.

The ability to so easily discover trademark infringement, both intentional and unintentional, has catapulted trademark law into one of the most active areas of litigation in the Internet arena. But the nature of trademark law itself has also added to the litigation explosion. As noted above, failure to properly police a mark can result in it becoming generic, and thus unprotected. Therefore, the same ease with which a trademark owner might uncover infringement may require that a trademark owner keep policing the Internet routinely and bring enforcement actions: If an infringement is known—or could be discovered through basic due diligence—and goes unchallenged, the trademark owner could lose control of its mark.

The requirement of constant policing of trademarks has, however, caused the unfortunate side effect of a growing number of heavy-handed actions against inexperienced web users, and still more enforcement actions that are brought in cases where a finding of infringement or dilution is highly unlikely. In many of these cases, well-intentioned individuals have been bullied by corporations over trademarks appearing on personal web pages. In some cases that have received significant media attention, sites created by fans of rock groups, automobiles, and movie stars have been threatened by the very entities that the sites were set up by their creators to honor.

Meta Tags

In recent years, several disputes have arisen over the use of trademarks in **meta tags** on Internet web pages. Web pages on the Internet are coded using a type of programming language called Hyper Text Markup Language, or HTML. The codes that are embedded in HTML documents, called tags, tell the browser how to display the information contained on the page, such as when to display words in bold, when to change fonts or font sizes, how to align tables, or where to place images. Web page designers can also include meta tags, which are special tags that contain information about the contents of the web page. Meta tags are used by search engines to find and rank pages so that more relevant search findings are displayed before less relevant ones.

In one of the first lawsuits over meta tags, *Oppedahl & Larson v. Advanced Concepts, et al.*, Civ. No. 97-CV-1592 (D.C. Colo., 1997), a Colorado law firm discovered that the defendants had put the law partners' names, "oppedahl" and "larson," in meta tags on several web pages. This was presumably done in hopes that searches for the respected law firm's name would gain more attention for the defendants' web pages. Suing under both the Lanham Act and the Federal Trademark Dilution Act, as well as state and common law unfair trade practice actions, the law firm won a permanent injunction against any further use of their names in meta tags on the defendants' web sites. Since that case, a number of other disputes have tested the extent to which trademarks may be used in meta tags and have largely resulted in prohibitions against uses by entities seeking to enhance site traffic by using the marks of competitors.

One of the issues that has arisen in meta tag disputes is the concept of "initial interest confusion." Initial interest confusion occurs when the use of another's trademark is done so in a manner reasonably calculated to capture initial consumer attention, even though no actual sale is finally completed as a result of the confusion. The case of *Brookfield Communications, Inc., v. West Coast Entertainment Corp.*, 174. F.3d 1036 (9th Cir. 1999), illustrates the issue. Brookfield operated a web site, MovieBuff.com, containing a movie database. West Coast, a video retailer, used the term "moviebuff" in meta tags on its web site. A court held that West Coast's use of term in meta tags led to "initial interest confusion," in which search engine users looking for MovieBuff.com's site might visit West Coast's site and stop looking for MovieBuff.com, even though there might never be any confusion over sponsorship of the two sites.

Not all cases in which meta tags were at issue have resulted in a ban on their use. For example, in the case of *Playboy Enterprises, Inc. v. Terri Welles*, 162 F.3d 1169 (9th Cir. 2002), a model who had posed as a Playboy Playmate of the Month was permitted to use "Playboy" and "Playmate" as meta tags for her web site. But new uses have created more confusion in this area. For example, in late 2003 and early 2004, several courts issued diverging opinions on the usage of trademarks to trigger various advertising "pop-up" advertisements and targeted advertisements keyed to trademarks appearing in search engines. Many of these cases are ongoing at the time this article is being written, and it is likely that confusion will continue until higher courts weigh in.

Deep Linking

Fundamental to the functioning of web pages on the Internet is the concept of a link. A link, short for hyperlink, is a tag coded within a web page that turns a piece of text (or in some cases an image) into a pointer to another document or page. Clicking on that link will typically cause the browser to follow the link and open the new page. While a simple link to the homepage of a web site will not typically run into trademark issues, some sites choose to create links to pages many levels down within a site. For example, instead of linking to the home page of a manufacturer, a web site designer might choose to create a link that goes directly to a page displaying one of the manufacturer's products. This practice is called **deep linking**.

Some site owners object to deep linking because it allows visitors to quickly bypass other contents of a web site, including advertisements, which they would normally see if they had to navigate step-by-step through the contents of a site. In several court cases, plaintiffs have charged that deep linking deprives them of the full benefits of having visitors explore their site, and have argued a variety of copyright, trademarks, and unfair competition claims. Proponents of deep linking counter that deep links are no different than footnotes or bibliographies, permitting readers to jump quickly to precise information. There are few clear court decisions on the trademark implications of deep linking, however many of the suits have focused on evidence of a defendant's bad faith, such as any appearance that the deep linking is intended to take unfair advantage of the other site's content, which will cut strongly in favor of the plaintiff.

In a related issue, there have been numerous disputes over the practice of "framing" Internet content. Framing is a technique in which content from one site is displayed within a "frame" appearing on another unrelated site. The use of framing often makes it appear that the content is owned or otherwise presented by an entity other than its actual owner or authorized user. Most disputes regarding framing have centered on copyright implications of unauthorized framing of content, however trademark issues also arise when there might be confusion as to the source of the content or its relationship to advertisements and other affiliations which might be suggested by the way in which the framed material appears.

DOMAIN NAMES

With the explosive growth of the Internet, both in its importance to global commerce and in the effect it has had on all aspects of our society, the importance of the domain names used on the Internet cannot be understated. The academic and non-commercial roots of the Internet caused many of its key functions, such as the Domain Name System, to be designed without some important safeguards. For example, domain names could then—and in many cases can still—be registered by anyone willing to pay the registration fee. In the early days of the Internet this fact caused something of a "land grab" mentality in which speculators rushed to purchase the rights to domain names that were expected to become valuable. Indeed, the domain name WallStreet.com, registered for under $100, was reportedly sold for over $1 Million (Bicknell, 1999).

Unfortunately however, some speculators also rushed in and purchased domain names that were identical (or in some cases merely similar) to valuable brand names. These so-called "cybersquatters" sought to gain financially by occupying the "virtual" real estate of someone else's trademark translated into a domain name. Because a domain name has become such an important part of a company's marketing identity, trademark owners have been forced to wage legal battles to retake control of their trademarks in cyberspace. Cybersquatting is discussed in detail in a later section, but it may be useful to look first at how domain names work and why they have become a trademark law battleground.

Domain Name System Basics

Generally speaking, each computer connected to the Internet requires a unique address, called an Internet Protocol ("IP") address, in order to distinguish it from all the other computers on the Internet. When computers communicate across the Internet, they use IP addresses in order to ensure that when a user on a particular computer requests data from another computer, the data gets delivered to the right place.

IP addresses are not very friendly to human eyes. Looking something like "192.168.27.145," it was quickly determined that it would be easier to assign names to stand in for those numbers, because many humans find it easier to remember names than to remember numbers. Thus, the designers of the early Internet developed the Domain Name System ("DNS") to permit the reliable association of names with IP addresses. As a result, with the help of DNS, when you tell your web browser that you want to check out the latest news at CNN.com, it is able to correctly direct your query to 64.236.16.116, which is one of the many web servers that answer to the busy CNN.com domain name.

Domain names, and their underlying numbers, are controlled by the Internet Corporation for Assigned Names and Numbers ("ICANN"). ICANN controls not only the allocation of IP addresses and the network of domain name registrars who control all domain names, but also delegate operation of the Root Servers. The Root Servers, the heart of the Domain Name System, are a collection of servers operated around the globe that manage all requests for information about the top level domains ("TLDs"). TLDs are simply a means of organizing domain names into broad categories.

As of this writing, there are 14 generic TLDs in which entities or individuals can register secondary domains, in some cases subject to certain restrictions. They include:

- .com for commercial sites
- .net for networks
- .org for non-profit organizations
- .gov for U.S. federal government sites
- .edu for educational institutions
- .int for entities created by international treaties
- .mil for U.S. military sites
- .biz for businesses
- .info for general use
- .name for personal use by individuals
- .pro for professional fields such as lawyers and accountants (this TLD was still inactive as of February 2003)
- .aero for the aerospace industry
- .coop for cooperatives
- .museum for museums

There are also over 200 country code TLDs (ccTLD), based upon the two-letter country codes for the worlds recognized nations. Examples include:

- .us for the United States
- .uk for the United Kingdom
- .ca for Canada
- .mx for Mexico
- .de for Germany
- .jp for Japan

When you enter a domain name into your browser (for purposes of this example we will use www.example.com) here is—in theory—how the Domain Name System works to assure you get to the web site you want:

- Your browser communicates your request for www.example.com, via your Internet connection, to the Domain Name Servers designated for your use by your Internet service provider.
- Your service provider's Domain Name Servers in turn ask the upstream DNS servers (and if necessary, eventually, the Root Servers) to search their database for the IP address of the Domain Name Servers that are authoritative for the TLD "com."
- Your query is then passed to the Domain Name Servers for "com," which then search their database for the IP address of the Domain Name Servers that are authoritative for the second-level domain "example" within the top level domain "com."
- Your query is then passed to the Domain Name Servers for "example.com," which then searches their database for the IP address of the server that answers to the subdomain "www" within that second-level domain.
- Once it locates the correct IP address, it tells your web browser what IP address to connect to, whereupon that server recognizes your request for a web page and transmits the appropriate data back to your computer.

This is "in theory" because in reality, this process can be simpler, or more complex, depending upon how your ISP chooses to manage its DNS requests. For example, some ISPs keeps a record of previous DNS requests in a "cache" file so that it can better manage time lag and server load issues by serving up IP addresses that it trusts are probably still correct since the looking them up a few hours earlier.

Domain Name Registration

The first challenge in registering a domain name is to identify a domain name that is suitable for your needs. Depending on the intended use of the domain name, there are many considerations, beginning with the choice of TLD that best suits your vision for your domain. Once you have decided on the TLD, you may have a choice of registrars delegated by ICANN to manage the process of domain name registration. For example, as of this writing there are several hundred ICANN-accredited registrars, not counting the designated registrars for all the country code TLDs.

Once you have selected a registrar, you will communicate to them what second-level domain you wish to register. In most cases, they will check their records and determine whether the domain name requested is already registered, or might have previously been reserved. Presumably you will have checked to see if there is a web site already operating at the domain name you have selected, however the absence of an active site is not determinative, as it is possible for a domain name to be registered, but not in active use.

If the second-level domain name you desire has not been previously registered, you will likely be given the choice of registering it. Upon providing contact and billing information, and paying the registrar's fee of course, you will also be asked to provide the IP addresses of a primary and a secondary Domain Name Server for your domain. While some registrars offer you the option of also hosting the domain on their own servers, you may need to have previously arranged with an ISP to establish the technical details necessary for operating DNS, web, and email services for your newly-chosen domain name. If you have set up these services in advance, however, then it is possible to have your new domain fully functional within just a matter of minutes or hours after completing the registration process.

Internet Domain Disputes

Far and away the greatest amount of trademark-related controversy on the Internet concerns use of domain names. Because of both the value of trademarks themselves, and the value of memorable domain names for maximizing the marketing and sales power of online operations, using popular trademarks as domain names has been an important issue for businesses beginning to make use of the Internet. Much to their consternation however, many companies have attempted to register domain names related to their company name or their trademarks only to discover that someone else has already registered those domain names.

In the course of many legal disputes over domain names, some consensus among the courts has developed. Most courts have applied trademark law in much the same fashion as they would in any other trademark dispute. For example, marks are assessed for the extent to which they are fanciful, arbitrary, suggestive, descriptive or generic. Disputes have also been judged on whether there is evidence of bad faith on the part of either party. In the Oppedahl & Larson case discussed above, there was no reasonable basis for the defendant to be making use of "Oppedahl" and "Larson" other than their desire to garner traffic attracted by someone else's mark.

The most common method of using a trademark in a domain name is the verbatim use of the mark in conjunction with the TLD, such as Pepsi.com. But a related form of trademark infringement comes in dilution through the registration of similar domains, or domains containing misspellings or common typographical errors. Disputes over domains such as "amazom.com" (instead of amazon.com), gateway20000.com (instead of gateway2000.com), and micros0ft.com (microsoft.com with the second letter "o" replaced with a zero), have almost uniformly resulted in court decisions or settlements transferring domain ownership to the aggrieved party. These and other cases of infringement have resulted in a new area of law—and even of legislation—focused on resolving trademark-related domain name disputes.

Cybersquatting

In the mid-1990s, Dennis Toeppen registered some 250 domain names that were either similar or identical to popular trademarks, including deltaairlines.com, eddiebauer.com, neiman-marcus.com, northwestairlines.com, and yankeestadium.com. In two cases considered pivotal among domain name trademark disputes, *Intermatic Incorporated v. Toeppen*, 947 F.Supp. 1227 (N.D. Ill. 1996), and *Panavision Int'l, L.P. v. Toeppen*, 945 F. Supp. 1296 (C. D. Cal., 1996), the plaintiffs successfully forced Toeppen to relinquish control of the domains intermatic.com and panavision.com, respectively.

The Panavision case in particular illustrates how many of the cybersquatting disputes play out. In 1995, Toeppen registered the domain name www.panavision.com and created a web site that contained photographs taken around the city of Pana, Illinois. When contacted by Panavision, a maker of motion picture cameras and photographic equipment, Toeppen offered to sell the domain name for $13,000. Panavision declined and brought suit under the Federal Trademark Dilution Act.

As discussed in an earlier section, the FTDA requires plaintiffs to demonstrate that their mark is "famous" and that the defendant is using a mark in commerce in a fashion that could cause dilution of the mark's distinctiveness. While Toeppen claimed that his use of the mark was non-commercial, the court held that having offered the domain name for sale indicated that he intended that the domain name itself be a commercial offering.

In the Intermatic case, Toeppen originally operated a web page at the intermatic.com address which described a piece of software he claimed to be developing called "Intermatic," later replacing it with information about Champaign-Urbana, Illinois, the community in which Toeppen lived. The Intermatic court held that despite these non-commercial uses, the registration of the domain name itself was dilutive of Intermatic's mark.

Anticybersquatting Consumer Protection Act

As the problem of cybersqatting grew throughout the 1990s, Congress responded in 1999 by enacting the Anticybersquatting Consumer Protection Act ("ACPA"), which amended the Lanham Act to include protections specific to Internet domain names. One change from past practice under the Federal Trademark Dilution Act, however, was the ACPA's removal of the requirement that the mark be used in commerce. This greatly expanded plaintiffs' ability to take control over domain names that had merely been registered but were not actually in use.

The ACPA states that cybersquatting occurs when the person registering a domain name containing a trademark "has a bad faith intent to profit from that mark" and "registers, traffics in, or uses" a domain name that is "identical or confusingly similar to or dilutive of that mark." The Act includes nine factors that courts may take into consideration when determining the existence of bad faith intent:

- the trademark or other intellectual property rights of the person, if any, in the domain name;
- the extent to which the domain name consists of the legal name of the person or a name that is otherwise commonly used to identify that person;
- the person's prior use, if any, of the domain name in connection with the bona fide offering of any goods or services;
- the person's bona fide non-commercial or fair use of the mark in a site accessible under the domain name;
- the person's intent to divert consumers from the mark owner's online location to a site accessible under the domain name that could harm the goodwill represented by the mark, either for commercial gain or with the intent to tarnish or disparage the mark, by creating a likelihood of confusion as to the source, sponsorship, affiliation, or endorsement of the site;
- the person's offer to transfer, sell, or otherwise assign the domain name to the mark owner or any third party for financial gain without having used, or having an intent to use, the domain name in the bona fide offering of any goods or services, or the person's prior conduct indicating a pattern of such conduct;
- the person's provision of material and misleading false contact information when applying for the registration of the domain name, the person's intentional failure to maintain accurate contact information, or the person's prior conduct indicating a pattern of such conduct;
- the person's registration or acquisition of multiple domain names which the person knows are identical or confusingly similar to marks of others that are distinctive at the time of registration of such domain names, or dilutive of famous marks of others that are famous at the time of registration of such domain names, without regard to the goods or services of the parties; and,
- the extent to which the mark incorporated in the person's domain name registration is or is not distinctive and famous.

The Act then indicates that bad faith cannot be found if the defendant "believed and had reasonable grounds to believe that the use of the domain name was a fair use or otherwise lawful."

The recent dispute over the domain name Nissan.com gives some insight into how courts are applying the ACPA and other aspects of traditional trademark law analyses. The domain name is at the center of a dispute between Nissan Motor Co., Ltd., a popular car manufacturer, and Nissan Computer Corporation, a small business in North Carolina operated by Mr. Uzi Nissan. In *Nissan Motor Co., Ltd v. Nissan Computer Corp.*, 61 U.S.P.Q.2d 1839 (C.D. Cal., 2002), the court noted that the defendant registered the domain in 1994 and has been operating his firm under the Nissan name since 1985. While the court found that the initial registration of the domain name was not in bad faith, the court did take issue with several aspects of Mr. Nissan's behavior, including his initial response to Nissan Motors complaint: an offer to sell the domain name for several million dollars. More recently, the court ordered Mr. Nissan to cease any commercial activities involving the site when it was discovered that Mr. Nissan was advertising automotive-related products on the site, despite his business being unrelated to automobiles. (Officialspin. com, 2002)

One of the innovative aspects of the ACPA is the way it deals with jurisdictional matters. Traditionally, legal disputes have always been subject to jurisdictional boundaries and national borders, and either the physical presence of the parties within those boundaries or evidence of the parties' contacts with the jurisdiction. Recognizing that in many cases cybersquatters go to some lengths to hide their identity or their location, the ACPA permits the trademark owner to take action against the domain name itself, rather than the domain owner personally. This permits aggrieved parties to locate the registrar and, although the registrar itself cannot be held liable for an infringing domain it permitted to be registered, the domain name itself can be attacked.

ICANN Domain Name Dispute Process

While the ACPA's jurisdictional elements have simplified matters somewhat for trademark owners with domains that have been registered within the United States, the global nature of the Internet has required a less geocentric dispute resolution process. To that end, ICANN as developed a Uniform Domain Name Dispute Resolution Policy ("UDRP") the provisions of which are in many respects similar to those of ACPA.

The UDRP process relies upon third-party, private dispute resolution mechanisms rather than the more expensive prospect of litigation in a court of law. For trademark owners who are seeking a quicker and cheaper resolution of domain disputes, the UDRP route has proven to be extremely popular, even though no monetary damages or injunctions are available. Indeed, the only remedies available under the UDRP are the cancellation or transfer of the domain name. Thus, for instance where the injury to the trademark owner is more serious, traditional litigation may yet be necessary.

The World Intellectual Property Organization ("WIPO") has attempted to define cybersquatting, and to establish guidelines for dispute resolution. In a 1999 report on the

Management of Internet Names and Addresses, the WIPO delegates discuss at great length the phenomenon of registering trademarks as domain names with the intent of profiting from the ownership, either by capitalizing on traffic brought in through the confusion, or by selling the domain to the trademark owner. In the end, WIPO's recommendations are very similar to those contained in the ICANN UDRP and the ACPA.

The UDRP, WIPO's recommendations, and the operations (and even the very existence) of ICANN are currently the subject of tremendous international debate. While the details of these arguments are too lengthy for inclusion in this brief article, many web sites (including ICANNWatch.org and UDRPinfo.com) chronicle the legal, technical, and political arguments over this emerging field.

CONCLUSION

As the Internet becomes an even more critical channel for businesses to reach out to consumers, the value of a well leveraged trademark has never been higher. At the same time, the pressures on trademark owners from infringing activities is requiring them to be ever more vigilant in their policing and prosecution of violators. In response to these pressures, courts and lawmakers have expanded and clarified traditional trademark protections, adding greatly to the remedies available to trademark owners who feel their rights have been violated. In this chapter we have covered the fundamentals of trademark law, and seen them applied to the unique new situations presented by Internet technologies. While the trademark space will continue to evolve, it is clear that the value of trademarks is as well-recognized as ever in the history of commerce.

If there is one conclusion to be drawn, it is that trademark is a very complex field of law and procedure, requiring expert guidance in order to provide maximum opportunity and protection. While this article may provide readers with a general overview of many current issues in trademark law, it is not a substitute for qualified legal counsel. As has been noted repeatedly throughout this article, successful use of trademark law depends upon many detailed analyses, procedural hurdles, and requires a significant commitment of time and resources in order to take full advantage. Trademark law provides robust protections to those who, with assistance from talented counsel, seek to protect their goods and services in the marketplace.

GLOSSARY

Blurring At type of dilution in which the distinctiveness of a mark is weakened through its identification with dissimilar goods.

Deep linking Creating a web page link that is tied directly to a document deep within the page hierarchy of a web site, rather than simply linking to the main home page of the site.

Dilution A lessening of the value of a famous trademark caused by an unauthorized use of the mark, regardless of whether any actual confusion, deception, or mistake occurred.

Distinctiveness The ability of a mark to distinguish the goods and services of the mark from the goods and services of another.

Domain Name An alphanumeric electronic address on the Internet.

Famous Trademark A court-determined trademark designation under 35 USC §1125(c).

Lanham Act Also known as the Trademark Act of 1946, it created a set of federal rules for governing the process of registering trademarks and established certain nationwide legal protections for trademark

Likelihood of Confusion The test of trademark infringement under the Lanham Act. A likelihood of confusion exists if a substantial number of reasonably prudent consumers are likely to be confused as to the source of the goods or services.

Infringement Use of a trademark in a way that is so similar to the owner's usage that an average consumer will be deceived, will mistake the infringing good for the original, or will experience confusion over the nature or origin of the product.

Initial Interest Confusion The use of another's trademark in a manner reasonably calculated to capture initial consumer attention, even though no actual sale is finally completed as a result of the confusion.

Intellectual property The concept of legal recognitions for property rights in intangible things such as ideas and intellectual creations.

Meta tags Hidden codes embedded in web pages that contain keywords related to the contents of a particular page, designed to only be seen by search engines.

Secondary meaning An association that has developed in the public's mind between the mark or trade dress of a product and owner of the mark or product.

Service mark A mark that is used to identify a service or the provider of a service rather than a tangible product, such as the name of a consulting firm, or the name of a proprietary analytical process used by that consulting firm.

Tarnishment A type of dilution in which the mark is used in an unflattering light, such as by associating it with inferior or distasteful products or services.

Trademark A mark that is used by a manufacturer or merchant to identify the origin or ownership of goods and to distinguish them from others and the use of which is protected by law.

Trade dress The overall image of a product, composed of the nonfunctional elements of its design, packaging, or labeling, including specific colors or color combinations, a distinctive package shape, or specific symbols or design elements.

U.S. Patent and Trademark Office (USPTO) The federal agency charged with managing the nationwide issuance of patents and registration of trademarks.

CROSS REFERENCES

See *Copyright Law; Legal, Social and Ethical Issues of the Internet; Patent Law; The Legal Implications of Information Security: Regulatory Compliance and Liability.*

REFERENCES

Bicknell, Craig (1999). Making a Mint on Wallstreet.com. Wired News. Available at: http://www.wired.com/news/business/0,1367,19285,00.html (Date of access: February 8, 2004)

Coca-Cola Co. v. Gemini Rising, Inc., 346 F. Supp. 1183 (E.D.N.Y. 1972)

Hormel Foods Corp. v. Jim Henson Productions, 73 F.3d 497 (2d Cir. 1996)

ICANN Uniform Dispute Resolution Policy (UDRP). Available at: http://www.icann.org/udrp/udrp.htm (Date of access: February 8, 2004)

Intermatic Incorporated v. Toeppen, 947 F.Supp. 1227 (N.D. Ill. 1996) Available at: http://www.loundy.com/CASES/Intermatic_v_Toeppen (Date of access: February 8, 2004)

Nissan Motor Co., Ltd v. Nissan Computer Corp., 61 U.S.P.Q.2d 1839 (C.D. Cal., 2002)

OfficialSpin.com (2002). Nissan Computer Corporation keeps domain name, for now. Available at: http://www.officialspin.com/main.php3?action=recent&rid=405 (Date of access: February 8, 2004)

Oppedahl & Larson v. Advanced Concepts, et al., Civ. No. 97-CV-1592 (D.C. Colo., 1997) Available at: http://www.patents.com/ac (Date of access: February 8, 2004)

Panavision Int'l, L.P. v. Toeppen, 945 F. Supp. 1296 (C.D. Cal. 1996) Available at: http://www.techlawjournal.com/courts/avery/19980417.htm (Date of access: February 8, 2004)

Playboy Enterprises, Inc. v. Terri Welles, 7 F. Supp. 2d 1098 (S.D. Ca. 1998), aff'd. in part, reversed in part, 162 F.3d 1169 (9th Cir. 2002)

Toys 'R' Us v. Akkaoui, 40 USPQ.2d 1836 (N.D. Cal. 1996).

Trademark Act of 1946 (also called the Lanham Act). (15 U.S.C. § 1051) Available at: http://www4.law.cornell.edu/uscode/15/1051.html (Date of access: February 8, 2004)

United States Patent and Trademark Office. Trademark Information. Available at: http://www.uspto.gov/main/trademarks.htm (Date of access: February 8, 2004)

Zatarains, Inc. v. Oak Grove Smokehouse, Inc., 698 F.2d 786 (5th Cir. 1983)